Handbook of Behavioral Assessment *edited by Anthony R. C[...]*
   Henry E. Adams

Counseling and Psychotherapy: A Behavioral Approach *by E[...]*

Dimensions of Personality *edited by Harvey London and John E. Exner, Jr.*

The Mental Health Industry: A Cultural Phenomenon *by Peter A. Magaro, Robert Gripp,*
   David McDowell, and Ivan W. Miller III

Nonverbal Communication: The State of the Art *by Robert G. Harper, Arthur N. Wiens, and*
   Joseph D. Matarazzo

Alcoholism and Treatment *by David J. Armor, J. Michael Polich, and Harriet B. Stambul*

A Biodevelopmental Approach to Clinical Child Psychology: Cognitive Controls and Cognitive
   Control Theory *by Sebastiano Santostefano*

Handbook of Infant Development *edited by Joy D. Osofsky*

Understanding the Rape Victim: A Synthesis of Research Findings *by Sedelle Katz and Mary*
   Ann Mazur

Childhood Pathology and Later Adjustment: The Question of Prediction *by Loretta K. Cass*
   and Carolyn B. Thomas

Intelligent Testing with the WISC-R *by Alan S. Kaufman*

Adaptation in Schizophrenia: The Theory of Segmental Set *by David Shakow*

Psychotherapy: An Eclectic Approach *by Sol L. Garfield*

Handbook of Minimal Brain Dysfunctions *edited by Herbert E. Rie and Ellen D. Rie*

Handbook of Behavioral Interventions: A Clinical Guide *edited by Alan Goldstein and Edna B.*
   Foa

Art Psychotherapy *by Harriet Wadeson*

Handbook of Adolescent Psychology *edited by Joseph Adelson*

Psychotherapy Supervision: Theory, Research and Practice *edited by Allen K. Hess*

Psychology and Psychiatry in Courts and Corrections: Controversy and Change *by Ellsworth A.*
   Fersch, Jr.

Restricted Environmental Stimulation: Research and Clinical Applications *by Peter Suedfeld*

Personal Construct Psychology: Psychotherapy and Personality *edited by Alvin W. Landfield*
   and Larry M. Leitner

Mothers, Grandmothers, and Daughters: Personality and Child Care in Three-Generation
   Families *by Bertram J. Cohler and Henry U. Grunebaum*

Further Explorations in Personality *edited by A.I. Rabin, Joel Aronoff, Andrew M. Barclay,*
   and Robert A. Zucker

Hypnosis and Relaxation: Modern Verification of an Old Equation *by*
   William E. Edmonston, Jr.

Handbook of Clinical Behavior Therapy *edited by Samuel M. Turner, Karen S. Calhoun, and*
   Henry E. Adams

Handbook of Clinical Neuropsychology *edited by Susan B. Filskov and Thomas J. Boll*

The Course of Alcoholism: Four Years After Treatment *by J. Michael Polich, David J. Armor,*
   and Harriet B. Braiker

Handbook of Innovative Psychotherapies *edited by Raymond J. Corsini*

The Role of the Father in Child Development (Second Edition) *edited by Michael E. Lamb*

Behavioral Medicine: Clinical Applications *by Susan S. Pinkerton, Howard Hughes, and W.W.*
   Wenrich

Handbook for the Practice of Pediatric Psychology *edited by June M. Tuma*

Change Through Interaction: Social Psychological Processes of Counseling and Psychotherapy
   by Stanley R. Strong and Charles D. Claiborn

Drugs and Behavior (Second Edition) *by Fred Leavitt*

(*continued on back*)

THE RORSCHACH: A COMPREHENSIVE SYSTEM

Volume
1

Second Edition

THE RORSCHACH
A COMPREHENSIVE SYSTEM
VOLUME 1: BASIC FOUNDATIONS
SECOND EDITION

JOHN E. EXNER, JR.

A WILEY-INTERSCIENCE PUBLICATION

JOHN WILEY & SONS, New York • Chichester • Brisbane • Toronto • Singapore

Library of Congress Cataloging in Publication Data:

Exner, John E.
   The Rorschach: a comprehensive system. Volume I,
Basic foundations.

   (Wiley series on personality processes)
   "A Wiley-Interscience publication."
   Includes indexes.
   1. Rorschach test.   I. Title.   II. Series.

BF698.8.R5E87   1986   155.2′842   85-17870
ISBN 0-471-80704-4

Printed in the United States of America

10 9 8 7 6

To My Sons and Daughter

John, Michael, Christopher, James, and Andrea

Series Preface

This series of books is addressed to behavioral scientists interested in the nature of human personality. Its scope should prove pertinent to personality theorists and researchers as well as to clinicians concerned with applying an understanding of personality processes to the amelioration of emotional difficulties in living. To this end, the series provides a scholarly integration of theoretical formulations, empirical data, and practical recommendations.

Six major aspects of studying and learning about human personality can be designated: personality theory, personality structure and dynamics, personality development, personality assessment, personality change, and personality adjustment. In exploring these aspects of personality, the books in the series discuss a number of distinct but related subject areas: the nature and implications of various theories of personality; personality characteristics that account for consistencies and variations in human behavior; the emergence of personality processes in children in adolescents; the use of interviewing and testing procedures to evaluate individual differences in personality; efforts to modify personality styles through psychotherapy, counseling, behavior therapy, and other methods of influence; and patterns of abnormal personality functioning that impair individual competence.

Irving B. Weiner

University of Denver
Denver, Colorado

Preface

If anyone present in 1970, during the assemblage of the first pieces of the *Comprehensive System,* which involved decisions concerning seating and instructions, had predicted that the project would still be ongoing more than 15 years later, they would not have been taken seriously. The task seemed straightforward, namely, to merge the empirically defensible features of other approaches into a standard format. It was naively assumed that almost all of the elements necessary for the understanding and use of the test already existed, thus no one could have foreseen the extended research odyssey that has evolved. In fact, even at the end of 1973, when the manuscript for the First Edition of this work was completed, much of that naiveté continued to exist. It was obvious that the issue of Special Scores was still to be resolved and that larger samples of data were required, and projects designed to accomplish those goals were already underway. But in effect, most of us who had worked at the task that I described in the Preface to the First Edition as "to present, in a single format, the best of the Rorschach," believed that we had completed most of the work necessary to accomplish that goal. But as it turns out, much of the "best" was yet to come.

As new projects were completed the data often raised more questions than were answered, thereby necessitating the design of many more studies than were originally anticipated. By early 1976, the breadth of data that continued to accumulate was much more extensive than could easily be scattered through a series of journal articles, and the decision to create Volume 2 was made. Although Volume 2 did provide an avenue through which to expand and clarify the basic work, focus on younger clients remained pitifully inadequate, and Volume 3 was a natural consequence, also providing a conduit for more expansion and clarification. But as the *System* has grown during the past 15 years, the original version of Volume 1 has become woefully outdated. Many new structural variables have been added since 1973 and the criteria for the application of some codings have been altered or expanded. More important, the continued accumulation of new data has added substantial information concerning the nature of the test and its interpretation. Thus this work is designed to bring together all of the components of the *System* as they have evolved to this point, so that Volume 1 can again be defined as the logical source from which one can learn about its application in using Rorschach's Test.

The basic objective of the project is the same—that is, to provide a method of using the test which is easily taught, manifests a high interscorer reliability, and for which the basic interpretive premises will withstand validation demands. The *System* remains free of any theoretical bent, although it is quite clear that many of the basic tenets of cognitive psychology are directly applicable to any viable understanding of how the test works, a finding indirectly predicted by Rorschach in his early explanation about the process of the test.

The *System* also remains comprehensive, that is, founded on an integration of the hard won wisdoms of those who developed and researched the test long before our project was initiated. In some ways the seeds of the idea for a single system were sown in my thinking more than 30 years ago when David Rapaport cautioned me to know *all* of the Rorschach. But they lay dormant until the late 1960s when Bruno Klopfer, after reading my comparative analysis of the five basic Rorschach Systems, suggested the possibility of a well-coordinated and extensive project to research each of the approaches to the test, a suggestion that was heartily endorsed by Samuel Beck, and later warmly encouraged by Marguerite Hertz and Zygmunt Piotrowski. These Rorschach giants provided much more than information. They offered suggestions, criticism, and, most of all, supportive friendships that served as a powerful motivation to persist at the task. If the project has been a success, it is largely because of their inspiration.

It would be foolhardy to suggest that the work is finished. The Rorschach continues to pose many unanswered questions. Some concern the nature of the stimulus figures, whereas others focus on establishing firmer conceptual links between some clusters of scores and their personality or behavioral correlates. Nonetheless, the *System,* as it stands, appears to have considerable usefulness in both clinical and research settings, and as such is a tribute to the hundreds who have been involved in its development. More than 600 examiners have participated in the many projects completed to date. Some have been professional psychologists or psychology graduate students, but more than half come from more varied backgrounds, ranging from a professional musician and a retired tailor, to an extremely talented high school senior. Other examiners have included physicians, dentists, nurses, social workers, educators, homemakers, and a few very adept secretaries who discovered that administering the Rorschach can sometimes be as boring as typing letters. The ability of these laypeople to learn to collect Rorschach data in a standardized format has been among the very reassuring aspects of the *System.*

There is another group of people who require special recognition here. These are the staff of the Rorschach Research Foundation (*Rorschach Workshops*) who have served variously as project directors and assistants with a seemingly tireless enthusiasm, and whose efforts often went well beyond what might have been expected.

Gerald Albrecht	Frederick Ehrlich
Doris Alinski	Gail Famino
Michael Allen	Ronda Fein
Franscesca Antogninni	Gary Fireman
Miriam Ben Haim	Roy Fishman
Jeffrey Berman	Jane Foreman
Carol Bluth	Benjamin Franklin
Peter Brent	Dorothy Frankmann
Richard Bruckman	Christy George
Edward Caraway	Katherine Gibbons
Eileen Carter	Nancy Goodman
Michael Coleman	Laura Gordon
Susan Colligan	Carolyn Hafez
William Cooper	Nancy Haller
Terry Cross	Doris Havermann
Robert Cummins	Dorothy Helinski
Mark Edwards	Lisa Hillman

Sarah Hillman
Milton Hussman
Geraldine Ingalls
Susan James
Marianne Johnston
Lester Jones
Mary Lou King
Richard Kloster
Beth Kuhn-Clark
Nancy Latimore
Carol (TC) Levantrosser
Arnold Lightner
Denise McDonnahue
Marianne McMannus
Louis Markowitz
Andrew Miller
Beatrice Mittman
Lynn Monahan
Ralph Nicholson
Michael O'Reilly
Carmen Penzulotta
George Pickering
Doris Price
Beth Raines
Virginia Reynolds

Felix Salomon
Joseph Schumacher
Whitford Schuyler
Barbara Seruya
Jane Sherman
Sherill Sigalow
Louise Stanton
Eva Stern
Sarah Sternklar
Robert Theall
Vicki Thompson
Peter Vagg
Alice Vieira
Donald Viglione
Edward Walker
Jane Wasley
Donna Wiener-Levy
Robert Wilke
Elizabeth Winter
Leslie Winter
Helen Yaul
Tracy Zalis
Nancy Zapolski
Mark Zimmerman

Still another group of people deserves very special mention. They have served as core staff or in senior advisory roles. Joyce Wylie served as our project coordinator between 1969 and 1978, and without her persistence, enthusiasm, and organizing talents we might well have faltered along the way. During that same period, Elaine Bryant oversaw most of our laboratory experiments and devised some remarkable innovations to improve on our designs.

Antonnia Victoria Leura was our recruiter for nearly nine years and during that time obtained nearly 8000 subjects for our various studies. I will never cease to be amazed at her ingenuity.

George Armbruster and Eugene Thomas have both served admirably in the role of "devil's advocate" on our research council. Both contributed much more than can be described in a few words, and both epitomize the best of psychology.

John Roger Kline was our first computer consultant and despite knowing little about the Rorschach, he impressed us enormously by the way he could manipulate data for us. Joel Cohen replaced John, and has been mainly responsible for the variety of sophisticated programs that we have developed during the past five years. He and Howard McGuire are also responsible for the development of our computer assisted interpretation program.

Vera Campo, Monserrat Ros, and Concepcion Sendin have been primarily responsible for testing the *System* in Spain, and Sendin has contributed substantially through the accumulation of a large Spanish sample to use for cross-cultural comparison.

Barbara Mason has also served as a jack-of-all-trades for us—as a trainer, teacher, researcher, and clinician. Her versatility is constantly impressive. S. Philip Erdberg has also been a key figure for us by his willingness to offer many of our continuing education workshops.

Luis Murillo has been a very special friend to Rorschach Workshops. He generously opened Stony Lodge Hospital to our efforts in 1970, and has continued to be very supportive of our research there ever since. He has been a close friend and a superb colleague.

Irving B. Weiner has also been a faithful friend, advisor, and critic since the inception of the project. He is directly responsible for much of the development of the *System,* and has often shared in many workshop ventures with me, thereby lightening the burden and increasing the enjoyment.

Finally, I must acknowledge an unpayable debt to my wife, Doris, who probably has often felt that she married an inkblot. She has been involved in almost every aspect of the work at Rorschach Workshops and has been a continuing source of support and encouragement to all of us.

JOHN E. EXNER, JR.

Bayville, New York
January 1986

Acknowledgments

Reproduction of the Rorschach Location Sheets for each of the protocols and of the blots to illustrate Location areas is by permission of Hans Huber Publishers, Bern, Switzerland.

Reproduction of Table 20, 28, C, and D from Beck, S. J., Beck, A. G., Levitt, E. E., and Molish, H. B. *Rorschach's Test. I: Basic Processes*. New York: Grune and Stratton, 1961, showing weighted and estimated values for organizing activity is by premission of Grune and Stratton.

Contents

PART I   THE HISTORY AND NATURE OF THE RORSCHACH

1. INTRODUCTION,   3

   Early History,   3
   The Rorschach Systems,   6
   The Concept of Projection and Projective Techniques,   14
   Intersystem Differences,   18
   The Comprehensive System,   20

2. THE NATURE OF THE RORSCHACH,   27

   Rorschach's Concept of the Method,   27
   The Rorschach as Problem-Solving Task,   28
   Decision Choices,   29
   The Response Process,   34
   A Summary of Operations in the Response Process,   51
   The Role of Projection in the Response,   51
   Summary,   53

PART II ADMINISTRATION AND SCORING

3. DECISIONS AND PROCEDURES,   59

   The Rorschach and the Test Battery,   60
   Procedures of Administration,   62
   The Problem of Lengthy Records,   68
   Recording the Responses,   69
   Inquiry Phase,   70
   The Location Sheet,   77
   Direct Inquiry and Testing of Limits,   77
   Comment or Response?,   78
   Summary,   78

4. SCORING: THE RORSCHACH LANGUAGE, 82

5. LOCATION AND DEVELOPMENTAL QUALITY: SYMBOLS AND
    CRITERIA, 90

The *W* Response (Wholes), 90
The *D* Response (Common Details), 91
The *Dd* Response (Unusual Details), 92
The *S* Response (White Space Details), 93
Location Coding for Multiple *D* Areas, 93
Coding for the Developmental Quality of the Response, 94

6. DETERMINANTS: SYMBOLS AND CRITERIA, 100

The Form Determinant (*F*), 103
The Movement Determinants, 103
Active-Passive Superscripts, 106
The Color Determinants (Chromatic), 110
The Color Determinants (Achromatic), 116
The Shading Determinants, 118
The Texture Determinant, 120
The Shading-Dimensionality Determinant (Vista), 123
The Diffuse Shading Determinant, 124
The Form Dimension Response, 127
Pair and Reflection Responses, 129
Summary, 133

7. BLENDS, ORGANIZATIONAL ACTIVITY, AND FORM QUALITY, 136

The Blend Response (.), 136
Organizational Activity (*Z*), 141
Form Quality, 146

8. CONTENT CATEGORIES AND POPULARS, 153

Content, 153
Popular Responses, 154

9. SPECIAL SCORES, 161

Unusual Verbalizations, 161
Deviant Verbalizations (*DV* and *DR*), 161
Inappropriate Combinations (*INCOM, FABCOM, CONTAM*), 163
Inappropriate Logic (*ALOG*), 164
Perseveration and Integration Failure, 164
Confabulation (*CONFAB*), 166
Special Content Characteristics, 166
Aggressive Movement (*AG*), 167

Morbid Content (*MOR*),   167
Personalized Answers,   167
Special Color Phenomena,   167

10. THE STRUCTURAL SUMMARY,   170

Sequence of Scores,   170
Frequency Tallies,   170
Ratios, Percentages, and Derivations,   177
Summary,   182

PART III   WORKING TABLES AND DESCRIPTIVE STATISTICS

11. WORKING TABLES,   187

Using Table A,   188

12. DESCRIPTIVE STATISTICS,   252

Rorschach Data and Descriptive Statistics,   252
Normative Samples,   255
Adult Sample,   255
Children and Adolescents,   257
The Psychiatric Reference Groups,   288

PART IV   INTERPRETATION

13. INTRODUCTION,   299

The Interpretive Process,   299
The Propositional Stage,   300
The Integration Stage,   301
Blind Interpretation,   302
Cookbooks and Computers,   306
Logical Progression in Interpretation,   307

14. STRUCTURAL DATA I—VALIDITY, CONTROLS, AND COPING
     STYLES,   311

Number of Responses (*R*),   311
R, Lambda, and Questions of Validity,   312
Stress Tolerance and Control,   315
The *D* Score,   315

The Adjusted D Score,   317
The Experience Actual (*EA*),   321
The Erlebnistypus (*EB*),   322
The Human Movement Response (*M*),   326
Chromatic Color Responses (*FC, CF, C*),   330
The Experience Base (*eb*),   333
The Form Dimension Response (*FD*),   342
The Experienced Stimulation (*es*),   344

15.   STRUCTURAL DATA II—COGNITION, IDEATION, AND AFFECT,   354

Cognitive Initiative and Complexity (*Zf, DQ,* Location, *Zd*),   354
Cognitive Rigidity and Dysfunction (*PSV, CONFAB*),   362
Conventionality and Perceptual Accuracy (*P*, $X+\%$, $F+\%$, $X-\%$),   364
Characteristics of Ideation (*a:p*, $M^a:M^p$, *M* Quality, SUM6 *Sp Sc*),   369
Characteristics of Affect (*FC:CF + C, Afr, S, CP,* Blends),   377

16.   STRUCTURAL DATA III—SELF-IMAGE AND INTERPERSONAL
      ATTITUDES,   392

Characteristics of Self Image ($3r + (2)/R$, *MOR, PER, Ab + Art, An + Xy*),   392
Interpersonal Perceptions (*H, Hd, Isolate:R, AG*),   401

17.   STRUCTURAL DATA IV—SPECIAL INDICES,   411

The Suicide Constellation (*S-CON*),   411
The Schizophrenia Index (*SCZI*),   416
The Depression Index (*DEPI*),   424

18.   THE FINISHED INTERPRETATION,   429

Analysis of the Sequence and Verbalizations,   429
The L.S. Protocol,   434
Summary,   441

PART V CLINICAL APPLICATIONS

19.   SOME ASSESSMENT ISSUES,   447

Protocol 1: A Question Concerning Tension and Depression,   447
Structural Interpretation,   455
Analysis of the Scoring Sequence,   457
Analysis of the Responses,   457
Analysis of the Inquiry,   458
Summary of Protocol 1,   458

Protocol 2: A Question of Adolescent Withdrawal,   460
Structural Interpretation,   468
Analysis of the Scoring Sequence,   471
Analysis of the Responses,   471
Analysis of the Inquiry,   472
Summary of Protocol 2,   473

Protocol 3: A Question of Psychosomatic Involvement,   473
Structural Interpretation,   480
Analysis of the Scoring System,   482
Analysis of the Responses,   483
Analysis of the Inquiry,   484
Summary of Protocol 3,   484

Protocol 4: A Question of Impulsiveness,   485
Stuctural Interpretation,   493
Analysis of the Scoring Sequence,   496
Analysis of the Responses,   496
Analysis of the Inquiry,   497
Summary of Protocol 4,   497

Protocol 5: A Question of Chronic Anxiety,   498
Structural Interpretation,   506
Analysis of the Scoring Sequence,   508
Analysis of the Responses,   508
Analysis of the Inquiry,   509
Summary of Protocol 5,   509

AUTHOR INDEX,   511

SUBJECT INDEX,   519

Tables

1   Average Number of Responses Given by Each of Five Groups During Four Intervals of Blot Exposure,   32

2   Means for $X + \%$ and Popular Responses for Each of Five Groups During Four Intervals of Blot Exposure,   33

3   Frequencies of Rankings for 10 Target Responses Given by Two Groups, with Ranks 1 and 2, and 4 and 5 Collapsed,   43

4   Correlation Coefficients for Nonpatient Groups of 50 Adults Retested after 12 to 14 Months and 100 Adults Retested after 36 to 39 Months,   46

5   Correlation Coefficients for 25 Nonpatient Eight-Year-Olds Retested after Seven Days, 35 Nonpatient Nine-Year-Olds, and 35 Nonpatient Adults Retested after Approximately Three Weeks,   47

6   Abbreviations Commonly Used for Recording Rorschach Responses,   70

7   Symbols Used for Coding the Location of Rorschach Responses,   91

8   Symbols and Criteria Used for Coding Developmental Quality,   96

9   Examples of Coding the Location Component,   98

10   Symbols and Criteria for Determinant Coding,   101

11   Results of an Active-Passive Word Study for Two Groups for 300 Items, Showing the Majority Score for Each Item for Each Group Plus the Number of Subjects Represented by that Majority, with * Indicating Group Disagreements,   107

12   Examples of the Three Types of Movement Responses,   111

13   Examples of the Four Types of Chromatic Color Responses,   114

14   Examples of the Different Types of Texture and Vista Responses,   125

15   Examples of Diffuse Shading Responses,   128

16   Examples of Form-Dimensional Responses,   130

17   Examples of Reflection and Pair Responses,   132

18   Percentage of Coder Agreement for Two Reliability Studies,   134

19   Examples of Blend Responses,   139

20   Organizational (Z) Values for Each of the Ten Cards,   143

21   Examples of Z Score Assignment for Responses to Each of the Ten Rorschach Cards,   144

22   Symbols and Criteria for Coding Form Quality,   148

23   Symbols and Criteria to be Used in Scoring for Content,   155

24   Popular Responses Selected for the Comprehensive System Based on the Frequency of Occurrence of at Least Once in Every Three Protocols Given by Nonpatient Adult Subjects and Nonschizophrenic Adult Patients,   158

25 Percentage of Coder Agreement for 12 Special Scores in Two Reliability Studies, 168

26 Scoring Sequence for Protocol L. S., 176

27 Structural Summary for Protocol L. S., 178

28 Best Weighted ZSum Prediction When *Zf* Is Known, 179

29 *EA-es D* Score Conversion Table, 180

30 Summary of Blind Analysis Studies Concerning the Rorschach, 304

31 Frequency Data for *m* and *Y* for Two Tests of Two Groups of Male Medical Patients, 320

32 Frequency of Cases Identified by Number of Positive Variables in a 12-Item Constellation from an Effected Suicide Group, Subdivided by Classification of Method Employed, Plus Three Control Groups, 415

33 Frequency of *SCZI* Identifications, Using Four or Five Variables Positive for Six Random Selections of 100 Subjects from Each of Five Groups, 423

34 Structural Summary—L.S. Protocol, 435

35 Scoring Sequence—L.S. Protocol, 437

36 Structural Summary—Protocol #1, 454

37 Scoring Sequence—Protocol #1, 455

38 Structural Summary—Protocol #2, 467

39 Scoring Sequence—Protocol #2, 468

40 Structural Summary—Protocol #3, 479

41 Scoring Sequence—Protocol #3, 480

42 Structural Summary—Protocol #4, 492

43 Scoring Sequence—Protocol #4, 493

44 Structural Summary—Protocol #5, 505

45 Scoring Sequence—Protocol #5, 506

A Figures Showing Common (*D*) and Unusual (*Dd*) Location Areas by Card, Listings of Ordinary (*o*), Unusual (*u*) and Minus Responses and Response Classes by Location Areas, Plus Populars and *Z* Values for Each Card, 189

B Illustrations of Responses That Should Be Coded *FQ+*, 249

C Organizational (*Z*) Values for Each of the ten Cards, 250

D Best Weighted ZSum Prediction When *Zf* Is Known, 250

E Popular Responses Used in the Comprehensive System, 251

F Distribution by Age and SES for 600 Nonpatient Adults, 256

G Descriptive Statistics for 69 Rorschach Variables for 600 Nonpatient Adults, 257

H Frequencies and Percentages Concerning Directionality for 18 Structural Variables for 600 Nonpatient Adults, 259

I Distribution of Demographic Variables, by Age, for 1580 Nonpatient Children and Adolescents, 260

J Descriptive Statistics for 69 Rorschach Variables for 1580 Nonpatient Children and Adolescents, by Age, 262

K Frequencies and Percentages Concerning Directionality for 18 Structural Variables for 1580 Nonpatients by Age Group from 5 Through 16, 286

L Descriptive Statistics for 69 Rorschach Variables for 320 Inpatient Schizophrenics, 288

M Frequencies and Percentages Concerning Directionality for 18 Structural Variables for 320 Inpatient Schizophrenics, 290

N   Descriptive Statistics for 69 Rorschach Variables for 210 Inpatient Depres-
     sives,   290
O   Frequencies and Percentages Concerning Directionality for 18 Structural Variables
     for 210 Inpatient Depressives,   292
P   Descriptive Statistics for 69 Rorschach Variables for 200 Outpatient Character
     Problems,   293
Q   Frequencies and Percentages Concerning Directionality for 18 Structural Variables
     for 200 Character Problems,   295

Figures

1   Visual Scanning by a 19-year-old Female During the First 500 ms of Blot Exposure,   35
2   Visual Scanning by a 23-year-old Male During the First 1100 ms After Blot Exposure,   36
3   Format for Recording Rorschach Responses,   71
4   Illustration of a Sequence of Scores,   88
5   Illustration of a Structural Summary,   88
6   Location Selections by L. S.,   171
7   *D* and *Dd* Areas for Card I,   195
8   *D* and *Dd* Areas for Card II,   200
9   *D* and *Dd* Areas for Card III,   209
10   *D* and *Dd* Areas for Card IV,   211
11   *D* and *Dd* Areas for Card V,   216
12   *D* and *Dd* Areas for Card VI,   222
13   *D* and *Dd* Areas for Card VII,   228
14   *D* and *Dd* Areas for Card VIII,   234
15   *D* and *Dd* Areas for Card IX,   241
16   *D* and *Dd* Areas for Card X,   248
17   Location Selections for Protocol 1,   453
18   Location Selections for Protocol 2,   466
19   Location Selections for Protocol 3,   478
20   Location Selections for Protocol 4,   491
21   Location Selections for Protocol 5,   504

THE RORSCHACH: A COMPREHENSIVE SYSTEM

Volume
1

Second Edition

PART I

The History and Nature of the Rorschach

CHAPTER 1

Introduction

The 10 inkblots that constitute the stimuli of the Rorschach test were first unveiled to the professional public in September 1921, with the release of Hermann Rorschach's famed monograph, *Psychodiagnostik*. Since that time the test has generated much interest, extensive use, and considerable research. For at least two decades, the 1940s and 1950s, its name was almost synonymous with clinical psychology. During those years the primary role of the clinician focused on assessment or psychodiagnosis. But even as the role of the clinician broadened and diversified during the 1960s and 1970s, the Rorschach remained among the most commonly used tests in the clinical setting, and that status continues today. It is a test from which considerable information can be derived if *properly* administered, scored, and interpreted. Some of this information is relevant to diagnostic decisions, the formulation of intervention plans, or making predictions. But most of the test data provide descriptive information about the psychological characteristics of the subject.

Although the test has become an important clinical tool, its history has been marked by much controversy. It has often proved baffling to researchers and very irritating to those advocating the stringent application of psychometric principles to any psychological test. Criticism of the test, some real and some unreal, became especially widespread during the 1950s and 1960s. During that period many openly judged its worth with contempt and advocated its abandonment as a test for clinical work (Jensen, 1958; Zubin, Eron, & Schumer, 1965). There is no question that many Rorschach advocates had overestimated its potential usefulness and often made unrealistic claims about its efficacy. Some even likened it to an X-ray of the mind in spite of a growing number of publications that appeared during the 1950s and 1960s, which reported negative findings for issues such as diagnostic accuracy, reliability, and validity. On the other hand, many of the criticisms were naive and unjust, often fomented from bias, ignorance, or simply a misunderstanding of the method and the principles that led to its exploration by Rorschach.

EARLY HISTORY

Rorschach did not conceive of his work as having yielded a test per se. Instead, he regarded his monograph as a report of findings from an investigation in perception that he believed might ultimately lend itself to a sophisticated diagnostic approach for the differentiation of schizophrenia. Obviously, he used inkblots as stimulus figures, but this was not an original Rorschach idea. Quite the contrary, there had been several attempts to use inkblots as some form of test well before Rorschach began his investigation. Binet and Henri (1895, 1896) had tried to incorporate them into their early efforts to devise an intelligence test. They were like many of their day, believing that the inkblot stimulus might be useful to the study of visual imagination. They abandoned the use of inkblot stimuli in their effort because of group administration problems. Several other investigators in the United States and Europe published articles about the use of inkblot stimuli to study imagination and creativeness (Dearborn, 1897, 1898; Kirkpatrick, 1900; Rybakov, 1911; Pyle, 1913, 1915; Whipple, 1914; Parsons, 1917). It is doubtful that any of this work stimulated Rorschach's original study, but it is quite likely that he became familiar with much of it before he wrote his monograph.

The reasons for Rorschach's decision to study the use of inkblots are not fully clear. There is little doubt that, like most children of his time, he often played the popular *Klecksographie* (Blotto) game as a youth. In fact, he even had the nickname "Klex" during his last two years in the Kantonsschule, which might have reflected his enthusiasm for the game or may simply have evolved from the fact that his father was an artist (Ellenberger, 1954). It is also clear that his continued close friendship with a classmate from the Kantonsschule, Konrad Gehring, played a role in stimulating his exploration of the use of inkblots with patients. The Blotto game had flourished in Europe for nearly 100 years by the time Rorschach began his psychiatric residency in 1909. It was a favorite of adults and children and had several variations. Inkblots (*Klecksen*) could be purchased easily in many stores or, as was more commonplace, players of the game could create their own. Sometimes the "game" was played by creating poem-like associations to the blots (Kerner, 1857). In another variation the blot would be the centerpiece for charades. When children played the game, they usually created their own blots and then competed in developing elaborate descriptions.

Konrad Gehring became a teacher at an intermediate school close to the Munsterlingen hospital where Rorschach did his residency, and he and his pupils often visited the hospital to sing for patients. Gehring had also discovered that if he contracted with his students to work diligently for a period of time and then permitted them to play the Blotto game, his classroom management problems were reduced considerably. Rorschach became intrigued with the management potential that the game seemed to offer, but was also interested in making comparisons between the Blotto responses of Gehring's male adolescent students and his own patients. Thus in a very casual and unsystematic manner, they worked together for a brief period, making and "testing out" different inkblots during 1911.

Probably little would have come from the Rorschach-Gehring "experiment" had not another event occurred during the same year. This was the publication of Eugen Bleuler's famed work on Dementia Praecox in which the term *schizophrenia* was coined. Bleuler was one of Rorschach's professors and supervisors. In fact, he directed Rorschach's "Doctor's Thesis," which concerned hallucinations. The Bleuler concepts intrigued the psychiatric community, but they also posed the very important issue of how to differentiate the schizophrenic from those forms of psychosis reflected an organically induced dementia. As almost a passing matter, Rorschach noted that patients who had been identified as schizophrenic seemed to respond quite differently to the Blotto game than did others. He made a brief report of this to a local psychiatric society, but little interest was expressed in his apparent finding. Thus Rorschach did not pursue the matter with any thoroughness for several years.

In 1910 he had married a Russian, Olga Stempelin, with plans to ultimately practice in Russia. He completed his residency in 1913 and moved on to Moscow, but for reasons unknown remained in Russia for only about seven months before returning to accept a position at Waldau; then, in 1915, he moved on to a position as Associate Director of the Krombach hospital in Herisau. It was at Herisau in late 1917 or early 1918 that Rorschach decided to investigate the Blotto game more systematically.

It is likely that the stimulus to that decision was the publication of the "Doctor's Thesis" of Syzmond Hens, a Polish medical student who studied under Bleuler at the Medical Policlinic in Zurich. Hens developed his own series of eight inkblots which he administered to 1000 children, 100 nonpatient adults, and 100 psychotic patients. His thesis focused on how the contents of responses were both similar and different across these three groups, and he suggested that a classification system for the contents of responses might be diagnostically useful. This approach to classification was quite different than the one Rorschach and Gehring had conceived of in their casual 1911 exploration. Whereas the Hens approach emphasized classifying content, Rorschach was more interested in classifying the more salient characteristics of the response. It seems clear that he was quite familiar with much of the literature on perception and apparently was especially intrigued with, and influenced by the concepts of Ach, Mach, Loetze, and Helmholtz, and particularly with the notion of an *apperceptive mass*. That concept is pervasive in much of his writing concerning his findings.

Rorschach used about 40 inkblots in his investigation, administering 15 of them much more frequently than the others. Ultimately, he collected data from 405 subjects of which 117 were nonpatients that he subdivided into "educated" and "noneducated." The sample also included 188 schizophrenics which were his basic target population. True to his casual 1911 observations, the schizophrenic group did respond to the inkblots quite differently than did the other groups. His major thrust avoided and/or minimized content, but instead focused on the development of a format for classifying responses by different characteristics. Thus he developed a set of codes, following largely from the work of the Gestaltists (mainly Wertheimer), that would permit the differentiation of response features. One set of codes, or scores as they have come to be called, was used to represent the area of the blot to which the response was given, such as W for the whole blot, D for large detail areas, and so on. A second set of codes concerned the features of the blot that were mainly responsible for the image perceived by the subject, such as F for form or shape, C for chromatic color, M for the impression of human movement, and so on. A third set of codes was used to classify contents, such as H for human, A for animal, An for anatomy, and so on.

By early 1921 the sample sizes of Rorschach's groups were sufficient for him to demonstrate that the inkblot method he had devised offered considerable diagnostic usefulness, especially in identifying the schizophrenic. But in the course of the investigation he had also discovered that clusterings of high frequencies of certain kinds of responses—mainly movement or color responses—appeared to relate to distinctive kinds of psychological and/or behavioral characteristics. Thus the method seemed to have both a diagnostic potential and the possibility of detecting some qualities of the person which, in the terminology of contemporary psychology, would probably be called personality traits, habits, or styles.

Several of Rorschach's colleagues were impressed with his findings, and Bleuler was particularly enthusiastic about its diagnostic potential. Collectively they encouraged him to publish his findings in a form from which others could learn to use the method. His first manuscript, based on the 15 blots that he used most frequently, was rejected by several publishers. One did accept it but with the proviso that the number of blots be reduced to six because of printing costs. Rorschach rejected this offer but continued with his investigation, adding more and more subjects to his sample. In 1920 he rewrote the manuscript to include his new data and again submitted it to several publishers. The work might not have been published if it were not for the efforts of Walter Morgenthaler, a colleague of

Rorschach's who became an informal solicitor on Rorschach's behalf. In 1920 Morgenthaler obtained a contract for Rorschach from a small publisher in Bern, The House of Bircher. But a compromise was necessary. Like other publishers, Bircher objected to the reproduction of 15 or more inkblots because of printing costs. Thus Rorschach agreed to rewrite the manuscript to include only 10 blots that he used most often. The manuscript was finally published in late June 1921, but with it came a new problem to be addressed. When the inkblots were reproduced, Bircher made them smaller and altered some of the colors slightly.

But another change was much more important. The blots that Rorschach used in his research contained no shading; they were all solid colors. When Bircher reproduced them, very marked differences in the saturation levels occurred. Shading differences appeared in almost every area of every blot, resulting in very different stimulus figures than Rorschach had used. But Rorschach is reported to have been more excited than dismayed with this printing error. According to Ellenberger (1954), "he was seized with a new enthusiasm, and understood at once the new possibilities that the prints offered." Thus he decided to continue his research using the new multishaded blots.

When he wrote the monograph, Rorschach chose to call his method a *Form Interpretation Test,* and cautioned that his findings were preliminary and stressed the importance of much more experimentation. It is apparent that he looked forward to much more research with the "method" and invested himself vigorously in it during the next several months. But then tragedy struck. On April 1, 1922 he was admitted to the emergency room at the hospital at Herisau after having suffered abdominal pains for nearly a week. He died the next morning! He was only 37 years old and had devoted less than four years to his investigation of the "Blotto Game." Had he lived to extend his work, the nature of the test and the direction of its development might have been much different than proved to be the case.

There is little doubt that Rorschach was disappointed about the indifference to his work that was apparent after the publication of *Psychodiagnostik.* The only Swiss psychiatric journal gave no review to it, and other European psychiatric journals did little more than publish brief summaries of the work. The monograph was a financial disaster for the publisher. Only a few copies were sold before Rorschach died and before the House of Bircher was to enter bankruptcy. Fortunately the subsequent auction of Bircher goods left the monograph and the 10 plates in the hands of a larger and highly respected publishing house in Bern, Verlag Hans Huber. Huber's reputation for quality publications plus a few favorable reviews of the monograph stimulated interest and the use of the method persisted. However, Rorschach's absence and the fact that a new set of blots had been created posed a significant problem for those who would try to continue his work. But that was only the beginning of the problem for those who became interested in developing and using Rorschach's method.

THE RORSCHACH SYSTEMS

Although several of Rorschach's colleagues continued to use his method after his death, none followed a systematic empirical approach to data collection as he had done. Instead, they attempted to focus on clinical and/or vocational applications of the method. Rorschach had deliberately avoided theorizing about the nature of his method and, as noted earlier, cautioned repeatedly in the monograph about the limitations of his data and the need for more research. He also tended to discount the importance of content per se, postulating that content analysis would yield little about the person. But this did not detract many users of the test from trying to apply it more directly to the increasingly popular Freudian theory.

Three of Rorschach's colleagues became the strongest advocates of the *Form Interpretation Test*. They were Walter Morgenthaler, Emil Oberholzer, and Georgi Roemer. At the beginning they based their advocacy on the premise that the method was well suited for the differentiation of schizophrenia, but like many others in the psychiatric community, felt that Rorschach's work was incomplete *mainly* because of the lack of content interpretation. Roemer tried to extend Rorschach's work by using a new set of blots and ultimately formulated several interesting but not well-received positions concerning the "test." Morgenthaler and Oberholzer remained quite faithful to Rorschach's blots and to his method for scoring answers, but each sought to extend his work by giving considerably greater emphasis to the use of the content. Oberholzer in particular was to play an important role in the ultimate expansion of the use and understanding of the test.

Actually, none of the early European users of the method exploited the use of content interpretation inordinately, but at the same time none seemed equipped, by reason of understanding or motive, to extend Rorschach's postulates concerning the perceptual properties of the method. No new scores were added to the format until 1932, when Hans Binder published an elaborate scheme for scoring achromatic and shading responses. But unlike Rorschach, Binder's scoring format was logically intuitive rather than empirically developed.

Many people and events were to become influential in determining the expansion and growth of Rorschach's method. Emil Oberholzer was among the first catalysts to that growth. By the mid-1920s he had become a widely respected psychoanalyst who included a specialty in children among his varied talents. Because of that reputation, an American psychiatrist, David Levy, petitioned for and received a grant to study with Oberholzer in Switzerland for one year. During his year with Oberholzer, Levy learned about Rorschach's work and on his return to the United States brought along several copies of the blot photos (they were not yet routinely mounted on cardboard), with the intent of exploring their use with children. Other interests deterred Levy from his intent to use and study the test but he did publish a translation of one of Oberholzer's papers about it in 1926. At that time Levy was a staff psychiatrist at the Institute of Guidance in New York City. The Institute was interdisciplinary and was a resource for the New York City schools to serve the needs of children, mainly those whose academic performances were substandard, but also to provide psychiatric consultation and service to disturbed children from the greater New York area. Thus it was a natural training facility for students in psychiatry and psychology.

In 1927, Samuel J. Beck, who was a graduate student at Columbia University, was awarded a student fellowship at the Institute. Typically, he worked a few hours each week, learning to administer and interpret various tests of intelligence, aptitude, and achievement. By 1929 Beck was actively searching for a research topic that might be acceptable for a dissertation. In a casual conversation one afternoon, Levy mentioned to Beck that he had brought copies of the Rorschach blots with him on his return from Switzerland; he showed them to Beck and loaned him a copy of Rorschach's monograph. Beck became intrigued with the method, as a test, and practiced with it under Levy's supervision at the Institute. Subsequently, with Levy's encouragement, Beck broached the idea of a standardization study to his dissertation advisor, the famous experimental psychologist Robert S. Woodworth. Woodworth was not specifically aware of Rorschach's work but was familiar with some of the experiments of the Gestaltists in which inkblots were used as a part of the stimulus field. After reviewing the test with Beck, Woodworth agreed that a standardization study using children as the subjects might contribute to the literature on individual differences. Thus nearly seven years after Rorschach's death, the first systematic investigation concerning his test was initiated, one which would launch Beck into a career that was to make him one of the truly great figures of the test.

Beck took nearly three years to collect and analyze the data for his study. It involved the testing of almost 150 children. During that period he maintained contact with two close friends who he had first met some 10 years earlier while working as a newspaper reporter in Cleveland; they were Ralph and Marguerite Hertz. It was shortly after Beck began his dissertation study that the Hertzes visited New York. At that time Marguerite Hertz was also a psychology graduate student, studying at Western Reserve University in Cleveland. During the visit Beck shared some of his notions about Rorschach's work with her and she was quick to recognize the vast potential of the method. As a result she also petitioned to do her dissertation about the test and devised a study similar to Beck's, but with several variations in sampling. Thus the second systematic investigation of the test began. Both dissertations were completed in 1932. After graduating, Hertz accepted a position involving a very elaborate multidisciplinary study of children at the Brush Foundation in Cleveland, whereas Beck took a joint position at the Boston Psychopathic Hospital and Harvard Medical School.

Neither Beck nor Hertz added any new components to Rorschach's format for coding or scoring answers in their dissertation works. Their findings did add important data concerning how children responded, but probably more important than the data as such was the breadth of experience each gained that led to a better comprehension of the conceptual framework used by Rorschach. Both completed their work with a marked awareness of how much more research was needed. If one were to have predicted the developmental future of the Rorschach Test at that time, it is doubtful that any anticipation of future controversy would have been mentioned. Both Beck and Hertz were trained in psychology programs with stringent empirical orientations. Many of their findings were similar as were most of the conclusions that they developed. But events of the world would ultimately alter this seemingly harmonious beginning very significantly.

Probably the most important of those events was the rise to power of Adolph Hitler in Germany. The ultimate chaos that was created affected the lives of three other psychologists markedly and, as a result, each became extensively involved with Rorschach's test. The first to experience the grave impact of the power of the Nazis in Germany was Bruno Klopfer. Klopfer had completed his Ph.D. in 1922 at the University of Munich. He became a specialist in children and focused much of his work on emotional problems as related to academic progress or lack thereof. Ultimately, he became a senior staff member at the Berlin Information Center for Child Guidance. It was an institute similar in design and scope to the Institute for Child Guidance in New York where Beck did his early research. But unlike Beck who by 1932 had become deeply interested in the test and its use, Klopfer had no interest in the Rorschach. Both his training and subsequent orientation were strongly phenomenological, and his abiding interest was in the Freudian and Jungian psychoanalytic theories. He had begun personal analysis in 1927 and training analysis in 1931, with the ultimate objective of becoming a practicing analyst. By 1933 the many directives from the government to the Berlin Information Center for Children concerning studies on, and services for Aryan and non-Aryan children, as well as the increasing pressure on Jews, led Klopfer to decide to flee the country. Klopfer's training analyst, Werner Heilbrun,[1] aided him in contacting many professionals outside of Germany, seeking assistance for him. One who responded positively was Carl Jung, who promised a position for Klopfer if he could reach Zurich, which he did during 1933.

The position that Jung found for Klopfer was that of a technician at the Zurich Psychotechnic Institute. The Institute served many functions, among which was psychological testing of candidates for various types of employment. The Rorschach test was among the techniques used routinely, and thus Klopfer was required to learn how to administer and score it. His instructor was another technician, Alice Garbasky. During the nearly nine months that he held this post, Klopfer became intrigued with some of the postulates offered by Rorschach in the monograph, *Psychodiagnostik,* but he did not become strongly interested in teaching or using the test. Instead, his first love remained psychoanalysis and his stay in Zurich provided the opportunity for considerable personal experience with Jung. His role of a technician was far less satisfying to him than had been his much more prestigious position as a senior staff member in Berlin. Consequently he persisted in soliciting other employment, both in Switzerland and other countries. Ultimately he was offered, and accepted a position as a research associate in the Department of Anthropology at Columbia University and immigrated to the United States in 1934. Interestingy, this was about the same time that Beck went to Switzerland, under a Rockefeller Fellowship, to study with Emil Oberholzer for a year. Beck anticipated that his study in Switzerland would lead him to a better understanding of Rorschach's concepts, and particularly of his notions concerning the use of the multishaded blots that had been created with the publication of the monograph.

By 1934 Beck had already published nine articles describing the potential merits of the Rorschach for the study of personality organization and individual differences. The first three of these appeared before Beck completed his dissertation, so that by 1934 considerable interest had began to develop about the test in the United States.[2] This interest was evident in both psychiatry and psychology and was similar to the interest that had developed in Europe during the first decade after Rorschach's death. But unlike the situation on most of the European continent, where the test had gradually gained widespread use, the American student of the test was faced with two problems. First Rorschach's monograph was not readily available, but even if a copy were located, the reader had to be quite skilled in reading German, because it was not translated into English until 1942. Second, and much more important at that time, was the fact that it had not gained the widespread use as was the case in Europe. Consequently, there were relatively few opportunities to learn the techniques of administration and scoring, or the principles of interpreting the results.

Beck had taught the method at Harvard Medical School and the Boston Psychopathic Hospital for about two years, and Hertz was teaching the method to technicians at the Brush Foundation and to students at Western Reserve University. David Levy left New York in 1933 to head a new children's unit at Michael Reese Hospital in Chicago, and he

[1] About four years after aiding Klopfer's flight from Germany, Heilbrun left his own practice to join the International Brigade in the Spanish Civil War. He was to become immortalized in some of Ernest Hemingway's writing as he was the model for ''the physician'' about who Hemingway wrote.

[2] Woodworth was very enthusiastic about Beck's project and pressed him to publish early and frequently about it. Beck admitted (Personal Communication, June 1963) that Woodworth's status as an editor for the *American Journal of Psychology* made this easy to do.

trained a few technicians there how to administer the test. But other than those three locations, no formal instruction in the test existed. Thus it was not uncommon for the interested student to experience some frustration, because formal training about the test was not readily available. It was this situation that would have a major impact on the career of Bruno Klopfer and ultimately lead him into a role as one of the most significant figures in the Rorschach community.

In late 1934 some of the graduate students at Columbia learned that Klopfer had gained considerable experience with the test in Zurich and petitioned their department chairman, Woodworth, for a seminar about the test to be conducted by the Research Associate from Anthropology. Woodworth was very reluctant to arrange a joint appointment for a relative unknown to his department, and instead suggested that he would try to arrange for some formal training in the test by Beck after Beck's return from Switzerland. The students were not to be deterred from their interest however, and enticed Klopfer to conduct an informal seminar in his apartment two evenings a week. Klopfer agreed to do so with the proviso that at least seven students would participate, each paying a small stipend for the 6-week seminar.

It had been Klopfer's intention to teach the fundamentals of administration and scoring during that first private seminar, but that format was subverted by the incompleteness of Rorschach's work. At almost every meeting, when participants would discuss responses that they had collected in their practice with the test, the lack of precise designations for the variety of blot areas—that is, whether an area being used was *common* or *unusual*—created much disagreement. More important, the lack of codes or scores to differentiate the variety of responses that emphasized the shading of the blots led to debates that would often continue well into the night. Klopfer readily perceived that the future of the test could easily hinge on the resolution of these problems. Klopfer was a masterful teacher and an excellent organizer, and as he found his own intrigue with the test rekindled by the enthusiasm of the students, he became excited about the challenge posed by the incompleteness of the test.

By the end of the six weeks the students had already decided to continue for a second six-week seminar, and other students from Columbia and New York University asked Klopfer to form a second group. The second led to a third and so on. In each of these seminars possible new scores for location designations, and to encompass those responses that included reference to the shading features were discussed, and decisions were made to add them to the existing scoring format. By late 1935 several new scores had been added, and more were being considered. The Klopfer groups approached the problem of the shading answers by drawing extensively from Binder's (1932) suggestions, but then re-defining some, and creating others.

By 1936 Klopfer was devoting most of his time to the test. It is quite important to note that during the time when Klopfer and his pupils were seeking to develop the test, the atmosphere was not readily conducive to new innovations. American psychology looked askance on phenomonology during that period, having established itself as closely aligned with the traditions of ''pure science.'' Behaviorism was a byword, and anyone willing to depart from the rigors of empiricism or unwilling to accept its tenets would often be regarded with a somewhat jaundiced eye. This was to create a significant problem for Klopfer and even more so for the development of the test.

Klopfer was quick to recognize the need to disseminate information about the Rorschach, especially because in each of his seminars new scores were being adopted or new formulations about the test evolved. In 1936 he began to publish a mimeographed newsletter that he called *The Rorschach Research Exchange,* which was later to become the *Journal of Projective Techniques,* and ultimately the *Journal of Personality Assessment.* Its basic purpose was to provide updates concerning the developments of the test, as they had evolved in the many seminars that Klopfer conducted privately and in the supervisory seminars he had begun teaching at Columbia. But there was another purpose. He perceived the *Exchange* as having the potential to serve as a vehicle to share data, ideas, and experiences with the test. In that context, he invited Beck, Levy, Hertz, and Oberholzer to contribute and anticipated that a dialogue among those experienced with the test would stimulate more rapid development. But this was not to be the case.

Shortly before the first issue of the *Exchange* appeared, an article was published by Beck (1936) in another journal that was extremely critical of some of the Swiss psychiatrists, especially Bleuler and his son Manfred, who were applying the test in ways Beck felt were far too subjective, especially in the way that the responses were being scored. The title of the article, "Autism in Rorschach Scoring," provides some indication of the vigor with which Beck attacked deviations from the coding or scoring format that Rorschach had developed. As he had done in previous articles, Beck pointed to the need for careful, systematic research that would lead to fixed standards for administration, scoring, and interpretation. It is not surprising then, in light of that firm position, to find that Beck reacted to Klopfer's movement to expand the scoring format for the test with very marked coolness. There is no question that the scoring format the Klopfer group developed, which was presented in the first issue of the *Exchange,* (Klopfer & Sender, 1936) was well organized and carefully thought through. But the absence of any data base plus the fact that the format diversified the scoring well beyond any points that Rorschach had conceptualized or defined, or that either Beck or Hertz had explored in their work, made it, at best, difficult and probably impossible for anyone committed to an empirical framework for the test to accept.

Things went from bad to potentially disastrous in early 1937. After Beck received an invitation to write for the *Exchange* in 1936, he sent a copy of a manuscript that he had been preparing for nearly two years. It was his first book, *Introduction to the Rorschach Method,* published as the first monograph of the American Orthopsychiatric Association in 1937, which later became known as "Beck's Manual." Klopfer decided to devote a major portion of a 1937 issue of the *Exchange* to a review of Beck's Manual (Klopfer, 1937). As might be expected, the review was more negative than positive, discussing Beck's reluctance to add scores and his criteria for the definition of good versus poor form quality responses. Naturally it provoked a reply from Beck, which Klopfer published in the second volume of the *Exchange* (Beck, 1937b). That article, "Some Rorschach Problems," was very critical of the Klopfer approach and clearly documents the fact that a very important schism existed between the two orientations. In the next issue of the *Exchange* a series of comments on the Beck article was published, most of which were written by followers of Klopfer or by those who tended to favor his orientation. Obviously many were very critical of Beck and some were openly hostile. Collectively they only served to strengthen Beck's resolve.

Marguerite Hertz, much to her disappointment, also became caught up in the controversy between Beck and Klopfer. Like Beck, she was among the earliest to identify the need for further development of the test and her commitment to that need never waned after her first contact with it. Her relation with Klopfer, first through correspondence and then personal contact, led her to take a positive stance toward his efforts for a consolidated approach to studying the test. But like Beck, she was committed to careful investigation.

When the Beck-Klopfer schism became so apparent in the *Exchange,* she attempted to assume the role of a mediator. Her first effort was put forth in a 1937 article that appeared in the *Exchange,* in which she noted the relatively limited data base from which Beck had drawn many of his conclusions, and at the same time criticized the Klopfer group for, "refining scoring to the extent of becoming involved in a maze of symbols. . . ." Although the article did little to reconcile Beck and Klopfer, it did point to the potential flaws of each approach. Nonetheless she remained hopeful for some more unified approach to the test and periodically would issue a new plea for reconciliation and compromise (Hertz, 1939, 1941, 1952).

In spite of the efforts of Hertz and others to strike some form of compromise between Beck and Klopfer, the schism continued to grow and by 1939 reached a point where reconciliation was no longer considered possible by either. After that time no further communication, verbal or written, was to occur between them. After his return from Switzerland, Beck was enticed by his old mentor, David Levy, to accept a joint appointment at the Michael Reese Hospital and the University of Chicago. During the period from 1944 to 1952 he published a three-volume series concerning the Rorschach, representing his approach to its use (Beck, 1944, 1945, 1952). Klopfer remained in New York, holding appointments at Columbia University and the City University of New York until the end of World War II. Then he accepted a professorship at the University of California at Los Angeles. His first book about the test appeared in 1942, coauthored by Douglas Kelley. Between 1954 and 1970 he and his colleagues also published a three-volume series which generally reflects the system he organized for using the test (Klopfer, Ainsworth, Klopfer, & Holt, 1954; Klopfer and others, 1956; Klopfer, Meyer, Brawer, & Klopfer, 1970).

Marguerite Hertz remained in Cleveland as a professor at Western University. She published more than 60 articles concerning the test plus a very elaborate set of frequency tables, which were revised several times, for use in scoring form quality (Hertz, 1936, 1942, 1951, 1961, 1970).[3] In effect, each went their own way, developing the Rorschach in the context of their own theoretical and/or empirical bias. As such the Rorschach became fragmented into three separate systems that were quite different from each other. But further diversification of the test was also to occur.

Among the participants in Klopfer's first seminar was Zygmunt Piotrowski, a postdoctoral fellow at the Neuropsychiatric Institute in New York. Piotrowski had been trained as an experimental psychologist, obtaining his Ph.D. in 1927 from the University of Poznan in Poland. He wanted to broaden his education by studying at a variety of universities, and after obtaining his degree spent two years at the Sorbonne in Paris; he then accepted a position as an instructor and postdoctoral fellow at the Columbia University College of Physicians and Surgeons. His primary objective in accepting that appointment was to learn more about neurology because, at that time he was very interested in the development of symbolic logic. He knew little about the Rorschach test, although he had been a

---

[3] Hertz began a manuscript describing her own approach to the test during the mid-1930s. It included large quantities of data collected at the Brush Foundation. When the Foundation closed, it was inadvertently destroyed, a tragedy that she described in personal correspondence (1968):

> One day it was decided to dispose of the material that was no longer in use and which the authorities felt was worthless. I was called and told that I may have my material. I went over at once with graduate students and a truck, but to my dismay I learned that my material had already been burned by mistake. All the Rorschach records, all the psychological data, all the worksheets, plus my manuscript went up in smoke. Of course the loss was irreparable.

subject, while a graduate student, for someone learning to use the test. From that experience, he had a vague notion about the nature of the test, but had little interest in it. As a postdoctoral fellow at Columbia he came into contact with many of the graduate students from psychology, and on the encouragement of one of them he decided to attend Klopfer's first seminar. The result of that somewhat casual decision was the onset of considerable intrigue with the test, not so much concerning its development as Klopfer encouraged, but more with the potential of the test to differentiate creativeness. He was especially interested in how those with neurologically related problems might function in the relatively ambiguous test situation. Piotrowski continued in a close relationship with Klopfer during the period of the first few Klopfer seminars, contributing ideas for some new scores that would become permanent fixtures in the Klopfer System. But as the Beck criticisms of the Klopfer approach became more intense, he backed away from the Klopfer group and devoted more time to studies of the neurologically impaired under the tutelage of Kurt Goldstein, and with the intent of returning to his homeland in 1939.

The German invasion of Poland, which began September 1, 1939, caused Piotrowski to alter his course and he accepted a position at the Jefferson Medical School in Philadelphia where he was able to continue his studies of the neurologically impaired and at the same time, test out some of his own ideas about the Rorschach method. Ten years later (1950) he published a monograph that contained the nucleus for his own unique approach to the test. Later he published an elaborate text about the use of the test, *Perceptanalysis* (1957), in which he integrated his own wisdoms about perceptual interpretation into a system for using the test. Thus a fourth approach to the Rorschach, different than Beck, Klopfer, or Hertz, came into being.

But even before Piotrowski completed his work with the test, another figure was to have a significant impact on the development and use of the Rorschach test in the United States. This was David Rapaport. Like so many others of his time Rapaport fled Europe in 1938, shortly after completing his Ph.D. at the Royal Hungarian Petrus at Pazmany. His orientation was strongly psychoanalytic and during his training he had become intrigued with the process of thinking, especially pathological thinking. He had some limited experience with the Rorschach, but no strong commitment to it or any other psychological test. His forte was theory, and primary among his professional dreams was to augment contemporary concepts about the functions of the ego in the classic analytic model. After coming to the United States he worked briefly at the Mount Sinai Hospital in New York and then took a position at a state hospital in Oswatomie, Kansas. His decision to accept the Kansas position came partly from financial need, but mainly because it brought him closer to the mecca of psychoanalytic thinking and practice, The Menninger Foundation. His position at Oswatomie afforded him frequent contact with Menninger's, and when a staff position opened there in 1940, he was appointed to it and became head of the psychology department two years later. His work with the Rorschach and other tests convinced him that they could be used to study ideational activity. He was also strongly influenced by the writing of Henry Murray (1938), concerning the process of projection and its relation to the study of personality.

On the encouragement of Karl Menninger he organized an elaborate project to study the efficacy of several psychological tests for the purpose of deriving a broad picture of the psychological functioning of the person. He was aware that his own training did not equip him well for psychometric research, but was able to surround himself with a brilliant research team, drawn both from the staff of the Foundation and from the graduate study body at the University of Kansas. This team included Merton Gill, who was a staff psychiatrist at the Foundation, and Roy Schafer who was an intern there and a graduate student at the University of Kansas. That project culminated in a masterfully written two-volume series, *Psychological Diagnostic Testing* (1946) which focused on the clinical applications of eight psychological tests, including the Rorschach. That work has been largely responsible for the notion that a battery or group of tests will provide the sorts of data from which an integrated and rich understanding of the person can evolve.

Rapaport was very aware of the dispute between Beck and Klopfer and took pains to avoid taking sides. The approach to the Rorschach that he ultimately selected is similar to Klopfer in some ways, yet also quite different from Klopfer and much more influenced by his allegiance to psychoanalytic propositions. The two volumes were frequented with charts and graphs that highlighted data, but the conclusions often ignored or went well beyond the data, reflecting much of Rapaport's logic about the psychology of the person. Had the Rapaport and Klopfer groups merged in their respective efforts to develop the test, the result might have been much more striking and ultimately influential concerning the use of the Rorschach; and some of Rapaport's tendencies to deviate markedly away from Rorschach's basic methodology might have been thwarted. But this was not to be, and by 1946 the seeds of a fifth approach to the test were firmly sown in ways that were incompatible with each of the other four approaches. Following the publication of the two volumes Rapaport was to drift away from psychological testing and back to his first love, developing a more detailed model about ego functioning. Nonetheless the system he had developed was to influence many users of the Rorschach and was to be marked once more by a classic work by Roy Schafer, published in 1954. That book, *Psychoanalytic Interpretation in Rorschach Testing*, not only added considerably to the basic Rorschach model that Rapaport had created, but also represents a milestone in the use of content analysis to derive a broad review of the dynamics of personality. In effect, what Rapaport began, Schafer extended enormously.

And thus during a period of slightly more than 20 years (1936–1957), five American Rorschach Systems developed. They were not completely different from one another, but most of the similarities among them consisted of the elements that each had incorporated from Rorschach's original work. Beyond those features the five systems were incredibly different, so much so in some respects that they defied comparison for many issues of scoring and the approach to interpretation (Exner, 1969). In spite of this the Rorschach *method* flourished as one of the mainstays in psychodiagnosis. Practitioners and researchers alike often tended to ignore the presence of five markedly different approaches to the method. Either they were not fully cognizant of the breadth of the differences that existed across the five separate systems, or they minimized those differences unrealistically. Most preferred to believe that a single test—*the* Rorschach—existed which could be described in laudatory or critical terms depending on one's perspective about it. That notion probably persisted because of another common thread that was to link the systems together by altering the way in which the method was characterized.

THE CONCEPT OF PROJECTION AND PROJECTIVE TECHNIQUES

During the first three decades of the twentieth century applied psychology was mainly involved with the use of tests to study intelligence, and operations related to intelligence, such as aptitudes, achievement levels, motor skills, and the like. There were methods devised to study some features of personality, but typically they were designed to measure single traits, such as introversion, dominance, flexibility, and so on. In those instances when a personality description or diagnosis was called for, a thorough interview and social history provided the bulk of data (Louttit, 1936). Tests that were used were constructed on traditional psychometric principles whereby specific scores could be judged against group means, with little or no regard for the contents of a subject's response.

Most of the early Rorschach research, such as that of Beck and Hertz, followed that same format. The concept of projection as applicable in psychological testing, had not really been formulated beyond the implications offered in Jung's Word Association Test (1910, 1918), which focused more on the issue of emotional arousal than projection as such. In Rorschach's experiment he concentrated on score frequencies to develop a psychogram. He noted that "occasionally" the content of responses might offer some information about the characteristics of the subject but expressed skepticism that this would be of major value in the method, stressing the fact that the task required adaptation rather than being one to evoke a stream of associations (pp. 122–123). It would be nearly *two decades* later before the notion of projection would be applied to Rorschach's method.

At about the same time that Klopfer began his first seminar, Morgan and Murray (1935) introduced the Thematic Apperception Test, which was based in part on the premise that people reveal something of their own personality when confronted with an ambiguous social situation. Three years later, Murray (1938) offered an elegant description of how the process of projection operates in an ambiguous stimulus situation. Murray's concept was, in part, derived from Freud's postulate about projection as a form of ego defense (i.e., the translation of internally experienced dangers into external dangers), thereby making them easier to deal with (Freud, 1894, 1896, 1911). Whereas Freud described the process as a defensive operation, Murray described it as a more natural process in which defense, as such, may or may not be relevant. Thus Murray's concept of projection was formulated simply as the tendency of people to be influenced by their needs, interests, and overall psychological organization in the cognitive translation or interpretation of perceptual inputs whenever the stimulus field included some ambiguity. This concept was neatly crystallized by Frank (1939) in a paper in which the term *projective hypothesis* was coined. Frank suggested the label "projective methods" for a variety of techniques useful to the clinician in evoking this kind of action. Obviously the Rorschach was cited as one technique with this potential.

The *Zeitgeist* of psychology and psychiatry was ripe for this movement, and very quickly the availability of methods such as the Rorschach and the TAT began to change the orientation of clinicians away from one based largely on nomothetic comparisons toward a more intense effort to study the idiography of the person. Psychodynamic theory was gaining in popularity and this change in direction, which emphasized the unique needs, interests, conflicts, and styles of the individual, afforded the clinician a new status among professionals. By the early 1940s case studies, research papers, opinions, and arguments concerning projective methods were appearing in the professional literature in a virtual torrent. During that decade and the next, many new projective techniques were developed. Louttit and Browne (1947) found that a 60% turnover occurred among the 20 tests used most frequently in clinical settings between 1935 and 1946. Sundberg (1961) repeated the Louttit and Browne survey using data through 1959, and found that the turnover rate between 1936 and 1959 had reached 76% for the 20 most frequently used tests. In the Louttit and Browne survey the Rorschach and TAT ranked fourth and fifth among the most frequently used instruments. In the Sundberg survey they ranked first and fourth, respectively. It seems clear that the emphasis on projective methodology became broadly pervasive in clinical testing during the 1940s and 1950s, and that emphasis has continued. Lubin, Wallis, and Paine (1971) collected data about test use through 1969 and found that the Rorschach ranked third and the TAT seventh. In a 1982 replication of that survey, Lubin, Larsen & Matarazzo (1984) found the Rorschach to rank fourth and the TAT fifth among the 30 most frequently used tests.

Although these surveys indicate the popularity of the Rorschach and of projective methods in general, they fail to illustrate the extensive controversy that has swirled around projective techniques. The controversy has been lengthy and often bitter, and unfortunately created a schism among many psychologists interested in measurement, individual differences, and personality assessment. One of the most unfortunate by-products of this controversy has been the tendency to categorize psychological tests into either of two classifications: (1) *objective* or (2) *projective*. The implication of this scheme is that objective tests have been developed in accord with fundamental measurement principles. In other words, they are scoreable, have been standardized, and have been demonstrated to have credible reliability and validity. Conversely, the implication regarding projective tests is that they lack some or all of the measurement features, and that data derived from them are interpreted more subjectively. Although there is some evidence for those implications, the dichotomy itself is grossly oversimplified.

Theoretically, any stimulus situation that evokes or facilitates the process of projection, as defined by Murray and Frank, can be considered a projective method. This is quite independent of whether or not the basic rules of measurement have been used in developing the test. Put more simply, any stimulus situation *that is not structured to elicit a specific class of response,* as are arithmetic tests, true-false inventories, and the like, *may evoke* the projective process. Intelligence tests are typically regarded as being objective tests because they are structured and developed in the basic psychometric framework. However, some intelligence tests include items, or whole sections, that permit a relatively open-ended form of response. For instance, several of the subtests in the Wechsler Scales are designed to permit open-ended responses. In the Comprehension subtest, the best answer to the question, "Why does the state require people to get a license before they get married?" is that it is for purposes of record keeping. If the response given is, "To prevent unsuspecting women from getting Herpes," the answer is not only less than satisfactory but also conveys some peculiarities about the respondent. A special interest or preoccupation has been projected into the response.

Many psychological tests have been designed to permit a broad range of responses, and the TAT is obviously one of them. The original Morgan and Murray format for its use included a technique of scoring for needs and presses in each story, using a scale from 1 to 5. But during the nearly 50 years since its publication, approaches to its use and interpretation have proliferated extensively. By the late 1940s at least 20 different approaches had been published, ranging from the strictly qualitative, emphasizing content analysis, to those that are more score oriented. Unfortunately, none of the latter have been pursued to the point of establishing a sturdy empirical basis for their use. Thus it is appropriate to identify the TAT as a projective test, and that is essentially what it was designed to be. But other tests, also designed to evoke the process of projection, such as some sentence-completion tests, also meet the standards for an objective test. For instance, the sentence completion developed by Rotter and Rafferty (1950) has included an elaborate format for scoring, and has been sufficiently researched to establish extensive normative data and address the issues of reliability and validity quite successfully. It is a projective technique, yet is it also an objective test, and to force classification into one or the other of the two categories is very misleading.

As noted earlier, the Rorschach was *not* designed as a projective method nor developed as such during the first two decades of use. But the nature of the test procedure and the ambiguity of its stimuli do permit a broad range of responses. And often the elaborations about responses can be very revealing about the subject. Consequently, it is not surprising that it became hailed as an important test in the projective movement of the early 1940s. As such, it was to also to become conspicuously listed among the projective tests in the objective-projective dichotomy. This does not mean that efforts to establish psychometric credibility for the test were abandoned. Beck and Hertz remained in the forefront among many researchers working toward that objective by studying the wide array of test variables. Their efforts were joined by many others who sought to demonstrate its efficacy as a projective method.

By the early 1950s, some of that research had a positive yield. Both Beck and Hertz had published useful normative data, and each had also published actuarially based tables for the discrimination of adequate form fit of responses. Several hundred very sound research articles had also appeared in the literature, offering data related to the validity of many of the scoring variables. But they constituted a very modest segment of Rorschach literature which, by that time, had burgeoned to more than 3000 books and articles. Many were clinical studies and many were research works containing negative or contradictory findings. Critics of projective methods often cited the latter as evidence for the conclusion that *the* Rorschach was of little use if gauged against psychometic or scientific standards.

Unfortunately, the rush into the projective movement had more or less overlooked the fact that there were five markedly different approaches to the test, or technique as some now prefer to call it. Both advocates and critics of the method ignored or downplayed those differences as being irrelevant to the larger issue of whether the method had merit. Many of the critics of the Rorschach, and of projective methods in general, were also critics of psychoanalytic theory and often naively linked the two. The erroneous assumption was that the process of projection, as formulated by Murray, was directly related to unconscious operations as defined in the Freudian concept (Lindzey, 1961; Sargent, 1945; Symonds, 1946; Wiggins, Renner, Clore, & Rose, 1971). Actually, very few projective methods are strictly theory based, least of all the Rorschach. But many clinicians trained during the 1940s and 1950s were strongly imbued with psychodynamic concepts and that model was commonly used as the framework for interpreting any test data.

Paul Meehl (1954) published an important work, *Clinical Versus Statistical Prediction,* that served to define and perhaps broaden the schism that was developing between those favoring a stringent psychometric approach and those aligned with a more global approach to assessment. He reviewed 20 studies, all but one of which showed that the actuarial method was equal to or better than the ''clinical'' technique, which customarily included the use of projective methods. He argued for an abandonment of the clinical approach to assessment, favoring less time-consuming techniques that are actuarilly based, such as the MMPI, to allow clinicians more time for other important work, especially psychotherapy. Later, Gough (1963) and Sawyer (1966) published surveys of predictive studies that appear to provide support for Meehl's argument, although Gough did observe that no adequate test of the clinician's forecasting skills had yet been carried out.

Holt (1958, 1970), in two excellent rejoinders to the Meehl argument, has pointed out that many of the studies cited by Meehl used extremely inadequate or even contaminated criteria. In his 1970 paper Holt called attention to the fact that another survey of predictive studies [Korman (1968)] reported positive findings for the clinical method. Holt noted, with a sense of dismay, that the Sawyer and Korman studies were published within two years of each other, but their respective bibliographies showed absolutely no overlap. That finding illustrates very well how a selective use of literature could be used to support almost any bias, and especially those concerning the objective-projective, or actuarial-clinical issues. Both Holt (1970) and Weiner (1972) have noted the focus of the Meehl position is prediction, whereas the major focus of the diagnostician is description and understanding.

In spite of the controversy, the use of the Rorschach continued to be widespread during the 1960s, a decade during which the very character of clinical psychology changed extensively. Through the 1950s the major role of the clinician was psychodiagnosis but with the early 1960s the profession began to broaden its scope and role. New models of behavior and intervention became popular, and most clinicians found themselves much more involved in planning and conducting intervention. Some universities had reduced or even discontinued training for assessment using tests by the end of the decade. But in the clinical settings *assessment* (a term that had come to replace psychodiagnosis) continued as a way of life for the professional, and the Rorschach remained one of the standard methods used. But to some extent it remained in a developmental state of limbo. In part this was because of the gradual deemphasis on psychological testing and the corresponding reductions in the number of broad-based studies that had marked the 1940s and 1950s. But the older *Rorschach problem* was probably much more responsible in fomenting this developmental lag.

INTERSYSTEM DIFFERENCES

All of the Rorschach Systems were firmly in place by 1957 and none of the systematizers were oriented toward integration or compromise. Some of the research published between 1950 and 1970 was system specific, but much was not. It was common for authors, readers, and practitioners to interpret almost any report in the literature, whether positive or negative, as applicable to *the* Rorschach. In effect, a substantial disregard for the differences among the systems existed.

A comparative analysis of the five approaches was ultimately published in *The Rorschach Systems* (Exner, 1969). That comparison was provoked by both Beck and Klopfer. Earlier, they had been encouraged to participate in a face-to-face discussion of their respective positions, but both declined. In doing so, however, each recommended that their differences be carefully reviewed in a journal article (Beck, 1961; Klopfer, 1961). That project seemed simple at the onset, yet the significant following of those trained in, or aligned with the Hertz, Piotrowski, or Rapaport-Schafer approaches to the use of the test argued for a broader comparison that would include the five approaches. Thus what was to be an article became a book and required nearly seven years to complete, because the literature concerning each of the systems was extensive, scattered, and sometimes very distorted.

The final yield of the comparison illustrated the enormous magnitude of the differences across the five Systems. For instance, only two of the five used the same seating arrangements and none of the five used the same instructions to the subject. In fact, none of the instructions to the subject, as given in one system, were even remotely similar to those used in any of the other systems. Obviously, each system collected the data of the test differently, making any comparison of the respective yields questionable. If the differences between the Systems had involved only seating and instructions, some resolution could have occurred easily through a systematic study of the effects of those differences on test performance. But the differences went far beyond these two easily studied variables.

Each systematizer had developed his or her own format for coding or scoring responses, and they were markedly different. All had included most of Rorschach's original scoring symbols, but most altered some or all of the criteria for their application. Ultimately, 15 different codes or scores were formulated among the five Systems to identify the *location* or area of the blot used in a response. *Not one* of those 15 codes was defined in the same way across all of the Systems. All five included Rorschach's scoring symbol *F* to denote that the form features or contours of the blot were important to the response, but each of the five used a different criterion to determine whether the form had been used accurately. *None* of the five scored the perception of movement the same as any of the other four, and each even defined the presence of a movement percept differently than the other four. Sixteen symbols existed among the Systems to code the presence of chromatic color in a response, but even when the same symbol appeared in more than one System, the criterion for its application was likely to be different than in the other Systems. The greatest disagreement for scoring among the Systems concerned the use of shading or achromatic color in a response. Each System had a relatively unique set of symbols and criteria for their application. This is not surprising because Rorschach's original work did not include this feature as his blots did not become shaded until the monograph was published.[4]

Obviously, the differences in scoring led to many differences concerning interpretation. They differed significantly about which scores should be calculated in a quantitative summary of the record and what relationships between scores would be important to interpretation. They differed concerning the meaningfulness of many variables and which configurations of variables might be interpretively important. In spite of their substantial differences, several interpretive postulates appeared in each of the Systems that were the same or similar. For the most part these were drawn from Rorschach's original work, but to the casual observer that common thread could easily convey the impression that the Systems were much more similar than was actually the case. Major differences existed across the Systems for issues about which Rorschach was not definitive or had offered no procedures or postulates.

The major conclusion drawn from the comparative analysis presented in *The Rorschach Systems* was that the breadth of differences among the Systems was so great that the notion of *the* Rorschach was more myth than reality. In effect, *five uniquely different Rorschach tests had been created.* They were similar only in that each used the same Swiss stimulus figures, and that each had included most of Rorschach's original scores and basic interpetive postulates, but even some of those had been uniquely embellished by some of the systematizers.

---

[4]Rorschach did become concerned with the need to score responses based on the shading features that appeared in the new blots which had been created by the publisher, Bircher. He began to use the score *(C)*, describing this in an unfinished paper that was published posthumously in 1923 on his behalf by Emil Oberholzer, and which has been included as a part of the monograph, *Psychodiagnostik* since 1942.

THE COMPREHENSIVE SYSTEM

Two questions were implicit in the yield of the comparative analysis of the five approaches to the Rorschach method: ''Which of the five demonstrated the greatest empirical sturdiness?'' and ''Which of the five had the greatest clinical utility?'' In 1968 the *Rorschach Research Foundation* was established to address those issues.[5] Among the first projects completed at the Foundation were three surveys, conducted to determine how clinicians were using the Rorschach method, and what problems in design and analysis were being encountered by those doing research with the method.

The first of the three surveys (Exner & Exner, 1972) involved the use of a relatively brief questionnaire, which was sent to 750 clinicians whose names were drawn randomly from the membership listings of the Division of Clinical Psychology of the American Psychological Association and the Society for Personality Assessment. The 30 items asked in which of the five Systems the respondent had received formal training, which of the five did he or she use in everyday practice, and a number of items pertaining to seating, instructions, scoring, and interpretation. A total of 395 (53%) usable questionnaires was returned and the results were very striking. Nearly three of every five responding had received some formal training in the Klopfer method and about one in every two in the Beck approach. Only about one in every five had received some formal training in the Piotrowski System, and about 10% had received training in either the Hertz or Rapaport methods. Although that distribution was not necessarily unexpected, two other findings were very much so.

First, nearly 22% of the respondents had abandoned scoring altogether. They used the method exclusively for the subjective analysis of contents. Second, 232 of the 308 respondents who did score the test admitted to *personalizing* the scoring, by integrating scores from one system to another system, and/or adding unique scores developed from personal experience with the test. An overwhelming majority also admitted that they did not necessarily follow the prescribed tactics for administration specified in the system from which they derived most of their scoring, and the same was true for interpretive postulates. In other words, one might administer the Rorschach using the Rapaport face-to-face seating (which was disavowed in all other systems), score responses using criteria drawn from Klopfer, Beck, and Piotrowski, and draw from at least as many sources to develop interpretive postulates concerning the resulting data.

Thus it was common to find that clinicians using the Rorschach method tended to piece together an assortment of features from the several Systems, and from their own experience with the test, to generate a final product that they identified as *the* Rorschach. The five major approaches to the method had become astronomically proliferated into almost as many different tests as there were test users.

In retrospect, the findings, although striking, should not have been surprising. Jackson and Wohl (1966) had conducted a survey of university Rorschach instructors. They found that 12% did not teach scoring, and that the variability of methods for administration, scoring, and interpretation was remarkable. They also found that approximately 60% of those teaching Rorschach in the university setting had little or no postdoctoral training with the test, and that 46% would have preferred to be teaching something else. The Jackson and Wohl data highlighted the failure to standardize the teaching of the test, emphasized that those teaching it at that time were often less well qualified to do so than

---

[5] Although the legal title, Rorschach Research Foundation, continues to exist, the Foundation has actually become more widely known by its nickname, *Rorschach Workshops*.

might be desired, and indicated that the generation of clinicians produced during the 1960s might be led to use the test in ways that could be substantially deviant from those for which the test was intended.

The second survey conducted by the Foundation involved the use of a more elaborate 90-item questionnaire, which was mailed to 200 Diplomates of the American Board of Professional Psychology. The return yielded 131 completed questionnaires, but 20 were discarded because the respondents indicated that they used the Rorschach fewer than 20 times per year. The remaining 111 questionnaires provided information about the practices and opinions of clinicians who used the test at least 20 times per year and who averaged 12 years of postdoctoral experience. Eighty-three of the respondents (75% had received formal training in at least two of the systems, usually either Beck or Klopfer plus one or two of the others, and 95 (85%) considered themselves knowledgeable in at least three of the systems. Only seven had discontinued scoring, but 62 (56%) admitted that they intermixed the procedures of administration and scoring from more than one system, and almost all used interpretive postulates drawn from more than one of the systems. In effect, the same broad proliferation of approaches indicated in the results of the first survey also existed among this group of highly qualified practitioners who were using the method with a substantial frequency. In fact, when the data from the two surveys were combined, it was revealed that only 103 of the 506 respondents (20%) faithfully followed any single system. Obviously, the divergence of Rorschach methodology into five major approaches, and the subsequent proliferation of those approaches, did little to promote a more thorough understanding of the method, as a test, or to enhance its development.

The third survey consisted of a 55-item questionnaire concerning issues of design and analysis in Rorschach research. It was mailed to 100 authors who had published research-based articles concerning the method between 1961 and 1969. The return yielded 71 usable replies. Nearly half of those responding, 34, had abandoned Rorschach research in favor of a different topic. Those persisting were typically focusing their efforts on the study of single scores or the development of new scores to address specific issues such as anxiety, body boundary, cognitive development, ego defense, and the like. The majority had received training in more than one system, but almost all were following research plans specific to a system. The results highlighted three broad areas of concern to most investigators.

The first concerned difficulties in recruiting subjects and/or the problem of requiring multiple examiners to avoid an experimenter bias effect. The second involved the complexities of data analysis, especially the applicability of parametric statistics to some data and/or the problem of controlling for the number of responses. The third represented the most common complaint, that of adequacy of control groups and/or the lack of extensive normative data to use for general comparisons. The respondents uniformly agreed that the complexities of the Rorschach often generated more discouragement than reinforcement to the researcher. Most identified important research objectives concerning the method, but many also elaborated on the difficulties that made the achievement of those goals seemingly impossible.

Concurrent with the three surveys, another project was completed at the Foundation in 1970 which involved a systematic review of all published Rorschach research. The purpose of the project was to categorize, cross-reference, and evaluate studies as they related to the variables of administration, scoring, and the interpretive postulates that had evolved in each of the five Systems. By 1970 the Rorschach literature consisted of more than 4000 articles and 29 books, plus Rorschach's monograph. In spite of that voluminous literature, a surprisingly large number of issues had not been researched systematically. For example, seating arrangements had never been subject to experimental manipulation and only one study compared different instructions, and for only two systems. No research had been published for 16 scoring variables and only a handful of studies had appeared concerning six other scores. Similarly, many interpretive postulates had not been addressed through research, and for many others, the data were equivocal because of problems in research design and/or data analysis. In fact, problems in design and/or analysis marked a very large number of the published research studies concerning the Rorschach.

About 2100 of the more than 4000 articles that had appeared concerning the Rorschach were purportedly research works. When scrutinized against *contemporary* standards for adequacy of design and/or data analysis however, more than 600 were judged to be seriously flawed to the extent that the conclusions probably were not valid. Another group of nearly 800 also contained flaws that rendered them of questionable value. It is important to emphasize that those findings should not be interpreted to mean that most Rorschach research was shoddy, incompetent, or illogical. The majority of studies reviewed in this project were published between 1938 and 1958, an era in which the tactics of design and data analysis for *all* of psychology were continually being improved so that works deemed adequate by the standards of one period might be considerably less sophisticated when compared with the methodology of another. This was especially the case for much clinical research. For instance, by 1970, 24 studies had been published addressing the issue of "blind analysis" in Rorschach interpretation. Although all were well intended, no more than nine of the 24 would meet contemporary standards for adequacy of design to test the issue. Similarly, 26 studies were published prior to 1970 focusing on the stimulus characteristics of the blots. Less than half would be considered to be free of flaws by contemporary standards.

It is also important to note that the project to evaluate the Rorschach literature yielded more than 700 research works which were clearly methodologically appropriate, and the data from those studies had been carefully and appropriately analyzed. Collectively, those works provided a data bank from which many elements of the various systems could be evaluated. The majority of these reported positive findings, but many also reported negative or equivocal results. In some instances, two or more adequately designed and analyzed studies reported contradictory findings. Many of these were works involving small samples, a finding that argued for replication using a larger number of subjects.

The most important project undertaken at the Foundation during the first two years was the creation of a data pool to permit direct comparison of the five Systems. By early 1970, that pool consisted of 835 Rorschach records. These protocols were submitted by 153 psychologists in response to a mailing request for 600 members of the Division of Clinical Psychology of the American Psychological Association and instructors of Rorschach courses at eight universities. The 835 were selected from more than 1300 that were submitted.[6] Each was accompanied by a data questionnaire concerning the demographic features of the subject, purpose of the examination, and information concerning the training and test procedures of the examiner. The protocols included 204 from nonpatient subjects and 631 from a variety of inpatient and outpatient psychiatric groups. When subdivided for the procedures of administration by system, the breakdown was: Klopfer, 329; Beck,

[6]Those selected to receive the mailing were professionals whose place of work was shown in the *Directory* of the American Psychological Association to be a hospital or clinic. A total of 1342 protocols was submitted but 507 were discarded because of illegibility, no completed data sheet, no inquiry, or because the procedures used in taking the record were grossly different from those recommended in any of the five systems.

310; Rapaport, 78; Piotrowski, 66; and Hertz, 52. Numerous comparisons of the records of each system with the others were completed and most of the results confirmed the main operational hypothesis, namely, that protocols of one system would be substantially different from those of the other systems in several ways. For instance, they differed significantly for the average number of responses, a finding that was not surprising because each system included instructions and procedures for administering the test that were different than each of the other systems.

By early 1971 the data accumulated at the Foundation tended to support three broad conclusions. First, that the intersystem differences in procedures did produce five relatively different kinds of records. Second, that each system included some scores, scoring criteria, and interpretive postulates for which no empirical support existed or for which negative findings had been discovered. Third, that each of the systems did include many empirically sturdy elements. In fact, if any system were applied faithfully for administration, scoring, and interpretation, a considerable positive yield would result. On the other hand, some of that positive yield might be offset by the flaws of the system, either in scoring or interpretation.

Those findings, plus the fact that the surveys concerning the use of the test indicated that fewer than 20% faithfully followed any single system, led to a decision to alter the main objective of the Foundation. The thrust was changed from one designed to study each system for its merits and liabilities to one designed to integrate the features of all systems for which empirically defensible data existed or could be established. During the next three years the pool of protocols was increased to nearly 1200, and more than 150 investigations were completed concerning the array of elements involved in the use of the Rorschach.

In the early phases of the project focus was on fundamental issues such as seating, instructions, recording and inquirying responses, and the selection of the codes or scores to be used. The issue of interscorer reliability was broached so that no scoring category was included in the "new" system unless a minimum .85 level could be achieved easily for groups of 10 to 15 scorers across at least 10 to 20 protocols in which the target score occurred frequently. Interestingly, this caused the initial rejection of many seemingly useful scores that have subsequently been added to the system by using a revision of the criteria for their application. Each of dozens of interpretive postulates was explored and no procedure or score was included in the new system unless it met fundamental requirements for validation. In the course of this research several new approaches to coding or scoring answers evolved, and several derivations of scores for interpretive purposes were discovered. Computer technology aided enormously to the search for *the* Rorschach. It permitted easy data storage and very complex analyses to be performed quickly, which only a decade earlier could have required inordinate periods.

The beginning of the final product was published in 1974 under the appropriate rubric, *Comprehensive System,* for indeed it does reflect an integration of the hard won, empirically demonstrable wisdoms that marked the growth of the test from the time of Rorschach's monograph in 1921 to the most current thinking and research of the early 1970s. It represents the works of all of the systematizers, plus the findings of many dedicated researchers who contributed to the study of a complex tactic used to generate information about personality structure and functioning.

As more information about the Rorschach method has evolved, a fundamental reality pervades. The method has not changed very much, if at all. The same 10 inkblots constitute the primary stimulus elements that were noted more than 60 years ago when Rorschach pursued his experiment. What has changed is that his experimental method has developed into a test. Its psychometric properties have been established and most of the other basic requirements for a psychological test have been met. Much of the research that has been conducted on and about it, especially during the past 15 years, indicates that it is *not* a magical x-ray of the mind, as some have purported it to be. Rather, it is a procedure that provokes many of the psychological operations of the subject. There is no question that the process of projection often occurs during the test, but it is misleading to label it simplistically as a projective technique. It is much more than that, and as the data concerning it have evolved through research, it has become clearer how the test stimuli provoke a complex set of psychological features into action. Some understanding of that process is necessary for the user of the test, because it helps to clarify why certain procedures are important, why scoring is crucial, and how interpretive postulates are generated.

REFERENCES

Beck, S. J. (1936) Autism in Rorschach scoring: a feeling comment. *Character & Personality*, **5**, 83–85.

Beck, S. J. (1937a) *Introduction to the Rorschach method: A manual of personality study*. American Orthopsychiatric Association Monograph, **1**.

Beck, S. J. (1937b) Some recent research problems. *Rorschach Research Exchange*, **2**, 15–22.

Beck, S. J. (1944) *Rorschach's Test I: Basic Processes*. New York: Grune & Stratton.

Beck, S. J. (1945) *Rorshach's Test II: A variety of personality pictures*. New York: Grune & Stratton.

Beck, S. J. (1952) *Rorschach's Test III: Advances in interpretation*. New York: Grune & Stratton.

Beck, S. J. (1961) Personal communication.

Binder, H. (1932) Die helldunkeldeutungen in psychodiagnostischen experiment von Rorschach. *Schweiz Archives Neurologie und Psychiatrie*, **30**, 1–67.

Binet, A., and Henri, V. (1895–1896) La psychologie individuelle. *Annuee Psychologie*, **2**, 411–465.

Dearborn, G. (1897) Blots of ink in experimental psychology. *Psychological Review*, **4**, 390–391.

Dearborn, G. (1898) A study of imaginations. *American Journal of Psychology*, **9**, 183–190.

Ellenberger, (1954) Hermann Rorschach, M.D. 1884–1922. *Bulletin of the Menninger Clinic*, **18**, 171–222.

Exner, J. E. (1969) *The Rorschach Systems*. New York: Grune & Stratton.

Exner, J. E. (1974) *The Rorschach: A Comprehensive system. Volume 1*. New York: Wiley.

Exner, J. E., and Exner, D. E. (1972) How clinicians use the Rorschach. *Journal of Personality Assessment*, **36**, 403–408

Frank, L. K. (1939) Projective methods for the study of personality. *Journal of Psychology*, **8**, 389–413.

Freud, S. (1894) The anxiety neurosis. *Collected papers*. Volume 1. London: Hogarth Press, 1953, 76–106.

Freud, S. (1896) Further remarks on the defense of neuropsychoses. *Collected papers*. Volume 1. London: Hogarth Press, 1953, 155–182.

Freud, S. (1911) Psychoanalytic notes on an autobiographical account of a case of paranoia. *Collected papers*. Volume 3. London: Hogarth Press, 1953, 387–396.

Gough, H. G. (1963) Clinical versus statistical prediction in psychology. In L. Postman (Ed.) *Psychology in the making*. New York: Knopf.

Hertz, M. R. (1936) *Frequency tables to be used in scoring the Rorschach ink-blot test*. Brush Foundation, Western Reserve University.

Hertz, M. R. (1937) Discussion on "Some recent Rorschach problems." *Rorschach Research Exchange*, **2**, 53–65.

Hertz, M. R. (1939) On the standardization of the Rorschach method. *Rorschach Research Exchange, 3,* 120–133.

Hertz, M. R. (1941) Rorschach: Twenty years after. *Rorschach Research Exchange, 5,* 90–129.

Hertz, M. R. (1942) *Frequency Tables for Scoring Rorschach Responses.* Cleveland: Western Reserve University Press.

Hertz, M. R. (1952) *Frequency Tables for Scoring Rorschach Responses.* Cleveland: Western Reserve University Press.

Hertz, M. R. (1952) The Rorschach: Thirty years after. In D. Brower, and L. E. Abt (Eds.) *Progress in Clinical Psychology.* New York: Grune & Stratton.

Hertz, M. R. (1961) *Frequency Tables for Scoring Rorschach Responses.* Cleveland: Western Reserve University Press.

Hertz, M. R. (1970) *Frequency Tables for Scoring Rorschach Responses.* Cleveland: Case Western Reserve University Press.

Holt, R. R. (1958) Clinical and statistical prediction: A reformulation and some new data. *Journal of Abnormal and Social Psychology, 56,* 1–12.

Holt, R. R. (1970) Yet another look at clinical and statistical prediction: Or, is clinical psychology worthwhile? *American Psychologist, 25,* 337–349.

Jackson, C. W., and Wohl, J. (1966) A survey of Rorschach teaching in the university. *Journal of Projective Techniques and Personality Assessment, 30,* 115–134.

Jensen, A. R. (1958) Personality. *Annual Review of Psychology, 9,* 395–422.

Jung, C. G. (1910) The association method. *American Journal of Psychology, 21,* 219–269.

Jung, C. G. (1918) *Studies in Word Association.* London: Heineman.

Kerner, J. (1857) *Klexographien:* Part VI. In R. Pissen (Ed.) *Kerners Werke.* Berlin: Boag & Co.

Kirkpatrick, E. A. (1900) Individual tests of school children *Psychological Review, 7,* 274–280.

Klopfer, B. (1937) The present status of the theoretical development of the Rorschach method. *Rorschach Research Exchange, 1,* 142–147.

Klopfer, B. (1961) Personal communication.

Klopfer, B., Ainsworth, M. D., Klopfer, W. G., and Holt, R. R. (1954) *Developments in the Rorschach Technique. I. Technique and Theory.* Yonkers-on-Hudson, N.Y.: World Book.

Klopfer, B. et al. (1956) *Developments in the Rorschach Technique. II. Fields of Application.* Yonkers-on-Hudson, N.Y.: World Book.

Klopfer, B., and Kelley, D. (1942) *The Rorschach Technique.* Yonkers-on-Hudson, N.Y.: World Book.

Klopfer, B., Meyer, M. M., Brawer, F. B., and Klopfer, W. G. (1970) *Developments in the Rorschach Technique. III. Aspects of Personality Structure.* New York: Harcourt Brace Jovanovich.

Klopfer, B., and Sender, S. (1936) A system of refined scoring symbols. *Rorschach Research Exchange, 1,* 19–22.

Korman, A. K. (1968) The prediction of managerial performance. *Personnel Psychology, 21,* 295–322.

Lindzey, G. (1961) *Projective Techniques and Cross Cultural Research.* New York: Appleton-Century-Crofts.

Louttit, C. M. (1936) *Clinical Psychology.* New York: Harper & Row.

Louttit, C. M., and Browne, C. G. (1947) Psychometric instruments in psychological clinics. *Journal of Consulting Psychology, 11,* 49–54.

Lubin, B., Wallis, R. R., and Paine, C. (1971) Patterns of psychological test usage in the United States: 1935–1969. *Professional Psychology, 2,* 70–74.

Lubin, B., Larsen, R. M., and Matarazzo, J. D. (1984) Patterns of psychological test usage in the United States: 1935–1982. *American Psychologist, 39,* 451–454.

Meehl, P. E. (1954) *Clinical Versus Statistical Prediction.* Minneapolis: University of Minnesota Press.

Morgan, C., and Murray, H. A. (1935) A method for investigating fantasies: The Thematic Apperception Test. *Archives of Neurology and Psychiatry, 34,* 289–306.

Murray, H. A. (1938) *Explorations in Personality.* New York: Oxford University Press.

Parsons, C. J. (1917) Children's interpretation of inkblots (A study on some characteristics of children's imagination). *British Journal of Psychology,* **9,** 74–92.

Piotrowski, Z. (1950) A Rorschach compendium: Revised and enlarged. In, J. A. Brussel et al. *A Rorschach Training Manual.* Utica, N.Y.: State Hospitals Press.

Piotrowski, Z. (1957) *Perceptanalysis.* New York: Macmillan.

Pyle, W. H. (1913) *Examination of School Children.* New York: Macmillan.

Pyle, W. H. (1915) A psychological study of bright and dull children. *Journal of Educational Psychology,* **17,** 151–156.

Rapaport, D., Gill, M., and Schafer, R. (1946) *Diagnostic Psychological Testing. Volumes 1 & 2.* Chicago: Yearbook Publishers

Rorschach, H. (1921) *Psychodiagnostik.* Bern: Bircher (Transl. Hans Huber Verlag, 1942).

Rotter, J. B., and Rafferty, J. E. (1950) *Manual: The Rotter Incomplete Sentences Blank.* New York: Psychological Corporation.

Rybakov, T. (1911) *Atlas for Experimental Research on Personality.* Moscow: University of Moscow.

Sargent, H. (1945) Projective methods: Their origins, theory, and application in personality research. *Psychological Bulletin,* **42,** 257–293.

Sawyer, J. (1966) Measurement and prediction, clinical and statistical. *Psychological Bulletin,* **66,** 178–200.

Schafer, R. (1954) *Psychoanalytic Interpretation in Rorschach Testing.* New York: Grune & Stratton.

Sundberg, N. D. (1961) The practice of psychological testing in clinical services in the United States. *American Psychologist,* **16,** 79–83.

Symonds, P. M. (1946) *The Dynamics of Human Adjustment.* New York: Appleton-Century-Crofts.

Weiner, I. B. (1972) Does psychodiagnosis have a future? *Journal of Personality Assessment,* **36,** 534–546.

Whipple, G. M. (1914) *Manual of Mental and Physical Tests.* Two volumes. Baltimore: Warwick & York.

Wiggins, J. S., Renner, K. E., Clore, J. L., and Rose, R. J. (1971) *The Psychology of Personality.* Reading, Mass.: Addison-Wesley.

Zubin, J., Eron, L. D., and Schumer, F. (1965) *An Experimental Approach to Projective Techniques.* New York: Wiley.

CHAPTER 2

The Nature of the Rorschach

It is very important for anyone using the Roschach test to understand how it works. How can the responses to 10 inkblots provide much information about an individual? This is an intriguing issue that has often baffled advocates of the test and has sometimes provided grist for the mill of the skeptic. At first glance it does seem incredulous. Such skepticism was probably increased as the projective movement reached its zenith. During that time major emphasis was on content analysis, and thus the test was usually conceptualized in terms of the projective process. Some attempted a direct symbolic interpretation of specific kinds of contents (Phillips & Smith, 1953). Others sought to equate the blot stimuli with universal symbolic meanings, generating faulty notions about a father card, mother card, sex card, interpersonal card, and so on (Halpern, 1953; Meer & Singer, 1950; Pascal, Ruesch, Devine, & Suttell, 1950). Although emphasis on projected material in interpretation served to enhance the usefulness of the test, it also detracted from a broader understanding of the true nature of the test, and detracted from the research on Rorschach's original thinking about the method.

RORSCHACH'S CONCEPT OF THE METHOD

The process of the test obviously intrigued Rorschach and he did formulate some hypotheses related to the response operation. He postulated that responses are formed through an integration of memory traces with the sensations created by the stimulus figure. He argued that this integration, or effort to match the sensations of the stimulus with existing engrams, is a *consciously realized* operation. In other words, the subject is aware that the blot is not identical to objects stored in memory. Consequently, the method requires a willingness by the subject to identify the blot, or blot area, as being something that it is not, but to which it has some similarity. He described this as an associational process. He postulated that differences in "thresholds" exist among people for the ability to assimilate or integrate the stimulus sensation with the existing engrams. He believed that the differences in threshold were the main cause for the broad array of responses that occurs. It was on this premise that he rejected the notion that unconscious elements might be influential in forming a response. He viewed the response process as one of perception and/or apperception.

He also argued, quite persuasively, that imagination had little or nothing to do with the *basic* process of the test, but that it could manifest in embellishments to responses. He felt that these reflected the creative quality of imagination. It seems likely that if Rorschach had lived long enough to consider Murray's concept of projection (1938), or Frank's formulation of the *Projective Hypothesis,* he would have been intrigued with them as relevant to the response process. But it is equally likely that he would have disavowed the concepts as representing a major component in the response process. Whatever might have been had Rorschach lived longer, there is no question that the nature of the test, and of the response process, were sorely neglected areas of research for several decades following his death. This neglect probably contributed substantially to the broad divergence that occurred among those attempting to develop the test. Interestingly, as that much-needed research has accumulated, considerable support for most of Rorschach's postulates has been generated. It would seem that he was correct in his basic hypotheses about the response process, but he probably oversimplified the cause for the great diversity that occurs for responses. The method, or test, is considerably more complex than he conceived of it. Numerous operations occur before a response is actually delivered, and they occur within a time frame that few recognized during the early days of the development of the test.

THE RORSCHACH AS A PROBLEM-SOLVING TASK

Rorschach was apparently correct in his assumption that the response is formulated after some awareness that the blot is not identical to existing memory traces. But the subject has some awareness of this well before the first blot is exposed. Cattell (1951) probably best described the task of the subject who is taking the Rorschach for the first time, in his effort to describe the projective situation. He noted that in this situation the subject is required to provide something that is not actually there. Essentially, the task requires the subject to "misperceive" the stimulus, according to Cattell, and through that misperception is encouraged to project something of himself or herself into the response.

Although Cattell may be correct in describing the projective situation, that description can be quite misleading when applied to the circumstances of the Rorschach, depending on whether the term *misperceive* is translated to mean how the stimulus is *translated* or how the stimulus is *identified*. This is a very important distinction, because the first implies that the subject neglects the fact that the stimulus is an inkblot, whereas the second does not carry that implication. Rorschach, of course, believed that identification is one of the essential operations in the response, but he also encountered subjects in his experiment who would concretely and redundantly name the blots. He concluded that they were so seriously debilitated by reason of intellectual limitations, neurological impairment, or active psychosis that the associational or integrative operations failed or decayed.

Most professionals who have used the Rorschach extensively will have encountered the kinds of subjects who are so impaired that they simply cannot respond to the task, or who are so detached from reality that they offer only hallucinatory type of responses when confronted with a blot (e.g., "My God, that sounds terrible, take it away."). But these are very rare subjects. The overwhelming majority of those who take the test are fully aware that they are responding to an inkblot. As noted earlier, that awareness is reinforced when the test is introduced.

Most examiners will usually alert the adult subject by saying something such as, "Now we are going to do the inkblot test." But even if the introduction to the test does not include the use of the word *inkblot,* as is commonly the case when testing younger clients, one would be hard-pressed to argue that the subject is not aware of the fact. For instance, when the records of 500 patient and nonpatient 5- and 6-year-olds were reviewed, it was found that 207 gave comments or responses at the onset implying an awareness of the nature of the stimulus (Exner, 1980). These varied from responses such as, ''It's an inkblot'' or ''It's a bunch of ink,'' to comments such as, ''I know how to make these'' or ''We make prettier ones than this.'' In reality, those children gave the only truly correct answer. The stimulus is only an inkblot! But if that correct answer is delivered as the *first* response, it is *not* accepted. Instead, the examiner encourages some other identification, usually by saying, ''Yes, I know. This is the inkblot test, but what might it be?''

In effect, the nature of the test situation forces the subject to convert the blot into something that it is not. A *problem-solving* situation is created which requires some violation of reality. At the same time the subject remains concerned with his or her own personal integrity. Thus the requirement to *misidentify* the stimulus provokes a complex of psychological operations into activity that ultimately culminates in decision making and the delivery of answers.

DECISION CHOICES

The problem posed by the need to misidentify the stimulus would be quite simple for most subjects if only one alternative to the answer ''inkblot'' occurred, but that is not the case. Many misidentifications, or potential answers, are formed very quickly after the blot is presented. Thus one component of the problem situation that the subject must address in taking the test is which of the potential answers to verbalize and which to discard.

Interestingly, for several decades after the test was published, most who used and researched it were unaware of the substantial frequency of potential answers that are available to most subjects. There are probably several reasons for this, beginning with Rorschach's report of his experiment. He noted that most subjects gave between 15 and 30 responses, with depressed, ''sullen or unobliging'' subjects tending to give the fewest. He noted that most subjects delay before giving answers and suggested that those who gave several responses very quickly were probably ''scattered'' in their perception or ideation. Rorschach did not record reaction times for first responses, or total times per blot, but his notion of ''scattered,'' plus another hypothesis concerning ''shock,'' caused those who followed him to stress the faithful recording of those times. As a result, many interpretive hypotheses were formulated about short and long records, and about reaction time data. The latter became particularly widespread across the several systems.

Rorschach used the term *color shock* to describe those instances in which a subject appeared to have considerable difficulty in forming a response to Card VIII, the first of the totally chromatic blots, although responding to the prior blots at a seemingly natural rate. He speculated that this apparent helplessness indicated some form of emotional repression. All of the systematizers, and many other researchers of the test were quick to incorporate and expand this concept to other chromatically colored blots, and also to formulate the notion of ''gray-black shock'' with regard to the achromatic blots. The latter was postulated to equate with forms of anxiety, whereas both were thought to represent neurotic characteristics (Beck, 1945; Klopfer & Kelley, 1942; Miale & Harrower-Erikson, 1940; Piotrowski, 1957). A variety of lists was developed that hypothetically identified those test characteristics related to color or gray-black shock. Although the lists differed, each included as the first or main feature a long reaction time for the first response to a blot. The implication, in both concepts, was that the subject was somehow traumatized by the blot features and therefore struggled to form a response.

A second factor that tended to mislead most Rorschachers about the availability of potential answers has been the variety of published norms. Although they have varied depending on the system employed, the mean number of responses for adults has generally ranged from about 22 to 32 responses, with standard deviations ranging from five to eight (Beck, Beck, Levitt, & Molish, 1961; Exner, 1974, 1978). The data concerning children yielded even lower means for R (Ames, Learned, Metraux, & Walker, 1952; Ames, Metraux, & Walker, 1971; Beck, 1961; Exner, 1978; Exner & Weiner, 1982). These data appeared to indicate that the average subject might be expected to find, or misidentify, two or three objects per blot, and few would have argued with the position that some subjects have difficulty formulating more than one answer to some of the blots. That conclusion was afforded further support by hundreds of research studies in which the average number of responses given by the subjects studied would generally fall within the "normal" range.

Another element contributing to the false notion that subjects of the test would formulate only a small number of answers per blot was the infrequent (but not uncommon) occurrence of card rejections—that is, instances in which subjects would report that they could not find or see anything other than the blot itself. Rorschach noted that some of his subjects did give "refusals" and suggested that this might be the result of an insurmountable blocking process. Klopfer and Kelley (1942) tended to agree with that postulate, but Beck (1945) argued that the rejection, or tendency to reject, might also be generated by problems in the perceptual organizing process, especially for the more "difficult" blots. This issue stimulated several interesting studies on card difficulty in which *reaction time* was used as an index of the difficulty or complexity of the stimuli (Dubrovner, Von-Lackum, & Jost, 1950; Matarazzo & Mensh, 1952; Meer, 1955; Rabin & Sanderson, 1947). Meer's findings were based on a transformation of reaction times and form accuracy data from 12 studies to formulate decisions about blot difficulty levels. Frequency data collected at the Rorschach Research Foundation suggest that most of his conclusions were correct concerning blot difficulty and/or complexity levels (Exner, Martin, & Cohen, 1983). However, findings such as those reported by Meer only served to reinforce the faulty notion that subjects often had to struggle to find or "misidentify" more than one object in each blot. Few practitioners or researchers entertained the notion that most subjects form potential answers quickly and with relative ease, yet this fact appears to be supported by a series of studies regarding the input-output process. Possibly the most important of these studies was not published until 57 years after Rorschach's monograph had been published.

The Range of Potential Responses   An issue of concern during the development of the Comprehensive System was the impact of the examiner on the subject. A considerable literature had evolved, suggesting that some features of Rorschach responses can be altered under conditions that vary from the standard procedures. For example, different instructional sets, such as asking the subject to find more things, find things moving, find more small objects, and so on, will usually produce more of the kinds of responses for which the set is established (Coffin, 1941; Hutt, Gibby, Milton, & Potthurst, 1950; Abramson, 1951; Gibby, 1951). Similarly, it has been demonstrated that differences among the basic instructions used by the various Rorschach Systematizers will produce significant differences in the average length of a record.

Goetcheus (1967) used 16 examiners in a crossover design to test for differences between the Beck and Klopfer instructions. Each examiner administered eight tests using the Beck instructions and eight using the Klopfer instructions. She found that the Beck instructions, which included, "Tell me everything you see," produced records that, on the average were six responses longer than those administered by the Klopfer format. One of the early studies at the Rorschach Research Foundation involved the comparison of 346 protocols representing the procedures used in the five different systems. The pool consisted of 75, each collected using the Beck and Klopfer procedures, 78 collected by the Rapaport method, 66 using the Piotrowski system, and 52 using the Hertz method. The Klopfer instructions, which are essentially the same as those used by Rorschach in his experiment, and also adopted for use in the Comprehensive System, produced the lowest average number of answers, 23.9. The other instructional formats, all of which encourage subjects to give more answers, turn cards, practice before beginning, or supplement information after each card, produced significantly more answers (Beck = 31.2, Hertz = 32.9, Piotrowski = 33.8, Rapaport = 36.4).

Several studies have also demonstrated that reinforcement, both verbal and nonverbal, can alter the frequencies of some kinds of responses (Wickes, 1956; Gross, 1959; Dinoff, 1960; Magnussen, 1960; Hersen & Greaves, 1971). As it turns out, all, or most all of these designs were tapping into the fact that most subjects generate many misidentifications, or potential responses when confronted with the blot. Although some hints of this fact can be culled from some of the early research on the response process, no one did so. It was not until the late 1970s that this fact became apparent, causing a much more careful review of the operations involved in the response process. This occurred somewhat serendipitously.

In a pilot investigation concerning the effects of reinforcement, two groups of 10 subjects each were instructed to give as many responses as they could, with a time limit of 60 seconds per blot (Exner & Armbruster, 1974). The subjects were reinforced with a payment of 10 cents per response, which was paid immediately as each response was delivered. The first group consisted of 10 nonpatients, and they averaged 104 answers to the 10 blots, with a range of 68 to 147 responses. The second group consisted of 10 nonschizophrenic outpatients. They averaged 113 responses, with a range of 71 to 164 answers. These strikingly large numbers of answers raised several questions. First, to what extent did the reinforcement of the dimes alter the Rorschach response process? Second, to what extent did the exposure time of 60 seconds force subjects to rescan the stimulus field, thereby forming responses that might not have been formulated under the standard administration conditions. Third, did the reinforcement condition cause subjects to violate the use of accurate form more frequently than might be typical? Finally, because only one examiner was used in the pilot, would subjects give unusually large numbers of responses if several examiners were used? These questions led to the design of a more sophisticated study.

Exner, Armbruster, & Mittman (1978) used 12 experienced examiners to administer the test to five groups of 20 subjects each: (1&2) 40 adult nonpatients, ranging in age from 20 to 41 years, subdivided into two groups of 20 each by a median split of their distribution of scores on the K Scale of the MMPI; (3) 20 nonpatient children, ranging in age from 11 to 13 years; (4) 20 inpatient depressives, aged 29 to 51 years; and (5) 20 inpatient schizophrenics, ranging in age from 24 to 42 years. None had been administered the Rorschach previously. The examiners were randomly assigned to subjects so that none tested more than four subjects from a single group or more than 10 subjects in all. All of the subjects had volunteered to participate in a *standardization* study concerning the inkblot test. The procedure followed the standardized method, except that prior to the onset of the association period each subject was told that he or she would have the blot for a 60-

second interval, which would be terminated by a beep from a timer, and that during that time the subject should report as many things as he or she could find in the blot.

The responses were audio recorded, and a silent signal was entered on the tape at 15-second intervals. The examiners would rewind the tape after the responses to all 10 cards had been given, and play them back, one at a time, to inquire for the location of the responses. This permitted a review of the answers for the accurate use of form. The average number of responses given by each group, to all 10 blots, is shown in Table 1, which also shows the average number given during the first 15-second interval, the second 15-second interval, and the last 30 seconds of exposure.

Table 1.   Average Number of Responses Given by Each of Five Groups During Four Intervals of Blot Exposure

	First 15 Seconds		Second 15 Seconds		Second 30 Seconds		Total 60 Seconds	
	M	SD	M	SD	M	SD	M	SD
Nonpatients, upper half, MMPI K scale $N = 20$	30.4	4.1	31.2	5.8	21.7	4.1	83.3[a]	9.2
Nonpatients, lower half MMPI K scale $N = 20$	38.1	6.8	32.2	6.1	30.4	7.8	100.6	10.4
Nonpatient children $N = 20$	38.9	7.1	30.7	4.3	24.5	8.3	94.1	9.8
Inpatient schizophrenics $N = 20$	22.7[b]	6.2	18.1[b]	5.1	22.4	6.7	63.2[b]	9.4
Inpatient depressives $N = 20$	14.8[b]	4.4	17.1[b]	5.7	19.3	7.8	51.2[b]	7.8

[a] Statistically fewer than nonpatient adult group scoring in the lower half of the MMPI K Scale distribution, $p < .05$

[b] Statistically significant difference from nonpatient groups, $p < .05$

The average number of responses given under *standard* procedures is about 22. The data in Table 1 indicate that all five groups gave more than two to four times that number under this experimental condition. The lowest average number was given by the depressed group, which under standard conditions would be expected to give fewer than 18 answers. The data are even more revealing when the average number of responses given during the first 15 seconds of blot exposure are examined. The three nonpatient groups all gave at least one-third more answers during that interval than is usually the case under the standard conditions of administration, in which most subjects retain the cards for between 40 and 55 seconds. Both psychiatric groups gave at least as many answers during the first 15 seconds of exposure to the blots as they would be expected to give when the test is administered under standardized conditions.

In addition to the striking finding that subjects can give many answers when instructed to do so, the data regarding the appropriate use of form are quite important. Table 2 shows the mean X + %'s for each of the groups for the total exposure period, plus those for the first and second 15 seconds, and last 30 seconds of exposure. Table 2 also includes the average number of Popular responses given by the groups during each of those intervals.

Table 2.   Means for X + % and Popular Responses for Each of Five Groups During Four Intervals of Blot Exposure

	First 15 Seconds		Second 15 Seconds		Second 30 Seconds		Total 60 Seconds	
	M	SD	M	SD	M	SD	M	SD
Nonpatients, upper half, MMPI *K* scale N = 20								
X + %	88.9	11.1	81.4	9.9	89.3	9.6	85.1	10.2
P	5.2	2.1	3.5	1.3	3.2	1.1	10.8	2.8
Nonpatients, lower half MMPI *K* scale N = 20								
X + %	83.2	9.7	79.6	7.6	78.1	8.7	79.9	9.8
P	5.0	1.9	2.4	1.1	1.9	0.9	9.3	3.1
Nonpatient children N = 20								
X + %	84.6	7.8	80.1	8.5	84.1	7.8	83.3	8.1
P	5.3	1.8	2.4	1.1	2.0	1.1	9.7	2.2
Inpatient schizophrenics N = 20								
X + %	63.2[a]	10.8	54.6[a]	11.7	49.3[a]	11.4	53.6[b]	12.7
P	2.4[a]	1.6	1.7	1.0	4.3[a]	1.7	8.4	3.8
Inpatient Depressives N = 20								
X + %	77.1	6.8	72.3	7.1	68.7	8.3	71.9	8.9
P	6.2	3.1	3.1	1.4	0.9	0.7	10.2	4.3

[a] Statistically significant difference from all other groups, $p < .05$.

As revealed in Table 2, none of the four nonschizophrenic groups violated form accuracy markedly during any of the intervals of exposure to the blots. The X + % does decline slightly for the Low K nonpatient group, but not significantly so. The High K nonpatient group and the nonpatient children actually show a higher mean X + % during the last 30 seconds of blot exposure than during the second 15-second interval. The depressives also declined slightly from the first 15 seconds to the last 30 seconds, as did the schizophrenics, but these reductions are not statistically or interpretively significant. In effect, each group gave about as many responses with well-defined and appropriate use of form during the first quarter minute as during the entire time of exposure, or stated differently, the significant majority of responses given by all but the schizophrenic group approximated the contours of the blot area used in the response.

The data concerning the Popular answers are also important in this context. Popular answers are the ones given most frequently. The criterion for a response to be defined as Popular is that it occurs at least once in every three records. At the time of this study 17 Popular responses were listed.[1] All of the nonschizophrenic groups averaged about eight Popular answers during the first 30 seconds of exposure, with about two-thirds of those

[1] Current norms show only 13 responses meeting the criterion for popularity. The number of Popular responses can be expected to differ slightly across cultures, and within a culture over extended time intervals.

occurring during the first 15 seconds with the blots. Thus with a relatively brief exposure period, the nonschizophrenic subjects gave as many or more answers than is customary when the test is given under standard conditions, and they also gave the types of answers that are commonly given under the standard conditions.

To say that these findings were surprising is an understatement! The average time for the first response to most blots for most of the groups was less than 2 seconds, a phenomenon Rorschach thought represented scattered perception or ideation; and none of the 100 subjects attempted to reject a blot! There is a considerable variance for the average number of answers per card, but even that performance is relatively consistent across groups when the ratio of responses to each card is considered in light of the total number of responses given. The most solid blots—IV, V, VI, and IX—generally yielded the lowest average number of answers for each group, whereas the most broken blots—III, VIII, and X—yielded the highest average number of answers.

The results of this study indicate that subjects, including those with severe pathology, can form multiple potential responses that are generally congruent with the blot stimuli, in a relatively brief interval after the blot is exposed. The shortest nonpatient record contained 56 answers, and the shortest patient record (from one of the depressed subjects) contained 34 answers. When the yield of responses to the 10 blots during the first 30 seconds of exposure is considered, the lowest number of answers from the nonpatient groups is 23, the highest being 89. One depressed patient gave only 10 responses during the first 30-second interval, but 32 of the 40 psychiatric subjects averaged 16 or more responses to the 10 blots in those intervals, the largest number being 51 given by a schizophrenic subject.

These findings are in sharp contrast with normative data which reveal that most adult groups average between 20 and 23 answers, and that most groups of adolescents and children average between 17 and 22 responses. This narrow range of means appears to be universal. For instance, in the United States, nonpatient adults average about 22 responses. Sendin (1981) has reported that the mean R for a large group of Spanish subjects is about 23. Nonpatient samples ranging in size from 40 to 150, collected in various countries by the Rorschach Research Foundation yield similar results (Canada = 21.6; Japan = 23.2; Malaysia = 22.4; Mexico = 21.2; Micronesia = 20.4; Phillippines = 21.3).

THE RESPONSE PROCESS

If subjects generate many potential answers to each blot, why is it they deliver far fewer than are available when the test is administered in the standardized manner? Extrapolating from the Exner, Armbruster, and Mittman study, it seems reasonable to suggest that many subjects will deliver fewer than 25% of the potential answers that they have available. Any attempt to understand why this occurs, and its importance to the interpretation of the test data, must include consideration of several elements involved in the response process. These include: (1) the input or encoding of the stimulus field, (2) the classification of the field and/or its parts, (3) discarding some potential answers by reason of economy and rank ordering, (4) discarding some potential answers through censorship, (5) selection from the remaining potential responses because of styles and/or traits, and (6) also selection of answers because of psychological states that are activated by the task demand.

1. *The Input Process.* Sometimes it is difficult to appreciate the capacities of the human being to process information. The Rorschach blots are, of course, a form of visual stimulation and the processing of visual information occurs quite rapidly. Although theories of visual processing remain open to discussion (Hochberg, 1981; Neisser, 1976; Pomerantz & Kubovy, 1981), an extremely large number of studies have demonstrated that pattern and/or picture recognition can occur very quickly (Fisher, Monty, & Senders, 1981). Although the number of studies concerning visual processing has increased dramatically during the last two decades (probably as a result of increasingly sophisticated technology), the methodology was not applied to Rorschach research until recently. Exner (1980, 1983) has studied the visual scanning activity of nonpatient adults to some of the blots. Figure 1 is a crude facsimilie of the eye-scanning activity of a 19-year-old female viewing Card I for approximately 500 ms.[2]

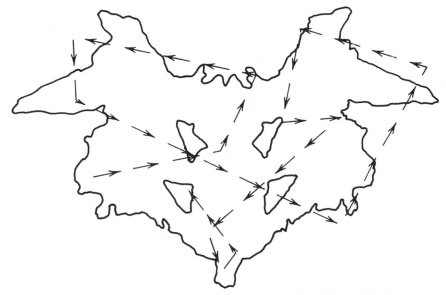

Figure 1.   Visual Scanning by a 19-Year-Old Female During the First 500 ms of Blot Exposure.

The arrows each represent the focal point of the visual field of the subject. It is not certain how far the peripheral visual field extends, but if a 1-inch area on either side of the centerpoint is used as a conservative estimate, it would appear that this subject has clearly viewed all of the blot, and some parts more than once. The importance of this finding is that the average reaction time for the first answer to Card I is 5.79 seconds ($SD = 2.38$) for 125 nonpatient adults, using a voice-accuated timer to insure precision. If this subject, or most like her, were allowed as much as twice the scanning time shown here (1000 ms) for the visual input and encoding of the stimulus field, slightly less than 5 seconds would

[2] A Gulf & Western Model 200 Eye Movement Monitor was used to record the scanning activity. The subject's head was held in a retainer to minimize random head movement. The blots were presented tachistoscopically on a small screen in the center of the subject's visual field. The eye movements were recorded through infrared sensors attached to spectacle frames worn by the subject and transmitted in an analog model to a computer and a digital model to a converter, which reproduced the activity on a video display.

remain before she might be expected to offer her first answer. Figure 2 is a crude fac-similie of the scanning action of a 23-year-old nonpatient male presented with Card III. It reflects his eye activity during the interval of 1100 ms after the blot was shown.

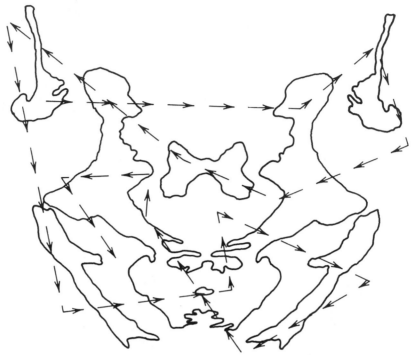

Figure 2.   Visual Scanning by a 23-Year-Old Male During the First 1100 ms After Blot Exposure.

This subject scanned Card III at about the same pace as other subjects in the study. A review of his eye activity indicates that he has viewed all of the features of this broken blot at least once, and some segments more than once during this interval. The average reaction time for the first response to this card is 7.74 seconds ($SD = 3.1$), indicating that the majority of subjects offer their first answer to the blot in a period of about 4.5 to nearly 11 seconds. In other words, an interval of between 5 and 9 seconds elapses *after* the input occurs until the first answer is given.

The importance of these findings is not so much that the subject is able to input the stimulus quickly; that information should have been obvious from the many studies on eye activity. The importance rests in confirmation of the *delay period* that exists between the input and the output. It is that critical interval of a few seconds, in which the many substantive operations take place, that lead to the decisions of how the subject will use the potential answers that he or she classified after being exposed to the stimulus.

2. *Classification of the Stimulus and/or Its Parts.* It seems quite probable, drawing from information concerning perception, that once the input is made it is encoded and held in a form of short-term storage, and the process of classification begins. Data from long-term storage are used as the basis for comparison to classify, or misidentify, the stimulus field and/or its parts. In some instances, the field as a whole, or some of its parts, may not be classified because of their apparent ambiguity to the subject. But almost all subjects,

with the probable exception of those with severe intellectual or neurologically related deficits, will classify some elements in the field as being sufficiently approximate to a known or imagined object to create potential answers.

It seems clear that some parts of the stimulus field have much more similarity to real or imagined objects than others. Thus they are easier to classify or misidentify. As a consequence, some whole blots or blots areas have a greater likelihood of being included among the responses that are actually delivered when the rank ordering and discarding procedures are completed. In some cases it seems likely that a greater effort will be made to classify some blot areas simply because the other areas are much more ambiguous. For example, the contours of the $D1$ area on Card VIII probably have a greater similarity to a known object, an animal, than any whole blot or any other areas of the blots. It has components that are very similar to the legs, body, and head of a four-legged animal. In addition, its location is somewhat discrete in relation to the remainder of the blot. Thus even though the coloring of this area (pink) is incongruous to a four-legged animal, the preciseness of the contours and its discrete location, plus the fact that other areas of the blot are less easily identified, a response to Card VIII that includes the use of this area as an animal is highly predictable. More than 90% of all nonpatient adults and children and more than 80% of all nonschizophrenic psychiatric subjects include the use of this area, as an animal, among their responses. Almost 65% of schizophrenics also give this type of response even though, as a group, they tend to give significantly fewer of the common or Popular answers on other blots.

There are also some characteristics of the blots that are critical to the formation of a potential answer—that is, bits or parts of the blots which have a high valence for belonging to a particular class of objects. The coloring of Card I and the contours of a relatively small area of the blot are a good illustration of this. The most frequently given answer to Card I is a bat, using the whole blot. Nearly 60% of all subjects, psychiatric and non-psychiatric, identify Card I as a bat. Exner (1959) demonstrated that if the achromatic coloring of the blot is changed to chromatic, holding all other features constant (size, shading, etc.), the frequency of the bat response is sharply reduced. In fact, some chromatic colors such as yellow and blue eliminate the bat response completely. Thus it can be surmised that the achromatic coloring of the blot is a stimulus bit that is quite important to the classification or misidentification of the stimulus field as a bat. But two other elements in the stimulus field are at least as important as the coloring, if not more so, to the formation of the bat response. These are the $Dd34$ projections that extend outward from either side of the top of the blot. Exner and Martin (1981) used a photographic technique to eliminate these areas and administered the entire test with the modified Card I to 30 adult nonpatient volunteer subjects. Not one bat response was given by the group and, in fact, the frequency of butterfly, moth, and bird responses all fell to nearly zero. Obviously, those projections play an important role in classifying the blot as a winged object.

Sometimes critical stimulus elements that contribute significantly to the classification process are not readily apparent. For instance, the most common answer given to the blue-colored $D1$ area in Card X (which is a multichromatic and broken stimulus field) is a spider. The response "crab" to this same area is the second most frequently given answer to this blot. For unknown reasons, schizophrenics do not give either of these responses very often. Exner and Wylie (1976), pursuing the hypothesis that the blue creates a dissonant effect, used a dye-coupling technique to alter the color of that blot area, making it a reddish-brown. The entire test was administered to two groups of 50 subjects each, one of nonpatients and one of schizophrenics. A random half of the subjects in each group were administered the standard Card X and the other half the altered version. The groups administered the altered version of Card X gave significantly fewer spider and crab responses than did the controls. This finding seemed puzzling until it was noted that the subjects in the experimental groups gave significantly more responses to another area of the blot, $D6$, which is colored blue. A 30-item questionnaire was hastily contrived and administered to the 50 nonpatient subjects who had participated in the experiment. It contained one critical item, "What is your favorite color?" Of the 50 subjects, 41 responded with the answer, "blue."

Thus it was hypothesized that although the contours of $D1$ can be judged as similar to those of a crab or spider, the blue coloring of the area increases the stimulus valence of the area, causing subjects to attend more to it during the classification process. Exner and Wylie (1977) created a completely achromatic version of Card X to test this hypothesis. They administered the entire test to 30 nonpatient volunteers, half of whom were administered the standard version of Card X and half the achromatic version. Only three subjects in the experimental group gave spider or crab responses to the $D1$ area, whereas 12 subjects in the control group did so.

There is still much to be learned about the cognitive activity involved in the classification procedure and, in turn, how that procedure relates to the total response process. It does seem clear that classification can occur very quickly after the blot is entered into the visual field of the subject. The first clue to this, generally disregarded by the Rorschach community, was evidenced in a study published in 1949 by Morris Stein. He presented the blots tachistoscopically to two groups of subjects, each of which was administered the test four times. The first, named the "ascending group," was shown the blots for intervals of 0.01 seconds in the first administration, 0.10 seconds in the second administration, 3.0 seconds in the third, and given an unlimited time exposure in the fourth. The control group, "descending," also received four administrations of the test, but with the exposure times reversed as compared with the ascending group (i.e., starting with the unlimited time exposure). Unfortunately the time intervals between testings were very brief and this rapid retest procedure probably confounded some of the results.

But some clues about the rapidity of the response formulation may be gleaned from the results for the ascending group. In their first trial, with the blots exposed for only 10 milliseconds, the subjects averaged nearly 10 answers, with a range of five to 14 responses. When the blots were exposed for a full 3.0 seconds, two trials later, the average number of answers had increased only slightly, to about 12, with a range of eight to 17. Stein noted that as the exposure times increased, so too did the frequencies of answers based exclusively or primarily on the contours of the blots. At the third trial, using the 3.0-second exposure, a significantly greater number of Popular responses were given than had been the case when the blots were exposed for the much briefer intervals. In other words, once the blots were exposed long enough to permit a full scan of the stimulus, considerable homogeneity occurred among the responses given.

In a related study, Horiuchi (1961) presented Cards III and VI tachistoscopically to groups of 80 nonpatients, 80 neurotics, and 80 schizophrenics for intervals of .10 seconds, .30 seconds, 1.0 second, and unlimited time. She found that 60 of the 80 nonpatients and nearly half of the neurotics and schizophrenics gave at least one response per blot with the exposure time of 100 ms. When the exposure time was increased to 300 ms, all of the nonpatients gave at least one response per blot, but the frequency of answers for the neurotic and schizophrenic groups did not increase. She also found that some subjects from the neurotic and schizophrenic groups continued to have difficulty forming a differentiated response when the blots were exposed for a full second. She concluded that some of the mediational activity necessary to form an answer is inhibited in conditions of psychopathology.

Colligan and Exner (1985) tested three groups of 36 subjects each—schizophreniform inpatients, orthopedic inpatients, and nonpatients—using a tachistoscopic presentation of the blots. They randomized each group into three subgroups of 12 subjects each and exposed the blots to one for 200 ms, the second for 400 ms, and the third for 600 ms. Subjects were instructed to give their responses after a tone sounded. The tone occurred 900 ms after the exposure to allow sufficient time for the decay of the icon. They found that 62 of the 72 nonpsychiatric subjects were able to give at least one response to each blot, and 9 of the 10 who gave refusals were in the subgroups with time exposures of 200 ms or 400 ms. Several of the nonpsychiatric subjects in each of the subgroups gave between 12 and 15 answers. There were many more refusals among the schizophrenic subjects at each of the exposure levels. In all, 17 of the 36 schizophrenics gave fewer than 10 answers. Eight of those 17 were in the 600 ms subgroup. These findings may support Horiuchi's postulate that mediational activity is impaired by psychopathology; however, it might be more accurate to suggest that the schizophrenics were much more defensive in the test situation. Six of the 19 schizophrenics who did not give refusals gave between 12 and 15 responses.

Another important finding from the Colligan and Exner study concerns the appropriate use of the blot contours. Nearly 70% of all responses given by the nonpsychiatric subgroups included an appropriate use of contours. An examination of those answers in which the contours of the blot were violated reveals that many occurred to the more broken blots—II, III, VIII, and X. Many of the answers given to those blots seem to reflect the principle of closure; that is, the subjects created an imaginary line to encompass the parts of the blots. For example, seven of the 72 nonpsychiatric subjects reported that Card III was a "face." Classification of this very broken blot in that way requires some closure operation. If such an answer occurs under the standardized procedures of administration, it is considered a serious violation of reality. The fact that it occurs with a considerable frequency among nonpsychiatric subjects faced with the task of classifying a field very quickly may provide a clue about why the female subject whose eye scan of Card I (Figure 1) was able to encompass almost all of the blot in about a half second, whereas the male subject scanning Card III (Figure 2) took approximately 1.1 seconds to complete a full scan of the blot. The more broken the stimulus field, the more time will be necessary for the procedure of encoding and classifying. This seems to confirm the notion that some blots or blot areas are classified very quickly and easily, whereas other blots or blot areas may require more scanning time.

Assuming that this is true, the differences in required scanning and classification time are not so substantial to account for the relatively lengthy delay that occurs between the presentation of the blot and the delivery of the first answer. Extrapolating conservatively from the eye-tracking data and the Stein, Horiuchi, and Colligan and Exner studies, it seems reasonable to assume that a period of 2 to 3 seconds after exposure is more than sufficient for encoding the stimulus and classifying at least three, if not more, potential answers. Why then, do most subjects take at least twice that time, and often much longer, before delivering their first answer? It seems probable that the procedures of ranking and discarding are mainly responsible for the delay.

3. *Discarding Potential Answers by Ranking.* The instructions to the subject are deliberately brief. No requirements or limits are implied concerning the number of responses that should be delivered. Subjects who give only one answer to Card I are encouraged to "Take your time and look a bit more and you'll probably find something else." The implication for that group is that only one response may not be sufficient. Subjects who give more than one response to Card I receive no confirmation that the yield is sufficient, except by the passive acceptance of the examiner. Some subjects seek direction by asking, "Is that enough?" "Do you want more?" or "How many should I give?" If only one answer has been given to Card I, the prompt is used, but if the subject has given more than one answer to Card I, the response to such queries remains open-ended: "It's up to you." This requires the subject to decide how many of the potential answers that have been formulated to deliver.

The majority of subjects appear to be influenced by an economy principle in their decisions about how many responses to give. There are occasional compulsive-like subjects who seem prepared to give an infinite number of answers to each blot, but they are deterred from this by withdrawing the card after the fifth response, if this occurs early in the test. But most subjects are much more conservative with their yield of answers, and this probably accounts for the fact that most groups average about 22 responses. Whether the orientation to economize is a simple matter of efficiency, or whether it is more a matter of defensive concealment is not certain, but probably both of these issues are involved. Practically all subjects, even children, have some conception of psychological testing, and often will have some vague awareness of the "inkblot test." Unfortunately, many of these concepts are based on faulty assumptions. People tend to think of testing in terms of educational models, which include right and wrong answers, high versus low scores, and passing or failing. Even when the competent examiner properly devotes time to an explanation of procedures and arranging for feedback with the subject, most will still approach the testing continuing to be influenced by prior sets and/or experiences of apprehension. The desire to complete the test quickly and effectively is natural in such a situation and probably contributes to some of the economy orientation.

A second factor contributing to the economy orientation is the rank ordering process. As noted earlier, some blots or blot areas are easier to classify than others. Quite often a single blot or blot area will be classified or misidentified more than once. For example, the whole Card I might be classified as a bat, a bird, and a butterfly. Some subjects elect to give two of those three potential answers, and occasionally a subject may give all three, or even more from the same general classification of winged objects. But most subjects will give only one of those responses. In doing so they withhold or discard the others. The selection of which of the three to deliver is based, at least in part, on some form of ranking, such as it looks more like a bat than either a bird or a butterfly. This same process occurs whether the multiple potential answers are generated from the same blot area or from a variety of areas. For instance, a subject might classify the whole Card I as a bat and a butterfly, the $D4$ area as a woman, the $D2$ area as an animal, the $D7$ area as a bird, and the $DdS29$ areas as triangles, but deliver only two or three of those six possibilities. This form of paired comparison rank ordering appears to contribute significantly to the process of selection and discarding. In a pilot study, Martin and Thomas (1982) presented the blots twice, using a slide projector, to a class of 28 high school students. In the first presentation each blot was exposed for 1 minute. The students were instructed to *write* three responses per blot on a form provided. After all 10 blots had been presented, they were shown again in the same order with exposure times of 15 seconds. Prior to the second exposure the students were instructed to look at the blots again and select one of the three answers they had written to be "scored," and also to write, in a space provided, a brief statement about why they selected that answer. Of the 280 statements, 159 could easily be catagorized under the heading, "It looks most like that." [3]

Although it seems clear that some form of paired comparison ranking, based on a similarity to known objects, does occur, it would be erroneous to assume that this procedure is *mainly* responsible for the selection of those answers to be delivered. There are at least three other elements that play a significant role in determining which of the potential answers will be delivered and which will be discarded.

4. *Discarding through Censorship.* As noted earlier, most subjects will approach psychological testing with some preconceptions or sets. Some of these may be specific to psychological testing or even to the Rorschach in particular. Generally they result from bits and pieces of information concerning testing that the subject has accumulated. However, many of the sets with which a subject approaches the test are derived from the more broadly based values that the subject has developed. Whatever the origins, this composite of attitudes will often be very influential on the procedures of discarding and selecting. For example, the MMPI *K* Scale has been demonstrated to have some relation to the orientation to make socially acceptable responses (Dahlstrom, Welsh, & Dalhstrom, 1972). In the Exner, Armbruster, and Mittman (1978) study, the 40 nonpatient adults were also administered the MMPI and subdivided into two groups based on a median split of the distribution of their scores on the *K* Scale. The results show that the 20 subjects scoring in the upper half of that distribution averaged 17 fewer responses than did those scoring in the lower half. In other words, those subjects more oriented toward making acceptable responses tended to withhold or discard more responses than did the subjects not so oriented. These findings have provoked several other studies regarding the circumstances in which subjects may be more or less prone to withhold or discard responses.

In a second study reported by Exner, Armbruster, and Mittman (1978), 10 therapists were asked to recruit two each of their own patients who had never taken the Rorschach. Those patients were randomized so that each therapist tested one of his or her patients and the patient of another therapist with whom the examining therapist had no prior contact. The results show that those patients tested by their own therapist averaged 10 more responses to the test than did the controls, including significantly more sex responses (4.3 versus 0.8). Leura and Exner (1978) trained 10 junior high school teachers to administer the test and then used them in the same design. Each teacher was asked to recruit two volunteers from his or her classes, the criterion for selection being that the students were progressing quite well in that class. All of the recruited students were from seventh-grade classes. As with the patients in the Exner, Armbruster, and Mittman study, they were randomized so that each teacher tested one of his or her own pupils and a student from another school with whom the examining teacher had no prior contact. Subjects tested by their own teacher averaged nearly 16 more responses than did the controls.

The results of these studies seem to indicate that subjects who feel emotionally and/or intellectually close to their examiner will deliver more and conceal less. This should not be translated to suggest that the well-trained examiner can or will have a significantly influential effect on how many responses are delivered. If the test is administered in the

---

[3] The comments for the total group varied considerably from "I don't know" to "I like those," but all categorized under the rubric of "It Looks Most Like That" ranged from form specified responses such as, "It has the wings and body like they are," to "It looks more like that than anything else there."

standardized manner, examiners can expect to obtain a normal distribution of responses from their subjects, unless they do a high frequency of testing with unusual populations such as the neurologically impaired, newly admitted criminals, and so on. Exner (1974) has demonstrated that some novice examiners may, because of their own difficulties and discomfort about learning the procedures of the test administration, cause fewer responses to be delivered than might ordinarily be the case. Apparently the discomfort of the examiner increases the apprehensiveness of the subject and leads to more withholding. But this is easily corrected with supervised experience in administration.

Goodman (1979) studied the effect of sex differences among examiners, using a design in which 10 male and 10 female examiners each tested two male and two female subjects. She also rated the examiners on an interpersonal "warmth" scale, using videotapes of them administering the TAT to a collaborator subject. Her results indicate no significant effects for the same-sex versus cross-sex pairings. She did find that the more experienced examiners, who also tended to be rated as "warmer" in their interactions with subjects, elicited a greater number of human responses than did the less experienced examiners. She also found that the experienced examiners obtained more records of average length (17 to 27 responses) than did the examiners who were still in graduate school training.

Although the element of rapport between the examiner and subject will contribute to censorship based discarding of potential answers, it seems likely that much censoring occurs because of sets about the test and value judgments concerning the acceptability of answers. Exner and Leura (1976) used 60 nonpatient adults, 30 males and 30 females, in a pilot study concerning the ease with which objects can be perceived in the blots. None had prior exposure to the test. They were randomized into two groups of 30 each and seated at opposite ends of a hotel ballroom, each at their own small table. The groups were separated by a thick sliding wall. Each subject was provided with a list of five answers per blot plus a location sheet on which all 50 answers were outlined. Each group of five answers was randomized for the ordering sequence so that no answer appeared at the same point in the list for more than six subjects in each group. Each group of five answers included a Popular response to the blot, two commonly given responses, and two others that are not given frequently. One of the five answers, the *target* response, had a content implying sexuality, injury, or violence.

For example, the five answers listed for Card I were, a bat, a mask, an animal, a bell, and the target answer, a naked woman. Subjects were instructed to look carefully at each blot as it was projected on a screen for an interval of 165 seconds, review the areas outlined on the location sheet, and decide the ease with which each could be recognized as compared with the remaining four answers, and assigning the rank of 1 for the easiest to see, 2 for the next easiest to see, and 5 for the one most difficult to see. The only difference between the two groups was that one was told that the responses they would be ranking were among those given *most frequently by normal subjects,* whereas the second group was told that the responses represented those given *most often by severely disturbed psychiatric patients.*

When the groups were compared for their rankings, a significant difference at .05 or less occurred for 22 of the 50 answers, including eight of the 10 target responses. For example, only four of the 30 subjects who thought the responses came from psychiatric subjects ranked the target response (naked woman) 1 or 2. In fact, 17 of the 30 ranked the target response 4 or 5, and 15 of those 17 assigned the rank of 5. Conversely, 19 of the 30 subjects told that the answers were given frequently by normal subjects ranked the target answer 1 or 2, and 14 of those 19 assigned the rank of 1. The responses listed for Card VI incuded an animal skin, a totem pole, a human profile, a dog, and the target response, a penis. One of the subjects set to believe that the answers came from psychiatric patients ranked the target answer 2, a second ranked the target answer 3, and the remaining 28 ranked the target answer 4 or 5, including 23 who assigned the rank of 5. In the group set to believe that the responses came from normal subjects, 19 ranked the target answer 1, and 4 others assigned the rank of 2. Only three subjects ranked the target answer 4 or 5.

Thomas, Exner, and Leura (1977) used another group of 60 nonpatients, naive to the test, in a modification of this same design. Again, the group was randomized into two groups of 30 each and seated at opposite ends of a ballroom separated by a sliding wall. They were provided with the same lists of five responses per blot used in the previous study, but with location sheets on which there were *no* outlines of the answers. These groups were given similar, but more distinctive sets concerning the origins of the responses. One group was told that the answers were given most commonly by *very successful businessmen*, whereas the second group was told that the responses were those given most often by *inpatient schizophrenics*. Instead of projecting the blots on a screen, each subject was provided with a set of the Rorschach cards. The subjects were instructed to study each blot carefully, using as much time as might be necessary, and *find* each of the objects listed and, using a black marking pen, to outline each on the location sheet. After locating and outlining all five, they were to decide which was the easiest to see, the next easiest, and so on, using the same rankings of 1 to 5 that had been used in the pilot investigation.

The results of this study are similar to those of the pilot study. The groups differed significantly for their rankings of 21 of the 50 responses, including nine of the 10 target responses. The 10 target responses and the frequencies for rankings are shown in Table 3. The ranks of 1 and 2, and 4 and 5 have been collapsed to represent the ''easier'' versus ''more difficult'' to see.

Table 3. Frequencies of Rankings for 10 Target Responses Given by Two Groups, with Ranks 1 and 2, and 4 and 5 Collapsed

			Group 1 Schizophrenia Set				Group 2 Businessmen Set		
						Rankings			
Card	Area	Responses	1–2	3	4–5		1–2	3	4–5
I	D4	Naked woman	5	4	16[a]		18[a]	9	3
II	D2	Blood smears	1	10	19		14[a]	5	11
III	D2	Blood running down	5	11	14		16[a]	6	8
IV	W	Monster looming	21	6	3		20	9	1
V	W	Rams fighting	7	15	8		18[a]	10	2
VI	D2	Penis	3	9	18[a]		21[a]	5	4
VII	D6	Vagina	0	7	23[a]		13[a]	9	9
VIII	W	Open chest cavity	4	7	19		14[a]	5	11
IX	D6	Buttocks	0	12	18[a]		11[a]	11	8
X	D9	Blood stains	5	13	11		15[a]	7	8

[a] Statistically significant larger number of this rank, $p < .05$.

In both of these studies *all* of the subjects could see the responses listed, whether outlined on the location sheet as in the pilot study, or not. The difference between the groups in each study lies in the rankings or weights assigned with regard to how *easily* each could be seen. It is important to note that all of the target responses involve larger and/or more discrete areas of the blots than others in the five response groupings and two of them *occur with a relatively high frequency when the test is administered under standard conditions.* These are the figure of the woman on Card I, and the anatomy response on Card VIII. The ''blood'' areas on Cards II, III, and X, and the penis area on Card VI are all very discrete blot areas. Because sets were employed concerning the origins of the responses, it seems logical to postulate that the negative set (i.e., the responses were given by psychiatric subjects) caused many to rank some responses as being more difficult to perceive, whereas those with the positive set felt less need to do so.

Although studies of this kind are inconclusive about the censoring operations that occur, they do appear to provide some clues about how the process may work. Thus even though the ranking operations might cause a potential answer to be ranked highly in terms of object similarity, the censoring operation might cause the response to be discarded because the subject places a negative value judgment on it in light of the test situation. But there are still two remaining elements that may override the ranking and censoring operations in the discarding and selection decisions.

5. *Styles and Traits and the Selecting Process.* It seems obvious that the basic psychological characteristics of the individual play a dominant role in determining which of the potential answers will be delivered. These are the features of people that cause them to be relatively consistent in many of their psychological operations and manifest behaviors. Historically, they have been identified as psychological habits, traits, styles, or dispositions. Whatever nomenclature is used, it represents the composite of the more dominant elements of the personality structure that breed behavioral preferences and create a tendency to redundancy in the selection of many coping responses.

These features are often reflected in the descriptions of a person rendered by those who know him or her well. For example, some people may be described as being quiet and reserved, whereas others may be described as more spontaneous and emotional. Some may be described as forceful or assertive, whereas others may be described as more passive. Some may be considered as strong in the face of stress and others as easily disorganized, and so on. If the person offering the description has frequent and close contact with the person being described, it is very likely that the description will be reasonably accurate.

These characteristics are especially influential to many of a person's decision operations that relate to coping and/or problem solving. In that the task of the Rorschach creates a form of problem-solving demand, it is only natural that the subject will be influenced by these characteristics in the final decisions concerning which responses to deliver. In effect, the tendency toward behavioral redundancy becomes manifest in Rorschach-related operations by creating a greater probability that certain classes of responses will be selected for delivery than other classes of responses that are also available. This creates one of the strengths of the Rorschach, as a test—its reliability over time.

During the often stormy history of the Rorschach, those who disavowed its usefulness as a test frequently pointed to problems of establishing satisfactory evidence of reliability. Unfortunately, most of the efforts to do so approached the issue by attempting to demonstrate that the test is internally consistent, using a split-half technique (Vernon, 1933; Hertz, 1934; Ford, 1946; Orange, 1953). Although most of the results were statistically significant, very few of the correlation coefficients fall into the .80 or higher range that would be required if a test is to be judged as truly internally consistent. The problem with this approach to reliability is the required assumption that the stimuli are equivalent, and will be equally likely to promote any class of response. The Rorschach blots are not equivalent stimuli. They differ for levels of complexity and are clearly different for the kinds of responses they are likely to generate. It was because of this problem that much of the work at the Rorschach Research Foundation has focused on the issue of reliability by studying the temporal consistency of classes of response. The operational hypothesis posed is that people do have preferred response styles that manifest in the majority of their responses, and evidence for those styles should be consistently evident in repeated testings.

Earlier, Holzberg (1960) had questioned the usefulness of the test-retest model as applied to the Rorschach, arguing that personality variables might not be consistent over time, and that a different set might occur during the second testing because of the memory input created by the earlier testing. Neither of these objections is very convincing. A host of data exist indicating that many so-called personality traits do remain consistent over time (London & Exner, 1978), and the findings of the Exner, Armbruster, and Mittman (1978) study suggest that if memory is an important variable, it is *less contingent on recalling what was seen, and more on recalling what was reported.*

By late 1983 more than 30 temporal consistency studies had been completed at the Rorschach Research Foundation, using many different groups of adults and children, patients and nonpatients. The intervals between first and second tests have varied from a few days to many months. When viewed in relation to the consistency of response styles or dispositions, the more important of these involve retesting after reasonably lengthy intervals. Data from two such studies are available and appear to support the consistency hypothesis. In the first, 100 nonpatient adults, 50 male and 50 female, were retested after 36 to 39 months (Exner, Armbruster, & Viglione, 1978). In the second, completed for this volume, 50 nonpatient adults, 25 male and 25 female, were retested after 12 to 14 months (Exner, Thomas, & Cohen, 1983). The retest correlations from each of these studies, for 25 variables, are show in Table 4.

An examination of the data for the 50 subjects retested after approximately 1 year reveals that two of the correlations exceed .90, and 13 others fall between .81 and .89. Only five of the correlations fall below .72, a finding that is not surprising, because all five relate to *state* rather than *trait* features. The data for the retests taken at approximately three years are quite similar. One of the correlations falls at .90, and 12 others are between .80 and .87. Again, only five, all related to state conditions, fall below .70.

The psychometric purist might argue, with some merit, that correlations falling below .80, or even below .85, are not sufficient to support a claim of stability or consistency for a variable. This argument is most relevant to those variables having retest correlations between .70 and .79. Five of these appear in the data for the 1-year retest, and seven in the data for the 3-year retest. Obviously the features and/or operations related to these variables are not as consistent as the features and operations related to the variables with higher retest correlations, yet each accounts for more than one-half of the variance. Thus it seems reasonable to postulate that these variables relate to characteristics having some considerable stability, but which are also more subject to influence by other conditions, including lengthy time intervals.

It is also important to note that none of the 18 single variables listed in Table 4, *taken alone*, have a critical impact on the interpretation of the test. The seven ratios and percentages shown in Table 4 have a much more important role in interpretation, and most of

Table 4. Correlation Coefficients for Nonpatient Groups of 50 Adults Retested After 12 to 14 Months and 100 Adults Retested After 36 to 39 Months

Variable	Description	1-Year Retest	3-Year Retest
		r	r
R	No. of Responses	.86	.79
P	Popular responses	.83	.73
Zf	Z Frequency	.85	.83
F	Pure Form	.74	.70
M	Human Movement	.84	.87
FM	Animal Movement	.77	.72
m	Inanimate Movement	.26	.39
a	Active Movement	.83	.86
p	Passive Movement	.72	.75
FC	Form Color Responses	.86	.86
CF	Color Form Responses	.58	.66
$C + Cn$	Pure Color & Color Naming	.56	.51
$CF + C + Cn$	Color Dominant Responses	.81	.79
$Sum\ C$	Sum Weighted Color	.82	.86
T	Texture Responses	.91	.87
C'	Achromatic Color Responses	.73	.67
Y	Diffuse Shading Responses	.31	.23
V	Vista Responses	.87	.81
Ratios & Percentages			
L	Lambda	.78	.82
$X + \%$	Extended Good Form	.86	.80
Afr	Affective Ratio	.82	.90
$3r + (2)/R$	Egocentricity Index	.89	.87
EA	Experience Actual	.83	.85
es	Experienced Stimulation	.64	.72
D	Stress Tolerance Index	.91	.83

those do have retest correlations of .80 or greater. Those having correlations of less than .80 are much more related to state influences.

Whereas the data in Table 4 indicate that most of the characteristics represented by Rorschach scores are very stable among nonpatient adults over long periods, the same is not true for children. Exner and Weiner (1982) have reported relatively low retest correlations for 6-year-olds who were retested at age 8, and for 9-year-olds retested when they were 12. The results of an 8-year longitudinal study of 57 nonpatient youngsters, tested first at age 8 and retested at each 2-year interval through the age of 16, show that retest correlations for most variables tend to remain low until the interval between 14 and 16 years of age (Exner, Thomas, & Mason, 1985). However, this should not be interpreted to mean that the traits or styles of the child are not stable over briefer intervals, or that those features will have little influence on the selection of responses. Retest correlations for most variables are quite high, for both childen and adults, when the second test is taken in less than 1 month. Table 5 includes the results of three such studies. One concerns 25 nonpatient 8-year-olds retested after 7 days (Exner & Weiner, 1982). In the other two, involving 35 nonpatient 9-year-olds and 35 nonpatient adults, the retest was administered after approximately 3 weeks (Thomas, Alinsky, & Exner, 1982).

Table 5.   Correlation Coefficients for 25 Nonpatient 8-Year-Olds Retested After 7 Days, 35 Nonpatient 9-Year-Olds, and 35 Nonpatient Adults Retested After Approximately 3 Weeks

Variable	Description	8-Year-Olds Seven-Day Retest	9-Year-Olds Three-Week Retest	Adults Three-Week Retest
		r	r	r
R	No. of Responses	.88	.87	.84
P	Popular responses	.86	.89	.81
Zf	Z Frequency	.91	.92	.89
F	Pure Form	.79	.80	.76
M	Human Movement	.90	.87	.83
FM	Animal Movement	.75	.78	.72
m	Inanimate Movement	.49	.20	.34
a	Active Movement	.91	.91	.87
p	Passive Movement	.86	.88	.85
FC	Form Color Responses	.90	.84	.92
CF	Color Form Responses	.76	.74	.68
C + Cn	Pure Color & Color Naming	.72	.64	.59
CF + C + Cn	Color Dominant Responses	.89	.92	.83
Sum C	Sum Weighted Color	.88	.87	.83
T	Texture Responses	.86	.92	.96
C'	Achromatic Color Responses	.77	.74	.67
Y	Diffuse Shading Responses	.42	.17	.41
V	Vista Responses	.96	.93	.89
Ratios & Percentages				
L	Lambda	.82	.84	.76
X + %	Extended Good Form	.95	.92	.87
Afr	Affective Ratio	.91	.91	.85
3r + (2)/R	Egocentricity Index	.94	.86	.90
EA	Experience Actual	.85	.87	.84
es	Experienced Stimulation	.74	.70	.59
D	Stress Tolerance Index	.93	.91	.88

The correlations for the 8-year-olds retested after 7 days include eight which are at .90 or greater and seven others between .81 and .89. Those for the 9-year-olds include eight at .90 or greater, and 11 others falling between .80 and .89. The correlations for the adults include three at .90 or greater and 14 between .81 and .89.

The large number of high correlations developed from these brief interval retest studies tends to favor the postulate that these styles and characteristics do play an important role in the selection of answers to be delivered. It could be argued, following from Holzberg (1960), that the memory factor may play a more important role when brief interval retesting is done, thereby causing some correlations to be spuriously elevated. But there is evidence to indicate that this is not the case.

Exner (1980) recruited 60 nonpatient 8-year-olds from four elementary schools under the guise of needing *practice* subjects for examiners in training. Thus each child volunteered for the study by his or her parents anticipated being tested at least twice, during regular school hours, in a five- to seven-day interval. Ten highly experienced examiners were used. None had any awareness of the nature of the study, assuming that they were collecting data in a rountine reliability investigation. When the first test was administered, the project director accompanied the child from the classroom to the testing room provided by the school and introduced the examiner. The second test was administered three or four days later. The 60 subjects had been randomized previously into two groups of 30 each, and the procedure for the Control subjects was the same for the second test as the first; that is, the project director accompanied the youngster from he classroom to the test location and introduced the new examiner. This procedure was altered for the subjects in the Experimental group. While accompanying them to the testing room, the project director would pause and ask the child to assist in the solution of an important problem concerning the training of the examiners. The "problem," as outlined quickly by the project director, was that the "trainees" were hearing the same answers repeatedly, and that the training would be enhanced consideraby if the child would "try hard" to remember the answers that he or she gave in the first test and promise not to repeat any of those in the test to be taken. In return, the project director offered a reward of 50 cents. All of the childen in the Experimental group promised to change their answers.

The retest correlations of the two groups are almost identical, with two exceptions. In the retest, the subjects in the Experimental group gave significantly fewer Pure Form responses than they had in the first test and significantly more responses that included the achromatic or shading features of the blots. Otherwise, the correlations are essentially no different for the two groups, and very similar to those shown in Table 5 for the eight-year-olds retested after only seven days. Five of the correlations for the Experimental group are at .90 or greater and eight others fall between .81 and .89. A critical issue for this study is whether or not the youngsters in the Experimental group actually gave different answers. This issue was addressed by randomizing the 60 pairs of records into three groups of 20 pairs each and assigning each group to one of three judges who were told that the records were from a reliability study. The judges were instructed to read each pair of records and check all responses in the second test that were the same (or nearly the same) as those in the first test. The comparisons revealed that 481 of the 546 responses (86%) given in the second test by the Control subjects were replications or near replications of answers that they had given in the first test. On the other hand, only 77 of the 551 answers (14%) given by Experimental subjects in the second test were the same or similar to the answers they had given in the first test. Thus even though the youngsters in the Experimental group generally did honor the promise to give different responses in the second test, the answers that they tended to select show a distribution of scores, subject by subject, similar to those of the first test.

There are other structural data, not shown in Tables 4 or 5, which are also important to the study of the consistency hypothesis as related to the selection of answers. These include three relationships, or ratio directions, that exist between data sets. Each is important to the interpretation of the test, either because of the directionality shown in the relationship (i.e., which of the data sets are greater) and/or the magnitude of the difference. The first, the *Erlebnistypus* (EB) was conceptualized by Rorschach and relates to the coping style of the subject. It involves the relationship of M (human movement) to the weighted sum of chromatic color responses (*Sum C*). Both direction and magnitude are important to the interpretation of this relationship. A minimum two-point difference is considered necessary before the data would be interpreted as indicating a preference in coping habits. In the one-year retest study of 50 adult nonpatients cited earlier, the first tests of 41 subjects showed an *EB* in which one side of the ratio was two or more points greater than the other side. In the second test, 38 of those 41 subjects continued to show at least a two-point difference in the EB, and *none* had changed for the direction of the difference. In the study involving the retest of 100 nonpatient adults after 3 years, 83 of the first test records showed at least a two-point difference in the *EB*. In the retest, 77 of those 83 continued to have the difference of two points or more and only two had changed directionality.

A second important ratio concerns the relationship between *FC* (Form Color Responses) and *CF + C + Cn* (Color Dominant Responses). It relates to the modulation or control of discharged emotion. Again, both direction and magnitude are important. In the one-year retest study, 36 of the 50 first records showed one side of that ratio to be two points or greater than the other side. The retests showed that 32 of those 36 subjects continued to have at least a two-point difference between these variables, and *none* had changed for directionality. In the 3-year retest study, 57 of the 100 first records had a difference of two points or more for this ratio. In he retest, 50 of the 57 continued to have the two or more point difference and none had changed directionality.

The third is the ratio of active (*a*) to passive (*p*) movement. In this relationship, more active movement is always expected but the magnitude of the difference is also important. It provides some information about the flexibility of thinking and/or values. In the 1-year retest study, 39 of the records from the first test showed a two or more point difference in this ratio, with 31 of the 39 being higher for active movement. The retest protocols showed that 30 of the 31 "high active" records remained two or more points greater on the active side, and all eight of those higher on the passive side in the first test also remained so. In the three-year retest, a two-point or more difference was noted in 76 of the first records, with 60 being higher for active movement. In the retest, 57 of those 60 were still two or more points higher on the active side, and 11 of the original 16 "high passive" records remained at least two points higher in that direction.

The composite of data regarding the consistency of Rorschach scores and ratios, during both lengthy and brief intervals, and even under conditions where different responses are generated, affords substantial support for the proposition that the traits or styles of the subject will be quite influential in the selection of which potential answers to deliver. Yet, there is still one more element that will often play a crucial role in the final decisions about which responses to deliver.

6. *Psychological States and the Selection Process*. The relative consistency of many personality characteristics and their consequent behaviors is contingent upon some relative consistency in the stimulus conditions that evoke them. In other words, the habits, traits, or response styles of a person are probabilistic. Certain classes of behaviors are likely to occur under certain classes of stimulus conditions. The stimulus conditions include *both internal and external elements*. The person who is an athletic-outdoor enthusiast may be far less likely to engage in such activities if the outside temperatures fall well below zero or above 115°. Sedentary activity may replace some of the common activities. That same person may also be less likely to engage in the athletic activities if his or her own temperature exceeds 101° or if an irritating stomach upset occurs. The person has not changed, but external or internal conditions have changed in a way to cause other behaviors to be evoked.

These changes, or alterations in behavior, may also result from changes in the psychological state of the individual. Increases or decreases in needs and/or emotions, or the unexpected experience of stress or the onset of various psychopathologial states can have the effect of evoking new behaviors that add to, or replace, preexisting orientations. In most instances, the basics of the person do not change, but some unexpected behaviors occur. In some cases, the behaviors of the person may shift slightly as in the instance of the normally sedate person who becomes flustered under recognition. In other instances, the deviations from expected behaviors may be much more marked as in the case of the individual who becomes panic-stricken and disorganized under moderate stress. These are *state* phenomenon, which tend to supersede the routine psychological functioning of the person, or at least will stimulate the addition of behaviors that are not ordinarily part of the psychological routine.

Rorschach responses can be viewed as a sampling of problem-solving behavior. Thus if a psychological state exists that will alter, or add to the routine functioning of the person, that state can also influence the selection of responses to be delivered during the test. For example, two of the scoring variables listed in Tables 4 and 5 show very low retest reliabilities, over both lengthy and brief retest intervals. These are *m*, scored for inanimate movement, and *Y*, scored for the articulation of diffuse shading. The means for both, from nonpatient samples, are quite low as are the standard deviations. Thus although either might occur once in a record, they are not expected to appear more frequently. Research has shown that both relate to situational stress (Shalit, 1965; Armbruster, Miller & Exner, 1974; Exner, Armbruster, Walker, & Cooper, 1975; Exner, 1978; Exner & Weiner, 1982). Thus if the frequencies for either or both are elevated in a protocol, it signals that the presence of some situationally related phenomenon that is stimulating the mental and/or emotional experiences which occur when concerns about loss of control and feelings of helplessness or paralysis exist.

Another illustration of how the selection of Rorschach answers may be influenced by a state condition is exemplified in the texture (*T*) responses. The average number of texture responses, for various age groups of nonpatients, is about 1.0, with a standard deviation of less than 1.0. This variable tends to distribute on a J-Curve. Approximately 80% of all nonpatient adults give one texture answer. For this reason, the retest reliabilities for texture responses usually range from the middle .80's to the low .90's in both short- and long-term retest studies. Less than 10% of nonpatient adults give more than one texture answer; however, if the subject has recently experienced a significant emotional loss, the average number of texture responses will usually increase significantly.

Exner and Bryant (1974) found an average of nearly *four* texture responses in the records of 30 nonpatient adults who had recently separated from close emotional relationships. The subjects were retested approximately 10 months later. Twenty-one of the 30 reported that they had established new relationships or reconstructed the one that had been fractured earlier. They gave substantially fewer texture responses in the second test than in the first. Conversely, the nine subjects who reported a continuing sense of loss all gave three or more texture responses in the second test.

Although many psychological states are transient, others can form a more enduring overlay to the primary personality structure. Many psychopathological states have this characteristic, and just as they influence a broad spectrum of behaviors, they are also quite influential in the selection of Rorschach answers. Severe and/or enduring depression is an example of this. Depressed patients tend to give much higher frequencies of vista (*V*) and achromatic color (*C*'s) responses than do other groups. They also have more answers that are marked by a clear morbidity (*MOR*), and are usually low on a index of self-esteem. Haller (1982) retested 50 first admission depressives three or four days after the first test had been administered. She asked a randomly selected half of the subjects to give different answers in the second test than in the first. She found that group repeated about one-third of their answers from the first test in the second, whereas her control subjects repeated nearly 70% of their first test responses in the second test. In spite of the fact that the experimental group gave more than 68% new answers in the second test, the retest reliabilities for both groups remained quite high, and did not differ significantly for any of the variables related to depression.

As the state endures, so does its influence, and the more severe the state may be, its impact on decision making will be greater. Exner, Thomas, and Mason (1985) found that the retest reliabilities for the major indices of depression remained very high among inpatient adolescents diagnosed as major depressive disturbance even after having been in treatment for nearly one year. On the other hand, as the state dissipates, so too does its influence on the selection of Rorschach answers. In a study completed for this work, Exner, Cohen, and Hillman (1984) retested 46 subjects, diagnosed initially using DSM-III criteria as major depressive disorder, at the termination of their treatment. All had begun treatment as inpatients and continued treatment as outpatients for a period averaging almost 2 years. The retest correlations for each of the variables related to depression were very low, ranging from .19 for the vista variable, to .33 for the presence of Morbid Content responses.

In effect, the psychological state of the person taking the Rorschach will contribute in the final selection of the answers that are delivered. The influence of the state in the selection process will probably be proportionate to its impact on the individual, and its continuing influence will be proportionate to its durability. It will not always supersede other influencing traits, styles, or habits, *but it may.*

A SUMMARY OF THE OPERATIONS IN THE RESPONSE PROCESS

It is in the very few seconds before a response is delivered that all of these operations occur. The bulk of data concerning information processing and cognitive activity support the notion that some overlap occurs between these six operations during the total process. Quite possibly, there is some merit in considering the six operations as they occur in three phases of the response process, because they probably occur before the delivery of the first answer.

Phase I: 1. Visual input and encoding of the stimulus and its parts.

         2. Classification of the stimulus and/or its parts and a rank ordering of the many potential responses that are created.

Phase II: 3. Discarding potential answers that have low rankings.

         4. Discarding other potential answers through censorship.

Phase III: 5. Selection of some of the remaining responses by reason of traits or styles.

         6. Selection of some of the remaining responses because of the state influences.

After these phases or operations have occurred, the delivery of the first answer to a blot is given.

THE ROLE OF PROJECTION IN THE RESPONSE

Does projection occur in the selection and/or discarding of all responses? That position could be argued *only* if the definition of projection is extended to include all decision operations, but this seems a simplistic and overinclusive position. If the selection of a response is based exclusively on the classification and rank ordering operations, it seems highly unlikely that projection is involved. The more common, somewhat simplistic responses that are formulated mainly by using the contours of the blots, such as a bat, two dogs, a butterfly, a tree, and so on, are the best examples of answers for which there is no evidence of projection. Similarly, much or all of the discarding that ensues, during and after classification, probably does not include much, if any, of the influences of the projective process. Most of this is directed more by attitudes and values of the subject, and his or her perception of the test situation.

In a similar context, it is difficult to reason that the traits or styles of the subject are significantly impacted by projection as such. To the contrary, these are enduring characteristics that will be influential in directing the projective process when it does occur. The same relationship exists between state influences and projection; that is, the presence of the state may give direction to the projective process *if* it occurs. In fact, when a state is intense and broadly encompassing, it can easily give rise to much rich projective material.

It is impossible, in light of the present state of knowledge concerning the test, to make fine discriminations concerning which words, or segments of verbalizations include projection and which do not. It is possible that some material included in movement responses may reflect some projected elements, because there is no movement in the stimulus field. Considerable caution should be exercised before making such a translation however, because the response styles or traits could promote a greater tendency by some subjects to classify an object in a movement perspective. This is especially true when human figures are involved. Similarly, the classification of animals or inanimate objects in a movement perspective is probably increased by need and/or stress states. In other words, if the characteristics of the blot are conducive to the classification of movement, it is less likely that the movement answer involves projection.

Conversely, some kinds of movement go well beyond the stimulus features of the blot and do seem to represent projected material. For instance, the response, "two people," to Card III is a simple classification answer. Most subjects report two human figures when responding to this blot, because the contours of a substantial part of it can easily be classified that way. If, instead of giving the simple classification response, the subject says, "two people picking something up," the element of movement has been injected, but it still could be based on the classification of the stimulus features and selected for delivery because of the traits or styles of the subject. However, if the answer is, "two people thinking about each other," the movement component goes beyond the stimulus features available. It represents some projected material.

The more obvious projected material usually appears in the form of embellishments to a response. For example, a derivation of the illustration used above could be, "two people struggling to pick something up like they are straining in great pain." It goes well beyond the stimulus features and clearly illustrates projected material. Any embellishments related to the response, which go beyond the basic answer and beyond the stimulus characteristics of the blot, are almost certain to be projections. Often they provide an important interpretive source when the content of the record is reviewed. In some instances the projected material is such that it may fall into one of the categories for Special Scores used in the System. For example, the scoring for morbid content (*MOR*) is based on a combination of the content of the response and how it is characterized. In other words, it usually represents some elaboration or embellishment to the basic answer. But although the scoring is important, it fails to capture the rich idiography that will often manifest in the projected material. This is why it is critical to review the verbal material in the record quite carefully during the interpretation.

It is important to recognize that not all of the responses, or all of the verbiage represents projected material. In fact, the majority of nonpatient records have more responses that contain *no* projections than those that do have that feature. It is less common, but not infrequent, to find records in which no projected material appears to exist. Usually these are closely guarded, relatively short protocols in which each response is limited to a few words. Those records are no less valid than the more elaborated protocols, but they do lack the rich, idiosyncratic features of the subject that tend to appear in projections and which, at times, contribute much in fleshing out a description of the subject.

SUMMARY

Although the process of the Rorschach is very complex, provoking an abundance of perceptual and cognitive operations, and laying open the psychological door for projection to occur, it is not a complicated assessment tool for the adept user. The procedures by which the data of the test are obtained are simplistic, but also delicate. If they are violated by intent or naiveté of the user, the method becomes reduced from a test to a composite of verbiage, the efficacy of which will depend largely on the clinical skills of the user plus a great deal of good fortune. Conversely, when the standard procedures for collecting the data are employed faithfully, the yield is very substantial. It provides information about habits, traits, and styles, and about the presence of states, and about many other variables that can be listed under the broad rubric encompassed by the term *personality*.

As noted earlier, the test is not an x-ray of the mind or soul, but it does afford, in a brief glimpse, a picture of the psychology of the person, as it is, and to some extent as it has been, and to some extent as it will be. It is not difficult to interpret the basics of the test, but the more sophisticated interpreter will always be able to glean more information from the data of the test because of his or her understanding of how the test works.

REFERENCES

Abramson, L. S. (1951) The influence of set for area on the Rorschach Test results. *Journal of Consulting Psychology,* **15,** 337–342.

Ames, L. B., Learned, J., Metraux, R. W., & Walker, R. N. (1952) *Child Rorschach Responses.* New York: Hoeber-Harper.

Ames, L. B., Metraux, R. W., and Walker, R. N. (1971) *Adolescent Rorschach Responses.* New York: Brunner/Mazel.

Armbruster, G. L., Miller, A. S., and Exner, J. E. (1974) Rorschach responses of parachute trainees at the beginning of training and prior to the first jump. Workshops Study No. 201 (unpublished), Rorschach Workshops.

Beck, S. J. (1945) *Rorschach's Test II: A Variety of Personality Pictures.* New York: Grune & Stratton.

Beck, S. J., Beck, A. G., Levitt, E. E., and Molish, H. B. (1961) *Rorschach's Test I: Basic Processes* (3rd Ed.) New York: Grune & Stratton.

Cattell, R. B. (1951) Principles of design in "projective" or misperceptive tests of personality. In

H. Anderson & G. Anderson (Eds.) *Projective Techniques*. Englewood Cliffs, N.J.: Prentice-Hall.

Coffin, T. E. (1941) Some conditions of suggestion and suggestibility: A study of certain attitudinal and situational factors in the process of suggestion. *Psychological Monographs, 53,* Whole No. 241.

Colligan, S. C. and Exner, J. E. (1985) Responses of schizophrenics and nonpatients to a tachistoscopic presentation of the Rorschach. *Journal of Personality Assessment, 49,* 129-136.

Dalhstrom, W. G., Welsh, G. S., and Dahlstrom, L. E. (1972) *An MMPI Handbook. Volume 1* (rev.) Minneapolis: University of Minnesota Press.

Dinoff, M. (1960) Subject awareness of examiner influence in a testing situation. *Journal of Consulting Psychology, 24,* 465.

Dubrovner, R. J., VonLackum, W. J., & Jost, H. (1950) A study of the effect of color on productivity and reaction time in the Rorschach Test. *Journal of Clinical Psychology, 6,* 331–336.

Exner, J. E. (1959) The influence of chromatic and achromatic color in the Rorschach. *Journal of Projective Techniques, 23,* 418–425.

Exner, J. E. (1974) *The Rorschach: A Comprehensive System. Volume 1.* New York: Wiley.

Exner, J. E. (1978) *The Rorschach: A Comprehensive System. Volume 2. Recent Research and Advanced Interpretation.* New York: Wiley.

Exner, J. E. (1980) But it's only an inkblot. *Journal of Personality Assessment, 44,* 562–577.

Exner, J. E. (1983) Rorschach Assessment. In I. B. Weiner (Ed.) *Clinical Methods in Psychology.* New York: Wiley.

Exner, J. E., and Armbruster, G. L. (1974) Increasing R by altering instructions and creating a time set. Workshops Study No. 209 (unpublished) Rorschach Workshops.

Exner, J. E., Armbruster, G. L., and Mittman, B. (1978) The Rorschach response process. *Journal of Personality Assessment, 42,* 27–38.

Exner, J. E., Armbruster, G. L., and Viglione, D. (1978) The temporal stability of some Rorschach features. *Journal of Personality Assessment, 42,* 474–482.

Exner, J. E., Armbruster, G. L., Walker, E. J., and Cooper, W. H. (1975) Anticipation of elective surgery as manifest in Rorschach records. Workshops Study No. 213 (unpublished) Rorschach Workshops.

Exner, J. E., and Bryant, E. L. (1974) Rorschach responses of subjects recently divorced or separated. Workshops Study No. 206 (unpublished) Rorschach Workshops.

Exner, J. E., Cohen, J. B., and Hillman, L. B. (1984) A retest of 46 major depressive disorder patients at the termination of treatment. Workshops Study No. 275 (unpublished) Rorschach Workshops.

Exner, J. E., and Leura, A. V. (1976) Variations in the ranking Rorschach responses as a function of situational set. Workshops Study No. 221 (unpublished) Rorschach Workshops.

Exner, J. E., and Martin, L. S. (1981) Responses to Card I when shown with Dd34 eliminated. Workshops Study No. 279 (unpublished) Rorschach Workshops.

Exner, J. E., Martin, L. S., and Cohen, J. B. (1983) Card by card response frequencies for patient and nonpatient populations. Workshops Study No. 276 (unpublished) Rorschach Workshops.

Exner, J. E., Thomas, E. E., and Cohen, J. B. (1983) The temporal consistency of test variables for 50 nonpatient adults after 12 to 14 months. Workshops Study No. 281 (unpublished) Rorschach Workshops.

Exner, J. E., Thomas, E. E., and Mason, B. (1985) Children's Rorschachs: Description and prediction. *Journal of Personality Assessment, 49,* 13–20.

Exner, J. E., and Weiner, I. B. (1982) *The Rorschach: A Comprehensive System. Volume 3: Assessment of Children and Adolescents.* New York: Wiley.

Exner, J. E., and Wylie, J. R. (1976) Alterations in frequency of response and color articulation as related to alterations in the coloring of specific blot areas. Workshops Study No. 219, (unpublished) Rorschach workshops.

Exner, J. E., and Wylie, J. R. (1977) Differences in the frequency of responses to the D1 area of Card X using an achromatic version. Workshops Study No. 237 (unpublished) Rorschach Workshops.

Fisher, D. F., Monty, R. A., and Senders, J. W. (Eds.) (1981) *Eye Movements: Cognition & Visual Perception.* Hillsdale, NJ: Erlbaum Associates.

Ford, M. (1946) *The Application of the Rorschach Test to Young Children.* University of Minnesota, Institute of Child Welfare.

Frank, L. K. (1939) Projective methods for the study of personality. *Journal of Psychology,* **8,** 389–413.

Gibby, R. G. (1951) The stability of certain Rorschach variables under conditions of experimentally induced sets: I. The intellectual variables. *Journal of Projective Techniques,* **15,** 3–26.

Goetcheus, G. (1967) The effects of instructions and examiners on the Rorschach. Unpublished M.A. Thesis, Bowling Green State University.

Goodman, N. L. (1979) Examiner influence on the Rorschach: The effect of sex, sex-pairing and warmth on the testing atmosphere. Doctoral Dissertation, Long Island University.

Gross, L. (1959) Effects of verbal and nonverbal reinforcement on the Rorschach. *Journal of Consulting Psychology,* **23,** 66–68.

Haller, N. (1982) The reliability of Rorschach depressive indices in major depressive disorder. Doctoral Dissertation, United States International University.

Halpern, F. (1953) *A Clinical Approach to Children's Rorschachs.* New York: Grune & Stratton.

Hersen, M., and Greaves, S. T. (1971) Rorschach productivity as related to verbal reinforcement. *Journal of Personality Assessment,* **35,** 436–441.

Hertz, M. R. (1934) The reliability of the Rorschach ink-blot test. *Journal of Applied Psychology,* **18,** 461–477.

Hochberg, J. (1981) Levels of Perceptual Organization. In M. Kubovy & J. R. Pomerantz (Eds.) *Perceptual Organization.* Hillsdale, NJ: Erlbaum Associates.

Holzberg, J. D. (1960) Reliability Re-examined. In M. Rickers- Ovsiankina (Ed.) *Rorschach Psychology,* New York: Wiley.

Horiuchi, H. (1961) A study of perceptual process of Rorschach cards by tachistoscopic method on movement and shading responses. *Journal of Projective Techniques,* **25,** 44–53.

Hutt, M., Gibby, R. G., Milton, E. O., and Pottharst, K. (1950) he effect of varied experimental ''sets'' upon Rorschach test performance. *Journal of Projective Techniques,* **14,** 181–187.

Klopfer, B., and Kelley, D. M. (1942) *The Rorschach Technique.* Yonkers-on-Hudson, NY: World Book.

Leura, A. V., and Exner, J. E. (1978) Structural differences in the records of adolescents as a function of being tested by one's own teacher. Workshops Study No. 265 (unpublished) Rorschach Workshops.

London, H., and Exner, J. E. (1978) *Dimensions of Personality.* New York: Wiley.

Magnussen, M. G. (1960) Verbal and nonverbal reinforcers in the Rorschach situation. *Journal of Clinical Psychology,* **16,** 167–169.

Martin, L. S., and Thomas, E. E. (1982) Selection of preferred responses by high school students. Workshops Study No. 278 (unpublished) Rorschach Workshops.

Matarazzo, J. D., and Mensh, I. N. (1952) Reaction time characteristics of the Rorschach Test. *Journal of Consulting Psychology,* **16,** 132–139.

Meer, B. (1955) The relative difficulty of the Rorschach cards. *Journal of Projective Techniques,* **19,** 43–53.

Meer, B., and Singer, J. L. (1950) A note on the "father" and "mother" cards in the Rorschach inkblots. *Journal of Consulting Psychology,* **14,** 482–484.

Miale, F. R., and Harrower-Erikson, M. R. (1940) Personality structure in the psychoneuroses. *Rorschach Research Exchange,* **4,** 71–74.

Murray, H. A. (1938) *Explorations in Personality.* New York: Oxford University Press.

Neisser, U. (1976) *Cognition and Reality.* New York: Appleton-Century-Crofts.

Orange, A. (1953) Perceptual consistency as measured by the Rorschach. *Journal of Projective Techniques,* **17,** 224–228.

Pascal, G., Ruesch, H., Devine, D., and Suttell, B. (1950) A study of genital symbols on the Rorschach Test: Presentation of method and results. *Journal of Abnormal and Social Psychology,* **45,** 285–289.

Phillips, L., and Smith, J. G. (1953) *Rorschach Interpretation: Advanced Technique.* New York: Grune & Stratton.

Piotrowski, Z. (1957) *Perceptanalysis.* New York: Macmillan.

Pomerantz, J. R., and Kubovy, M. (1981) Perceptual Organization: An Overview. In M. Kubovy & J. R. Pomerantz (Eds.) *Perceptual Organization.* Hillsdale, NJ: Erlbaum Associates.

Rabin, A. I., and Sanderson, M. H. (1947) An experimental inquiry into some Rorschach procedures. *Journal of Clinical Psychology,* **3,** 216–225.

Sendin, C. (1981) *Respuestas Populares al test de Rorschach in sujetos Espanoles.* Proceedings of the 10th International Rorschach Congress, Washington, D.C.

Shalit, B. (1965) Effects of environmental stimulation on the *M., FM,* and *m* responses in the Rorschach. *Journal of Projective Techniques and Personality Assessment,* **29,** 228–231.

Stein, M. I. (1949) Personality factors involved in the temporal development of Rorschach responses. *Rorschach Research Exchange,* **13,** 355–414.

Thomas, E. E., Alinsky, D., and Exner, J. E. (1982) The stability of some Rorschach variables in 9-year-olds as compared with nonpatient adults. Workshop Study No. 441 (unpublished) Rorschach Workshops.

Thomas, E. E., Exner, J. E., and Leura, A. V. (1977) Differences in ranking responses by two groups of nonpatient adults as a function of set concerning the origins of the responses Workshop Study No. 251 (unpublished) Rorschach Workshops.

Vernon, P. E. (1933) The Rorschach inkblot test. II. *British Journal of Medical Psychology,* **13,** 179–205.

Wickes, T. A. (1956) Examiner influence in a testing situation. *Journal of Consulting Psychology,* **20,** 23–26.

PART II

Administration and Scoring

CHAPTER 3

Decisions and Procedures

Before laying hand to the Rorschach cards, the person responsible for the assessment must make some important decisions. One of the most important of these concerns the appropriateness of the Rorschach for the task at hand. The Rorschach *does not* provide data from which answers to all questions can be derived. The data that unfold from the test are essentially descriptive in substance. The data represent a report from the subject of what he or she has seen or imagined when confronted with the 10 inkblots. That report is a complex specimen of behavior which, when scored and compared with norms and studied for its apparent idiosyncracies, can be translated into a series of descriptive statements concerning the subject. This description can be quite lengthy, converging on such features as response styles, affectivity, cognitive operations, motivations, preoccupations, and interpersonal-interenvironmental perceptions and response tendencies. Ordinarily, the description will include reference both to overt and covert behaviors, the characterization of either being determined mainly by the richness of the protocol. Many statements may be made with considerable sureness, whereas others may be more speculative; but most will represent the subject as he or she is, rather than how the subject may have been, or will be. It is common for the description to include some information concerning etiological factors, and possibly to offer predictions, but generally these kinds of statements are derived less directly from the data of the protocol. More likely they are the product of using inductive and deductive logic to integrate the data from the record with other available information concerning the subject. As such, they are more speculative and rely heavily on the accumulated knowledge of the interpreter regarding personality, response styles, psychopathology, and behavior. Rorschach data can be used legitimately for some speculations about the past or the future. For instance, piecing together data concerning the variety of assets and liabilities of the subject, *as manifest* in Rorschach data, can lead to logical recommendations about intervention objectives and alternatives. Similarly, an evaluation of the apparent strengths and/or relationships of certain responses tendencies can generate logical speculation about the chronicity, or even the origins of such tendencies.

But speculation can be carried on *ad absurdum*. It would seem that, too frequently, clinicians have been enticed by the intrigue of questions (or by their own grandiosity) into issuing verdicts about people and their behaviors, after reviewing a Rorschach, which have little relevance to the data found in the record. In good assessment practice, it follows that the assessor will use procedures appropriate to the questions for which answers are being sought. For instance, questions concerning parent interaction, religious preference, hobbies, supervisor or teacher ratings, sibling relationships, sexual preference, or the frequency of intercourse can be relevant in some cases. Any or all may be important questions but at best, most Rorschach data will be only indirectly related to any of them. There are much better methods than the Rorschach to gain these kinds of information. A good interview or a thorough social history should provide most of it. Just as questions of this sort are inappropriate to the Rorschach, so too are certain classes of prediction, such as success or attrition in some types of training, marital success, ultimate family size, length of hospitalization, or the probability of parole violation. Most of these are intelligent questions and the well-equipped psychologist, given appropriate information and adequate criterion measures, might attack them with considerable success, *but not from the Rorschach alone, and possibly not using the Rorschach at all.*

There are other questions often asked of the clinician that may seem more compatible with the Rorschach method but are not necessarily so. These are questions concerning intellectual functioning and problems of neurological involvement. Both have been considered in research with the Rorschach and some positive relationships have been found. Some elements in the Rorschach do correlate positively with indices of intelligence, but not to the extent that the Rorschach can be used in a reliable and valid manner to substitute for an intelligence test. Similarly, there are some elements in the Rorschach that have a reasonably high probability of occurrence in some conditions of neurologically related dysfunctioning, but *none* have proven to be diagnostically differentiating except in those cases where the dysfunction is so severe that it can easily be detected by visually observing the subject. Thus if the primary purpose of the assessment relates to questions of intelligence or cognitive functioning, the Rorschach is not the test of choice. It may be useful in the overall assessment of the subject, but as an adjunct to provide some information concerning the personality of the subject if that seems relevant.

THE RORSCHACH AND THE TEST BATTERY

The strength of the Rorschach rests with its yield concerning some of the psychological functioning of the subject. In many cases it is important to integrate this yield with data and information from other sources. In some instances, the yield may be sufficient to address the assessment issues that have been raised.

In the historical framework of psychodiagnostics or assessment, the clinician usually is inclined to use multiple procedures. The mainstay of this approach has been the interview and the "test battery." The latter sometimes may include as few as two or three tests, but not uncommonly it has been comprised of more than three, and often more than five. The rationale for the use of the test battery has been expounded considerably (Rapaport, Gill, & Schafer, 1946; Piotrowski, 1958; Harrower, 1965). The premises underlying the test battery approach are essentially twofold. The first is that no test is so broad in its scope to test everything. Different tests focus on different dimensions or functions of the subject, and thus the test battery provides a broader data base from which to evaluate the *total* person. Second, various tests do overlap to some extent, thereby affording the possibilities of cross-validating information derived from any single test. The test battery procedure is argued to minimize error and maximize accuracy. Proponents of the test battery approach have suggested that it can be viewed as multiple samples of behavior, noting that data from a single instrument will generate greater speculation, whereas the composite of data from several instruments provides for greater certainty in conclusions.

The positions supporting the test battery approach have been challenged in several studies (Sarbin, 1943; Kelly & Fiske, 1950; Gage, 1953; Kostlan, 1954; Giedt, 1955). Data from each point to the fact that clinicians often do not use all of the data available to them, or if they do, they are prone to weigh some segments inordinately. These critics also argue that a ceiling of predictive accuracy is usually reached quickly and adding more data provides only slight, if any, increase in the predictive correlation. Several studies appear to refute these criticisms about the test battery approach, demonstrating that it does work well in the clinical situation (Vernon, 1950; MacKinnon, 1951; Stern, Stein, & Bloom, 1956; Luborsky & Holt, 1957). In each, validity is increased as the data are increased. Holt (1958, 1970) has probably offered the most cogent arguments about the additive process and how it can be essential for some kinds of descriptive or predictive conclusions.

Support for the test battery approach does not mean that it should be used always; nor does it mean that the same composite of tests should be used when a battery is required. One of the most important decisions in the assessment process concerns which procedures to use. This decision usually will evolve from consideration of the questions to be addressed, but the decision does not always end there. In some situations a subject may react to a procedure in a very unpredicted manner, providing new questions and forcing the assessor to alter the planned procedures. For example, a subject whose WAIS performance is extremely bizarre and psychotic-like probably need not be administered the Rorschach if the prime question to be answered concerns the presence of a psychotic state. Similarly, the subject rendering 25 rich Rorschach responses might not be administered the TAT unless important unanswered questions remain after the Rorschach has been examined, and which the TAT might best address. Many clinicians are prone to administer both the MMPI and the Rorschach to their clients on the premise that they are complimentary, but offer data derived from different task sources (i.e., self-report and cognitive-perceptual activity). Although it is true that they compliment each other, there may be many instances when the MMPI alone may suffice, or other instances where the Rorschach might be the preferred instrument because of the nature of the questions posed.

Unfortunately, there remain far too many instances where a clinician perseverates in the use of a "standard" test battery no matter what the appointed task, and no matter what data become available during the testing process. This tactic of assessment harks back to the 1940s and 1950s when the primary role of the clinician was diagnostics and much less was known about tests, procedures, personality, and psychopathology. It may have been important then, to provide a sort of security blanket for those confronted with the task, but that is no longer true. Great chunks of data are not necessarily required for most assessment goals. It is also clear that the amount of time consumed in administering test after test is often disproportionate to the objectives of the process, a situation that is made even worse when the clinician does not use all of the data obtained from the lengthy procedure. Unfortunately, hospital and clinic files have become filled with psychological test reports of varying lengths, many of which replay information given in the interview and provide little description from the test data even though 5 to 10 hours of testing occurred. No clinician should insult the dignity of the subject with such a piece of work. If a test battery is used, then all of the data obtained should be interpreted.

Another important decision that must be made by the assessor is the placement of each procedure in the process. For instance, Van de Castle (1946) found that test order could alter the incidence of human content responses in the Rorschach. Grisso and Meadow (1967) reported differences in WAIS performances depending on whether the WAIS was administered prior to or after the Rorschach. Exner and Hark (1979) studied 200 WAIS records, 100 of which were administered prior to the Rorschach and 100 administered after the Rorschach. No significant differences were found for any of the WAIS subtest scores *or* for the distributions of Rorschach scores. Nonetheless, good judgment should be exercised in the placement of any test in an assessment process. For example, Exner and

Hark (1980) found that Rorschachs administered after three hours of prior testing do have a significantly lower average number of responses than those administered after only 90 minutes of prior testing. It is also probable, although not proven, that Rorschach productivity will be affected by almost any procedures in the assessment process that are stressful to the subject.

For example, subjects with some cognitive dysfunctioning will often have difficulties on the Categories Test, or the Tactual Performance Test of the Halstead-Reitan Battery. Thus it is probably not wise to administer the Rorschach *immediately* after either of these procedures unless the subject has performed quite well on them. Similarly, it is probably best not to administer the Rorschach *immediately* after the MMPI. Although the MMPI can yield very important information concerning a subject, it can also produce a fatigue effect that could impact Rorschach performance.

Whenever a test battery approach is selected, the time factor can be critical. Usually, when neuropsychological issues are not involved, the total assessment process can be completed within a three-hour time frame. Weiner (1966) presented an exceptionally fine summary of those indicators relevant to the diagnosis of schizophrenia using a test battery that should take less than three hours. In contemporary assessment that would be targeted toward a reasonably full picture of the person, three tests might best be considered as forming the nucleus of the assessment procedure: (1) one of the Wechsler Intelligence Scales, (2) the Rorschach, and (3) the MMPI. Each is empirically sturdy and each provides a wealth of information from which the sophisticated clinician can generate many important and meaningful hypotheses concerning the subject.

None of the foregoing should be interpreted to mean that the Rorschach should always be used as a part of a test battery. It can stand alone quite well and provide much data concerning a subject, descriptive data which ordinarily will go well beyond that extracted from other tests. One need only to review the extensive literature concerning the yield of the test to gauge the wealth of information that it can provide, either from the quantitative analysis or from the qualitative analysis of the projected material (Beck, 1937, 1945, 1952, 1960; Exner, 1969, 1978; Klopfer & Kelly, 1942; Klopfer et al., 1954; Hertz, 1969; Piotrowski, 1958, 1969; Schafer, 1954). In this context, the assessor should not be adverse to using the Rorschach alone if the assessment questions are specific to the yield of the test.

It is also important to reaffirm that some questions are unanswerable from any assessment procedure, whether Rorschach, interview, observation, or other tests. Other questions can only be addressed in a speculative manner. If, however, the prime question conerns a description of the psychological operations, needs, styles, habits, and so on of the subject, the Rorschach is probably the best instrument to accomplish that task, of those procedures currently available. It is a worthy but sometimes delicate method that will generate great amounts of information about its subject if used wisely. The interpretation of the test requires much training. It is not a simplistic, "this equals that" technique, but with appropriate training the clinician should be able to provide a broad spectrum of information about the subject of the test.

PROCEDURES OF ADMINISTRATION

Once the decision to use the Rorschach in the assessment process has been made, it is vitally important that the test be used appropriately. Factors such as seating, instructions, recording responses, and Inquiry all become critical to generating the data bank from which many conclusions will be reached. Sometimes these items seem incidental to the task at hand, but they are not. The procedures employed with the inkblots can often dictate whether a protocol is truly valid or whether it should be reduced to the level of a free-wheeling interview. Alterations in procedure can influence such elements as the number of answers and the characteristics of the response as reported. These serve only to minimize the ultimate data available to the interpreter and, in the instance of the more naive user, can create some alterations in the final description rendered.

Seating   The preferred seating for Rorschach administration is where the subject and examiner *sit side-by-side*. This can be done at a table, or using two comfortable chairs with a small table between them, or any of several variations of this. There are two reasons for the side-by-side seating. The first, and most important, is to reduce the effects of inadvertent and unwanted cues from the examiner that may influence the subject. Second, the side-by-side position affords the examiner a much better view from which to see the features of the blot as they are referred to by the subject.

Rorschach apparently had some awareness of the potential for examiner influence and used side-by-side seating in his experiment. However, the systematizers who extended his work varied the seating arrangement in accord with their own positions concerning the test. Klopfer and Hertz continued to use the side-by-side seating; Piotrowski also recommended the side-by-side position, but stressed that it should not be used if it necessitated a change in the regimen used in interviewing or prior testing; Beck preferred to sit behind the subject; and Rapaport recommended a face-to-face seating on the assumption that it is the most natural for interviewing and testing. Actually, there is no psychological test that requires the face-to-face arrangement. Even when materials must be laid before the subject, as in some intelligence testing, the examiner can sit next to the subject.

The impact of the examiner, or cues given by the examiner, should not be regarded lightly in any testing situation, and especially one in which the Rorschach is involved. Coffin (1941) demonstrated that when factors intended to provoke projection exist (such as the ambiguity and novelty of the Rorschach situation), an increase in the subject's susceptibility to influence or suggestions is likely to occur. Schachtel (1945) was among the first to offer a major conceptual position concerning this element. He stressed the subject's problem in reacting to the total test situation, which includes apparent freedom yet simultaneous control, compounded by the relationship between the examiner and subject. He argued that the subject tends to create a ''subjective definition'' of the situation. Schafer (1954) extended this idea considerably, emphasizing the interaction between the subject and the dynamics of the situation. He suggested that factors such as required levels of communication, violation of privacy, the lack of situational control, and the danger of premature self-awareness arouse anxiety and defensiveness from which specific reactions to the examiner evolve. Neither Schachtel nor Schafer posited that the Rorschach performance can be altered completely by the examiner-subject relationships, but both warned that many of the test variables can be affected.

Research on the subject of examiner influence has revealed some important findings. Lord (1950) used three female examiners in a counterbalanced design to test 36 male subjects. Each subject was tested three times, once by each of the examiners who varied their examiner roles across three models. One was designed to make the subject feel accepted and successful, a second to make the subject feel rejected and a failure, and the third a more standard procedure of affective neutrality. Her results were clouded by the complexity of the retest design, but many significant differences did occur across the different rapport models; however, the largest and most frequent differences occurred across examiners, regardless of the rapport model that they employed.

Baughman (1951) studied the protocols obtained from 633 subjects by 15 examiners. He found that the records obtained by most of the examiners were highly comparable, but that records obtained by some examiners continually deviated quite markedly. He attributed those deviations to variations in procedure *or* to the examiner-subject relationship. Gibby, Miller, and Walker (1953) also found substantial differences among examiners for length of protocol and certain classes of scores, especially pure Form, color, and shading.

Masling (1965) hypothesized that unintentional reinforcement by examiners could be a major factor underlying the observation that subjects produce different responses for different subjects. He created an especially clever design to test this proposition, using 14 graduate students, naive to the Rorschach, who volunteered for special training in the test which would be quick and efficient. Randomized into two groups, all received identical instruction except that one group was given the set that experienced examiners always elicit more human than animal responses. The second group of trainees were given the opposite set. After the training sessions were completed, each student tested two subjects. The sessions were audio recorded with the expectancy of finding evidence for verbal conditioning by the student examiners. The two groups did differ in the predicted direction for the ratio of human to animal responses, *but no evidence* was found for verbal conditioning. Masling logically concluded that the examiners influenced subjects with postural, gestural, and facial cues.

Exner, Leura, and George (1976) used a modification of the Masling design to test the impact of seating on the outcome. They trained 24 student volunteers, randomized into four groups of six each, to administer the test. Two of the groups used a face-to-face seating, whereas the second two groups were trained to sit side-by-side. One face-to-face group and one side-by-side group were given the set that competent examiners obtain more human responses and the other two groups were set to believe the opposite. After the training was complete, each student examiner tested three subjects and the sessions were videotaped. The two groups using the face-to-face seating did differ from each other in the predicted direction for the ratio of human to animal responses, and behavioral ratings of the videotapes confirmed Masling's hypothesis that more postural, gestural, and facial cues would occur when the subject gave a response related to the set. Similar differences in the behavioral ratings for postural, gestural, and facial activity were found for the two groups giving the test using the side-by-side seating, *but they did not differ for the ratio of human to animal response.*

The foregoing should not be interpreted to suggest that all, or most all Rorschach variables can easily be altered through some subtle set given either to the examiner or the subject. As noted earlier in the Exner (1980) and Haller (1982) studies, the distributions of most scores do not differ even though subjects, by instruction, give different responses in a retest than they did in the first test. In the same context, Fosberg (1938) found no major differences in a retest design in which subjects were asked to give their best and worst impressions. Carp and Shavzin (1950) used the same technique and obtained similar results. Similarly, the basic features of the protocol do not change as a product of ego-altering sets (Cox & Sarason, (1954); by requests to respond as quickly as possible (Williams, 1954); when the test is introduced as one of imagination (Peterson, 1957), or when the subject is led to believe that there are right and wrong answers (Phares, Stewart, &

Foster, 1960). Even when the face-to-face position is used, some variables are not affected although sets are given to the examiner concerning desirable responses. In two studies (Strauss, 1968; Strauss & Marwit, 1970) examiners were "set" to expect records in which a higher number of human movement (M) or a higher number of chromatic color responses (FC, CF, C) would occur, and also created an expectancy for long or short records. The results indicate no significant differences for any of the sets. On the other hand, the results of the Goodman (1979) study, described in the preceding chapter, indicate that more experienced examiners will generally be rated as warmer in their interactions with a subject, and will also be more likely to obtain records in which an average number of answers occur.

It would be folly to assume that the side-by-side seating eliminates all examiner influence, but it does reduce the prospect of the subject being influenced inordinately by the nonverbal behaviors of the examiner, and this is probably true of any test. Unfortunately, the accumulated information concerning behavior modifying techniques has made considerably less impact on assessment procedures than should logically have been the case. The examiner who fails to weigh the potential impact of those behaviors in the assessment situation only makes his or her task more difficult and may even provide a disservice to the subject.

Introducing the Test   Ordinarily, no special elaboration concerning the nature of the Rorschach should be required *if the subject has been prepared properly for the overall assessment process*. In most cases this will be done after a relatively brief interview, during which the examiner seeks to insure that the subject has a reasonable awareness of the purpose of the assessment. Most subjects are aware of the general purpose of assessment, but unfortunately much of that awareness includes some negative or erroneous assumptions. In instances when a subject is self-referred the responsibility for clarifying the purpose will rest with the examiner. In cases where the subject is referred for assessment by someone else, it is the responsibility of that person to explain why the referral has been made. Similarly, it is the responsibility of the examiner to provide the subject with an overview of the procedures in the assessment process.

An important purpose in providing the introductory overview concerning procedures is to ease any mistrust or anxiety that the subject may have about the situation. But beyond that, the subject is entitled to know what will be happening and what will be done with the results—when they will be available and who will receive them. The routine should be honest, but the description of the procedures need not be overly elaborate. The purpose is to describe the procedures, not how they are interpreted. For example, if a Bender Gestalt and a WAIS are planned as a part of the routine, the examiner might say, "I am going to have you copy some designs and then we will do a test that has several different parts. In one I'll ask you to remember some numbers, in another I'll ask you create some designs using some blocks, in another I'll ask you to tell me what different words mean, and so on."

In the course of the overview a statement such as, "And we will be doing the inkblot test, maybe you've heard of it" can be included. The brevity of the statement is not meant to circumvent a longer explanation about the test and sometimes more information may be required. But most subjects are "test-wise," because testing has become an integral part of the culture, and most will have taken tests for different reasons, such as job placement and academic achievement. Similarly, most subjects will have some familiarity with the inkblot method, whether it is the child who has made inkblots in the first grade or the adult who has formulated some ideas about the test through the media, educational experience, games, or relationships with others who have been administered the Rorschach.

If the subject expresses naiveté about inkblots, and wants to pursue the issue of why the test is to be used, the response should be honest (e.g., "It is just some inkblots that I'll show you and ask you what they might be.") Depending on the circumstances, a statement can be added to the effect that it is a test that provides some information about some of the characteristics of a person or, it helps us to understand something about the personality of an individual. Occasionally a subject may want to discuss some of the procedures in greater detail, including the Rorschach and especially how it works. It is probably best to avoid more detailed explanations of any of the procedures prior to testing, and instead offer the subject an opportunity to raise more questions after all of the data have been collected.

Assuming that the seating is appropriate, and that the subject has been prepared for testing, the procedure of administering the Rorschach becomes relatively simple. Some sort of alert to the subject is in order (e.g., "Now we are going to do the inkblot test."). The specific content of the alert will depend largely on what dialogue ensued when the examiner did the overview of all procedures. Thus there are some instances when the test might be identified as the Rorschach, but the term *inkblot* will probably be preferable in most cases, and can be used freely. In a few instances some explanation about how inkblots are made is appropriate, especially if the subject is a young child. In other instances the particularly anxious subject may ask something about correct answers, and the standard response should be to the effect that people see all sorts of things in the blots. But this kind of commentary should be avoided whenever possible and, most specifically, *it should not* include any reference to card turning, right or wrong answers, or any statement that might create a set about the quantity of answers to be given. The ultimate nature of the pretest phase of Rorschach administration must be left to the judgment of the examiner. No two subjects or testing situations will be completely identical; however, it is important that the examiner accomplish the pretest procedures as smoothly as possible within the realities of the test situation.

Usually, the blots will be visible to the subject, stacked *face down,* and in the appropriate order, with Card I on top. They should be within easy reach of the examiner *but not* of the subject. The Location Sheet that will be used during the Inquiry phase of the test should not be visible at this time. Because all responses will be recorded verbatim, the examiner should be well prepared with plenty of paper, and an extra pen or pencil can sometimes prove very important.

Instructions The test begins by handing the subject the first blot and asking, *"What might this be?"* That is the basic instruction to the subject and nothing need be added.

If, in spite of the pretest preparation, the subject comments, "It's an inkbot," the examiner should counter with an acknowledgment plus a restatement of the basic instruction, such as, "That's right. This is the inkblot test, and I want you to tell me what it might be."

The Response (Association) Phase The period during which the subject is giving responses to the blots has often been called the Free Association (Exner, 1974, 1978; Exner & Weiner, 1982), but that label can be misleading because the subject is not really associating to the blot. Instead, he or she is defining it and selecting responses for delivery from those definitions. Whatever the nomenclature, it is a time when the examiner's responsibilities become somewhat more complex than during the pretest preparation. The examiner must record all verbal material *verbatim*, quickly and efficiently, field questions on occasion, and in some instances provide a nondirective form of encouragement. The examiner must avoid injecting any set, bias, or direction into the situation except in those few instances when encouragement is required. Silence by the examiner is the rule, interrupted only during the exchange of cards or when a comment is necessary, but even then the verbalizations from the examiner should be formulated with care. As noted earlier, it is the perfunctory utterance that has the potential to impinge on the ambiguity of the situation. Even the most simple response, such as "mmm-hmm," can operate as a significant influence without any awareness by the subject.

The subject should *hold the card*. If some reluctance to do so is manifest, the examiner should say, "Here, take it." If the subject opts to place the card on the table, the examiner should not interfere, but initially it should be placed in the subject's hand.

Questions and Encouragement   It is not uncommon for subjects to ask a variety of questions, especially early into the test. The response from the examiner should be nondirective, conveying the general notion that people respond to the blots in different ways. The following are examples of questions commonly asked, and responses that would ordinarily be appropriate.

S: Can I turn it?

E: It's up to you.

S: Should I try to use all of it?

E: Whatever you like. Different people see different things.

S: Do you want me to show you where I see it?

E: If you like. (It is probably best at this point to avoid any mention of the Inquiry.)

S: Should I just use my imagination?

E: Yes, just tell me what you see. (It is more appropriate to use the word *see* rather than *reminds you of* to questions of this sort, stressing perception rather than association.)

S: (After giving a response) Is that the kind of thing you want?

E: Yes, just whatever it looks like to you.

S: Is that the right answer?

E: There are all sorts of answers.

S: Does it look like that to you?

E: Oh, I can see a lot of things.

S: How can you make anything out of what I see?

E: Why not wait until we are done and I'll try to explain it a bit more.

S: Do you buy these or just make them?

E: We buy them.

S: Do you always show people the same ones?

E: Yes.

S: How many of these are there?

E: Just 10.

S: How long will this take?

E: Not very long.

There is another class of question, the response to which will depend on the point at which it occurs in the Response Phase. These are questions concerning how many responses should be given. Often, before giving any answers or after giving only *one* response to Card I, a subject will ask, "How many things should I find?" The standard response by the examiner should be, *"If you take your time I am sure that you will find more than one."* If the subject gives only *one* response to Card I and then attempts to return the card to the examiner, a similar prompt is employed, *"If you take your time and look some more I think that you will find something else, too."*

The objective of the prompt is to "set" the subject to give a record of sufficient length to permit a valid interpretation. If, however, the subject fails to give a second answer to Card I, the examiner should *accept* that decision. If the subject does give *more than one* response to the first card and then asks, "How many should I see?," the standard response is, *"It's up to you."* This same response should be used if the subject raises a question about the quantity of answers while viewing cards *after* Card I.

Potential Rejections   In a few cases, especially with very resistant subjects, an attempt is made to reject the card. Usually the subject will say, "It doesn't look like anything to me" or, "I just don't see anything there" or, "All I can see is an inkblot, nothing else." If this occurs in responding to Card I, or to Card II after the subject has given only one answer to Card I, it may be an indication that the examiner has not created sufficient rapport with the subject during the overview of purposes and procedures. If this is true, it will be necessary to stop the administration and review the purpose of the assessment with the subject once again. Conversely, some subjects simply do not want to be tested and, unfortunately, there is no magic formula that will insure their cooperation. If this proves to be the case, efforts to administer the Rorschach should be abandoned. The latter is usually a very unusual instance that occurs with the extremely guarded and hostile subject, or occasionally with some who are extremely disorganized because of the psychological chaos created by an active psychotic state. The subject who is chaotically psychotic should not have been referred. As for the angry and guarded subject, the judgment and skills of the examiner must dictate the matter of disposition.

The most common attempts to reject cards do not occur with Cards I or II. Instead, they tend to occur later in the test, and quite often with Card IX, which seems to have the highest level of difficulty. If a subject has been giving responses to the preceding cards, the attempted rejection can be taken as an indicator of the discomfort that the subject is experiencing as the task proceeds. But it *does not mean that the subject cannot respond.* To the contrary, it suggests that he or she is having difficulty in the discarding and selection operations. Some reassurance can be helpful such as, *"Take your time, we are in no hurry."* If the subject persists in the rejection attempt, the examiner should be more firm, responding with, *"Look, take your time, everyone can find something. We've got all day if we need it."* This sort of pressure should be applied only in the exceptional circumstance where no other tactic can be used to avoid the rejection. It is likely that the remainder of the record will be brief and possibly more guarded than might otherwise be the case, but unfortunately, the alternative is to have a record that is missing responses to one or more cards, and it will probably not be valid.

THE PROBLEM OF LENGTHY RECORDS

Whereas the most common problem in Rorschach administration involves the excessively short record, some subjects become overly involved in the task, and because of their obsessive style, will give endless numbers of answers if permitted to do so. In the early days of the Rorschach, and extending through the 1960s, examiners had no guidelines to use to halt a subject if he or she seemed determined to provide very large numbers of answers to each blot. Exner (1974) found that the Beck tactic of encouraging for more than one response on each of the first five blots yielded an increase in the average R of nearly 10 responses; however, the majority of the increase consists of answers in which a common detail area (D) is used, that are based on pure form (F), and involve animal (A) content. In effect, the increased number of responses does not contribute significantly to the interpretive yield.

In a study completed for this work, protocols from various patient and nonpatient groups, ranging in length from 45 to 85 answers, were drawn from the data pool for study: Each of these 135 records were retyped, but including no more than the first five responses per blot. Both sets of records, the original full-length one and the reduced one, were interpreted by at least two of a group of six judges, working independently of each other, and they were also processed through a computer interpretation program. When the interpretive descriptions and conclusions were examined in pairs (i.e., one derived from the original and one derived from the reduced version for each subject), the interpretations were strikingly similar. In some instances, the longer record produced a more firm conclusion that the subject was obsessive or pedantic, but few other differences evolved, and they were not consistent. These findings suggest that it is reasonable to limit the number of answers that a subject is permitted to deliver, *under some circumstances*.

If a subject delivers *six* responses *to the first blot*, the examiner should intervene and take the blot from the subject. Subsequently, *if the same subject* delivers *five* answers to Card II, the same procedure should be employed, and so on. However, *anytime the subject delivers fewer than five answers to a blot, no further intervention should occur*.

This tactic has some hazards, and should be employed cautiously. For instance, the calculations for both the Affective Ratio and the Egocentricity Index may be affected as R is being controlled. Several other ratios and percentages might also be afffected, and the application of normative data, even though done proportionally, may be of questionable use for some variables. This procedure is a trade-off to replace the inordinately long rcord, which may be extremely time-consuming to administer and score, and equally problematic to interpret. It is important to note that if the subject gives fewer than *six* answers on Card I, *no intervention* will occur, *regardless of the number of answers on any subsequent blot*.

RECORDING THE RESPONSES

All responses must be recorded verbatim. This may seem like a difficult feat, especially for the Rorschach novice, but it is not as arduous as it might appear. Most Rorschachers use a relatively common scheme of abbreviations in recording answers. These combine the use of phonetics, the coding abbreviations for response content, and some logically derived abbreviations not unlike those found in speed writing. Some of the more common abbreviations are shown in Table 6.

There are two reasons that responses must be recorded verbatim. First, the examiner must be able to read them later to decide on the coding (scoring) for the response. The codes or scores are based on the presence of specific words or phrases. Responses that are not recorded verbatim cannot be coded accurately, and the record will not be valid. Second, the verbatim recording creates a permanent record of the test so that others can also

Table 6.   Abbreviations Commonly Used for Recording Rorschach Responses

Phonetically Derived		Logically Derived		Derived from Scores	
Abbreviation	Meaning	Abbreviation	Meaning	Abbreviation	Meaning
b	be	abt	about	h	human
c	see	a.t.	anything	a	animal
g	gee	bc	because	bl	blood
o	oh	bf	butterfly	cg	clothing
r	are	cb	could be	cl	cloud
u	you	dk	don't know	ex	explosion
y	why	e.t.	everything	fd	food
		frt	front	fi	fire
		j	just	ge	geography
		ll	looks like	hh	household
		mayb	may be	ls	landscape
		ss	some sort	na	nature
		st	something	sc	science
		wm	woman	sx	sex
		-g	ing	xy	x-ray

read the record and know *exactly* what the subject said. This is important for purposes of consultation, be even more so if the subject is retested at another time to cross-validate the findings, or to review changes that may have occurred as the result of treatment. The latter cannot be overestimated in importance. If the responses in the first administration are illegible, or not recorded verbatim, the comparison of the two records becomes difficult or impossible.

It is also important for the examiner to record the position of the blot when the response is given. The use of carat marks for this purpose were suggested by Loosli-Usteri (1929), using the peak of each angle to represent the direction of the top of the card, <, V, >, with no mark entered when the card is upright. A circle (0) may also be useful in noting instances when the subject has rotated the card completely *without stopping,* but this should not be confused with those instances when a subject deliberately turns the card to each side and examines each view before giving a response, <, V, >.

The format for recording responses should not vary from examiner to examiner. It is best to use 8½ by 11-inch paper, which is easiest to file, and to record the responses on the sheet *horizontally* rather than vertically, that is, with the 11-inch margin at the top. This provides ample room to record the Response Phase and the Inquiry Phase and still have room for recording the card number and a column for entering the scores. This format is illustrated in Figure 3.

INQUIRY PHASE

The procedure for administering the Rorschach becomes more complex for the examiner during the Inquiry. It is conducted *after* all responses are given to all 10 cards. The purpose of the Inquiry is to gain whatever additional information is necessary in order to score the response accurately, *as it occurred.* In other words, the Inquiry is *not* used to

Card	Response	Inquiry	Scoring
I	1. Ths ll a bat 2 me	E: U said ths ll a bat to me	
		S: Yeah, it has the wgs & som feelrs	
		E: I'm not sur where u r seeing it	
		S: Oh, all of it	
	(S wants to return card)		
	E: I thk if u tak ur time u'll c sthg else too		
	< V >		
	2. I supp ths cb a wm in the cntr	E: And then u said I supp this cb a wm in the cntr	
		S: Yeah, c here (outlines), her shape, & she's got her hands up. lik she's waving or sthg	
		E: I'm not sur wht maks it ll tht	
		S: Just the way it is, curvy, lik a wm, c her legs r here & the hands up here	
II	v3. Ths way it ll an ex	E: Here u said it ll an ex	
		S: Yeah, c ths part here (points)	
		E: I'm not sur I'm see-g it the way u r	
		S: C the way the lines go out, kinda up, lik an ex, lik a blast	
		E: A blast?	
		S: Its all red lik a blast is, lik fire	
	That's all I c		

Figure 3. Format for recording Rorschach Responses.

generate new information from the subject, but simply to clarify what was perceived during the Response Phase. But this is easier said than done, and the procedure requires the examiner to work within some very narrow parameters to avoid injecting new sets into the situation.

First, it is *critically important* that the subject be prepared for the Inquiry. This is best accomplished if the examiner explains the procedure and its purpose clearly. The preface to the Inquiry will vary slightly, depending on the characteristics of the subject, but it should generally follow this format:

> *O.k., we've done them all. Now we are going to go back through them. It won't take long. I want you to help me see what you saw. I'm going to read what you said, and then I want you to show me where on the blot you saw it and what there is there that makes it look like that, so that I can see it too. I'd like to see it just like you did, so help me now. Do you understand?*

The crux of these instructions is that the examiner wants to see the object, *as the subject sees it*. If that happens, the response is scored easily.

Once the subject implies an understanding of the Inquiry procedure, it can begin. Card I is handed to the subject and the examiner says, "All right, here you said. . . ," and finishing the statement with a *verbatim* reading of what was given in the first answer. If the subject has understood the nature of the task, he or she will proceed to point out the main features of the object reported. Conversely, if the subject simply replies with, "Yes that's right," the examiner should reaffirm the Inquiry purpose by saying something such as, *"Wait now, remember why we are doing this. I want to see it like you do. So help me. Show me where it is and what there is that makes it look like that."*

Each response should be inquired by first rereading, verbatim, the subject's answer. The reasonably cooperative subject will comprehend the task quickly and will usually provide the examiner with enough information to score the response accurately. Under these optimal conditions, very few questions or comments from the examiner will be required, and in some circumstances the need for questions is eliminated. In fact, there are occasions when the ideally cooperative subject is sufficiently articulate during the Response Phase that an answer need not be inquired, but before making this decision the examiner should review the response carefully to insure that information about the location and determinant(s) has been given.

Obviously, the examiner must know how to code a response to conduct the Inquiry properly. As the subject elaborates on the answer the examiner must review the information given in light of all scoring possibilities. Nothing should be assumed, and codes are assigned *only* when warranted by the articulations of the subject. Unfortunately, the Inquiry sometimes has been the most misunderstood and abused features of the test. When done correctly, it enhances the richness of the data. When it is done in a negligent or distorted manner however, it can muddle the record terribly. It must not be done hastily, and the decision to inject a comment or question should be weighed intelligently.

Appropriate Questions   In considering whether to inject a question during the Inquiry, the examiner focuses on the three major components of coding: (1) Location (Where is it?), (2) Determinants (What makes it look like that?), and (3) Content (What is it?). Most problems for the novice examiner occur arise from the second of the three determinants, because the subject will usually say where it is and the response itself indicates what it is.

But why it looks like that can be another matter. Objects may be perceived in the blots because of the shape of the contours, color, shading, apparent movement, or any combination of these. The report of the subject should reveal which of these elements has been important to the formulation of the answer. It would simplify the process if the subject could be asked directly about each of the elements, but several studies indicate that the number of answers based exclusively on the form features will decrease, and the number of answers that include the use of color, movement, or shading will increase if this direct method is employed (Gibby & Stotsky, 1953; Klingensmith, 1956; Baughman, 1958, 1959; Zax & Stricker, 1960). Only one study suggests that this will not be the case (Reisman, 1970). The Rapaport et al. (1946) approach to the test included the Inquiry after each card. When records taken using that method were compared with those employing the Inquiry after all 10 cards, a significant increase was found in the frequencies of movement, color, and shading answers (Exner, 1974). Thus the traditional method of using subtle, nondirective questions, free of any cues, should always be followed.

In most instances, routine kinds of questions can be used. *"I'm not sure that I'm seeing it as you are,"* is a standard form of prompting to remind the subject of the task at hand. It should not, however, be repeated endlessly and thus other nondirective questions should also be employed. *"I'm not sure I know where you are seeing it,"* is a standard prompter when the location is in doubt. *"I'm not sure what there is there that makes it look like that,"* focuses on the determinant issue by asking the subject for clarification.

Occasionally, a very resistive subject will be extremely vague during the Inquiry, by saying, "It just looks like that." Here, the examiner must also be resistive and not permit the subject to be evasive. Again, it may be necessary to restate the purpose of the procedure, but sometimes a comment such as, *"I know it looks like that to you, but help me see it too,"* may suffice. If a subject is vague about location, there can be some value in directing, *"Run your finger around it and show me some of the parts."* As a last resort some examiners may feel that it is appropriate to ask the subject to trace the object on the Location Sheet with a pen or pencil, but this is not an ideal tactic, and if it is used, the examiner should make sure that the subject does not draw on the blot itself.

There is another category of questions that is sometimes required in instances when a subject has used a *key word* in the response, or spontaneously at the onset of the Inquiry. Most key words are adjectives, but not always, and the examiner must be alert to any word that implies the presence of a determinant. For instance:

RESPONSE	INQUIRY
It cb a very pretty flower	*E:* (Repeats S's response verbatim)
	S: Yes, ths cb the stem & here r the petals

At this point the subject has provided the basic location and has implied the use of contours in forming the answer, but a key word has occurred in the Response that must be pursued. The word is *pretty,* implying the possible use of color in the response.

E: U mentioned that it is pretty

If the subject had not used the word *pretty* in the response, the examiner would not have posed any question in the Inquiry, *even if the response were given to a chromatically colored area of the blot.* Inquiry questions are posed only when there is a substantial implication that an unarticulated determinant exists. Consider another example:

RESPONSE	INQUIRY
It 11 2 peopl doing sthg at nite	*E:* (Repeats *S*'s response)
	S: Yes, c here thy r, their heads and legs & thes r the arms

Again, the location and form features have been delineated, and movement has also been given. But even though the response already includes the movement determinant, two issues remain in doubt. There is no indication about whether the movement is active or passive, and the subject has used the word *night,* implying the possible use of the achromatic features of the blot. It is usually best to avoid addressing both of these issues in a single question such as, "You said doing something at night?" Instead, it would be more appropriate to separate the issues into two questions, "You said they are doing something?" and, if no clarification about the word night is generated, to ask a second question, "You also said it was at night?"

In some cases the key word does not occur in the response, but does occur, *spontaneously,* in the Inquiry. The decision to pursue it must be conservative. If the word occurs at the onset of the Inquiry, the issue is not in doubt and the word should be pursued. But if the word occurs in response to a question, the examiner must proceed very cautiously in asking another question. For example:

RESPONSE	INQUIRY
That 11 2 bears to me	*E:* (Rpts *S*'s response)
	S: Yeah, c 1 here & 1 here, like they r fighting

The word *fighting* signals active movement and the score should be assigned to the response, but the word *fighting* also raises the issue about whether color might be involved. Because the word is offered spontaneously, it should be questioned, "You said like they are fighting?" And if the subject replies, "Yes, that red looks like blood, like they are hurt," the score for color would be assigned. However, presume that the answer is given in the following manner:

RESPONSE	INQUIRY
That 11 2 bears to me	*E:* (Rpts *S*'s resp)
	S: Yeah, c 1 here & 1 here, like thyr do-g sthg
	E: Doing sthg?
	S: Yeah, maybe thyr fit-g or sthg

In this instance, the score for the active animal movement would be assigned, but the indecisiveness of the subject suggests that the issue should not be pursued further. Conversely, had the subject said, "Well it looks like they are hurt so they've probably been fighting," a question concerning the word *hurt* would clearly be in order.

The rule about whether or not to pose a question when a key word appears in the Inquiry is more ambiguous than might be desired. If the key word relates to something said in the original response, it should be questioned. If there is reason to believe that the subject is simply reporting something that he or she saw during the Response Phase, it should be questioned. On the other hand, if the examiner has been asking many questions as the Inquiry proceeds, the issue of whether those questions may have provoked *new* information, not present in the original response, must be weighed by the examiner. It is clear that if the subject is simply reexamining the response in an effort to assist the examiner in seeing the object reported, no further questioning should ensue. These decisions are never made easily, but conservatism should always be the guideline.

Inappropriate Questions   There are some classes of question that should never be posed during the Inquiry. These are the direct or leading questions, or questions that are oriented to elicit material that is not related directly to the coding issue. Direct questions such as, "Did the color help?" or "Are they doing anything?" can only serve to cloud the scoring issue and create unwanted sets about the procedure. The same is true of leading questions such as, "Which side of the skin is up?" or "Can you tell me anything else about it?" which create the same sort of unwanted sets. It is sometimes very tempting to ask a subject to elaborate on a response such as, "Are they males or females?" or "Why do you think he feels sad?" These are questions that are completely foreign to the coding issue, and although the answers might appear to be clinically useful, the questions only serve to contaminate the test.

The Inquiry should be viewed as a delicate procedure. It is the "soft underbelly of the test," and it is a procedure in which the examiner has several tasks. The verbiage must be recorded *verbatim*, the Location Sheet must be completed, and the material must be carefully reviewed with an eye to whether questioning is necessary. It is a crucial segment of the test that can be likened to an Achilles' heel and botched badly when done by the unskilled or casual examiner. There is no absolute cookbook listing of questions to be asked. The examiner should not feel compelled to ask about the possible presence of every determinant. Brevity should be the rule, and the questions must be nondirective. And finally, the examiner must be aware that the subject is now operating under a new set of guidelines which Levin (1953) has likened to a second test. In some instances it can promote a sense of relief for the subject as the task is now more well defined. If this occurs it is not uncommon for subjects, especially children, to offer new responses during the Inquiry. Those *additional* answers should be faithfully recorded, because they may have some qualitative usefulness, but they are not coded or used directly in the basic interpretation of the test. Conversely, the new guidelines of the Inquiry can provoke a sense of threat in other subjects because of the perceived need to justify the responses that were reported earlier. In some such cases the subject may accuse the examiner of a recording error such as, "I didn't say that. You must have wrote it wrong." In other instances a subject may attempt to avoid a response by saying either, "That's not what I really saw," or "It doesn't look like that now," or "I can't find it now."

The examiner who encounters this form of resistance in the Inquiry should proceed tactfully but firmly. In the case where the subject denies the response, the examiner should counter with something such as, "No, I'm sure I wrote every word, here look at what I wrote. Now let's find it so you can show it to me." If the subject states that it does not look like that now, or worse, reports that it cannot be found, the examiner should be firmly reassuring, saying something such as, "Sometimes things look different when you look again, but let's try to see it like you did before. Take your time, and let me tell you again what you said."

The following are some illustrations of how resistence during the Inquiry might be handled:

RESPONSE PHASE	INQUIRY
Maybe sk of animal	*E:* (Rpts *S*'s resp)
	S: I dk, mayb here (vaguely outlines)
	E: I'm not sur I c it
	S: Just there
	E: Wait now, I kno u c it but help me c it
	S: Ok, the head & legs here

(This is sufficient and no further questions are required.)

A face	*E:* (Rpts *S*'s resp)
	S: I don't c it now
	E: Take ur time, u saw it once I'm sur u can find it again
	S: Nope, its not there
	E: Keep trying, don't hurry
	S: It's not there
	E: Do u remember what kind of face?
	S: I dk, an A I guess
	E: Try a little longer

(If *S* continues to deny the response, the Inquiry effort concerning the response should be abandoned and a minus form quality score assigned such as, *Ddo* F- Ad.)

Maybe an airplane	*S:* (Rpts *S*'s resp)
	S: Yeah it could b
	E: Show me where u c it
	S: All of it
	E: I'm not sur what makes it ll an airplane
	S: It just does
	E: I kno it does to u but help me c it too
	S: I dk it just does
	E: Show me some parts of it
	S: C the wgs lik a plane

(This is sufficient and no further questions are required.)

A parachute	*E:* (Rpts *S*'s resp)
	S: It doesn't ll tht now, it ll a tree
	E: Ok, we'll talk about the tree in a minute, but first let's try & c it as a parachute
	S: But its not lik that now

> *E:* I kno, but it did before, let's try to c it tht way 1st
>
> *S:* Well I thot of ths big top here
>
> *E:* Run ur finger around it 4 me
>
> *S:* (Outlines)

(This should be sufficient to score, and at this point the examiner should record and inquire about the additional tree response.)

Although redundant, it seems important to reaffirm the importance of preparing the subject for the Inquiry. If this is accomplished skillfully, the examiner will be free to use a greater latitude in questioning the subject that otherwise might provoke extreme resistence to the process by the subject.

THE LOCATION SHEET

Another important task of the examiner during the Inquiry is recording the locations used for the responses. This is done on the Location Sheet that has been developed for use with the test. It is a single page on which the blots are reproduced in miniature. The recording is done by outlining the area designated by the subject on the miniature, using an ink or a felt-tip pen, and recording the number of the response close to the outline. If the whole blot has been used, the scoring symbol *W* is recorded on the Location Sheet together with the number of the response.

The importance of completing the Location Sheet carefully cannot be overstated. It provides a permanent record that will be used when the test is scored, and is available later for others to review the test with an awareness of which blot areas have been used. The competent examiner will also take the time to identify some of the features of the object reported *if* they are not obvious to the casual observer. The less common the response, the greater the likelihood that these added notations will be important during the scoring or in a later review of the protocol.

If the response involves a human or animal, some notation concerning the areas in which the nose, legs, or arms have been identified can be helpful. Similarly, some responses include several separate objects such as, "a man riding a bicycle with a child running in front of him as they are passing a pond." Here, each of the four features (man, bicycle, child, and pond) should be noted on the Location Sheet.

DIRECT INQUIRY AND TESTING OF LIMITS

There are instances when information developed during the Inquiry may seem insufficient even though several questions have been posed to the subject. Thus the examiner is faced with the dilemma of asking too many questions or abandoning an issue prematurely. Usually these are instances when a subject has been overly vague about a response in spite of one, two, or even three questions. It will also often occur when the form quality of the response is minus. The decision about whether to pursue the matter further should be made conservatively. In a few cases, added questions may seem critical, but when this is not the case, the examiner should proceed to the next response. *After* the Inquiry has been completed, an examiner still troubled by this quandary can opt to return to the issue, using either a direct questioning method (Zax & Stricker, 1960), or a more subtle paired-comparison form of question (Baughman, 1958) to attempt to resolve the issue. Although the new information may be clinically useful, however, it *should not be used in coding the response*. The reason this added information should not be used in the coding decision is that it is collected under questioning which is much too directive to insure that the new material is truly reflective of the cognitive operations that occurred originally, as the response was formulated and delivered.

A second form of post-Inquiry questioning may be much more important. This is the Testing-of-Limits procedure, recommended originally by Klopfer and Kelley (1942). It was designed to test out hypotheses that responses (objects) may have been classified but later rejected in the response process. The procedure can be taken to extremes and, as such, has no useful purpose to the interpretation of the record. Nonetheless, there are instances, especially with schizophrenic subjects, when a very low number of Popular responses have been delivered in the record and the question arises about whether the subject did not classify, *or* simply failed to report the commonly reported object. This is especially important to differentiate the subject whose perceptual processes are so impaired to cause a marked perceptual distortion versus those who discard the obvious in favor of more idiosyncratic answers.

Testing-of-Limits proceeds with the examiner selecting blots to which the most common Popular response ordinarily occur, but have not in a particular protocol, and simply asking the subject if he or she might see that object there. The directions are simplistic— *"Sometimes people see . . . here. Do you see anything that looks like that?"* Often this procedure will provide valuable information, useful in discriminating perceptually impaired persons from those who are less prone to offer the conventional responses. These findings can be especially important for the treatment planning for schizophrenics.

COMMENT OR RESPONSE?

Occasionally a subject will say something when viewing a blot that may be a response, but might simply be a comment. For instance, if a blot has chromatic coloring, a subject might say, "Oh, blue and pink," which, if a response, would be coded as color naming (*Cn*) but if a comment about the blot, would not be pursued in the Inquiry. Or a subject might say, "That's an ugly-looking thing," raising the issue of whether this is comment concerning the blot or the identification of an ugly-looking object. In instances such as this the examiner should, at the appropriate point in the Inquiry, read what the subject said verbatim and ask, "Did you mean that as an answer?" Most subjects will offer clarification quickly and the examiner should proceed accordingly.

SUMMARY

The task of administering the Rorschach is not simple, but it is not difficult to learn. The key to the procedure is proficiency in coding. As noted earlier, no one can be competent in the tactics of administering the Rorschach unless they can code responses easily and accurately. Once the decision is made that the data of the Rorschach will be relevant to the assessment issues, the examiner becomes committed to a complex procedure that relies heavily on coding expertise. But competent administration of the Rorschach is not contingent *only* on that skill. Good examiners also exercise good judgment in the process of administering the test, and deal with their subjects in a tactful, sensitive, and very human manner.

REFERENCES

Baughman, E.C. (1951) Rorschach scores as a function of examiner differences. *Journal of Projective Techniques,* **15,** 243–249.

Baughman, E. E. (1958) A new method of Rorschach Inquiry. *Journel of Projective Techniques,* **22,** 381–389.

Beck, S. J. (1937) *Introduction to the Rorschach Method: A manual of personality study.* American Orthopsychiatric Association Monographs, No. 1.

Beck, S. J. (1945) *Rorschach's Test. II: A variety of personality pictures.* New York: Grune & Stratton.

Beck, S. J. (1952) *Rorschach's Test. III: Advances in interpretation.* New York: Grune & Stratton.

Beck, S. J. (1960) *The Rorschach Experiment: Ventures in blind analysis.* New York: Grune & Stratton.

Carp, A. L., and Shavzin, A. R. (1950) The susceptibility to falsification of the Rorschach diagnostic technique. *Journal of Consulting Psychology,* **3,** 230–233.

Coffin, T. E. (1941) Some conditions of suggestion and suggestibility: A study of certain attitudinal and situational factors influencing the process of suggestion. *Psychological Monographs,* 53, Whole No. 241.

Cox, F. N., and Sarason, S. B. (1954) Test anxiety and Rorschach performance. *Journal of Abnormal and Social Psychology,* **49,** 371–377.

Exner, J. E. (1969) *The Rorschach Systems.* New York: Grune & Stratton.

Exner, J. E. (1974) *The Rorschach: A Comprehensive System. Volume 1.* New York: Wiley.

Exner, J. E. (1978) *The Rorschach: A Comprehensive System. Volume 2. Current research and advanced interpretation.* New York: Wiley.

Exner, J. E. (1980) But it's only an inkblot. *Journal of Personality Assessment,* **44,** 562–577.

Exner, J. E., and Hark, L. J. (1979) Order effects for WAIS and Rorschach scores. Workshops study No. 262 (unpublished) Rorschach Workshops.

Exner, J. E., and Hark, L. J. (1980 Frequency of Rorschach responses after prolonged cognitive testing. Workshops study No. 271 (unpublished) Rorschach Workshops.

Exner, J. E., Leura, A. V., and George, L. M. (1976) A replication of the Masling study using four groups of new examiners with two seating arrangements and video evaluation. Workshops study No. 256 (unpublished) Rorschach Workshops.

Exner, J. E., and Weiner, I. B. (1982) *The Rorschach: A Comprehensive System. Volume 3: Assessment of children and adolescents.* New York: Wiley.

Fosberg, I. A. (1938) Rorschach reactions under varied instructions. *Rorschach Research Exchange,* **3,** 12–30.

Gage, N. L. (1953) Explorations in the understanding of others. *Educational and Psychological Measurement,* **13,** 14–26.

Gibby, R. G., Miller, D. R., and Walker, E. L. (1953) The examiner's influence on the Rorschach protocol. *Journal of Consulting Psychology,* **17,** 425–428.

Gibby, R. G., and Stotsky, B. A. (1953) The relation of Rorschach free association to inquiry. *Journal of Consulting Psychology,* **17,** 359–363.

Giedt, F. H. (1955) Comparison of visual, content, and auditory cues in interviewing. *Journal of Consulting Psychology,* **18,** 407–416.

Goodman, N. L. (1979) Examiner influence on the Rorschach: The effect of sex, sex pairing and warmth on the testing atmosphere. Doctoral Dissertation, Long Island University.

Grisso, J. T., and Meadow, A. (1967) Test interference in a Rorschach-WAIS administration sequence. *Journal of Consulting Psychology,***31,** 382–386.

Haller, N. (1982) The reliability of Rorschach depressive indices in major depressive disorder. Doctoral Dissertation, United States International University.

Harrower, M. (1965) Differential diagnosis. In B. Wolman (ed.) *Handbook of Clinical Psychology.* New York: McGraw-Hill.

Hertz, M. R. (1969) A Hertz interpretation. In J. E. Exner *The Rorschach Systems.* New York: Grune & Stratton.

Holt, R. R. (1958) Clinical and statistical prediction: A reformulation and some new data. *Journal of Abnormal and Social Psychology,***56,** 1–12.

Holt, R. R. (1970) Yet another look at clinical and statistical prediction. *American Psychologist,* **25,** 337–349.

Kelly, E. L., and Fiske, D. W. (1950) The prediction of success in the V.A. training program in clinical psychology. *American Psychologist,* **4,** 395–406.

Klingensmith, S. W. (1956) A study of the effects of different methods of structuring the Rorschach inquiry on determinant scores. Doctoral Dissertation, University of Pittsburgh.

Klopfer, B., and Kelley D. M. (1942) *The Rorschach Technique.* Yonkers-on-Hudson, N.Y.: World Book.

Klopfer, B., Ainsworth, M. D., Klopfer, W. G., and Holt, R. R. (1954) *Developments in the Rorschach Technique. I: Technique and theory.* Yonkers-on-Hudson, N.Y.: World Book.

Kostlan, A. A. (1954) A method for the empirical study of psychodiagnosis. *Journal of Consulting Psychology,* **18,** 83–88.

Levin, M. M. (1953) The two tests in the Rorschach. *Journal of Projective Techniques,* **17,** 471–473.

Loosli-Usteri, M. (1929) Le test de Rorschach applique a differents groupes d'enfants de 10-13 ans. *Archives de Psychologie,* **21,** 51-106.

Lord, E. (1950) Experimentally induced variations in Rorschach performance. *Psychological Monographs,* **60,** Whole No. 316.

Luborsky, L., and Holt, R. R. (1957) The selection of candidates for psychoanalytic training. *Journal of Clinical and Experimental Psychopathology,* **18,** 166–176.

MacKinnon, D. W. (1951) The effects of increased observation upon the accuracy of prediction. *American Psychologist,* **6,** 311 (abstract).

Masling, J. (1965) Differential indoctrination of examiners and Rorschach responses. *Journal of Consulting Psychology,* **29,** 198–201.

Peterson, L. C. (1957) The effects of instruction variation on Rorschach responses. Unpublished M.A. Thesis, Ohio State University.

Phares, E. J., Stewart, L. M., and Foster, J. M. (1960) Instruction variation and Rorschach performance. *Journal of Projective Techniques,* **21,** 28–31.

Piotrowski, Z. A. (1958) The psychodiagnostic test battery: Clinical application. In D. Brower, and L. E. Abt (Eds.) *Progress in Clinical Psychology.* Vol. 3. New York: Grune & Stratton.

Piotrowski, Z. A. (1969) A Piotrowski interpretation. In J. E. Exner *The Rorschach Systems.* New York: Grune & Stratton.

Rapaport, D., Gill, M., and Schafer, R. (1946) *Diagnostic Psychological Testing.* Vol 1. Chicago: Yearbook.

Reisman, J. M. (1970) The effect of a direct inquiry on Rorschach scores. *Journal of Projective Techniques and Personality Assessment,* **34,** 388–390.

Sarbin, T. R. (1943) A contribution to the study of actuarial and i dividual methods of prediction. *American Journal of Sociology,* **48,** 593–602.

Schachtel, E. G. (1945) Subjective definitions of the Rorschach test situation and their effect on test performance. *Psychiatry,* **8,** 419–448.

Schafer, R. (1954) *Psychoanalytic Interpretation in Rorschach Testing.* New York: Grune & Stratton.

Stern, G. G., Stein, M. I., and Bloom, B. S. (1956) *Methods in Personality Assessment.* Glencoe, Ill.: Free Press.

Strauss, M. E. (1968) Examiner expectancy: Effects on Rorschach Experience Balance. *Journal of Consulting Psychology,* **32,** 125–129.

Strauss, M. E., and Marwit, S. J. (1970) Expectancy effects in Rorschach testing. *Journal of Consulting and Clinical Psychology,* **34,** 448.

Van de Castle, R. L. (1964) Effect of test order on Rorschach human content. *Journal of Consulting Psychology,* **28,** 286–288.

Vernon, P. E. (1950) The validation of civil service selection board procedures. *Occupational Psychology,* **24,** 75–95.

Weiner, I. B. (1966) *Psychodiagnosis in Schizophrenia.* New York: Wiley.

Williams, M. H. (1954) The influence of variations in instructions on Rorschach reaction time. *Dissertation Abstracts,* **14,** 2131.

Zax, M., and Stricker, G. (1960) The effect of a structured inquiry on Rorschach scores. *Journal of Consulting Psychology,* **24,** 328–332.

CHAPTER 4

Scoring:
The Rorschach Language

The full value of the Rorschach is realized only from the complete sum of its parts. A neglect of any available Rorschach data, whether quantitative or qualitative, is an abuse of the test and a disservice to the subject. This principle has been emphasized by all of the Rorschach Systematizers. Beck (1945, 1967), Klopfer. (1942, 1954) and Rapaport-Schafer. (1946, 1954) have each stressed the importance of using the total *configuration* of the record. Hertz (1952, 1963) has accented the same principle in her "interactionist approach" and Piotrowski (1957) has elaborated on this in his "principle of interdependent components." In essence, the concept of *total* Rorschach acknowledges that few if any single test variables will have a consistently high correlation with any internal or external behavior. Instead, this concept is predicated on the notion that an understanding of any feature of an individual can be useful only when it is judged in the context of other features. It is the knowledge of how the characteristics of a person merge together in a series of complex interrelationships that breeds a reasonable understanding of that person.

Much rich information concerning the characteristics of a person, and the interrelationship of those characteristics, is derived from the scoring summary of the Rorschach. These are the data that provide the nucleus of interpretation. The issue of scoring and the symbols to be used have been topics of much discussion in the literature. In fact, it was the scoring issue that formed the original seeds of divergence among the various systematizers and ultimately led them in different directions in extending Rorschach's work (Exner, 1969). It was also on this issue that the major criticisms of the Rorschach unfolded during the 1950s and 1960s. Much of the research published during that period focused on single variables rather than constellations or configurations of variables. The result was a sizable body of literature concerning the test which reported negative or equivocal findings, provoking some, such as Zubin et al. (1965), to argue that the test should not be considered in the "measurement" framework at all.

To some extent, critics such as Zubin have been correct in the assumption that all Rorschach "scores" do not meet some of the psychometric characteristics that are common in most psychological tests. For instance, many scores are not normally distributed, making the application of parametric statistics at best, difficult. Others are valid but not temporally consistent, and some have levels of temporal consistency or reliability that account for less than one-half of the variance. Moreover, the test is open-ended; that is, all protocols are not of the same length. Even when the total number of responses is the same for two records, it is highly unlikely that the distribution of codes or scores to each of the 10 cards will be the same. This is both an asset and a liability for the test. It is a liability because it restricts the full usefulness of normative comparisons and thus makes for greater difficulty is establishing useful normative data (Cronbach, 1949). Holtzman, et al. (1961) pointed out, "Providing a subject with only ten inkblots and permitting him to give as many or as few responses as he wishes characteristically results in a set of unreliable scores with sharply skewed distributions."[1] The Cronbach-Holtzman criticism concerning the variability of the number of responses cannot be denied, but they erred in suggesting that this makes the test psychometrically unapproachable. It is quite true that this composite of *measurement* problems constitutes a difficult problem for the statistician, and a virtual nightmare for the psychometric purist, but none have been unresolvable in the context of contemporary statistical methods plus the use of reasonably large samples of data.

As noted in Chapter 2, much of the criticism of the test was fomented by a lack of understanding about the nature of the test. But some of the misunderstanding was also generated by a misuse or overgeneralization of the term *score*. The procedure of translating Rorschach responses into Rorschach symbols traditionally has been called scoring. Unfortunately, the use of the word *score* carries with it, in the realm of psychology, some concepts of measurement that are not always useful or appropriate to Rorschach scoring. Once a protocol has been collected from a subject, each response is *coded*. The coding is called scoring, but most of the code assigned does not involve numbers. They are not ordinal scores as used in an intelligence or achievement test. In effect, the coding procedure reduces the response into a logical and sytematic format, a special Rorschach language. It is like a system of shorthand used to record various components that exist in a response. It is only in very rare instances that the score or code for any single response becomes interpretively important. For instance, a response scored *Do Fo A* simply indicates that the subject responded to a common detail area of the blot, and gave a frequently reported animal response using the contours of the blot to delineate the animal.

The Rorschach scores that are crucial to interpretation are the frequency scores for each of the codes and the numerous percentages, ratios, and other metrically useful derivations that are calculated from them. Collectively, they represent the *Structural Summary* of the record. Thus although some substance of the response is lost in the coding or scoring translation from words to symbols, the data derived from those codes allow an evaluation of response styles and other psychological features of the subject that otherwise would not be possible. Obviously, the procedure of scoring or coding each response is critically important, because each contributes to the Structural Summary of the protocol.

The codes that have been selected for use in the Comprehensive System represent a combination of those derived from other systems for which empirical support has been established, plus some new codings that have evolved as the System has matured. Most of Rorschach's original symbols are included. He recognized the importance of coding responses and devised a simplistic format for doing so that consisted of five categories: (1) Location (to which feature(s) of the blot did the subject respond?), (2) Determinant (What features of the blot contribute to the formulation of the answer?), (3) Form Quality (Is the object described appropriate for the blot contours used?), (4) Content (What is the class of content to which the response belongs?), and (5) Popular (Does the response occur with a

---

[1] In fact, Holtzman devised an inkblot test consisting of 45 blots in which subjects are permitted to give only one response per blot. By controlling for the number of responses, statistical manipulations are accomplished more easily and the use of a psychogram is appropriate. Although considerable normative and reliability data have been reported for the Holtzman Inkblot Method, data concerning validity are somewhat more limited.

high frequency in the general population?). Each of the systematizers retained this basic format in their own systems and it has proved useful.

Beck (1937) and Hertz (1940) added a sixth category for Organizational Activity, to account for responses involving the meaningful integration of blot features. Rapaport et al. (1946) also added a category of Special Scores designed to note strange verbiage and pathognomic features in responses. The work of Friedman (1952) has led to the development of an eighth category related to the location selection, which concerns the Developmental Quality of that selection. Although the number of specific codes or scores within each category has increased or decreased as the result of research findings, each of these eight categories remains useful to the ultimate richness of interpretation that is derived from the structural data. Some responses are scored or coded for as few as five of these categories, whereas others will be marked by coding from six, seven, or all eight.

There is only one symbol (*P*) if the response is Popular, used for each of 13 very high frequency answers. Each of the remaining seven categories has multiple symbols. There are three symbols for the Location, *W* (whole blot), *D* (common detail area), and *Dd* (unusual detail area), and the symbol *S* is added to any of the three if white space is also involved. One of four Developmental Quality symbols is added to the Location coding. Many more options exist when coding the Determinants. Symbols are used to denote the use of form, chromatic color, achromatic color, each of three kinds of shading, and each of three kinds of movement. One of four symbols is used to signify the appropriateness of the form use. The symbols for coding the content of the responses are logical abbreviations, such as *H* for human, *A* for animal, *Bt* for botany, and so on. When responses involve integrating or organizing the blot or blot areas in a complex manner, a score for Organizational Activity, a numerical value, is also assigned to that answer. Two kinds of Special Scores are used. They are also abbreviations. One kind notes the presence of cognitive slippage in the response, such as *DV,* which is the abbreviation for deviant verbalization. The second set of Special Scores is used to note unique characteristics of the response, such as *Ag,* which is employed for movement answers in which the action is aggressive.

The constancy of the Rorschach language permits interpreters to recognize the same characteristics in a single record, and across records. The composite frequencies for each code yield a base of data, and when those frequencies are numerically translated into ratios and percentages, the breadth of information concerning personality features and/or psychopathology becomes very substantial.

The *cardinal rule* of coding (or scoring) Rorschach responses is that the code (or score) should represent the cognitive operation that occurred at the time the subject gave the answer. Obviously this is a very difficult objective to achieve, and this is the main reason that the Inquiry creates some hazards to the overall process. Nonetheless, the objective of coding *only* the process reflected in the original response cannot be emphasized enough, particularly to the Rorschach novice. The coder-interpreter must resist the temptation to consider the original response and the information developed in the Inquiry as being continuous, for this is an illogical assumption. Many events transpire between the original response and the Inquiry and, as noted earlier, the latter occurs under a much different structure than the former.

Although the *cardinal rule* in coding is easy to understand (although not always easy to apply), the second most important rule in coding is that *all of the components that appear in the response should be included in the coding.* Rorschach endorsed this principle, although his scheme for coding was much less elaborate than developed by those following in his footsteps.[2] Each of the Rorschach Systems developed after his death made some provision for this, although Klopfer later deviated from this principle.[3]

Some illustrations of the coding process may be useful before addressing the complexities of each of the eight coding categories. Each of these illustrations involves a relatively common or Popular response to Card III.

RESPONSE	INQUIRY
III Ths 11 a person, mayb a man I guess	*E:* (Rpts *S*'s response)
	S: Yes, right here (points to *D9*)
	E: I'm not sure I'm seeing it lik u r, help me.
	S: Here is his head & body & legs

This is a very simplistic response. The subject has reported only one figure, whereas most people report two in this blot. Nonetheless, it is still a very common answer. The coding for this answer is:

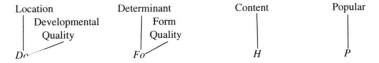

Location	Determinant	Content	Popular
Developmental Quality	Form Quality		
Do	*Fo*	*H*	*P*

The coding of *Do Fo H* indicates that the subject used a common detail area of the blot (*D*) and identified it as a single or unitary object (*o*). The Determinant of *F* indicates that only the form or contours of the blot area were identified to justify the object. The Form Quality code (*o*) indicates that the use of the form was acceptable, and the Content of the response (*H*) signifies that is human. The code *P* indicates that it is a frequently given response.

A second response to Card III shows how the coding will become more complex as the response increases in complexity.

RESPONSE	INQUIRY
III Ths 11 2 wm stirring sthg in a pot	*E:* (Rpts *S*'s response)
	S: That's right, thy r here (points to *D1*) & ths 11 a pot tht thy r stirring sthg in

[2] Rorschach's format for coding is considerably briefer than developed by other systematizers for two reasons. First, his premature death left much of his work incomplete, but possibly even more important is the fact that the blots used in his investigation contained no shading. The shading components that exist in the blots now used were apparently created through a printing error at the time his monograph was published. In the subsequent development of the test several newer codes have been required in consideration of responses that include the use of the shading.

[3] In the early 1940s Klopfer, out of concern that determinants were being scored too liberally, decided to adopt the position that only one determinant should be given full weight in the interpretation. Thus instead of using the principle of blended determinants that had been suggested by Rorschach, he moved to a tactic of scoring only one determinant as the "main" determinant, and all others in a response were called "additional" and quantitatively assigned half weight. In a private interview in 1965 at Asilomar, California, Klopfer expressed some regret about that decision. He did maintain, however, that the Main-Additional dichotomy he created did, in fact, preclude the interpreter from overemphasizing determinants that may not have existed in the response proper but which might have been provoked by questioning in the Inquiry.

In this example, the subject provides most of the information necessary for coding the response when giving the response. He or she reports the commonly identified human figures in the blot and includes the frequently reported human movement associated with them. The Inquiry to the response correctly begins with the repeating of the subject's response and, in this instance, is designed to confirm the location of the objects reported, but with the awareness that the subject may *spontaneously* add other features not previously reported. If this occurred, they would be pursued in the Inquiry. This subject did not add any features to the original response that would be related to the coding, thus the code will be:

Location   Determinant   Contents   Popular   Organization
Developmental   Form   Pair   Activity
Quality   Quality
$D+$ M^ao (2) H, Hh P 3.0

This code (or score) also shows that the subject used a common detail area of the blot (*D*, and that in doing so, some form of synthesizing activity occurred (+); that is, the subject mentally broke up the area into separate objects and then organized them in a meaningful way. The Determinant of M^a indicates that the response was form based and involved active human movement. The notation of a pair (2) indicates that the subject reported two similar objects, using the symmetrical features of the blot as the basis for this impression. The Contents of the response are human (*H*) and household (*Hh*). It is a Popular response, and because it is complex, it is assigned an Organizational Activity score of 3.0, which is the value used when the objects organized are in adjacent detail areas on this blot. Some responses will have multiple determinants, and can have more than one Special Score as in the following example.

RESPONSE	INQUIRY
III It's a cpl of skeletons in a battle, really vicious	E: (Rpts S's response)
	S: Yeah wow, c here thy r (points to *Dl*) c the heads & legs
	E: U said in a battle, really vicious
	S: Yeah, its lik thy r fighting w eo & thy got bld all over ths wall in the back, c the red splotches r lik bld on the wall

This response is a good illustration of how, at times, information developed spontaneously in the Inquiry will contribute to the coding of the response. It is not until after the examiner has asked for clarification (U said in a battle, really vicious), that the subject reveals the presence of two determinants that were not obvious in the basic response. Because they have been given without provocation, they will be included in the Determinant coding of the response. When multiple determinants occur in a response, each is separated from the next by a dot (.) which notes a determinant *Blend*. The complete coding or scoring for this response is:

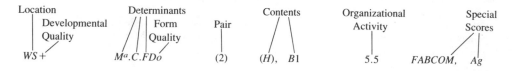

Location   Determinants   Contents   Organizational   Special
Developmental   Form   Pair   Activity   Scores
Quality   Quality
$WS+$ $M^a.C.FDo$ (2) $(H), Bl$ 5.5 $FABCOM, Ag$

In the response the subject used the entire blot (W), plus white space (S. Thus the Location scoring is WS. There is synthesis of the reported objects and so a Developmental Quality code of $+$ is added to the location scoring, $WS+$. There are three determinants in the response, active human-like movement (M^a), the use of chromatic color without including any form features in its use (C), and dimensionality, the blood is on a wall in the background (FD). Thus the blend of $M^a.C.FD$. Although the response is strange, the use of the form features is appropriate, and the Form Quality code of o (ordinary) has been added to the Determinant code, $M^a.C.FDo$. There are two similar objects reported (skeletons), using the symmetry of blot as the basis, and so a 2 is included to note the pair. The Content codes are (H), used to denote human-like figures, and Bl for blood. There is organizing activity involved and a score for that, 5.5, has also been entered. Finally, there are two Special Scores assigned. The first identifies the highly implausible relationship of the skeletons that has been reported. Skeletons do not fight, except in cartoons and there is no implication that this is a cartoon. Also skeletons do not bleed. When these sorts of highly implausible relationships are reported, they are called Fabulized Combinations, and scored as $FABCOM$. The second Special Score is used to note the characteristic of the movement. It is clearly aggressive, and the score Ag is included in the coding.

In most instances the coding for a single response will have little or no interpretive significance, regardless of whether it is simple and uncomplicated as in the first illustration, or quite complex as in the last example. As noted earlier, these codes are converted into frequency data, and from those frequencies a variety of ratios and percentages is derived. The frequencies are derived by first listing each of the codes or scores separately in consecutive sequence. This is called the Sequence of Scores. A computer printout of a scoring sequence for a protocol is shown in Figure 4. The numbers that have been entered after the Location codes identify which area of the blot has been used for the response.

The Sequence of Scores makes it easy to tally the frequency for each of the variables, and they are entered in the upper section of the Structural Summary. The ratios and percentages that form the basis of the interpretive process are then calculated and entered in the lower section of the Structural Summary. A printout of the Structural Summary, derived from the Sequence of Scores shown in Figure 4, is presented in Figure 5.

When completed, the Structural Summary provides a wealth of information concerning some of the psychological characteristics of the subject. Obviously, it is vital that each of the codes be applied accurately. They have been selected and defined to minimize ambiguity and to maximize the research yield concerning each variable. Numerous studies have been conducted at the Rorschach Research Foundation to insure adequate interscorer reliability for each variable, using a *minimum* standard of 90% agreement among coders or a .85 intercorrelation. Two such studies have been completed for the revision of this work, one involving 20 "scorers" and 25 nonpatient records and the second involving 15 scorers and 20 psychiatric records. The results of these studies are included in the various sections of the next several chapters, in which the codes (or scores) that constitute this special Rorschach language are described in detail for each of the eight basic categories.

```
                           SEQUENCE OF SCORES
===================================================================================
CARD NO. LOC.  #    DETERMINANT(S)     (2) CONTENT(S) POP  Z     SPECIAL SCORES
===================================================================================
  I   1 W+    1 Ma.FC'o          2 H,(H)            4.0  AG,MOR
      2 Wo    1 FYo                Xy                1.0

 II   3 D+    2 FMau             2 A                5.5  AG
      4 DS+   5 FC'o               Id               4.5

III   5 D+    1 nao              2 H,Id         P   3.0  AG

 IV   6 Wo    1 FYo                Xy                2.0

  V   7 W+    1 Mpo              2 H                2.5  PER

 VI   8 Do    2 Fu                Sc
      9 Do   12 FDo               La

VII  10 D+    2 Mao             2 Hd           P   3.0  AG,PSV
     11 Do    2 Fo                A

VIII 12 Do    3 Fo                An
     13 Wv    1 CFo               An,Bl                  MOR

 IX  14 Dd+  99 Mao             2 (H),Id,Cg    P   2.5  AG
     15 DS+   8 mp.FVo            Id                5.0

  X  16 D+   11 FMao            2 (A)              4.0
     17 Do    3 FCo               Bt                     MOR
===================================================================================
(C)1976, 1983 BY JOHN E. EXNER, JR.
```

Figure 4. Illustration of a Sequence of Scores.

```
                          STRUCTURAL SUMMARY
===================================================================================
  R = 17    Zf = 11    ZSum = 37.0    P = 3    (2) = 7    Fr+rF = 0

LOCATION           DETERMINANTS           CONTENTS      S-CONSTELLATION
FEATURES            BLENDS       SINGLE                    (ADULT)
                                          H   = 3, 0   NO..FV+VF+V+FD>2
 W   =  5       M.FC'        M   =  4     (H)  = 1, 1   NO..Col-Shd Bl>0
 (Wv  =   1)    m.FV         FM  =  2     Hd   = 1, 0   NO..Ego<.31,>.44
 D   = 11                    m   =  0     (Hd) = 0, 0   NO..MOR > 3
 Dd  =  1                    C   =  0     A    = 2, 0   NO..Zd > +- 3.5
 S   =  2                    Cn  =  0     (A)  = 1, 0   YES..es > EA
                             CF  =  1     Ad   = 0, 0   NO..CF+C+Cn > FC
    DQ                       FC  =  1     (Ad) = 0, 0   NO..X+ < .70
 ........(FQ-)               C'  =  0     Ab   = 0, 0   NO..S > 3
                             C'F =  0     Al   = 0, 0   NO..P < 3 or > 8
  +  =  9 ( 0)               FC' =  1     An   = 2, 0   NO..Pure H < 2
 v/+ =  0 ( 0)               T   =  0     Art  = 0, 0   NO..R < 17
  o  =  7 ( 0)               TF  =  0     Ay   = 0, 0    1.....TOTAL
  v  =  1 ( 0)               FT  =  0     Bl   = 0, 1
                             V   =  0     Bt   = 1, 0   SPECIAL SCORINGS
                             VF  =  0     Cg   = 0, 1    DV    =  0
                             FV  =  0     Cl   = 0, 0    INCOM =  0
                             Y   =  0     Ex   = 0, 0    DR    =  0
                             YF  =  0     Fi   = 0, 0    FABCOM=  0
       FORM QUALITY          FY  =  2     Fd   = 0, 0    ALOG  =  0
                             rF  =  0     Ge   = 0, 0    CONTAM=  0
  FQx       FQf      M Qual. Fr  =  0     Hh   = 0, 0    --- WSUM6 = 0
                             FD  =  1     La   = 1, 0    AG    =  5
  +  =  0    +  =  0   +  =  0  F = 3     Na   = 0, 0    CONFAB=  0
 o  = 15    o  =  2   o  =  5             Sc   = 1, 0    CP    =  0
 u  =  2    u  =  1   u  =  0             Sx   = 0, 0    MOR   =  3
 -  =  0    -  =  0   -  =  0             Xy   = 2, 0    PER   =  1
none=  0   none=  0  none=  0             Idio = 2, 2    PSV   =  1
===================================================================================

                RATIOS, PERCENTAGES, AND DERIVATIONS

ZSum-Zest =  37.0 - 34.5     FC:CF+C  =  1: 1    W:M      =  5: 5
                                 (Pure C =  0)
Zd           =  2.5                                W:D      =  5:11
                             Afr      =  0.55
.----------------------.                          Isolate:R =  2:17
:EB = 5: 1.5  EA =  6.5:     3r+(2)/R =  0.41
:            >D=  0                                Ab+Art    =  0
:eb =  3: 5   ea =  8  :     L        =  0.21
'----------------------'                          An+Xy     =  4
(FM= 2 " C'= 2 T= 0) (Adj D=  0)  Blends:R =  2:17
(m = 1 " V = 1 Y= 2)                              H(H):Hd(Hd) =  4: 1
                             X+%      =  0.88      (Pure H =  3)
a:p      =  6: 2             (F+%     =  0.67) (HHd):(AAd) =  1: 1
                             X-%      =  0.00
Ma:Mp    =  4: 1                                 H+A:Hd+Ad =  7: 1
----------------------------------------------------------------------
        SCZI = 0         DEPI = 1              S-CON = 1
===================================================================================
(C)1976,1983 BY JOHN E. EXNER, JR.
```

Figure 5. Illustration of a Structural Summary.

REFERENCES

Beck, S. J. (1937) *Introduction to the Rorschach Method*. American Orthopsychiatric Association Monograph No. 1

Beck, S. J. (1945) *Rorschach's Test. II: A variety of personality pictures*. New York: Grune & Stratton.

Beck, S. J., and Molish, H. B. (1967) *Rorschach's Test. II: A variety* of personality pictures. (2nd Ed.) New York: Grune & Stratton.

Cronbach, L. J. (1949) Statistical methods applied to Rorschach scores: A review. *Psychological Bulletin*, **46**, 393–429.

Exner, J. E. (1969) *The Rorschach Systems*. New York: Grune & Stratton.

Friedman, H. (1952) Perceptual regression in schizophrenia: An hypothesis suggested by the use of the Rorschach test. *Journal of Genetic Psychology*, **81**, 63–98.

Hertz, M. R. (1940) *Percentage Charts for use in computing Rorschach scores*. Cleveland: Brush Foundation and the Department of Psychology, Western Reserve University.

Hertz, M. R. (1952) The Rorschach: Thirty years after. In D. Brower, and L. E. Abt (Eds.) *Progress in Clinical Psychology*. New York: Grune & Stratton.

Hertz, M. R. (1963) Objectifying the subjective. *Rorschachiana*, **8**, 25–54.

Holtzman, W. H., Thorpe, J. S., Swarz, J. D., and Herron, E. W. (1961) *Inkblot Perception and Personality*. Austin: University of Texas Press.

Klopfer, B., and Kelley, D. M. (1942) *The Rorschach Technique*. Yonkers-on-Hudson, N.Y.: World Book.

Klopfer, B., Ainsworth, M. D., Klopfer, W. G., and Holt, R. R. (1954) *Developments in the Rorschach Technique. I: Technique and Theory*. Yonkers-on-Hudson, N.Y.: World Book.

Piotrowski, Z. (1957) *Perceptanalysis*. New York: Macmillan.

Rapaport, D., Gill, M., and Schafer, R. (1946) *Diagnostic Psychological Testing: The theory, statistical evaluation, and diagnostic application of a battery of tests. Volume II*. Chicago: Yearbook Publishers.

Schafer, R. (1954) *Psychoanalytic Interpretation in Rorschach Testing*. New York: Grune & Stratton.

Zubin, J., Eron, L. D., and Schumer, R. (1965) *An Experimental Approach to Projective Techniques*. New York: Wiley.

CHAPTER 5

Location and Developmental Quality: Symbols and Criteria

The first, and probably easiest, of the coding decisions concerns the location of the response; that is, to which part of the blot did the response occur? The open-endedness of the test permits either of two approaches in formulating answers. The subject may decide to use the entire blot or may select only a portion of it. When the former occurs, it is a *whole* response and the coding is simple and straightforward, using the symbol *W*. In the latter case it is a *detail* response, and the symbol used in coding the location will depend on whether the area selected is one that is commonly used. If so, the symbol *D* will be employed to note this. Conversely, if the area selected is not among those used frequently by subjects, the symbol *Dd* is employed. As noted in the preceding chapter, whenever the subject includes use of the white space (ground), the symbol *S* is added to the location code.

The symbols and criteria used in the Comprehensive System for coding location are essentially those described in the Beck methodology, which follows from Rorschach's suggestion. The discrimination between *D* and *Dd* has been based on empirical findings, thus avoiding some of the arbitrary or overinclusive features that exist in some of the other approaches to coding location.

In some instances the information necessary for deciding on the location code will be given in the response, such as, ''Well the whole thing looks like . . . ,'' or ''If I use only this upper part it could be . . .'' When this occurs, only a brief verification concerning location area is required in the Inquiry. In many responses, however, the subject does not specify the area of the blot being used during the response, and this matter becomes an important target during the Inquiry. Ordinarily, it is easily derived, especially when the subject has been prepared properly for the Inquiry, which will include mention of this objective. Nonetheless, some subjects remain vague about location and when that occurs, the examiner must persist by using instructions such as, ''Run your finger around it carefully,'' or ''Point to some of the features so that I can see it, too.''

The four symbols used in coding location and the criterion for each are shown in Table 7.

THE *W* RESPONSE (WHOLES)

The criterion for coding or scoring *W* constitutes an either-or issue. Either the subject uses the entire blot, or less than the entire blot. Only the former is coded *W*. It is quite important that the examiner verify that the entire blot has been used in a response. Occasionally, a subject will report a response that is like those commonly given to the whole, but in fact,

Table 7.   Symbols Used for Coding the Location of Rorschach Responses

Symbol	Definition	Criterion
W	Whole response	Where the entire blot is used in the response. All portions must be used.
D	Common detail response	A frequently identified area of the blot
Dd	Unusual detail response	An infrequently identified area of the blot
S	Space response	A white space area is used in the response (scored only with another location symbol, as in *WS, DS,* or *DdS*)

the subject has not used the entire blot in forming the answer. For example, the response, "bat," is the most frequently given answer to both Cards I and V. About 97% of subjects who give either of those responses use the entire blot, but a small minority exclude some portions of the blot in order to be more precise about the answer. Those kinds of responses are *not* coded as *W* even though only a few small segments are omitted.[1]

Under the routine conditions of administration there should be no reason for misidentification of whole answers. In two interscorer reliability studies, one involving 20 scorers and 25 records and the second involving 15 scorers across 20 records, the percentage of agreement for coding *W* is 99% in both, with the disagreements resulting from scorer error.

THE *D* RESPONSE (COMMON DETAILS)

The criterion for coding *D* follows the suggestion of Rorschach. He referred to these as "Normal" details of the plates. He suggested that the differentiation of these areas from other areas of the blots should be based on the frequency with which subjects respond to them. During the early development of the Rorschach, several efforts were made to codify the obvious detail areas with numerical designations to provide easy identification of the areas. These efforts were not always based on the same format for decision making, nor did those involved always agree on Rorschach's intent. The result was several schemes for identifying the different blot areas. When the nucleus of the Comprehensive System was formulated in 1972, it was decided to use the Beck method of coding detail areas. That decision was based on three considerations. First, Hertz (1970) had compared her format for designating details with that used by Beck, Piotrowski, and Klopfer. She noted that she and Beck agreed on 90 of 97 areas, which she had designated as being appropriate for scoring *D*. Second, the Beck scheme includes the designation of 25 other areas that Hertz does not consider. Third, in two surveys of Rorschach practitioners (Exner, 1974; Exner

---

[1] Two of the systematizers, Klopfer and Hertz, added a second type of *W* response, that of the cut-off whole, using the symbol *W* for coding. The rationale was that Rorschach sometimes coded a *W* for Card III even though the outside red areas were omitted in the response. Klopfer later defined the cutoff whole as any response using at least two-thirds of the blot. Investigation of this code revealed low interscorer reliability, and no empirical basis for interpreting it differently than *Dd* responses. Thus it was excluded from those variables integrated into the Comprehensive System.

& Exner, 1972) it was noted that considerably more were already familiar with the Beck format.

In preparation for the revision of this volume, two random samples, each consisting of 1500 records drawn from a much larger protocol pool, were used to review the frequency of responses by subjects to each of the 103 blot areas designated as D by the Beck format. One sample included 750 nonpatient adults and children and 750 nonschizophrenic adult and children outpatients. The second sample consisted of 750 psychiatric inpatients, including 150 schizophrenics, and 750 nonpatient adults and children. The distribution of the responses by the various groups, including schizophrenics, is not significantly different from those given by any of the other groups. Because the purpose of the review was to provide some cross-validation for the Beck format of distinguishing common (D) from uncommon (Dd) detail areas, a cutoff criterion of 5% was established. Therefore an area would continue to be designated as D if at least 5% of the *subjects* gave at least one response to the area. The results of this review indicate that 29 of the 103 areas designated by Beck as D fall short of the 5% criterion. This is not too surprising, because Beck apparently tended to number D areas in terms of the frequencies that he observed in his relatively small samples. In other words, he assigned the designation $D1$ to the area most frequently used, $D2$ to the next most frequently used, and so on. Most of the D areas specified by Beck that do not meet criterion involve higher numbers, such as $D7$, $D8$, and so on.

In addition to the discovery that 29 areas previously specified as D should be reclassified as Dd, it was also found that there are five areas, one each on Cards IV, VI, VII, VIII, and IX, that had not been numbered by Beck to which more than 5% of subjects respond. These have been added to the listing of D areas. Thus the current format for the Comprehensive System includes 79 blot areas that are designated as D areas. Obviously, some are used much more frequently than others; that is, they have a higher valence as discrete or semidiscrete stimuli in the field, or they may be areas that are more easily misidentified as possible responses because of their similarity to known or imagined objects. For instance, about 95% of all subjects taking the test include the selection of the card VIII, $D1$ area as a separate object, usually an animal. It is both discrete and has contours that are very similar to an animal. The $D1$ and $D2$ areas on Card VII, and the $D1$ areas on Cards II and III are also used in forming answers by a very high percentage of subjects taking the test.

Many D areas encompass large segments of the blot, but this is not always the case. Several involve only small portions of the total blot. The numbering of the D areas is shown for each of the 10 cards in figures included in Table A of this work.

THE *Dd* RESPONSE (UNUSUAL DETAILS)

The Dd coding is afforded responses that are given to areas of the blots which are used infrequently. A criterion of less than 5% of use by *subjects* has been established to define Dd areas. It could be argued that a cutoff of 5% is too low. Although that is possible, it is important to note that most D areas are selected by 20% or less of the subjects taking the test. It is true there is a rather sharp demarcation differentiating a few D locations that are selected by a high percentage of subjects (40% or more), from a second grouping that are selected for use by between 15% and 20% of the subjects. In fact, this second grouping is also significantly different for selection frequency from a third grouping of D areas that is selected by between 5% and 10% of the subjects. This finding could be used as a basis to favor a differentiation of two or three types of common details. But there is no empirical support for such a differentiation. Klopfer attempted this, but research conducted in relation to the formation of the Comprehensive System indicates that such a differentiation has no empirically based interpretive usefulness. It is conceivable that, at some future time, a subclassification of the *D* areas might be found to relate to different forms of information processing, but that is very speculative at this time.

None of the areas identified as *Dd* approach the 5% selection frequency criterion. A few are selected by as many as 3% of subjects, but most have selection frequencies of 1 or 2%, and many are selected by less than 1% of the subjects taking the test. These are areas that attract little attention for the overwhelming majority of subjects taking the test, or if they do attract attention, the potential responses generated from them are apparently discarded with a very high frequency. Beck (1937, 1944) found it useful to provide numerical designations for some *Dd* areas. His listing has been expanded in the Comprehensive System by adding to it those areas that he had specified as *D,* but which do not meet the 5% criterion, plus some other areas that have been studied in the research at the Rorschach Research Foundation.

The majority of *Dd* areas involve small segments of the blots, but size is not necessarily a determining factor. In many instances, a subject may deliberately eliminate some small areas of the whole blot, or of a common detail area in an effort to be more precise. This creates a *Dd* area. The majority of *Dd* selections used by subjects are *not* included among those afforded numerical designations in Table A. Indeed, they are so rare that they have not been recorded systematically. Obviously, any response that is not a *W* or a *D* is coded as *Dd.*

THE *S* RESPONSE (WHITE SPACE DETAILS)

The symbol *S* is included in the Location coding whenever a white space area of the card is included in the response. The use of white space can occur in either of two ways. The subject may integrate the white space with other blot areas, or may elect to deliver a response that involves only a white space area. Regardless of which form of space use occurs, the *S* is never scored alone as a location code. Instead it is always used in conjunction with one of the three primary location codes, as in *WS, DS,* or *DdS.* The rationale for using *S* only with another location code is to maintain consistency in evaluating the three primary types of location selections. Some space answers, particularly on Cards I, II, and VII occur with a much greater frequency than space answers on other cards. If the *D* versus *Dd* criteria are applied, it is clear that some *S* responses are clearly *DS,* whereas most will be *DdS.*

LOCATION CODING FOR MULTIPLE *D* AREAS

Some responses will involve the use of two or more *D* areas. In some of these responses, the appropriate coding will be *D,* whereas in other instances the coding of *Dd* is correct. Some *D* areas are, in fact, a combination of other *D* areas. For example, the *D*1 area on Card III is actually the composite of the two *D*9 areas plus *D*7. Similarly, the composite of *D*1 and *D*3 on Card IX equals the *D*12 area. Naturally, a response to any area listed as *D* will be coded as *D*. However, there are instances when subjects will combine *D* areas to form a new area that is not commonplace. *If* that combination involves only one object, the answer will be coded *Dd*. Conversely, if the subject is using each of the combined *D* areas to identify a separate object, the appropriate location code will still be *D* even though more than one common detail area is involved. These are synthesized responses and will be noted as such by the coding for Developmental Quality.

For example, on Card III a subject might report a person (*D9*) working on some pottery (*D7*). In this answer the integrity of each *D* area is maintained by reporting separate objects, one being used for the person and one for the pottery. On the other hand, the same two areas might be integrated more uniquely if the response were a person (*D9*) with a grotesque hand (*D7*). Here, the subject is reporting the composite of the two areas as a single area, a very uncommon event, and requiring the coding of *Dd*.

Once a coder has become familiar with the *D* areas, as identified in Table A, misidentifications of *D, Dd,* and *S* should not occur unless the coder is negligent. In the two interscorer reliability studies mentioned previously, the percent agreement for *D* is 99%, for *Dd* is 99%, and for *S* is 98%. When disagreement occurred, it was the result of coder neglect.

CODING FOR THE DEVELOPMENTAL QUALITY OF THE RESPONSE

The full interpretive value of the data concerning location selection is increased substantially by the addition of a second code to differentiate the *quality* of the area specification. All whole responses are not selected or organized in the same manner. Neither are the specifications involved in the selection of common or unusual details, or the use of space in forming a response. Rorschach recognized these differences and discussed them as "Apperceptive" approaches (*Erfassungstypen*), suggesting that some subjects manifest a "keen imagination" in forming responses, whereas others approach the blot in a more simplistic or even concrete manner. All of those involved in the development of the test after Rorschach's death have described these differences in cognitive processing, using such words as unorganized, simple, organized, combinatory, and superior.

For example, the unorganized response is one in which the subject uses the blot in a manner that does not require specifications of features. Responses such as clouds, blood, paint, dirt, an island, and so on are examples of this concrete and somewhat nonchalant use of the stimulus field. It has been identified in a manner that circumvents the necessity to organize specific stimulus features in meaningful relationships. A cloud, an island, a skin, and so on can take any of a broad variety of external shapes and, similarly, there are no specific form demands concerning the internal characteristics of the object.

At a higher, but still somewhat simplistic and economical level, the blot is defined as a single object that requires greater specificity, such as, a bat, a person, a maple tree, the skin of a leopard, the island of Barbados, and so on. In these types of answers the cognitive activity includes the necessity of organizing some of the stimulus features in a meaningful way. Combinatory or superior responses require a much higher level of cognitive action, such as "two people picking up a large boulder," or "a woman running after a child up a small hill," or "a submarine gliding through the water with its shadow being cast in the moonlight." The location codes do not provide information concerning the quality of the specification involved in the response. Consequently, a second code is necessary to identify this characteristic.

Meili-Dworetzki (1939, 1956) was among the first to recognize the potential in the Rorschach for differentiating levels of mental complexity and flexibility. She studied levels of location selection in children of various ages, designing her investigations based on the assumptions of Rorschach (1921), Piaget (1924), and Beck (1933). She found a general "enrichment" in location selection and integration with increasing age levels, and suggested the possibility of studying cognitive development through a differentiation of various types of location responses. Rapaport et al. (1946) obviously perceived the same potential and suggested an experimental approach to differentiate types of W responses. Friedman (1952, 1953) developed the most elaborate method for differentiating location specification. His work is based on Werner's (1948, 1957) theory of cognitive development. It is similar to, but much more inclusive than the Rapaport approach, being applicable to both whole and detail responses. The Friedman approach employs six categories for evaluating location specification, three of which are considered "developmentally high" codes or scores, and three reflecting "developmentally low" scores. The research on the Friedman method has been considerable and appears to establish that the technique can be useful for the study of developmental levels of cognitive functioning.[2]

Early attempts to integrate the Friedman approach for coding developmental quality into the Comprehensive System encountered three problems. First, two of the categories tend to overlap for criteria, creating considerable difficulty in establishing adequate levels of interscorer reliability. Second, two other categories are based on a questionable assumption that five of the blots are markedly different than the remaining five in terms of stimulus unity. Third, and possibly most important, one of the developmentally low categories is directly correlated with the inaccurate use of the blot contours—that is, the form quality of the response. The developmental quality codes relate the levels of cognitive functioning, whereas the coding for form quality relates to perceptual accuracy or conventionality. Although there is probably some relationship between the two, it is far less than is implied by the direct correlation used in the Friedman method.

When the Comprehensive System was first published (Exner, 1974), no solution to the overlap problem between developmental quality and form quality was readily apparent; however, the other two issues were resolved by reducing the number of categories from six to four. The four categories were represented by the symbols $+$ (synthesis), o (ordinary), v (vague), and $-$ (arbitrary). The arbitrary code $(-)$ is the one that correlated directly with form quality, and considerable research ensued during the next several years to resolve the interpretive problem created by that spurious relationship. The issue was ultimately resolved by reviewing findings concerning levels of cognitive activity that had been differentiated in a series of problem-solving studies, plus data that had been collected using the Halstead-Reitan neuropsychological test battery. Each data set was divided into quartiles and the first and fourth quartiles compared with special attention to responses that had been coded either v or $-$ for developmental quality, but which also included some synthesis activity. Those types of answers were assigned either of two experimental developmental quality scores, $v/+$ or $-/+$ (Exner, 1983). As hypothesized, subjects with a higher frequency of synthesized responses $(+, v/+,$ and $-/+)$ fall significantly more often in the upper quartile; that is, they demonstrate higher levels of performance in analysis-synthesis operations in problem solving, concept formation, and have better per-

---

[2] Although the Friedman method does distinguish differences in children, as identified by chronological and mental age, it probably deals more specifically with general cognitive operations. Thus the concept of development, as used traditionally in psychology in the study of children, is not directly applicable.

formances on the conceptual tests in the Halstead-Reitan battery. Conversely, subjects with few synthesis responses and a higher than average frequency of $-$ and v responses in their Rorschachs, fall in the lowest quartile of the distribution based on these kinds of performance.

The second step in this analysis was to determine if the presence of the arbitrary code, $-$, contributed significantly to the differentiation of subjects in the first and fourth quartiles of the distribution. The results are essentially negative; that is, the arbitrary DQ codings do occur only slightly, but not significantly more often among subjects in the lowest quartile.

These data led to the elimination of the arbitrary code for developmental quality, and the addition of another code to signify synthesis activity occurring in responses that previously would have been coded as v (vague). The new code is $v/+$. It is designed to identify answers in which some synthesizing activity has occurred, but the objects reported have no form demand. Thus four developmental quality codes remain in the Comprehensive System. The criterion for each is presented in Table 8. In the two previously cited studies concerning interscorer reliability, the percent agreement for the $+$ code is 95%, for the $v/+$ is 94%, for the o is 96%, and for the v is 95%. As with the coding for location selection, interscorer disagreements occurring in the two studies cited resulted from scorer neglect.

Some elaboration concerning the criteria for the DQ coding is in order, because there are some key words in each. For each of the two types of synthesis ($+$ and $v/+$) responses the criterion statement includes, "... separate but related." More than one object must be involved *and* it must be reported in a meaningful relationship to the other objects in the response. For example, "two birds sitting on a fence" would be coded $+$ because there are three objects in the response and all are interrelated. The two birds are sitting on the fence. If the response had been, "two birds," alluding to the symmetry of the blot, the DQ code would be o (ordinary) because there is no meaningful relationship between them. No integration has occurred. If the separate objects involve clothing on a figure, the clothing *must* be identified in a way that alters the natural contour of the figure, or be a discrete blot area itself.

Table 8. Symbols and Criteria Used for Coding Developmental Quality

Symbol	Definition	Criterion
$+$	Synthesized response	Unitary or discrete portions of the blot are articulated and combined into a single answer. Two or more objects are described as separate but related. At least *one* of the objects involved must have a specific form demand, or be described in a manner that creates a specific form demand.
$v/+$	Synthesized response	Unitary or discrete portions of the blot are articulated and combined into a single answer. Two or more objects are described as separate but related. None of the objects involved have a specific form demand, or are articulated in a way to create a specific form demand.
o	Ordinary response	A discrete area of the blot is selected and articulated so as to emphasize the outline and structural features of the object. The object reported has a natural form demand or the description of the object is such to create a specific form demand.
v	Vague response	A diffuse or general impression is offered to the blot or blot area in a manner that avoids the necessity of articulating specific outlines or structural features. The object reported has no specific form demand, and the articulation does not introduce a specific form demand for the object reported.

For example, subjects often report one or two human figures on Card III. Occasionally the figure is described as wearing a tuxedo, which is defined because the figure is dark in coloring. This is *not* coded + because the same blot area is being used for both the figure and the clothing. Conversely, if the figure (D9) were described as wearing big mittens (Dd16), a + would be appropriate because discrete blot areas have been used.

Some other very important key words in the criteria are, "specific form demand." This means that the object being reported generally has a consistent form; that is, when the noun identifying the object is used, some specific shapes are implied. For example, the words *man, bird, butterfly, spider, lion, ship, house,* and so on each identify a class of objects that has some specific form characteristics even though some variations may exist within each class. Men may be short or tall, thin or fat, and so on, but men cannot take an infinite number of shapes. On the other hand, words such as *cloud, lake, island, foliage, blood, paint, desert,* and so on represent classes of objects that can take any of a wide variety of shapes. There is no specific form demand. Thus if the object reported does have a form demand, the *DQ* coding must be *o* (ordinary) or + (synthesis) if it is meaningfully combined in relation to another object, *regardless of whether the other object has form demand.* If the object reported has no specific form demand, the *DQ* coding will be *v* (vague), or *v/+* (synthesis) if it is meaningfully combined with another object *that also has no form demand.*

It is important to note that, at times, a subject will report an object that has no specific form demand, but in elaborating on the object may inject a form demand. For example, the response, "cloud" will usually be coded *v*; however, a subject might elaborate, "like the kind that build up in a funnel shape, like those dangerous storm clouds." This elaboration has injected a form demand, requiring the coding of *o* rather than *v*. Similarly, the response, "a lake" that is not elaborated for specification will be coded *v*, but Lake Michigan, which does have a specific shape, would be coded *o*.

Examples   The location component of each response will always include two symbols—one for the area used and the second for the developmental quality. Some examples of the various types of codings are shown in Table 9.

Accuracy in coding location is essential. Although the criteria are reasonably straightforward, the process may seem to be more simplistic than is actually the case, and caution is always in order. The overall impact of the location coding to the interpretation of the protocol can be considerable. Several interpretive hypotheses concerning cognitive functioning, perceptual scanning, needs for achievement, awareness of convention, and proneness to economize are often based on the composite of these data. If they are accurate, so too will be the interpretive postulates, but if they are inaccurate, the interpretive yield can suffer significantly.

Table 9.   Examples of Coding the Location Component

Card	Response	Location Coding
I	Two witches dancing around a woman (W)	W+
	A piece of coral (D1)	Dv
	Two ghosts (DdS30) climbing up a hill (Dd24)	DdS+
II	Two dogs rubbing noses (D6)	D+
	Some sort of colorful map (W)	Wv
	Icicles (Dd25)	Ddo

Table 9   (Continued)

Card	Response	Location Coding
III	Some pieces of a puzzle (*W*)	*Wv*
	A person seeing his reflection in a mirror (*D1*)	*D+*
	A catfish (*D2*)	*Do*
IV	A man sitting on a tree stump (*W*)	*W+*
	Some storm clouds coming together (*W*)	*Wv/+*
	A couple of boots, one on each side (*D6*)	*Do*
V	A bat (*W*)	*Wo*
	An x-ray of some insides (*W*)	*Wv*
	A map of the United States (*W*)	*Wo*
VI	A piece of torn fur (*D1*)	*Dv*
	A bearskin rug (*D1*)	*Do*
	Some shrubs or something on a hill (*D3*)	*Dv/+*
VII	A necklace (*W*)	*Wo*
	An island in the ocean (*WS*)	*WSv/+*
	A bird (*Dd25*) gliding toward his nest (*D6*)	*Dd+*
VIII	A brightly lit chandelier (*W*)	*Wo*
	Some insides of a dissected animal (*W*)	*Wv*
	Some torn cloth hanging on a stick (*D5*)	*Dv/+*
IX	A big explosion (*W*)	*Wv*
	An atomic explosion with the mushroom cloud (*W*)	*Wo*
	A dried-up bloodstain (*Dd28*)	Ddv
X	A lot of underwater creatures swimming around these rocks, like fish and eels (*W*)	*W+*
	A whole lot of things like you see in the water, like fishes (*D2*) and crabs (*D1*) and other things (*W*)	*Wo*
	A Buddha (*DdS29*) with a jewel for a navel (*D3*)	*DdS+*

REFERENCES

Beck, S. J. (1933) Configurational tendencies in Rorschach responses. *American Journal of Psychology,* **45,** 432–443.

Beck, S. J. (1937) *Introduction to the Rorschach Method: A Manual of Personality Study.* American Orthopsychiatric Association, Monograph No. 1.

Beck, S. J. (1944) *Rorschach's Test. I: Basic Processes.* New York: Grune & Stratton.

Exner, J. E. (1974) *The Rorschach: A Comprehensive System. Volume 1.* New York: Wiley.

Exner, J. E. (1983) *1983 Alumni Newsletter.* Bayville, N.Y: Rorschach Workshops.

Exner, J. E., and Exner, D. E. (1972) How clinicians use the Rorschach. *Journal of Personality Assessment,* **36,** 403–408.

Friedman, H. (1952) Perceptual regression in schizophrenia: A hypothesis suggested by the use of the Rorschach test. *Journal of Genetic Psychology,* **81,** 63–98.

Friedman, H. (1953) Perceptual regression in schizophrenia: An hypothesis suggested by the use of the Rorschach test. *Journal of Projective Techniques,* **17,** 171–185.

Hertz, M. R. (1970) *Frequency Tables for Scoring Rorschach Responses.* (5th Ed.) Cleveland: Case Western Reserve Press.

Meili-Dworetzki, G. (1939) Le test Rorschach et l'evolution de la perception. *Archives de Psychologie,* **27,** 111–127.

Meili-Dworetzki, G. (1956) The development of perception in the Rorschach. In B. Klopfer et al.

Developments in the Rorschach Technique. II: Fields of Application. Yonkers-on-Hudson, N.Y: World Book.

Piaget, J. (1924) *Le Judgement et le Raisonnement chez l'Enfant.* Neuchatel: Delachaux & Niestle.

Rapaport, D., Gill, M., and Schafer, R. (1946) *Diagnostic Psychological Testing. Volume 2.* Chicago: Yearbook Publishers.

Rorschach, H. (1921) *Psychodiagnostik.* Bern. Blicher.

Werner, H. (1948) *Comparative Psychology of Mental Develoment.* (Rev. Ed.) Chicago: Follett.

Werner, H. (1957) The concept of development from a comparative and organismic point of view. In D. B. Harris (Ed.) *The Concept of Development.* Minneapolis: University of Minnesota Press.

CHAPTER 6

Determinants:
Symbols and Criteria

The most important, and possibly the most complex, of the coding decisions concerns the response determinant, that is, the blot features that have contributed to the formation of the percept. The object of determinant coding is to provide information concerning the complex perceptual-cognitive process that has produced the response. There are many stimulus characteristics in the blots, each of which generally falls into one of three descriptive classifications: (1) those involving form, (2) those involving color, and (3) those involving the shading features. Determinant coding would be a relatively easy task if all responses could be discretely identified as falling into one of these three categories, but that is not ordinarily the case. In many instances, more than one of the three categories is involved as in, "a yellow rose with a long stem," or "a man in the shadows." The first involves both form and color, whereas the second involves both form and shading. In other instances, a broad classification of stimulus characteristics fails to differentiate the ways in which the stimulus is used. For example, form features can be used to create the impression of movement as in "a person bowing," or "a bat flying." Sometimes the symmetry of the blot is used as a reflection as in, "a woman seeing herself in a mirror." In still other instances the form may be used simply for purposes of identification as in, "It looks like a bat because of the shape of the wings and the body."

The numerous ways in which the stimulus characteristics of the blots can be used to create responses have continually posed a challenge to those seeking to offer a systematic coding for the test. Recommendations for determinant codes have varied considerably from system to system and have often been focal points of Rorschach controversy. Rorschach had originally suggested five symbols for the scoring of determinants, one for form (*F*), one for human movement (*M*), and three for color (*FC, CF,* and *C*), two of which were selected to indicate the relative importance of form in the color answer (1921). It was a relatively simple system which discounted the importance of separate codings for responses marked by animal or inanimate movement, perceived dimensionality, reflections, or the use of the achromatic coloring as color. It obviously contained no codes for shading type responses because the blots with which Rorschach did most of his work *did not* contain shading. He did begin working with shaded blots shortly before his death, and introduced a sixth scoring symbol (*C*) in his last, posthumously published, paper (1923), to be used for "chiaroscuro" responses. The six symbols provided the base from which others continued to study and refine the test. Unfortunately, each Rorschach systematizer preferred to use symbols and criteria, which, more often than not, are different than those selected by another systematizer, and in some instances even different than those that Rorschach had suggested. The end product was an astonishing lack of agreement. Even where the same symbol appears in two or more systems, the criterion for the use of that symbol probably differs. In fact, there is no single symbol the criterion for which is agreed upon by all five American Rorschach systems, and there are only a few determinant symbols the criteria for which were agreed upon even by two of the systems (Exner, 1969). For example, 16 different symbols representing 12 different types of color response have been suggested. An even greater number of symbols have been recommended for the shading responses.

The selection of the symbols and criteria for determinants in the Comprehensive System would be relatively uncomplicated if any one system could be demonstrated as clearly superior to the others, but that is not the case. Some are overly elaborate, including components without the logic of a sound empiric base or providing "subscorings" that tend to misrepresent summary data. Others have omitted important components, or have altered component criteria in such a way as to be inconsistent with symbol definitions. Consequently, the symbols and criteria selected for the Comprehensive System constitute a composite of several systems. Each of the possibilities from each system has been considered and evaluated against research findings. The result of this process has yielded 24 symbols, representing nine determinant categories. These nine categories are: (1) Form, (2) Movement, (3) Color (chromatic), (4) Color (achromatic), (5) Texture (shading), (6) Dimensionality (shading), (7) General Shading, (8) Dimensionality (form), and (9) Pairs and Reflections. The symbols used in each of these categories, plus the criterion for the symbol, are presented in Table 10.

Table 10.   Symbols and Criteria for Determinant Coding

Category	Symbol	Criteria
Form	F	*Form answers.* To be used separately for responses based exclusively on form features of the blot, or in combination with other determinant symbols (*except M & m*) when the form features have contributed to the formulation of the answer.
Movement	M	*Human movement response.* To be used for responses involving the kinesthetic activity of a human, or of an animal or fictional character in human-like activity.
	FM	*Animal movement response.* To be used for responses involving a kinesthetic activity of an animal. The movement perceived must be congruent to the species identified in the content. Animals reported in movement *not* common to their species should be coded as *M*.
	m	*Inanimate movement response.* To be used for responses involving the movement of inanimate, inorganic, or insensate objects.
Chromatic Color	C	*Pure color response.* To be used for answers based exclusively on the chromatic color features of the blot. *No* form is involved.
	CF	*Color-form response.* To be used for answers that are formulated *primarily* because of the chromatic color features of the blot. Form features *are* used, but are of secondary importance.
	FC	*Form-color response.* To be used for answers that are created mainly because of form features. Chromatic color is also used, but is of secondary importance.
	Cn	*Color naming response.* To be used when the colors of the blot or blot areas are identified *by name,* and with the intention of giving a response.
Achromatic Color	C'	Pure achromatic color response. To be used when the response is based exclusively on the gray, black, or white features of the blot, when they are clearly used as color. *No* form is involved.

Table 10 (Continued)

Category	Symbol	Criteria
	$C'F$	Achromatic color-form response. To be used for responses that are formulated *mainly* because of the black, white, or gray features, clearly used as color. Form features *are* used, but are of secondary importance.
	FC'	*Form-achromatic color response.* To be used for answers that are based *mainly* on the form features. The achromatic features, clearly used as color, are also included, but are of secondary importance.
Shading-Texture	T	*Pure texture response.* To be used for answers in which the shading components of the blot are translated to represent a tactual phenomenon, with no consideration to the form features.
	TF	*Texture-form response.* To be used for responses in which the shading features of the blot are interpreted as tactual, and form is used secondarily, for purposes of elaboration and/or clarification.
	FT	*Form-texture response.* To be used for responses that are based *mainly* on the form features. Shading features of the blot are translated as tactual, but are of secondary importance.
Shading-Dimension	V	*Pure vista response.* To be used for answers in which the shading features are interpreted as depth or dimensionality. *No* form is involved.
	VF	*Vista-form response.* To be used for responses in which the shading features are interpreted as depth or dimensionality. Form features are included, but are of secondary importance.
	FV	*Form-vista response.* To be used for answers that are based *mainly* on the form features of the blot. Shading features are also interpreted to note depth and/or dimensionality, but are of secondary importance to the formulation of the answer.
Shading-Diffuse	Y	*Pure shading response.* To be used for responses that are based exclusively on the light-dark features of the blot that are completely formless and do not involve reference to either texture or dimension.
	YF	*Shading-form response.* To be used for responses based primarily on the light-dark features of the blot. Form features are included, but are of secondary importance.
	FY	*Form-shading response.* To be used for responses that are based *mainly* on the form features of the blot. The light-dark features of the blot are included as elaboration and/or clarification and are secondary to the use of form.
Form Dimension	FD	*Form based dimensional response.* To be used for answers in which the impression of depth, distance, or dimensionality is created by using the elements of size and/or shape of contours. *No* use of shading is involved in creating this impression.
Pairs & Reflections	(2)	*The pair response.* To be used for answers in which two identical objects are reported, based on the symmetry of the blot. The objects must be equivalent in all respects, but must *not* be identified as being reflected or as mirror images.
	rF	*Reflection-form response.* To be used for answers in which the blot or blot area is reported as a reflection or mirror image, because of the symmetry of the blot. The object or content reported has no specific form requirement, as in clouds, landscape, shadows, etc.
	Fr	*Form-reflection response.* To be used for answers in which the blot or blot area is identified as reflected or a mirror image, based on the symmetry of the blot. The substance of the response is based on form features, and the object reported has a specific form demand.

It will be obvious to the experienced Rorschacher that, in addition to including the five original Rorschach symbols (*F, M, FC, CF, C*) and his criteria for them, many of the symbols are drawn from the Beck and Klopfer systems. The familiarity of the symbol, however, does not necessarily mean that the criterion is identical. This is not the case in some instances, particularly where a symbol has been used in two or more systems with different criteria. This matter is clarified as each of the symbols, its criterion, and reason for selection is discussed more extensively.

THE FORM DETERMINANT *(F)*

The selection of the symbol *F* for the Form answers should require little explanation. It was used by Rorschach to denote answers based on form and has been incorporated into all subsequent systems, using essentially the same criterion. The Form answer has been the focus of some intersystematizer disagreements, but the issues have not concerned the basic criterion. Rather, these disagreements have centered on methods of evaluating form quality (which are discussed in the next chapter), or have related to other determinant criteria, the inclusion or exclusion of which determines what is a ''Pure'' Form answer. *F* is coded for any response which includes Form as one of the determinant features, and is coded separately when no other determinant is involved.

Generally, the inclusion of Form as a response determinant is easily identified. Subjects frequently use the words *form* or *shaped,* or, in some cases, describe the details of the object perceived so as to emphasize the form features. For instance, in elaborating on the response of ''a bat'' to Card I, the subject may add, ''These outer parts look like wings and the center looks like the body part,'' Even without further elaboration it seems clear that the Form features of the blot have been used. Responses based exclusively on the Form features usually comprise the largest single determinant category in a record, and ordinarily Form features will be included in more than 95% of all responses given.

THE MOVEMENT DETERMINANTS

Three kinds of movement responses may occur in the Rorschach, (1) those involving humans or human-like behaviors, (2) those involving animals, and (3) those involving inanimate or inorganic objects or forces. Rorschach scored for only one type of movement, that involving humans or human behaviors. He specifically discounted animal movement as having the same meaning as human movement, and thus provided no scoring for it. Beck (1937, 1944, 1961) vigorously defended Rorschach's position, and also excluded any formal scoring for animal or inanimate movement in his method. Klopfer (1936, 1942, 1954), Hertz (1942, 1951, 1970), and Piotrowski (1937, 1947, 1957) have each taken the opposite position and include scorings for animal and inanimate movement, using the same scoring symbols but with differing criteria for the scoring of inanimate movement.

An examination of each of these positions seems to indicate that both are at least partially correct. There is very little empirical evidence to suggest that the three types of movement all represent different levels of the same psychological process as has been implied by Klopfer and Piotrowski. Quite the contrary, work which has been reported encourages the notion that the three types of responses represent relatively different psychological operations. In that context, Rorschach and Beck have been correct in discouraging separate scorings for animal and inanimate movement so as not to confuse the interpretation of human movement responses. On the other hand, animal and inanimate responses do occur, the former with considerable frequency. Research findings indicate that, just as they are different from human movement responses, they are different from answers based only on form.

Human Movement *(M)*   The symbol *M,* and its criterion, is derived from Rorschach's original work. Each of the systems developed after Rorschach includes this symbol for human movement answers and three of those (Beck, Klopfer, and Hertz) use Rorschach's criterion. The Piotrowski (1947, 1957) and Rapaport-Schafer (1946) systems each include modifications of Rorschach's criterion. Piotrowski restricts the scoring of *M* to responses occurring to an area sufficiently ambiguous as to make any type of movement or posture equally plausible. It is a caution designed to avoid scoring *M* falsely, as in responses where movement is injected to explain form features. Rapaport restricts the scoring of *M* to responses which include complete, or nearly complete, human figures. Neither of the arguments for these criterion restrictions follows from an empirical base, nor is the logic strongly persuasive. The Piotrowski position appears to depend excessively on subjective judgments concerning the intent of the subject in his use of movement. The Rapaport restriction appears to eliminate the scoring of *M* in some instances where *M* does occur. It is quite true that movement perceived to whole human figures is interpreted differently than in movement perceived in partial human figures, but in each, the movement has been perceived and should be scored.

The *M* is scored for human activity. The movement may be active such as in running, jumping, fighting, and arguing, or it may be passive, such as in sleeping, thinking, smiling, and looking. In either instance *M* is scored.

The symbol *F* is *not used* when *M* is scored. The *M* assumes form, even when the content is abstract such as "Depression," or "Happiness." The existence of *M* should not be assumed simply because human figures are perceived. The movement itself must be articulated for a response to be scored *M.* In *most cases,* the movement is reported during the Association. In *fewer instances,* the movement is not reported in the Association, but instead is reported *spontaneously* at the onset of the Inquiry to the response. For example, a subject might respond to Card III, "It looks like two people here." This response appears to be based on form only and would not be scored *M.* If, however, after the examiner begins the Inquiry to the response by simply restating *S*'s response and *S* offers, "Yes, they are right here, it looks like two people doing something," it seems logical to assume that movement had been perceived during the Association but had not been articulated. Spontaneity must be the guideline and *M should never be scored* if there is reason to believe that the movement was provoked by the Inquiry questioning of the examiner. This rule holds true for all determinants.

Although most *M* responses involve human figures, *M* may also occur where the content is animal, but only when the movement described involves a human activity which is not common to the animal species. For example, "two beetles arguing" would be coded *M,* as would "two bears playing gin rummy." Conversely, "two beetles fighting over something," or "two bears playing together," *would not* be scored *M,* but instead would be coded using the symbol for animal movement, *FM.*

Animal Movement *(FM)*   This coding was originally suggested by Klopfer and Sender (1936). His justification for the use of *FM* was based primarily on Rorschach's 1923 article, in which Rorschach referred to a special consideration for responses that are essentially form based but which also tend toward the use of movement or color. Because some of Rorschach's examples included animals in movement, it was natural for Klopfer to include designation of animal movement in this category. By 1942, Klopfer had decided to use a different symbol to represent "tendencies toward" ($\rightarrow$), and selected *FM* for use exclusively in animal movement responses. The criterion selected for use in the comprehensive system is that of Klopfer. It is to be scored for any response involving animals in activity which is common to the species, such as "a dog barking," "a bat flying," and "a leopard stalking its prey." In extremely rare instances, an animal will be perceived in an animal activity which is not common to its species, such as "a snake flying along in the air." In these cases, *M* is entered as the determinant to reflect the human fantasy that has been involved in forming the answers.

Although most *FM* answers include a whole animal, some will involve only a partial animal figure such as "two animals scampering behind a bush, you can only see their legs," on Card V. Occasionally, the content of the animal movement response will be a mythological animal such as a dragon or a unicorn. The scoring in these unusual types of responses continues to be *FM* and the uniqueness of the animal is accounted for in the Content scoring. The scoring of *FM*, like that of *M*, is contingent on the spontaneous reporting of movement by the subject.

Inanimate Movement (*m*)   The third type of movement response which may occur in the Rorschach involves inanimate, inorganic, or insensate objects. The symbol *m*, which has been selected to denote such responses, was first suggested by Piotrowski (1937) during a time when he was closely identified with Klopfer's efforts to develop the Rorschach. Klopfer and Hertz continued to use the symbol in their systems of the test, but with a substantially broader criterion than is used by Piotrowski, including in it phallic forces, facial expressions, and human abstracts.

It is essentially the Piotrowski criterion and method which have been selected for the coding of inanimate movement in the Comprehensive System. The criterion is reasonably precise and does not overlap with either the *M* or *FM* categories, as does the broader criterion of Klopfer and Hertz. Thus *m* is scored for any movement perceived which involves nonhuman and nonanimal objects. The most common types of inanimate movement responses include fireworks, explosions, blood dripping, water falling, and trees bending. Some other types of inanimate movement which occur with considerably less frequency include, skins stretched tightly, a leaf floating, seaweed drifting, a bullet smashing, and such. The *m* is scored for any of these or similar responses. In very rare cases, inanimate objects are perceived in human-like activity, such as "trees dancing a waltz." In this kind of response the scoring should be *M*, rather than *m*.

In the studies concerning interscorer agreement, the 20 coders working with 25 protocols have a 96% agreement for *M*, 97% for *FM*, and 93% for *m*. In the group of 15 coders and 20 records, the percent agreement for *M* is 96%, for *FM* is 98%, and for *m* is 95%. Most of the disagreements concerning *M* and *FM* were caused by coder error; however, some legitimate disagreements occurred about coding *M* or *FM* for science fiction creatures in human-like behavior. Most of the disagreements concerning *m* involved answers in which an object was reported in a form of passive or static movement, such as a coat hanging on a post, which should be coded *m* because of the unnatural tension state, or a rug lying on the floor, which should not be coded as *m* because no unnatural tension state exists.

ACTIVE-PASSIVE SUPERSCRIPTS

A second important coding that must be added to *all* movement answers is a superscript that notes whether the movement is active or passive (^{a} for active, ^{p} for passive). Rorschach suggested the importance of evaluating movement answers in terms of "Flexion" (moving toward the center of the blot) or "Extension" (moving away from the center of the blot). Beck et al. (1961) called attention to a third movement stance, *static*. Piotrowski (1957, 1960) has studied various kinds of movement answers extensively and suggested differentiations such as active-passive, cooperative-noncooperative, aggressive-friendly, and so on. Research findings generated from several studies designed to test some of Piotrowski's hypotheses indicate that the active-passive dimension provides the most consistently valid interpretive yield.

One of the more frustrating issues associated with the development of the Comprehensive System has involved attempts to establish precise criteria for the application of the ^{a} and ^{p} superscripts. That objective has not been achieved. Nevertheless, most people do seem able to agree on the meaning of the terms *active* and *passive* when applied to movement answers. Reliability studies, in which trained coders are instructed to differentiate large numbers of movement answers as either active or passive, have a surprisingly positive yield. For example, 10 postdoctoral fellows show a 93% agreement for 150 movement answers, whereas 10 briefly trained high school students show a 94% agreement for the same 150 answers (Exner, 1978). In another study, 20 nonpatient adults (none trained in psychology) and 20 second-year psychology graduate students, completing a course in assessment that included training in Rorschach, were asked to code 300 words, most of them verbs, as either active or passive. The lay group was provided with a few examples to create a conceptual framework, such as "leaping," "brawling," and "zooming" to illustrate active movement and "gliding," "thinking," and "languishing" to illustrate passive movement. The students were asked to code in the context of their Rorschach training. The majority of subjects from both groups agreed on the coding for 275 of the 300 words. The students agreed unanimously on 213 of the 300 words, whereas the lay group agreed unanimously on only 112. More important, the overall percentage of agreement among the student group was 95% and for the lay group was 86%. In other words, even when coding occurs *without the context of the full response*, there is very high agreement among those with formal training, and very substantial agreement among those who have no training.

Table 11 shows the 300 words used in this study, and includes the coding for each agreed to by the majority of subjects, plus the actual number of subjects in each group that constitute that majority. It has been included here as a *general reference* for those learning to make the active-passive differentiation; *however, it should not be considered as absolutely definitive*. The final decision to code active or passive must be made in the context of the complete response. The table can be used as a guideline, but there will be responses for which the final decision may be difficult and equivocal. Usually they will involve words that are in Table 11, but for which the two groups disagreed, or for which the number constituting the majority is modest. Most Rorschachers using the Comprehensive System set a comparative reference to use as a guideline. At the Rorschach Research Foundation that reference is "talking," which is always coded *passive*. It serves as a benchmark against which questionable issues are judged. In that context, "whispering," "standing," "looking," and the like are easily defined as passive, whereas "yelling" and "arguing" are easily defined as active.

Table 11. Results of an Active-Passive Word Study for Two Groups for 300 Items, Showing the Majority Score for Each Item for Each Group Plus the Number of Subjects Represented by that Majority, with * Indicating Group Disagreements

Item	Lay Group N = 20 Score	N	Students N = 20 Score	N	Item	Lay Group N = 20 Score	N	Students N = 20 Score	N
Abandoned	p	19	p	18	Challenging	a	18	a	20
Accelerating	a	20	a	20	Charging	a	20	a	20
Accusing	a	20	a	19	Chasing	a	20	a	20
Acting	a	17	a	18	Chewing	a	18	a	20
Admonishing	a	19	a	20	Clapping	a	19	a	20
Aggravated (looks)	a	18	a	16	Climbing	a	20	a	20
Aggressive	a	20	a	20	Clinging (helplessly)	p	20	p	20
Agitated	a	18	a	19	Clutching	a	18	a	20
Ailing	p	16	p	19	Composed (looks)	p	16	p	18
Aimless (feeling)	p	20	p	20	Confused (looks)	p	17	p	20
Alarmed	a	18	a	20	Creeping (animal)	a	18	a	20
Amazed (looks)	p	14	p	15	Crouched (animal)	p	16	p	20
Amused (looks)	p	15	p	18	Crying	p	17	p	20
Anchored	p	20	p	20	Cuddled	p	18	p	20
Angry (looks)	a	20	a	20	Dancing	a	20	a	20
Anguished (looks)	p	16	p	14	Dealing (cards)	a	18	a	20
Animated	a	15	a	18	Deciding	a	14	a	17
Annoyed (looks)	p	14	p	16	Defensive (looks)	p	15	p	19
Anxious	a	17	a	15	Defeated (looks)	p	19	p	20
Apologizing	p	16	p	14	Demanding	a	20	a	20
Arguing	a	20	a	20	Demoralized	p	18	p	20
Ascending (smoke)	p	19	p	20	Depressed	p	20	p	20
Aware (looks)	p	14	p	13	Deprived (looks)	p	17	p	20
Bad (looks)	a	11 *	p	12	Deteriorating	p	20	p	20
Baffled	p	16	p	17	Determined (looks)	a	17	a	19
Baking	p	18	p	16	Determined (feels)	a	19	a	20
Balancing (a top)	a	17	a	20	Disappointed (feels)	p	18	p	20
Basking (in the sun)	p	19	p	20	Discussing	a	17	a	20
Bathing	a	14	a	16	Disturbed (upset)	a	14 *	p	13
Battering	a	20	a	20	Dreaming	p	16	p	20
Battling	a	20	a	20	Dripping (water)	p	20	p	20
Beaming (the sun)	p	16	p	20	Drowning	a	13 *	p	18
Bending (in wind)	p	19	p	20	Dropping (leaf)	p	20	p	20
Bewildered (looks)	p	18	p	20	Dying	p	20	p	20
Bleeding	p	20	p	20	Ejecting	a	16	a	18
Blissful (looks)	p	17	p	20	Embarrassed	p	13	p	17
Blowing (hair)	p	18	p	20	Erect (penis)	a	19	a	20
Boasting	a	20	a	20	Euphoric (looks)	a	14	a	15
Bouncing (ball)	a	20	a	17	Excited	a	20	a	20
Breaking	a	18	a	16	Exhausted	p	20	p	20
Bumping (balls)	p	14	p	15	Exploding	a	20	a	20
Burning (fire)	p	13	p	17	Facing	p	14	p	20
Calmly	p	19	p	20	Falling	p	20	p	20
Calling	a	20	a	20	Feeling (physical)	a	16	a	14
Carrying	a	20	a	20	Feeling (mental)	p	18	p	16
Carving	a	18	a	20	Ferocious	a	20	a	20
Casual (looks)	p	17	p	20	Fighting	a	20	a	20
Catching	a	20	a	20	Filling (a pool)	p	14	p	19
Celebrating	a	20	a	20	Firm (muscle)	a	15	a	18

Table 11 (Continued)

Item	Lay Group N = 20 Score	N	Students N = 20 Score	N	Item	Lay Group N = 20 Score	N	Students N = 20 Score	N
Fixing	a	20	a	20	Leading	a	17	a	20
Flapping (in wind)	p	20	p	20	Leering (a wolf)	a	15	a	20
Flapping (bird)	a	18	a	20	Leaning (against)	p	17	p	20
Fleeing	a	20	a	20	Lifting	a	20	a	20
Floating	p	20	p	20	Limping	a	14	a	13
Flowing (river)	p	19	p	20	Loading (cargo)	a	20	a	20
Flying	a	20	a	20	Longing (looks)	p	14	p	18
Frightened (looks)	p	18	p	20	Loosely (held)	p	11	p	16
Gambling	a	16	a	20	Loving (2 people)	a	18	a	20
Gasping (for breath)	a	17	a	12	Lustful (looks)	a	15	a	20
Gazing	p	18	p	20	Lying (down)	p	20	p	20
Glaring (at someone)	a	17	a	20	Mad (looks)	a	17	a	20
Graciously (standing)	a	14 *	p	16	Magical	a	14 *	p	13
					Making (a cake)	a	20	a	20
Grinding	a	17	a	19	Mashing	a	20	a	20
Growing (plant)	a	15 *	p	14	Mean (looks)	a	16 *	p	15
Hallucinating	a	13 *	p	17	Meditating	p	14	p	20
Hammering	a	20	a	20	Menstruating	p	16	p	20
Hanging (man)	p	18	p	20	Miserable (looks)	p	20	p	20
Happy (looks)	a	17	a	19	Mixing	a	20	a	20
Harassed (looks)	p	14	p	17	Modeling (standing)	p	14	p	20
Helping	a	20	a	20	Modeling (clay)	a	11	a	18
Hesitant	p	15	p	19	Mounting	a	20	a	20
Holding	a	17	a	20	Moving	a	20	a	20
Hostile (looks)	a	20	a	17	Mugging	a	20	a	20
Hunting	a	20	a	20	Murdering	a	20	a	20
Hurting	a	20	a	20	Musing (alone)	p	15	p	20
Idle	p	19	p	20	Nervous (feels)	a	13 *	p	18
Imagining	a	13 *	p	18	Nervous (looks)	p	12	p	20
Impatient (looks)	a	14 *	p	14	Nodding (to sleep)	p	20	p	20
Impulsive	a	18	a	20	Noticing (someone)	a	17 *	p	20
Inclining	p	13	p	20	Numb (feels)	p	18	p	20
Inert	p	20	p	20	Objecting	a	20	a	20
Injured	p	20	p	20	Oblivious	p	20	p	20
Inspecting	a	16 *	p	14	Observing	p	16	p	20
Intercourse	a	20	a	20	Offensive (looks)	a	13 *	p	14
Interested	a	13	a	17	Oozing	p	20	p	20
Isolated (feels)	p	18	p	20	Opening (a door)	a	16	a	20
Jeering	a	20	a	20	Opposing	a	18	a	20
Jerking	a	19	a	20	Outraged	a	20	a	20
Jogging	a	20	a	20	Pacing	a	20	a	20
Joining (2 people)	a	18	a	20	Painful (feels)	p	14	p	20
Jovial (looks)	a	17	a	18	Panting (a dog)	p	13 *	a	16
Jumping	a	20	a	20	Passing	a	20	a	20
Kidding (2 people)	a	20	a	19	Peaceful (looks)	p	20	p	20
Killing	a	20	a	20	Perplexed (looks)	p	15	p	20
Knowingly (looks at)	p	14 *	a	17	Picking up	a	20	a	20
Laboring	a	20	a	20	Playing	a	20	a	20
Landing (plane)	a	18	a	16	Pleased (feels)	p	13	p	17
Laughing	a	15	a	13	Pleased (looks)	p	15	p	20
Laying	p	20	p	20	Pondering	p	12	p	20

Table 11 (Continued)

Item	Lay Group N = 20 Score	N	Students N = 20 Score	N	Item	Lay Group N = 20 Score	N	Students N = 20 Score	N
Preaching	a	20	a	20	Smoking (fire)	p	17	p	20
Pretending (sleep)	p	11	p	16	Smoking (person)	a	18	a	20
Prowling	a	20	a	20	Sniffing	a	11 *	p	19
Puffed (balloon)	p	14	p	20	Speaking	a	16	a	14
Pulling	a	20	a	20	Spilling (water)	p	14	p	20
Pushing	a	20	a	20	Springing	a	16	a	20
Putting (golf)	a	20	a	20	Squall (rain)	a	14	a	18
Queer (looks)	p	16	p	20	Stabbing	a	20	a	20
Querulous (looks)	p	15	p	20	Standing	p	13	p	20
Quiet	p	20	p	20	Steaming water	p	18	p	20
Quivering	a	13 *	p	14	Stormy	a	13	a	20
Racing	a	20	a	20	Stroking	a	11	a	16
Raging (river)	a	20	a	20	Struggling	a	20	a	20
Raising (a log)	a	20	a	20	Stuck (in mud)	p	20	p	20
Ramming (2 cars)	a	20	a	20	Subdued (looks)	p	16	p	20
Rapturous	a	16 *	p	18	Suffering	a	13 *	p	17
Reaching	a	20	a	20	Suspicious (looks)	p	12	p	20
Ready (to run)	a	20	a	20	Swimming	a	20	a	20
Reckless (looks)	a	12 *	p	20	Taking	a	18	a	20
Refreshed	p	13	p	11	Talking	a	13 *	p	18
Remorseful	p	15	p	17	Tapping	a	20	a	20
Reposing	p	20	p	20	Tearful	p	17	p	20
Resigned	p	16	p	20	Telling	a	14 *	p	18
Resolute (looks)	a	13	a	15	Terrorized (feels)	p	16	p	20
Reticent (looks)	p	11	p	17	Thrilled	a	14	a	13
Revolving	a	17	a	20	Throwing	a	20	a	20
Riding (a horse)	a	20	a	20	Thumping	a	20	a	20
Ringing (bell)	a	14	a	18	Tilted	p	14	p	20
Ripping fabric	a	20	a	20	Toasting (people)	a	17	a	20
Roaring (lion)	a	20	a	20	Tormented (feels)	p	15	p	20
Roaring (water)	a	13 *	p	18	Touching (2 people)	a	14	a	17
Rolling (ball)	p	17	p	20	Tranquil (looks)	p	20	p	20
Rowing	a	20	a	20	Troubled (looks)	p	13	p	20
Running	a	20	a	20	Turning (around)	a	20	a	16
Sad (looks)	p	18	p	20	Unconscious	p	20	p	20
Sad (feels)	p	20	p	20	Unsteady	p	14	p	20
Sagging	p	16	p	20	Upset (feels)	p	13	p	20
Sailing (boat)	p	14	p	20	Vaulting (animal)	a	18	a	20
Satisfied (feel)	p	13	p	19	Vibrating	a	20	a	20
Screaming	a	20	a	20	Vigorous	a	20	a	20
Seated	p	17	p	20	Violent	a	20	a	20
Seeing	p	15	p	20	Waiting	p	16	p	20
Seething	a	16	a	20	Walking	a	20	a	20
Shaking	a	16	a	18	Wanting	p	11	p	16
Shocked	p	13	p	20	Watching	a	13 *	p	20
Singing	a	20	a	20	Weary (feels)	p	15	p	20
Sinister (look)	a	13	a	16	Whirling	a	20	a	20
Skimming	a	17	a	14	Wounded	p	17	p	20
Sleeping	p	20	p	20	Writing	a	20	a	20
Slipping	p	15	p	20	Yielding	p	18	p	20
Smelling	a	12 *	p	17					

Some movement responses are always coded as *passive*. They are the answers in which the movement reported is *static*. The static feature of the response is usually created by qualifying the answer to make it an abstract, a caricature, or a picture. These are all coded p regardless of the description of the movement reported. Many static responses involve inanimate movement such as, "an abstract of fireworks exploding on the Fourth of July." The described movement, "exploding," is clearly active but it is qualified by the word *abstract* and thus would be scored m^p. Similarly, "a painting of two people struggling to lift something," or "a drawing of two lions climbing a mountain" both involve active movement that has become static because of the qualifications of "a painting . . ." and "a drawing . . ." These responses would be coded M^p and FM^p, respectively. It is important to make sure that the subject has qualified the response rather than simply used a qualifying word as a manner of articulation. Children often use the words *picture* or *painting* in their responses. Differentiation between the static response and the articulation style is sometimes difficult, but in most cases involving articulating style, the subject will use the same qualifying word in other responses that do not include movement.

Some examples of the three types of movement answers and the active-passive coding are shown in Table 12. Most include only the original response, although critical parts of the Inquiry are included in parentheses when essential to the coding decision

THE COLOR DETERMINANTS (CHROMATIC)

The symbols used for coding chromatic color responses are the same as used by Rorschach, and the criteria for them are very similar to those that he prescribed. He observed that subjects frequently are impressed with the chromatic colors and use them as factors in forming their responses to the five blots that contain chromatic features. He differentiated these responses into three basic categories: (1) those based exclusively on the color features (*C*), (2) those based primarily on the color features but also involving form (*CF*), and (3) those based primarily on form but also involving color (*FC*). He also used a special scoring (*CC*) in one of his example protocols to note an instance of color naming. Each of the Rorschach systematizers incorporated Rorschach's three basic scoring categories for chromatic color responses into their respective systems, but some have altered the criteria for their application. Beck remained most faithful to the Rorschach criteria and Klopfer and Rapaport have deviated most from them.

Each of the systematizers, except Beck, also proliferated the chromatic color scoring categories somewhat extensively. Special scorings for "color projections," "color denial," "crude color," "color description," "color symbolism," "arbitrary color," and "forced color" are found in the various systems. All of the systems except Beck also include color naming, although the criterion varies from system to system. There are no empirical findings to support the usefulness of the variety of proliferated categories for coding chromatic color answers, with the possible exceptions of color naming and color projection. The data concerning color projection suggest that it should be coded separately rather than as a determinant. Thus the Comprehensive Systems include four symbols for coding responses that include the use of chromatic color, *C* (Pure Color), *CF* (Color-Form), *FC* (Form Color), and *Cn* (Color Naming).

The Pure Color Response *(C)*   The *C* response is based exclusively on the chromatic features of the blot. It occurs with least frequency of any of the three basic types of color

Table 12. Examples of the Three Types of Movement Responses

Card	Location	Response	Coding
I	D4	A wm stndg w her arms raised	M^p
I	W	Two witches dancing arnd some symbol	M^a
I	W	A bf glidding along	FM^p
I	W	A bat zoomg in to strike	FM^a
I	Dd24	A church bell ringing (Dd 31 is clapper)	m^a
I	W	A fallen leaf disintegrating (S: Ths little pieces out to the sides r prts fallg off)	m^p
II	W	Two clowns dancing in a circus	M^a
II	D3	Menstruation	M^p
II	D6	Two dogs fighting	FM^a
II	D4	An erect penis	M^a
II	DS5	A top spinning	m^a
III	D1	Two people leaning over something	M^p
III	D1	Two people picking something up	M^a
III	D3	A bf flyg between two cliffs	FM^a
III	D2	A bat hanging upside down, asleep	FM^p
III	D2	Blood running down a wall	m^p
IV	W	A man sitting on a stump	M^p
IV	W	A giant looming over you	M^a
IV	D1	A caterpillar crawling along	FM^a
V	W	A bf floating along	FM^p
V	W	Someone dressed up like a bunny doing a ballet dance	M^a
V	W	Two people resting against each other	M^p
VI	D3	An erect penis	M^a
VI	<D4	A ship passing silently in the night	m^p
VI	Dd19	A speedboat racing up a river	m^a
VII	D2	A little boy looking in the mirror	M^p
VII	∨W	Two wm dancing	M^a
VIII	Dd	(Half of blot including D1) An animal climbing up something	FM^a
VIII	D4	A frog leaping over something	FM^a
VIII	D5	Two flags waving in the breeze	m^a
IX	W	Intercourse (D9 male, remainder of blot female)	M^a
IX	>D1	A wm running after a child	M^a
IX	∨W	An atomic explosion	m^a
IX	DS8	A waterfall	m^p
X	D1	A crab grabbing something (D12)	FM^a
X	D2	A collie dog sitting down	FM^p
X	Dd	(Upper D9 each side) Two boys talking to each other	M^a
X	∨D10	Someone swinging in a swing (D5 is the person, D4 is the swing)	M^a
X	∨D6	Two people reaching out to each other	M^a
X	W	Fireworks	m^u
X	D7	A deer jumping	FM^a
X	D3	A seed dropping to earth	m^p
X	W	A lot of seaweed floating along	m^p
X	Dd	(Center parts including D9, D3, D6, and D10) A flower that is opening up to the sun	m^p
X	D11	Two animals trying to climb a pole	FM^a

answers and is identified by the complete lack of form. The decision to code pure *C* is usually based on the fact that color alone has been specified or implied in the Association with no attempt to articulate form features. Among the more common examples of the pure *C* response are blood, paint, water, and ice cream. Any of these might be articulated in such a manner as to include form, such as "blood running down" (Card III), and when such an articulation occurs the coding is *CF* rather than *C*. In that the clarification of the use of color is not commonly offered during the Association, it is especially important that the Inquiry be cautious but specific to this point such as, "I'm not sure why it looks like that." The examiner must rely on the "spontaneity" of the Inquiry material and, for responses such as "blood" given in the Association, the *C* should be coded unless a form clarification is spontaneously offered *at the onset of the Inquiry*. Ordinarily, when a pure color response has been given in the Association, the subject simply verifies the location of his answer at the onset of the Inquiry. Conversely, where form has also been involved, the subject usually concentrates on the form features at the onset of the Inquiry. Two similar responses, extracted from the protocol pool, serve as good examples. Both are whole responses to Card X.

ASSOCIATION	INQUIRY
X Gee, a lot of paint	*E:* (Rpts *S*'s response)
	S: Yeah, all over like somebody threw a lot of paint there
	E: I'm not sure why it looks like paint.
	S: All those colors, that's like paint

In this response the absence of form is implied in the Association and confirmed immediatly in the Inquiry, and a score of *C* is appropriate. The second example is somewhat different even though the Association is extremely similar.

ASSOCIATION	INQUIRY
X Oh a lot of paint	*E:* (Rpts *S*'s response)
	S: Yes, all of it ll an abstract of somesort
	E: An abstract?
	S: Yes, it's the same on both sides as if to give each of the colors a double meaning, as if the painter was trying to convey s.t. by the design that he selected which is very pretty by the way

In this response the subject spontaneously injects the form features of the blot at the onset of the Inquiry. In most instances the form quality of the blot would have been implied in the Association, such as "oh, an abstract painting," but this particular subject did not do so. Assuming that there has been no set offered by the examiner during the Inquiry which would produce a form orientation, this response would be coded *CF* rather than *C*. It has been suggested previously that questionable *M* responses might best be decided in light of the overall record. This principle also holds for the questionable *C* responses; namely, if other pure *C* responses have occurred, the questionable response should probably be coded as *C*, and vice versa. Again, caution should be exercised in the use of this guideline. It is not a hard-and-fast rule, but simply one tactic that may assist the examiner who is confronted with a coding dilemma.

Quite often, the Rorschach novice finds it difficult to discriminate the pure *C* response, being overly influenced by the fact that everything has some form. Although that fact is unrefutable, it is not an issue here. The issue is whether the subject *processes and articulates the use of the form features in creating and selecting the response.* The failure to articulate those features of the stimulus field signals some disregard and/or dysfunction in processing, mediating, or integrating the stimulus characteristics that are present. For instance, a drop of blood has a contour, but that contour can take an infinite number of shapes. If a subject identifies a drop of blood, and adds no more, the cognitive operations have, in effect, discarded or disregarded the possible use of contours. Conversely, a subject might identify "an almost perfectly round drop of blood," or "a drop of blood that looks like it has splattered outward." In each of these responses, the subject has included some meaningful, albeit not necessarily definitive, use of contour in the response and the appropriate coding is *CF*.

The Color-Form Response *(CF)*   The *CF* response is one based primarily on the color features of the blot and which also includes reference to form. These are very often answers the content of which does not require a specific form. In many instances the presence of form articulation differentiates them from pure *C* responses as in "two scoops of ice cream sherbet" (Card VIII), or "orange flames from a forest fire" (Card IX). In other responses, the vagueness of form articulation differentiates them from the *FC* type answer as in "a lot of flowers" (Card X). Most flower responses are *FC* because the form characteristics such as petals, leaves, and stems are mentioned. In the example above, however, the subject offers no further form differentiation in the Inquiry ("Yeah, just a lot of different colored flowers"). The distinction of *CF* from *FC* is often difficult because of the vagueness or inarticulation of subjects. A seemingly large number of *CF* responses involve objects which have ambiguous form requirements such as lakes, maps, meat, foliage, minerals, or underwater scenes. Any of these contents can be *FC* if the subject provides sufficient justification by his emphasis on form. Conversely, many responses, such as the example to Card X, which carry specific form requirements, and which usually will be *FC* when color is used, might be *CF* if form is deemphasized by the subject.

Some Rorschach authorities, such as Klopfer and Hertz, have suggested a more definitive criterion for differentiating *FC* from *CF* by using the form requirements of the content as a guide. Thus all flowers, which have a relatively common form, are *FC*, whereas all lakes, which have only ambiguous form requirements, are *CF*. Although the intent of these differentiations is clearly worthwhile, the logic is not altogether sound, for it assumes that all subjects interpret color equally if they use the same content. This is probably no more the case for differentiating *CF* from *FC* than it would be for differentiating *C* from *CF*. Consequently, the articulation of the subject must be weighed carefully and a cautious but nondirective Inquiry is always in order. Where doubt remains, the examiner may use the remainder of the protocol as a basis for decision making.

The Form-Color Response *(FC)*   The *FC* response represents the most controlled use of color. It involves an answer where the form features of the blot are primary in forming the percept and color is also used for purposes of elaboration or clarification. The overwhelming majority of *FC* responses have specific form such as in "a red butterfly" (Card

III), "an anatomy chart with the lungs (D1), the rib cage and the lower organs" (Card VIII), or "daffodils" (Card X). These form features are also given considerable elaboration, either in the Association or in the Inquiry. Some inarticulate subjects do not offer much elaboration regarding form features but do mention color. Here, as with decisions about other determinants, the total protocol proves a useful guide and the limited articulation will be noted in noncolor responses. If the issue remains in doubt, a conservative approach to coding *CF* versus *FC* is in order, because one is generally interpreted to mean a more limited affective control than the other. In either instance, it is quite important that the *FC not be rejected* simply because the content reported does not have a specific form requirement. Numerous contents of ambiguous form requirement such as anatomy, foliage, sea animals, and even blood cells can be offered in a manner that emphasizes the form features while also including reference to color. In such cases, the code is *FC*.

The Color Naming Response *(Cn)*   Rorschach gave little attention to color naming other than to score it *CC* and to note that he observed it in the records of deteriorated epileptics. Piotrowski (1936) introduced the use of the symbol *Cn* for color naming in his studies of the protocols of organics. He does not consider it to be a genuine color response but rather an acknowledgment of the presence of color. The research which has been reported on color naming suggests that it can be an important diagnostic clue and that it does occur with sufficient frequency among the more severely disturbed to warrant special scoring. The criterion adopted for *Cn* in the comprehensive system follows Klopfer and Rapaport; that is, that it is intended as a response. Naturally, it is important that *Cn,* as is the case with any other unique or dramatic response, be interpreted in the context of the total configuration of the protocol. Thus a *Cn* response followed by a *CF* response, using the same or nearly the same blot areas, will be interpreted differently than will be a *Cn,* which is the only response given to a card. In either instance, the *Cn* should be scored, provided that the subject actually identifies one or more chromatic areas by name (red, green, blue, etc.) and intends that identification as a response. The examiner should not confuse occasional spontaneous comments which some subjects give when presented with chromatically colored cards, with color naming. Comments such as "Oh, how pretty," or "My, look at all the colors," *are not* color naming. They are interpretively important comments but should not be considered as the same, or even similar, to the *Cn* answer. Most *Cn* responses are given with an almost mechanical or detached flavoring, manifesting the difficulties which the subject has in cognitively integrating the complex stimulus material.

Some examples of the four types of chromatic color responses are provided in Table 13. The Inquiry material included consists *only* of that which is relevant to the coding decision, so that in some instances, the Inquiry is omitted and in other instances only a portion of the Inquiry is shown.

Table 13.   Examples of the Four Types of Chromatic Color Responses

Card	Location	Association		Inquiry	Coding
II	D3	This red ll blood	S:	Its all reddish	C
II	D3	A red bf			FC
II	D2	A fire, like a bonfire	S:	Well its all red like a bonfire sort of blazing upward	CF.m[a]

Table 13 (Continued)

Card	Location	Association		Inquiry	Coding
II	W	Two clowns, in a circus	S:	I thought of a circus because of the red hats	FC
III	D2	Bad meat	S:	The color makes it look spoiled to me	C
III	VD2	Blood running down a wall or s.t.	S:	Its red & u can c it like its running down	CF.m^p
III	D3	A hair ribbon	S:	Its a pretty red one	FC
VIII	W	A dead animal	S:	It looks like the insides, all decayed	CF
			E:	Decayed?	
			S:	Yes all the different colors ll decay & u can c some bones	
VIII	D5	Two blue flags			FC
VIII	W	Pink and orange & blue			Cn
VIII	D4	A frog	S:	Well the legs r out & it has a froggy like body & it has a froggy like color to it	FC
VIII	D2	An ice cream sundae	S:	It ll orange & raspberry ice cream, like two scoops	CF
IX	W	A forest fire	S:	Well the fire here (D3) is coming up over ths trees & stuff	m^a.CF
			E:	Trees & stuff?	
			S:	C, the green here cld b trees & ths other cld b bushes	
IX	D9	Pink here	S:	Right down here	Cn
IX	D4	A newborn baby	S:	U can c the head, that's all, it must b newborn because its pinkish	FC
IX	VW	An atomic explosion	S:	The top prt is the mushroom cld & dwn here the orange is the fire blast & the green area cld b smoke	m^a.FC
X	VD4	A seahorse	S:	It has that shape & its green	FC
X	D9	Coral	S:	Its colored like coral	C
X	W	Some sort of really neat abstract	S:	Well the artist has taken pains to make it the same on both sides & then he's represented his different thoughts with different colors, really neat	FC
X	W	An abstract painting of some kind	S:	Just a lot of colors to represent an abstract thought I guess, its pretty good	CF
X	D13	A potato chip	S:	Well it's kind of shaped like a potato chip & it has the same color as one	FC
X	D15	A flower	S:	I don't kno what kind, it is a pretty yellow, there isn't much of a stem tho u can only c the flower part itself, like the petals and that	FC
X	D12	A leaf	S:	Its green like a leaf	CF

The decision to code color is sometimes complicated by the approach of the subject to the test. Under ideal conditions, subjects will identify color responses by a statement, such as "It looks like that because of the color." Unfortunately, many subjects are not that cooperative or articulate. For example, a subject may give a response such as "blood" to the D3 area of Card III. When the response is inquired, the subject may state, "Yes, here in this red part." The question is legitimately raised concerning the necessity to inquire further to verify the actual use of color. It is indeed a rare subject who would give a blood response to a red area and then deny that color was influential; however, it does happen occasionally. These rare instances do necessitate some inquiry approach by the examiner to establish the fact that color is used. It is *not*, however, necessary for the examiner to repeat the same Inquiry routine to evoke the word *color* to every response which apparently involves color. The skilled examiner will detect the pattern of articulation early in the Inquiry, and it is appropriate for him or her to use that information wisely in forming subsequent Inquiry questions. The use of good judgment by the examiner will save both time and probably avoid some irritation to the subject. Thus if a subject gives several color responses in a protocol but does not articulate the word *color* easily in the Inquiry, the examiner should rely on the consistency of articulation as a guide once the color element has been established as being important. This is not to imply that color should be automatically assumed in one response because it has been used in another response, for that should never be the case. It is, however, necessary for the examiner to manifest some flexibility in his or her communications with the subject. The inflexible examiner takes the risk of creating a "color set" for the subject so that, as the questioning is repeated and prolonged, the tendency to articulate color to the last three cards is exaggerated, and color may be offered as an elaboration when, in fact, color was not used in the Association.

The examiner must also be careful not to assume the use of color simply because the subject identifies a location area by its color, as in "This red part looks like a butterfly," or "This blue reminds me of a crab." These *are not* color responses as they stand. Naturally, if there is reason to believe that color might be used, it should be inquired; however, the use of color to specify location should not be confused with the use of color as a response determinant.

THE COLOR DETERMINANTS (ACHROMATIC)

Rorschach did not suggest a special scoring for responses which include the use of achromatic color as color in determining a response. The first formal scoring for these kinds of responses was devised by Klopfer and Miale (1938), using the symbol C'. Klopfer's decision to create a separate scoring for the achromatic color response was, at least in part, based on Rorschach's apparent disregard of the determinant, plus the subsequent writing of Binder (1932), who proposed an elaborate system for evaluating "chiaroscuro" responses. Binder, like Rorschach, did not suggest a separate scoring for the achromatic color response, but did imply that they are interpretively different than responses using the light-dark features as "shading." Klopfer defined the C' response as one in which the black, gray, or white areas of the blot are used as color. This symbol and criterion were adopted by Rapaport and variations of it are in the Piotrowski and Hertz methods.

Campo and de de Santos (1971) reviewed the literature regarding approaches to coding responses based on the light-dark features of the blots and concluded that the *C'* type of answer is discrete from other categories. Similarly, the accumulation of research findings indicate that *C'* responses represent different operations than do the shading responses, and as such, the coding provides useful interpretive information. In that context, the symbols and criteria employed by Klopfer to identify these responses have been incorpo rated into the Comprehensive System, and follow a form-related continuum similar to that used for the coding of the chromatic color answers.

The Pure Achromatic Color Response *(C')*   The *C'* response is one based exclusively on the achromatic features of the blot. It is very uncommon and is identified by the complete absence of form. In some instances, the achromatic color will be used directly in the Association, as in "white snow" (*DS*5 area of Card II). In most cases, a formless content is offered in the Association and elaborated as having been perceived by the achromatic color in the Inquiry. Two responses, both to Card V, serve as good examples.

	ASSOCIATION	INQUIRY
V	It ll mud to me	*E:* (Rpts *S*'s response)
		S: Yeah, it's black
		E: I'm not sure I c it as u do
		S: All of it here, its black just like mud
V	Some coal	*E:* (Rpts *S*'s response)
		S: Its dark
		E: Im not sure I c it as u do
		S: It must b coal, its dark like coal

In each of these responses the subject has made no effort to develop the form characteristics and, in each case, has offered achromatic color spontaneously. If the second response had been "a piece of coal," *accompanied* by some attempt at form differentiation, the coding would not be *C'* but rather *C'F*.

The Achromatic Color-Form Response *(C'F)*   The *C'F* response is one based primarily on the achromatic color features and form is used secondarily for purposes of elaboration or clarification. In almost all of these responses it is clear that the answer would not have been formulated without the achromatic features of the blot being involved and the form features are vague and often undifferentiated.

	ASSOCIATION	INQUIRY
I	A black sky with white clouds	*E:* (Rpts *S*'s response)
		S: Its all black & ths thgs r like white clouds (*DdS*26)
VII	Pieces of black coral	*E:* (Rpts *S*'s response)
		S: There r 4 of them, thyr black like pieces of coral, black coral, they mak jewlry out of it

In the first example the differentiation, by content, of the blackness of the whole blot from the white spaces is a vague form use, sufficient to warrant scoring $C'F$ rather than C'. In the second example, the differentiation of blot into "pieces" also justified the inclusion of F into the scoring. Occasionally, subjects will perceive "smoke" because of the achromatic color and, depending on the extent of form use, the scoring will be C' or $C'F$. Most "smoke" responses, however, are perceived because of the shading features rather than the achromatic color and the scoring decision must be formulated carefully, with regard to the report of the subject. It is not uncommon for subjects to use the word *color* to articulate shading features and, in even more frustrating circumstances, subjects may include the specific achromatic element, such as "the blackness of it." This is not necessarily an achromatic color answer and the examiner needs to ensure that it is not simply a way of describing the shading features.

The Form-Achromatic Color Response *(FC')*   The FC' response is one in which form is the primary determinant and achromatic color is used secondarily, for elaboration or clarification. It is the most frequent of the achromatic color responses and is usually easy to identify because of the emphasis on specific form features offered by the subject. Among the more common FC' responses are "a black bat" (Cards I and V); "Halloween figures in ghost costumes" ($DdS26$ area of Card I), clarified as ghost costumes because they are white; "African figures" (Card III), elaborated as being African because they are black or dark; a silhouette of a tree (Card IV), elaborated as being a silhouette because it is black or dark; and ants or insects ($D8$, Card X), elaborated as being gray or dark.

The *key* words on which any of the achromatic color codings are based are black, white, gray, dark, and light. Unfortunately, these same words are sometimes used to specify the location of an object, as in, "This black part looks like . . ." Obviously, it is important to insure that the word is being used to denote the use of the achromatic feature as color before applying the C' coding. It is also unfortunate but true that some of these words are also used to note the use of shading rather than achromatic color, as in ". . . it is blacker here, like it would be deeper" (vista), or ". . . it is lighter up here like the top of a cloud" (diffuse shading). The examiner's decision to use one of the C' symbols is usually not difficult, for the majority of these responses will include the words *black, white,* or *gray* in a manner conveying the use of the achromatic color, *as color,* quite clearly. Greater difficulty in the decision is encountered when the words *dark* or *light* are employed. The decision to use one of the C' symbols versus one of the symbols for diffuse shading should be made cautiously, and following the rule that *the intent of the subject is clear and unequivocal.* If that is not true, the code for diffuse shading should be used.

THE SHADING DETERMINANTS

The coding of responses in which the light-dark features of the blot are used as a determinant has been one of the most controversial aspects of the Rorschach. Although discussed extensively, it has been the least researched of the major determinant categories. It has been previously noted that Rorschach made no mention of shading or "chiaroscuro" features in his original monograph because the cards on which his basic experiment was based contained no variations in hue. These characteristics of the blots were created through a printing error, and according to Ellenberger (1954), Rorschach immediately perceived the possibilities created by the new dimension. Rorschach, during the brief period in which he worked with shaded cards, scored all references to shading as (C) to denote the *Hell-Dunkel* interpretations. Binder (1932) was the first systematically to develop a more extensive scoring for the shading features, following from some of the inferences that had been offered by Rorschach. The Binder approach differentiates four basic types of shading responses but suggests scorings for only two of these. The two which Binder codes are Helldunkel (scored using the symbol *Hd*), which includes answers based on "the diffuse total impression of the light and dark values of the whole card," and *F(Fb)* responses in which shading is differentiated within the blot area used. Binder also noted that subjects sometimes use the shading contour as form-like, or use the light-dark features as achromatic color. Because neither meet his criteria for *Hd* or *F(Fb)*, he offers no special codings for them.

Binder's work has been quite influential to the decisions of the systematizers in their respective approaches to shading answers. Piotrowski, in addition to coding for achromatic color, used two categories for shading responses. One, *c* or *Fc*, is for shading and/or texture responses prompted by the light shades of gray. The second, *c'* or *Fc'*, is used where the dark nuances of the blot are involved, or when a dysphoric mood is expressed. Rapaport also included two categories for shading. The first, *Ch, ChF,* or *FCh*, represents all shading responses except those falling into the second category. The second, scored *(C)F* or *F(C)*, is for the chiaroscuro answer in which the shading components specify important inner details, or for Color-Form responses which include reference to texture.

Hertz includes three categories of shading response, in addition to achromatic color. The first, *c, cF,* or *Fc*, is for responses in which the shading features produce a textural, surface, or reflective quality. The second, employing the symbols *(C), (C)F,* and *F(C)*, is for answers where shading precipitates the interpretation of a three-dimensional effect. The third, *Ch, ChF,* or *FCh*, is used for all other shading responses. Beck also used three categories for shading responses. One, *T, TF,* or *FT*, denotes answers in which the shading features create the impression of texture. The second, *V, VF,* or *FV*, is for responses in which shading contributes to the interpretation of depth or distance, and the third, *Y, YF,* or *FY*, is used for all other types of shading responses and is also used when achromatic color is involved.

The Klopfer approach to shading is the most complex. Klopfer was actually the first, after Binder, to formulate multiple categories for the coding and interpretation of shading responses. In addition to *C'* for achromatic color, Klopfer formulated four categories of shading. The first, *c, cF,* or *Fc*, is used for responses in which shading is interpreted to represent textural, surface, or reflective qualities. It is the same coding and criterion incorporated by Hertz and the criterion is nearly the same as used by Beck in his coding of *T*. The second utilizes the symbols *K* and *KF* to note responses in which the shading is perceived as diffuse. It is very similar to Binder's *Hd*, the Rapaport and Hertz *Ch*, and the Beck *Y*. The third, *FK*, represents instances where shading is used for vista, linear perspective, reflections and landscapes. Some components of this criterion are similar to the Hertz use of *(C)* and the Beck *V*. These three shading categories appeared in Klopfer's original 1936 work. In 1937, Klopfer added a fourth category, *k, kF,* or *Fk*, defined as a three-dimensional expanse projected on a two-dimensional plane. The *k* category, as used in the Klopfer system, applies to X-ray or topographical map responses. The Klopfer approach to the shading responses is made considerably more complex by a number of idiomatic rules for specific types of responses. The product of these rules is that some responses are provided a shading code, even though the response determinant does not meet the criterion for the category. The majority of these idiomatic rules require the use of the *Fc,* although some call for the use of *FK.* For example, "transparencies" are *Fc,* as are answers in which achromatic color is interpreted as "bright" color. Similarly, most responses that emphasize "roundness" are *Fc* rather than *FK,* and *Fc* is also used when the "fine differentiations" in shading are designated to specify parts of objects. The *FK* idioms include both vista and reflection responses *even though* shading is not mentioned.

The selection of symbols and criteria for the coding of shading responses in the Comprehensive System is based on several considerations. The first concerned the possible use of the Klopfer method because it is the most comprehensive. Campo and de de Santos, in their evaluation of the various approaches to the scoring of shading, make a strong logical argument favoring the Klopfer method, but they neglect the complications created by the variety of idiomatic scorings. These scoring idioms not only tend to violate the scoring criteria but also imply the feasibility of interpreting relatively different types of responses as the same. The empirical data available concerning shading responses are somewhat complex, because it is difficult to translate findings derived by one method of coding to another coding approach. It is clear, however, that reflection answers are interpretively different from vista responses, and that percepts that include an emphasis on roundness are different from transparencies. A notable lack of empirical support for the separate *k* category also argues against the Klopfer approach. Data which have been reported suggest that the kind of shading perceived in x-ray responses is different than that used in topographical maps, the former being either achromatic color or diffuse shading, the latter involving the use of shading as vista.[1]

The factors that argue against the Klopfer system also argue in favor of an approach in which the criteria are distinct, which avoids idiomatic scorings, and which neatly differentiates the various types of shading responses. None of the systems accomplish these tasks completely. The three category approach appears clearly preferable to the two category method of Binder, Piotrowski, and Rapaport. The symbols selected for the Comprehensive System are those of Beck (*T, V,* and *Y*), but the criteria for two of these three are *more restricted* than that suggested by Beck. The *V* category includes *only* responses in which shading is present, and the *Y* category *excludes* achromatic color responses.

THE TEXTURE DETERMINANT

The shading features of the blots are often interpreted to represent "tactual" stimuli. In these types of answers the subject elaborates on the composition or texture of the object. The elaboration carries with it, explicitly or implicitly, the conceptualization that the object is differentiated by its tactual features such as soft, hard, smooth, rough, silky, grainy, furry, cold, hot, sticky, and greasy. Texture is coded when the shading components of the blot area are used to justify or clarify these kinds of associations. Texture *should not* be assumed simply because words such as those listed above are used. They are legitimate clues to the probability that shading is involved but this is not always the case; thus Inquiry skill of the examiner is often extremely important. It is not uncommon, for example, to obtain responses in which words such as *rough, shaggy,* or *furry* are used as

[1] Klopfer remarked during a 1964 interview with me that he had been continuously dissatisfied with the various criteria for the scoring of shading responses in his system, especially the *k* category. He quickly added, however, that he felt his own approach was superior to others developed, and expressed the belief that it would be unrealistic to attempt to change his own system in that it had been in use for 30 years by that time.

form elaborations, with no concern for shading features. Similarly, objects may be perceived as "hot" or "cold" because of color. In the optimal situation the subject will indicate the use of shading when giving the response, but this is the exception rather than the rule. In most cases the association will contain some clue that texture may be included, such as using words like *shaggy, furry, hot,* and so on, or the nature of the object itself may raise the possibility as in a rug, a coat, some ice, and such. These clues form the basis of Inquiry questions if they are required. Some subjects, especially children, will actually *rub* the blot but not necessarily articulate the shading. *This is sufficient evidence of the tactile impression to code texture.* The texture determinant is coded in one of three ways, depending on the extent of form involvement.

The Pure Texture Response *(T)*   The *T* response is the least common of the three kinds of texture. It is used for answers in which the shading components of the blot are represented as "textural" with no form involvement. The criterion for differentiating a *T* from a *TF* answer is essentially the same as for differentiating *C* from *CF*. In other words, no effort is made by the subject to use the form features of the blot, even in a secondary manner. Responses such as "wood, flesh, ice, fleecy wool, grease, hair, and silk" all represent examples which *might* be scored *T* provided shading is involved and has been perceived as texture, *and* no form is used. Where the form configuration of the blot area is included, even though it is relatively ambiguous or formless, the coding should be *TF* rather than *T*.

The Texture-Form Response *(TF)*   The *TF* response is one in which the shading features are interpreted as texture and form is used secondarily for purposes of elaboration and/or clarification. In most instances the object specified will have an ambiguous form such as "a chunk of ice," "an oily rag," "a piece of fur," or "some very hard metal." Less commonly, a specific form is used but it is clear, from the Association or information offered spontaneously in the Inquiry, that the shading features precipitated the response; for example, "Something breaded, like a,—well like shrimp, yeah, that's it, fried shrimp" (Card VII). Usually this response will be scored *FT,* because most subjects giving it emphasize the form features and mention the texture as a clarification. In this example, however, the subject, responds first to the texture and then integrates the form in a meaningful way. The scoring of *TF* for objects of specific form must meet the criterion requirement that the interpretation of shading as texture is primary in the response, and that the form features have been used secondarily in the percept. In most cases, the issue is clarified by the Association material, and that must be considered before information given in the Inquiry is weighed. In some situations, the first information given in the Inquiry elaborates shading. This should not automatically be interpreted by the examiner to mean that shading was perceived as the primary feature in forming the response, particularly if the Association is such to suggest that the response might have been form determined. Three very similar responses to Card VI provide examples of how form and texture may vary in importance.

ASSOCIATION	INQUIRY
VI Gee, ths is a funny one, I guess it could b a skin, like an A skin.	*E:* (Rpts *S*'s response) *S:* Well, yeah its all kinda fuzzy and spotted, ths here cld b legs

In this example, there is no indication in the Association that form has been primary. Quite the contrary, the subject is somewhat vague in the response formulation and uses the word *skin* first, and then clarifies it as an animal skin. In addition, the first material offered in the Inquiry concerns shading ("kinda fuzzy"), and only after that is some reference to form injected. This response is *TF*. In a second example, the response is similar but the coding is different.

ASSOCIATION	INQUIRY
VI It ll an A skin to me	*E:* (Repeats *S*'s response)
	S: Well it has a very furry appearance to it and the edging is very rough like an A skin wld b & there is the distinct impression of legs and & the haunch part too

The appropriate code for this response is *FT*, even though the shading features are mentioned first in the Inquiry. The decision to code *FT* rather than *TF* is based on the fact that the Association is reasonably definitive and *could be* form dominated, and the bulk of the *spontaneously given* Inquiry material is form oriented. The necessity of weighing the possibility of form domination in the Association response is demonstrated by a third example.

ASSOCIATION	INQUIRY
VI Well, it cld b an A skin	*E:* (Rpts *S*'s response)
	S: Yes, its not very well done either, it ll the skinner didn't get as much of the front prt as he could have
	E: I'm not sure what u see that ll an A skin
	S: Well all of it except ths top part looks that way, here r the rear legs & I suppose ths r the ft legs

This response involves no shading, or at least the subject has not articulated shading. The total emphasis of the subject is on the form features and the coding must be *F*. The Rorschach skeptic may argue that, because most animal skin responses to Card VI do involve the use of shading as texture, the coder would be justified in scoring *FT*, even though it is not articulated. Empirical findings argue against such a procedure. Baughman (1959) obtained animal skin responses to cards presented in silhouette form and to those in which shading features had been eliminated. It has also been demonstrated (Exner, 1961) that the frequency of "skin" responses to Card IV and VI is not altered if the gray-black features of the cards are made chromatic.

The Form-Texture Response *(FT)*   *FT* is used for responses in which form is the primary determinant and the shading features, articulated as texture, are used secondarily for purposes of elaboration and/or clarification. Most responses coded as *FT* will involve objects that have specific form requirements. For example, the commonly perceived animals on Cards II and VIII are sometimes elaborated as "furry" because of the light-dark features. Similarly, the human figure often reported to Card IV is frequently perceived as wearing a "fur coat." There is, however, a glaring exception to the guideline that *FT* will ordinarily involve objects of specific form requirement. This is the animal skin response to Card VI, which is the most frequently given of all texture responses. A random selection from the protocol pool at the Rorschach Research Foundation of 250 adult nonpatient records and 850 records of adult nonschizophrenic patients yielded 22,311 responses, of which 851 have a texture coding. The 851 include 364 responses (43%) to Card VI, of which 337 are the common animal skin responses and 318 of those are coded *FT*. The distribution of texture responses to Card IV is the second largest for this group, constituting 202 (24%) of the answers, of which 161 are *FT*, about equally divided between animal skin responses and human or human-like figures with fur or fur coats. Only 112 of the texture responses (13%) occurred to Cards I, II, III, and V, whereas 173 of these answers (20%) occurred to Cards VII, VIII, IX, and X. A total of 727 of the 851 texture responses (85%) are coded as *FT*, 107 (13%) are *TF*, and only 15 (2%) are pure *T*.

THE SHADING-DIMENSIONALITY DETERMINANT (VISTA)

The least common use of the light-dark features of the blot involves the interpretation of depth or dimensionality. These responses are marked by the use of the shading characteristics to alter the flat perspective offered by the blot stimulus. The most frequent type of vista response is one in which the contours created by the shading are used to convey the general impression of depth. Three codings are used for the vista responses.

The Pure Vista Response *(V)*   The pure *V* answer is extremely rare. The coding of *V* requires that the subject report depth or dimensionality based exclusively on the shading characteristics of the blot, with no form involvement. These responses, when they occur, are somewhat dramatic because they ignore the form qualities of the stimulus. Some examples are "depth," "perspective," "deepness," and "It's sticking out at me." Any of these similar responses might have some elaboration which involves the form features of the blot. When this occurs, the coding is *VF* rather than *V*.

The Vista-Form Response *(VF)*   The *VF* responses include primary emphasis on the shading features to represent depth or dimensionality and incorporate the form features of the blot for clarification and/or elaboration. Most *VF* responses have contents of nonspecific form requirement, such as "one of those maps like you use in a geography class with the mountains and plateaus shown," "rain clouds, one behind the other," or "a deep canyon with a river running in there." If the topographical map were to be more specifically defined, such as "a topographical map of the western part of the United States," or the canyon and river were more specifically defined, as in "an aerial view of the Colorado River," wherein the form features are given greater emphasis, the coding would be *FV* rather than *VF*. The *VF*, like *TF*, is contingent on the primary emphasis being given to the shading features.

The Form-Vista Response *(FV)*   The *FV* response is one in which form is the primary feature and the shading component is used to represent depth or dimensionality for purposes of clarification and/or elaboration. Most *FV* responses will have contents with a relatively specific form requirement but that is not necessarily an adequate guideline for differentiating the *FV* and *VF* answers. For example, "a well" has a reasonably specific form requirement, yet most "well" responses are *VF* rather than *FV,* the differentiation being based on whether primary emphasis is given to the form characteristics or the shading. The response which is *FV* will generally include considerable emphasis or elaboration on form. Almost any content, ranging from frequently perceived human or animal figures to very unusual answers, may involve vista. Bridges, dams, and waterways are among the more frequently given *FV* responses; however, the vista component may be reported in almost any form dominated response. For example, the human figure often reported to the center *D* of Card I is sometimes perceived as "behind a curtain" because of the shading difference, or the lower center *D* area of Card IV is often perceived as a worm or caterpillar "coming out from in under a leaf." Both are scored *FV, provided* shading contributes to the percept. The *FV* answer is the most common of the three types of vista.

Some examples of the different types of texture and vista responses are provided in Table 14. The Inquiry material included consists *only* of that which is directly relevant to the scoring decision; therefore, in some instances the Inquiry is omitted, and in other instances, a portion of the Inquiry is presented.

The differentiation between texture and vista answers is not always precise and can make for difficult decisions. For example, a response such as "the convolutions of the brain" to the center area of Card VI will ordinarily be scored *VF* because of the emphasis on dimensionality. The same response, however, might be elaborated as "It looks bumpy, like if you touched it you could feel the bumps." This elaboration, which emphasizes the tactual interpretation, meets the criterion for the scoring of *TF.* The guideline that should be used for the scoring decision requires consideration of the "interpretive emphasis" offered by the subject. If, in the example cited, the elaboration on "bumpy" features appears to have been injected for purposes of clarification, the scoring remains *VF.* Conversely, if the tactual emphasis is injected in the Association, or is offered spontaneously *at the onset* of the Inquiry, the scoring should be *TF.* Fortunately, in most cases, the subject provides material from which the "interpretive emphasis" can be identified easily. For example, "rough mountain peaks" (vista) is easy to differentiate from "a rough piece of sandpaper" (texture). The word *rough* occurs in each, but mountain peaks are not associated tactually, and sandpaper is not perceived dimensionally. In those few responses where doubt may remain after the Inquiry has been completed, the examiner should review the remainder of the record with concern for the occurrence of other texture or vista answers. If the record contains no other vista responses but does have texture answers, the texture code should be used, and *vice versa.* Accurate coding of vista and texture is quite important, because each carries significantly different interpretive assumptions.

THE DIFFUSE SHADING DETERMINANT

A frequent use of the shading features of the blots is in a nonspecific, more general manner than is the case in either vista or texture answers. It is this type of shading response with which Rorschach concerned himself in developing the scoring of (*C*). The shading features may be used in this way as primary to the formation of a percept, or secondary to provide greater specification to a form answer. The coding for diffuse shading incorporates all shading answers which are neither vista nor texture.

Table 14. Examples of the Different Types of Texture and Vista Responses

Card	Location	Association		Inquiry	Coding
I	W	A dried up leaf	S:	Pts r missing & fallg off & its crinkly	FT
			E:	Crinkly?	
			S:	It looks rough, the way the colors are there	
I	D4	A wm behind a curtain	S:	U can't c all of her, just the lowr prt of her body (D3) & ths is like a curtain u can c thru	FV
I	W	An old torn rag w oil spots on it	S:	Its all black and oily looking to me	TF
II	D4	A circumcised penis	S:	U can c the folds left thr in the cntr	FV
II	D1	A teddy bear	S:	It has that shape & it has all that fur ther	FT
II	DS5	Somethg deep, lik a hole mayb	S:	U can c the round edges ther, like a bottomless pit, at least I don't c any bottom	VF
III	D1	Two gentlemen in velvet suits	E:	U mentioned velvet suits	FT
			S:	Yes, it looks velvet to me, dark shiny velvet	
III	D3	A bow tie	S:	It has a big bulging knot ther in the middl of it	FV
IV	W	Hunters boots prop'd up against a post	S:	The post is behind them u can tell bec it looks further away	FV
			E:	Further away?	
			S:	Well u c where they come together the color is different like the post was further back	
IV	W	An old bearskin	S:	It looks like the fur is pretty well worn	FT
IV	Dd30	A red hot spike	S:	Its a lot lighter on the outside like very hot metal	FT
V	W	A person in a fur cape	S:	U c mostly the cape, it looks like fur to me (rubs fingers on card)	FT
V	W	It looks sticky if u touched it	S:	Ugh, it just ll a sticky mess	T
V	W	The rite half is lower than the left	S:	Thers a deep crack rite dwn the cntr & it ll the rite side is lower	V
V	W	A rabbits head behnd a big rock	S:	Its here (D6), u can't c much of it, just the outline, the drkr prt is the rock in frt	FV
VI	D1	An irrigation ditch	S:	Its dwn in the cntr ther U can c how the diffrnt amounts of waterg have effected the land @ it	FV

125

Table 14 (Continued)

Card	Location	Association		Inquiry	Coding
VI	D4	A chunk of ice	S:	Its cold lookg like ice wld b, all grey	TF
VI	W	A skinned A, the head is still on	S:	Most of it ll the furry skin & u can still c the head prt here (points)	FT
VI	∨Center Dd	A deep gorge	S:	Ths prt (D12) is the bttm & u can c the sides comg up to the top	VF
VII	>D2	A scotty dog	S:	He has more fur on his chin & ft legs, where its drkr	FT
VII	W	Rocks	S:	It just ll 4 rocks next to e.o., u can c that they r round, especially the bottom 2	VF
VII	Dd25	It ll a dam back in there	S:	Well the dam is here, ths liter prt (Dd25 ceter) & the frt prt is like the water-fall part, or mayb a river comg ths way	FV
VII	∨W	Hair, a lot of hair	S:	It all looks hairy to me	T
VIII	D5	An aerial view of a forest	S:	Yeah, thes drkr prts wld be the bigger trees stckg up	VF
VIII	D2	Ice cream sherbet	S:	It looks grainy like sherbet is grainy	TF
IX	D6	Cotton candy, its al fluffy	S:	It has like rolls, like it was fluffy like cotton candy is fluffy	VF
IX	DS8	There's a plant inside a glass	S:	U can just c the stem (D5) & it looks hazy like u were seeg it inside the glass or bowl	FV
IX	DS8	Like u were lookg into a cave or s.t.	S:	It ll an opening & u can c back into it, like the cave mouth	VF
X	D9	Ths pink part ll a map of a chain of mts	S:	Its like a map that is used in schls or s.t. to show the way mts r formed, some r higher than others	VF
X	D13	A piece of leather	S:	Its rough, like it hasn't been tanned	TF
			E:	Rough?	
			S:	U c the different colors there, they make it ll that	
X	D3	A maple seed	S:	The pods r a drkr color, like they r thicker, round like	FV

The Pure Shading Response *(Y)*   The scoring of *Y* is used for percepts based exclusively on the light-dark features of the blot. No form is involved, and the content used typically has no form feature as in mist, fog, darkness, and smoke. A response in which pure *Y* is the only determinant is quite rare.

The Shading-Form Response *(YF)*   The *YF* response is one in which the light-dark features of the blot are primary to the formation of the response and form is used secondarily for purposes of elaboration and/or clarification. The content of the *YF* answer ordinarily has an ambiguous or nonspecific form requirement as in clouds, shadows, nonspecific types of X-rays, and smoke associated with a specific form object such as "smoke coming out of this fire." The main factor that differentiates *YF* from pure *Y* is the intent of the subject to delineate form features, even though vague, in the response. Similarly, the *YF* response is usually differentiated from the *FY* answer by the lack of specificity or emphasis on form. Contents having a specific form requirement are rarely coded *YF*, occurring only in those cases where the shading features are clearly of primary importance to the formation of the percept.

The Form-Shading Response *(FY)*   The *FY* code is used for responses in which form characteristics are primary to the formation of the percept, and shading is used for purposes of specification and/or elaboration. Shadows associated with specific content, X-rays, and elaborations concerning characteristics of form specific objects, such as dirty face, are among the more commonly reported *FY* responses. Ordinarily, the *FY* response can be identified by the fact that the content could be given as a pure form response, whereas this is not usually the case in the *YF* or pure *Y* answer. A notable exception to this rule is the "cloud" response *which can be* based purely on form. When the shading features are associated with the cloud answer, the code is usually *YF*, but in some instances, such as "cloudiness," may be pure *Y,* and in other cases, where form is strongly emphasized, may be *FY*.   .

Some examples of the various types of diffuse shading responses are provided in Table 15. The Inquiry material included consists only of that related to the scoring decision. It is important to emphasize that, at times, the shading features of the blots are used as form contour. For example, the *D*3 area of Card I is sometimes perceived as the lower part of a person and delineated by "these dark lines." Similarly, a dark spot may be sometimes identified as an eye. These *are not* shading responses per se and should be scored as form answers. They do have interpretive importance because the subject has chosen to respond to the "internal" form features of the blot, but they should not be confused with the shading answer.

The Form-Dimension Response *(FD)*   This is a new category, developed out of the research related to the formation of the Comprehensive System. There is no coding comparable to it in the other Rorschach systems, although both Beck and Klopfer have noted the existence of such answers. Klopfer had idiomatically included such responses in the *FK* category, even though no shading is involved. Beck has been prone to score these answers *FV*, but only in instances where the unarticulated use of shading seems very probable. Beck specifically avoided the scoring of *FV* for perspective or dimensionality based on size discrimination.

The potential usefulness of a separate scoring for dimensional responses based exclusively on form was first noted during some System related research concerning the mean-

Table 15. Examples of Diffuse Shading Responses

Card	Location	Association		Inquiry	Coding
I	*W*	An x-ray of a pelvis			*FY*
I	< *D*8	A Xmas tree at night	*S:*	Its dark like it wld b at night	*FY*
I	*W*	Ink	*S:*	It's just all dark like ink is dark[a]	*Y*
II	*D*3	A very delicate bf	*E:*	U mentioned that it is delicate	*FY*
			S:	You can c the differnt colors, their shades I guess, in the wgs	
II	*D*4	A church steeple	*S:*	It looks like light is in the top, it's lighter there as if the sun was shining on it	*FY*
III	*D*7	Some sort of x-ray	*S:*	It is different colors like an an x-ray	*YF*
IV	*W*	Darkness	*S:*	It just ll darkness to me, I can't tell u why	*Y*
IV	*D*3	A multi-colored flower	*S:*	It has different colors in it, like the petals r a different color fr the middle part	*FY*
V	*W*	A piece of rotten meat	*S:*	Some of it is more rot'd than the rest	*YF*
			E:	More rotted?	
			S:	The colors r different	
VI	*D*2	A highly polished bedpost	*S:*	Its very shiny lookg	*FY*
VI	*D*4	It ll a sailing ship cruising in the nite	*S:*	Its all darkish so it must be in the nite	*m[a].FY*
VII	*W*	It could be clouds I guess	*S:*	Its pretty irregular like clouds would be & it has dark and lite color to it like clouds, mayb like cumulus clouds	*FY*
VII	*W*	Storm clouds	*S:*	They'r dark like a storm cloud formation is dark	*YF*
VII	*D*2	A granite statue	*S:*	Its dark like granite	*FY*
VIII	*D*1	An animal with dirt all over its face	*S:*	This drkr part is the circle around the eye like dirt, ther's more there too, more dirt	*FY*
IX	∨ *W*	A lot of smoke and fire	*S:*	The orange part is the fire & the rest is the smoke, u can see how the colors go together	*CF.YF*
X	*D*11	Some bones that r drying out	*S:*	It ll bones drying up, ths prt is lighter so it must be drier	*YF*

[a] Had the subject indicated that it is *black* like ink the scoring would be *C'*.

128

ingfulness of vista answers. This research, which is presented in detail in chapters on interpretation, included examination of 60 protocols obtained from subjects prior to suicide or a suicidal gesture. It was noted that a significant number of form determined dimensional-perspective responses occur in this group when compared with a non-psychiatric group. A closer inspection of an additional 150 protocols revealed that the *FD* type of answer occurs with considerable frequency in the records of a variety of subjects, both psychiatric and nonpsychiatric. The number of *FD* answers is greater than the number of vista answers for most groups. When it is interpreted in the context of other information in the protocol, it appears related to factors such as introspectiveness and self-awareness.

The *FD* is for responses which include perspective or dimensionality based *exclusively* on form, interpreted by size or in relation to other blot areas. The most common *FD* is the Card IV human figure, seen as "leaning backward," or "lying down." The elaboration to this response usually includes mention that the "feet" portion is much larger; thus the head must be further away. Although the *FD* response occurs most frequently to Card IV, it has been noted in every card. In some answers, such as "leaning backward" on Card IV, another determinant is involved, but in most instances only the form features are used. Some examples of *FD* responses are provided in Table 16.

Many of the examples offered in Table 16 are of responses in which the dimensionality or perspective is based on the size of the blot area used. In other instances, the relationship between two blot areas creates the effect, wherein the "absence" of features is interpreted to support a percept of dimensionality or perspective. For example, the response to Card V, shown in Table 16, notes the leg of an animal is showing, whereas the larger portion of the blot is interpreted as a bush. The interpretation is of an animal jumping behind a bush because only the leg is obvious. Whether or not this is the same type of percept as "a person lying down" to Card IV is still open to investigation. At this time, it seems appropriate to code both responses as *FD* because both imply perspective.

PAIR AND REFLECTION RESPONSES

Another category incorporated in the Comprehensive System, which is not found in any of the other Rorschach systems, is related to the reflection response. This category, like the *FD* scoring, was discovered somewhat accidentally during an investigation regarding "acting out," which was conducted during 1966 and 1967. In that investigation, which included the collection of a large number of protocols from patients in an installation for the "criminally insane," it was noted that overt homosexuals and "psychopaths" tend to offer a significantly greater number of reflection responses than do other psychiatric subjects or nonpsychiatric subjects. Originally, these data were interpreted as an index of "narcissism" (Exner, 1969, 1970); however, because of the complexity of the concept narcissism, it seems more appropriate to use the concept of *egocentricity*. A sentence completion test, patterned after one developed by Watson (1965), was developed to study the characteristic of egocentricity in greater detail, and to relate those findings to the occurrence of reflection answers in the Rorschach. This work has confirmed a high correlation between a high "self-centeredness" score on the sentence completion blank and the reflection answer in the Rorschach. A variety of independent measures of egocentricity (or self-centeredness) has been used, and the results seem clearly to indicate that subjects who are highly egocentric or self-focusing tend to give significantly more reflec-

Table 16. Examples of Form-Dimensional Responses

Card	Location	Association		Inquiry	Coding
I	< D2	A tree off on a hill	S:	Its a lot smaller so it must be far off	FD
II	D4 + DS5	Some sort of temple at the end of a lake	S:	This (DS5) is the lake & here (D4) is the temple, u have to thk of it in perspective	FD
III	V Dd20	Two trees off on a hill with a path leading up to them	S:	These (D4) r the trees & this (D11) is the path	FD
			E:	U said off on a hill	
			S:	It doesn't hav to b a hill, its just that they'r small & the path is pretty wide so they r off a ways	
IV	W	A person laying down	S:	His feet r out in front, like toward me & his head is way bk there, like he was flat on his back	M^p.FD
V	D4	An animal jumping behnd a bush, u only c his leg	S:	Well here is where the bush ends & ths is the leg so it has to be behind	FM^a.FD
VI	W	A religious statue on a hill-top	S:	Well its a lot smler so it wld b off in the distance like ths cld b a hill here if u stretch u'r immagin	FD
VII	Dd19	A city off in the distance	S:	U can c the bldgs there	FD
			E:	U said off in the distn.	
			S:	Its so small, it must b a long ways off	
VIII	D4	Two people stndg off on a hill	S:	U can c the people here (Dd24) & this wld b the hill	M^p.FD
IX	< Dd26	A person stndg out on a ledge	S:	Yeah, here's a ledge (most of D3) & there's this person way out there, leaning up against a tree or s.t., its quite far out there	M^p.FD
			E:	Quite far?	
			S:	He's so small, it's fairly hard to even see him	
X	V D6	Two men pushing s.t. out in front of them	S:	Their bodies r shaped like they were bending forward & their arms r extended outward like they were pushing this thing in front of them	M^a.FD

tion responses than do subjects who are not highly egocentric. These types of reflection answers are based *on the symmetry of the blot,* and are different from the extremely rare reflection answer that does not use symmetry. The nonsymmetrical reflection ordinarily involves shading, and thus is usually scored either *V* or *Y*.

Numerous studies have been completed to validate the usefulness of the sentence completion blank as an index of egocentricity (Exner, 1973), and to investigate the reflection answer in more detail. During the course of these investigations, which are described in detail in the chapters on interpretation, a second Rorschach phenomenon was discovered that appears to be related to the reflection answer. This is the *pair* response, in which the perceived object is reported as two identical objects because of the card symmetry. The pair type of response occurs with considerable frequency in most records, usually including about one-third of the responses. The pair frequency increases significantly in the more egocentric subjects and is almost nonexistent in the protocols of subjects who have little regard for themselves.

The selection of appropriate symbols to record the reflection and pair answers created some problem because, like the *FD* answer, they are based on the form of the blot, and yet the form is used somewhat differently than in selection of content. The symbol *r* seems a logical choice. The symbol selected for the pair response is the Arabic numeral 2. Because the pair answer occurs with considerable frequency, it was decided that the coding should be entered apart from the regular determinant scoring and in parentheses, so as to avoid "cluttering" the determinant code and also to make the number of pair answers easy to tabulate for the Structural Summary. There is only one coding for the pair answer (2), whereas two are used for different types of reflection answers.

The Reflection-Form Response *(rF)*   The *rF* is used for responses in which the symmetry features of the blot are primary in determining the answer, and form is used nonspecifically, or ambiguously, as an object being reflected. The *rF* type of reflection is very uncommon, and always involves content with nonspecific form requirements such as clouds, rocks, shadows, and rain. In some instances, the subject may select a content that is nonspecific in form requirements, but provides sufficient articulation of the perceived object to warrant the scoring of *Fr* rather than *rF*. The most common example of this is when landscape is perceived as being reflected in a lake or pond. In almost all of these cases the appropriate code is *Fr*.

The Form-Reflection Response *(Fr)*   *Fr* is for responses in which the form of the blot is used to identify specific content, which, in turn, is interpreted as reflected because of the symmetry of the blot. In many cases, movement is also associated with the reflection as in "a girl seeing herself in the mirror." The critical issue in coding either *rF* or *Fr* is that the subject *uses* the concept of reflection. This may be manifest directly through the use of the word *reflection* or it may be implied by other wording such as *mirror image,* and "seeing himself in the lake." The identification of "one on each side" or "there is two of them" is *not a reflection* answer and is coded simply as a pair response.

The Pair Response (2)   The symbol (2) is used whenever the symmetry features of the blot precipitate the report that "two" of the perceived object are present. The pair is independent of form specificity or the form quality used in the answer. The pair coding (2) *is not* used when the object is interpreted as being reflected, because the reflection code already denotes that two of the objects are being seen. The articulation of pairs varies considerably among subjects. Some will actually use the word *pair,* but more commonly the word *two* is used, and in many responses, the subject comments, "There is one here and one here." The pair code is used *only* when the symmetry is involved; thus clarification of the location areas used is important. It is not uncommon, for example, for a subject, looking at Card X, to report, "A couple of bugs." The response appears to be a pair, but the Inquiry reveals that he is using the upper $D1$ area as one bug, and the side $D7$ area as a second bug.

Some examples of pair and reflection responses are provided in Table 17. It will be noted that either the reflection or pair answers can occur in responses which have other determinants as well.

The percentage of agreement among coders in the two reliability studies completed for this work, for each of the Determinant codes, and by category, is shown in Table 18.

As will be noted from examination of Table 18, the agreement levels in both studies are quite respectable for all variables. As might be expected, the greatest percentage of disagreement occurs in coding the *active-passive* dimension of movement. Most important, however, is the fact that when a total category is reviewed—that is, was texture coded, regardless of whether it was coded *FT, TF,* or *T,* or was chromatic color coded, regardless of whether the coding was *FC, CF,* or *C*—the agreements are very high. These data indicate that trained examiners, as were used in these studies, will generally apply the same coding to the same responses. Some will err, and some will disagree from time to time, but overall the levels of agreement fall well within acceptable limits for a task as complex as coding Rorschach determinants.

Table 17.   Examples of Reflection and Pair Responses

Card	Location	Association		Inquiry	Coding
I	< $D2$	A couple of donkeys, there's one on each side			$F(2)$
I	$D1$	Two little birds who r peeking their heads out of a nest			$FM^a(2)$
II	< $D6$	A rabbit sliding on an ice pond, he's being reflected in the ice	S:	Ths white is the ice & u can c his reflection in it	$FM^a.Fr$
II	W	Two bears doing a circus act	S:	They have red hats on like a circus act & they have their paws touchg	$FM^a.FC(2)$
III	$D1$	Two people picking s.t. up			$M^a(2)$
III	$D1$	A person inspecting himself in the mirror	S:	He's bending forward like he's looking at himself	$M^p.Fr$
IV	< W	If u turn it ths way it ll a reflection of s.t., mayb a cloud	S:	Well all of ths on one side is being reflected here, its like a cloud I guess	$YF.rF$
			E:	I'm not sure how u c it as a cloud	
			S:	Well its all dark like a cld at nite. There's not much shape to it	

Table 17 (Continued)

Card	Location	Association	Inquiry	Coding
IV	D6	A pair of boots		F (2)
V	W	Two people laying back to back		M^p (2)
VI	>W	All of ths is the same down here	S: I don't kno what it is, mayb rocks of s.t., it's the same on both sides like a reflection	rF
VI	<D1	It ll a submarine in the nite being reflected in the water	S: Its all black like nitetime, u can c the conning tower & the hull & here its all reflected	FC'.Fr
VII	D2	Ths ll a little girl, there's one on each side		F (2)
VII	D2	A little girl looking in the mirror		M^p.Fr
VIII	D5	A pair of flags		F (2)
VIII	<W	An A crossing over some rocks or s.t. like in a creek, u can c his reflection there, he's looking down at it		FM^a.Fr
IX	<D5	Its like u r out in the water & u can c ths coastline off in the distance	S: Well, its being reflected in the water, c here is the waterline (points to midline), its all so small it must b way off in the dist. U really can't make much out, mayb some trees or s.t. like that	FD.rF
IX	D3	Two halloween witches	S: They r colored like for halloween, all orangish & they'r leaning back like they r laughing	M^a.FC (2)
X	D1	A couple of crabs	S: There's one on each side, they'r the same on both sides	F (2)
X	D7	Deer, like they'r jumping	S: One here & one here, they'r the same, w. their legs outstretched like they were jumpg	FM^a (2)

SUMMARY

The 26 symbols that are used for coding the nine major determinant categories contribute much to the nucleus of the structural data of the Rorschach. None have exacting correlations with behavior or with personality characteristics, but collectively they are used to form a caricature of response styles and personality characteristics. There are still other features of the response that, when coded or scored accurately, add considerably to the structural data. Three of these are described in the next chapter.

Table 18.   Percentage of Coder Agreement for Two Reliability Studies

Variable	20 Coders 25 Records	15 Coders 20 Records
	% Agreement	% Agreement
M	96%	96%
FM	96%	98%
m	93%	95%
Movement coded	97%	98%
a	90%	91%
p	88%	89%
C or Cn	89%	91%
CF	90%	92%
C or CF	95%	96%
FC	97%	96%
Chromatic Color Coded	98%	99%
C'	98%	97%
C'F	91%	90%
FC'	94%	96%
Achromatic Color Coded	96%	95%
T	99%	99%
TF	96%	94%
FT	94%	91%
Texture Coded	97%	97%
V	—	99%
VF	98%	96%
FV	97%	95%
Vista Coded	99%	98%
Y	89%	90%
YF	87%	89%
FY	94%	92%
Diffuse Shading Coded	95%	97%
FD	97%	95%
rF	92%	94%
Fr	93%	93%
(2)	98%	99%
F	90%	91%

REFERENCES

Baughman, E. E. (1959) An experimental analysis of the relationship between stimulus structure and behavior on the Rorschach. *Journal of Projective Techniques,* **23,** 134–183.

Beck, S. J. (1937) *Introduction to the Rorschach Method: A Manual of Personality Study.* American Orthopsychiatric Association Monograph, No. 1.

Beck, S. J. (1944) *Rorschach's Test: Basic Processes.* New York: Grune & Stratton.

Beck, S. J., Beck, A. G., Levitt, E. E., and Molish, H. B. (1961) *Rorschach's Test. I: Basic Processes.* (3rd Ed.) New York: Grune & Stratton.

Binder, H. (1932)   Die Helldunkeldeutungen im psychodiagnostischen experiment von Rorschach. *Schweizer Archiv fur Neurologie und Psychiatrie.* **30,** 1–67, 232–286.

Campo, V., and de de Santos, D. R. (1971) A critical review of the shading responses in the Rorschach I: Scoring problems. *Journal of Personality Assessment, 35,* 3–21.

Ellenberger, H. (1954) The life and work of Hermann Rorschach. *Bulletin of the Menninger Clinic, 18,* 173–219.

Exner, J. E. (1961) Achromatic color in Cards IV and VI of the Rorschach. *Journal of Projective Techniques, 25,* 38–40.

Exner, J. E. (1969) *The Rorschach Systems.* New York: Grune & Stratton.

Exner, J. E. (1969) Rorschach responses as an index of narcissism. *Journal of Projective Techniques and Personality Assessment, 33,* 324–330.

Exner, J. E. (1970) Rorschach manifestations of narcissism. *Rorschachiana, IX,* 449–456.

Exner, J. E. (1973) The self focus sentence completion: A study of egocentricity. *Journal of Personality Assessment, 37,* 437–455.

Exner, J. E. (1978) *The Rorschach: A Comprehensive System. Volume 2: Current research and advanced interpretation.* New York: Wiley.

Hertz, M. R. (1942) *Frequency Tables for Scoring Rorschach Responses.* Cleveland, Ohio: The Press of Western Reserve University.

Hertz, M. R. (1951) *Frequency Tables for Scoring Rorschach Responses.* (3rd Ed.) Cleveland, Ohio: The Press of Western Reserve University.

Hertz, M. R. (1970) *Frequency Tables for Scoring Rorschach Responses.* (5th Ed.) *Cleveland, Ohio: The Press of Case Western Reserve University.*

Klopfer, B., and Sender, S. (1936) A system of refined scoring symbols. *Rorschach Research Exchange, 1,* 19–22.

Klopfer, B. (1937) The shading responses. *Rorschach Research Exchange, 2,* 76–79.

Klopfer, B., and Miale, F. (1938) An illustration of the technique of the Rorschach: The case of Anne T. *Rorschach Research Exchange, 2,* 126–152.

Klopfer, B., and Kelley, D. (1942) *The Rorschach Technique.* Yonkers-on-Hudson, N.Y.: World Book.

Klopfer, B., Ainsworth, M., Klopfer, W., and Holt, R. (1954) *Developments in the Rorschach Technique. I: Theory and Technique.* Yonkers-on-Hudson, N.Y.:' World Book.

Piotrowski, Z. (1936) On the Rorschach method and its application in organic disturbances of the central nervous system. *Rorschach Research Exchange, 1,* 148–157.

Piotrowski, Z. (1947) A Rorschach compendium. *Psychiatric Quarterly, 21,* 79–101.

Piotrowski, Z. (1957) *Perceptanalysis.* New York: Macmillan.

Piotrowski, Z. (1960) The movement score. In M. Rickers-Ovsiankina (ed.) *Rorschach Psychology.* New York: Wiley.

Rapaport, D., Gill, M., and Schafer, R. (1946) *Diagnostic Psychological Testing.* Vol. 2. Chicago: Yearbook Publishers.

Rorschach, H. (1921) *Psychodiagnostik.* Bern: Bircher.

Rorschach, H., and Oberholzer, E. (1923) The application of the form interpretation test. *Zeitschrift fur die Gesamte Neurologie und Psychiatrie, 82.*

Watson, A. (1965) Objects and objectivity: A study in the relationship between narcissism and intellectual subjectivity. Unpublished Ph.D. Dissertation, University of Chicago.

CHAPTER 7

Blends, Organizational Activity, and Form Quality

Three very important elements, for which all Rorschach responses must be evaluated, are (1) the blend, wherein two or more determinants have been used in an answer; (2) the organizational activity, which represents those responses in which some synthesis of the blot stimuli has occurred; and (3) the form quality, which is an evaluation of the "fitness" of the blot features to the object described. Each of these response characteristics carries considerable interpretive significance, especially because they are *not common* to all responses. A modest proportion of the answers in most records have multiple determinants. Similarly, it is unusual to find a large proportion of the responses marked by the synthesis features of organizational activity. Conversely, most responses will be evaluated for form quality. These response features yield important data concerning the idiographic dimensions of the subject; thus accurate evaluation of responses for their presence is vital.

THE BLEND RESPONSE (.)

The term *blend* signifies that more than one determinant has been used in the formulation of a response. When this occurs, each determinant should be entered, separated from each other by a dot (.), as in *M.YF*, which represents the answer containing both human movement and a shading-form component. The frequency of blend responses varies considerably from record to record. A sample of 2000 protocols, for example, shows that slightly more than 20% of the responses are blends, but the variance is considerable, with some records yielding more than 50% blends and others containing no blend answers. Any combination of determinants is theoretically possible in a response, and each should be scored. The majority of blend answers contain two determinants, but in unusual instances three, and even four, separate determinants may occur.

There has been some disagreement among Rorschach systematizers concerning the appropriate method for scoring and evaluating the blend answer. Most have followed Rorschach's lead in the scoring procedure. He simply scored multiple determinants together when they occurred, as in *MC* (1921). The protocols published by Rorschach contain relatively few blend responses, mainly because his basic work was accomplished using blots which contained no shading features. Klopfer (1942, 1954) deviated most from Rorschach's approach to the multiple determined responses. He postulated that only one determinant can be "primary" to the formation of a percept, and subdivided the "Main" or primary determinant, from other determinants, coded as "Additional." Accordingly, Klopfer weighs the interpretive importance of the Main determinants differently than Additionals. This procedure is possibly one of the major limitations to the

Klopfer system, and is compounded by the fact that a somewhat arbitrary "hierarchical" scheme is used to distinguish Main from Additional determinants in answers where the relative importance is not clear; M is given preference, with chromatic color, texture, and achromatic color ranked in that order of importance. Klopfer did not begin his Rorschach system with the Main-Additional distinction. He originally followed Rorschach's technique of entering multiple scores but, as his recommended technique of Inquiry became more elaborate, and as the number of scoring categories was proliferated, he perceived the fact that large numbers of multiple determinant scores would create much difficulty in interpretation. In addition, he became convinced that determinants relevant only to a part of a concept, or those given somewhat reluctantly in the Inquiry, were not as important to the "basic" personality as the "primary" determinant. By this time (1938), he began scoring some of the "questionable" determinants as Additional, although he continued to use multiple determinant scores where the issue seemed clear. Subsequently, he decided that it was impractical to expect all scorers to be consistent in these decisions and by the time his first text on the Rorschach was published (1942), he had settled on the principle of giving only one score for the Main determinant.[1]

The other systematizers differ only slightly from each other, and from Rorschach, in scoring multiple determined answers. Beck (1937) introduced the use of the dot (.), as a convenient method of identifying and tabulating the blend response. In each of the systems except Klopfer's, all determinants are given equal weight in forming interpretive postulates.

The decision to include the Blend in the Comprehensive System is based on two elements. First, four of the five Rorschach systems endorse this approach. Second, and more important, is a series of three studies completed to gather more data concerning the multiple determinant answer. The first of the three was designed to evaluate the relationship of the multiple determinant response to intelligence. The protocols of 43 nonpsychiatric subjects, for whom Otis Intelligence Test scores were also available, were rescored using the Comprehensive System by one of three scorers. These subjects were selected because the I.Q. scores manifest a considerable range, 84 to 122, with a median of 103. The Rorschach protocols were divided on the basis of an I.Q. median split, with the midranking protocol discarded, thus creating two groups of 21 each. The mean I.Q. for the upper half is 113.4, and for the lower half 93.7. The number of blend responses was tallied for each protocol and the data subjected to chi-square analysis, which indicates that subjects in the upper half give significantly more blend answers than do subjects in the lower half. In fact, 17 of the 21 protocols of subjects in the upper half contain at least one blend, whereas only eight of the 21 protocols in the lower half contain at least one blend. The number of blends in a given protocol does not correlate highly with I.Q. ($r = .32$), but the tendency to give a blend answer apparently does require at least average intellectual ability. In view of these findings, a second study was undertaken using 28 psychiatric outpatients for whom WAIS I.Q. scores were also available. These I.Q.'s ranged from 97 to 132, with a median of 110. Using the same procedure of a median split and tallying the number of blend answers for upper and lower half, the resulting chi-square *was not* significant. Twelve of the subjects in the upper half gave blend answers, whereas 10 of the 14

[1] In a private interview in 1965 at Asilomar, California, Klopfer expressed some regret concerning that decision. He alluded to the fact that the interpreter, relying "too heavily" on the psychogram, could be misled in some instances. He maintained, however, the belief that the Main-Additional dichotomy in determinant scoring did, in fact, preclude the interpreter from "overemphasis" of determinant scores which might be developed in the inquiry.

protocols in the lower group contained blends. An interesting by-product of these two investigations is the fact that the psychiatric group tended to give proportionally more blends per protocol than did the subjects in the upper half of the nonpsychiatric group (31% versus 19%). This finding generated a third study, using two protocols from each of 21 "neurotic" outpatients. The first protocol from each subject was collected at the onset of intervention, whereas the second was taken at intervention termination, which varied from 9 to 17 months later. A comparison of the pre- and posttreatment protocols for total number of blends *is not* significantly different, although there is a tendency toward decrease. Conversely, when the actual number of pre- and posttreatment records containing blend answers is compared, a significant difference is discovered. Twenty of the 21 pretreatment protocols contain blend responses as contrasted with 13 of the 21 posttreatment records. It is possibly of even greater interest to note that the kinds of determinants used in the blend answers change substantially when the pre- and posttreatment records are compared, the former containing more shading blends, and more determinants in which form is secondary such as *CF* and *TF*. The latter records yield fewer shading blends, more *FD* type determinants, and more determinants in which form is primary. These data appear to indicate that the blend, although somewhat related to intellect, is very possibly a useful index of the complexity of the subject's psychological process. This interpretation is generally consistent with Beck's hypothesis concerning the blend (1944, 1961), and argues for a method of coding multiple determinant answers which gives equal weight to each of the determinants involved. The Beck procedure has been incorporated into the Comprehensive System.

The symbols entered in the blend *are the same* as would be used if any of the determinants were scored separately. Some examples of blend responses are shown in Table 19.

The majority of blend responses involve complex answers, and typically, but not always, the whole blot or a large segment of it is used. The coding of *F* (pure Form) in a blend is *extremely rare*. A review of nearly 15,000 protocols in the pool at the Rorschach Research Foundation yields only 26 such responses. Almost all are in records collected from neurologically impaired or intellectually limited subjects. They are responses in which two or more separate contents are identified, at least one of which is based exclusively on form, *and which is not reported in relation to the other(s)*. These responses occur with the greatest frequency to Card III, such as "There are two people, and a butterfly, and they are picking something up." The answer sounds like two responses, people picking something up as one, and the butterfly as the second, and if the subject does not distinguish them as separate answers in the Inquiry, or organize them meaningfully (it's flying between them), the examiner should ask, *"Did you mean that all as one answer?"* If the subject answers, "yes," and still fails to integrate the objects reported, the *F* should be included in the blend with the other determinant. In this example, the coding will be $M^a.F$. These responses indicate a significant cognitive dysfunction in either processing or mediating the stimulus field. Any examiner deciding to code an *F* in a blend should review the responses very carefully, because they are extremely unusual and interpretively quite significant.

Most blends containing multiple objects will include a proximate and/or meaningful relation between the objects as in, "a woman standing with smoke all around her" to Card I. In this response, both proximity and direct relationship are present. Here the coding is $M^p.YF$, and if the response had been "a woman with smoke all around her," with no inference of movement offered in the Association or spontaneously in the Inquiry, the coding would be simply *YF*.

Table 19. Examples of Blend Responses

Card	Location	Association	Inquiry	Coding
I	W	A wm stndg in the cntr w her arms raised w a lot of smk around her	E: (Rpts S's resp) S: Rite here, ths r her arms & ths is her body & all ths (points to each side) is all dark & hazy like smoke	$M^p.YF$
II	W	Two bears fitg, they'v got ther paws togethr & ther's bld on ther heads & feet	E: (Rpts S's resp) S: C, heads, paws, bodies, feet & the red ll bld	$FM^a.CF$
III	W	Ths ll 2 butlers bowing to e.o.	E: (Rpts S's resp) S: Its like at a party, thes red thgs cld b s.s. of decoration & ths r the butlers in their formal suits sort of bending frwd like they were bowing E: Formal suits? S: Yes, they'r black, like a tuxedo.	$M^a.FC.FC'$
IV	∨W	Ths ll a snake or a worm crawling out from in under a leaf	E: (Rpts S's resp) S: Well u can just c the head, I thk its a snake bec it has the different markgs on it E: And the leaf? S: Yeah, all the rest of it ll a leaf, its dead and dried up E: Dead & dried up? S: Yeah, its all black like dead leaves get after a while E: U said it was crawling out from in under the leaf S: Yeah, the way it is there he must be under it bec u can only c the head	$FM^a.FY.C'F.FD$
IV	W	A guy sitting on a stump in a fur coat, like an old raccoon coat	E: (Rpts S's resp) S: He's leaning backward, like he was laughg or s.t., c heres the feets, big feets & his head & little arms E: U mentioned a fur coat, like an old raccoon coat S: Yeah, it looks all furry to me	$M^p.FT.FD$
VI	D1	Its a deep gorge with a river I guess, it must b cause it overflowd not too long ago	E: (Rpts S's resp) S: This cntr looks really deep, c how dark it is & yet all the land around it looks differnt colors like it was partly water	$FV.YF$

Table 19 (Continued)

Card	Location	Association	Inquiry		Coding
VII	D2	A cpl of kids w mud or dirt on their faces like they r makg faces at e.o.	*E:* *S:* *E:* *S:*	(Rpts *S*'s resp) U just c the upper part of 'em, 2 little girls I guess stickg their lips out like makg a face U mentioned that they hav mud or dirt on their faces Its all dark like dried mud or dirt wld b	*MP.FY*
VIII	D2	Down here it ll some strawberry & orange Italian ices	*E:* *S:* *E:* *S:*	(Rpts *S*'s resp) See here is the pink like strawberry & the orange U said they ll ices Rite, I did. They look icy to me, not like real ice cream, more like ice chips	*CF.TF*
IX	VW	Wow, an explosion w a lot of fire & smoke	*E:* *S:* *E:* *S:*	(Rpts *S*'s resp) Yeah, its all shootg up & u c the fire here, its orange & all ths green ll the smoke I'm not sure why it ll smoke Well u c how the diff colors come togethr, like fire & smoke all mixed together	*mᵃ.CF.YF*
X	D9	Ths ll bld thats dryg	*E:* *S:*	(Rpts *S*'s resp) Well its blood o.k., there's no question about that & u can tell that its drying because these outside parts r darker	*mP.C.Y.*

One further scoring caution concerning the blend answer seems important, particularly for the novice. This concerns the shading determined responses. The light-dark features of the blot, when used to delineate a feature of a percept, are usually perceived as only one of the three types of shading. Responses containing multiple shading determinants are quite unusual and, when they do occur, a vista component is frequently involved. When shading blends occur, they are identifiable by the fact that different contents, or different characteristics of a single content, are articulated, for example, "muddy fields on each side of a deep gorge" (Card VI). In this response two contents, muddy fields and deep gorge, are offered, each of which includes a shading determinant, yielding a coding of *YF.FV*. Obviously, the possibilities exist for any combination of shading determinants to be given in a single response so that blends such as *FV.FY, V.T, FT.YF,* or even *YF.TF.VF* are noted occasionally. It is quite important, however, that the coder not confuse the shading blend with the sometimes complex articulation of a single shading determinant; for instance: "These dark differences in the shading make it look bumpy, like velvet. Its all very soft looking like it is the soft folds in a blanket" (Card IV). Even though the articulation is complex, including words relevant to each of the three types of shading (dark differences, bumpy like velvet, soft looking), the content is essentially singular and only one use of the shading is manifest. Thus the response is scored only once, for texture. A similar response is, in fact, a shading blend: "This looks like a piece of material, something very fuzzy, that has been bunched together, like it was pleated, these lies here are the folds.'' The Inquiry to this answer confirms that the subject perceives both texture (fuzzy) and vista (folds) and the scoring is *TF.VF*.

ORGANIZATIONAL ACTIVITY *(Z)*

The scoring for organizational activity has been one of the most neglected of the Rorschach components. At least three factors appear to contribute to the general lack of interest among Rorschachers in this type of scoring. First, the systems differ considerably in approaching this feature. Beck was the first to introduce an organizational score (1933), using a scheme of weighing organized responses depending on the type of organization and the complexity of the stimuli involved (Z score). Hertz used a method in which all organized responses are weighed equally (*g* score, 1940), whereas Klopfer (1944) included some recognition of organizational activity in his Form Level Rating but also included other elements in this score; thus it does not represent organizational activity per se. The other systems do not include a formal scoring for organization activity, nor did Rorschach, although he appears to have offered some description of the process in his discussion of *Assoziationsbetrieb*. Second, most of the literature concerning a scoring for organizational activity focuses on the Beck Z score, the procedure for which sometimes appears to be much more complicated than is actually the case. Third, and possibly most important, is the *misconception* that the clinical utility of a scoring for organizational activity is centered mainly on estimates of I.Q. Unfortunately, Beck's own words, ''These totals (ZSums) vary directly as the intelligence of *S*,'' (1945), plus the fact that a considerable segment of the research on organizational activity scores has concerned the relationship to intelligence test performance, seems to have encouraged this misconception.

There is no question but that organizational activity scores, whether weighed as in Beck or unweighed as in Hertz, do correlate positively with some components of intelligence testing. A variety of positive correlations have been reported for both types of scoring, some of which are statistically significant well beyond the .01 level. Wishner (1948) reports a .536 correlation between Wechsler-Bellevue I.Q. and the weighted Z score. Sisson and Taulbee (1955) obtained correlations of .43 and .52 between Wechsler I.Q. and weighted and unweighted ZSums, respectively. Blatt (1953) found correlations of .49 and .46 between weighted ZSums and the verbal and reasoning sections of the Primary Mental Abilities Test. The Wishner findings seem especially important to understanding the kind of relation that seems to exist between organizational activity and intellect. He reports correlations for each of the individual subtests in the Wechsler-Bellevue, including data both for the regular weighed Z scores and using a method that eliminates Z scores for the so-called unorganized Whole answers such as the Bat response on Cards I and V. The standard Beck ZSum correlates significantly with two verbal subtests (vocabulary .605 and information .365) and two performance subtests (picture completion .346 and digit symbol .308) with other correlations ranging as low as .102 for block design. The modified ZSum correlates quite differently with the Wechsler subtests, ranging from a high of .306 for similarities to −.059 for object assembly. In other words, these data seem to suggest that the weighted method of assigning Z scores, as used by Beck, does correlate significantly with some types of intellectual operations but not with others. Even this issue is cast in some doubt when it is noted that Wishner's data are collected from only 42 psychiatric (neurotic) cases. Hertz (1960) has reported substantially lower correlations between the Beck ZSum and Otis I.Q. (.174) and Stanford-Binet M.A. (.113) for 12-year-olds. She also reports low positive correlations between her g score and I.Q. and M.A. (.256 and .249). At the lower end of the intellectual spectrum, Jolles (1947), using "feebleminded" subjects, found correlations of .08 between weighted ZSum and Binet I.Q. and .15 with Wechsler I.Q. Kropp (1955), in reviewing most of the studies on the Z score, concluded that it relates highly to W, and to M, but that it does not relate to intelligence as operationally defined by intelligence tests.

Obviously, intelligence appears to have some relationship to organizational activity, but this relationship apparently varies with certain response styles, a variation which is especially notable in some instances of psychopathology. Schmidt and Fonda (1953) have shown that Z scores are significantly higher in manics than in schizophrenics. Varvel (1941) and Hertz (1948) both report lower levels of organizational activity in depressed patients, whereas Beck (1952) and Molish (1955) find high organizational activity in patients prone to "project conflicts" in a systematized delusional operation. It would seem that intelligence is prerequisite to organizational activity, but other factors influence the frequency and characteristics of the organizing activity.

The variety of empirical data seems to argue in favor of including some form of organizational activity scoring in the Comprehensive System. A major question appears to be whether such a scoring should include weighing different kinds of responses as suggested by Beck, or considering all organized responses equally as purported by Hertz. An interesting work, published by Wilson and Blake (1950), appears to support the Hertz approach. They correlated Z scores, as weighed in the Beck method, using a count of *one* for each organized response, with the weighed ZSums for 104 subjects, and derived a .989 correlation. However, the Wilson and Blake sample included 81 "normals" and only 23 psychiatric cases of which only eight were psychotic. The sample limitations in their study appeared to suggest that a larger psychiatric group would be worthwhile to study. In this context, two groups of 60 protocols each were randomly selected from the protocol pool, one representing nonpsychiatric subjects and the second a psychiatric group comprised of 26 schizophrenics and 34 nonschizophrenics. Each of the protocols was rescored using the Beck weighted Z score method and also with the Wilson-Blake method of assigning a value of 1 to each response manifesting organizational activity. The correlation for the "normal group" was consistent with the Wilson-Blake findings, .984; however, the correlation for the psychiatric group was considerably lower, .708. A closer examination of the data from the group of psychiatric protocols revealed that in approximately 25% of the cases, the sum of Z differed from the Wilson-Blake estimated sum of Z by four or more points. In fact, using an arbitrary cutoff value for a difference score (d) of 3.0, nearly one-third (32%) of the psychiatric group is identified, whereas only two of the "normal" subjects fall in this range.

Following the discovery that the Wilson and Blake table of estimated ZSums is significantly less accurate in predicting the *actual* ZSum for psychiatric subjects than for nonpatients, a series of studies concerning this issue have been completed at the Rorschach Research Foundation (Exner, 1978). The findings from these studies indicate that those subjects with a ZSum greater than $+3.0$, or less than -3.0 from the estimated ZSum (*Zest*), derived from the Wilson and Blake table, do exhibit markedly different features in scanning and/or processing visual or auditory information. The former exert much more effort in processing and tend to be overly thorough and cautious, whereas the latter are often hasty and negligent in the scanning effort. In view of these findings, the Beck method of assigning weights for responses that are marked by organizational activity has been incorporated into the Comprehensive System.

A Z score is assigned to any response that *includes form and meets at least* one of the following criteria: (1) it is a *W* response that has a *DQ* coding of +, v/+, or o (answers that are *Wv* are not assigned a Z score); (2) it is a response that *meaningfully* integrates two or more adjacent detail areas; (3) it is a response that *meaningfully* integrates two or more nonadjacent detail areas; or (4) it is a response in which white space is *meaningfully* integrated with other details of the blot. Form *must always* be involved to score Z; thus pure *C, T, Y,* or *V* answers *are never scored Z.*

The specific Z score assigned to an organized response will depend on which of the scoring criteria have been met, and to which card the response has been given. The weighted Z values for each of the four types of organizational activity are shown, by card, in Table 20.

Table 20.   Organizational (Z) Values for Each of the Ten Cards

| Card | Type of Organizational Activity | | | |
	W (DQ+, v/+, o)	Adjacent Detail	Distant Detail	White Space with Detail
I	1.0	4.0	6.0	3.5
II	4.5	3.0	5.5	4.5
III	5.5	3.0	4.0	4.5
IV	2.0	4.0	3.5	5.0
V	1.0	2.5	5.0	4.0
VI	2.5	2.5	6.0	6.5
VII	2.5	1.0	3.0	4.0
VIII	4.5	3.0	3.0	4.0
IX	5.5	2.5	4.5	5.0
X	5.5	4.0	4.5	6.0

Source: This table is taken from Beck, S. J., Beck, A., Levitt, E., and Molish, H. *Rorschach's Test,* Vol. 1. New York: Grune & Stratton, 1961. Those familiar with the Beck system will note that Beck's special z scoring for W with Adjacent Detail, which Beck uses for some responses to Cards III, VI, and VII, has been omitted in preference for criteria that are consistent across all cards.

Whenever a response meets *two or more* of the criteria for scoring Z, the higher of the values is assigned. For example, a *W* response to Card I is ordinarily assigned a Z score of 1.0; however, if the whole blot is used in a manner so that adjacent detail areas are specifically organized as in "a woman standing in the center with two creatures dancing around her," the value of 4.0 (Adjacent Detail weighted score) would be assigned.

The issue of meaningfulness of organization in responses is critically important to the decision to score Z, in both whole and detail responses. It should be obvious that the component parts of the blot used in the response are related to each other in some meaningful way. For instance, "two figures, pointing in different directions" on Card VII is not scored Z, because the response does not manifest any *meaningful* relationship. The same two figures, ". . . arguing about which way to go," is scored Z in that a meaningful relation does obviously exist. Some examples of organizational activity scores are provided in Table 21. Inquiries are included only where they are relevant to the decision concerning the Z score.

Table 21. Examples of Z **Score Assignment for Responses to Each of the Ten Rorschach Cards**

Card	Association	Inquiry	Z Scoring
I	A bat	(Confirms W)	1.0
I	A halloween mask	*S:* The white parts are the eyes & mouth so the rest is a mask	3.5
I	A dead leaf lying on the snow	*S:* U can c the snow thru the holes in the leaf	3.5
I	Two big birds, thy'r lookg at a couple of mountains off in the distance ($D2$ = Birds; $Dd22$ = Mountains)		6.0
II	Two clowns kicking e.o.	[The lower ($D3$) area represents the kick]	4.5
II	Two dogs rubbing noses		3.0
II	A rocket ship taking off w the fire coming out	(Confirms $DS5 + D4$ is rocket, $D3$ is flame)	4.5
II	Two hens getting ready to fite, lik fiting cocks	($D2$)	5.5
III	Two witches brewing s.t. in their den w trophies hung all over	(W)	5.5
III	Two wm pickg up a basket	($D1$)	3.0
III	Two wm looking at e.o.	($D9$ only, $D7$ not includ)	4.0
IV	A big giant sitting on a stump	($D1$ is stump)	4.0
IV	A bear hide	(W)	2.0
IV	∨Two witches arguing w e.o.	($Dd26$)	3.5
IV	∨Like Hansel & Gretel taking a bite off a candy tree	($DdS24$ are Hansel & Gretel, $D1$ is the candy tree)	5.0[a]
V	A butterfly	(W)	1.0
V	An alligator's head, there's one on each side		No Z score
VI	Ths ll a totem pole sitting high up on a mountain	($D3$ is totem, the rest of the card is the mt)	2.5
VI	I c a submarine being reflectd	($D4$ is the submarine)	2.5
VI	∨There r 2 littl birds in a nest	($Dd28$)	2.5
VI	∨There r 2 birds calling to e.o.	($Dd21$)	6.0
VI	Ths whole thg cld b an island	(W)	No Z score[b]
VII	Two wm smiling at e.o.	($D1$)	3.0
VII	Two wm talkg to e.o. standg behind ths rock	(W, $D2$ are wm, $D4$ is rock)	1.0
VII	∨Two can-can dancers	*S:* Their heads r touchg here & u can only c one leg bec the other is kicked out:	3.0[c]
VII	A mountain range and a lake	*S:* Ths white part ($DS7$) is the lake & the rest r mountains, like u were lookg thru them to see the lake down below	4.0
VIII	Two rats climbing up a garbage heap of s.s.	(W)	4.5

Table 21 (Continued)

Card	Association	Inquiry	Z Scoring
VIII	Two animals, one on each side		No Z score
VIII	A bear climbing a tree	(D1 is a bear, D4 is tree)	3.0
VIII	∨A milk bottle balanced on a log	(Center small white space is milk bottle, D5 is the log)	4.0
VIII	Somebody splattered paint here	(W) Names colors	No Z score[d]
IX	∨The whole thg ll an atomic explosion	(W, with D6 being the cloud, the green area being smoke, & the orange area being fire)	5.5
IX	A man playing a saxaphone	(D1, with the man being the major portion of the area used and the saxaphone the remaining part):	2.5[e]
IX	Two witches having a good joke together	(D3) S: They are leaning backward as if they are laughing about a joke	4.5
IX	Like an explosion on the sun where gas is shot off	(Top of D8 is sun, Dd25 is the gas shooting off) S: U can c the space in between the sun and where the gas rises (DdS32)	5.0
X	An artist's abstract, its symmetrical with each pair of object having a special significance	(W)	5.5
X	A lot of paint, like s.b. thru alot of paint on it	(W)	No Z score[f]
X	A fraternity paddle	(D11 is the handle, upper DdS30 is the paddle, D3 is a design on on the paddle)	6.0
X	Two dogs, they'r each sitg up	(D2)	No Z score
X	Two dogs, they'r both sitg w their heads raised as if they r howling at the moon	(D2)	4.5
X	Two creatures trying to climb a pole	(D8 are animals, D14 is the pole)	4.0
X	A lot of undersea things, I c 2 crabs and 2 lobsters & 2 fish:	(D1 are crabs, D7 are lobsters, D13 are fish)	No Z score[g]

[a]Hansel and Gretel alone would be assigned the value for distant detail (3.5); however, the fact that they are related meaningfully to the "candy tree" requires the value of 5.0 (space integrated with detail).

[b]The Developmental Quality coding for a nonspecific island will be v. Wv responses are not assigned a Z score.

[c]The Z value for distant detail is assigned here because the figures are not perceived as adjacent even though the portions of the blot used actually do touch.

[d]No Z score is assigned as no basic form is used.

[e]This is an example of an organizational activity which involves a break-up and synthesis of a single D area. In this instance the Z value for "adjacent detail" is assigned.

[f]In the first example to Card X the response clearly includes reference to meaningful relationships of the component detail. In the second example no such reference occurs.

[g]This response, although similar in basic content to W responses of "an underwater scene" which would have a Z score of 5.5, is essentially three separate detail responses. The whole blot is not used nor is there any indication of a meaningful synthesis of the pairs of "undersea things" identified.

An accurate scoring of organizational activity in the Rorschach protocol, both in terms of frequency of Z and the sum of Z scores, can provide very useful data from which some aspects of cognitive activity can be evaluated.

FORM QUALITY

The issue of "goodness of fit" of the response to the area of the blot used was, during the time of the Rorschach's development, a major point of contention. Each of the systematizers has agreed that form quality or "fit" is one of the most important of the "quantifiable" elements of the test. They have also generally agreed that responses can be differentiated into two basic categories—those with good form and those with poor form. This is consistent with Rorschach's recommendation. Beyond these two basic points of agreement, the systematizers differ concerning the "best" method of evaluating the appropriateness of the form used in the response. Beck et al. (1961) and Hertz (1970) followed Rorschach's suggestions most closely. They, like Rorschach, used the symbol + for good form answers, and the symbol − for poor form answers. The assignment of the plus or minus symbols is, essentially, based on the statistical frequency with which any given type of response occurs to specific location areas.

Kinder, Brubaker, Ingram, and Reading (1982) have traced the development of Beck's decisions concerning the assignment of the + and − symbols, and suggest that many of Beck's decisions were more subjectively based than may have been implied in Beck's description of his work. Both Beck and Hertz have published elaborate tables, by card and location areas, to define which responses are + and which are −. The two differ in that they do not always use the same location areas, but Hertz has reported a relatively high agreement level between her table and that of Beck.

Piotrowski (1957) and Rapaport both endorse the concept of using statistical frequencies to determine the adequacy of form fit, but neither has developed frequency distributions for use. In Klopfer's early work he also used the symbols + and −, but he was generally opposed to statistical frequency as a determining criterion. Rather, he preferred to defend the appropriateness of the subjective evaluation of the examiner in determining the goodness of form fit of the response. Ultimately, he discarded the plus-minus symbols in favor of a Form Level Rating (Klopfer & Davidson, 1944).

Early in the development of the Comprehensive System it was decided that decisions concerning form quality should be based on an empirical approach to insure intercoder reliability, and to maintain a consistency in evaluating form fit that could be subject to a variety of validation studies. A method based on statistical frequency, such as that of Beck and Hertz, has broad applicability and appears to be effective in assuring high interscorer reliability. This seems especially important in that the proportion of good and poor form answers in a protocol is often an important clue in some differential diagnoses (Weiner, 1966). Statistical frequency methods are, however, somewhat limited by the fact that all + responses are not of equal quality, nor are all − answers equally poor in form fit. Rapaport (1946) noted this in his work, and suggested that form quality might be differentiated into six categories (plus, ordinary, vague, minus, special plus, and special minus). Rapaport argued that such a differentiation of form quality would provide a clearer understanding of the "reality testing" operations of the subject.

Mayman (1966, 1970), following from Rapaport's suggestion, developed a method of evaluating form quality which has six categories ranging from exceptionally good form to exceptionally poor form. The categories and criterion for each are as follows:

$F+$ (highest level):   Representing a successful combination of imagination and reality congruence.

Fo (ordinary level):   Representing the obvious, easily noticed answers, requiring little or no creative effort. This category includes almost all responses that would be considered commonplace.

Fw (weak level):   Representing a significant shift away from the reality adherence characteristic of the $F+$ or Fo answers. Mayman suggests that some Fw answers border on the adequate (scored $Fw+$) when the general contours do not clash with the answer, whereas other Fw answers are less than adequate (scored $Fw-$) when some of the blot area used makes the form fit somewhat incongruous.

Fv (vague level):   Representing answers in which the content avoids the necessity of specific shape.

Fs (spoiled level):   Representing an essentially adequate use of form that has been spoiled by an oversight or distortion.

$F-$ (minus level):   Representing the wholly arbitrary percept where there is substantial disregard for the structural properties of the blot areas used.

Mayman has been able to demonstrate that this method of differentiation of form quality yields data of substantially greater diagnostic usefulness than does the simple plus and minus differentiation. He reports very respectable correlations with ratings of health, tolerance for anxiety, motivation, ego strength, and quality of interpersonal relations. He also reports a reasonably high level of agreement between scorers for most of the six categories.

At first glance it appeared that the Mayman method for evaluating form quality might be appropriate for the Comprehensive System, especially if it could be integrated with a format based on statistical frequency. A pilot study concerning its usefulness was conducted in which four predoctoral clinical psychology interns were given approximately 90 minutes of instruction in the Mayman method, plus preinstructional readings, and asked to code independently 20 protocols randomly selected from the protocol pool. Their codings were only for form quality, and they were also permitted to use the Beck Tables of Good and Poor Form as a guideline. The results were somewhat disappointing in that the levels of agreement among the four scorers ranged from 41 to 83%. Checking the levels of agreement among only three of the four scorers yielded only slightly higher percentages. An analysis of the discrepancies rendered some insight into the low reliability problem. First, there was considerable disagreement in the scoring of responses as $Fw+$ or $Fw-$. Second, there was substantial disagreement in the use of the Fv category, partly because some of the responses that might be scored Fv in the Mayman scheme are listed as $+$ by Beck, whereas others are listed $-$ by Beck, and partly because the levels of articulation varied considerably in these types of responses. Mayman also reported the lowest level of agreement for this category. Third, there was considerable disagreement for the scoring of Fs versus $F-$. As a consequence of these findings, it was decided to investigate a modification of the Mayman method, in which Fv and Fs would be eliminated from the format, and all Fw answers would be considered as a single score rather than attempt to differentiate $Fw+$ and $Fw-$. The same four predoctoral interns independently scored a second set of 20 randomly selected protocols, using this modified format. The results of this scoring were quite encouraging. The percentage of agreement among all four scorers ranged from 87 to 95%. It was even more encouraging to discover that almost all instances of disagreement occurred either between the scoring of Fw or $F-$, or between the scoring of $F+$ or Fo. In other words, if the $F+$ and Fo answers are all considered as representing "good" form, the scorers agreed in 99% of the responses. Similarly, if the Fw and $F-$ answers are all considered as representing "poor" form, the scorers agreed in 98% of the responses. These high levels of agreement were generated essentially through the use of Beck's Tables of Good and Poor Form, with instances of disagreement occurring where the response in question did not appear on the Beck listing.

These findings promoted a decision to select a method of form quality evaluation for the Comprehensive System which utilizes the frequency distribution method favored by Beck and Hertz, and which *also* permits some differentiation regarding the goodness or poorness of the form used in the response. This format consists of four categories, derived from Mayman's work, two of which represent form which is used appropriately with good fit, one of which accounts for responses in which the appropriate use of form is not violated significantly, but which has a content reported by a very low frequency of subjects, and the fourth that represents those answers in which the form use has been inappropriate and/or distorted. These four categories and the criterion for each are shown in Table 22.

Table 22.   Symbols and Criteria for Coding Form Quality

Symbol	Definition	Criterion
+	Superior-overelaborated	The unusually precise articulation of the use of form in a manner that tends to enrich the quality of the response without sacrificing the appropriateness of the form use. The + answer need not be original, but rather unique by the manner in which details are defined and by which the form is used and specified.
o	Ordinary	The obvious, easily articulated use of form features to define an object reported frequently by others. The answer is commonplace and easy to see. There is no unusual enrichment of the answer by overelaboration of the form features.
u	Unusual	A low-frequency response in which the basic contours involved are not significantly violated. These are uncommon answers that are seen quickly and easily by the observer.
−	Minus	The distorted, arbitrary, unrealistic use of form in creating a response. The answer is imposed on the blot structure with total, or near total disregard for the structure of the area being used in creating the response. Often arbitrary contours will be created where none exist.

The appropriate symbol for form quality is entered at the end of the determinant coding. For instance, responses based exclusively on form will be coded as $F+$, Fo, Fu, or $F-$. Similarly, when determinants other than pure Form are present in the answer, the placement of the form quality coding remains the same, as in $M^a o$, TFu, $FC.FD-$, $FM^p.FC'+$.

The decision process concerning which symbol to employ will begin with an examination of Table A, which is one of the working tables included in Part III. Table A provides a listing of responses, card by card, and by location areas. It was constructed using 7500 protocols that include 162,427 responses. These include the records of 2500 nonpatient adults (56,478 responses), 2500 nonschizophrenic outpatients (57,898 responses), and 2500 nonschizophrenic-nonpsychotic inpatients (48,051 responses). It replaces an earlier version that was published in the first edition of this work, which had been constructed using only 1200 records containing slightly more than 26,000 responses.

Each item in Table A is identified as *ordinary (o), unusual (u),* or *minus* (−). If the item is designated as *ordinary (o),* and involves a W or D area, this signifies that the object was reported in at least 2% (150 or more) of the 7500 records, and that it involves blot contours that do exist. If the item listed as *o* involves a *Dd* location, this signifies that the *area* was used by at least 50 subjects, that the object was reported by no fewer than two-thirds of those using the area, and involves blot contours that do exist. If the response is listed as *ordinary* in Table A, the coding for form quality must always be either *o* or + . Most of these responses will be coded *o,* because the frequency of + responses is quite low in all groups. Responses that should be coded + are usually easy to distinguish, because the subject identifies many more form details than is commonplace. Nonetheless, the decision to code + versus *o* includes the subjective judgment of the coder.

If the item in Table A is designated as *unusual (u),* and involves a W or D area, this indicates that it was reported by fewer than 2% of the 7500 subjects, but in the unanimous opinion of at least three judges, working independently of each other, the object is seen quickly and easily and is appropriate to the contours that are used. If the item designated as *u* involves a *Dd* area, this signifies that it was reported by fewer than 50 subjects, but in the unanimous opinion of at least three judges, working independently of each other, it is seen quickly and easily and is appropriate to the contours that are involved. Although Table A encompasses a large number of items, it does not include all possible responses. Generally, if an item is not included in Table A, it is a minus response; however, subjects can often be quite original in using the blot features uniquely without violating the contours of the area involved.

If an examiner-coder is confronted with a unique response that is not in Table A, a judgment call is required. The criteria for distinguishing *u* from − answers should be reviewed carefully and faithfully. If the response can be seen *quickly and easily,* it should be coded *u.* Otherwise it should be coded − . Some examiners are loath to code a response − , apparently influenced by a faulty impression that a minus answer will have great interpretive significance. This is not true, however. The overwhelming majority of subjects from all groups give one or more minus responses. Minus answers become interpretively important when the frequency is significantly high, or in some cases, when they all involve a single content.

The items listed as *minus* in Table A generally are those that occur with low frequencies and are not congruent with the contours of the blots. But all are not necessarily low-frequency answers for all groups. For instance, the response of a face, using all of Card X inverted, is relatively commonplace among some groups of adolescents, both patients and nonpatients. It is a curious phenomenon that is not well understood, and which apparently occurs because those subjects tend to perceptually "close" the broken figure. Nonetheless, it is properly coded as − because the subject must create contours that do not exist in the blot. The majority of minus answers do have some contours that are congruent with the object reported, but the overall "fit" of the object(s) tends to violate the contours considerably. As a rule of thumb it is best to code questionable responses as − , following the principle that one or two minus responses will not contribute significantly to the overall interpretation of the record.

It is practical to question the cut-off of 2% in determining the *ordinary* responses in Table A for *W* and *D* location areas, and the requirement of at least 50 answers to a *Dd* location area, with two-thirds including the reported object to be designated ordinary or commonplace. These are somewhat arbitrary cut-off points, but they are not drawn randomly or carelessly. As noted earlier, the frequency of responses to the *D* areas is somewhat bimodal. Some *D* areas attract a great deal of attention, with response rates well into the hundreds, whereas other areas designated as *D* are used for considerably fewer responses. An examination of all of the responses included in Table A reveals that some occur with frequencies greater than 1000. These are typically responses defined as *Popular* in the next chapter. A second group of answers has frequencies ranging between 150 and 500. The majority of items listed in Table A as *o* have such frequencies. Interestingly, there are very few items listed in Table A that have response frequencies falling between 125 and 150. To the contrary, most with frequencies of less than 150 occur less than 100 times. Thus the mark of 150 seems to be a good breakpoint.

A second factor arguing in favor of the 150 cut-off concerns the protocols of antisocial or asocial subjects. Nearly 400 of these subjects are included among the 2500 outpatients and nearly 500 are included among the 2500 inpatients used in the construction of Table A. Antisocial and asocial people typically do not violate reality. Instead, they interpret it in a way to coincide with their own needs and orientation toward unconventionality. This is reflected in the *unusual* response. *Practically all subjects* give some unusual answers, and this represents their individuality. But if the premise is true, that antisocial and asocial people do this to an extreme, they should have a significantly higher frequency of *u* answers as contrasted with *o* or − responses. An analysis of the records of 868 subjects in the Table A construction pool, who meet the DSM-III criteria for antisocial or asocial personalities, reveals that the use of "good" form quality, (i.e., *o* or +) is significantly lower than for nonpatients, but the frequency of − answers is not significantly greater than for nonpatients. In other words, they give substantially more unusual answers.

A third factor that tends to support the construction principles used in creating Table A is derived from data concerning the protocols of schizophrenics and psychotic subjects. *None* of these were used in constructing Table A on the premise that either group—but especially the schizophrenic group—might have a high frequency for some responses that would not appear among the nonpatient, or nonschizophrenic groups. One of the characteristics of schizophrenics, and many psychotic subjects, is perceptual inaccuracy. They distort the perceptual input in translating it, or possibly their psychological disarray causes them to dysfunction during the input operation. In either event, they do not interpret reality adequately in many more instances than is true for nonpatients or nonschizophrenics. When taking the Rorschach, they tend to give significantly more minus responses than do other groups (Exner, 1978, 1981; Weiner, 1966). The protocols of 320 first admission schizophrenics, drawn randomly from the protocol pool at the Rorschach Research Foundation, were recoded for form quality, using Table A as the guideline. They were compared with equal-sized groups of nonpatients and nonschizophrenic inpatients, drawn randomly from the Table A construction pool. The results show that an average of 31% of the responses from schizophrenics are minus, as contrasted with an average of 15% minus responses among the nonschizophrenic inpatients, and only 6% of minus responses among the nonpatients.

The two studies regarding interscorer reliability indicate that considerable agreement does occur when Table A is used as a guideline for coding form quality. For the group of 20 coders and 25 records the percentages of agreement are: + = 93%, *o* = 97%, *u* =

94%, and $-$ = 94%. For the group of 15 coders and 20 records, the percentages of agreement are: $+$ = 96%, o = 97%, u = 95%, and $-$ = 93%.

Mayman (1970) has offered an important caution to all Rorschachers concerning the coding of form quality. He states,

> Many clinicians seem to feel that there is little they can learn from form level scores that they do not already know from their impressionistic scanning of Rorschach protocols. Those who do score form quality often settle for a rough-and-ready classification of responses as either "acceptable" or "poor" . . . The form quality of Rorschach responses indicates in microcosm the attitude with which a person maintains his hold on is object world.

Presumably, the modification of Mayman's technique for coding form quality included in the Comprehensive System goes well beyond the "rough-and-ready" classifications to which Mayman alludes. It will afford a more sophisticated glimpse into the world of the subject and his object relations than do the more simplified methods of good form–poor form that have been used in the past.

REFERENCES

Beck, S. J. (1933) Configurational tendencies in Rorschach responses. *American Journal of Psychology,* **45,** 433–443.

Beck, S. J. (1937) *Introduction to the Rorschach Method: A Manual of Personality Study.* American Orthopsychiatric Association Monograph, No. 1.

Beck, S. J. (1944) *Rorschach's Test. I: Basic Processes.* New York: Grune & Stratton.

Beck, S. J. (1945) *Rorschach's Test. II: A Variety of Personality Pictures.* New York: Grune & Stratton.

Beck, S. J. (1952) *Rorschach's Test. III: Advances in Interpretation.* New York: Grune & Stratton.

Beck, S. J., Beck, A., Levitt, E., and Molish, H. (1961) *Rorschach's Test. I: Basic Processes.* (3rd Ed.) New York: Grune & Stratton.

Blatt, H. (1953) An investigation of the significance of the Rorschach z score. Unpublished Ph.D. dissertation, University of Nebraska.

Exner, J. E. (1978) *The Rorschach: A Comprehensive System. Volume 2. Current research and advanced interpretation.* New York: Wiley.

Exner, J. E. (1981) The response process and diagnostic efficacy. 10th International Congress of Rorschach and Projective Techniques. Washington, D.C.

Hertz, M. (1940) *Percentage Charts for Use in Computing Rorschach Scores.* Brush Foundation and Department of Psychology, Western Reserve University.

Hertz, M. (1948) Suicidal configurations in Rorschach records. *Rorschach Research Exchange,* **12,** 3–58.

Hertz, M. (1960) Organization Activity. In Rickers-Ovsiankina, M. (Ed.), *Rorschach Psychology.* New York: Wiley, pp. 25–57.

Hertz, M. (1970) *Frequency Tables for Scoring Rorschach Responses.* (5th Ed.) Cleveland: Case-Western Reserve University Press.

Jolles, I. (1947) The diagnostic implications of Rorschach's Test in case studies of mental defectives. *Genetic Psychology Monographs,* **36,** 89–198.

Kinder, B., Brubaker, R., Ingram, R., and Reading, E. (1982) Rorschach form quality: A comparison of the Exner and Beck systems. *Journal of Personality Assessment,* **46,** 131–138.

Klopfer, B., and Tallman, G. (1938) A further Rorschach study of Mr. A. *Rorschach Research Exchange,* **3,** 31–36.

Klopfer, B., and Kelley, D. (1942) *The Rorschach Technique.* Yonkers-on-Hudson, N.Y.: World Book.

Klopfer, B., and Davidson, H. (1944) Form level rating: A preliminary proposal for appraising mode and level of thinking as expressed in Rorschach records. *Rorschach Research Exchange,* **8,** 164–177.

Klopfer, B., Ainsworth, M., Klopfer, W., and Holt, R. (1954) *Developments in the Rorschach Technique. I: Technique and Theory.* Yonkers-on-Hudson, N.Y.: World Book.

Kropp, R. (1955) The Rorschach "Z" score. *Journal of Projective Techniques,* **19,** 443–452.

Mayman, M. (1966) Measuring reality-adherence in the Rorschach test. American Psychological Association Meetings, New York.

Mayman, M. (1970) Reality contact, defense effectiveness, and psychopathology in Rorschach form-level scores. In Klopfer, B., Meyer, M., and Brawer, F. (Eds.), *Developments in the Rorschach Technique. III: Aspects of Personality Structure.* New York: Harcourt Brace Jovanovich, pp. 11–46.

Molish, H. (1955) Schizophrenic reaction types in a naval hospital population as evaluated by the Rorschach Test. Bureau of Medicine and Surgery, Navy Department, Washington, D.C.

Piotrowski, Z. (1957) *Perceptanalysis.* New York: Macmillan.

Rapaport, D., Gill, M., and Schafer, R. (1946) *Diagnostic Psychological Testing.* Vol. 2. Chicago: Yearbook Publisher.

Rorschach, H. (1921) *Psychodiagnostics.* Bern: Bircher (Transl., Hans Huber Verlag, 1942).

Schmidt, H., and Fonda, C. (1953) Rorschach scores in the manic states. *Journal of Projective Techniques,* **17,** 151–161.

Sisson, B., and Taulbee, E. (1955) Organizational activity of the Rorschach Test. *Journal of Consulting Psychology,* **19,** 29–31.

Varvel, W. (1941) The Rorschach Test in psychotic and neurotic depressions. *Bulletin of the Meninger Clinic,* **5,** 5–12.

Weiner, I. (1966) *Psychodiagnosis in Schizophrenia.* New York: Wiley.

Wilson, G., and Blake, R. (1950) A methodological problem in Beck's organizational concept. *Journal of Consulting Psychology,* **14,** 20–24.

Wishner, J. (1948) Rorschach intellectual indicators in neurotics. *American Journal of Orthopsychiatry,* **18,** 265–279.

CHAPTER 8

Content Categories and Populars

Another task in coding the Rorschach response involves two steps. First, an appropriate symbol must be selected to represent the content of the response. Second, the response should be checked against a listing of "Popular" answers, that is, those given quite frequently in Rorschach records. Neither of these procedures is complex, but both are quite important for the interpretive process.

CONTENT

All responses are coded for content. The symbol used for the content score should be reasonably representative of the object or of the class of objects reported in the response. Rorschach (1921) used only six different symbols for content scoring. They are *H* (Human), *Hd* (Human Detail), *A* (Animal), *Ad* (Animal Detail), *Ls* (Landscape), and *Obj* (Inanimate Objects). In the early development of the test it became obvious that these six categories did not provide adequate differentiation of many frequently reported classes of objects. Therefore each of the Rorschach systematizers has expanded Rorschach's original listing considerably to provide for a greater discrimination among responses. There is considerable agreement among the systems concerning the more commonly appearing contents; however, the agreement is far from unanimous. The lists of categories vary considerably, differing notably in length. Beck used the longest (35 categories), and Klopfer and Davidson (1962) the shortest (23 content categories). Slight variations also occur across the listings regarding the actual symbol to be used. For instance, Beck used the symbol *An* to score anatomy content, whereas Klopfer used the symbol *At* for the same category.

The list of content symbols used in the Comprehensive System was developed in three phases. First, a random sample of 600 protocols was selected from the protocol pool. These records constitute 13,542 responses, each of which was coded for content using the Beck listing of symbols, because that list is the longest for any of the systems. A frequency tally was then derived for each of the 35 content scores, and any category that did not show a frequency of 20 or more was deleted form the list. This procedure reduced the length of the Beck listing from 35 to 21 content categories.[1] The rationale for this procedure is that any content occurring with very limited frequency is probably quite "idiographic" when it does occur; thus it is better represented in a summary of codes in

---

[1] The 14 Beck Content scorings eliminated by this procedure are *Aq* (Antiquity), *Ar* (Architecture), *As* (Astronomy), *Dh* (Death), *Im* (Implement), *Mn* (Mineral), *Mu* (Music), *My* (Mythology), *Pr* (Personal), *Rc* (Recreation, *Rl* (Religion), *Ru* (Rural), *Tr* (Travel), and *Vo* (Vocational).

written-out form. For example, contents such as a candle, a milk bottle, ice tongs, and flags appear in Rorschach records very infrequently. Although each could be coded in a general category, such as object *(obj)*, the full uniqueness of the content would not be readily evident in a summary as it would be in written-out form.

The second phase in developing the list of content scorings was comprised of a reexamination of the 21 remaining content categories to determine if any one might be including two or more frequently occurring, but relatively different, classes of objects. Two such categories were discovered. The scoring of Anatomy *(An)* included 179 responses of anatomy and 97 X-ray responses. Although Beck had decided to score both under the single rubric of *An,* it was decided to create a separate scoring for X-ray. Similarly, the scoring of Fire *(Fi)* include two relatively separate kinds of answer. The most frequent was "explosion" $(N = 248)$, approximately half of which included reference to fire. A somewhat different kind of response, also scored *Fi,* is "fire," involving no explosion $(N = 69)$. These findings seem to warrant a separate content scoring for explosion answers. These decisions increased the number of content scoring categories to 23.

In addition, many of the human and animal responses were of fictional and mythological humans or animals, such as witches, giants, monsters, unicorns, and devils. More than 20% of the human content responses and more than 10% of the animal content responses in the sample of 600 records are of this variety. Thus it seemed logical, following the approaches of Klopfer, Piotrowski, and Rapaport, to add four categories—*(H), (Hd), (A),* and *(Ad)*—to account for these types of contents.

The final listing selected for use in the Comprehensive System is comprised of 27 categories. These categories and the symbol and criterion for each are shown in Table 23.

Table 23.   Symbols and Criteria to be Used in Scoring for Content

Category	Symbol	Criterion
Whole Human	*H*	Involving or implying the percept of a whole human form.
Whole Human (fictional or mythological)	*(H)*	Involving or implying the percept of a whole human form of a fictional or mythological basis, that is, gnomes, fairies, giants, witches, King Midas, Alice in Wonderland, monsters (human like), ghosts, dwarfs, devils, and angels.
Human Detail	*Hd*	Involving the percept of an incomplete human form, that is, a person but the head is missing, an arm, fingers, two big feet, and the lower part of a woman.
Human Detail (fictional or mythological)	*(Hd)*	Involving the percept of an incomplete human form of a fictional or mythological basis, that is, the hand of God, the head of the devil, the foot of a monster, the head of a witch, and the eyes of an angel.
Whole Animal	*A*	Involving or implying the percept of a whole animal form.
Whole Animal (fictional or mythological)	*(A)*	Involving or implying the percept of a whole animal form of a fictional or mythological basis, that is, unicorn, flying red horse, black beauty, Jonathan Livingston Seagull, and a magic frog.
Animal Detail	*Ad*	Involving the percept of an incomplete animal form, that is, the hoof of a horse, the claw of a lobster, the head of a fish, the head of a rabbit.

Table 23 (Continued)

Category	Symbol	Criterion
Animal Detail (fictional or mythological)	(*Ad*)	Involving the percept of an incomplete animal form of a fictional or mythological basis, that is, the wing of the bird of prey, Peter Rabbit's head, the head of Pooh Bear, the head of Bambi, and the wings of Pegasus.
Abstraction	*Ab*	Involving the percept which is clearly an abstract concept, that is, fear, depression, elation, and anger, abstract art, or any form of symbolism.
Alphabet	*A*1	Involving percepts of arabic numerals, such as 2, 4, and 7, or the letters of the alphabet, such as A, M, and X.
Anatomy	*An*	Involving the percept of anatomy (internal organs) of either human or animal content, that is, a heart, lungs, stomach, a bleached skull of a cow, a brain of a dog, and the insides of a person's stomach.
Art	*Art*	Involving percepts of paintings, plus other art objects, that is, a family crest, the seal of the president, and a sculpture of a bird.
Anthropology	*Ay*	Involving percepts which have a specific cultural relationship, that is, a totem pole, a helmut like those used by Romans, a viking ship, or Lindberg's airplane.
Blood	*B*1	Involving the percept of blood, either human or animal.
Botany	*Bt*	Involving the percept of any plant life, that is, flowers, trees, bushes, and seaweed.
Clothing	*Cg*	Involving the percept of any clothing ordinarily associated with the human, that is, hat boots, jacket, trousers, and tie.
Clouds	*C*1	Involving the percept of clouds. Variations of this category, such as fog, mist, and so on, should be scored as *Na*.
Explosion	*Ex*	Involving percepts of an actual explosion, occurring most commonly to Card IX, as an atomic explosion or blast. The determinant for inanimate movement (*m*) should always accompany this content. Percepts of an explosion "aftermath" such as, "A blast has just occurred and things are lying all over the place," should be coded for other content, or written out in complete form.
Fire	*Fi*	Involving percepts of actual fire, smoke, burning candles, flame given off from a torch, and such. These percepts will ordinarily involve the determinant scoring of *m* to denote the inanimate movement of the "fire" association.
Food	*Fd*	Involving the percept of any edible, such as ice cream, fried shrimp, chicken legs, a piece of steak, etc. The intent or meaning of the association must be clearly associated with "everyday" consumer produce, as in the instance of lettuce, cabbage, carrots, fried foods, etc., or must be presented in such a manner as to suggest that the object perceived is identified as a food substance, that is, "looks like a chicken like we used to have for Sunday dinner."

155

Table 23 (Continued)

Category	Symbol	Criterion
Geography	*Ge*	Involving percepts of any maps, specified or unspecified, that is, a map of Sicily, or a map of an island, peninsula, and continent. The percepts of *Ge do not* include the actual percept of definite or indefinite land masses which are "real" rather than representations. These type of percepts are scored as *Ls* (Landscape) or written out in rare instances.
Household	*Hh*	Involving percepts of interior household items, that is, chairs, beds, bedposts, plates, silverware, and rugs.
Landscape	*Ls*	Involving percepts of landscapes or seascapes, neither of which would be scored as *Bt* or *Ge*. A tree or a Bush, might legitimately be scored as *Bt*, whereas "trees," or "a bunch of shrubs" are more ordinarily scored *Ls*. This category includes some underwater scenes where specific animals are not identified, or in some instances as a secondary score as in Card X where a few specific animals may be cited but the bulk of the percept is left vague.
Nature	*Na*	Involving percepts of a wider natural scope than are included in *Bt*, *Ge*, or *Ls*, usually including sky, snow, water, racing sea, a storm, night, ice, rainbow, sun, night, etc.
Science	*Sc*	Involving percepts that are ordinarily associated with science or science fiction such as bacteria, germs, science fiction monsters, ray guns, rockets, rocket ships, spaceships, etc. In some instances, the symbol *Sc* will be used as the primary content but in other responses, especially those involving science fiction objects, the symbol (*A*) or (*H*) may be assigned as primary and *Sc* as secondary.
Sex	*Sx*	Involving percepts of sex organs or activities related to sex function, that is, intercourse, erect penis, menstruation, vagina, testes, and breasts.
X-ray	*Xy*	Involving percepts of x-ray, most of which pertain to bone structure, that is, the x-ray of a pelvis, the x-ray of some bones, but may also involve x-rays of organs or organ like structures, that is, an x-ray of the stomach and an x-ray of the intestines. *Shading is always* involved in these percepts.
Vocational (supplementary)	(*Vo*)	Involving percepts which *may* be interpreted as related to the occupation of the subject. This scoring is *never* used as the primary or main content score but may be included as secondary or additional so as to alert the interpreter of a vocational or occupational percept.

POPULAR RESPONSES

Rorschach made no mention of the commonly given, or Popular, answers in his original work (1921). He did, however, call attention to these types of responses in his posthumously published 1923 paper, referring to them as "Vulgar" answers. Rorschach defined the Vulgar or Popular responses as those occurring at least once in every three protocols, suggesting that they represent the capability for conventional perception. Each of the Rorschach systematizers has included the Popular, or P, scoring as an important feature of the test; however, there exists considerable variation across the systems concerning the listings of responses to be scored P. These intersystem differences have generally been created by disagreements concerning the criterion of P, although in some instances sampling differences have contributed to the variations. Most of the systematizers broadened Rorschach's criterion of limiting the P scoring to answers occurring at least once in three records. Rapaport et al. (1946) recommended the scoring of P for responses occurring once in every four or five records. Beck et al. (1961) list as Popular, responses occurring at least three times as frequently as the next most commonly occurring answer to a blot, provided that it is given not less than once by at least 14% of his adult sample. Piotrowski (1957) included responses given at least once in every four records. Hertz (1970) used the broadest criterion, defining as Popular any answer which occurs at least once in six protocols, and presents the longest listing of Populars, although not substantially longer than that developed by Beck. The Klopfer et al. (1962) listing of Populars has considerably fewer answers, having been developed from "clinical experience," using Rorschach's guideline of responses occurring once in three protocols.

The absence or deficiency of Popular answers has been noted in several empirical works (Rickers-Ovsiankina, 1938; Rapaport et al. 1946; Beck, 1954; Bloom, 1962), and is a consistent finding across systems. Unfortunately, the interpretive conclusions concerning the incidence of high or low numbers of Popular answers is often system-specific and not easily generalized.

Because the concept of *Popular* reflects the *very* conventional answers, it was decided to use Rorschach's suggestion to define them as any response occurring at least once in every three records. The 7500 protocols used in the construction of Table A (2500 nonpatient adults, 2500 nonschizophrenic outpatients, and 2500 inpatient nonschizophrenic and nonpsychotic patients) were computer tallied for response frequencies. Any specific response that occurred at least 2500 times in this sample is designated as *Popular* in the Comprehensive System. The analysis yielded 13 Popular responses, which are shown in Table 24 with the percentage of nonpatient and nonschizophrenic groups that gave each response also included.

The listing in Table 24 replaces the 13 *classes* of Popular responses that were published in the first edition of this work. The 1974 list combined the bat and butterfly responses to Cards I and V and the spider and crab responses to Card X. The current list eliminates five responses that were found to be Popular a decade ago, and includes two answers that meet the Popular criterion now. Interestingly, the current listing, with the exception of the Card IX Popular, is essentially the same as reported by Sendin (1981), using a sample of 294 Spanish adult patients and nonpatients.

The one-in-three criterion may seem somewhat stringent to some. It is true that there is great variation in the frequencies by which each of the 13 answers are reported. The least frequent of the 13, however, the Popular for Card IX, occurs significantly more than the next most frequent response in the sample, which is the female figure reported in the

Table 24. **Popular Responses Selected for the Comprehensive System Based on the Frequency of Occurrence of at Least Once in Every Three Protocols Given by Nonpatient Adult Subjects and Nonschizophrenic Adult Patients**

Card	Location	Criterion	% Nonpatient Reporting	% Nonschizophrenic Reporting
I	W	Bat. The response always involves the whole blot	48	38
I	W	Butterfly. The response always involves the whole blot.	40	36
II	D1	Animal forms, usually the heads of dogs, bears, elephants, or lambs; however, the frequency of the whole animal to this area is sufficient to warrant the scoring of P.	34	35
III	D1 or D9	Two human figures, or representations thereof, such as dolls and caricatures. The scoring of P is also applicable to the percept of a single human figure to area D9.	89	70
IV	W or D7	A human or human-like figure such as giant, monster, science fiction creature, etc.	53	41
V	W	Butterfly, the apex of the card upright or inverted. The whole blot *must* be used.	46	43
V	W	Bat, the apex of the card upright or inverted, and involving the whole blot.	36	38
VI	W or D1	Animal skin, hide, rug, or pelt.	87	35
VII	D1 or D9	Human head or face, specifically identified as female, child, indian, or with gender not identified. If D1 is used, the upper segment (D5) is usually identified as hair, feather, etc. If the response includes the entire D2 area, P is coded if the head or face are restricted to the D9 area. If Dd23 is included as part of the human form, the response is *not* coded as P.	59	47
VIII	D1	Whole animal figure. This is the most frequently perceived common answer, the content varying considerably, such as bear, dog, rodent, fox, wolf, and coyote. All are P. The P is also coded when the animal figure is reported as part of the W percept as in a family crest, seal, and emblem.	94	91
IX	D3	Human or human-like figures such as witches, giants, science fiction creatures, monsters, etc.	54	24
X	D1	Spider with all appendages restricted to the D1 area.	42	34
X	D1	Crab with all appendages restricted to the D1 area. Other variations of multilegged animals are not P.	37	38

center D4 area to Card I. In that context, the selection of the one-in-three criterion can be justified on a statistical basis. The female figure to D4 in Card I occurred in 25% of the total sample and, as such, does meet a one-in-four criterion, but it does not occur significantly more often than five other answers that have response frequencies between 18 and 24%. They are an animal face or mask to WS on Card I (24%), a rocket ship to DS5 on Card II (19%), a butterfly to D3 on Card III (21%), an animal skin to the whole of Card IV

(22%), and a totem pole to D3 on Card VI (18%). In addition, there are more than 50 other responses that have frequencies of between 13 and 17%.

Piotrowski (1957) has suggested that the listing of Populars may vary across cultures. Some support for this hypothesis is noted by the failure of the Card IX Popular to reach the criterion frequency in Sendin's sample of Spanish adults, and by the findings of Fried (1977) who found that subjects in Finland deliver the response "Christmas elves" to Card II with a Popular frequency. These differences are more likely to exist among the Popular answers that barely meet criterion in one culture, but it is unlikely that the higher frequency answers will differ cross-culturally. Some support for this postulate is derived from the examination of a group of 293 protocols that were collected in 12 countries for the Rorschach Research Foundation (Argentina = 15, Australia = 25, France = 37, India = 9, Italy = 16, Japan = 14, Malaysia = 22, Mexico = 60, Micronesia = 33, Philippines = 40, Switzerland = 8, and New Zealand = 14). None of these samples is large enough to test for Populars, but when combined, 11 of the 13 Populars listed in Table 24 occur in at least 40% of the records. The two that fall below the one-third criterion are the Populars on Cards II and IX, with percentages of 31 and 26%, respectively.

The high frequencies with which the Popular responses occur suggest that they represent the most distinctive contours or other stimulus features of the blots, and thus are most easily misidentified. Nonetheless, there are some marked differences in response rates among patients and nonpatients for the Populars on Card VI and Card IX, which merit further study. Similarly, there are also some subtle sex differences for some of the Populars that do reach levels of statistical significance. They warrant further study. Females report the Popular butterfly responses on both Cards I and V more frequently than males, whereas males report the bat responses on Cards I and V more frequently than females. Similarly, males report the Card X crab with a higher frequency than females, whereas the reverse is true for the Card X spider response. On Card VII, females identify the Popular human figures as women much more often than they report children or Indians. The reverse is true for male subjects. The same pattern of difference occurs for the Card VIII Popular. Males report larger and nondomestic animals most often, whereas females report smaller and domestic animals more frequently.

The two interscorer reliability studies show percentages of agreement for both groups for coding P to be 99%. There is no room for error in coding P. Similarly, high percentages of agreement occurred for both groups in coding *primary* content, that is, the basic content of the response. The 20 coders and 25 records yielded a 95% agreement for primary content, whereas the 15 coders and 20 records had a 96% agreement. However, the percentage of agreement for both groups was considerably lower for the coding of *secondary* contents. In the past, and in the first edition of this work, little emphasis has been afforded the importance of coding secondary contents. Research during the past decade indicates that they are much more important than implied heretofore. In the reliability study involving 20 coders and 25 records, a very modest 78% agreement occurred for secondary content, and only slightly better, 82%, for the 15 coders and 20 records. The disparity for each group was created much more by omissions rather than actual disagreements. Several contents such as Abstract *(Ab)*, Art, Botany *(Bt)*, Clothing *(Cg)*, Fire *(Fl)*, Nature *(Na)*, Landscape *(Ls)*, and Science *(Sc)* occur far more frequently as secondary contents than as primary contents. The conscientious examiner will scan each answer carefully and code for each additional content that may exist. In many cases the presence of secondary contents will add very little to the interpretive yield, but in some instances the accumulated frequencies for one or two, or for some combinations of contents, will contribute significantly to the overall interpretation.

REFERENCES

Beck, S. J. (1954) *The six schizophrenias.* American Orthopsychiatric Association. Research Monograph No. 6.

Beck, S. J., Beck, A. Levitt, E., and Molish, H. B. (1961) *Rorschach's Test. I: Basic Processes.* (3rd ed.) New York: Grune & Stratton.

Bloom, B. L. (1962) The Rorschach Popular response among Hawaiian schizophrenics. *Journal of Projective Techniques,* **26,** 173–181.

Fried, R. (1977) Christmas elves on the Rorschach: A Popular Finnish response and its cultural significance. 9th International Congress of Rorschach and Projective Techniques. Fribourg, Switzerland.

Goldfried, M. R., Stricker, G., and Weiner, I. B. (1971) *Rorschach Handbook of Clinical and Research Applications.* Englewood Cliffs, N.J.: Prentice-Hall.

Hertz, M. R. (1970) *Frequency Tables for Scoring Rorschach Responses.* (5th ed.) Cleveland: The Press of Case Western Reserve University.

Klopfer, B., and Kelley, D. (1942) *The Rorschach Technique.* Yonkers-on-Hudson. N.Y.: World Book.

Klopfer, B., and Davidson, H. (1962) *The Rorschach Technique. An Introductory Manual.* New York: Harcourt Brace Jovanovich.

Piotrowski, Z. (1957). *Perceptanalysis.* New York: Macmillan.

Rapaport, D., Gill, M., and Schafer, R. (1946) *Diagnostic Psychological Testing.* Vol. 2, Chicago: Yearbook Publishers.

Rickers-Ovsiankina, M. (1938) The Rorschach Test as applied to normal and schizophrenic subjects. *British Journal of Medical Psychology,* **17,** 227–257.

Rorschach, H. (1921) *Psychodiagnostics.* Bern: Bircher (Transl. Hans Huber Verlag, 1942).

Rorschach, H., and Oberholzer, E. (1923) The application of the interpretation of form to Psychoanalysis. *Zeitschrift fur gesamte Neurologie und Psychiatrie,* **82,** 240–274.

Schafer, R. (1954) *Psychoanalytic Interpretation in Rorschach Testing.* New York: Grune & Stratton.

Sendin, C. (1981) Identification of Popular responses among Spanish adults. 10th International Congress of Rorschach and Projective Techniques. Washington, D.C.

Weiner, I. B. (1966) *Psychodiagnosis in Schizophrenia.* New York: Wiley.

CHAPTER 9

Special Scores

The final task in coding the Rorschach response is to determine whether the answer has any of the features that require the addition of a *Special Score*. Like most other components in the Rorschach language, Special Scores are actually codes, rather than numerical scores, which signal the presence of an unusual characteristic in the response. The use of Special Scores permits quantification of many features of responses that have been interpreted more qualitatively in the past.

Rapaport et al. (1946) were the first to recognize the importance of systematically identifying unusual features of answers, and they devised 25 special categories for this purpose. Unfortunately, as Rapaport cautioned, many had overlapping criteria and, as a consequence, the interscorer reliability for most has been modest. As a result the issues of validation have been quite difficult to approach. Currently, there are 12 Special Scores in the Comprehensive System, 10 of which are derivations from one or more of Rapaport's categories. Six concern unusual verbalizations, two are used for perseverations and integration failure, two involve special characteristics of content, one is used when the answer is personalized, and one is used for a special color phenomenon. None of the 12 was included when the Comprehensive System was first published (Exner, 1974) because of problems with criteria, interscorer reliability, or a lack of convincing validation data. The first five, all dealing with unusual verbalizations, were published approximately two years later (Exner, Weiner, & Schuyler, 1976), developed from the works of Rapaport, Schafer (1954) and Weiner (1966). Two each were added with the publications of Volume 2 (Exner, 1978) and Volume 3 (Exner & Weiner, 1982). The remaining three have been developed since that time for inclusion here.

UNUSUAL VERBALIZATIONS

Unusual verbalizations are an important element in the study of cognitive processing, and more particularly, cognitive slippage. When some form of cognitive disarray occurs, whether momentary or for a longer interval, it will often manifest verbally. It is evidenced in Rorschach responses in any of three ways: (1) Deviant Verbalizations, (2) Inappropriate Combinations, or (3) Inappropriate Logic. Six Special Scores are used to note the presence of these sorts of disarray in Rorschach answers, two for the Deviant Verbalizations, three for the Inappropriate Combinations, and one for Inappropriate Logic.

DEVIANT VERBALIZATIONS (*DV* AND *DR*)

There are two Special Scores for Deviant Verbalizations, one of which is restricted to the brief form of slippage and the second which concerns a larger segment of the response.

Both are characterized by idiosyncratic modes of expression that impede the subject's ability to communicate clearly.

1. Deviant Verbalization (DV) DV is assigned to those answers that have either of two characteristics, both of which create the impression of oddity in the answer.

    a. *Neologism.* Involving the use of an incorrect word, or neologism, in place of a correct word that falls well within the subject's verbal capacity. Examples are: "A woman with a *disretheal* air about her," "Some bacteria you might see under a *telescope*," "A cat sticking her *purr* up," "The *pubic* arch of somebody."

    b. *Redundancy.* Involving the odd use of language that cannot be justified in terms of subcultural idioms or limited vocabulary skills, in which the subject identifies *twice* the nature of the object(s) reported. Examples are: "The two *twin* lips of a vagina," "A pair of *two* birds," "The backward *reversed* propeller of an airplane," "A *trio* of three people," or "A matched *brace* of lungs." *DV* responses are usually easy to detect because the inappropriate word stands out quite markedly.

2. Deviant Response (DR). *DR* is assigned to answers that have a strange or peculiar quality. This may be manifest in either of two ways.

    a. *Inappropriate Phrases.* Involving the inclusion of phrases that are inappropriate or completely irrelevant to the response. For example: "A bird, *but I was hoping to see a butterfly*," "Some kind of bug but I've never seen one like it, *neither has anyone else for that matter*," "It's a womb, *it's not nice this way 'cause the baby is gone*," "A dancer with a pink robe, a blue bra and a green G-string, *she's perfectly anonymous cause you can't see her body*," "An abstract of President Carter *if you look at it from a Democratic perspective*."

    b. *Circumstantial Responses.* Involving answers that are fluid or rambling in which the subject becomes inappropriately elaborative or has marked difficulty in achieving a definition of the object. Examples are: "I'm not sure what this could be, something like an animal nose, maybe equine or bovine, *like in that play that was so filled with passions and psychological drama and thrills and so many tensions. I had to see it twice.* Yes, the nose of a horse." "It looks like a map of two continents, *I can tell because I've traveled a lot and that middle line is something like the Arabs would do, dividing it all up like a map that represents darkness and light.* It's probably a map of Africa and Eastern Asia." "*I'm a scientist.* I can see legs, a head, and a tail like an insect *but I'm having trouble seeing it. I see unilateral and bilateral symmetry and it's very interesting in the phylogenetic scheme of things, but I don't see what I know.* I'll just say an insect." "It could be part of a crab, *I'm just trying to think of the angle we're looking at it from, maybe it's a stone crab, I really like those. If you are ever in Maine try them, the only thing you ever get is the leg 'cause they're only allowed to harvest the legs.*"

Caution should be exercised to avoid confusing the circumstantial *DR* response with the elaborate but appropriate answer. In the latter, the subject remains *on target* and simply verbalizes the organization of the answer. For example: "These might be some flowers and a walkway, like it is in a garden or a park, and you know this part in the top could be like a tower or a fountain if you look at it in perspective. In fact you could even think of it as the Eiffel Tower as you might see it across a park with many pretty flowers lining the walkway."

In the *DR* response the subject tends to wander *off target*, sometimes aimlessly, and may never actually return to the response object. For example: "Oh dear, I know I've seen something like that in a magazine, like a person from Samoa or someplace like that, *I'm always doing a lot of reading because it sharpens your mind and you can learn a lot of things about people and the world if you devote yourself to self-improvement by making sure to read something new every day without fail.*" The circumstantial verbiage in the *DR* answer is not necessarily bizarre. In the preceding example the commentary about reading and self-improvement might be quite appropriate in a different situation, but is inappropriate for the task at hand. Rapaport suggested that responses such as these indicate a loss of distance from the task.

Most examiners find the circumstantial *DR* easy to identify because so much of the verbiage has little if any relevance to the actual response. Some *DR* answers will also contain a *DV*. When this occurs, *only* the *DR* is coded.

INAPPROPRIATE COMBINATIONS (*INCOM, FABCOM, CONTAM*)

These combinative responses involve the inappropriate condensation of impressions and/or ideas into responses that violate realistic considerations. They are answers in which unreal relationships are inferred between images, objects, or activities attributed to objects. There are three types of inappropriate combinations, each of which has a separate code.

1. Incongruous Combination (*INCOM*). Involving the condensation of blot details or images that are inappropriate merged into a single object. For example: "A *four*-legged chicken," "A butterfly with his *hands* out," "A frog with a *mustache*," or "A woman with the *head of a chicken*." Sometimes the incongruity will be manifest by the inappropriate combination of color and form as in "*Red* bears," "*Black* snow," or "An *orange* man." The *INCOM* is coded *only* when the combination involves a single object.

2. Fabulized Combination (*FABCOM*). Involves an implausible relationship that is posited between two or more objects identified in the blot. These answers *always* include two or more discrete details of the blot. Examples are: "Two chickens holding *basketballs*," "A woman attacking a *submarine*," "Mice biting the *fingers of a martian*," or "Two ants fighting over a *baseball bat*." *FABCOM* is also coded for implausible transparencies such as "There is a big man sitting there and you can see his *heart pumping*," or "This is a vagina and here are her *fallopian tubes*."

3. Contamination (*CONTAM*). This is the most bizarre of the inappropriate combinations. The *CONTAM* represents two or more impressions that have been fused into a single response in a manner that clearly violates reality. The process of fusion causes impairment to the adequacy of either impression in contrast to the situation where they might be reported separately. Whereas the *INCOM* answers fused impressions from discrete blot areas into a single implausible object, the *CONTAM* response involves the use of a single discrete area. One response has been psychologically overlaid above another as in a photographic double exposure. Contaminations often (but not always) include the use of a neologism or other peculiar verbalizations to describe the object. A classic illustration of the neologistic *CONTAM* is the condensation of the front view of a bug and the front view of an ox into "*The face of a bug ox*." Another involves carefully viewing Card III upright, and then inverted, and then concluding that the D3 area is "*No doubt, a butterflower*," apparently fusing the impressions of a flower and a butterfly. In other instances, the strained logic that apparently characterizes the *CONTAM* is more directly manifest as in *"It looks like blood here, and an island, it must be a bloody island,"* or *"It must be a bird dog 'cause it's got the body like a dog and the nose of a bird."*

In the past it has been suggested that all *CONTAM* responses be assigned a form quality coding of − , but this is a faulty rule. Form quality concerns perceptual accuracy, whereas the *CONTAM* signals cognitive or ideational impairment that may or may not involve perceptual distortion. If the object reported is nonexistent, as a bug-ox or a butterflower, it will obviously be coded as − for form quality. If the form is appropriate to the blot area used, however, the form quality may be *u,* or in some cases may be *o.*

INAPPROPRIATE LOGIC *(ALOG)*

The *ALOG* is used whenever the subject, *without prompting,* uses strained reasoning to justify his or her answer. The logic involved is clearly not conventional, representing, rather, a form of loose thinking. Usually the *ALOG* response is easily identified because the subject calls attention to size features or spatial elements of the blot. For example, "This is a very small lion *because it is only a part of the picture,"* or "This green must be lettuce *because it's next to the rabbit,"* or "It must be a man and a woman *because they're together,"* or "It's the North Pole *because it's at the top."* In each of these statements, the reasoning becomes attached to, and dependent upon, the size, positioning, or number of objects included in the response.

It is important to reemphasize that *ALOG* is coded *only* when the impaired logic is offered *spontaneously.* There are instances when a subject may offer a complex answer, and in the attempt to use the entire card, or as much as possible, includes features in a more "qualified" way, as in the statement ". . . and I suppose this could be a . . . if you stretch your imagination." These kinds of qualifications are *not* scored *ALOG.* Similarly, it is not uncommon for some "strained" logic to be manifest in the inquiry *after* the examiner has asked for clarification of a percept. *ALOG* would not be scored in these instances, inasmuch as the element of spontaneity has been removed by the examiner's questioning.

PERSEVERATION AND INTEGRATION FAILURE

In some records two or more almost identical responses will be given to the same blot. In other cases, a response given previously will be alluded to again to a different blot. In some records, the same answer will be offered redundantly across several blots, and in still other instances an answer will be overgeneralized to the whole blot by using only an area of the blot. These sorts of answers represent a form of cognitive dysfunction or a marked psychological preoccupation. Two Special Scores are included in the System to indicate the presence of these answers.

PERSEVERATION *(PSV)*

There are at least three types of perseveration that may occur. Although they are different, all are assigned the same Special Score *(PSV).*

Within Card Perseveration The within card *PSV* responses are those that use *exactly* the *same* location, the *same* determinant(s), the *same* content, the *same DQ* and *FQ,* and the *same Z* scoring if it has been involved, *as the preceding response.* The content may change slightly, but it will remain in the same general content category. The most common examples of this form of *PSV* response occur in Cards I and V, when the subject gives two Popular answers in *consecutive* order. For instance:

1. "This could be a bat." (described by form and to the *W* and coded *Wo Fo A P* 1.0) followed by,

2. "Or, it could be a butterfly, too." (described by form and to the *W* and coded *Wo Fo A P* 1.0 *PSV*)

It is quite important to establish the fact that the subject *does* mean to give two responses and not simply an alternative, as is often the case. Usually, when the alternative type of answer is intended, it will be revealed by the selection of one of the two answers as being most appropriate, as in "Well the more I look at it it seems like a butterfly rather than a bat." In other instances, a subject may give an alternative type response, "Well it might be a bat, or it could be a butterfly too," but then will clearly differentiate the two in the inquiry. For example, "Well it really could be a bat because it's all black too," *Wo FC'o A P* 1.0; and "Of course it would be a good butterfly if you ignore the coloring," scored *Wo Fo A P* 1.0.

The real issue in a within card form of *PSV* is that the subject does deliver essentially the same answer *in the context* of the coding, with *no intervening answers.*

Content Perseveration Whereas within card *PSV* is only for consecutive answers within a card, Content Perseveration characterizes responses that are not necessarily within the same card or to consecutive cards; but the content is *identified as the same seen earlier.* The coding of the new response may be quite different than for the answer in which the object was initially perceived, but the subject makes it quite clear that it is the same object(s). For instance, a subject may identify "Two people in a fight" on Card II, and to Card III report, "Oh, there are those *same* two people but the fight is over now and they're bowing to each other." It is not uncommon for some subjects, especially children, to see a bat on one card, usually Card I or V, and then report, "Oh, there's *that bat again*" to a subsequent card.

Mechanical Perseveration A third type of perseverative response is seen more frequently among subjects who are intellectually handicapped and organically impaired. For the most part, this kind of perseveration is noted in very brief records, and it is easily identified because the subject gives essentially the same answer over and over, in an almost mechanical way. For example, a subject with severe organic impairment gave the answer "A bat" to each of the first seven cards, with no other responses intervening. When Card VIII was presented, he said, "Oh, this bat is colored," and finally on Card IX said, "Where did it go; it's not there anymore." These subjects will often inadvertently emphasize their perceptual rigidity by saying, "Oh, another . . . ," or "This one looks like a . . . too," or "My, they all look like . . . to me." Typically, subjects who manifest this form of perseveration are not good candidates for the Rorschach, and because they are so mechanistic, they are usually distinguished easily from the very resistive subject who is more clearly uncooperative and attempting to conceal through comments such as, "Man, they just don't look like nothing. They all look the same, all bats or something."

CONFABULATION *(CONFAB)*

In rare instances, a subject attends only to a detail area of the blot, but generalizes a response from that detail to a larger area, or to the entire blot. In most of these responses the contours of the detail selected will be used and/or described appropriately, but the overall response will be inappropriate for the total area involved. For instance, a subject might focus on the $D1$ area of the Card I and respond, "It's a claw, it's a lobster." In the Inquiry the subject establishes that the entire blot is included for the response, but when the examiner pursues the features of the response, the subject persists in justifying the answer because of the presence of the claw. There is no meaningful integration of the remainder of the blot even though the subject insists that the entire blot is included in the answer. The coding for this response would be *Wo F− A CONFAB*. A *Z* score is *not* assigned to the Confabulated answer.

It is important that the examiner insure that integration failure has truly occurred. Some very resistive subjects, especially adolescents, become irritated and/or threatened by the requirements of the Inquiry. If asked, "What is there that makes it look like . . . ?" they often respond, "I don't know, it just does," and are quite vague about any details of the object or the location used. Occasionally these subjects will point out one feature such as, "There's a foot there," for a response involving a whole human or whole animal. These are *not* typically *Confabulated* responses, but rather instances of lazy or resistive articulation. Usually, a caution to the subject by the examiner will clarify the issue as in, "Look, I know it looks like that to you, but you have to help me see it, too. Take your time. We are in no hurry. Now show me . . . ."

The true *CONFAB* is more mechanistic, and often the subject will seem mystified by the fact that the examiner does not appear to understand. A hint to the possible presence of a *CONFAB* sometimes will occur in the original association such as, "A claw, a lobster." The response has a stilted quality that strikes the ear of the listener. Unfortunately, some *CONFAB* answers are not identified as such until the Inquiry, because the subject gives only a single-word response in the original association. For example, a subject might give the response, "A lobster," and in the Inquiry report, "Sure, see the claw?" It is only when the examiner pursues the matter further that the *CONFAB* becomes apparent, because the subject will persist in focusing the single detail such as, "Look, see the claw, it's a lobster." Sometimes the subject will even manifest the very strained *ALOG*-like reasoning in attempting to defend the answer: "It's got a claw, it must be a lobster 'cause they have claws." Even if the *ALOG* is manifest it is *not* coded, because the *CONFAB* coding reflects the serious pathognomic quality of the answer and the perceptual-cognitive impairment that it includes.

SPECIAL CONTENT CHARACTERISTICS

Some of the studies completed at the Rorschach Research Foundation have focused on the special issues of content, and especially those features of responses that can be argued to reflect the characteristics of *projection*. In other words, those features of an answer that go beyond the level of classification. Although criteria to define various codes for this purpose are relatively easy to establish, the matter of validating their interpretive usefulness is more difficult to achieve. Sufficient work has been completed to warrant the incorporation of two of these codes into the Comprehensive System. Each relates to issues of self-image and interpersonal relationships.

AGGRESSIVE MOVEMENT *(AG)*

The *Ag* coding is used for any movement response (*M, FM,* or *m*) in which the action is clearly aggressive, such as fighting, breaking, tearing, stalking, exploding, arguing, looking angry, and so on. The aggressive action must be occurring. Caution should be exercised to avoid coding *Ag* for responses in which the object *has been* subjected to aggression, such as a bear that has been shot, or a ship that has been bombed. These are *not Ag* responses. Similarly, an explosion per se is not *Ag,* but something being destroyed by an explosion *is Ag.*

MORBID CONTENT *(MOR)*

The *MOR* coding is used for any response in which an object is identified by either of two classes of characteristics:

1. Identification of the object as dead, destroyed, ruined, spoiled, damaged, injured, or broken (e.g., a broken mirror, a dead dog, a worn out pair of boots, a bear that is hurt, a ripped piece of cloth, a wound, a torn coat, a decaying leaf, and so on).

2. Attribution to an object of a clearly dysphoric feeling or characteristic (e.g., a gloomy house, a sad tree, an unhappy person, a person crying, depression, and so on.)

PERSONALIZED ANSWERS

Many responses contain personal pronouns such as I, me, my, or we. Most are used naturally in the course of articulating a response such as, "It looks like a bat to me," or "I think that it looks like two people." There are, however, instances in which these forms of self-reference are used somewhat differently, and when that occurs, a Special Score is required because it signals a form of defensiveness.

Personal *(PER)*   The *PER* code is assigned to any response in which the subject refers to personal knowledge or experience as part of the basis for justifying and/or clarifying a response. Examples are: "We had one like that once," "I see them all the time in the yard," "I used to make them like this," "My father showed me some once," "I remember seeing one in a magazine," and so on.

Ordinarily the *PER* response will include the use of a personal pronoun—I, me, my, or we—but in some instances the personal knowledge or experience may be conveyed without a personal pronoun being employed. For instance, "It's an amoeba, if you ever took a biology course you've seen them," or "They make you wear ones like this in the Army." In either case the examiner should be convinced that the subject is injecting personal knowledge or experience rather than commentary. Comments such as "They used them a long time ago, I think," or "I've never seen one but I think they are like that," or "I think they are popular among children" are *not PER.*

SPECIAL COLOR PHENOMENA

In most instances subjects identifying chromatic colors will do so correctly—that is, red as red, green as green, and so on. In rare instances some subjects misidentify chromatic colors. If this occurs, the examiner should pursue the issue cautiously in the Inquiry to determine whether a verbal lapse may have occurred. If the subject makes an appropriate correction, the response should be coded *DV* to indicate the verbal slip. Conversely, if no correction is made, an appropriate examination for color vision should be conducted. If color vision is intact, the response is a *DV*.

There is another special phenomenon involving color for which a Special Score exists.

Color Projection *(CP)*　The *CP* coding is assigned to any response in which a subject identifies an achromatic blot or blot area as being chromatically colored. These are rare responses, occurring most frequently to Cards IV or V. In most, the chromatic coloring is hinted at but not specified in the original response, such as "Oh, what a beautiful butterfly." Obviously, the key word *beautiful* should be pursued in the Inquiry, and some subjects do report that the blot has "a pleasant purple coloring," or "different yellows and blues" and the like. There are no data to suggest that responses such as these are related to deficiencies in color vision, and research suggested by Piotrowski (1957) indicates that they do have a special interpretive significance.

CP is coded only when the subject specifically identifies the presence of chromatic coloring in the achromatic blot area. Most subjects who give *CP* answers tend to delineate the chromatic colors by using the shading features of the blot, thus requiring a determinant coding for diffuse shading (*FY, YF,* or *Y*).

The percentages of agreement in the two interscorer reliability studies, for each of the 12 Special Scores, are shown in Table 25.

Table 25.　Percentage of Coder Agreement for 12 Special Scores in Two Reliability Studies

Special Score	Symbol	20 Coders 25 Records % Agreement	15 Coders 20 Records % Agreement
Deviant Verbalization	DV	96%	97%
Deviant Response	DR	94%	95%
Incongruous Combination	INCOM	97%	97%
Fabulized Combination	FABCOM	98%	97%
Inappropriate Logic	ALOG	93%	95%
Contamination	CONTAM	99%	99%
Perservation	PSV	None present	99%
Confabulation	CONFAB	None present	None present
Aggressive Movement	Ag	97%	96%
Morbid Content	MOR	98%	99%
Personal	PER	96%	97%
Color Projection	CP	99%	None present

REFERENCES

Exner, J. E. (1974) *The Rorschach: A Comprehensive System. Volume* 1. New York: Wiley.

Exner, J. E. (1978) *The Rorschach: A Comprehensive System. Volume 2. Current Research and Advanced Interpretation.* New York: Wiley.

Exner, J. E., and Weiner, I. B. (1982) *The Rorschach: A Comprehensive System. Volume 3. Assessment of Children and Adolescents.* New York: Wiley.

Exner, J. E., Weiner, I. B. and Schuyler, W. (1976) *A Rorschach Workbook for the Comprehensive System.* Bayville, N.Y.: Rorschach Workshops.

Piotrowski, Z. (1957) *Perceptanalysis.* New York: Macmillan

Rapaport, D., Gill, M. M., and Schafer, R. (1946) *Diagnostic Psychological Testing. Volume II.* Chicago: Yearbook Publishers.

Schafer, R. (1954) *Psychoanalytic Interpretation in Rorschach Testing.* New York: Grune and Stratton.

Weiner, I. B. (1966) *Psychodiagnosis in Schizophrenia.* New York: Wiley.

CHAPTER 10

The Structural Summary

The objective of coding each response accurately is to be able to complete the *Structural Summary*. The Summary represents the composite of code frequencies plus many ratios, percentages, and numerical derivations. They are the data base from which Rorschach interpretation begins, and from which many important postulates concerning psychological functioning are generated. There are three simple procedures involved in creating the Structural Summary: (1) listing the Sequence of Scores, (2) recording frequencies for each variable, and (3) performing various calculations required to obtain the ratios, percentages, and derived scores. The protocol of a 26-year-old male has been included here to illustrate each of these steps.

SEQUENCE OF SCORES

The first step is the listing of the codes for each response in the order of occurrence, that is, Card by Card and with the responses numbered consecutively. This consolidation of the coding makes it easier to do the frequency tallies that are required, and the Sequence itself is often an additional source of important interpretive data. The Sequence of Scores page of the *Structural Summary Blank* includes columns for Card number, response number, and each of the major categories of coding used. It *also* has a column after the *Location* section headed *No.* that can be used to record the Location number involved in the response, such as *D3*, *DdS26*, and so on. If an area used is not numbered in Table A, the number 99 is used. The listing of location numbers in the Sequence of Scores will, occasionally, contribute to the interpretation of individual records, but generally they are much more useful for research purposes, and essential if a computer interpretation of the Structural Summary is to be generated. The Sequence of Scores for the protocol of L.S. is shown in Table 26.

FREQUENCY TALLIES

The second step in preparing the Structural Summary is the entry of frequency tallies for each of the codes on the *Structural Summary Blank*.

1. Location Features. Each of the three basic location codes is tallied separately. Spaces are also included to enter the frequencies of *Wv* and *S* responses, although *neither* of these frequencies is subtracted from the tallies for the three basic location codes of *W*, *D*, or *Dd*. Frequencies are also entered for each of the developmental quality codes, disregarding the type of location used.

2. Determinants. Each of the determinants is tallied separately, *except* when occurring in a blend. Each blend is entered in its entirety in the separate section under *Blends*,

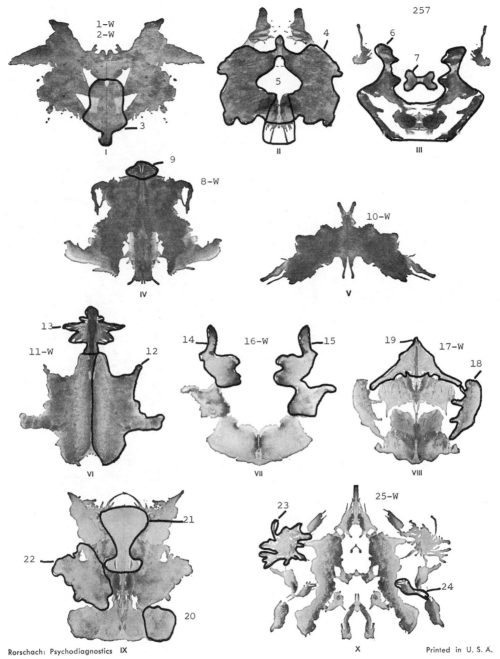

257

Figure 6. Location Selections by L.S.

Card	Response	Inquiry	Scoring
I	1. ll a bat gliding along	*E:* (Rpts *S*'s resp) *S:* It has the outstrchd wgs & the small ft feet & ths cntr part wld b the body	*Wo* FM^po *A* *P* 1.0
	2. It cld also b a modrn dance of s.s. w a wm in the cntr w her hands in the air & 2 creatures dancg around her	*E:* (Rpts *S*'s resp) *S:* Yes, it ll her hands r raised in sort of supplication & ths creatures on the side reprsnt s.t. symbolic of whatever she's doing *E:* Symbolic *S:* They rem me of those wgd *A*'s in Greek mythology, I can't rem the name.	*W+* M^ao (2) *H, (A), Ab* 4.0
	3. Say, ths lowr prt c.b. a bell	*E:* (Rpts *S*'s resp) *S:* It has a pretty good shape of one w the clapper here	*Ddo* *Fo* Bell
II	4. It cld b a cpl of dogs touchg noses	*E:* (Rpts *S*'s resp) *S:* Its ths drkr areas (points), it ll the upper prts of dogs, thr noses r touchg, ths wld b the ear *E:* Upper parts? *S:* Its just the neck & head, u can't c the rest of the body	*D+* FM^po (2) *Ad* *P* 3.0
	5. The cntr cld b a rocket ship taking off & ths red cld b the exhaust fire	*E:* (Rpts *S*'s resp) *S:* It has a delta shape & the way the color is there u get the impression of firey exhaust & upward motion	*DS+* $m^a.CFo$ *Sc, Fi* 4.5
III	6. A cpl of men bendg ovr to lift s.t. up	*E:* (Rpts *S*'s resp) *S:* U can c the gen outlins of thm, it ll thy'r about to lift s.t. up but I can't tell what it is	*D+* M^ao (2) *H* *P* 3.0

7. The cntr red area c.b. a bowtie

E: (Rpts S's resp)
S: Well, the red attracted my attention to it, made me thk of those big red bowties that clowns wear sometimes

Do FCo Cg

IV

8. It cld b a gorilla sittg on a stump

E: (Rpts S's resp)
S: Yeah, it looks all furry lik a big A, lik a gorilla w the feet here (points), sorta lik he's leaning bkward bec the ft r so much bigger
E: U said it looks furry
S: Yes, all of the color variation makes it ll that

W+ FMp.FT.FDo A,Bt P 4.0

9. A delicate flower

E: (Rpts S's resp)
S: I don't kno the name, my wife grows them, they almost ll velvet w ths contour & coloring effect
E: Coloring effect?
S: Yes, all the different shades in there

Do FYo Bt PER

V

10. It cld b a bat or a bf, I thk more a bf now that I look at it bec I said bat before.

E: (Rpts S's resp)
S: Well it has the wgs & antennae & the split tail lik som bf's hve
E: I'm not sure where u see it
S: All of it I suppose, the W thg

Wo Fo A P 1.0

VI

11. Wld u believe an A skin?

E: (Rpts S's resp)
S: I don't kno what kind of A, prob from the cat family bec of the stuff around the head
E: The stuff around the head?
S: Well actually, the W thg looks furry & spotted, lik from a tiger or s.t. & ths r whiskers

Wo FTo Ad P 2.5

Card	Free Association	Inquiry			Scoring		
	<12. Ths c.b. a submarine crusg along in the drkness	E: (Rpts S's resp) S: It has a pretty good shape of a sub, & the fact its all blk makes me thk of darknss, like at night, the blacknss is like a shadowy effect, lik a nite, u get a good effect of the superstructure, the conning tower part here (points) & the long bow (points)	Do	$m^p.FY+$		Sc	
	13. U kno, tht c.b. a totem too	E: (Rpts S's resp) S: The gen form of it rem me of kind of carving u mite c on a totem, usually a wgs effect like ths has to it	Do	Fo		Ay	
VII	14. A cpl of kids	E: (Rpts S's resp) S: Just the heads, lik they hav feathers in their hair E: I'm not sure why they ll tht S: U can c the gen features, chins, noses, foreheads, that sort of thg	$D+$	Fo	(2)	Hd	P 1.0
	<15. Ths way the side ll a scotty dog	E: (Rpts S's resp) S: It has the blunt nose, thes r the short legs, & here's the tail	Do	Fo		A	
	V16. Ths way it ll a cpl of wm doing the can-can	E: (Rpts S's resp) S: Thy hav big hairdos & r dancg on one leg, sort of throwg their heads backward	$W+$	$M^a o$	(2)	H 3.0	
VIII	17. The W thg cld b an emblem	E: (Rpts S's resp) S: Yes, its like a family crest of s.s., beig symmetrical & quite colorful	Wo	FCo		Art	4.5
	18. Ths thg on the side c.b. A's of s.s.	E: (Rpts S's resp) S: There's 2 of 'em, one on each side E: Can u tell me how u c them S: Well thy c.b. mice or s.t. of the ro-	Do	Fo	(2)	A	P

dent family, c (points) here r the legs
& head & tail

19. U kno, ths top prt c.b. a sand crab, lik it was leapg forward, going away from u

   E: (Rpts S's resp)
   S: The pincers r here (points) & the area where the eyes r & it has the legs extended lik it was leaping out, prob going away fr u the proportions give that effect

   Do $FM^a.FDu$ A

IX 20. Ths ll T. Roosevelt's head

   E: (Rpts S's resp)
   S: Rite here in the pink, its got the mustache & the flat forehead, its just the head, it really ll tht

   Do Fo Hd

21. Tht cntr prt c.b. a vase

   E: (Rpts S's resp)
   S: Its just shaped lik a vase to me

   Do Fo Hh

<22. U kno, ths way it ll a person on a motorcycle or bike

   E: (Rpts S's resp)
   S: Ths W green prt, most of it ll the person, I guess a heavy set man, & he's holdg the handlebars. The bike isn't too clear but the way his head is formed there u can get the impression of his hair flying bk in the breeze

   $D+$ $M^a.m^p+$ $H, bike$ 2.5

X 23. Ths blue thg ll crabs

   E: (Rpts S's resp)
   S: Thy just giv tht impress w all the legs

   Do Fo (2) A P

24. Ths brwn c.b. a deer jumpg

   E: (Rpts S's resp)
   S: The legs r outstrchd & u can c the antlers here (points)

   Do FM^ao A

∨25. Ths way it ll a floral scene, w a huge flower in the cntr & smaller flwrs around it

   E: (Rpts S's resp)
   S: Well, the cntr flwr made me thk of it & I stretched it abit about the other thgs
   E: I'm not sure what u were seeing
   S: Its very colorful, the pink c.b. a daffodil & the blue pom poms but I can't really identify the rest. Its very pretty tho like a floral display

   $W+$ FCo Bt 5.5

175

Table 26.   Scoring Sequence for Protocol L.S.

```
===========================================================================
CARD  NO. LOC.  #    DETERMINANT(S)    (2)  CONTENT(S) POP   Z    SPECIAL SCORES
===========================================================================
  I    1  Wo    1  FMpo                  A              P   1.0
       2  W+    1  Mao               2  H,(A)               4.0
       3  Ddo  24  Fo                   Id

 II    4  D+    1  FMpo              2  Ad             P   3.0
       5  DS+   5  ma.CFo               Sc,Fi              4.5

III    6  D+    1  Mao               2  H              P   3.0
       7  Do    3  FCo                  Cg

 IV    8  W+    1  FMp.FT.FDo           A,Bt               4.0
       9  Do    3  FYo                  Bt                       PER

  V   10  Wo    1  Fo                   A              P   1.0

 VI   11  Wo    1  FTo                  Ad             P   2.5 MOR
      12  Do    4  mp.FY+               Sc
      13  Do    3  Fo                   Ay

VII   14  D+    1  Fo                2  Hd,Id          P   1.0
      15  Do    2  Fo                   A
      16  W+    1  Mao               2  H                  3.0

VIII  17  Wo    1  FCo                  Art                4.5
      18  Do    1  Fo                2  A              P
      19  Do    4  FMa.FDu              A

 IX   20  Do    4  Fo                   Hd
      21  Do    8  Fo                   Hh
      22  D+    1  Ma.mp+               H,Id               2.5

  X   23  Do    1  Fo                2  A              P
      24  Do    7  FMao                 A
      25  W+    1  FCo                  Bt                 5.5
===========================================================================
(C)1976, 1983 BY JOHN E. EXNER, JR.
    ABBREVIATIONS USED ABOVE:
       FOR DQ: "/" = "v/+"; FOR CONTENTS: "Id" = "IDIOGRAPHIC CONTENT"
       SPECIAL SCORES: "INC" = "INCOM", "FAB" = "FABCOM", "CON" = "CONTAM"
                       "CFB" = "CONFAB"
```

and the determinants are not counted again as each of the frequencies for single determinants are entered.

3. Form Quality. There are three distributions to be entered concerning form quality. The first, shown by the heading on the Structural Summary Blank as *FQx* (Form Quality Extended), includes *all* of the responses in the record. It includes spaces to enter the tallies for each of the four types of form quality, plus one for the frequency of responses in which no form quality has been coded. The second is headed as *FQf* (Form Quality-Form) on the Summary. It is for the *FQ* frequencies of those responses in which pure *F* is the only determinant. The third is headed *M Quality,* and is for the distribution of *FQ* for all of the Human Movement responses.

4. Contents. The column headed Contents includes each of the 27 categories. In some instances, *two* entries are required for a single category, one indicating the frequency of responses in which the category represents *the primary content* and the second, separated from the first by a comma, representing the frequency of responses in which the category has been used as *an additional or secondary content*. For example, two responses may have Botany (*Bt*) as the primary content, such as "A tree," and "Some flowers," but a third response may have *Bt* as an additional content, such as, "A man sitting on a tree

Table 27. Structural Summar for Protocol L. S.

```
==================================================================
 R = 25     Zf = 13     ZSum = 39.5     P =  8     (2) =  7    Fr+rF = 0
```

LOCATION FEATURES	DETERMINANTS BLENDS	SINGLE	CONTENTS	S-CONSTELLATION (ADULT)

```
LOCATION        DETERMINANTS              CONTENTS     S-CONSTELLATION
FEATURES          BLENDS      SINGLE                      (ADULT)
                                          II  = 4, 0   NO..FV+VF+V+FD>2
W   = 8         m.CF          M  = 3     (H)  = 0, 0   NO..Col-Shd Bl>0
  (Wv  =   0)   FM.FT.FD      FM = 3     Hd   = 2, 0   YES..Ego<.31,>.44
D   = 16        m.FY          m  = 0     (Hd) = 0, 0   NO..MOR > 3
Dd  = 1         FM.FD         C  = 0     A    = 8, 0   NO..Zd > +- 3.5
S   = 1         M.m           Cn = 0     (A)  = 0, 1   YES..es > EA
                              CF = 0     Ad   = 2, 0   NO..CF+C+Cn > FC
   DQ                         FC = 3     (Ad) = 0, 0   NO..X+ < .70
........(FQ-)                 C' = 0     Ab   = 0, 0   NO..S > 3
                              C'F= 0     Al   = 0, 0   NO..P < 3 or > 8
 +   =  9 ( 0)                FC'= 0     An   = 0, 0   NO..Pure H < 2
v/+  =  0 ( 0)                T  = 0     Art  = 1, 0   NO..R < 17
 o   = 16 ( 0)                TF = 0     Ay   = 1, 0    2.....TOTAL
 v   =  0 ( 0)                FT = 1     Bl   = 0, 0
                              V  = 0     Bt   = 2, 1   SPECIAL SCORINGS
                              VF = 0     Cg   = 1, 0     DV    =  0
                              FV = 0     Cl   = 0, 0     INCOM =  0
                              Y  = 0     Ex   = 0, 0     DR    =  0
                              YF = 0     Fi   = 0, 1     FABCOM=  0
       FORM QUALITY           FY = 1     Fd   = 0, 0     ALOG  =  0
                              rF = 0     Ge   = 0, 0     CONTAM=  0
 FQx       FQf      M Qual.   Fr = 0     Hh   = 1, 0     --- WSUM6 =  0
                              FD = 0     Ls   = 0, 0     AG    =  0
 +  =  2   +  = 0   +  =  1   F  = 9     Na   = 0, 0     CONFAB=  0
 o  = 22   o  = 9   o  =  3              Sc   = 2, 0     CP    =  0
 u  =  1   u  = 0   u  =  0              Sx   = 0, 0     MOR   =  1
 -  =  0   -  = 0   -  =  0              Xy   = 0, 0     PER   =  1
none=  0           none=  0              Idio = 1, 2     PSV   =  0
==================================================================
```

```
             RATIOS, PERCENTAGES, AND DERIVATIONS

ZSum-Zest =  39.5 - 41.5        FC:CF+C  = 3: 1     W:M      = 8: 4
                                   (Pure C =  0)
Zd        = -2.0                                    W:D      = 8:16
                                Afr      = 0.56
.----------------------------.                      Isolate:R = 3:25
:EB =  4: 2.5   EA = 6.5:       3r+(2)/R = 0.28
:                      >D= -2                        Ab+Art   = 1
:eb =  8: 4     es = 12 :       L        = 0.56
'----------------------------'                       An+Xy    = 0
(FM= 5 " C'= 0 T= 2) (Adj D= 0) Blends:R  = 5:25
(m = 3 " V= 0 Y= 2)                                 H(H):Hd(Hd)= 4: 2
                                X+%      = 0.96        (Pure H =  4)
a:p       =  7: 5                 (F+%    = 1.00)   (HHd):(AAd) = 0: 0
                                X-%      = 0.00
Ma:Mp     =  4: 0                                   H+A:Hd+Ad = 12: 4
--------------------------------------------------------------------
          SCZI = 0        DEPI = 1        S-CON = 2
==================================================================
```

stump.'' Thus the entry for the *Bt* category will be *Bt* = 2,1. A second column of blank lines is included on the Summary to enter the idiographic contents.

5. Organizational Activity. Two entries are required at the top of the Summary for organizational activity. The first, *Zf (Z Frequency),* is the number of times a Z response has occurred in the record. The second, *ZSum,* is for the summation of the weighted Z scores that have been assigned.

6. Populars, Pairs, and Reflections. There are three other entries at the top of the Summary. One represents the number of Popular answers, the second (2) is for the total number of pair responses, and the third, $Fr + rF$, is for the number of reflection responses in the protocol.

7. Special Scores. The last set of frequencies to be entered includes those for each of the 12 Special Scores, and a calculation is required to enter a *Weighted Sum* for the first six (*WSUM6*). The values assigned are: Each $DV = 1$, each $DR = 3$, each $INCOM = 2$, each $FABCOM = 4$, each $ALOG = 5$, and each $CONTAM = 7$.

The Structural Summary for the protocol of L. S. is shown as Table 27, illustrating how each of the frequencies has been entered in the upper portion, and how various ratios, percentages, and derivations are entered in the lower section.

RATIOS, PERCENTAGES, AND DERIVATIONS

Once the data have been organized into frequencies, the Structural Summary can be completed by doing the various calculations required for the entries in the lower portion of the Summary. The *S-Constellation, Depi, and Sczi are completed last.*

1. Zsum − Zest. This is a basic calculation required to obtain the *Zd* score. The *ZSum* has already been entered at the top of the Summary and should be reentered here. The *Zest* is a prediction of the ZSum taken from the Wilson and Blake (1950) table of estimates, which is shown here as Table 28. The Zest value taken from Table 28 is the one corresponding to the *Zf* for the protocol. In the L. S. protocol the *Zf* is 13, which yields a Zest from Table 28 of 41.5.

2. Zd. The Zd score is the difference obtained by subtracting ZSum − Zest, with the appropriate sign also recorded. In the L. S. protocol ZSum − Zest = 39.5 − 41.5, yielding a *Zd* of −2.0.

3. EB (Erlebnistypus). This is a relationship between two major variables, human movement (*M*), and the *weighted* sum of the chromatic color responses. It was originally suggested by Rorschach (1921) and is a major element in interpretation. It is entered as Sum *M:* Sum weighted Color. The Sum of weighted Color is obtained by assigning one of the following values to each of the *three* commonly given chromatic color responses: *FC* = 0.5, *CF* = 1.0, and *C* = 1.5. *Color naming* (Cn) responses are not included in the weighted sum. The L. S. protocol contains four *M* responses, three *FC* determinants, and one *CF* answer, yielding an *EB* of 4:2.5.

4. EA (Experience Actual). This is a derivation suggested by Beck (1960) and relates to available resources. It is obtained by adding the two sides of the *EB* together, that is, *Sum M + Sum weighted Color.* In the L. S. protocol it is 4 + 2.5 = 6.5.

5. eb (Experience Base). This is a relationship comparing all nonhuman movement determinants with the shading and achromatic color determinants. It was developed from research suggested by Klopfer (1954). It provides information concerning stimulus demands experienced by the subject. It is entered as *Sum FM + m: Sum C' + T + Y + V.* The data in the right side of the ratio include *all* determinants in which any of the four components exist, such as *FC', TF, FY,* and so on. In the L. S. protocol, as indicated by the entries made just below the *eb*, there are five *FM* and three *m* determinants, plus two *FT* and two *FY* responses. Thus the *eb* is 8:4.

6. es (Experienced Stimulation). This is a derivation obtained from the data in the *eb*. It relates to current stimulus demands. It is obtained by adding the two sides of the *eb* together, that is, *Sum FM + m + C' + T + Y + V.* In the L. S. record it is 8 + 4 = 12.

7. D (Unadjusted D Score). The D score provides important information concerning

Table 28.   Best Weighted ZSum Prediction When _Zf_ Is Known[a]

Zf	Zest	Zf	Zest
1	*	26	88.0
2	2.5	27	91.5
3	6.0	28	95.0
4	10.0	29	98.5
5	13.5	30	102.5
6	17.0	31	105.5
7	20.5	32	109.0
8	24.0	33	112.5
9	27.5	34	116.5
10	31.0	35	120.0
11	34.5	36	123.5
12	38.0	37	127.0
13	41.5	38	130.5
14	45.5	39	134.0
15	49.0	40	137.5
16	52.5	41	141.0
17	56.0	42	144.5
18	56.0	42	144.5
18	59.5	43	148.0
19	63.0	44	152.0
20	66.5	45	155.5
21	70.0	46	159.0
22	73.5	47	162.5
23	77.0	48	166.0
24	81.0	49	169.5
25	84.5	50	173.0

[a]Taken from Beck, S. J., Beck, A., Levitt, E., and Molish, H. _Rorschach's Test I: Basic Processes_ (3rd ed.) New York: Grune & Stratton, 1961.

the relationship between _EA_ and _es_. This relates to stress tolerance and elements of control. It is obtained by first calculating the raw score difference between the two (i.e., _EA_ − _es_) and including the appropriate sign. The raw difference score is then converted into a scaled difference score, based on standard deviations, in which each _SD_ has been rounded to equal 2.5. Thus if the raw score of _EA_ − _es_ falls between +2.5 and −2.5, there is no significant difference between the two values and the _D_ score is 0. If the raw score of _EA_ − _es_ is greater than +2.5, the _D_ score will increase by units of +1 for each 2.5 raw score points. If the raw score of _EA_ − _es_ yields a value of less than −2.5 the _D_ score will increase by units of −1 for each 2.5 points. Table 29 is the Conversion Table for obtaining the _D_ score.

8. _ADJ D_ (Adjusted _D_ Score). Whereas the _D_ score provides information concerning stress tolerance and available resources, it is important to determine whether the score has been influenced by situational elements. This is done by subtracting from the _es_ raw score, elements that are related to situational phenomena. The tactic is simple. All but one _m_ and one _Y_ (including _FY_ and _YF_) are subtracted from the _es_, and the adjusted _es_ is substituted in the _EA_ − _es_ formula. In the L. S. record there are three _m_ and two _Y_ responses. Whereas the basic raw score for _ES_ − _es_ is −5.5, subtracting a value of 3 from _es_ reduces the raw score to −2.5, which yields an _ADJ D_ of 0.

9. _a:p_ (Active:Passive). This relationship concerns flexibility in ideation and attitudes.

Table 29.   *EA − es D* Score Conversion
Table

$EA - es$ Raw Score	D Score
+ 13.0 to + 15.0	+ 5
+ 10.5 to + 12.5	+ 4
+ 8.0 to + 10.0	+ 3
+ 5.5 to + 7.5	+ 2
+ 3.0 to + 5.0	+ 1
− 2.5 to + 2.5	0
− 3.0 to − 5.0	− 1
− 5.5 to − 7.5	− 2
− 8.0 to − 10.0	− 3
− 10.5 to − 12.5	− 4
− 13.0 to − 15.0	− 5

It is entered as the total number of *Active* movement answers on the left and the total number of *Passive* movement responses on the right. *All* movement responses are included. The L. S. record shows an *a:p* of 7:5.

10. $M^a:M^p$ **(Active: Passive for** *M***).** This variable concerns some characteristics of thinking. It includes *only* human movement responses with total Active entered on the left and total Passive entered on the right. The L. S. record has an $M^a:M^p$ of 4:0.

11. *FC:CF + C* **(Form-Color Ratio).** This ratio relates to the modulation of affect. It is entered as shown, with the total number of *FC* determinants on the left and the sum of the *CF + C + Cn* determinants on the right. Each of the chromatic color determinants is weighed equally in this ratio as contrasted with the weighted Sum *C* used in the *EB* and *EA*. The L. S. protocol contains three *FC* responses and one *CF* which occurred in a blend, yielding an *FC:CF + C* of 3:1.

12. *Pure C.* This also relates to the modulation of affect. The entry consists of the sum of *C + Cn*, which is 0 for L. S.

13. *Afr* **(Affective Ratio).** This is a ratio that compares the number of answers to the last three cards with those given to the first seven cards. It relates to interest in emotional stimulation. It is calculated:

$$\frac{\text{Sum } R(\text{VIII + IX + X})}{\text{Sum } R(\text{I + II + III + IV + V + VI + VII})}.$$ L. S. gave nine responses to the last three cards and 16 responses to the first seven cards. Calculating $\frac{9}{16}$ yields an *Afr* of .56.

14. $3r + (2)/R$ **(Egocentricity Index).** This index relates to self-centeredness. It represents the proportion of reflection and pair responses in the total record, with each reflection determinant weighed as being equal to three pair responses. It is calculated:

$$\frac{3 \ (rF + Fr) + \text{Sum} \ (2)}{R}$$ The L. S. protocol contains no reflection responses and seven pair responses leading to an Egocentricity Index of .28.

15. *L* **(Lambda).** This is a ratio that compares the frequency of pure *F* responses with all other answers in the record. It relates to issues of economizing the use of resources. It is calculated: $\frac{\text{Sum F}}{\text{Sum } R - F}$. In the L. S. protocol there are nine pure *F* responses and 16 answers with other determinants, which yields an *L* of .56.

16. Blends:*R* (Complexity Index). This relationship is usually not reduced to a ratio, but instead is entered as indicated with the total number of blends on the left and the total number of responses on the right. It concerns the psychological complexity of the subject. L. S. has five blends in his record.

17. $X + \%$ (Conventional Form). This variable concerns perceptual accuracy for the total record. It is calculated: $\frac{\text{Sum } FQ + \text{ and } o}{R}$. In the L. S. protocol, 24 of the 25 responses have a form quality of $+$ or o, yielding an $X + \%$ of 96.

18. $X - \%$ (Distorted Form). This variable concerns the proportion of perceptual distortion that has occurred in the record. It is calculated: $\frac{\text{Sum } FQ -}{R}$. L. S. has no $-$ responses in his protocol.

19. $F + \%$ (Conventional Pure Form). This variable concerns perceptual accuracy among the Pure F responses, calculated: $\frac{\text{Sum } F + \text{ and } Fo}{\text{Sum } F}$. The L. S. record contains nine Pure F responses, all of which have a form quality of o, yielding an $F + \%$ of 100.

20. $W:M$ (Aspirational Index). This relationship is usually not reduced to a ratio, but instead entered as indicated with the total number of W responses on the left and the total number of M responses on the right. In the L. S. record the $W:M$ is 8:4.

21. $W:D$ (Economy Index). This relationship is not reduced to a ratio. It concerns economy of approach to the blots, and is entered as shown with the number of W's on the left and the total number of D locations on the right. In the L. S. protocol, the $W:D$ is 8:16.

22. *Isolate:R* (Isolation Index). This variable is related to social isolation. It is entered as the sum of the *primary and secondary* contents in the five categories, $Bt + Cl + Ge + Na + Ls:R$. Some examiners may prefer to reduce the Index to a percentage by dividing the sum of the five contents by R. In the L. S. record, the Bt category contains two primary and one secondary entries, and no entries in any of the other four categories; thus the Index is entered as 3:25.

23. *Ab + Art:R* (Intellectualization Index). This index provides information concerning the tendency to approach issues in an intellectualized manner. It is entered as the sum of the *primary and secondary* contents in the two categories, $Ab + Art:R$. It should not be reduced to a ratio or proportion. The L. S. record contains one *Art* content and the entry is 1:25.

24. *An + Xy* (Body Concern). This entry concerns the presence of those contents that may signify some unusual body concern or preoccupation. It is recorded as the sum of *primary and secondary* contents for each of the two categories. The L. S. record has none of either, and thus the entry of 0:25.

25. *H + (H):Hd + (Hd)* (Human Interest). This is a recording of the total number of human contents, with whole human or human-like figures on the left and human detail responses on the right. In the L. S. protocol there are four whole human contents and two human detail contents, and thus the entry is 4:2.

26. *Pure H* (Conceptions of People). This subentry is designed to provide a quick review of how many *Pure H* answers appear in the record. *Only primary contents are entered.* The L. S. protocol shows that all four whole human contents are *Pure H*.

27. *(H) + (Hd):(A) + (Ad)*. This is also a summary entry designed to provide information concerning the frequencies of parenthesized human and animal contents. *Only primary contents are counted* in the entry. It is entered as shown. The L. S. protocol does not contain any parenthesized contents.

28. *H + A:Hd + Ad*. This is also a summary entry, providing information concerning the frequencies of whole human and whole animal responses as contrasted with the frequencies of human and animal detail answers. *Only primary contents are entered.* The Sum of $H + (H) + A + (A)$ is entered on the left, and the Sum of $Hd + (Hd) + Ad + (Ad)$ is entered on the right. The L. S. record contains four H and eight A contents, and two Hd and two Ad responses, yielding an entry of 12:4.

29. S-Con (Suicide Constellation—Adult). The 12 variables that comprise the Suicide Constellation for adults are listed in the upper portion of the Structural Summary. A checkmark should be entered in the space provided next to each variable in the list for which the data meet the criterion shown. The sum of the number of positive variables is then entered at the bottom of the column in the space provided. The sum should also be entered in the lower portion of the Summary in the space at *S-Con*. One variable in the S-Constellation has not been specifically mentioned before. It is the *Color-Shading Blend (Col-Shd Bl).* It is any response that contains *both* a chromatic color determinant and an achromatic color *or* shading determinant, such as *FC.FC', CF.TF,* or *C.Y.* The L. S. protocol contains two of the variables that are positive.

30. DEPI (Depression Index). This entry represents the sum of the variables that are *positive* for criterion for each of five items in a cluster that relates to major affective disturbance. The five variables are:

1. Sum $FV + VF + V > 0$
2. Color-Shading Blend > 0
3. $3r + (2)/R < .30$ for an adult, or lower than 1 *SD* from the appropriate age mean for children.
4. Sum $FC' + C'F + C' > 2$
5. Sum $MOR > 3$

The L. S. record has one positive variable from this cluster.

31. SCZI (Schizophrenia Index). This entry represents the sum of the number of variables that are *positive* for criterion in a cluster of variables related to problems in thinking and perceptual accuracy. The variables are:

1. $X + \% < .70$
2. Sum $FQ - >$ Sum FQu *or* $X - \% > .20$
3. $M - 0$ *or* $WSUM6 > 11$
4. Sum $DV + DR + INCOM + FABCOM + ALOG + CONTAM > 4$
5. Sum $DR + FABCOM + ALOG + CONTAM >$ Sum $DV + INCOM$ *or* $M - > 1$

None of these variables are positive in the L. S. protocol.

SUMMARY

Once the Structural Summary has been completed, the interpretation can proceed. It is not a lengthy process, but the interpretive yield is directly dependent on the element of accuracy—accuracy in coding each response, accuracy in entering each of the frequencies, and accuracy in completing the variety of calculations necessary to generate the ratios, percentages, and derivations. *If* the total data base is accurate, the resulting interpretation of the record is far less likely to be blemished by inappropriate or inaccurate conclusions.

The novice Rorschacher may find the procedures required to collect, collate, and complete the calculations cumbersome and time-consuming, but the time requirements are reduced quickly as experience builds. The experienced Rorschacher will ordinarily devote little more than 30 minutes to code the responses in an average length record, even though some of the responses are quite complex. Completing the Structural Summary should take little more than 10 to 15 minutes for those who are comfortable with the procedures, and the interpretation, although involving many principles and rules, can usually be completed in considerably less than 1 hour.

PART III

Working Tables
and Descriptive Statistics

CHAPTER 11

Working Tables

This chapter contains five tables, each of which is used frequently in coding decisions concerning responses. The first, Table A, includes figures of each of the 10 blots showing the revised location numbering system for the common and unusual detail areas. Approximately 70% of those location numbers are extracted directly from Beck's work, with the remaining 30% generated by the procedures described in Chapter 5. The bulk of Table A is comprised of listings of responses, by card and location area. Each is designated as *o* (ordinary), *u* (unusual), or − (minus), depending on whether it meets the frequency or judgment criteria described in Chapter 7.

Table A could be expanded considerably with the addition of a large number of minus answers, selected either from the more than 162,000 responses against which the frequency criteria were applied, or from psychotic or schizophrenic records not included in that data base. The overwhelming majority of those answers occur with an extremely low frequency, however, typically less than once per 1000 records. Their inclusion would probably detract (more than assist) from the usefulness of the table by making it much longer. Thus a frequency criterion of 10 or more has been used in selecting the minus responses that are included for the *W* and *D* areas, and three or more for inclusion in the listings for *Dd* areas.

As noted in Chapter 7, decisions to code a response as *FQ*+ involves some subjective judgment. They reflect an unusual detailing of form features that may be very creative, or may simply represent a tendency toward greater preciseness. Table B provides a few illustrations of responses in which the form features have been articulated extensively, thus warranting the *FQ* coding of +. All could be delivered with less emphasis on the specific form elements and, if so, would be coded as *o*. In each of these examples the subject has gone well beyond the necessities of form elaboration to enrich the answer. It is important to restrict the coding of + to answers that, with less elaborate form articulation, would be coded *o*. The vast majority of responses in the *FQ* data base that include an unusual elaboration of form elements also meet the criterion to be coded *o*. It is true that unusual answers, especially those that are very creative, may include a precise and/or elaborate articulation of the form features. Even so, the *FQ* coding of *u* is required. Some examiners may wish to note the unusual form elaboration by using the experimental coding of *u*/+ to denote the superior use of the form. If the *u*/+ code is assigned, however, the response should continue to be treated as *u* in all of the Structural calculations.

The *Z* values by card have also been entered in Table A. Table C has been included here to provide the entire array of those values. Table D provides the estimated weighted ZSum (*Zest*) from which the *Zd* score is derived.

The criterion for Popular responses is also included, by card, in Table A. Table E provides the entire listing of Populars.

USING TABLE A

It has been noted in Chapter 7 that the listing of responses in Table A should be fairly inclusive because of the size of the sample involved in its construction. Nonetheless, some objects may not appear in the table with the same specificity that occurs in a response. Obviously, it is appropriate to attempt *conservative* extrapolation from the Table A data when that occurs. For example, some specific animals may appear in a listing for a given location area, but "cougar" may not be in the list. If this is the case, it should not be difficult to extrapolate from the available items to the appropriate coding decision for "cougar." If the scanning of the list reveals an animal similar to a cougar, such as a tiger or cat, it is appropriate to assign the code listed for them for the cougar response. Conversely, if the specific animals listed are not comparable in form to cougar, the coding decision will remain more subjective, using the following principles that are derived from the *FQ* criteria: (1) If a specific item is not listed and extrapolation does not occur easily, it should be coded either as u or $-$ by applying principles 2 or 3; (2) if a specific item does not appear in the list, but can be perceived *quickly and easily,* and involves no substantial contour distortions, it should be coded u; (3) if a specific item does not appear in the list, and can be perceived only with difficulty, or not at all, it should be coded as $-$.

Sometimes it may be necessary to review the listings for more than one location area before making a decision concerning extrapolation. For instance, a response might involve two or three different anatomy items. The list for the total area used might indicate a *FQ* code for anatomy "(Unspecified)." In this case, the listings for the areas used for each of the specific anatomy components should be reviewed to determine if codes are available for any of those items.

Some responses containing multiple objects will also require a review of more than one location listing to insure that the *FQ* codes for each of the items are comparable. If that is not the case, *the lowest FQ value should be assigned to the response.* For example, on Card III, the *D*9 areas are Popular for a human, and assigned an *FQ* code of *o* or $+$ depending on the extent of form elaboration. If *D*1 (which includes both *D*9 areas plus *D*7) is reported as "two people holding a butterfly," the response will be coded as $-$ because the *D*7 area is listed as $-$ for a butterfly.

Caret marks ($< v >$) have been included for some responses to indicate the direction for the apex of the blot. If no caret mark appears next to an item, it signifies that the *FQ* coding listed is appropriate only when the apex of the card is in the upright position.

Table A.   Figures Showing Common (*D*) and Unusual (*Dd*) Location Areas by Card, Listings of Ordinary (*o*), Unusual (*u*) and Minus (−) Responses and Response Classes by Location Areas, Plus Populars and Z Values for Each Card

CARD I

P Is to W.   Bat or Butterfly

Z Values:		W = 1.0	Adjacent = 4.0			Distant = 6.0	Space = 3.5

Location	FQ	Category	Location	FQ	Category
W	−	Abalone		o	Bug (Winged)
	−	Abacus		−	Bullet
	−	Abdomen		o	Butterfly
	u	Abstract drawing		u	v Cabin
	u	Airplane (Top view)		u	Cocoon
	−	Airplane (Front view)		−	Cactus
	−	Albacore		−	Cage
	u	Amoeba		−	Cake
	−	Anchor		u	v Cap (Snow)
	o	Angel		u	Cape
	−	Animal (Not winged)		−	Car
		(*Note:* This class of response includes a		−	Cart
		large group of animals that do not have		u	v Castle
		wings or flappers such as bear, cat,		−	Cat
		dog, lion, etc.)		u	v Catamaran (Front view)
	u	Animal (Winged but unspecified)		−	Cattle (Herd)
	−	Ant		u	Cave
	−	Anteater		o	v Chandelier
	u	v Astrodome		−	Chest
	−	Australia		−	Chevron
	−	Baboon		−	Chinese Art
	o	Badge		u	Cinder
	o	Bat		u	v Circus Tent
	−	Battleship		−	Cistern
	−	Bear		−	Citrus Tree
	−	Beard		−	Clamp
	u	Bee		−	Clitoris
	u	Beetle		u	Cloak
	−	Bell		−	Clock
	u	v Bellows		u	Cloud(s)
	−	Bib		−	Clove
	o	Bird		u	Coal (Piece)
	−	Blanket		−	Coat
	−	Boat		u	Coat of Arms
	−	Body		−	Codfish
	−	Body (Split)		u	Coral
	−	Book		−	Cow
	−	Bookmark		o	Crab
	u	Bone (Skeletal)		−	Crate
	u	Bowl (With handles)		−	Crater
	−	Brain		u	Crawfish
	u	Brain (Cross section)		u	Crow
	−	Breast		o	v Crown
	−	Bridge (Man-made)		o	Dancer (In costume or cape)
	u	Bridge (Natural)		−	Dandelion
	−	Buckle		u	Demon (Caped)
	−	Bug (Unspecified, not winged)		u	Design

Table A (Continued)

Location	FQ	Category	Location	FQ	Category
	—	Dirigible		u	Fog
	u	Dirt		—	Foliage
	o	Disc (Anatomy)		—	Food
	u	v Dome		—	Forest
	—	Door		u	Fossil
	u	Dracula		o	v Fountain
	—	Dragonfly		—	Frog
	—	Dream		u	Fur (Piece)
	—	Dress		u	Fuzz (Piece)
	—	Drill		u	Gnat
	—	Drillpress		—	Garden
	u	Duck		u	v Gazebo
	u	Dust (Speck)		o	Girls (Dancing or standing in a circle)
	o	Eagle			
	—	Egg		u	v Hair (Styled)
	—	Elves (Group)		o	v Hat (Woman's)
	o	Emblem			Head (See face)
	—	Explosion		o	v Headdress
		Face		—	Helicopter

(*Note:* Most faces are *o* or *u*, provided *Dd*34 is used as ears, and *DDS*29 and 30 are used for eyes & mouth and the content is *(Hd), Ad, or (Ad);* however, some faces are inappropriate for the contours. A partial list is given below.)

Location	FQ	Category	Location	FQ	Category
				o	v Helmet
				u	v Hill
				—	Hive (Insect)
				u	v House
				—	Human
	u	Abstract		o	Human (Winged or caped)
	o	Animal (Unspecified)		u	Humans (2 facing midline)
	—	Ant		—	Humans (2 turned away)
	u	Bear		o	Humans (3)
	—	Bird		—	Ice
	o	Cat		u	Inkblot
	u	Cow		—	Insect (Not winged)
	u	Dog		o	Insect (Winged)
	—	Fish		u	Island
	o	Fox		—	Jellyfish
	—	Goat		—	Keel (Boat)
	—	Horse		—	Kidney(s)
	—	Human		—	Lamp
	u	Monster		u	Landscape

(*Note:* This category includes rocks, rocky terrain, and broad landscape expanse such as a mountainside.)

Location	FQ	Category	Location	FQ	Category
	u	Mouse		o	Leaf
	—	Racoon		—	Lungs
	u	Robot		—	Map (Specific)
	—	Seal		u	Map (Unspecified)
	o	Tiger		o	Mask
	—	Turtle			
	o	Wolf			

(*Note:* This category includes a wide variety of animal, Halloween, monster, party, voodoo, etc., masks.)

Location	FQ	Category	Location	FQ	Category
	—	Fan		—	Mat (Door)
	—	Fern		—	Meat
	—	Fiddle		u	Medusa
	—	Fire		—	Melon
	—	Flag		u	Monster
	u	Flea			
	u	Fly			

Table A (Continued)

Location	FQ	Category	Location	FQ	Category
	u	v Mountain		u	v Train (As D4 crossing a trestle)
	u	Mosquito		—	Tree
	ʋ	Moth		—	Tuning Fork
	u	Mud		—	Turtle
	—	Neck		u	Urn
	—	Neckbone		—	Valve
	—	Nest		u	Vase
	—	Net		—	Washing Machine
	—	Nose		u	Wasp
	—	Note (Musical)		—	Wave
	o	Opera Singers (2 or 3)		—	Weathervane
	o	Ornament		—	Weed
	—	Owl		o	Witches (2 or 3)
	—	Pau (Cooking)		o	Woman (Winged or caped)
	—	Parking Meter		—	Wood
	o	Pelvis		o	X-ray (Chest)
	—	Pick (Guitar)		—	X-ray (Heart)
	—	Plant		—	X-ray (Lungs)
	—	Plymouth Emblem		o	X-ray (Pelvis)
	—	Pot		—	X-ray (Stomach)
	—	Printing Press		o	X-ray (Unspecified)
	—	Rib(s)		—	Yacht
	—	Roadmap			
	u	Robot	D1	—	Angels
	u	v Rock		—	Ants
	u	v Rocketship		o	Antennae
	u	Rower (In boat)		u	Antlers
	—	Rudder		—	Apes
	—	Rug		—	Birds
	—	Sailboat		o	Bird Heads
	—	Sawhorse		—	Bones
	o	Sea Animal (With D2 or Dd34 as		—	Bugs
		flappers)		u	Butterflies
	—	Seed		o	Claws
	—	Ship		—	Clip
	—	Shrimp		—	Crabs
	—	Skeleton (Unspecified)		—	Dancers
	o	Skull (Human or animal)		u	Duck Heads
	—	Smile		u	Eagle Heads
	—	Snowflake		—	Elves
	u	Spaceship		o	Feelers
	—	Sperm		o	Fingers
	—	Spider		—	Flags
	—	Sponge		—	Fork
	—	Spring (Metal)		u	Ghosts
	o	Statues (2 or 3)		—	Gun
	—	Steeple		o	Hands
	u	Stone (Carved)		—	Heads (Animal)
	—	Stove		o	Heads (Birds)
	—	Sundial		u	Heads (Monster)
	—	Tank (Army)		u	Heads (Reptile)
	u	v Tent		o	Horns
	o	Totem (Winged)		o	Humans
	—	Tornado		—	Insect

Table A (Continued)

Location	FQ	Category	Location	FQ	Category
	o	Mittens		−	Pig
	u	Monsters		−	Rodent
	−	Penis		−	Sky
	o	Pincers		−	Tree
	u	Puppets		u	< Tree(s) & Foliage
	u	Rock		o	Wing(s)
	−	Rocket		−	Wolf
	−	Roots		u	Woodpecker (Profile)
	u	Sculpture (Abstract)		−	X-ray (Specified or unspecified)
	−	Shrimp			
	−	Tooth	D3	u	Alligator
	u	Thumb		u	Alligator (Reflected)
	−	Tree		o	v Bowling Pin
	−	Waves		−	Brain Stem
				−	Candle
D2	o	Acrobat		−	Candle Holder
	−	Airplane		−	Face
	−	Anatomy		−	Gun
	o	Angel		o	Human (Lower half)
	o	Animal (Specified as long-eared, such as donkey, elephant, some varieties of dogs.)		−	Insect
				o	Legs
				o	Mummy Case
	−	Animal (Specified as short-eared, such as cat, cow, and some varieties of dogs.)		−	Nose
				−	Ornament
				−	Penis
	o	Animal (Cartoon)		u	Robot
	u	Animal (Unspecified)		−	Snake
	−	Bat		u	Spaceship
	−	Beetle		u	Spinal Cord
	o	Bird (With Dd34 as wings)		o	Statue
	u	Bug (With Dd34 as wings)		o	Totem Pole
	−	Bug (Not winged)		−	Tree
	−	Cat		−	Vagina
	−	Chicken		o	Vase
	−	Cow		u	Violin
	u	Cloud			
	o	Dancer	D4	−	Alligator
	o	Demon		−	Anatomy
		Dog (See Animal)		−	Animal (Unspecified)
	−	Dragon		−	Ant
	o	Face (Animal, Bird Cartoon, or Monster with Dd34 as nose)		u	Baboon
				o	Beetle
	−	Face (Animal, Bird, Cartoon or Monster with Dd34 as ear)		−	Bird
				−	Bone Structure
	−	Face, Human		o	Bug (With D1 as antennae or feelers)
	−	Fish			
	o	Head, Bird		−	Bullet
	o	Human		−	Cat
	o	Human-like Figure		o	Cello
	o	Landscape		−	Centipede
	u	Map (Unspecified)		−	Clitoris
	−	Map (Specified)		−	Crab
	o	Pegasus		u	Crown (Ceremonial)

Table A (Continued)

Location	FQ	Category	Location	FQ	Category
	−	Door		u	Pot (Dd34 as handle)
		Face		u	Rock
	−	Fish		−	Skull
	−	Frog		o	Sphinx
	o	Gorilla		o	Statue (Bird)
	o	Human (Whole)		u	Weathervane
	o	Human (Headless)		o	Wings
	o	Humans (2)	Dd21	−	Anatomy
	o	Insect (Unspecified with D1 as antennae or feelers)		o	Bug (D1 as feelers)
	−	Island		u	Crab
	u	Jack-in-the-Box		−	Foliage
	−	Lamp		−	Heart
	−	Lobster		−	Jellyfish
	o	Monster		u	Landscape
	u	Monument		o	Nest
	−	Nose		−	Sea Animal
	−	Plant		u	Shield
	−	Reptile		−	Statue
	u	v Rocket	Dd22	−	Balls
	u	v Rocketship		u	Breasts
	−	Spider		u	Boulders
	o	Statue		−	Buttocks
	−	Turtle		−	Heads (Animal)
	u	v Tree		u	Heads (Human)
	−	Wasp		o	Hills
	o	Woman		u	Labia
	u	Vase		o	Mountains
	u	Viola		−	Trees
D7	−	Animal (Not winged)	Dd23	−	Airplanes
	o	Animal (Winged)		u	Birds
	u	Arrowhead		−	Dots
	o	Bird		−	Flies
	−	Bone		u	Insects
	u	Cliff		o	Islands
	u	Cloud		−	Notes (Musical)
	o	Crow		−	Symbols
	u	Duck	Dd24	o	Bell
	o	Eagle		−	Bug
	u	Face, Animal (With Dd34 as nose)		o	Cello
	u	Face, Cartoon (With Dd34 as nose)		u	Emblem
	−	Face, Human		−	Head
	−	Hat		u	Helmet
	−	Insect (Not winged)		−	Human (Whole)
	u	Insect (Winged)		u	Human figure (Lower half)
	o	Landscape		u	Lamp
	−	Map (Specific)		u	Lantern
	u	Map (Unspecified)		u	Monster
	u	Nest		−	Plant
	−	Plant			

Table A (Continued)

Location	FQ	Category	Location	FQ	Category
	u	Skirt		—	Lungs
	—	X-ray		u	Snow
Dd25	—	Animal		—	Trees
	—	Animal Rump	Dd31	u	Feet
	o	Face, Human-Abstract		—	Hammer
	u	Face, Human		u	v Head (Rabbit)
	—	Trees		—	Head (Unspecified)
				—	Nose
DdS26	o	Clouds		—	Root
	o	Eyes		—	Skull
	o	Ghosts		u	Tooth
	o	Mask Details			
	u	Snow	DdS32	u	Bay
	—	Trees		—	Bird
				u	Canyon
Dd27	u	Boat (With midline)		—	Mask
	o	Buckle		—	Vase
	u	Elevator (With midline)			
	—	Face	Dd33	—	Ball
	—	Head		—	Bell
	—	Heart		—	Bone
	u	Shield		—	Head (Animal)
	u	Spaceship		u	v Head (Human)
	—	Top		—	Lamp
	—	Ulcer		u	v Mushroom
				u	Tail
Dd28	u	Arrowhead		o	v Tree
	—	Bird (Whole)			
	u	Hat	Dd34	u	Arrowhead
	—	Head (Animal)		u	Blade (Knife)
	o	Head (Bird)		o	Cliff
	—	Head (Human)		—	Face
	—	Pole		o	Fin
	—	Shoe		u	< Ghost
	u	Tree		—	Head
				—	Insect
DdS29	o	Eyes (Abstract)		o	< Mountain
	—	Eyes (Human)		u	Nose (Cartoon)
	u	Flying Saucers		u	Rock
	o	Ghosts		u	Saw
	o	Holes		u	< Seal
	u	Mountains		u	< Shrub
	u	Pyramids		u	< Tower
	u	Snow		o	< Tree (Fir)
	u	Spaceships		u	< Tree (Unspecified)
	u	Triangles		u	< Umbrella (Closed)
	u	Tents			
	u	Wings	Dd35	u	< Dog
				—	Face (Animal)
DdS30	o	Eyes		—	Face (Bird)
	o	Ghosts		u	v Face (Human)
	u	Human (In costume)			

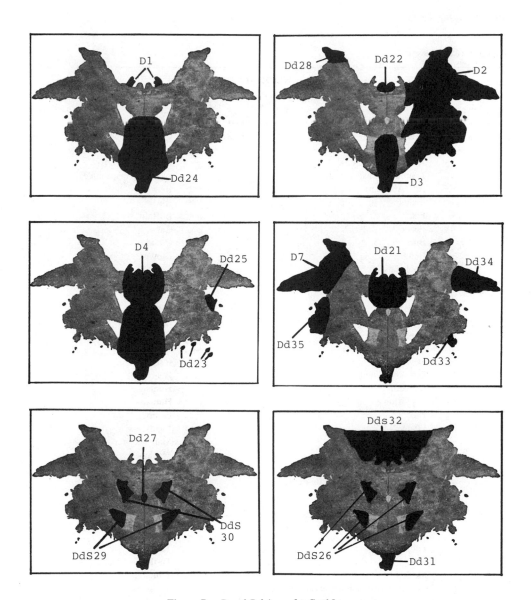

Figure 7. *D* and *Dd* Areas for Card I.

Table A (Continued)

CARD II

P Is to *D*1: Bear, Dog, Elephant or Lamb, Head or Whole Animal

Z Values: W = 4.5   Adjacent = 3.0   Distant = 5.5   Space = 4.5

Location	FQ	Category	Location	FQ	Category
W	−	Anatomy (Specific)	D1	−	Amoeba
	u	Anatomy (Unspecified)		u	Animal (Unspecified)
	u	Art (Abstract)		o	Bear
	−	Badge		−	Bird
	−	Bat		u	< Buffalo
	o	Bears		o	< Cat
	−	Bird		u	Cloud
	−	Body		−	Clown
	u	Bookends		u	v Coat
	−	Bug		o	Cow
	u	v Bug (Winged)		u	v Demon
	o	v Butterfly		o	Dog
	u	Cave		o	Elephant
	o	Dancers		−	Fish
	u	Design (Abstract)		u	v Gorilla
	o	Devils		−	Hat
	−	Disc (Anatomy)		−	Heart
	u	Emblem		−	Human
	o	v Explosion		o	v Human
	−	Face		o	Lamb
	o	Fire & Smoke		u	Landscape
	−	Fly		−	Map
	u	Gorillas		−	Machine
	−	Heart		o	v Mountain(s)
	o	Humans or Human-like figures		−	Monument
	−	Insect		o	v Monster
	u	Insect (Winged)		o	< Rabbit
	−	Intestines		u	Rock
	−	Kidneys		−	Sponge
	−	Lungs		−	Tree
	−	Map		−	Turtle
	u	Mask		−	Wing
		(*Note:* This category includes a variety of animal, cartoon, Halloween, party, etc., masks)	D2	u	Angel
	−	Meat		o	Bird
	−	Mouth		o	Blood
	o	Ornament		−	Boot
	u	v Pelvis		−	Bug (Not winged)
	−	Plant		u	Bug (Winged)
	−	Rectum		o	Butterfly (Side view)
	−	Spaceship		o	Cap
	o	Statues		−	Candle
	−	Stomach		−	Cell (Blood)
	−	Throat		u	Chicken
	u	v Torches (With smoke)		o	Creature (Cartoon)
	−	Vagina		u	Devil
	u	Volcano		u	Finger Painting
	−	X-ray		−	Finger Print
				u	Footprint

Table A (Continued)

Location	FQ	Category	Location	FQ	Category
	−	Hand		−	Head (Bird)
	o	Hat		−	Head (Human)
	−	Head (Animal)		u	v Headset (Radio)
	u	Head (Bird)		−	Heart
	−	Head (Human)		u	Insect
	u	Head (Human-like)		u	Jellyfish
	u	v Holster		−	Kidney
	u	v Italy (Map)		−	Lobster
	−	Kidney		−	Lung
	−	Lantern		u	Manta Ray
	u	Lava		−	Mask
	−	Leg		u	Monster
	o	Mask (Animal, bird, cartoon, human-like)		u	Meat
				u	Menstruation
	−	Mitten		u	Moth
	−	Penis		−	Octopus
	o	Puppet (Hand)		o	Paint
	u	Rabbit		u	Plant
	−	Rat		u	Snail
	o	Seal		u	Spaceship
	−	Shoe		o	v Sun
	u	Snail		o	v Torch
	u	v Sock		o	Vagina
	u	v South America (Map)		−	Uterus
	−	Tongue			
	−	Tooth	D4	o	Arrow
	o	Torch		o	Arrowhead
	−	Vase		−	Bat (Baseball)
	−	Worm		−	Bell
				−	Bottle
D3	u	Anemone (Sea)		o	Bullet
	−	Ant		u	Candle
	−	Anus		o	Capsule (Space)
	−	Beetle		u	Castle
	o	Blood		−	Crucifix
	−	Bug (Not winged)		−	Crucifixion
	o	Bug (Winged)		u	Dome
	o	Butterfly		u	v Drill
	−	Clamp		−	Face
	u	Coral		u	Hands (Praying)
	o	Crab		u	Hat
	−	Crawfish		−	Head
	u	Embryo		u	Helmet
	o	v Explosion		−	Knife
	−	Face (Animal)		o	Missile
	u	Face (Devil or monster)		u	Monument
	−	Face (Human)		−	Mountain
	u	Fan		−	Nose
	o	Fire		u	Penpoint
	−	Fish		u	Penis
	u	Flower		u	Pliers
	−	Fly		u	Pyramid
	−	Head (Animal)		o	Rocket

Table A (Continued)

Location	FQ	Category	Location	FQ	Category
	—	Snake		—	Animal
	o	Spaceship		u	Animals (2 unspecified)
	u	Spear (Tip)		o	Animals (2, each meeting
	o	Steeple			criterion for o as D1)
	—	Tail		—	Bat
	o	Temple		—	Bird
	o	Tower		u	Butterfly
	u	Tree (Fir)		u	Cloud(s)
	—	Tree (Unspecified)		—	Insect (Not winged)
	—	Vase		u	Insect (Winged)
				u	Island
DS5	o	Airplane		—	Lungs
	u	Archway		—	Map (Specific)
	u	Basket		u	Map (Unspecified)
	—	Bat		u	Moth
	u	Bell		o	v Pelvis
	—	Bird		—	Rug
	—	Boat		u	Spinal cord (Slice, may include
	u	Bowl			DS5)
	—	Butterfly		o	v X-ray (Pelvic)
	o	Castle (May include D4)		—	X-ray (Specific other than pelvic)
	o	Cave		u	X-ray (Nonspecific)
	o	Chandelier			
	o	Church	Dd21	—	Beak
	u	Crown		—	Bird
	u	Dome		—	Ear
	—	Dress		—	Frog
	u	Fountain		o	Head (Animal)
	u	Goblet		—	Head (Bird)
	u	Hat (Woman's)		—	Head (Fish)
	—	Heart		—	Head (Human)
	u	Helmet		o	Mountain
	o	Hole		—	Nest
	u	Island		—	Seal
	u	Kite		—	Shrub
	o	Lake		—	X-ray
	o	Lamp			
	o	Light	Dd22	o	v Bush
	—	Mask		—	Chicken
	o	Missile		—	Head (Animal)
	—	Mouth		u	v Head (Human)
	o	Ornament		u	v Rabbit
	u	Pendant		u	v Rock
	o	Rocket		—	Tree
	o	Spaceship			
	u	Steeple	Dd23	u	Bush
	u	Sting Ray		—	Frog
	—	Stomach		—	Head
	o	Top		u	v Mountain
	o	Tunnel		u	v Rock
	u	Vagina		—	Tree
	o	Vase			
			Dd24	u	Anus
D6	—	Anatomy		u	Bowling Pin

Table A (Continued)

Location	FQ		Category	Location	FQ		Category
	u		Bullet		u		Claw
	u		Candle		−		Nail
	−		Doorway		−		Tail
	−		Face		−		Wall
	u		Ghost				
	−		Human	Dd28	u		Bloodstain
	u		Human-like Figure		−		Head
	u		Penis		−		Turtle
	u		Rocket		u		Varnish
	−		Tooth		u		Wood (Stained)
	u		Totem		−		X-ray
	o		Vagina				
	u	v	Waterfall	DdS29	u		Cave
					u		Cup
Dd25	o		Antennae		u		Dome
	o		Antlers		u	v	Goblet
	u		Feelers		u		Pottery
	o		Horns		u		Tunnel
	u		Icicles				
	u		Needle	DdS30	−		Clam
	u		Spike		−		Eyes
	u		Spear		−		Head
	u		Spike		u		Inlet
	u		Stick		−		Oyster
	−		Tail				
	−		Tusk	Dd31	u		Beak
					−		Claw
Dd26	o		Blood		u	v	Ears (Animal)
	u		Caterpillar		−		Head (Animal)
	o		Fire		u		Head (Human)
	u		Sunset		u		Head (Human-like)
	−		Walrus		u	<	Mountains
	u		Worm		u		Stone Sculpture
					−		Trees
Dd27	u		Bridge (Draw)				

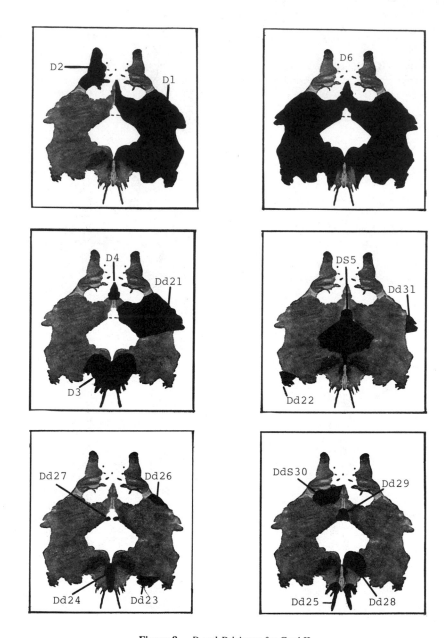

Figure 8. *D* and *Dd* Areas for Card II.

Table A (Continued)

CARD III

P Is to D1 or D9: Human Figure or Representation Thereof

| Z Values: | W = 5.5 | Adjacent = 3.0 | Distant = 4.0 | Space = 4.5 |

Location	FQ	Category	Location	FQ	Category
W		(*Note:* Most W responses that involve a single object will be coded – as the blot is broken. In a few instances, response frequencies argue in favor of a *u* coding for answers that conform to the contours and are not largely dependent on arbitrarily created contours. W responses coded *o* will usually involve multiple objects.)		*u*	v Monster
				–	Noose
				–	Rib Cage
				–	Skeleton
				–	Spider
				u	v Vase (With handles and design)
				–	X-ray
	–	Anatomy	D1	–	Animal
	–	Animal		*u*	Animals (2 Unspecified)
	o	Animals (As D1 in a scene with other objects, such as in a circus. All other objects included must be codable as *o* if reported separately.)		–	Ant
				u	v Arch
				–	Bird
				o	Birds (2)
				o	Bone Structure
	–	Ant		–	Bug
	u	Art (Abstract)		*u*	v Cave Entrance
	u	Badge		–	Dog
	o	Birds (As D1 in a scene with other objects such as in a cage. All other objects included must be codable as *o* if reported separately.)		*o*	Dogs (2 with D7 as separate object)
				o	Dolls (2)
				–	Human
				o	Humans (2 with D7 as separate object)
	u	Bowl (With handles and design)		*u*	v Humans (With D5 as arms)
	–	Bug		–	Insect
	–	Butterfly		*u*	Keel (Boat with D5 as supports)
	–	Cat		*o*	v Landscape
	u	Chandelier		–	Lobster
	–	Crab		–	Map (Specific)
	u	Emblem		*u*	Map (Unspecified)
	–	Face		*o*	Monkeys (With D7 as separate object)
	–	Flower			
	–	Fly		*u*	Monster
	–	Gorilla		*o*	Ostrich (2)
	–	Human		*o*	Pelvic Structure
	o	Humans or Human-like Figures (As D1 in a scene with other objects each of which would be coded as *o* if reported separately, such as in ceremonies, parties, playgrounds, etc.)		*o*	Sheep (2, or Lambs)
				–	Skeleton
				–	Skull
				–	Spider
				–	Trees
				u	Vase
	–	Insect		*o*	X-ray (Pelvis)
	u	v Islands		*u*	X-ray (Unspecified)
	–	Jack-O-Lantern	D2	–	Anchor
	–	Jellyfish		*u*	Amoeba
	u	v Landscape		*o*	Animal (Long-Tailed)
	–	Map (Specific)		–	Animal (Not long-tailed)
	u	Map (Unspecified)			

Table A (Continued)

Location	FQ	Category	Location	FQ	Category
	−	Artery		o	Pot (Hanging)
	o	Bird		o v	Puppet
	o	Blood		−	Rabbit
	−	Bone		u	Robot
	−	Brain		u	Sea Horse
	−	Bug		−	Snail
	−	Cocoon		−	Snake
	u	Chandelier		u	Statue (Abstract)
	o	Chicken (Hanging)		u	Statue (Animal)
	u	Coral		o	Statue (Human)
	−	Club		−	Stick
	o	Decoration (Unspecified)		u	Stomach
	o	Devil		o	Symbol (Abstract)
	−	Dog		u v	Tree
	−	Dragon		o	Umbilical cord (With placenta)
	−	Duck		−	Vase
	o	Embryo			
	u	Esophagus	D3	−	Antennae
	o	Fire		−	Antlers
	−	Fish		−	Bird
	−	Flesh		u	Bellows
	u v	Flower		−	Bat
	−	Fly		−	Bird
	u	Germ		−	Brain
	u	Guitar		o	Blood
	o	Hat (Clown or costume)		u	Bone
	−	Head (Animal)		o	Bow
	−	Head (Bird)		o	Bowtie
	−	Head (Human)		u	Brassiere
	u	Head (Human-like)		−	Breasts
	−	Heart		−	Breastbone
	u	Hook		o	Butterfly
	o	Human (This class of response includes many variations of the human figure such as acrobat, child, gymnast, etc.)		−	Crab
				u	Dam (Between hills)
				o	Decoration (Unspecified)
				−	Dragonfly
				u	Dumbbell
	o	Human-like Figure (This class of response includes many variations of cartoon, mythological, or science fiction figures such as devil, dwarf, elf, imp, etc.)		u	Emblem (Abstract)
				u	Eye Shades
				−	Eye Glasses
				u	Exercise Apparatus
				o	Fire
				−	Fly
	−	Insect		u	Fossil
	−	Intestine		−	Girdle
	u	Island		u	Hang Glider
	u	Kidney		−	Heart
	−	Lung		−	Helmet
	o	Meat (Hung)		−	Human(s)
	o	Monkey		−	Insect (Not winged)
	o	Neuron		u	Insect (Winged)
	u	Note (Musical)		u	Island
	o v	Parrot		−	Intestine
	u v	Pipe		u	Kidney
	u v	Plant		−	Lips

Table A (Continued)

Location	FQ	Category	Location	FQ	Category
	o	Lungs		—	Buckle
	—	Mask		—	Butterfly
	u	Mosquito		—	Cactus
	o	Moth		o	Cauldron
	—	Mouth		u	Coal (Piece)
	—	Nose		o	Crab
	—	Oranges		u	Drum
	o	Pelvic Structure		—	Eye Glasses
	o	Ribbon		—	Face
	—	Seed		o	Fireplace
	—	Skeleton		u	Gate
	u	Spinal Cord (Cross section)		—	Head
	u	Sun Glasses		—	Heart
	—	Testicles		u	Island
	u	Wasp		—	Kidney
	u	Wing		—	Lungs
	—	Wishbone		u v	Mushrooms
				o	Nest
D5	u	Arm		o	Pelvis
	u	Arrow		o	Rock(s)
	—	Bird		u	Shadows
	u	Bomb		u	Smoke
	—	Bone		—	Stomach
	—	Bug		o v	Trees
	u	Bullet		—	Vagina
	u	Claw		u	Vertebrae
	u	Club		o	X-ray (Pelvis)
	o	Fish		—	X-ray (Specific other than pelvis)
	—	Gun		u	X-ray (Unspecified)
	—	Hand			
	u	Island	D8	o	Bones
	o	Leg (Animal)		—	Brain Stem
	o	Leg (Bird)		—	Chest
	o	Leg (Human)		u	Crab
	u	Limb (Tree)		—	Dragon
	u	Log		u	Hour Glass
	—	Map		u	Lamp
	u	Missile		u	Lake (In mountains)
	u	Peninsula		u	Monster
	u	Rocket		—	Pumpkin
	o	Shark		o	Ribs
	—	Snake		u	Skeletal (Specific other than ribs)
	u	Spaceship		o	Skeletal (Unspecified)
	u	Spear		u	Stone
	u	Stick		u v	Torch
	u	Torpedo		—	Vagina
	—	Tree		u v	Vase
	—	Vine		u v	Wine Glass
				—	X-ray
D7	—	Anatomy			
	—	Animal	D9	—	Anatomy
	o	Basket		u	Animal (Unspecified)
	—	Beetle		—	Ant
	o	Bones		o	Bird

Table A (Continued)

Location	FQ	Category	Location	FQ	Category
	−	Bug		u	Cloud
	o	Cartoon Figure		u	Ghost
	u	Chicken		−	Head
	u	Cloud		u	Water
	u	Demon			
	o	Dog	DdS24	u	Bowl
	o	Doll		−	Face
	u	Duck		−	Head
	−	Foliage		u	Lake
	u	Ghost		u	v Lamp
	o	Human		u	v Mushroom
	−	Insect		u	Snow
	u	Jack-In-The-Box		u	v Statue
	−	King Kong		u	Vase
	o	Lamb			
	u	v Landscape	Dd25	u	Esophagus
	o	Monkey		−	Face
	u	Monster		−	Head
	u	v Mountain		u	Root
	u	Parrot		−	Spear
	o	Puppet		u	Stick
	−	Rabbit		u	String
	−	Root		u	Tail
	o	Sheep		−	Tool
	u	Skeleton		u	Tube
	−	Spider		u	Umbilical cord
	u	Statue		u	Worm
	−	Tree			
	o	Witch	Dd26	u	Fin
	−	X-ray		−	Head
				−	Leg
Dd21	u	Bird		o	Penis
	−	Bomb		u	Stump
	u	Cliff			
	−	Dog	Dd27	o	Breast
	−	Head (Animal)		−	Building
	o	Head (Bird)		o	Head (Animal)
	o	Head (Fish)		o	Head (Bird)
	−	Head (Human)		u	Head (Fish)
	u	Landscape		−	Head (Human)
	o	v Mountain		u	< Mountain
	u	Pensula		u	Nose
	u	v Tree		−	Skull
Dd22	−	Animal	Dd28	u	Corset
	o	Bird		u	Dam
	−	Bone		u	Doors (Swinging)
	u	Cloud		−	Face
	u	Human (Upper half)		−	Head
	u	v Landscape		u	Net
	−	Rodent		−	Tooth
	u	Statue			
			Dd29	−	Airplane
DdS23	u	Bird		−	Arrow

Table A (Continued)

Location	FQ	Category	Location	FQ	Category
	u	Arrowhead		−	Ball
	u	Bird		u	Clam
	u	Breast		u	Coconut
	u	Butterfly		−	Egg
	u	Cartoon Character		−	Eye
	−	Fetus		−	Fish
	−	Head		−	Head (Animal)
	−	Heart		o	Head (Bird)
	−	Human		o	Head (Human)
	−	Insect		u	Mask
	−	Tent		u	Oyster
	u	< Valentine		u	Rock
				u	Statue
Dd30	u	Arm			
	−	Club	Dd33	u	Claw
	−	Foot		u	Finger
	−	Hand		u	Foot
	−	Head		−	Fork
	u	Icicle		u	Hand
	−	Missile		−	Head (Animal)
	u	Log		u	Head (Bird)
				−	Head (Human)
Dd31	−	Anatomy		o	Hoof
	u	Animal		−	Penpoint
	o	Ball		o	Shoe
	u	Balloon		−	Spear
	o	Basket			
	u	Bones	Dd34	−	Animal
	u	Cloud		o	Bird
	−	Earmuffs		−	Fish
	−	Embryo		o	Human (Upper part)
	−	Eyes		−	Insect
	−	Face		o	v Landscape
	u	Gourd		o	v Mountains
	−	Hat		−	Skeletal
	−	Head (Animal)		−	X-ray
	o	v Head (Human)			
	o	v Head (Skeletal)	Dd35	u	Arch
	u	Kettledrums		o	Birds (2)
	−	Lamp		u	Bones
	−	Lungs		u	Bowl
	u	Mittens		−	Crab
	−	Mountains		−	Frog
	o	Pot		u	Islands
	o	Skeletal		o	v Landscape
	o	v Skull		u	Mountains (Aerial view)
	o	Stones		o	Pelvis
	o	v Trees		−	Trees
	−	Turtle		o	X-ray (Pelvis)
	−	Womb		−	X-ray (Specific other than pelvis)
Dd32	−	Animal		u	X-ray (Unspecified)

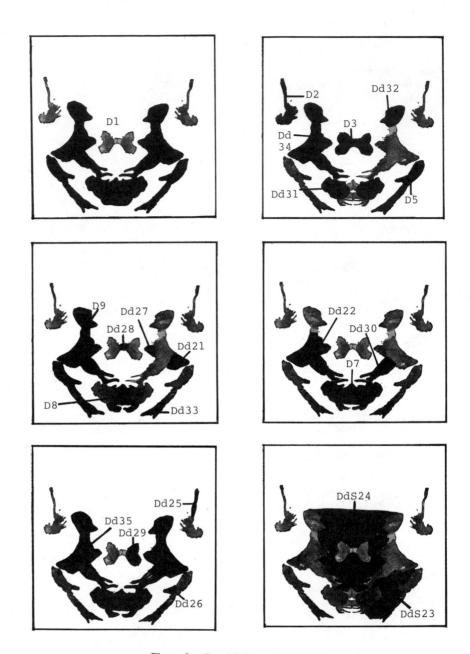

Figure 9. *D* and *Dd* Areas for Card III.

Table A (Continued)

CARD IV

P Is to W or D7: Human or Human-Like Figure

Z Values:	W = 2.0	Adjacent = 4.0	Distant = 3.5	Space = 5.0

Location	FQ	Category	Location	FQ	Category
	−	Amoeba		u	Kite
	o	v Anchor		o	< Landscape (Reflected)
	o	Animal		o	Leaf
	o	v Badge		−	Lettuce
	o	v Bat		−	Lobster
	u	Bell		−	Lung(s)
	u	v Bird		−	Map (Specific)
	o	Boots (On pole)		o	Map (Topographic, nonspecific)
	−	Brain		u	Map (Unspecified)
	−	Bug		u	Mask
	−	Bull		o	Monster
	o	Bush(es)		u	v Moth
	o	Butterfly		u	Mountain
	−	Candle		−	Mud
	u	Carcass (Animal)		o	Pelt
	u	v Chandelier		o	v Pelvis
	u	Cloud(s)		o	Plant
	o	Coat (On pole)		u	Robe
	−	Coral		u	Rock
	−	Crab		−	Root
	o	v Crest		o	Rug
	u	Design (Abstract)		o	Sea Animal
	u	v Eagle		u	Sea Weed
	o	v Emblem		o	Skin (Animal)
	−	Embryo		u	Smoke
	−	Face		−	Snail
	u	Flower		−	Snowflake
	u	Fountain		u	Sponge
	u	Fossil		u	Squid
	u	Frog		u	Squirrel (Flying)
	o	Giant		u	Statue
	o	Gorilla		o	v Sting Ray
	u	Head (Animal)		u	Temple
	−	Head (Bird)		o	Tree
	−	Head (Human)		u	v Urn
	−	Helmet		o	X-ray (Pelvis)
	o	Hide (Animal)		−	X-ray (Specific other than pelvis)
	o	Hunchback		u	X-ray (Unspecified)
	o	Human	D1	−	Alligator
	(Note: This class of response may		−	Animal
	involve W as the human figure or D7 as		u	Bug
	the human figure with D1 as a second		o	Bush(es)
	object, such as bike, seat, stump, etc.		o	v Cactus
	The card *must* be upright.)		u	v Candle
	u	Ice Cream Cone		u	v Castle
	−	Insect		u	Caterpillar
	u	Island (Unspecified)		−	Crab
	−	Jello		−	Crawfish
	−	Jellyfish			

Table A (Continued)

Location	FQ		Category	Location	FQ		Category
	u	v	Crown		–		Map (Specific other than Africa
	–		Fish				or South America)
	o	v	Head (Animal, horned or horse)		u		Map (Unspecified)
	–	v	Head (Animal, specific not		u		Peninsula
			horned or horse)		o	<	Pig
	u	v	Head (Animal, not specific)		u		Rock
	u	v	Head (Bird)		o	<	Seal
	–	v	Head (Human)		o		Shoe
	o	v	Head (Insect)		u		Sphinx
	u	v	Head (Monster)		u		Statue
	–	v	Head (Reptile other than turtle)		u	<	Totem
	u	v	Head (Turtle)		u		Wing
	–		Human		–		X-ray
	u		Hydrant				
	o		Insect	D3	–		Anus
	–		Intestines		u		Brain
	–		Lamp		o		Bud (Flower)
	u	v	Lighthouse		u		Bush
	u		Medulla		u		Butterfly
	–		Penis		u		Cabbage
	–		Shell		u		Clam
	o		Shrub		u		Crown
	u		Skull		–		Face
	u		Snail		u		Fan
	–		Snake		o		Flower
	o		Spinal Cord		o		Head (Animal, flat-faced such as
	o		Stool				cat, monkey, owl, etc.)
	o		Stump		–		Head (Animal, specific but not
	u		Tail				flat-faced)
	o		Tree Trunk		u		Head (Animal, unspecified)
	o		Vertebrae		u		Head (Bird)
	–		X-ray		–		Head (Human)
					u		Head (Monster or science fiction)
D2	o	<	Bear		–		Insect (Not winged)
	–		Boat		u		Insect (Winged)
	–		Bone		u		Mushroom
	u		Cliff		u		Leaf
	u		Cloud		o		Sea Shell
	–		Cow		u		Shrub
	o	v	Dog		u		Tam o' Shanter
	–		Emblem		u		Vagina
	o		Foot				
	o	<	Head (Animal, flat or stubby	D4	–		Animal
			nose such as bear, dog, pig, seal,		u		Arm
			etc.)		–		Arrow
	u	<	Head (Animal, not specific)		o		Bird (Long-necked)
	–		Head (Bird)		o		Branch (Tree)
	u	v	Head (Camel)		u		Cap (Stocking)
	o	<	Head (Human)		o		Claw
	–		Head (Insect)		o		Diver (Back flip)
	–		Head (Reptile)		–		Ear
	u		Landscape		u		Eel
	u		Map (Africa or South America)		–		Fish

Table A (Continued)

Location	FQ	Category	Location	FQ	Category
	o	Handle		—	Sea Animal
	—	Head (Animal)		*u*	Shoe
	o	Head (Bird)		*u*	Smoke
	u	Horn (Animal)		*u*	Wing
	o	Human (Bending or diving)			
	o	Icicle	D7	*u*	v Anchor
	—	Leg		*o*	Animal
	o	Lizard		*u*	v Badge
	u	Nail (Bent)		*o*	v Bat
	u	Peninsula		*u*	Bird
	—	Penis		—	Bug
	u	Root		—	Crab
	o	Snake		—	Face
	u	Tail		*u*	Fossil
	u	Trunk (Elephant)		*o*	Giant
	o	Vine (Hanging)		*o*	Gorilla
				—	Head
D5	*o*	Bone (Skeletal)		*u*	Helmet
	o	Canyon		*o*	Hide (Animal)
	o	Column		*o*	Hunchback
	—	Crayfish		*o*	Human
	u	Drill		*u*	Island
	—	Fish		*o*	Mask
	u	v Fountain		*o*	Monster
	o	Gorge		*u*	Mountain
	—	Insect		*o*	v Pelvis
	o	Pole		*u*	Statue
	o	River			
	u	Rocket	Dd21	—	Apple
	o	Spinal cord		*u*	Crown
	—	Statue		*o*	Face (Human, profile)
	u	Totem		—	Head (Animal)
	—	Tree		*o*	Head (Human)
	o	Vertebrae		*u*	Hut
	o	Waterway		*u*	Landscape
	u	X-ray (Specific other than spine)		*u*	Temple
	o	X-ray (Spine)		*u*	Tent
	u	X-ray (Unspecified)		—	Wart
D6	*o*	Animal (As D2 on hill or rock)	Dd22	—	Eye
	o	Boot		—	Face
	—	Face		—	Head
	o	Foot		—	Moon
	u	v Head (Camel)		—	Shrub
	u	v Head (Cartoon animal)			
	o	< Human (As D2 sitting in chair or on a hill)	Dd23	*u*	Beak
				—	Head (Animal)
	u	Italy		*o*	Head (Bird)
	o	Leg		—	Head (Human)
	o	Map (Italy)		*u*	Head (Reptile)
	—	Map (Specific other than Italy)			
	u	Map (Unspecified)	DdS24	*u*	Clouds
	u	Rudder		*u*	Ghosts

Table A (Continued)

Location	FQ		Category	Location	FQ		Category
	−		Head(s)		u		Flower
	u		Snow		−		Heart
					−		Human
Dd25	−		Face		u		Nail
	−		Human(s)		o	v	Rocket
	−		Human-like Figure(s)		u		Tack
	u		Landscape (Aerial view)		u		Tee (Golf)
					−		Tongue
Dd26	−		Clitoris		u		Tooth
	u		Feet		u		Waterfall
	u		Fingers				
	u	v	Ghosts	Dd31	−		Animal
	−		Heads (Animal)		−		Bird
	u		Heads (Bird)		u		Ghost
	−		Heads (Human)		−		Head (Animal)
	−		Human		−		Head (Bird)
	u	v	Human-like Figures		−		Head (Human)
	u		Legs		u	v	Head (Human-like)
	u		Snakes		−		Human
	−		Teeth		−		Rock
	−		Trees		−		Root
	u		Worms		u	v	Seal
					u	v	Statue
Dd27	u		Bridge		−		Tree
	u		Cliff		u	v	Witch
	−		Foot				
	−		Tail	Dd32	−		Fist
					u	v	Head (Animal with flat or stubby nose)
Dd28	o		Antennae				
	−		Claws		u	v	Head (Human)
	−		Feet		u		Rock
	u		Horns		u		Toe
	−		Legs				
	−		Roots	Dd33	o		Bone (Skeletal)
					o		Canyon
DdS29	u		Clouds		u		Drill
	u		Ghosts		o		Gorge
	u		Lakes		u		Pole
	u		Monsters		o		River
					o		Spine
Dd30	u		Beak		o		Waterway
	−		Face				

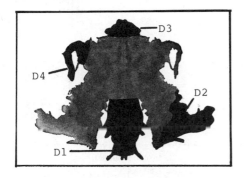
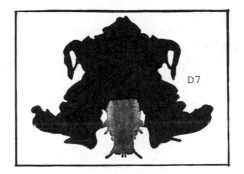
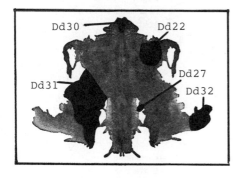
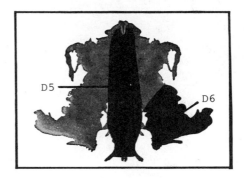
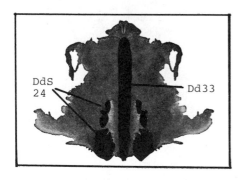
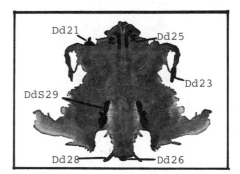

Figure 10. *D* and *Dd* Areas for Card IV.

Table A (Continued)

CARD V

P Is to *W*: Bat or Butterfly

Z Values:			$W = 1.0$	Adjacent = 2.5		Distant = 5.0	Space = 4.0

Location	FQ		Category	Location	FQ		Category
	u	v	Acrobat (Doing handstand)		o		Insect (Winged)
	u		Airplane		–		Kangaroo
	–		Anatomy		u		Kite
	–		Anchor		–		Kidney
	u		Angel		o		Landscape
	–		Animal		u		Leaf
	o		Animals (2 butting heads)		–		Lung(s)
	–		Badge		–		Machine
	o		Bat		–		Map
	u		Bee		–		Microorganism
	–		Beetle		u		Monster
	o		Bird		u		Mosquito
	u		Bookends		o		Moth
	–		Bug (Not winged)		u		Mustache
	u		Bug (Winged)		–		Neckbone
	o		Butterfly		u		Ornament
	u		Cape		u		Ostrich
	–		Cat		u		Pelvis
	u		Cloth (piece)		o	v	Pelvis
	u		Cloud(s)		–		Propeller
	–		Clove		–		Pump
	u		Coal (Piece)		–		Ribs
	–		Coat		u		Rower (In boat)
	–		Coral		–		Sailboat
	u		Crow		–		Skeleton
	o		Dancer (In costume)		u	v	Smoke
	u		Demon		u		Spaceship
	o		Dracula		–		Spider
	u		Duck		u		Stole (Fur)
	u		Eagle		u		Stone
	–		Elves		–		Tent
	–		Explosion		u	<	Tornado (Reflected)
	–		Fern		–		Umbrella
	–		Flag		o		Vampire
	u		Fly		o		Vulture
	u		Flea		u		Wings
	u		Flower		u	v	Wok (Cooking)
	u		Foliage		o		X-ray (Pelvis)
	–		Gnat		–		X-ray (Specific other than pelvis)
	–		Grasshopper		u		X-ray (Unspecified)
	–		Hairpiece				
	–		Head	D1	u		Arm
	u		Hill (With trees)		–		Arrow
	–		Human		o		Bone
	o		Human (In costume)		–		Cylinder
	o		Humans (Back to back)		–		Eel
	u		Human-like Figure (Specified with giant arms or wings)		–		Fish
					u		Foot (Animal)
	–		Ice		–		Foot (Human)
	–		Insect (Not winged)		–		Head (Animal)

Table A (Continued)

Location	FQ	Category	Location	FQ	Category
	u	Head (Cartoon animal)		o	Head (Animal, with horns or
	–	Head (Human)			long ears)
	o	Head (Reptile)		u	Head (Animal)
	o	Leg (Animal)		o	Head (Insect)
	o	Leg (Human)		–	Head (Human)
	u	Limb (Tree)		o	Head (Human, in costume or
	u	Log			with mask)
	u	Muscle		u <	Head (Reptile)
	–	Nose		u	Insect (With antennae)
	u	Root		u	Pliers
	u	Skull (Animal)		u v	Robot
	–	Spear		u v	Sawhorse
	u	Stick		u	Scissors
	–	Wrench		u	Slingshot
				u	Statue
D4	o	Animal (With head at D7)		–	Tuning Fork
	–	Anteater		–	Vase
	u	Blanket		u	Wishbone
	o	Bush(es)			
	u	Cloud	D7	o	Animal (Horned or long-eared)
	–	Crab		–	Animal (Not horned or long-
	–	Driftwood			eared)
	u	Fan		–	Beetle
	–	Head (Animal)		–	Bone
	–	Head (Bird)		u	Bug (With antennae)
	o	Head (Human, profile)		o	Demon
	o	Human (Reclining)		o	Devil
	–	Insect		–	Fish
	–	Jellyfish		–	Human
	–	Kangaroo		o	Human (In costume)
	u	Landscape		u	Humans (2, with arms raised)
	–	Leaf		u	Insect (With antennae)
	–	Leg		u	Monster
	u	Leg (Chicken or turkey cooked)		o	Rabbit
	–	Mud		–	Skeleton
	u	Plant		–	Tree
	o	Rock			
	u	Shoulder Pad (Football)	D9	u	Beak
	–	Skin		u v	Bells
	u	Sleeping Bag		u v	Brooms
	o v	Smoke		v v	Birds (2, long-necked)
	–	Tree		u	Chopsticks
	u	Weed		u	Clamp
	u	Wing		u	Cleaners (Vacuum)
				–	Feet (Animal)
D6	u	Antennae		o	Feet (Bird)
	u	Badge		–	Feet (Human)
	–	Bird		o v	Flamingos
	u	Clippers		o v	Geese
	u v	Elves		–	Head
	o	Face (Animal, long-eared)		u	Heads (2, Birds)
	–	Face (Human)		–	Insect(s)
	o	Face (Human with mask)		u	Legs (Animal)
	u	Hat (Mickey Mouse)		o	Legs (Bird)

Table A (Continued)

Location	FQ	Category	Location	FQ	Category
	—	Legs (Human)	Dd25	u	Cannon
	o	Swans		—	Hat
	u	Tail(s)		—	Penis
	o	Tweezers		u	Rock
	—	Vagina		—	Thumb
	o	Wishbone		—	Tree
D10	u	Bones	Dd26	u	v Bird (In flight)
	—	Coral		u	Branch (Tree)
	—	Head (Animal)		—	Head
	u	Head (Bird)		—	Reptile
	u	Head (Cartoon)		—	Tree
	o	Head (Reptile)	DdS27	u	Cone
	—	Insect		u	Ghost
	u	Legs (Animal)		u	Inlet
	—	Legs (Bird)		u	Tower
	u	Legs (Human)		u	Spike
	—	Nose		u	v Vase
	u	Peninsula	DdS28	u	Cup
	u	Pipewrench		—	Helmet
	o	Roots		u	v Hill
	u	Wood (Driftwood, logs, or		u	Inlet
		sticks)		u	v Mountain
Dd22	o	Arrow		u	Vase
	u	Bayonet	DdS29	u	Inlet
	u	Crutch		u	River
	—	Finger		—	Snake
	—	Head (Animal)	Dd30	—	Ball
	u	Head (Bird)		—	Face (Animal except cat or
	—	Head (Human)			rabbit)
	—	Insect		u	Face (Bird)
	o	Limb (Tree)		u	Face (Cat)
	—	Leg (Animal)		—	Face (Human)
	u	Leg (Bird)		u	Face (Rabbit)
	—	Leg (Human)		u	Head (Animal)
	o	Reptile		u	Head (Bird)
	o	Spear		—	Head (Human)
	o	Sword		o	Mask
	o	Tail		—	Skull
Dd23	u	Coastline	Dd31	o	Bone
	—	Head (Animal)		o	Ear (Animal)
	—	Head (Human)		u	Elf
	u	Landscape		u	Finger
Dd24	u	Bird		—	Foot
	—	Breast		—	Head
	u	Ghost		—	Human
	—	Human		u	Leg
	u	Monster		u	Penis
	u	Nipple		u	Stick
	u	Tent			
	u	Tree			

Table A (Continued)

Location	FQ		Category	Location	FQ		Category
	−		Tree		u		Clippers
	u		Worm		u		Elves
					−		Heads (Animal)
Dd32	u		Antenna		−		Heads (Birds)
	o		Beak		−		Heads (Human)
	o	v	Bird (Long-necked)		u		Heads (Insect)
	u		Bone		u		Heads (Reptile)
	u		Club		o		Horns
	−		Finger		−		Humans
	o		Head (Bird)		u		Human-like Figures
	−		Match		u		Legs
	−		Root		u	<	Mouth (Animal or bird)
	−		Snake		u		Pliers
	o	v	Swan		u		Scissors
	−		Tree		u		Stool
					u	v	
					−		Trees
Dd33	−		Breast	Dd35	−		Breast
	−		Head (Animal)		−		Head (Animal)
	−		Head (Human)		−		Head (Bird)
	u		Head (Human-like)		o		Head (Human, profile)
	o		Hill		u		Human (Sitting or lying)
	o		Mountain		o		Landscape
	o		Shrub(s)		u		Mask (Profile)
					o		Mountains
Dd34	o		Antennae		−		Nose
	u		Bones		u		Rocks

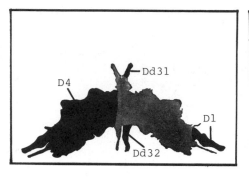

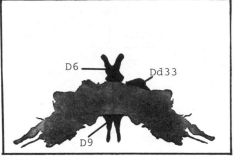

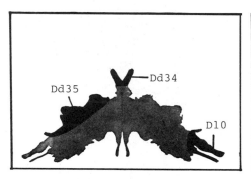

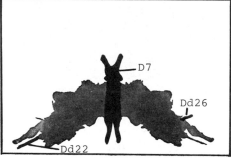

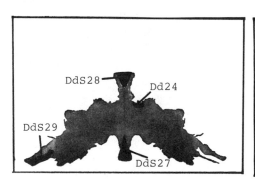

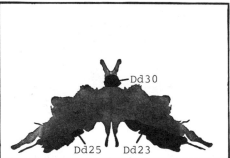

Figure 11. *D* and *Dd* Areas for Card V.

Table A (Continued)

CARD VI

P Is to *W* or *D*1: Animal Skin, Hide, Pelt, or Rug

Z Values:			*W* = 2.5	Adjacent = 2.5	Distant = 6.0	Space = 6.5

Location	FQ		Category	Location	FQ		Category
W	u		Abstract Drawing		—		Frog
	u		Airplane		o		Fur Pelt
	—		Amoeba		—		Genitals (Male)
	—		Anchor		—		Gnat
	u		Animal (In natural form, canine or feline, such as cat, dog, lynx, tiger, wolf, etc.)		u		Guitar
					—		Hair
					o	<	Iceberg (Reflected)
	—		Animal (In natural form, *not* canine or feline, such as anteater, elephant, giraffe, etc.)		—		Insect (Not winged)
					u		Insect (Winged)
					u		Island
	o		Animal (In unnatural form such as flattened, skinned, etc.)		—		Lamp
					o	<	Landscape (Reflected)
	o		Animal Pelt or Skin		u		Leaf
	—		Artichoke		u		Leather (Piece)
	—		Badge		—		Lungs
	—		Bat		—		Map (Specific)
	—		Bear		u		Map (Unspecified)
	o		Bearskin		u		Mask (Science fiction)
	—		Bee		u	v	Mirror (Hand)
	—		Beetle		o		Missile Launch (With missile at *D*6 and pad or smoke at *D*1)
	u		Bird				
	—		Body		u		Monster (Animal)
	—		Brain		u		Monster (Sea)
	—		Brainstem		—		Mosquito
	—		Bug (Not winged)		—		Moth
	u		Bug (Winged)		—		Mud
	—		Butterfly		—		Note (Musical)
	o		Candle (With *D*1 as base)		—		Pan
	—		Chest		o		Pelt
	o	v	Coat (Hanging on post)		u	v	Plant
	—		Club		—		Pot
	—		Crab		o		Rocket Launch (With rocket at *D*3 and pad or smoke at *D*1)
	—		Crow				
	—		Doll		u		Rudder
	—		Dragonfly		o		Rug
	u	v	Drill		u	v	Scarecrow
	—		Duck		u	v	Shield
	u	v	Duster (With handle)		o	<	Ship (Reflected with *D*3 as second object(s))
	—		Emblem				
	u		Explosion		—		Shrimp
	—		Face		o		Skin (Animal)
	o	v	Fan		—		Snail
	—		Fish		—		Spider
	u	v	Flag		u	v	Sponge
	—		Flea		u	v	Statue
	u	v	Flower		u	v	Sting Ray
	—		Fly		o		Totem (As *D*3 with *D*1 as hill or expanse)
	u		Forest (Aerial view)				
	u		Fountain (Abstract)		o	v	Tree

Table A (Continued)

Location	FQ	Category	Location	FQ	Category
	o	Waterway (As *D*5 with other areas landscape)		*u*	Map (Topographic)
				u	Map (Unspecified)
	−	X-ray (Specific)		*u*	v Monkeys (Back to back)
	u	X-ray (Unspecified)		*u*	v Monsters
				o	< Mountain Range (Reflected)
*D*1	*u*	Amoeba		*u*	Mud
	−	Anatomy		*u*	Ornament
	−	Animal		*o*	Pot (With handles)
	u	v Animals (Back to back)		*u*	Rock
	−	Artichoke		*o*	Rug
	u	Badge		−	Shell
	u	Bib		*u*	Shield
	o	Blanket		*o*	Ship (Reflected)
	−	Body		*o*	Skin (Animal)
	u	Bookends		−	Skull
	u	Bowl (With handles)		*u*	Smoke
	−	Brain		*u*	Sponge
	−	Bug		−	Star
	−	Butterfly		−	Starfish
	u	v Cape		*o*	Statues
	−	Chest		−	Turtle Shell
	u	Cloak		*u*	Urn
	u	Cloud(s)		*o*	Waterway (As *D*5 with other areas as landscape)
	u	Coal (Piece)		−	X-ray (Specific)
	o	Coat		*u*	X-ray (Unspecified)
	u	v Crown			
	−	Disc (Anatomy)			
	u	Doors (Swinging)	*D*2	*o*	Alligator
	u	Emblem		−	Animal
	−	Face		*o*	Banister Spindle
	u	Face (Monster)		*o*	Bedpost
	u	Filet (Fish or meat)		*u*	Bone
	−	Flesh		−	Bug
	−	Flower		*o*	Candle
	u	Foliage (Aerial view)		*o*	Candlestick
	u	Forest (Aerial view)		−	Caterpillar
	u	Gate		*u*	Club
	−	Head		*u*	Crocodile
	−	Heads (Animal)		*u*	Drill Bit
	u	Heads (Human, profile, back to back)		*u*	Eel
				−	Fish
	u	v Hive (Bee)		*o*	Giant
	−	Human		*o*	Human
	u	Humans (Back to back)		*o*	Human-like Figure
	u	Ice		−	Insect
	o	v Iceberg (Reflected)		*u*	Knife
	u	Island		*o*	Lamp (Ornamental)
	u	v Jacket		*o*	Lamp Post
	o	Landscape		*o*	Lamp (Street)
	o	Leaf		*o*	Missile
	−	Liver (Anatomy)		*u*	Nail
	−	Lung(s)		−	Needle
	−	Map (Specific)		−	Penis

Table A (Continued)

Location	FQ	Category	Location	FQ	Category
	u	Piston		o	Totem Pole
	u	Reptile		u	Tree
	o	Rocket		−	Valve
	o	Statue (Human-like)		u	Wasp
	u	Sword	D4	o	< Aircraft Carrier
	u	Thermometer		u	v Animal
	o	Totem Pole		o	< Animal (As Dd24 and remainder
	u	Train (Aerial view)			as another object)
	−	Vertebrae		o	< Bathtub (With Dd24 as another
	−	X-ray (Specific)			object)
	u	X-ray (Unspecified)		o	< Battleship
D3	u	Airplane		o	< Boat (In some instances Dd 24
	−	Anatomy			may be reported as a separate
	−	Animal (Not winged)			object)
	u	Animal (Winged)		−	Building
	o	Bird		−	Cocoon
	u	Bug (Not winged)		u	Cloud
	o	Bug (Winged)		o	< Cloud
	u	Butterfly		u	Coral
	o	Cross (Abstract or modern)		u	< Explosion
	o	Crucifix (Abstract)		u	< Gun (Science fiction)
	u	Crucifixion		−	Head (Animal)
	o	Duck (Flying)		−	Head (Bird)
	o	Emblem		o	Head (Human, profile)
	−	Face		u	v Human
	u	Flower		u	v Human-like Figure
	u	Fly		o	Iceberg
	u	Flying Fish		−	Insect
	o	Goose (Flying)		o	Landscape
	u	Head (Animal, with whiskers)		−	Map (Specific)
	−	Head (Bird)		u	Map (Unspecified)
	−	Head (Human)		o	Mask
	−	Head (Insect)		o	< Mountain(s)
	−	Head (Reptile)		o	Rock
	−	Human		o	< Rower (In boat)
	o	Human (Abstract)		o	< Sailboat
	o	Human (In costume)		o	< Ship
	o	Human-like Figure		o	Statue
	u	Insect (Not winged)		o	< Submarine
	o	Insect (Winged)		u	< Tank (Army)
	o	Lamp	D5	−	Animal
	o	Match (With fire)		o	Backbone
	o	Ornament		o	Bone
	−	Owl		o	Canal
	−	Penis		o	Canyon
	u	Pole (Electric or telephone)		−	Caterpillar
	u	Rocket		−	Eel
	o	Rocket (With fire or smoke)		−	Fern
	o	Scarecrow		u	Foliage (Aerial view)
	u	Shrub(s) (Reflected)		o	Gorge
	−	Skull		−	Human
	o	Statue			

Table A (Continued)

Location	FQ	Category	Location	FQ	Category
	−	Insect		o	Cross (On hill)
	−	Knife		o	Crucifix (Abstract)
	o	Missile Launch (With missile as		o	Crucifixion (On hill)
		D2 or D6 and remainder as		o	Flower (In pot)
		smoke and/or fire)		o	Fountain
	u	Pole		u	Head (Animal, whiskered)
	u	Reptile		−	Head (Bird)
	o	River		−	Head (Human)
	o	Road		−	Head (Reptile)
	o	Shaft		o	Lighthouse
	u	Spear		−	Map
	o	Spinal cord		o	Plant
	u	Thermometer		o	Scarecrow
	−	Tree		−	Spinal cord
	u	Tube		o	Statue (Human-like)
	o	Waterway		o	Totem Pole
	u	Worm		u	Tree
	−	X-ray (Specific other than spine)		−	Turtle
	o	X-ray (Spine)		−	X-ray
	u	X-ray (Unspecified)			
			D12	−	Arrow
D6	−	Animal		u	Burner (Bunsen)
	u	Arm (With fist at Dd23)		o	Canal
	o	Bullet		o	Candle
	u	Carving		o	Canyon
	u	Club		o	Gorge
	u	Cylinder		−	Human
	u	Eel		u	Missile
	−	Fish		−	Needle
	−	Head		u	Pencil
	−	Human		−	Penis
	u	Insect		−	Rectum
	u	Log		u	Road
	o	Missile		o	River
	u	Mummy Case		u	Rocket
	−	Neck		o	Shaft (Mine)
	u	Parking Meter		u	Spear
	o	Penis		u	Spinal cord
	o	Pole		u	Vagina
	o	Reptile		o	Waterway
	u	Road			
	o	Rocket	Dd21	o	v Claw
	−	Skull		−	Hand
	u	Statue		−	Head (Animal)
	−	Valve		o	v Head (Bird)
	u	Weapon (Unspecified)		−	Head (Human)
				o	v Head (Reptile)
D8	−	Animal		u	v Horn
	u	Airplane		o	v Pincer
	u	Bird (Statue)		o	v Tongs
	−	Bug			
	u	Bug (Winged, crawling from	Dd22	−	Arms
		object)		u	Birds (2, Profile)
	−	Butterfly		u	Branch(es)

Table A (Continued)

Location	FQ	Category	Location	FQ	Category
	u	< Cactus		−	Reptiles
	o	Feathers		u	Sticks
	u	Flames		u	Whiskers
	−	Flowers			
	u	Geese (Flock)	Dd27	−	Anatomy
	−	Ice		−	Buttocks
	u	Light Rays		u	v Eggs
	−	Pelt		−	Eyes
	u	v Shrub(s)		−	Heads
	−	Tree(s)		−	Humans
	o	Water (Splashing)		−	Testicles
	o	Whiskers		−	Vagina
				u	v Waterfall
Dd23	−	Bug			
	−	Eyes	Dd28	u	v Claws
	u	Fist		−	Heads
	u	Hands (Clasped)		u	v Reptiles
	−	Head (Animal)		−	Trees
	u	Head (Bird)			
	−	Head (Human)	Dd29	u	Coastline
	u	Head (Monster)		−	Head
	u	Head (Reptile)		−	Human Profile
	−	Heads (2)			
	u	Nob (Door)	DdS30	−	Cup
	−	Nose		u	Inlet
				−	Vase
Dd24	u	v Animal (Sitting)			
	−	Boot	Dd31	u	Bird
	u	v Castle		−	Head
	o	Cliff		−	Human
	u	v Head (Animal, with upper body)		u	Iceberg
	−	Head (Bird)		−	Nose
	−	Head (Human)		u	Shaker (Salt or pepper)
	−	Leg			
	−	Paw	Dd32	u	Boat
	o	Peninsula		−	Brain
	o	Rock		u	Butterfly
	o	< Seal		−	Egg
	o	< Smokestack		−	Eyes
	u	< Statue		u	Flames
	u	< Walrus		−	Kidney(s)
				−	Lung(s)
Dd25	u	Carving		u	Shell (Opened)
	u	Doll		−	Tonsils
	u	Foot (Human)		u	Waterwings
	−	Head			
	u	Human	Dd33	u	v Canyon (May include waterfall)
	−	Mountain		u	Inlet
	u	Paw		u	Landscape
	−	Penis		o	v Nest
	u	Shoe		u	Tongs
	u	Statue		u	Tweezer
				u	Vagina
Dd26	u	Antennae			

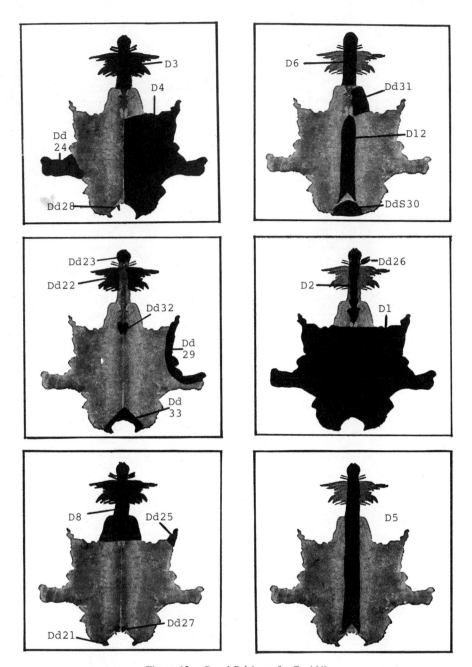

Figure 12. *D* and *Dd* Areas for Card VI.

Table A (Continued)

CARD VII

P Is to *D*1 or *D*9: Human Heads or Faces

Z Values:	*W* = 2.5	Adjacent = 1.0	Distant = 3.0	Space = 4.0

Location	FQ	Category	Location	FQ	Category
W	u	Abstract Drawing		o	Food (Breaded or fried)
	−	Amoeba		−	Frog
	−	Anchor		u	Froglegs (Food)
	−	Anatomy		−	Giant
	−	Animal		o v	Girls
	u	Animals (2, cartoon with each as one-half of the blot)		o	Harbor (Includes *DS*7)
	−	Animals (2, real, with each as one-half of the blot)		u	Horseshoe
				−	Human
	o	Animals (2, as *D*2 and identified as cat, cartoon monkey, or rabbit, with *D*4 as a separate object)		u	Humans (2)
				o	Humans (As *D*2 with *D*4 as separate object)
		(*Note:* If the animals reported as *D*2 are not cat, cartoon, monkey, or rabbit, they should be coded as *u* if the contours are used in an appropriate way, or − in other cases. Examples of *u* include flat-faced animals such as some dogs. Examples of − include fox, elephant, horse, lion, etc.)		o v	Humans (2)
				−	Insect
				o	Island(s)
				−	Keel (Boat)
				u v	Lamp (Ornamental)
				−	Leaf
	u v	Arch		u	Leaf (Torn)
	−	Beard		−	Legs
	−	Bird		−	Map (Specific)
	−	Body (Lower half)		u	Map (Unspecified)
	−	Body (Split)		u	Monument
	u	Bones (Unspecified)		−	Moth
	−	Bug		−	Mouth
	−	Butterfly		−	Neck
	o	Canyon		−	Neckbone
	u v	Cap (With ear flaps)		u	Necklace
	u	Carving		−	Plant
	u v	Cave		u	Puzzle
	o v	Chair (Includes use of *DS*10)		u	Reef
	o	Cloud(s)		u	Rocks
	−	Coat		u	Rocking Horse
	−	Cookie (Includes broken)		−	Sea Animal
	−	Conch Shell		u	Sculpture
	−	Cracker (Includes broken)		−	Shrimp
	u	Crown		u	Shrimps (4)
	o v	Dancers (2)		−	Shrub(s)
	−	Dogs		−	Skull
	u	Dolls		u	Smoke
	o	Dolls (As *D*2 with *D*4 as separate object)		u	Spaceship
				o	Statues (As *D*2 with *D*4 as base)
	u v	Doorframe		u	Stool
	o	Elves (As *D*2 with *D*4 as separate object)		u	Swing
				−	Table
	−	Face		−	Vagina
	u v	Face (Photo negative and includes use of *DS*7 or *DS*10)		u	Vase
				u v	Wig
				−	Womb
				−	X-ray (Specific)
				u	X-ray (Unspecified)

Table A (Continued)

Location	FQ	Category	Location	FQ	Category
D1	−	Anatomy		−	Animal (Large)
	−	Animal		−	v Animal
	u	v Animal (Small, long-tailed with nose at Dd24)		u	v Animal (Cartoon)
	u	< Animal (Cartoon with D5 as long nose or beak)		−	Bird
				u	Bush
	u	Art (Abstract)		o	Cherub
	−	Bird		−	Chicken
	u	Cactus		u	Chicken Wings (Breaded or fried)
	u	v Cap (Coonskin)			
	−	Cat		o	Cloud(s)
	u	Chair		−	Cow
	−	Chicken		o	< Dog
	o	Cliff		−	Dragon
	o	Cloud(s)		−	Donkey
	u	Commode		o	Dwarf
	−	Eagle		o	v Elephant (Cartoon or toy)
	−	Fish		−	Fish
	u	Fist (With finger pointing upward)		u	Food (Breaded or fried)
				−	Fox
	u	Foliage		−	Frog
	o	Head (Animal, as cat, cartoon, monkey, or rabbit)		−	Head
				u	Hill
		(*Note:* If animal head reported is not cat, cartoon, monkey, or rabbit, it should be coded as *u* if the contours are used appropriately, as for some dog heads, or − if that is not the case.)		−	Horse
				o	Human (Child, Indian, female, or unspecified, may be whole human or head and upper body)
	u	v Head (Animal, with D5 as trunk)		u	Human (Adult male)
	o	Head (Human, as child, Indian, female, or unspecified)		o	Human-like Figure
				o	Island(s)
	u	Head (Human, adult male)		u	Lamb
	o	Head (Human-like)		u	Landscape
	−	Horse		−	Meat (Raw)
	−	Insect		u	Mountains
	u	Ladle		o	Rabbit
	u	Landscape		u	Shrimp (2, breaded or fried)
	−	Map (Specific)		o	Snowman
	u	Map (Unspecified)		o	Statue
	u	Mask		−	Tiger
	−	Mountain		o	Toy (Human or animal)
	o	Rabbit (With nose as D8)		−	Tree(s)
	u	v Rudder		−	X-ray
	−	Sea Animal	D3	−	Animal
	o	Shrimp (Breaded or fried)		−	Beard
	o	Statue		u	Candy (Cotton)
	−	Tree		−	Cap
	−	X-ray		u	Cleaver
D2	o	Angel		u	Cliff
	o	Animal (Small, with D5 as ear and Dd 21 as tail, such as cat, dog, monkey, rabbit)		u	Cloud
				−	Cup
				−	Dog
	o	Animal (Cartoon)		u	Fish (Tail as Dd21)
				u	Fist (Thumb as Dd21)
				−	Hairpiece

Table A   (Continued)

Location	FQ	Category	Location	FQ	Category
	−	Ham		u	Kite
	−	Hand		u	Landscape
	o	Head (Animal, with Dd21 as ear		−	Lung(s)
		or horn)		−	Map (Specific)
	u	v Head (Animal, with Dd21 as		u	Map (Unspecified)
		nose or trunk)		−	Mountain(s)
	o	Head (Animal, cartoon or toy)		u	Paper (Torn)
	u	v Head (Bird, with Dd21 as beak)		o	Pelvis
	−	Head (Human)		u	Plateau (Aerial view)
	u	Head (Human-like)		−	Rib Cage
	−	Head (Reptile)		o	Rock(s)
	−	Insect		−	Sea Animal
	u	Island		−	Shell
	u	Kite (With Dd21 as tail)		−	Shoes
	u	Landscape		−	Shrub(s)
	−	Map		−	Skull
	o	Mask		−	Tent
	−	Nest		−	Vagina
	u	Peninsula		u	Wings
	u	Rock		o	X-ray (Pelvis)
	−	Sack		−	X-ray (Specific other than pelvis)
	u	Shrimp (Breaded or fried)		u	X-ray (Unspecified)
	−	Shrub			
	u	Statue	D5	−	Animal
	−	Tree		−	Arrow
	−	X-ray		u	Arrowhead
				−	Bird
D4	−	Anatomy		o	Blade (Knife)
	−	Animal(s)		u	< Boat
	o	v Bat		u	Bone
	o	Bird		u	< Canoe
	u	Bookends		u	Caterpillar
	−	Boots		u	Claw
	o	Bow		u	Comb (Decorative)
	u	Bowtie		−	Drill
	−	Bowl		−	Eel
	−	Bridge (Man-made)		o	Feather
	u	Bridge (Natural)		u	Finger
	−	Bug (Not winged)		−	Gun
	u	Bug (Winged)		u	Hair (Groomed or styled as in
	o	Butterfly			hairpiece or pony tail)
	−	Buttocks		−	Head
	−	Chest		u	Headdress
	o	Cloud(s)		u	Horn
	u	Cushion(s)		−	Human
	u	Doors (Swinging)		u	v Icicle
	−	Emblem		−	Insect
	−	Fly		u	Leg
	u	Hang Glider (May include D6 as		−	Log
		person)		−	Penis
	−	Head		u	Pick (Guitar)
	−	Human		u	Plant
	−	Insect (Not winged)		−	Rifle
	u	Insect (Winged)		u	Sabre

Table A (Continued)

Location	FQ	Category	Location	FQ	Category
	—	Sausage		*u*	v Helmet
	u	Saw		*u*	Lake
	—	Smoke		*o*	v Lamp
	u	Stalamite		*o*	v Mushroom
	u	Sword		*u*	v Pagoda
	u	Tail		*u*	Pot
	u	Totem		*o*	v Sphinx
	—	Tree		*o*	v Statue
	u	Wing		—	Tree
	—	Worm		*u*	Vase
*D*6	—	Animal	*D*8	*u*	City (In distance)
	u	Anus		*u*	Cliff(s)
	—	Bone		—	Dragon
	—	Bug		*o*	Forest
	o	Canal		—	Head
	o	Canyon		*u*	Humans (Several on cliff or hill)
	—	Caterpillar		*u*	v Icicles
	u	Clitoris		*o*	Landscape
	u	Crack		*u*	Nest
	u	Dam		*u*	Sea Animal
	u	Doll		*u*	Snail
	—	Drill		*u*	Stalagmites
	—	Fish		*u*	Towers (Electric)
	o	Gorge		*u*	Trees
	—	Head		*o*	Village
	o	Hinge (Door)		*u*	Whale
	o	Human			
	o	Human-like Figure	*D*9	*u*	Cliff
	—	Insect		*u*	Cloud
	u	Missile (Often with *Dd*28 as pad or smoke)		*o*	Head (Animal, small such as cat, dog, monkey, etc.)
	u	Monster (Animal)		—	Head (Animal, large)
	—	Penis		*u*	v Head (Animal)
	o	River		—	Head (Bird)
	u	Rocket (Often with *Dd*28 as pad or smoke)		*o*	Head (Human)
				o	Head (Human-like)
	—	Spine		—	Insect
	—	Tower		*u*	Landscape
	—	Tree		—	Sea Animal
	o	Vagina		*o*	Statue (Bust)
	o	Waterway			
			*DS*10	*o*	Bowl
*DS*7	—	Anatomy		*u*	Entrance
	u	Arrowhead		—	Face
	—	Bell		*o*	Harbor
	o	Bowl		*o*	v Hat (Historical)
	—	Cloud		—	Head
	u	Entrance		*o*	Helmet
	—	Face		*u*	Lake
	o	Harbor		*o*	Lampshade
	u	v Hat (Historical)		*u*	Mushroom (Cap)
	—	Head		*u*	Tent

Table A (Continued)

Location	FQ	Category	Location	FQ	Category
Dd21	−	Ant		−	Cloud
	u	Arm		u	Dirt
	−	Bird		−	Head
	u	Caterpillar			
	−	Face	Dd25	u	Bird
	o	Finger		u	Landscape
	−	Head		u	Seagull
	u	Horn		−	Vagina
	u	Paw		u	Waterfall
	u	Peninsula			
	−	Penis	Dd26	o	Canyon
	−	Rifle		o	Gorge
	u	Tail		u	Human
	u	Thumb		u	Human-like Figure
	u	Trunk (Elephant)		o	River
				o	Statue
Dd22	−	Animal		o	Vagina
	u	Animal (Cartoon or toy)			
	−	Bones	Dd27	−	Animal
	u	v Doll		u	Anus
	u	Human		−	Human
	o	Human-like Figure		−	Teeth
	u	v Human		−	Vagina
	u	Puppet		−	Window
	u	Statue			
			Dd28	−	Animal
Dd23	−	Animal		−	Bird
	u	Brick		−	Buttocks
	u	Cloud		u	Face (Animal)
	u	Hat (Fur)		−	Face (Human)
	−	Head (Animal except bear or dog)		u	Face (Monster)
				u	Humans (2)
	o	Head (Animal, bear or dog)		u	v Parachute (With D6 or Dd26 as person)
	−	Head (Human)			
	u	Pillow		−	Plant
	u	Rock		u	Statue(s)
	−	Shoe		u	Water
				o	v Waterfall
Dd24	u	Cave		u	v Waves

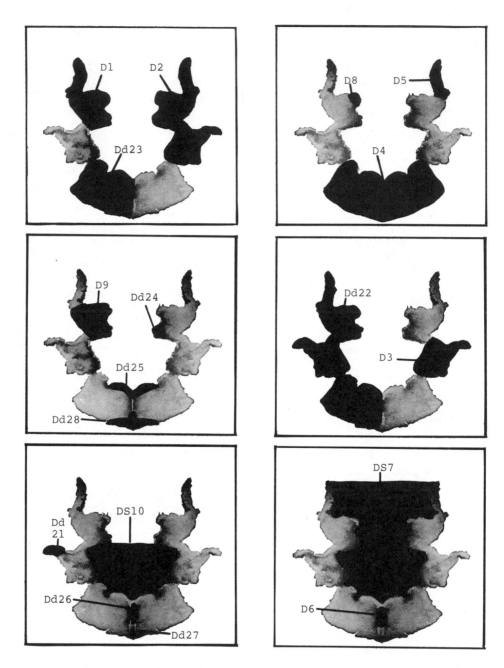

Figure 13. *D* and *Dd* Areas for Card VII.

228

Table A (Continued)

CARD VIII

P Is to *D*1: Whole Animal Figure

| Z Values: | | *W* = 4.5 | Adjacent = 3.0 | Distant = 3.0 | Space = 4.0 |

Location	FQ	Category	Location	FQ	Category
W	—	Airplane		u	Island(s)
	—	Anatomy (Specific)		—	Jacket
	o	Anatomy (Unspecified)		—	Jellyfish
	—	Animal		—	Kidney(s)
	o	Animals (As *D*1 with other areas identified as object(s) that are consistent with contours)		u	Kite
				u	Lamp (Decorative)
				o	Landscape (Often as aerial view)
	o	Art (Abstract)		u	Lantern (Oriental)
	u	Badge		u	Leaf
	—	Bat		u	Lights (Colored as created by strobes)
	—	Bird			
	—	Bones (Skeletal)		—	Lobster
	o	Bowl (Ornamental)		—	Lung(s)
	—	Brain		—	Machine
	—	Butterfly		—	Map (Specific)
	u	Cage (Bird)		u	Map (Unspecified)
	o	Carousel		u	Mask
	—	Cake		—	Meat
	o	Chandelier		o	Medical Illustration (Parts are representative rather than real)
	u	Christmas Tree			
	u	Circus Tent		u	Monument
	—	Cloud(s)		—	Moth
	o	Coat-of-Arms		u	Mountain
	u	Coral		o	Ornament
	—	Crab		u	Pagoda
	u	Crown		—	Pelvis
	o	Design (Abstract)		o	Plant (Often in pot)
	o	Emblem		o	Poster (Abstract)
	—	Explosion		o	Poster (Nature)
	—	Face		—	Pyramid
	—	Fish		u	Robot
	u	Flag		u	Rocket
	o	Floral Design		u	Rubbish
	o	Flower		—	Sea Animal
	u	Foliage		u	Sea Shell
	o	Fountain		o	Ship (With sails, view from end)
	—	Frog		—	Skeleton
	u	Garden		—	Skull
	u	Gazebo		—	Snowflake
	—	Head (Animal)		—	Spider
	—	Head (Bird)		u	Statue
	—	Head (Human)		—	Stomach
	—	Head (Insect)		u v	Torch
	u	Head (Monster)		u	Totem Pole
	u	Headdress (Ornamental)		—	Tree
	u	Helmet (Science fiction)		u	Tree (Abstract or cartoon)
	—	Human		u	Vegetation (Tropical)
	—	Insect		u	Vegetation (Underwater)
	—	Intestines		u	Vase

Table A (Continued)

Location	FQ	Category	Location	FQ	Category
	u	Volcano (Erupting)		–	Crown
	–	X-ray		–	Disc (Spinal)
				–	Dog
D1	–	Anatomy		–	Emblem
	o	Animal (Four-legged, and appropriate to contours. This class of response includes a wide variety of animals, including some considered to be prehistoric. The most commonly reported include badger, bear, cat, dog, gopher, lion, mouse, possum, rat, and wolf. Four-legged animals that are not appropriate for the contours should be coded as –, such as elephant, giraffe, horse, kangaroo, etc.)		u	Fire
				–	Flesh
				o	Flower
				–	Frog
				–	Hat
				u	v Head (Animal, short-eared or horned)
				–	Head (Animal, not short-eared or horned)
				–	Head (Bird)
				–	Head (Human)
				–	Head (Insect)
				u	Head (Monster)
				o	Ice Cream
	–	Bird		–	Insect
	u	Blood		u	v Jacket
	–	Camel		u	Jell-O
	–	Dolphin		u	Landscape
	–	Fish		o	Lava
	–	Flower		u	Leaf
	–	Frog		–	Meat
	u	Iguana		u	Mountain(s)
	–	Insect		u	Painted Desert
	u	Lizard		–	Pelvis
	–	Lung		u	Pot
	u	Petal (Flower)		u	Rock(s)
	–	Porpoise		u	Rug
	–	Reptile (Other than iguana or lizard)		u	Scab
				u	Slide (Biological)
	–	Seal		–	Stomach
	–	Shrimp		–	Vagina
	–	Tree		–	Vertebrae (Cross section)
	–	Turtle			
	–	X-ray	D3/DS3	u	< Animal (Reflected)
				–	Badge
D2	–	Anatomy		o	Bone Structure
	–	Animal		–	Cave
	–	Bat		u	Corset
	u	Bowl (Decorative)		–	Door
	–	Brain		–	Face
	u	Bug		–	Head
	o	Butterfly		u	Ice
	–	Buttocks		o	Mask
	u	Cake		–	Net
	u	Canyon		o	Rib Cage
	u	v Cape		u	Skeleton
	–	Chest		o	Skull (Animal)
	u	v Coat		–	Skull (Human)
	u	Coral		u	Snow
	–	Crab		u	v Spaceship

Table A (Continued)

Location	FQ		Category	Location	FQ	Category
	u	v	Tepee	D5		(*Note:* D4 + D5 = D8)
	u	v	Tent		−	Animal
	u	v	Tree (Fir)		*u*	Bat
	o		Vertebrae		*u*	Bird
	−		Web		*o*	Bird (Prehistoric or science fiction)
D4			(*Note:* D4 + D5 = D8)		−	Bone
	u		Airplane		*o*	Butterfly
	−		Animal		*u*	Cliff(s)
	u	v	Antlers		*o*	Cloth
	−		Bat		*u*	Cloud(s)
	−		Bridge (Man-made)		−	Face
	−	v	Bridge (Natural)		*o*	Flags
	u		Boomerang		−	Flower
	−		Butterfly		−	Head(s)
	u		Castle (On mountain)		*o*	Ice
	u		Cliff(s)		−	Kidney(s)
	−		Cloud		*o*	Landscape (Often as aerial view)
	u		Crab		−	Leaves
	−		Crawfish		−	Lung(s)
	−		Crown		−	Pelvis
	−		Face		*u*	Pillow(s)
	u		Face (Science fiction)		−	Rib Cage
	−		Fish		*u*	Sails
	o		Frog		−	Skull(s)
	−		Head		−	Sky
	u		Head (Science fiction)		*o*	Water
	−		House		−	X-ray
	−		Human(s)			
	u		Ice	D6	−	Anatomy (Specific)
	u		Iceberg		*o*	Anatomy (Unspecified)
	u		Insect		*u*	Art (Abstract)
	−		Jellyfish		−	Bird
	−		Lobster		−	Bones
	u		Mask (Science fiction)		−	Brain
	o		Monster		*u*	Chandelier
	o		Mountain		*u*	Christmas Tree
	−		Octopus		−	Crab
	u	v	Pelvis		−	Face
	u		Robot		*o*	Flower
	u		Rocket		*u*	Glacier
	o		Roots		−	Head
	u		Sea Animal		*u*	Helmet (Science fiction)
	−		Scorpion		−	Human
	u		Shrub(s)		*u*	Island(s)
	−		Skull		*o*	Landscape (Often aerial view)
	o		Spaceship		*u*	Mask
	u		Spider		*o*	Mountain
	u		Stump (Tree)		*u*	Ornament
	u		Temple		*u*	Pagoda
	u		Tent		*o*	Plant
	u		Tree		*u*	Ship (With sails, view from end)
	u		Vine		*u*	Statue
	u		Waterfall		*u*	Vegetation

Table A (Continued)

Location	FQ	Category	Location	FQ	Category
D7	—	Animal		u	Feet (Animal)
	—	Bird		u	Glove
	o	Blood (Usually dried)		u	Hand
	—	Buttocks		u	Horn (Animal)
	u	Canyon		u	Root
	—	Chest			
	—	Face	Dd23	u	Anus
	—	Head		u	Canyon
	o	Ice Cream		—	Face
	u	v Jacket		u	Flask
	u	Jello		—	Head
	u	Landscape		—	Human(s)
	u	Leaf (Autumn)		u	Vagina
	—	Mountain		u	Waterfall
	u	Painted Desert			
	o	Rocks	Dd24	u	Antennae
	u	v Vest		—	Birds
				u	Feelers
D8	(Note: D4 + D5 = D8)			u	Fingers
	—	Anatomy		u	Horns
	u	Bird		—	Human(s)
	—	Butterfly		u	v Legs (Human)
	u	v Chandelier		u	Pincers
	—	Crab		u	Roots
	—	Face		—	Teeth
	u	Floral Display		o	Trees
	—	Flower			
	u	Glacier	Dd25	u	Alligator
	—	Head		—	Animal
	u	Helmet (Science fiction)		—	Bird
	u	Landscape		—	Fish
	u	Pagoda		—	Human
	o	Plant		u	Island
	—	Shell		—	Penis
	o	Spaceship		u	Spaceship
	u	Tent		u	Statue
Dd21	—	Animal	Dd26	u	v Cliff
	o	Bone (Skeletal)		u	< Dog
	—	Esophagus		u	< Head (Animal)
	—	Human		—	Head (Bird)
	u	Knife (And case)		—	Head (Human)
	u	v Missile Launch		u	Rock
	o	River		u	< Statue
	u	Rockets (Separating stages)			
	—	Spear	Dd27	u	Alligator
	o	Spinal cord		u	Bone
	u	Stick(s)		u	Drill Bit
	u	Waterfall		u	Hypodermic
	o	Waterway		u	Knife
				u	Missile
Dd22	—	Animal		—	Needle
	o	Arm (Human)		u	Pen
	u	Branch		u	Rocket

Table A (Continued)

Location	FQ	Category	Location	FQ	Category
	u	Spear		—	Crab
	—	Worm		—	Insect
				u	Monster (Animal-like)
DdS28	u	Cloud(s)		—	Reptile
	u	Snow		u	Root(s)
	u	Water		—	Wing
DdS29	u	v Bottle (Milk)	Dd32	u	Albatross
	u	v Bowling Pin		o	Bird
	—	Ghost		u	Butterfly
	u	v Salt Shaker		o	Gull
	—	Statue		o	Snow
	—	Tooth		u	Water
	u	v Triangle (Music)			
	u	< Whale	Dd33	—	Anatomy
Dd30	u	v Cane		u	Butterfly
	u	Gorge		—	Face
	u	River		u	Flower(s)
	o	Spinal Cord		u	Head (Animal)
	o	Stick		—	Head (Bird)
	—	Sword		—	Head (Human)
	u	Waterfall		u	Ice Cream
Dd31	—	Animal		—	Lung(s)
				u	Rock(s)

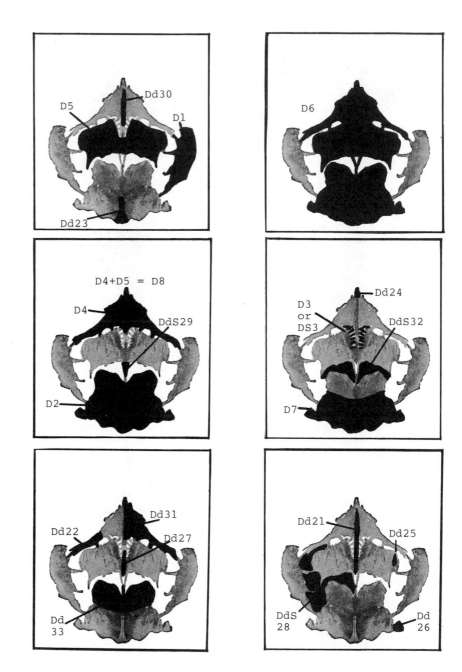

Figure 14. *D* and *Dd* Areas for Card VIII.

Table A (Continued)

CARD IX

P Is to *D*3: Human or Human-like Figures

Z Values:		W = 5.5	Adjacent = 2.5		Distant = 4.5	Space = 5.0

Location	FQ	Category	Location	FQ	Category
W	—	Anatomy		o	Illustration (Medical)
	u	Anchor		—	Insect
	—	Ant		u	Island
	o	Art (Abstract)		u v	Jellyfish
	u	Badge		u v	Lamp (Ornamental)
	—	Bird		o	Landscape
	o v	Birds (As D3 under tree)		—	Leaf
	o	Bowl (Ornamental)		—	Lung(s)
	—	Bug		—	Machine
	—	Butterfly		—	Map (Specific)
	u	Cactus		u	Map (Unspecified)
	u	Cake (With candles as D3)		o	Mask
	u	Candle (With D6 as base)		u	Monster
	o	Canyon (As D8 with other areas as foliage and/or landscape)		u	Ornament
				o	Paint
	u v	Cape (Theatrical)		o	Pallet (Artist's)
	u	Chair (Winged with D6 as base or swivel)		o	Plant (Sometimes with D6 as pot)
	u v	Clothing (Woman's)		u v	Robot
	—	Cloud(s)		—	Sea Animal
	—	Cocoon		u	Seaweed
	o	Coral		—	Seed
	—	Crab		—	Skull
	u	Crater (As D8 with other areas as foliage and/or landscape)		u	Spaceship
				—	Throat
	u	Decoration		u v	Tree
	u v	Dummy (Dressmaker's)		—	Vagina
	u	Emblem		o	Vase
	o	Explosion		o	Waterfall (As D5 with other areas as foliage and/or landscape)
	—	Face			
	u	Face (Clown)			
	u	Face (Monster)		—	X-ray
	o	Fire (Usually with smoke as D1)			
	o	Floral Arrangement	D1		(*Note:* D1 + D1 = D11)
	o	Flower (Often with D6 as pot)		—	Anatomy
	—	Fly		—	Animal
	o	Foliage		u <	Animal (Unspecified)
	o	Fountain		o <	Ape
	o	Garden		o <	Bear
	u	Hat		—	Bird
	—	Head (Animal)		—	Bone
	—	Head (Human)		—	Bug
	—	Head (Insect)		—	Butterfly
	u	Head (Monster)		—	Cat
	o	Headdress (Ceremonial)		u	Cloud
	u	Helmet (Science fiction)		u	Coral
	—	Human		u <	Dog
	u v	Human (In costume)		—	Elephant
	u v	Human-like Figure		u	Fern

Table A (Continued)

Location	FQ	Category	Location	FQ	Category
	—	Fish		—	Cloud(s)
	o	Foliage		u	Coral
	u	Forest (Usually aerial view)		—	Crab
	—	Frog		o	Crater (As D8 with other areas as
	o	< Giant			foliage and/or landscape)
	o	Grass		u	Emblem
	—	Hat		u	Explosion
	u	Head (Animal, with snout at the		—	Face
		D5 centerline)		o	Face (Clown)
	o	Head (Animal, with snout at		u	Face (Monster)
		Dd24, often with DdS25 as eye)		o	Fire (As D3 with other areas as
	o	v Head (Animal, with snout at D5			smoke)
		centerline or at DdS25)		o	Flower
	—	Head (Bird)		—	Fly
	u	< Head (Human or human-like		o	Foliage
		with chin at Dd24)		u	Fountain
	—	Head (Insect)		u	Garden
	—	Heart		—	Head (Animal)
	—	Human		—	Head (Human)
	o	< Human (With Dd24 as head)		u	Head (Human-like)
	—	Insect		—	Head (Insect)
	o	Landscape		o	Headdress (Ceremonial)
	u	Leaf		u	Helmet
	—	Lion		—	Human
	—	Lung		u	Illustration (Medical)
	—	Map		—	Insect
	u	< Monkey		u	v Jellyfish
	u	< Monster		o	Landscape
	—	Mushroom		u	Leaf (Autumn)
	u	v Pig		—	Map
	u	Plant		o	Mask
	u	< Rabbit		u	Ornament
	—	Sea Animal		o	Plant
	o	Shrub		—	Sea Animal
	u	Smoke		—	Skull
	u	Sponge		o	v Tree
	u	< Statue		u	Vagina
	—	Tree		o	Vase
	—	Wing		u	v Waterfall (As D5 with other
	—	X-ray			areas as foliage and/or
					landscape)
D2	—	Anatomy			
	o	Anchor	D3	—	Anatomy
	u	Art (Abstract)		o	Animal (Antlered or horned)
	u	Badge		—	Animal (Not antlered or horned)
	—	Bird		u	Bird
	o	v Birds (As D3 under bush)		o	v Bird
	o	Bowl		u	Blood
	—	Bug		—	Bone
	—	Butterfly		—	Bug
	o	Canyon (As D8 with other areas		u	Carrot
		as foliage and/or landscape)		o	Cliff
	u	Chair (Wing)		u	Cloud
	—	Clothing		o	Clown

Table A (Continued)

Location	FQ	Category	Location	FQ	Category
	−	Club		−	Eye
	u	Crab		−	Fish
	o	Dancer (In costume)		u	Flower
	o	< Deer		u	Head (Animal)
	o	Demon		o	Head (Human)
	−	Dog		u	Mask
	u	Dragon		−	Meat
	−	Face		−	Pot
	o	Fire		o	Raspberry
	−	Fish		u	Rock
	o	Flower		−	Sperm
	o	Ghost		u	Sponge
	o	v Gnome		u	Strawberry
	o	Head (Animal, antlered or horned)		−	Turtle
	−	Head (Animal, not antlered or horned)	D5	−	Anatomy
				−	Animal
	o	Head (Human)		u	Arrow
	o	Head (Human-like)		o	Bone
	−	Head (Insect)		o	Candle
	o	Hill		u	Cane
	u	Human		u	Drill Bit
	o	Human-like Figure		−	Esophagus
	−	Insect		u	Flame
	o	Landscape		u	Geyser
	o	Lava		u	Gorge
	−	Leg		−	Head
	u	Lobster		−	Human
	−	Lung		−	Insect
	u	Map (Unspecified)		o	Landscape
	−	Meat		o	Match
	u	v Owl		−	Peninsula
	o	v Parrot		−	Penis
	u	Plant		u	Reptile
	−	Rodent		u	River
	o	Sand		u	Road
	−	Sea Animal		u	Sand Bar
	−	Shrimp		o	< Shoreline
	−	Skull		o	Skewer
	u	Statue		o	Spinal Cord
	u	Sun Spot		u	Stalagtite
	u	Torch		u	Stem
	o	Toy (For punching)		u	Sword
	−	Tree		−	Tree
	u	Wing		o	Waterfall (With D8 as background)
	o	Witch		u	Waterway
D4	−	Anatomy			
	o	Apple	D6	−	Anatomy
	o	Ball		−	Animal(s)
	u	Blood		o	Apples (4)
	−	Bug		o	Babies (2)
	o	Candy (Cotton)		o	Balloons
	−	Cocoon		−	Bird

Table A (Continued)

Location	FQ	Category	Location	FQ	Category
	o	Blood		u	v Human-like Figure
	u	v Butterfly		u	Keyhole
	–	Buttocks		u	v Lamp
	o	Candy (Cotton)		o	Light Bulb
	o	Cloud (Including mushroom cloud)		u	v Mask
				u	v Monster
	o	Embryos (2)		u	Nose (Cow or horse)
	–	Face		u	Parking Meter
	u	v Face (Insect)		u	v Robot
	u	v Face (Science fiction)		o	v Salt Shaker
	u	Fire		–	Skull
	u	Flower(s)		u	Sky
	–	Head (Animal)		–	Tree
	u	v Head (Elephant or rodent)		u	Tornado
	o	< Head (Human, reflected)		–	Vagina
	–	Human		o	Vase
	o	< Human (Sitting, reflected)		u	Violin
	–	Insect		o	Water
	–	Island		o	Waterfall
	u	Marshmallows		–	Womb
	–	Meat			
	u	v Mushroom	D9	–	Animal
	–	Pot(s)		u	Chandelier
	u	Powder Puff		u	v Corkscrew
	u	Raspberries		–	Drill
	o	Sherbet		–	Head (Animal other than elephant)
	u	v Shoulders (Human)			
	–	Skin		u	Head (Elephant)
	u	Smoke		–	Head (Human)
	u	Strawberries		–	Head (Insect)
	–	Vagina		u	v Heron (On one leg)
	–	Wing		–	Human
				o	v Flower
D8/DS8	–	Anatomy		o	Fountain
	–	Animal		u	v Lamp
	u	Blender		o	Spindle (Office)
	o	Bottle		u	v Tree
	o	Canyon		o	v Umbrella
	o	Cave		u	v Valve
	u	Chandelier			
	–	Chest	D11	–	Anatomy
	u	v Dress		u	Bat
	u	v Dummy (Dressmaker's)		u	Bird
	–	Face (Animal)		u	Bookends
	–	Face (Human)		o	Butterfly
	u	v Face (Monster)		–	Ear Muffs
	u	v Flask		–	Earphones
	o	v Ghost		o	Foliage
	–	Head (Animal)		–	Head
	–	Head (Human)		–	Human
	u	v Head (Monster)		–	Insect
	o	Hourglass		u	Insect (Winged)
	–	Human		–	Lungs

Table A (Continued)

Location	FQ	Category	Location	FQ	Category
	o	Pelvis	Dd24	u	Cliff
	u	Plant		u	Head (Animal)
	u	Shrubs		u	< Head (Human)
D12	—	Animal	Dd25	u	Claws
	u	< Dragon		u	Feelers
	o	Fire (Forest)		—	Fingers
	o	< Human (As D1 with D3 as other		u	Roots
		object such as hill, sand, etc.)		u	Tentacles
	o	< Landscape		—	Trees
	u	Leaves		u	Weeds
	—	Monster			
	—	Tree	Dd26	—	Animal
				u	Claw
Dd21	o	Claws		o	Finger
	o	Finger		—	Foot
	u	v Fins		u	Gun (Often science fiction)
	u	v Horns		u	Hose (Nozzle)
	—	Humans		—	Human
	u	Icicles		u	Key
	—	Rake		—	Nose
	u	v Rockets (Group)		u	< Scarecrow
	—	Spears		u	< Statue
	u	Stalagtites		u	Trumpet
	—	Trees			
			Dd27	—	Animal
Dd22/	u	Bowl		—	Face
DdS22	—	Candles		—	Head
	u	Cavern		—	Human
	—	Cup		u	< Tent
	—	Door(s)		u	< Top
	—	Eyes			
	—	Face (Animal)	Dd28	—	Blood
	—	Face (Human)		u	Breast
	—	Face (Insect)		u	Egg
	o	Face (Monster)		—	Head
	—	Head		u	Insect (Hard-shelled)
	—	Jar		—	Scab
	—	Jellyfish		u	Shell
	u	Lake(s)		—	Stomach
	o	Mask			
	u	Nose (Animal)	DdS29	o	Bell
	o	Pumpkin (Halloween)		—	Bug
	—	Skull		u	Eye
				—	Face
DdS23	u	Caves		o	Ghost
	u	Eyes		—	Human
	o	Holes		u	Human-like Figure
	u	Islands		u	Lake
	u	Lakes			
	u	Nostrils (Animal)	Dd30	u	Candlewax
	—	Pillows		u	Caterpillar
	—	Shells		—	Intestine

Table A (Continued)

Location	FQ	Category	Location	FQ	Category
	−	Penis	Dd34	−	Animal
	−	Reptile		u	Antlers
Dd31	u	Breast		u	Branches
	u	v Cover (Pot)		u	Bridge (Natural)
	u	< Face (Animal)		u	Cannon (Usually science fiction)
	u	< Face (Human)		u	Claw(s)
	u	Foliage		o	Drawbridge (Often opening)
	−	Tree(s)		u	Horns
				u	Hose
DdS32	u	v Bowl		−	Human(s)
	u	Dome		u	Lightning Flash
	−	Helmet		u	Roots
	u	Moon (Upper half)		−	Skeletal
	u	Shell		−	Trees
	u	Sun (Upper half)			
	u	Sunspot	Dd35	−	Animal
	u	Tent		u	Bathysphere
				−	Bird
Dd33	o	< Alligator		u	Buttocks
	o	< Crocodile		u	Furnace
	u	Foliage		−	Head
	u	< Head (Animal)		−	Lung(s)
	−	Head (Human)		−	Mask
	u	< Head (Reptile)		u	Pot
	u	Log		u	Rock(s)
	−	Mountain(s)		u	Stove (Iron)
	−	Tree			

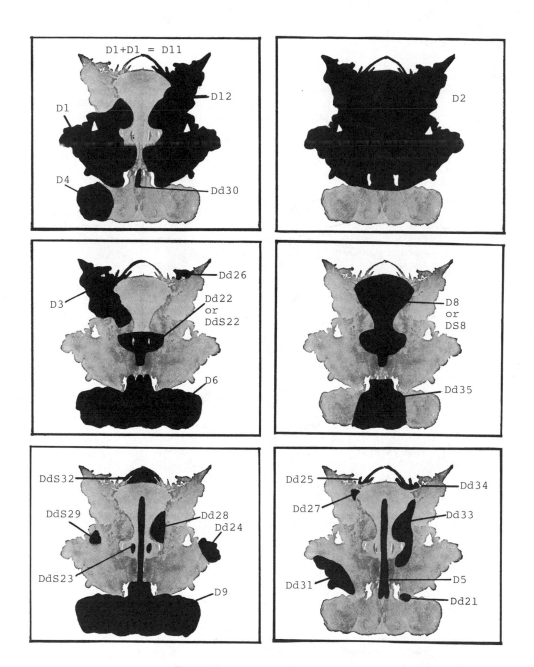

Figure 15. *D* and *Dd* Areas for Card IX.

Table A (Continued)

CARD X

P Is to *D*1: Spider or Crab

Z Values:		$W = 5.5$	Adjacent $= 4.0$		Distant $= 4.5$		Space $= 6.0$

Location	FQ	Category				
W	−	Anatomy		−		Sea Animal
	o	Animals (Marine, unspecified, or if specified, meeting appropriate contour requirements)		o		Underwater Scene
				o		Walkway (As center space and other areas as flowers and/or shrubbery)
	u	Animals (Not marine but meeting contour requirements)				
	o	Art (Abstract)	D1	o		Amoeba
	o	Aquarium		−		Animal
	u	v Aviary		u		Bug
	u	Bacteria		u		Cell (Biological)
	−	Birds		−		Cockroach
	−	Bones		u		Coral
	u	Chandelier		o		Crab
	u	Children's Play Park (With all areas included as play equipment)		u		Dragon
				u		Earring
				−		Face
	−	Christmas Tree		u		Fern
	−	Clouds		−		Fish
	u	Costume (Theatrical, hanging on wall)		u		Flower
				−		Hat
	u	Design (Abstract)		−		Head
	u	v Explosion		u		Insect
	−	Face		u		Island
	u	Fireworks Display		−		Jellyfish
	o	Floral Design		u		Landscape
	o	Flower Garden		−		Leaf
	o	v Flowers (Bouquet)		u		Lobster
	o	Garden Scene (With some areas as flowers or shrubbery and areas such as D11 and/or D6 as sculpture or architecture)		−		Map
				−		Mask
				u		Monster
				o		Octopus
	−	Headdress		u		Pom Pom
	−	Human		−		Reindeer
	o	Insects (Unspecified, or if specified, meeting appropriate contour requirements)		u		Roots
				o		Scorpion
				−		Sea Shell
	u	Islands		u		Snowflake
	u	Kaleidoscope		o		Spider
	u	Lights (Created by strobe)		o		Water (Drop)
	−	Map (Specific)		−		Web
	u	Map (Unspecified)		u		Weed
	−	Mask				
	u	Mobile (Abstract)	D2	u		Amoeba
	−	Pagoda		u		Animal (Unspecified)
	o	Painting (Modern)		−		Bee
	u	Painting (Finger)		u		v Bird
	u	Pallet (Artist's)		u		Bug
	u	Plants		u		Cat
	o	Poster (Abstract)		o		Cell (Biological)
	u	Puzzle (Pieces)		−		Chicken

Table A (Continued)

Location	FQ	Category	Location	FQ	Category
	o	Dog		o	Wishbone
	o	Egg (Broken or fried)		u	v "V"
	—	Eye			
	—	Face	D4	—	Anatomy
	u	v Fish		—	Animal
	o	Flower		u	v Animal (Prehistoric)
	u	Frog		—	Arm
	—	Head		u	Boot (Jester)
	u	Insect		—	Bug
	u	Island		o	Caterpillar
	u	Leaf		—	Cucumber
	o	Lion		o	Eel
	—	Monkey		—	Fish
	—	Monster		—	Head (Animal)
	u	Plant		u	v Head (Animal, prehistoric)
	—	Sea Animal		—	Head (Bird, except peacock or
	u	Seal			swan)
	—	Sperm		—	Head (Human)
				u	v Head (Peacock)
D3	—	Airplane		u	v Head (Swan)
	o	v Antennae (Radar or TV)		u	Horn
	u	Antennae (Insect)		—	Insect
	o	v Balloons (Weather)		u	Plant
	—	Bird		u	v Saxophone
	u	Buds		o	v Sea Horse
	—	Bug		u	Smoke
	o	Cherry Pits		u	Snail
	—	Crab		o	Snake
	u	Ear Muffs		u	Tail (Bird)
	u	Earphones		—	Tree
	—	Eyes		—	Wing
	—	Flower(s)			
	o	Governor (On motor)	D5	o	v Angel
	—	Head		—	Bug
	—	Human		u	Clothespin
	o	Instrument (Weather, for D5		u	v Crucifix
		wind velocity)		u	v Devil
	u	Instrument (Medical)		—	Face
	u	Knocker (Door)		o	Head (Animal, long-eared)
	u	Lights (Electric)		—	Head (Animal, not long-eared)
	—	Lungs		—	Head (Human)
	u	v Necklace		u	Head (Insect, with antennae)
	—	Notes (Musical)		o	v Human
	—	Ovaries		u	v Human-like Figure
	—	Parachutist		—	Insect
	o	Pawnbroker Symbol		o	Mask
	—	Rower (In boat)		u	v Tack
	—	Scissors		u	v Tooth
	o	Seed Pod (Maple)		u	Tweezers
	u	Spaceship			
	—	Stethoscope	D6	—	Anatomy
	—	Testicles		—	Animal
	u	Tongs (Ice)		o	v Anthropoids
	u	Twig		u	Bagpipes

Table A (Continued)

Location	FQ	Category	Location	FQ	Category
	–	Bat(s)		–	Sea Animal
	u	Birds		u	Seed Pod
	u	Brassiere		u	Spider
	–	Breasts		–	Turtle
	o	Bridge (Natural)		u	Weed
	–	Cloud(s)			
	u	Coral	D8	–	Animal
	u	v Dolls		u	Animal (Cartoon or prehistoric)
	u	Ducks		o	Ant
	–	Eyeglasses		u	Bee
	–	Face(s)		o	Beetle
	u	v Flowers		o	Bug
	o	v Ghosts		–	Cat
	o	v Gorillas		–	Chicken
	–	Hands		u	Chipmunk
	u	v Heads (Animal)		u	Crab
	u	Heads (Bird)		o	Dragon
	–	Heads (Human)		u	Dwarf
	u	v Humans		u	Elf
	o	v Human-like Figures		u	Emblem
	–	Insect(s)		–	Face
	–	Jaw		–	Fish
	–	Kidneys		u	Frog
	–	Lungs		u	Gnome
	o	v Monsters		–	Goat
	u	Nest		–	Head (Animal)
	–	Nose		o	Head (Animal-like creature)
	–	Ovaries		–	Head (Human)
	u	Pipes (Smoker's)		u	Head (Human-like creature)
	u	Skeletal		o	Head (Insect)
	u	Water		–	Human
				o	Insect
D7	o	Animal (Leaping)		–	Lizard
	o	Ant		u	Mask
	–	Bird		–	Monkey
	–	Clam		o	Monster (Animal)
	u	Claw		o	Monster (Human-like)
	o	Cockroach		u	Parrot
	u	Cocoon		u	Rodent
	o	Crab		u	Roots
	o	Crayfish		–	Sea Animal
	o	Deer		–	Shrimp
	–	Dog		–	Skeletal
	–	Face		–	Spider
	–	Fish		u	Unicorn
	–	Frog		–	Witch
	o	Grasshopper			
	–	Human	D9	–	Anatomy (Except intestine)
	–	Kidney		–	Animal
	u	Lobster		u	Animal-like Creature
	o	Nest		u	Bacon
	u	Preying Mantis		o	Blood
	u	Rodent (With head toward D9)		u	Bone
	o	Roots		–	Bug

Table A (Continued)

Location	FQ	Category	Location	FQ	Category
	o	Caterpillar		—	Centipede
	u	Cloud		o	Eiffel Tower
	o	Coral		—	Face
	—	Dolphin		u	Face (Monster)
	u	Eel		u	v Flower
	o	Elf		u	v Funnel
	o	Fire		o	Helmet (Science fiction)
	—	Hair		—	Human
	—	Head		o	Insects (As D8 and D14 as
	u	Human			another object)
	o	Human-like Figure		—	Intestines
	u	Insect		—	Lungs
	u	Island		u	Mask
	—	Map		o	Missile (With smoke or on pad)
	u	Map (Topographic)		u	Mistletoe
	o	Mermaid		—	Nervous System
	o	Microorganism		u	Plant
	u	Mountain Range (Often as aerial		o	Rocket (With smoke or on pad)
		view)		o	Roots
	o	Mummy		u	Skeletal
	—	Porpoise		—	Skull
	u	Sea Horse		o	Spaceship
	o	Worm		u	Statue
				o	v Torch
D10	o	Arbor		u	v Tree
	o	Arch		—	X-ray (Specific)
	—	Anatomy		u	X-ray (Unspecified)
	u	Angel			
	—	Animal	D12	u	Bean
	u	v Bird		—	Bird
	u	v Comb (Ornamental)		o	Buffalo
	o	v Door Knocker		o	Bull
	—	Flower		o	Bug
	u	Fountain		u	Claw
	—	Funnel		o	Cow
	u	v Head (Animal, horned)		u	Dog
	—	Head		—	Fish
	o	v Horns		u	Goat
	o	v Human (As D5 with other area as		u	Grasshopper
		flags, smoke, streamers, swing,		o	Insect
		etc.)		u	Lamb
	—	Insect		o	Leaf
	u	Lyre		—	Plant
	o	v Parachutist		o	Ram
	u	v Pelvis		—	Rodent
	o	Shrub(s)		u	Seed Pod
	u	v "U"		o	Unicorn
	o	Wishbone		u	Whale
D11	u	Airplane	D13	o	< Animal (Usually lying or
	—	Animal			jumping and includes a wide
	—	Broom			variety, such as bear, buffalo,
	o	Candle (With holder)			cat, dog, lion, etc.)
	u	Castle		—	Ant

Table A (Continued)

Location	FQ	Category	Location	FQ	Category
	−	Bird		−	Jellyfish
	u	Bug		o	Rose
	u	Cloud		−	Seal
	−	Face		−	Smoke
	u	Fish		−	Walrus
	−	Flower		u	Wing
	−	Head			
	−	Human	Dd21	−	Animal(s)
	u	Insect		u	v Antennae
	u	Leaf		u	Arch
	u	Mat		u	v Bird (Flying)
	o	Potato Chip		−	Boomerang
	u	Rock		o	v Butterfly (Front view)
	−	Sea Shell		u	Canyon
	u	Sponge		u	v Chevron
	−	Tree		o	v Flower (Sometimes including D6)
D14	−	Animal		−	Human(s)
	u	Artery		−	Insect
	u	Baton		u	v Keel (Boat)
	o	Bone		u	Landscape
	o	Candle		u	v Ornament
	o	Chimney		u	Reef
	u	Crowbar		−	Tuning Fork
	−	Face		u	v Wishbone
	−	Finger			
	u	Handle	DdS22	−	Anatomy
	−	Head		u	Design (Abstract)
	−	Human		−	Face
	−	Knife		−	Head
	u	Log		u	Islands
	o	Missile		−	Map (Specific)
	u	Pencil		u	Map (Unspecified)
	u	Penis		u	Underwater Scene
	o	Post			
	o	Rocket	Dd25	u	Coastline
	u	Root		−	Head (Animal)
	u	Ruler		o	Head (Human)
	u	Shotgun		o	Head (Human-like)
	o	Spinal Cord			
	u	Statue	Dd26	−	Breast
	o	Stove Pipe		−	Face (Animal)
	u	Sword		u	Face (Human, profile)
	u	Test Tube		u	Face (Human-like, profile)
	u	Vase			
			Dd27	−	Face
D15	−	Animal		u	Insect
	o	Bird		−	Seaweed
	o	Bud (Flower)		−	Trees
	u	Butterfly			
	−	Cloud	Dd28	−	Clown
	o	Flower		u	Insect
	−	Head		u	Puppet
	−	Insect		u	Roots

Table A (Continued)

Location	FQ	Category	Location	FQ	Category
DdS29	o	Buddha	Dd33	o	Acorn
	–	Face		u	Ball
	o	Fan (With D11 as handle)		–	Eye
	u	Lantern (Sometimes with D11 as handle)		–	Head
				u	Orange
	u	Paddle (With D11 as handle)		u	Sun
				o	Walnut
DdS30	–	Skeleton			
	u	Water	Dd34	u	Basket
				–	Bullet
Dd31	u	v Head (Animal)		–	Head
	u	v Head (Caterpillar)		–	Skull
	–	Head (Human)		u	Tooth
	u	v Head (Human-like)			
			Dd35	–	Animal
Dd32	–	Animal		u	People (On a cliff)
	u	Head (Animal)		–	Reptile
	–	Head (Human)		u	Trees (On a cliff)

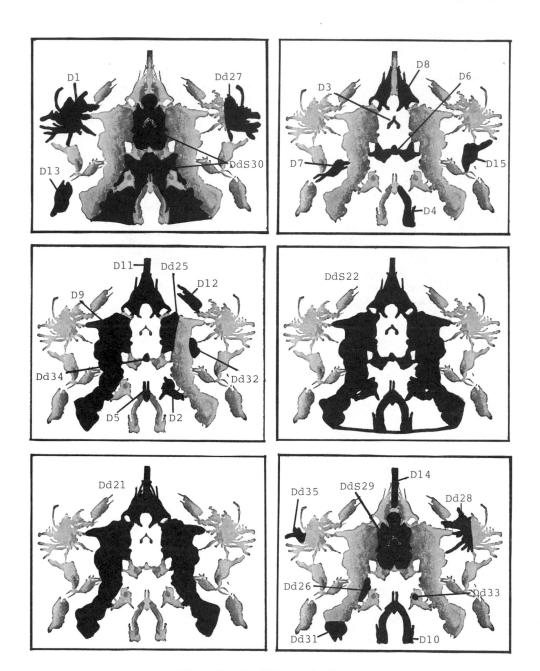

Figure 16. *D* and *Dd* Areas for Card X.

Table B. Illustrations of Responses That Should Be Coded _FQ_+

Card	Response		Inquiry
I	Ths 11 one of those exotic bf's, it has the irregular edges & the markings & the little antennae	E:	(Rpts S's resp)
		S:	Yes, well most bf's have wings that r straighter, but some of the one's that r rare have a more irregular structure like this. And there r the triangular white markings & here r the very small antennae & the little round nobs at the head & the tail is here
I	There is s.o. standg in the cntr & people dancing arnd her with large flowg capes on, thy have little caps on too	E:	(Rpts S's resp)
		S:	Ths is the person, the legs, the waist & up here r her hands, her head is not apparent, mayb she's dancing too & her head is back & on each side there r other dancers, thy hav thes long flowing capes out here & their heads r here & it almost looks lik thy all have their feet down here, together, mayb its a balancing act or dance, thy seem to hav little caps on too, c up here
IV	Ths 11 a fellow like sorta hunched over riding a bike or a motorcycle, he has a little helmet on & he's stickg his feet out forward	E:	(Rpts S's resp)
		S:	Here r his big legs, comg out this way & the cntr is the tire of the motorcycle & thes r the handlebars, c how thy come to points as thy r bent downward & ths is his body & up here is lik his head only u can only c the helmet, here
V	Ths 11 2 people, sittg on the ground resting back to back, lik mayb thy hav ski caps on & thy r covered with blankets	E:	(Rpts S's resp)
		S:	Thy r back to back, here is their heads & thes 11 tassled caps lik skiers wear sometimes & their legs r out here, c the outline of them but the bodies look too full, lik they r covered lik w a blanket, u can c the bulges lik where their arms and knees might be
VI	< Ths 11 a submarine in a battle, u can c the conning tower & the bomb blasts out in front of it	E:	(Rpts S's resp)
		S:	Here is the conning tower & the bow & ths is the waterline & the hull & out here is a blast like effect, lik it was being shelled, c the splash effect here
VII	Ths is lik 2 littl childrn on a see-saw, little girls w their pony tails bouncg up in the air	E:	(Rpts S's resp)
		S:	Yes, one here & here, c the head, the little nose & mouth & ths is the pony tail & ths is like a bar tht thy lean against & thy r lik squatting & down here is the base of the thg sorta curved upward lik the see-saw
VIII	Ths is a carousel, mayb a painting of one, lik an elaborate painting with each part detailed by a a diff color	E:	(Rpts S's resp)
		S:	Well it has the two animals on the sides, lik standg on their hind legs & this blue square part would b the machinery & the top the tent lik effect & the round base dwn here
VIII	< Ths 11 an animal that is walking over some rocks & thgs stickg up from the water to get from ths rock to ths stump here & its all reflected down here	E:	(Rpts S's resp)
		S:	Here, the pink, c the head & the legs and the tail, c the pointed nose & ths orange is lik a big boulder & he's stepping on these smaller rocks & his front paw is on ths stump that is stickg up here & the blue is the water and all of the details r reflected dwn here
IX	< Ths 11 a heavy set person chasing a littl kid up ths hill here	E:	(Rpts S's resp)
		S:	Well here is the person, it 11 a woman, sorta bulky, c the head & the body & ths is her arm & out in front of her is the kid, c the head & her body, her hair is lik flyg in the breeze & this is lik a hill, going up, mayb a sand dune caus its got the orange color, lik mayb thy r running in the sand

Table B (Continued)

Card	Response		Inquiry
X	It ll the inside of an aquarium	E:	(Rpts S's resp)
		S:	There r alot of undersea creatures. The blue & this brown both ll crabs, thy hav a lot of legs sticking out, & the green ll vegetation & the pink is lik logs or coral & ths green dwn here is lik two seahorses, c the curved heads & the yellow r lik amoeba sort of thgs, not amoeba but bigger with the rounded cntr & ths brown cb sk of shell

Table C.   Organizational (Z) Values for Each of the Ten Cards

Card	W	Type of Organizational Activity		
		Adjacent Detail	Distant Detail	White Space With Detail
I	1.0	4.0	6.0	3.5
II	4.5	3.0	5.5	4.5
III	5.5	3.0	4.0	4.5
IV	2.0	4.0	3.5	5.0
V	1.0	2.5	5.0	4.0
VI	2.5	2.5	6.0	6.5
VII	2.5	1.0	3.0	4.0
VIII	4.5	3.0	3.0	4.0
IX	5.5	2.5	4.5	5.0
X	5.5	4.0	4.5	6.0

Table D.   Best Weighted ZSum Prediction When Zf Is Known

Zf	Zest	Zf	Zest
1	*	26	88.0
2	2.5	27	91.5
3	6.0	28	95.0
4	10.0	29	98.5
5	13.5	30	102.5
6	17.0	31	105.5
7	20.5	32	109.0
8	24.0	33	112.5
9	27.5	34	116.5
10	31.0	35	120.0
11	34.5	36	123.5
12	38.0	37	127.0
13	41.5	38	130.5
14	45.5	39	134.0
15	49.0	40	137.5
16	52.5	41	141.0
17	56.0	42	144.5

Table D (Continued)

Zf	Zest	Zf	Zest
18	59.5	43	148.0
19	63.0	44	152.0
20	66.5	45	155.5
21	70.0	46	159.0
22	73.5	47	162.5
23	77.0	48	166.0
24	81.0	49	169.5
25	84.5	50	173.0

Table E.   Popular Responses Used in the Comprehensive System

Card	Location	Criterion
I	W	Bat, the response *always* involving the whole blot.
I	W	Butterfly, the response *always* involving the whole blot.
II	D1	Animal, specifically identified as bear, dog, elephant, or lamb. The response is usually the head or upper body; however, responses involving the whole animal are also coded P.
III	D9	Human figure or representations thereof such as dolls, caricatures, etc. If D1 is used as two human figures, D7 should not be reported as part of the human figure if the coding P is to be applied.
IV	W or D7	Human or human-like figure such as giant, monster, science fiction creature, etc.
V	W	Bat, the apex of the blot upright or inverted and *always* involving the whole blot.
V	W	Butterfly, the apex of the blot upright or inverted and always involving the whole blot.
VI	W or D1	Animal skin, hide, rug, or pelt.
VII	D1 or D9	Human head or face, specifically identified as female, child, or Indian, or with gender not identified. If D1 is used, the upper segment (D5) is usually identified as hair, feather, etc. If the response includes the entire D2 area, P is coded if the head or face is restricted to the D9 area. If Dd23 is included as a part of the human form, the reponse is not coded as P.
VIII	D1	Whole animal figure, usually of the canine, feline, or rodent varieties.
IX	D3	Human or human-like figure such as witch, giant, monster, science fiction creature, etc.
X	D1	Crab, with all appendages restricted to the D1 area.
X	D1	Spider, with all appendages restricted to the D1 area.

CHAPTER 12

Descriptive Statistics

This chapter contains several tables of normative and comparative data. They are important to the understanding and utilization of the test. Two, Tables G and H, contain normative data generated from the protocols of 600 nonpatient adults, stratified for geographic distribution, and partially stratified for socioeconomic level. A second pair, Tables J and K, present the normative data for 1580 nonpatient children and adolescents, ages 5 through 16, which were published originally in Volume 3 of the series on the Comprehensive System (Exner & Weiner, 1982). Those data have been updated in accord with changes in coding criteria that have evolved since 1982. They are partially stratified on the basis of geographic and socioeconomic distributions. The normative data for adults and children, used correctly, can provide the interpreter with useful baseline information from which to make comparisons.

Tables L through Q include data for the same variables listed in the normative tables for three groups of adult psychiatric subjects. They represent a random selection of approximately 25% of larger samples available in the protocol pool at the Rorschach Research Foundation. Tables L and M present data for 320 schizophrenics selected from 1289 protocols. Tables N and O include data for 210 inpatient depressives, selected from a total protocol pool of 839 subjects. Tables P and Q contain data for 200 outpatient character problems, selected from 756 protocols. Although the data have been randomly selected from larger samples, no attempt has been made at stratification except to distribute relatively equal samples of private and public hospital subjects among the two psychiatric inpatient groups. The data for the three psychiatric groups should not be regarded as "normative" in any sense. Rather, they afford a *comparative* review of these samples with the adult normative findings. Such a review can be useful in establishing a conceptual framework concerning each of the groups, but is by no means diagnostically practical.

RORSCHACH DATA AND DESCRIPTIVE STATISTICS

Several issues confront those who use normative data in professional practice. Included among those are the integrity of the normative sample and issues of cross-validation. However, a much more important issue concerns application, that is, how best to use the data. Normative data can be abused much more easily than is readily apparent, and this is especially true for Rorschach normative data. Norms are meant to provide descriptive information about groups. They offer reference points against which individual subjects can be compared. Unfortunately, in many cases, some reference points do not provide adequate information from which meaningful judgments concerning conformity or deviation can be derived. Most norms are presented in terms of arithmetic means and standard deviations. In theory, these measures of central tendency provide useful reference points that are easily interpreted. But means and standard deviations are also easily misinterpreted. While providing some information about scores, they can be misleading with regard to the nature of the distribution of scores. Thus issues concerning deviation can become clouded quite easily.

Means and standard deviations are possibly most revealing when the distribution of scores approaches the Gaussian or normal-shaped curve. As distributions deviate from normality, the possibilities increase that the mean and standard deviation will not provide a good representation of the true distribution. This is especially the case when scores fall on a J-curve, that is, one in which most of the values fall on one, two, or three data points of the curve and very few deviate from those points. The distributions for many Rorschach variables fall on J-curves, and this event considerably reduces the usefulness of mean and standard deviation data when considering those variables. In fact, the frequencies for some Rorschach variables have such a restricted range that efforts at scaling or smoothing the distribution are futile. This is not to suggest that means and standard deviations are useless when working with Rorschach data. To the contrary, they provide a very accurate picture for many variables, but their usefulness can be enhanced considerably if other methods are also used to describe frequency and score distributions.

Among the variety of descriptive statistics available, which can be useful in approaching the issue of variables that are not normally distributed, are the frequency, range, mode, skewness, and kurtosis. The frequency provides information concerning the number of subjects who have given a particular kind of response. The range describes the spread of the values for a variable, whereas the mode indicates which value appears most frequently in a distribution. The values for skewness and kurtosis concern the actual shape of the curve. The perfectly bell-shaped normal distribution will have a skewness value of .00. If the curve is positively skewed, that is, with the greater proportion of the scores being low or to the left of center, the skewness value will be positive. If the curve is negatively skewed, the value will be shown as a minus. The kurtosis value indicates something about the height of the curve. In the perfect bell-shaped distribution the kurtosis is .00. If the curve is *leptokurtic,* that is, with a piling up of scores in one region, the kurtosis will be positive, whereas if the curve is *platykurtic,* with the scores being more or less evenly distributed over a broad range, the kurtosis value will be minus.

The composite of these seven measures—mean, standard deviation, mode, range, frequency, skewness, and kurtosis—should provide a much better picture of Rorschach frequencies and scores than any one used alone, or even a composite of two or three. For example, the data in Table G show that the texture variable (FT + TF + T) has a mean of 1.16 and a standard deviation of .80. Technically, this suggests that two-thirds of the 600 subjects gave between .36 and 1.96 texture responses. Because it is impossible to give a fractional texture response, it is reasonable to postulate that those subjects all have values of 1 for texture. That postulate appears supported by the fact that the mode is 1, even though the range is 0 to 5. The frequency data show that 538, or about 90%, of the 600 subjects gave at least one texture response. The composite of these data suggests the probability of a J-curve distribution. That notion is supported by the data concerning skewness and kurtosis. The skewness is + 1.62, indicating a sharp positive distribution, whereas the kurtosis is + 6.42, indicating that a marked clustering of scores exists. They confirm the presence of a J-curve. In reality, 79% of the subjects gave one texture response, 5% gave two, 6% gave more than two, and 10% had no T answers.

In the example concerning the texture variable, the possibility of a J-curve distribution was evident early on. The Table G data for the C' variable illustrate circumstances in which such a finding is not nearly as obvious. Table G shows a mean for the C' variable as 1.31 and a standard deviation of 1.28. This suggests that two-thirds of the 600 subjects gave between .08 and 2.59 C' responses. In other words, one or two C' responses would be considered as average. But that is not consistent with other data. The mode is 1, but the range is extensive, from 1 to 10, and the frequency is 447, indicating that 25% of the sample gave *no C'*. The skewness is $+2.84$, indicating a large number of low scores, and the kurtosis is $+6.42$, revealing a large cluster of scores at one or two data points. The skewness is very marked and the kurtosis quite extreme. The fact that 25% of the sample gave no C' responses, and the mode is 1, indicates that more than half of the total sample have C' values of either 0 or 1. Adding those findings to the indications provided by the skewness and kurtosis values leaves little doubt that a J-curve exists.

The issue that remains unanswered is whether a C' value of 2 should be regarded as "average" or "deviant." Although an exact answer is not easily derived, the magnitude of the standard deviation, plus the values of the range, suggests an answer. The broad range tends to magnify the standard deviation, and the curve is markedly lopsided. Because more than half of the subjects have C' values of 0 or 1, the most conservative conclusion is that a value of 2 should be considered as "unusual," and possibly deviant.

The data in Tables H and K are included to add descriptive information concerning the distributions of scores, especially those that are used in ratios or as critical cutoffs. Some descriptive statistics can be misleading even though several measures are included among them. The distribution for the *Erlebnistypus (EB)* is probably the best illustration of this. It is entered in the Structural Summary as the Sum M on the left, and the Weighted Sum C on the right. A difference of 2 or more points is considered critical in defining coping styles. Table G shows a mean for M of 4.19 with a standard deviation of 2.04 and a mode of 3. Table G shows a mean for the Weighed Sum C of 4.23 with a standard deviation of 1.82 and a mode of 3. If one were to predict the distribution of the *EB* from these composite data, a logical conclusion is that the majority of subjects should have an *EB* in which the value on the left is similar to the value on the right—that is, having less than a 2-point difference. The means and standard deviations are very similar and the modes are identical.

The values for skewness and kurtosis offer some clue to the possibility that the overlap of the two curves is not as great as might be suspected. The distribution for M is skewed to the left and slightly flatter than a normal curve, whereas the distribution for the Weighted Sum C is skewed slightly to the right and also is flatter than a normal curve. In reality, as indicated by the data in Table H, only 23.8% of the sample have scores for Sum M and Weighted Sum C for which there is less than a 2-point difference. Slightly more than 40% have a Sum M that is 2 or more points greater than the Weighted Sum C, and 36% have a Weighted Sum C of 2 or more points greater than the Sum M.

If the descriptive measures that have been included here are applied carefully, the likelihood of interpretive error concerning the data should be reduced significantly. One added caution seems in order before describing the normative samples. Obviously, it is an error to assume that norms reflect normality. Deviations from the norm do indicate uniqueness but, often, uniqueness can be an asset rather than a liability. Some idiographic features are expected in most people. Experienced Rorschachers are well aware of records in which all of the scores important to interpretation fall well within the average range, yet the conclusion reached is that the personality is impoverished in some way. On the other hand, it is equally possible to find records in which many scores fall outside the average range, yet the interpretive conclusions find the subjects to be quite well adjusted.

NORMATIVE SAMPLES

Almost any normative sample will have limitations, and those presented here are no exceptions. The data for nonpatient adults in Tables G and H, and for the younger subjects in Tables J and K have been collected as faithfully as possible by competent examiners, working within the constraints of problems created by subject recruitment and sample sizes. It seems reasonable to argue that the data do reflect coding and scoring distributions that would be very similar to those obtained from different groups of nonpatients, provided those groups have geographic and socioeconomic distributions that are similar to those here.

All of the subjects are, in one sense or another, volunteers. None had special reasons to be examined and none have any admitted psychiatric history. Among the provisions of agreement before the testing occurred was one discounting any possibility of feedback concerning results. All were informed that the project concerned standardization of the test. The majority of the 600 adult subjects—396—volunteered through their places of work, usually under conditions of encouragement by supervisors or union leaders, and typically were provided with time away from work for the testing. An additional 162 adult subjects volunteered through social or interest organizations to which they belonged, such as the PTA, local Audubon groups, bowling leagues, and so on, and the remaining 42 were recruited through the assistance of social service agencies. None were financially reimbursed for their participation, although all received greeting cards of appreciation.

The 1580 nonpatient children were recruited through schools and social organizations such as Cub Scouts, Little Leagues, 4H Clubs, and such. They were "volunteered" by their parents and about 75% were tested in schools during school hours. Ideally, all of the sample sizes for each of the age groups should be larger. The original goal was to obtain a minimum of 150 subjects at each of the 12 age levels, but that objective was achieved for only three of the 12 groups.

THE ADULT SAMPLE

As noted earlier, this sample of 600 was randomly selected from a larger group of 1225 adult nonpatient records that were available. The final selection was stratified so that 120 subjects were choosen from each of five geographic areas—Northeast, South, Midwest, Southwest, and West. Although the population of the United States is not equally distributed among those regions, it seemed more important to avoid loading the sample from any given area. Attempts were made to insure equal numbers of male and female subjects for each geographic subgroup; however, this was not possible because the total pool contained more female than male subjects. The most marked deviation from an even gender split occurred for the Southwest subgroup, which contains 71 females and 49 males. Overall, the sample contains 336 females and 264 males, with an age range of 18 to 64. The mean age is 29.18 (SD = 8.08), and 63% of the sample are between the ages of 18 and 39. It includes 498 whites and 102 nonwhites.

The subjects in the sample average 13.15 years of completed education with a range from 8 to 19. Fifty-one subjects completed between 8 and 11 years of education, 199 are high school graduates, 201 have completed between 1 and 3 years of higher education, 133 are college graduates, and 18 have completed 1 or more years of graduate school.

The distribution of the 1970 U.S. Census was used in an attempt to achieve some partial stratification for urban-suburban-rural residence, and for socioeconomic level in selecting subjects. Unfortunately, the total pool of 1225 was much too small to permit exacting selections for these variables. Therefore, 219 (36.5%) are from urban areas, 237 (39.5%) are from suburban areas, and 143 (23.8%) are from rural areas. The classification of socioeconomic levels was defined using a nine-point variation of the Hollingshead and Redlich scale. It includes three subdivisions for each of the categories: upper, middle, and lower. Essentially, it is a scheme of classification based mainly on income. Thus SES 2 represents the middle-upper class, SES 5 the middle-middle class, and SES 9 is for the lower-lower class and restricted to subjects exclusively on public assistance. The SES distribution, by age groupings, is shown in Table F.

Table F.   Distribution by Age and SES for 600 Nonpatient Adults

Age Group	SES							
	2	3	4	5	6	7	8	9
18 to 25	0	5	9	24	19	15	18	21
26 to 33	2	8	11	31	21	22	26	16
34 to 40	7	8	17	26	28	23	16	7
41 to 48	5	7	16	23	17	17	3	8
49 to 56	3	12	9	26	18	9	2	0
57 to 64	2	0	5	18	18	2	0	0
Totals	19	40	67	148	121	88	65	52

It will be noted from examination of Table F that no SES class 1 subjects (upper-upper) are included, and that the majority (56%) are from the three middle-class groups, 4, 5, and 6. The three lower-class groups comprise 35% of the sample, whereas the two upper-class groups represent slightly less than 10% of the sample. A basic multivariate model was used to search out possible differences among scores between the three broad categories— upper, middle, and lower—and among several pairs of the subcategories. The only consistently significant difference found is when the SES 9 (lower-lower) group is compared with other individual subcategories. Those records have a significantly higher average Lambda than do the records of any other SES subcategory. Consequently, they also have lower mean values for most of the other determinants. Interestingly, the inclusion of the SES 9 group in the sample does not alter the means and standard deviations for any of the 69 variables in Table G significantly. Apparently this is because the N for the group is modest (52), representing only 8% of the sample. It is also important to note that the distribution of scores for the SES 8 group (middle-lower) does not differ significantly from the other SES groups, with the exception of SES 9. Similarly, when SES groups 4, 5, and 6 are collectively compared with the composite of SES groups 7, 8, and 9, no significant differences (other than those that can be discarded as spurious) are found.

A series of parametric and nonparametric analyses was calculated to determine whether the distributions of scores for the 498 white subjects differ significantly from those for the 102 nonwhite subjects. The nonwhite subjects did give a significantly larger number of chromatic color responses ($p < .02$), and this creates a significant difference among the groups in the average Weighted Sum C ($p < .05$). As might be suspected from these data, the nonwhites also show a larger proportion, although not statistically significant, of *EB*'s in which the right side value is greater than the left side value. Other than this one exception, the two groups did not differ significantly for the distributions of any other variables.

Table G. Descriptive Statistics for 69 Rorschach Variables for 600 Nonpatient Adults

Variable	Mean	SD	Mode	Min	Max	Freq	SK	KU
R	22.57	5.54	23	10	39	600	2.81	0.70
P	6.66	1.66	6	2	11	600	−0.62	−0.16
W	8.58	2.66	9	2	20	600	3.67	5.49
D	12.59	4.74	14	0	24	594	−1.85	−0.01
Dd	1.73	2.74	0	0	14	398	8.23	9.53
S	1.84	1.66	1	0	9	540	3.58	5.85
DQ+	6.90	2.25	6	2	14	600	0.77	−0.06
DQv/+	0.33	0.62	0	0	2	152	1.03	1.53
DQo	13.66	4.89	15	3	33	600	3.36	2.89
DQv	1.66	1.49	0	0	8	443	1.62	1.88
FQ+	0.87	0.85	0	0	4	351	0.37	−1.03
FQo	17.19	4.22	18	5	28	600	−1.18	0.44
FQu	2.94	2.12	3	0	12	557	3.92	5.75
FQ−	1.30	1.10	1	0	8	499	2.30	7.92
M	4.19	2.04	3	0	10	597	1.11	−0.41
M^a	2.82	1.60	2	0	8	586	0.50	−0.48
M^p	1.35	0.99	1	0	5	490	0.82	1.23
M−	0.09	0.45	0	0	4	38	3.43	72.97
FM	3.51	1.51	4	1	9	600	1.40	1.73
m	1.25	1.06	1	0	6	451	1.02	1.60
a (Active)	6.25	2.30	5	2	13	600	1.52	0.05
p (Passive)	2.70	1.69	3	0	9	548	1.26	0.85
FC	3.87	2.06	5	0	9	566	0.16	−0.55
CF	2.07	1.21	3	0	5	537	−0.02	−0.75
C+Cn	0.12	0.43	0	0	2	53	1.51	11.15
Wgt Sum C	4.23	1.82	3	0	8	597	−0.17	−0.94
FC'+C'F+C'	1.31	1.28	1	0	10	447	2.84	10.18
FT+TF+T	1.16	0.80	1	0	5	538	1.62	6.42
FV+VF+V	0.48	0.93	0	0	5	163	1.94	4.29
FY+YF+Y	0.98	1.60	0	0	10	280	4.28	8.65
Sum Shad'g	3.81	3.36	2	0	23	583	7.46	6.62
Fr+rF	0.12	0.46	0	0	4	47	2.29	29.07
(2)	8.44	2.65	8	1	17	600	0.11	0.78
FD	1.15	1.09	1	0	8	448	2.46	8.99
F	8.17	3.27	8	1	18	600	1.10	0.51

Table G (Continued)

Variable	Mean	SD	Mode	Min	Max	Freq	SK	KU
Zf	11.22	2.96	11	5	23	600	3.10	3.02
Zd	0.84	3.11	+1	−8.5	9	600	0.28	0.69
EA	8.28	2.56	9	1.5	15	600	−0.56	−0.40
es	8.71	4.68	6	3	31	600	7.33	3.84
D Score	0.02	1.83	0	−10	3	600	−4.00	6.22
ADJ D	0.31	1.37	0	−6	4	600	−2.21	3.30
Afr	0.66	0.19	0.50	0.19	1.29	600	0.08	0.36
$3r + (2)/R$	0.39	0.11	0.32	0.03	0.84	600	0.01	2.91
Lambda	0.59	0.28	0.67	0.04	2.25	600	0.53	6.82
Blends	5.02	2.21	5	1	12	600	0.92	−0.13
Col-Sh $B1$	0.51	0.69	0	0	4	254	1.06	3.48
$X + \%$	0.80	0.09	0.86	0.48	1.00	600	−0.11	2.04
$F + \%$	0.76	0.17	1.00	0	1.00	600	−0.13	1.27
$X - \%$	0.06	0.05	0.04	0	0.43	499	0.16	14.38
$A \%$	0.45	0.10	0.42	0.15	0.92	600	0.09	2.60
$Prim\ Cont$	7.13	1.75	8	2	11	600	−1.15	0.22
$Pure\ H$	3.07	2.00	2	0	9	578	2.12	0.58
All H Cont	5.12	1.86	4	0	10	597	0.56	−0.27
S-Constell	2.07	2.11	0	0	9	433	2.31	0.43
$SCZI$	0.40	0.78	0	0	4	161	1.81	2.49
$DEPI$	0.95	1.08	0	0	4	322	0.95	−0.13
DV	0.36	1.20	0	0	4	101	2.79	11.43
DR	0.51	1.31	0	0	4	206	2.02	5.84
$INCOM$	0.54	0.79	0	0	5	258	1.90	8.45
$FABCOM$	0.18	0.56	0	0	4	70	2.20	17.64
$ALOG$	0.09	0.35	0	0	3	43	1.72	30.16
$CONTAM$	0.01	0.07	0	0	1	3	0.99	194.35
$SUM6\ SP\ SC$	1.64	2.09	1	0	11	449	6.72	14.55
$WSUM6\ SP\ SC$	3.96	1.76	2	0	23	449	5.34	8.13
AG	0.72	0.84	0	0	4	304	0.83	4.42
$CONFAB$	0.00	—	0	0	0	0	—	—
CP	0.01	0.11	0	0	1	7	0.98	80.45
MOR	0.70	0.94	0	0	6	283	1.67	4.80
PER	1.06	1.01	1	0	5	406	1.25	2.38
PSV	0.05	0.22	0	0	1	32	0.89	13.75

Table H   Frequencies and Percentages Concerning Directionality for 18 Structural Variables for 600 Nonpatient Adults

Variable	Freq	%
FR Style		
M − WSUM $C \geqslant 2$ (Introversive)	241	40.1
M − WSUM $C = +1.5$ to -1.5 (Ambient)	143	23.8
WSUM C − $M \geqslant 2$ (Extratensive)	216	36.0
EA − *es Differences:* Overload		
D SCORE < 0	126	21.0
ADJ D SCORE < 0	97	16.2
Zd Score $> +3.0$ (Overincorporator)	107	17.8
Zd Score < -3.0 (Underincorporator)	42	7.0
Form Quality Deviations		
$X + \% < .70$	60	10.0
$F + \% < .70$	157	26.1
$X - \% > .15$	20	3.3
S-Constellation $\geqslant 8$	11	1.8
Schizophrenia Index		
$SCZI = 5$	0	—
$SCZI = 4$	6	1.0
Depression Index		
$DEPI = 5$	0	—
$DEPI = 4$	14	2.3
Miscellaneous Variables		
$FM + m <$ Sum Shading	117	19.5
$a < p$	17	2.8
$M^a < M^p$	71	11.8
$3r + (2)/R < .30$	56	9.3
$Afr < .55$	157	26.1
Lambda $\geqslant 1.5$	8	1.3
Pure $H < 2$	118	19.7
Isolation Index $> \frac{1}{4}R$	85	14.2

CHILDREN AND ADOLESCENTS

Three guidelines were applied in selecting the samples included in the normative data for children and adolescents: (1) that he samples at each age would contain enough subjects to be psychometrically meaningful, (2) that relatively equal numbers of males and females would be included at each age, and (3) that the samples would be stratified, to the extent possible, on the basis of socioeconomic level and geographic distribution. The 1970 U.S. Census figures were used as a reference for the stratification. Optimally, each age group should consist of 75 males and 75 females, of which 65% would be drawn from urban and suburban areas and 35% from rural areas, with 16% from SES 2 and 3, 54% from SES 4, 5, and 6, and 30% from SES 7, 8, and 9.

The final total sample does not always meet these optimal objectives, but they are approximated reasonably well for several age groups. The 1580 records were collected by 47 examiners, for an average of 13 records each. Eleven examiners did collect between 20 and 23 records each, but no examiner collected fewer than eight protocols. Eighty-four school districts are represented in the sample, with no one district yielding more than 37 subjects, and none contributing more than 11 records for any given age level. The protocols of the 229 minority subjects were collected almost exclusively from the Northeast, Southwest, and West. Table I provides the frequency data, by age group, for each of the variables used in attempting to stratify the sample. The objective of 150 subjects per age was achieved for only three groups—9, 11, and 16—but among the 11-year-olds, the lower two socioeconomic levels are not adequately represented. SES 2 is underrepresented at almost every age.

Table I   Distribution of Demographic Variables, by Age, for 1580 Nonpatient Children and Adolescents

| | Age Groups | | | | | | | | | | | |
	5	6	7	8	9	10	11	12	13	14	15	16
Total Sample	110	105	145	140	150	130	150	140	125	115	120	150
Male	51	48	74	72	74	61	75	63	59	47	60	75
Female	59	57	71	68	76	69	75	77	66	68	60	75
White	94	92	124	122	124	109	126	120	110	99	107	127
Minority	16	13	21	18	26	21	24	20	15	16	13	23
SES Levels												
2	10	4	8	6	8	10	11	9	6	4	7	9
3	19	16	21	18	17	17	19	16	14	13	15	18
4	21	22	26	21	29	24	28	23	21	19	21	24
5	17	16	24	30	27	21	33	27	29	25	14	23
6	19	15	21	14	24	26	22	24	19	18	19	26
7	11	14	15	17	19	13	19	16	22	14	21	21
8	7	9	15	20	14	9	8	11	8	10	14	13
9	6	9	15	14	12	11	6	14	6	12	9	16
Geographic Distribution												
Urban	38	30	42	38	50	32	48	39	40	27	47	49
Suburban	34	36	49	51	51	44	54	59	46	49	41	53
Rural	38	39	54	51	49	54	48	42	39	39	32	48
Northeast	23	31	41	30	35	42	38	36	33	22	30	52
Southeast	18	10	23	19	20	14	21	18	15	27	12	18
Midwest	30	28	25	18	32	31	31	28	41	17	29	36
Southwest	19	17	18	29	28	17	22	29	10	23	20	19
West	20	19	38	44	35	29	38	29	26	26	29	35

As with the adult sample, a series of multivariate and nonparametric analyses was employed to search for differences by sex, SES, or geographic distribution. In that each of the potential cells, as illustrated in Table I, contains relatively small N's, except for gender, contiguous cells were often combined to make the analyses more meaningful. For example, sample sizes prohibit any direct comparison between SES 2 and SES 9. Thus SES 2 and 3 were combined and compared with SES 8 plus 9. Many differences were discovered but were not consistent across age groups. For instance, females of ages 5 to 7 gave significantly more chromatic color responses than the males of those ages. Similarly, children of both sexes in the age range 10 through 14, from the Southwest and West, gave significantly more $CF + C$ than the children of the same ages from any other region. Children from the Northeast and Midwest, at ages 8, 10, and 11, gave significantly more C' responses than the children from any other region. Differences of this variety are probably spurious, but also might be explored to some logical conclusion.

The largest number of significant differences were found when the combined SES groups $8 + 9$ were compared with other groups. Children of ages 5 through 11 from those groups gave significantly fewer M responses and significantly more F answers than any other group or combination of groups. For ages 7, 9, and 10, children from SES $8 + 9$ have significantly lower egocentricity indices than children in SES groups 2 through 5. For ages 13 through 15, children from SES $8 + 9$ gave significantly fewer W responses and more DQV answers than any of the other groups. Interestingly, when the SES groups were combined into three larger groups— $2 + 3$, $4 + 5 + 6$, and $7 + 8 + 9$—most of the differences disappeared. This finding is especially important, because the majority of the minority group children fall into the SES groups 6, 7, and 8 at most of the age levels. The absence of more differences suggests that the samples, by age, are reasonably homogeneous, and as such constitute a useful normative base.

Table J   Descriptive Statistics for 69 Rorschach Variables for 1580 Nonpatient Children and Adolescents, by Age

Variable	Mean	SD	Age 5 − N = 110 Mode	Min	Max	Freq	SK	KU
R	15.27	5.54	14	10	26	110	3.41	0.87
P	3.54	3.72	3	1	8	110	−0.71	−0.07
W	9.21	3.78	9	2	17	110	1.64	2.29
D	5.63	2.07	6	1	18	110	−0.57	−0.43
Dd	0.48	0.32	0	0	4	11	6.13	21.48
S	0.74	0.77	0	0	5	52	4.18	9.57
DQ+	2.61	1.74	1	0	6	91	2.38	6.47
DQv/+	0.69	0.84	0	0	3	61	5.59	11.77
DQo	7.18	3.64	6	2	16	110	2.63	2.26
DQv	4.84	2.34	4	2	11	110	0.19	1.08
FQ+	0	—	0	0	0	0	—	—
FQo	12.31	3.15	11	5	16	110	−1.24	−0.26
FQu	2.09	2.89	2	0	7	89	2.87	6.31
FQ−	0.71	0.81	0	0	4	61	4.10	9.06
M	0.83	0.60	1	0	5	93	4.16	8.67
Ma	0.69	0.77	1	0	5	93	5.02	10.08
Mp	0.24	0.64	0	0	2	19	7.37	22.16
M−	0.06	0.81	0	0	1	18	9.11	24.09
FM	2.84	1.23	2	0	9	106	2.49	3.96
m	0.16	0.13	0	0	2	7	4.81	31.22
a	2.64	1.30	2	1	11	110	2.93	5.71
p	1.14	0.69	1	0	4	71	4.26	8.91
FC	0.52	0.84	0	0	4	52	4.19	9.83
CF	1.91	0.65	1	0	5	104	3.06	1.89
C+Cn	0.92	0.70	1	0	3	77	7.19	10.24
Wgt Sum C	3.54	1.71	3.5	0	9.5	110	2.96	1.81
FC'+C'F+C'	0.56	0.47	0	0	3	56	5.67	9.38
FT+TF+T	0.81	0.44	1	0	3	101	3.43	6.94
FV+VF+V	0	—	0	0	0	0	—	—
FY+YF+Y	0.38	0.33	0	0	2	21	6.78	19.04
Sum Shad'g	1.64	1.09	1	0	4	103	4.71	7.31
Fr+rF	0.74	0.51	0	0	2	54	6.16	16.28
(2)	7.33	3.31	6	3	14	110	1.01	−0.29
FD	0.02	0.02	0	0	1	16	9.36	31.84
F	8.18	2.91	8	4	16	110	0.46	1.13

Table J (Continued)

Variable	Mean	SD	Mode	Min	Max	Freq	SK	KU
Zf	8.26	3.37	7	1	14	110	2.06	2.71
Zd	− 1.14	2.61	1.5	9.5	6	110	1.27	0.39
EA	3.96	1.89	4	1	8.5	110	− 0.28	0.79
es	5.03	2.11	3	1	14	110	2.97	3.27
D Score	− 1.06	1.02	− 1	− 3	3	110	1.31	5.27
ADJ D	− 1.01	0.78	− 1	− 3	3	110	0.89	6.23
Afr	1.07	0.31	0.88	0.38	1.59	110	2.09	− 0.84
3r+(2)/R	0.61	0.15	0.56	0.28	1.00	110	2.56	− 0.49
Lambda	1.14	0.39	0.96	0.37	3.15	110	2.91	4.31
Blends	1.89	0.73	2	0	7	88	3.17	3.93
Col-Sh *B*1	0.37	0.21	0	0	2	17	1.87	9.39
X+%	0.81	0.11	0.80	0.45	1.00	110	0.23	2.64
F+%	0.83	0.12	0.78	0.33	1.00	110	0.49	3.10
X−%	0.05	0.04	0.03	0	0.25	61	1.03	12.41
A%	0.54	0.13	0.48	0.28	1.00	110	2.17	− 0.19
Prim Cont	4.23	2.13	4	2	11	110	0.39	2.19
Pure H	1.61	0.87	1	0	4	93	2.17	5.86
All *H* Cont	3.38	1.34	3	0	7	95	3.01	3.21
S-Constell (Child)	2.86	2.01	3	0	6	66	3.87	6.17
SCZI	0.73	0.84	1	0	4	42	4.67	7.93
DEPI	1.06	0.78	1	0	4	79	0.27	6.57
DV	1.03	1.21	1	0	3	101	0.07	9.17
DR	1.61	1.32	2	0	4	107	− 0.48	3.26
INCOM	1.14	0.68	1	0	4	88	1.81	6.72
FABCOM	0.64	0.29	0	0	3	67	2.39	9.05
ALOG	1.21	0.49	1	0	4	102	0.88	3.16
CONTAM	0.01	0.09	0	0	1	3	8.84	34.69
SUM6 SP SC	5.84	2.76	4	1	11	110	1.07	− 0.19
WSUM6 SP SC	13.72	5.02	12	2	25	110	1.44	− 0.36
AG	1.23	0.74	1	0	6	93	3.25	6.97
CONFAB	0.02	0.02	0	0	1	2	0.21	46.38
CP	0.03	0.12	0	0	2	5	0.35	27.93
MOR	1.46	0.86	1	0	4	102	1.31	8.97
PER	4.38	0.86	2	0	11	93	3.81	3.01
PSV	0.89	0.62	0	0	4	53	2.99	8.71

Table J (Continued)

Variable	Mean	SD	Age 6 − N = 105 Mode	Min	Max	Freq	SK	KU
R	16.13	4.33	15	10	25	105	4.01	1.06
P	4.24	3.51	4	2	9	105	0.51	−0.62
W	8.63	3.11	7	0	14	104	0.96	1.08
D	6.09	2.71	7	3	16	105	−1.22	−0.14
Dd	1.39	0.78	1	0	4	61	4.87	13.16
S	1.43	0.74	1	0	5	68	4.39	8.82
$DQ+$	2.64	1.87	2	0	8	96	3.21	5.27
$DQv/+$	1.33	1.54	0	0	4	50	6.87	10.16
DQo	7.85	3.73	7	4	17	105	0.89	0.94
DQv	4.31	2.53	3	1	8	105	2.23	1.46
$FQ+$	0.02	0.04	0	0	1	4	7.72	28.35
FQo	13.85	4.41	13	9	17	105	0.33	−0.27
FQu	1.25	1.01	1	0	6	54	1.89	8.46
$FQ-$	1.03	0.71	0	0	4	72	3.86	5.13
M	1.43	0.57	1	0	4	101	2.99	4.62
M^a	1.13	0.67	1	0	4	99	3.03	3.23
M^p	0.30	0.41	0	0	2	17	7.26	14.91
$M-$	0.13	0.08	0	0	1	11	8.89	20.06
FM	2.94	1.58	2	0	8	101	2.86	5.62
m	0.28	0.51	0	0	2	19	8.36	9.48
a	3.31	1.39	3	0	8	103	2.93	5.34
p	1.27	0.74	1	0	2	70	1.08	12.64
FC	0.84	0.64	1	0	3	71	1.88	8.59
CF	2.62	1.36	2	0	6	102	−0.24	6.11
$C+Cn$	0.74	0.58	0	0	3	52	2.86	6.29
Wgt Sum C	4.92	2.13	3.5	0.5	8.5	105	1.59	0.69
$FC'+C'F+C'$	0.62	0.54	1	0	3	66	3.16	8.72
$FT+TF+T$	0.97	0.58	1	0	2	94	2.94	7.03
$FV+VF+V$	0	—	0	0	0	0	—	—
$FY+YF+Y$	0.24	0.36	0	0	2	21	4.04	9.11
Sum Shad'g	1.74	0.86	1	0	4	105	2.29	5.38
$Fr+rF$	0.72	0.48	0	0	3	49	2.18	4.73
(2)	8.62	2.38	9	1	15	105	−0.18	1.01
FD	0.18	0.23	0	0	1	19	8.90	21.63
F	7.72	3.58	7	3	14	105	0.87	0.46

Table J (Continued—Age 6)

Variable	Mean	SD	Mode	Min	Max	Freq	SK	KU
Zf	9.86	3.53	8	1	14	105	2.94	2.17
Zd	−1.23	2.71	−1.5	−8.5	5	105	3.08	0.18
EA	4.99	2.01	4	0	9	105	−0.58	−0.07
es	5.14	2.34	4	0	11	105	1.48	1.68
D Score	−0.44	1.83	−1	−2	2	105	1.37	1.12
ADJ D	−0.24	1.69	−1	−2	3	105	1.23	1.48
Afr	0.91	0.24	0.83	0.25	1.75	105	3.04	0.89
3r+(2)/R	0.60	0.13	0.55	0.18	1.00	105	2.37	−0.18
Lambda	0.91	0.28	0.86	0.26	4.15	105	0.91	−0.71
Blends	3.12	1.69	3	0	5	83	2.77	3.10
Col-Sh B1	0.41	0.48	0	0	2	29	1.89	8.79
X+%	0.86	0.11	0.82	0.38	1.00	105	1.13	1.24
F+%	0.89	0.09	0.80	0.33	1.00	105	1.06	2.75
X−%	0.06	0.08	0.06	0	0.22	72	−0.21	8.91
A%	0.57	0.09	0.50	0.20	1.00	105	2.16	0.31
Prim Cont	5.06	2.18	4	2	10	105	1.83	2.02
Pure H	2.03	0.87	1	0	5	93	2.45	4.89
All H Cont	3.86	1.59	4	0	6	94	2.12	2.82
S-Constell (Child)	2.01	1.47	2	0	7	54	1.86	5.21
SCZI	0.89	1.23	1	0	4	61	−0.37	4.98
DEPI	1.23	0.85	1	0	4	48	3.14	7.01
DV	1.32	0.78	1	0	5	78	2.69	1.44
DR	0.99	0.72	1	0	6	70	−0.26	3.79
INCOM	1.69	0.93	2	0	5	101	1.06	6.29
FABCOM	0.73	0.44	0	0	4	59	3.66	5.28
ALOG	1.43	0.72	2	0	4	86	−0.34	3.11
CONTAM	0	—	0	0	0	0	—	—
SUM6 SP SC	6.07	2.35	3	1	9	105	2.71	7.21
WSUM6 SP SC	14.41	5.96	11	2	30	105	1.03	−0.63
AG	1.03	0.85	1	0	4	100	0.73	4.12
CONFAB	0.01	0.01	0	0	1	1	0.03	31.97
CP	0.14	0.12	0	0	1	11	0.18	21.33
MOR	1.08	1.02	1	0	6	99	0.57	8.46
PER	4.07	2.23	4	0	6	95	0.77	4.24
PSV	0.73	0.58	0	0	3	38	4.04	8.87

Table J (Continued)

Variable	Mean	SD	Age 7 − N = 145 Mode	Min	Max	Freq	SK	KU
R	18.33	4.72	17	11	29	145	1.94	0.44
P	4.04	1.82	5	2	9	145	0.84	−0.71
W	9.12	3.08	8	4	17	145	2.91	3.97
D	7.61	2.39	8	3	20	145	−0.70	−0.11
Dd	1.57	0.84	0	0	4	79	5.19	8.03
S	2.13	0.93	1	0	6	131	4.21	4.06
DQ+	3.90	1.77	3	0	8	122	2.16	3.29
DQv/+	1.12	1.04	0	0	4	69	3.99	5.89
DQo	9.73	3.62	9	4	24	145	1.26	2.36
DQv	4.03	2.53	3	0	7	145	2.84	4.29
FQ+	0.52	0.69	0	0	3	13	6.13	16.29
FQo	14.83	2.93	15	11	26	145	−0.81	0.27
FQu	1.89	1.51	1	0	6	133	4.92	4.62
FQ−	1.18	0.73	0	0	5	77	6.07	7.27
M	1.72	0.64	1	0	4	133	2.48	3.67
M^a	1.38	0.58	1	0	4	133	3.16	4.02
M^p	0.44	0.37	0	0	2	41	6.29	8.15
M−	0.57	0.27	0	0	1	23	7.13	9.84
FM	3.64	1.78	3	0	10	140	1.24	1.67
m	0.31	0.28	0	0	2	21	6.77	9.03
a	3.92	1.62	4	0	10	144	1.09	−1.16
p	1.37	0.56	0	0	4	78	4.16	1.81
FC	1.21	0.54	1	0	5	116	3.89	4.02
CF	2.64	1.29	3	0	7	138	2.08	−0.16
C+Cn	0.61	0.33	0	0	4	69	5.01	6.62
Wgt Sum C	4.13	2.32	4	0	11.5	143	0.78	1.26
FC'+C'F+C'	0.78	0.63	1	0	4	117	−0.06	4.18
FT+TF+T	0.82	0.49	1	0	3	119	1.04	5.44
FV+VF+V	0.01	0.07	0	0	1	2	14.38	39.68
FY+YF+Y	0.46	0.38	0	0	3	47	5.21	7.01
Sum Shad'g	1.83	0.84	2	0	7	126	−0.62	6.12
Fr+rF	0.74	0.41	0	0	5	71	2.11	5.93
(2)	9.14	2.72	10	3	19	145	−0.28	1.03
FD	0.32	0.24	0	0	2	41	3.95	11.06
F	8.73	2.53	8	2	15	145	0.81	0.94

Table J (Continued—Age 7)

Variable	Mean	SD	Mode	Min	Max	Freq	SK	KU
Zf	10.57	2.73	9	3	15	145	2.81	3.11
Zd	−0.94	2.41	−1 0	−9 0	6	145	−0.89	−0.08
EA	4.98	2.89	4.5	0	11	145	−0.75	−0.06
es	5.78	2.03	5	1	16	145	1.09	3.67
D Score	−0.32	2.17	−1	−3	3	145	2.47	2.04
ADJ D	−0.19	2.60	−1	−3	3	145	2.26	1.99
Afr	0.84	0.18	0.78	0.20	1.20	145	3.07	0.26
3r+(2)/R	0.61	0.14	0.60	0.15	0.96	145	1.38	3.62
Lambda	0.91	0.25	0.95	0.22	2.75	145	−0.41	1.16
Blends	3.48	1.69	4	3	7	145	2.13	3.42
Col-Sh *B*1	0.51	0.48	0	0	3	38	3.27	5.13
X+%	0.84	0.12	0.78	0.33	1.00	145	0.73	6.91
F+%	0.86	0.11	0.75	0.20	1.00	145	2.83	4.77
X−%	0.07	0.53	0.04	0	0.33	86	1.66	2.86
A%	0.51	0.12	0.45	0.15	0.87	145	1.81	0.28
Prim Cont	6.03	2.11	5	2	12	145	1.26	3.78
Pure H	1.89	1.12	1	0	8	134	3.00	5.34
All *H* Cont	4.12	2.34	4	0	10	136	0.93	2.89
S-Constell (Child)	1.96	1.23	0	0	7	73	2.38	5.89
SCZI	1.01	0.80	1	0	5	89	0.67	3.29
DEPI	1.33	1.23	2	0	5	79	2.07	5.22
DV	1.42	0.73	1	0	5	91	1.68	3.04
DR	1.01	0.58	1	0	3	64	0.33	4.26
INCOM	1.12	0.59	1	0	3	114	0.71	6.91
FABCOM	0.79	0.52	1	0	3	101	−0.55	5.78
ALOG	0.93	0.68	2	0	4	106	−0.38	2.94
CONTAM	0.01	0.01	0	0	1	1	0.08	16.29
SUM6 SP SC	5.27	2.81	5	2	11	145	1.79	2.95
WSUM6 SP SC	13.36	5.39	10	4	36	145	2.02	−0.78
AG	0.98	0.81	1	0	7	102	2.41	5.83
CONFAB	0.01	0.01	0	0	1	1	0.12	31.94
CP	0.01	0.03	0	0	1	3	0.07	24.28
MOR	1.24	0.62	1	0	5	112	1.53	10.03
PER	3.61	1.39	3	0	6	122	1.31	2.84
PSV	0.41	0.28	0	0	2	40	1.77	12.08

Table J (Continued)

Variable	Mean	SD	Age 8 − N = 140 Mode	Min	Max	Freq	SK	KU
R	19.61	4.63	19	12	30	140	2.11	0.56
P	4.62	2.14	4	2	9	140	0.89	− 0.14
W	8.92	3.11	8	3	13	140	2.17	4.79
D	9.23	3.18	10	4	19	140	− 0.38	− 0.14
Dd	1.49	1.02	1	0	6	129	6.13	7.29
S	1.74	0.68	2	0	5	97	− 1.09	4.96
DQ +	4.08	2.33	3	0	8	122	1.85	3.97
DQv/ +	2.03	1.14	1	0	4	81	3.46	5.19
DQo	10.63	3.64	10	6	24	140	3.59	1.79
DQv	3.89	1.96	3	1	7	140	4.06	4.29
FQ +	0.48	0.77	0	0	2	7	7.89	13.71
FQo	16.13	3.98	15	10	28	140	− 1.26	0.09
FQu	2.01	0.97	2	0	4	131	2.27	5.84
FQ −	0.99	0.68	0	0	6	101	1.63	6.27
M	1.93	0.83	1	0	7	127	2.11	4.42
M^a	1.23	0.86	1	0	7	126	3.09	5.12
M^p	0.71	0.41	0	0	3	37	3.38	5.74
M −	0.51	0.38	0	0	4	26	4.92	13.61
FM	3.44	1.81	3	1	10	140	1.89	7.31
m	0.59	0.44	0	0	3	68	5.11	11.21
a	3.82	1.19	3	1	9	140	3.06	4.11
p	2.08	0.88	0	0	4	71	3.99	6.41
FC	1.33	0.58	1	0	4	123	2.67	4.17
CF	2.72	1.22	3	0	6	136	− 0.16	1.94
C+Cn	0.41	0.33	0	0	3	49	4.76	6.23
Wgt Sum C	4.84	2.06	4	2.0	9.5	140	− 0.31	0.66
FC'+C'F+C'	0.73	0.63	1	0	5	91	− 0.46	4.62
FT+TF+T	0.93	0.40	1	0	3	116	− 0.18	7.71
FV+VF+V	0.01	0.06	0	0	1	7	7.38	26.98
FY+YF+Y	0.28	0.41	0	0	2	44	5.12	6.82
Sum Shad'g	1.74	0.89	2	0	9	118	− 0.07	5.49
Fr+rF	0.70	0.47	0	0	2	70	1.38	9.61
(2)	8.69	3.13	9	2	19	140	0.17	0.83
FD	0.61	0.29	0	0	3	74	1.49	7.34
F	9.11	2.68	8	2	22	140	1.94	0.80

Table J (Continued—Age 8)

Variable	Mean	SD	Mode	Min	Max	Freq	SK	KU
Zf	10.77	2.94	10	0	15	138	2.31	0.37
Zd	−0.67	2.08	−10	−10.5	6	140	1.68	−0.37
EA	5.23	2.50	4.5	0.5	10	140	1.08	−0.81
es	5.89	2.39	6	1	13	140	0.46	2.83
D Score	−0.68	2.16	−1	−4	3	140	1.89	2.50
ADJ D	−0.38	2.28	−1	−3	3	140	1.98	3.02
Afr	0.79	0.15	0.78	0.10	0.90	140	1.39	0.07
3r+(2)/R	0.56	0.13	0.50	0.18	0.92	140	1.32	1.48
Lambda	0.86	0.24	0.88	0.15	2.25	140	0.52	2.39
Blends	3.91	1.89	3	0	7	126	3.28	5.12
Col-Sh *B*1	0.47	0.22	0	0	2	37	3.04	4.87
X+%	0.85	0.14	0.80	0.33	1.00	140	0.95	3.56
F+%	0.85	0.16	0.80	0.25	1.00	140	1.73	4.25
X−%	0.08	0.05	0	0	0.30	77	2.01	3.11
A%	0.53	0.10	0.46	0.30	0.72	140	2.41	2.61
Prim Cont	5.89	2.18	6	3	11	140	−0.33	2.79
Pure H	2.18	1.24	2	0	5	109	1.92	2.65
All *H* Cont	4.47	2.19	5	0	8	132	−0.07	1.21
S-Constell (Child)	1.41	1.18	0	0	7	71	2.47	4.63
SCZI	0.89	0.78	1	0	4	81	0.13	4.28
DEPI	0.74	0.83	0	0	4	58	1.79	5.06
DV	0.68	0.51	1	0	4	72	0.79	3.25
DR	1.31	1.09	1	0	4	109	0.48	3.98
INCOM	0.84	0.61	1	0	4	81	−0.28	4.10
FABCOM	1.03	0.72	1	0	4	119	0.31	4.37
ALOG	0.83	0.69	1	0	5	101	−0.19	3.31
CONTAM	0	—	0	0	0	0	—	—
SUM6 SP SC	4.46	2.05	4	1	13	140	1.09	1.52
WSUM6 SP SC	10.64	4.90	10	2	41	140	1.61	−0.50
AG	1.13	0.83	1	0	6	107	0.48	4.03
CONFAB	0.01	0.03	0	0	1	2	0.04	28.99
CP	0.02	0.03	0	0	1	4	0.07	24.38
MOR	1.05	0.62	1	0	5	118	0.28	8.61
PER	3.48	1.41	3	0	8	112	2.06	1.91
PSV	0.49	0.44	0	0	3	61	2.28	10.46

Table J   (Continued)

Variable	Mean	SD	Mode	Min	Max	Freq	SK	KU
			Age 9 − N = 150					
R	20.27	4.53	19	12	29	150	1.96	0.38
P	4.71	1.23	5	2	10	150	−0.71	−1.05
W	9.82	3.04	10	4	18	150	0.77	1.37
D	9.92	2.86	9	2	22	150	0.94	3.74
Dd	0.63	0.92	1	0	3	106	4.47	5.19
S	1.31	0.82	1	0	4	104	2.16	4.39
$DQ+$	4.92	1.62	5	0	10	139	−0.39	3.16
$DQv/+$	1.17	0.86	1	0	4	84	3.18	6.26
DQo	11.56	3.36	13	8	24	150	2.49	1.89
DQv	3.62	2.09	2	0	11	149	3.91	5.11
$FQ+$	0.94	1.03	0	0	3	68	2.58	4.10
FQo	16.15	4.88	15	10	26	150	0.26	0.77
FQu	2.06	1.31	1	0	9	144	2.58	1.79
$FQ-$	1.06	0.56	1	0	6	126	3.13	5.91
M	1.74	0.83	1	0	5	146	1.93	3.37
M^a	1.11	0.62	1	0	5	146	2.54	4.14
M^p	0.63	0.57	0	0	2	64	4.16	5.89
$M-$	0.27	0.48	0	0	1	18	5.78	14.73
FM	3.64	1.69	4	0	11	149	−0.12	1.13
m	0.33	0.20	0	0	3	34	7.13	12.45
a	3.44	1.51	4	0	9	149	−0.18	0.98
p	2.08	0.66	1	0	9	82	4.06	1.74
FC	1.53	0.67	1	0	5	129	3.01	3.89
CF	2.04	0.77	2	0	6	146	1.73	4.88
$C+Cn$	0.39	0.59	0	0	2	38	4.64	10.35
Wgt Sum C	3.67	2.01	3.5	0.5	8.0	150	1.74	3.89
$FC'+C'F+C'$	0.56	0.51	0	0	4	74	4.96	8.18
$FT+TF+T$	0.89	0.72	1	0	3	131	−0.21	8.03
$FV+VF+V$	0	—	0	0	0	0	—	—
$FY+YF+Y$	0.26	0.41	0	0	2	37	6.19	9.27
Sum Shad'g	1.64	0.77	1	0	7	139	1.79	5.86
$Fr+rF$	0.44	0.22	0	0	2	36	7.24	14.11
(2)	9.53	2.89	10	4	17	150	−0.67	1.09
FD	0.47	0.27	0	0	3	69	3.34	9.64
F	8.84	3.14	8	3	22	150	0.96	0.81

Table J (Continued—Age 9)

Variable	Mean	SD	Mode	Min	Max	Freq	SK	KU
Zf	10.68	3.93	10	0	17	144	1.35	2.13
Zd	−0.07	2.77	−0.5	−8.0	8	150	1.66	−0.41
EA	5.39	2.55	5	1	10.5	150	1.27	0.38
es	5.73	2.48	6	0	15	149	−0.17	1.95
D Score	−0.26	2.27	0	−4	3	150	0.03	2.82
ADJ D	0.08	2.39	0	−3	3	150	−0.13	2.63
Afr	0.77	0.15	0.80	0.15	1.05	150	2.67	−0.35
3r+(2)/R	0.52	0.10	0.50	0.10	0.82	150	0.81	0.94
Lambda	0.78	0.19	0.75	0.18	1.85	150	0.99	2.07
Blends	3.84	1.31	3	0	6	137	2.49	2.93
Col-Sh *B*1	0.83	0.64	0	0	3	59	1.96	3.88
X+%	0.84	0.09	0.80	0.25	1.00	150	0.49	1.85
F+%	0.84	0.11	0.75	0	1.00	150	1.48	2.77
X−%	0.05	0.04	0.05	0	0.33	79	1.81	2.92
A%	0.47	0.10	0.42	0.25	0.75	150	2.03	2.45
Prim Cont	6.07	2.94	6	3	12	150	0.18	2.51
Pure H	2.71	1.28	2	0	6	139	1.69	2.37
All *H* Cont	4.22	1.94	5	0	10	144	−0.27	1.34
S-Constell (Child)	1.35	0.94	1	0	7	99	1.16	4.07
SCZI	1.38	0.78	1	0	4	86	−0.19	3.10
DEPI	1.03	0.89	1	0	5	93	0.57	3.98
DV	1.02	0.89	0	0	4	73	2.09	3.61
DR	0.99	0.71	1	0	3	112	0.07	3.15
INCOM	0.93	0.57	1	0	4	83	0.22	3.87
FABCOM	0.81	0.73	1	0	3	101	−0.04	3.92
ALOG	0.58	0.28	0	0	2	57	1.37	4.06
CONTAM	0	—	0	0	0	0	—	—
SUM6 SP SC	4.23	2.31	4	1	9	150	0.89	0.96
WSUM6 SP SC	9.76	3.87	8	2	27	150	0.83	1.62
AG	1.23	0.87	1	0	6	119	1.18	3.62
CONFAB	0.01	0.01	0	0	1	1	0.02	46.78
CP	0.01	0.01	0	0	1	1	0.02	46.78
MOR	1.17	0.93	1	0	6	121	−0.23	0.89
PER	3.26	1.61	2	0	8	119	1.18	1.52
PSV	0.38	0.23	0	0	2	31	1.06	9.40

Table J (Continued)

Variable	Mean	SD	Age 10 − N = 130 Mode	Min	Max	Freq	SK	KU
R	20.22	4.39	20	12	30	130	2.97	0.56
P	5.34	1.61	6	3	10	130	−0.77	−0.41
W	9.29	2.93	9	5	14	128	0.21	1.98
D	9.41	3.60	10	4	21	130	−1.12	0.89
Dd	1.51	0.57	2	0	7	99	−0.11	7.89
S	1.43	0.66	1	0	4	91	1.96	4.82
DQ+	5.43	2.41	5	0	8	123	1.11	3.26
DQv/+	0.84	0.88	0	0	3	88	3.61	6.48
DQo	11.97	3.94	12	6	26	130	1.82	3.19
DQv	2.03	0.98	1	0	7	113	3.87	2.94
FQ+	0.85	0.67	0	0	2	57	4.12	6.39
FQo	15.64	4.97	16	12	25	130	−0.04	0.71
FQu	2.81	1.47	3	0	7	126	−0.39	1.84
FQ−	0.91	1.01	1	0	6	101	3.84	8.13
M	2.03	1.12	2	0	5	122	1.16	5.09
M^a	1.45	0.89	1	0	5	118	1.97	6.04
M^p	0.57	0.63	0	0	3	37	4.21	8.18
M−	0.31	0.52	0	0	1	19	6.26	12.80
FM	3.09	0.92	2	0	10	127	2.79	2.08
m	0.19	0.23	0	0	2	24	7.01	11.46
a	3.92	1.39	3	0	13	129	1.86	2.63
p	1.38	0.61	1	0	4	59	1.18	3.89
FC	1.42	0.77	1	0	6	113	0.59	4.04
CF	2.08	0.74	2	0	5	104	0.44	5.27
C+Cn	0.38	0.19	0	0	2	36	7.73	11.11
Wgt Sum C	3.38	1.63	3.0	0.5	7.5	130	0.94	2.84
FC′+C′F+C′	0.62	0.52	1	0	4	73	−0.88	6.17
FT+TF+T	0.91	0.34	1	0	3	118	−0.48	6.83
FV+VF+V	0.13	0.09	0	0	1	10	8.33	23.61
FY+YF+Y	0.26	0.39	0	0	3	34	4.91	9.64
Sum Shad'g	1.82	0.78	1	0	7	118	3.06	4.34
Fr+rF	0.44	0.24	0	0	3	39	5.37	6.13
(2)	9.51	2.63	9	5	23	130	0.52	2.14
FD	0.68	0.37	0	0	2	83	2.93	7.83
F	9.03	2.90	8	2	18	130	1.07	1.46

Table J (Continued—Age 10)

Variable	Mean	SD	Mode	Min	Max	Freq	SK	KU
Zf	10.21	3.73	9	0	15	128	0.87	2.01
Zd	−0.12	2.89	0	−7.5	10	130	0.39	−0.41
EA	5.67	2.48	5	0.5	11	130	1.12	0.29
es	5.32	2.71	5	2	14	130	0.69	3.00
D Score	0.17	1.91	0	−4	3	130	0.28	1.98
ADJ D	0.30	1.68	0	−3	3	130	0.14	2.03
Afr	0.79	0.14	0.80	0.10	1.00	130	1.79	1.60
3r+(2)/R	0.51	0.10	0.46	0.08	0.90	130	0.15	0.79
Lambda	0.81	0.16	0.78	0.10	3.20	130	1.73	1.43
Blends	3.71	1.27	3	0	7	111	1.88	2.06
Col-Sh B1	0.91	0.78	0	0	3	63	2.06	4.01
X+%	0.82	0.09	0.78	0.25	1.00	130	0.57	0.96
F+%	0.83	0.11	0.80	0.33	1.00	130	1.19	2.54
X−%	0.06	0.04	0.05	0	0.30	101	1.75	2.31
A%	0.48	0.10	0.45	0.10	0.75	130	1.83	2.39
Prim Cont	5.94	2.69	6	3	13	130	−0.11	2.37
Pure H	2.88	1.54	2	0	8	117	1.61	2.02
All H Cont	4.18	1.67	4	0	7	123	0.81	1.19
S-Constell (Child)	1.95	1.07	2	0	7	108	0.16	2.87
SCZI	1.23	1.31	1	0	5	90	2.16	3.91
DEPI	1.22	0.94	1	0	4	81	−0.13	1.86
DV	0.51	0.54	0	0	3	78	2.49	4.71
DR	0.49	0.46	0	0	3	58	2.17	3.86
INCOM	0.81	0.57	1	0	3	89	1.36	4.02
FABCOM	0.77	0.43	0	0	3	71	2.07	3.18
ALOG	0.56	0.24	0	0	2	58	1.76	4.20
CONTAM	0	—	0	0	0	0	—	—
SUM6 SP SC	3.58	1.68	3	0	7	114	1.42	2.61
WSUM6 SP SC	7.33	2.73	6	0	18	114	2.09	0.74
AG	1.03	0.77	1	0	3	102	0.89	4.18
CONFAB	0	—	0	0	0	0	—	—
CP	0	—	0	0	0	0	—	—
MOR	1.20	0.83	1	0	5	117	−0.12	3.02
PER	2.28	1.09	2	0	5	80	1.17	1.39
PSV	0.31	0.18	0	0	1	27	1.06	14.75

Table J (Continued)

Variable	Mean	SD	Age 11 − N = 150 Mode	Min	Max	Freq	SK	KU
R	19.63	4.33	20	12	28	150	2.13	0.49
P	5.78	1.94	6	3	11	150	0.38	−0.34
W	8.18	3.32	9	3	15	150	−0.29	3.27
D	9.61	3.38	9	2	20	150	0.46	−0.19
Dd	1.76	0.84	1	0	6	124	2.41	5.76
S	1.58	0.51	1	0	5	136	1.84	3.89
DQ+	5.12	2.30	6	0	13	147	−0.84	1.19
DQv/+	1.27	1.83	0	0	4	81	3.29	6.19
DQo	11.71	3.54	13	6	26	150	1.03	2.88
DQv	1.52	0.73	1	0	7	124	3.18	6.28
FQ+	0.96	0.82	0	0	3	69	4.54	7.07
FQo	14.91	3.81	13	9	24	150	−0.13	−0.38
FQu	2.33	1.05	3	0	8	144	1.59	4.16
FQ−	1.40	0.82	0	0	5	83	3.03	5.14
M	2.64	1.28	2	0	6	139	1.38	4.28
M^a	1.78	0.91	2	0	5	139	1.89	5.47
M^p	0.86	0.71	0	0	3	71	3.27	5.01
M−	0.37	0.53	0	0	2	24	5.47	12.93
FM	3.09	0.84	2	0	7	149	1.89	2.24
m	0.23	0.39	0	0	3	26	6.83	10.07
a	4.04	1.14	4	0	11	149	1.47	1.13
p	1.92	0.58	1	0	6	79	1.36	2.09
FC	2.02	0.74	1	0	5	146	0.36	2.74
CF	2.14	0.88	2	0	4	138	1.87	2.40
C+Cn	0.43	0.39	0	0	3	35	2.81	11.74
Wgt Sum C	3.42	1.84	3.0	0	8.5	146	0.74	1.16
FC'+C'F+C'	0.71	0.67	1	0	4	104	0.95	4.12
FT+TF+T	0.91	0.54	1	0	4	138	−0.08	7.27
FV+VF+V	0.01	0.03	0	0	1	9	4.11	22.84
FY+YF+Y	0.42	0.31	0	0	2	61	4.76	6.96
Sum Shad'g	2.04	0.86	2	0	8	138	2.89	2.59
Fr+rF	0.30	0.23	0	0	2	27	3.67	24.71
(2)	8.94	2.88	9	3	19	150	0.41	1.03
FD	0.81	0.37	1	0	3	114	2.61	6.01
F	9.22	3.39	10	3	20	150	0.92	−0.46

Table J (Continued—Age 11)

Variable	Mean	SD	Mode	Min	Max	Freq	SK	KU
Zf	9.92	3.12	9	2	17	150	1.96	1.83
Zd	0.02	2.84	0.5	−6.5	9	150	−0.19	0.66
EA	6.23	2.89	6	0.5	12.5	150	0.07	0.33
es	5.43	2.60	6	1	13	150	0.61	1.73
D Score	0.23	1.06	0	−3	4	150	0.71	2.46
ADJ D	0.31	1.01	0	−3	4	150	0.50	2.17
Afr	0.75	0.17	0.75	0.27	1.10	150	0.48	0.85
3r+(2)/R	0.50	0.11	0.48	0.10	0.88	150	0.56	1.01
Lambda	0.88	0.21	0.76	0.12	1.75	150	0.64	0.91
Blends	3.44	1.23	4	0	6	147	2.08	2.41
Col-Sh *B*1	0.73	0.61	0	0	3	84	2.69	3.28
X+%	0.81	0.11	0.75	0.30	1.00	150	−0.04	0.26
F+%	0.84	0.09	0.80	0.20	1.00	150	1.28	1.91
X−%	0.08	0.05	0.05	0	0.33	83	0.66	9.23
A%	0.46	0.13	0.40	0.15	0.78	150	1.72	2.11
Prim Cont	6.12	2.42	6	3	12	150	−0.07	2.71
Pure *H*	3.26	1.19	3	0	9	140	−0.57	1.34
All *H* Cont	4.51	2.08	4	0	11	142	1.22	3.62
S-Constell	2.07	1.48	1	0	8	119	2.81	3.14
(Child)								
SCZI	1.12	0.98	1	0	4	97	2.34	6.12
DEPI	1.31	0.71	1	0	5	89	2.57	4.12
DV	0.59	0.37	0	0	2	76	1.38	4.93
DR	0.42	0.39	0	0	3	52	2.81	5.71
INCOM	0.92	0.68	1	0	2	103	−0.15	4.67
FABCOM	0.68	0.49	1	0	2	79	−0.48	6.11
ALOG	0.47	0.46	0	0	3	68	1.92	8.47
CONTAM	0	—	0	0	0	0	—	—
SUM6 SP SC	3.18	1.58	3	0	8	119	2.07	3.45
WSUM6 SP SC	6.90	2.03	5	0	15	119	2.34	1.62
AG	0.93	0.89	1	0	3	104	0.81	4.27
CONFAB	0	—	0	0	0	0	—	—
CP	0.14	0.17	0	0	1	11	1.87	8.96
MOR	1.22	0.89	1	0	4	113	1.09	5.41
PER	1.96	0.89	1	0	4	129	2.22	7.34
PSV	0.21	0.19	0	0	2	19	1.78	12.79

Table J   (Continued)

Variable	Mean	SD	Age 12 $-$ N = 140 Mode	Min	Max	Freq	SK	KU
R	20.23	4.48	20	13	31	140	1.71	0.31
P	6.22	2.08	6	3	11	140	-0.11	-0.49
W	7.74	3.58	8	4	14	140	0.97	2.29
D	11.13	3.06	10	6	23	140	0.22	-0.46
Dd	1.38	0.72	1	0	7	122	3.84	7.93
S	1.48	0.83	1	0	4	119	2.75	6.42
$DQ+$	5.79	2.64	6	0	10	139	2.94	4.31
$DQv/+$	0.97	0.96	1	0	3	86	2.46	7.89
DQo	11.37	4.02	12	8	27	140	-0.71	1.23
DQv	2.10	0.77	2	0	6	136	1.09	6.44
$FQ+$	0.51	0.82	0	0	2	49	3.16	5.86
FQo	16.06	3.34	17	12	25	140	-0.28	-0.09
FQu	2.64	1.07	3	0	9	134	-0.21	4.31
$FQ-$	1.01	0.79	1	0	5	99	0.81	5.61
M	2.70	1.02	2	1	6	140	0.93	4.38
M^a	1.89	0.95	2	0	6	138	1.17	4.91
M^p	0.81	0.72	1	0	4	79	0.73	6.21
$M-$	0.17	0.23	0	0	2	18	2.12	14.19
FM	3.22	1.08	3	1	11	140	1.46	2.28
m	0.34	0.28	0	0	4	38	3.86	10.07
a	4.31	1.93	5	1	13	140	-0.57	2.87
p	1.89	0.71	2	0	5	108	1.88	0.93
FC	2.63	1.30	3	0	7	137	1.02	0.72
CF	2.49	1.72	2	0	5	139	1.13	0.89
$C+Cn$	0.22	0.10	0	0	2	24	1.34	13.56
Wgt Sum C	4.31	2.11	3.5	0.5	10.0	140	0.64	-0.29
$FC'+C'F+C'$	0.73	0.53	1	0	5	83	-0.89	5.19
$FT+TF+T$	1.01	0.54	1	0	4	127	0.13	4.89
$FV+VF+V$	0.34	0.42	0	0	2	37	3.14	7.28
$FY+YF+Y$	0.38	0.41	0	0	4	46	2.87	6.19
Sum Shad'g	2.24	0.91	2	0	7	138	2.12	4.62
$Fr+rF$	0.41	0.19	0	0	2	56	3.17	9.87
(2)	9.11	2.73	9	4	21	140	0.46	0.67
FD	0.61	0.38	0	0	4	80	2.03	6.27
F	9.33	3.09	10	3	19	140	0.89	0.56

Table J (Continued—Age 12)

Variable	Mean	SD	Mode	Min	Max	Freq	SK	KU
Zf	10.26	3.09	9	3	16	140	1.57	1.76
Zd	0.29	2.61	0	−5.5	7	140	0.43	0.79
EA	7.01	3.11	6	1.5	13	140	0.71	−0.14
es	5.92	2.75	5	1	12	140	0.95	1.28
D Score	0.49	1.57	0	−3	4	140	0.42	1.86
ADJ D	0.58	1.49	0	−3	4	140	0.78	2.03
Afr	0.71	0.15	0.75	0.14	1.05	140	1.30	−0.21
3r+(2)/R	0.51	0.13	0.45	0.15	0.85	140	3.06	0.67
Lambda	0.85	0.18	0.80	0.20	1.45	140	1.93	0.27
Blends	3.42	1.33	3	0	7	136	2.49	2.05
Col-Sh B1	0.67	0.51	0	0	2	81	3.54	4.06
X+%	0.82	0.12	0.75	0.35	1.00	140	0.89	1.58
F+%	0.85	0.11	0.80	0.33	1.00	140	0.72	1.46
X−%	0.09	0.04	0.05	0	0.33	99	0.82	7.26
A%	0.48	0.14	0.40	0.15	0.72	140	1.36	1.08
Prim Cont	6.89	3.02	6	2	11	140	0.88	1.87
Pure H	2.68	1.14	2	0	7	129	0.53	1.64
All H Cont	4.27	1.81	5	0	10	137	0.13	1.09
S-Constell (Child)	1.69	1.02	1	0	6	103	1.26	3.89
SCZI	0.89	0.67	0	0	4	79	1.84	4.27
DEPI	1.03	0.71	1	0	4	97	0.38	6.44
DV	0.47	0.29	0	0	3	52	1.03	5.78
DR	0.31	0.26	0	0	2	50	0.93	6.24
INCOM	0.79	0.34	1	0	3	91	−0.18	3.16
FABCOM	0.34	0.12	0	0	2	36	0.47	8.13
ALOG	0.42	0.34	0	0	2	52	0.71	6.91
CONTAM	0	—	0	0	0	0	—	—
SUM6 SP SC	2.34	1.36	3	0	7	108	−0.23	1.78
WSUM6 SP SC	6.31	2.24	6	0	17	108	0.95	1.09
AG	1.13	0.71	1	0	4	110	0.58	4.61
CONFAB	0.01	0.01	0	0	1	1	0.21	34.62
CP	0.01	0.01	0	0	1	3	0.34	27.52
MOR	1.07	0.73	1	0	4	112	0.89	5.36
PER	1.87	0.91	1	0	3	105	1.63	4.82
PSV	0.29	0.22	0	0	2	41	0.57	13.58

Table J (Continued)

Variable	Mean	SD	Age 13 — N = 125 Mode	Min	Max	Freq	SK	KU
R	20.62	4.79	19	11	28	125	2.31	0.81
P	6.08	2.44	7	2	10	125	−0.11	−0.53
W	7.19	2.18	7	2	14	125	1.31	3.06
D	11.74	3.38	13	6	20	125	−0.34	−0.85
Dd	1.71	0.68	1	0	7	119	3.16	6.28
S	0.89	0.43	1	0	3	114	1.29	7.73
DQ+	5.41	2.16	6	1	10	125	0.97	−0.03
DQv/+	0.86	0.57	0	0	5	49	4.21	7.91
DQo	12.68	4.02	11	5	21	125	1.38	1.26
DQv	1.67	0.91	1	0	5	113	2.23	5.06
FQ+	0.36	0.52	0	0	1	22	0.88	11.24
FQo	16.32	4.27	15	10	24	125	0.19	0.39
FQu	2.95	1.31	3	0	8	118	1.28	3.43
FQ−	0.99	0.67	1	0	5	74	2.67	8.73
M	3.13	1.19	2	1	8	125	0.86	0.12
M^a	2.04	0.88	2	0	8	123	1.21	1.06
M^p	1.09	0.49	1	0	5	96	0.58	4.38
M−	0.36	0.28	0	0	2	14	1.94	16.25
FM	3.64	1.52	4	1	9	125	0.93	1.41
m	0.42	0.18	0	0	4	41	3.18	7.61
a	4.84	1.62	5	1	10	125	−0.36	2.07
p	2.28	0.89	2	0	6	109	1.67	0.78
FC	2.03	1.14	2	1	8	125	0.69	1.49
CF	2.33	1.19	2	0	5	124	0.74	0.28
C+Cn	0.41	0.36	0	0	2	46	2.89	6.81
Wgt Sum C	4.02	1.78	3.0	0.5	9.0	125	−0.87	−0.59
FC'+C'F+C'	0.62	0.67	1	0	6	81	−0.29	5.01
FT+TF+T	0.93	0.68	1	0	2	108	0.25	6.29
FV+VF+V	0.42	0.29	0	0	2	47	2.79	5.61
FY+YF+Y	0.35	0.31	0	0	3	51	1.89	4.42
Sum Shad'g	2.14	1.03	2	0	10	117	1.59	3.86
Fr+rF	0.29	0.24	0	0	2	36	1.14	18.23
(2)	8.84	2.94	9	3	21	125	0.19	0.59
FD	0.84	0.38	1	0	4	94	1.79	5.26
F	8.73	3.13	9	3	11	125	0.81	0.31

Table J (Continued—Age 13)

Variable	Mean	SD	Mode	Min	Max	Freq	SK	KU
Zf	9.48	1.89	9	2	15	125	1.32	1.52
Zd	−0.31	2.53	0	−6.6	7	125	0.79	0.95
FA	7.15	3.28	8	1.5	12	125	1.04	0.53
es	6.74	2.80	6	1	16	125	0.68	1.44
D Score	0.14	1.07	0	−4	3	125	0.20	2.03
ADJ D	0.38	1.02	0	−3	3	125	0.47	1.98
Afr	0.73	0.15	0.66	0.20	0.95	125	1.17	−0.09
3r+(2)/R	0.47	0.09	0.45	0.15	0.88	125	1.03	0.38
Lambda	0.73	0.12	0.68	0.18	1.35	125	1.86	0.29
Blends	3.92	1.41	4	1	8	125	1.16	2.02
Col-Sh B1	0.71	0.59	1	0	2	88	−0.15	5.67
X+%	0.81	0.10	0.77	0.45	1.00	125	0.53	1.94
F+%	0.83	0.09	0.75	0.25	1.00	125	0.73	1.66
X−%	0.05	0.04	0.04	0	0.25	74	0.38	8.27
A%	0.43	0.08	0.40	0.15	0.70	125	0.84	1.21
Prim Cont	6.51	2.47	6	3	12	125	1.31	2.01
Pure H	2.38	1.24	2	0	5	121	0.89	1.38
All H Cont	4.43	1.74	5	1	12	125	−0.16	0.31
S-Constell (Child)	1.93	1.71	2	0	8	107	0.22	−0.48
SCZI	0.78	0.51	0	0	3	68	1.29	5.11
DEPI	1.71	1.01	1	0	5	114	0.98	1.87
DV	0.54	0.40	0	0	3	61	0.29	5.89
DR	0.27	0.31	0	0	2	33	0.46	7.29
INCOM	0.92	0.42	1	0	3	91	0.26	3.15
FABCOM	0.39	0.23	0	0	2	46	0.39	9.28
ALOG	0.44	0.34	0	0	2	42	0.61	7.89
CONTAM	0	—	0	0	0	0	—	—
SUM6 SP SC	2.54	1.29	2	0	8	81	0.68	1.39
WSUM6 SP SC	6.13	2.57	6	0	16	104	0.73	0.89
AG	0.89	0.91	1	0	4	93	0.29	5.75
CONFAB	0	—	0	0	0	0	—	—
CP	0.01	0.01	0	0	1	1	0.08	28.85
MOR	1.02	0.89	1	0	4	108	0.46	8.16
PER	1.38	0.64	1	0	3	96	1.03	4.81
PSV	0.21	0.24	0	0	1	23	0.49	15.48

Table J (Continued)

Variable	Mean	SD	Age 14 − N = 115 Mode	Min	Max	Freq	SK	KU
R	21.57	5.12	20	12	31	115	2.01	−0.14
P	6.31	2.24	6	2	11	115	−0.02	−0.54
W	7.76	2.81	8	3	14	115	1.16	2.96
D	11.68	3.23	12	5	22	115	−0.61	−0.32
Dd	2.14	1.11	1	0	8	102	4.51	8.49
S	0.79	0.54	1	0	4	88	3.21	6.38
DQ+	5.91	2.27	6	1	11	115	0.12	−0.08
DQv/+	0.83	0.72	1	0	3	69	1.71	9.63
DQo	13.54	3.66	14	7	24	115	1.23	2.34
DQv	1.33	0.73	1	0	4	79	3.67	6.81
FQ+	0.59	0.49	0	0	3	39	0.98	6.74
FQo	17.12	3.39	17	12	25	115	0.39	1.89
FQu	2.89	1.21	3	0	7	108	−1.03	5.43
FQ−	1.01	0.83	1	0	6	77	0.67	6.03
M	2.92	1.19	2	1	9	115	1.07	−0.46
M^a	1.88	0.93	2	0	8	113	1.29	−0.17
M^p	1.04	0.71	1	0	5	86	0.87	3.16
M−	0.28	0.41	0	0	1	14	2.26	4.36
FM	3.24	0.91	3	1	9	115	1.15	1.03
m	0.21	0.34	0	0	4	21	2.27	5.68
a	4.12	1.79	4	1	12	115	0.57	−0.13
p	2.23	0.84	2	0	7	97	1.08	3.16
FC	2.07	1.23	2	1	6	115	0.11	2.83
CF	2.42	1.28	3	0	5	111	−0.41	−0.16
C+Cn	0.21	0.34	0	0	2	23	1.84	7.29
Wgt Sum C	3.77	1.57	4.0	1.0	8.0	115	−0.26	−0.09
FC'+C'F+C'	0.48	0.31	0	0	4	49	1.58	8.64
FT+TF+T	0.81	0.51	1	0	2	89	−0.16	7.87
FV+VF+V	0.34	0.27	0	0	1	28	0.98	14.63
FY+YF+Y	0.35	0.39	0	0	2	31	1.12	6.48
Sum Shad'g	1.73	0.58	1	0	5	102	2.11	4.05
Fr+rF	0.21	0.08	0	0	1	16	0.24	18.69
(2)	8.70	2.89	9	3	17	115	0.38	1.06
FD	0.87	0.62	1	0	3	101	1.49	4.89
F	9.37	2.51	10	3	22	115	−0.29	0.73

Table J (Continued—Age 14)

Variable	Mean	SD	Mode	Min	Max	Freq	SK	KU
Zf	9.13	2.61	9	3	14	115	0.99	1.87
ΣU	0.19	2.64	0	−3.3	8	115	0.67	1.03
EA	6.69	2.91	6	1.5	13.5	115	1.31	0.22
es	5.18	3.01	6	2	15	115	1.12	0.53
D Score	0.41	0.93	0	−4	4	115	0.67	1.39
ADJ D	0.49	0.83	0	−3	4	115	0.71	1.26
Afr	0.72	0.09	0.67	0.17	1.05	115	0.55	0.39
3r+(2)/R	0.43	0.09	0.45	0.10	0.92	115	0.07	0.51
Lambda	0.77	0.17	0.70	0.24	2.00	115	2.71	−0.24
Blends	3.37	1.12	3	1	6	115	0.90	2.49
Col-Sh B1	0.56	0.58	0	0	2	54	1.09	2.73
X+%	0.82	0.09	0.84	0.33	1.00	115	−0.02	1.70
F+%	0.82	0.11	0.75	0.20	1.00	115	0.72	1.19
X−%	0.07	0.06	0.06	0	0.22	77	0.17	7.35
A%	0.47	0.08	0.40	0.12	0.85	115	1.23	1.68
Prim Cont	7.02	2.48	6	3	12	115	1.04	1.96
Pure H	2.78	0.99	3	1	6	115	−0.12	4.23
All H Cont	4.72	1.93	5	2	12	115	−0.38	1.20
S-Constell (Child)	2.18	1.06	2	0	7	81	1.44	0.68
SCZI	0.48	0.67	0	0	3	49	1.37	2.01
DEPI	1.19	0.85	1	0	4	83	0.70	1.93
DV	0.56	0.38	0	0	3	54	0.35	5.09
DR	0.26	0.41	0	0	2	21	0.28	6.73
INCOM	0.81	0.57	1	0	3	83	−0.08	4.28
FABCOM	0.49	0.32	0	0	2	55	0.23	5.47
ALOG	0.38	0.22	0	0	2	23	0.26	8.76
CONTAM	0	—	0	0	0	0	—	—
SUM6 SP SC	2.41	1.18	2	0	7	90	0.67	2.31
WSUM6 SP SC	5.71	2.38	6	0	14	90	0.28	1.83
AG	1.02	0.89	1	0	3	81	0.23	4.79
CONFAB	0	—	0	0	0	0	—	—
CP	0	—	0	0	0	0	—	—
MOR	0.95	0.71	1	0	4	97	0.07	5.25
PER	1.19	0.64	1	0	3	89	0.11	4.37
PSV	0.28	0.24	0	0	1	26	0.58	12.62

Table J (Continued)

Variable	Mean	SD	Age 15 − N = 120 Mode	Min	Max	Freq	SK	KU
R	21.52	5.39	20	12	29	120	1.39	0.08
P	6.64	1.45	6	3	11	120	0.83	−0.57
W	8.19	3.04	8	1	13	120	1.13	1.72
D	11.52	3.36	12	4	21	120	−0.34	−0.06
Dd	1.77	0.93	1	0	6	109	3.19	4.47
S	0.69	0.43	1	0	3	78	5.18	8.28
DQ+	5.71	1.94	5	2	9	120	−0.72	−0.16
DQv/+	0.74	0.69	1	0	3	66	0.95	4.12
DQo	13.13	3.43	13	7	24	120	1.01	0.57
DQv	1.94	0.87	2	0	7	102	−0.62	3.82
FQ+	0.48	0.39	0	0	2	29	2.81	5.31
FQo	17.01	4.31	16	10	23	120	0.89	0.27
FQu	3.13	1.14	3	0	8	115	0.63	2.82
FQ−	0.90	0.83	1	0	4	91	−0.18	7.08
M	2.81	1.19	3	0	6	119	−0.44	1.84
M^a	1.93	0.96	2	0	6	118	1.22	3.87
M^p	0.88	0.98	1	0	4	73	−0.76	2.49
M−	0.31	0.19	0	0	1	18	2.62	9.82
FM	3.34	1.33	3	1	11	120	1.04	0.78
m	0.43	0.29	0	0	4	41	3.07	6.96
a	4.12	1.28	5	1	13	120	−1.03	2.34
p	2.37	0.68	2	0	6	97	1.81	1.49
FC	2.24	0.94	2	0	7	117	0.17	1.80
CF	1.93	0.78	1	0	5	114	−0.67	0.23
C+Cn	0.19	0.23	0	0	2	21	2.04	6.89
Wgt Sum C	3.48	1.52	4.0	1.0	10.0	120	−0.93	−0.44
FC'+C'F+C'	0.54	0.47	1	0	4	41	1.32	7.94
FT+TF+T	0.93	0.63	1	0	3	105	−0.12	5.89
FV+VF+V	0.32	0.28	0	0	2	23	2.88	7.18
FY+YF+Y	0.21	0.14	0	0	2	20	3.97	10.15
Sum Shad'g	1.81	0.91	1	0	6	110	2.08	3.91
Fr+rF	0.41	0.26	0	0	1	33	1.87	21.94
(2)	8.33	2.19	8	1	16	120	−0.18	1.58
FD	1.02	0.74	1	0	4	104	0.08	4.13
F	9.52	2.78	9	2	24	120	0.67	0.07

Table J (Continued—Age 15)

Variable	Mean	SD	Mode	Min	Max	Freq	SK	KU
Zf	10.37	2.93	10	2	16	120	0.89	2.46
Zd	0.06	2.91	0	−6	8	120	0.58	0.91
EA	6.29	2.63	6	1	14	120	0.87	0.30
es	5.58	2.76	5	1	16	120	1.23	1.01
D Score	0.19	1.02	0	−4	3	120	0.44	0.92
ADJ D	0.28	0.87	0	−2	3	120	0.76	1.09
Afr	0.70	0.17	0.70	0.14	0.90	120	0.63	−0.28
3r+(2)/R	0.44	0.09	0.45	0.15	0.87	120	0.13	0.83
Lambda	0.79	0.11	0.68	0.18	1.45	120	1.39	0.47
Blends	3.81	1.53	3	0	6	119	1.06	2.58
Col-Sh B1	0.53	0.61	0	0	3	57	1.23	2.53
X+%	0.81	0.09	0.74	0.30	1.00	120	0.49	1.16
F+%	0.82	0.12	0.70	0.20	1.00	120	0.69	1.38
X−%	0.08	0.05	0.06	0	0.30	91	0.28	6.49
A%	0.42	0.09	0.35	0.10	0.75	120	1.04	1.54
Prim Cont	6.99	2.79	6	2	11	120	1.27	2.03
Pure H	2.41	0.93	3	1	7	120	−0.41	3.86
All H Cont	4.73	1.89	5	2	12	120	−0.57	0.85
S-Constell (Child)	1.91	2.07	2	0	7	89	1.32	0.59
SCZI	0.54	0.49	0	0	3	33	1.08	2.86
DEPI	1.20	0.91	1	0	5	94	0.58	2.15
DV	0.28	0.14	0	0	3	21	0.46	10.48
DR	0.25	0.18	0	0	2	16	0.33	12.38
INCOM	0.62	0.38	1	0	2	68	−0.21	6.97
FABCOM	0.41	0.25	0	0	2	30	0.46	8.76
ALOG	0.34	0.29	0	0	2	26	0.41	9.81
CONTAM	0	—	0	0	0	0	—	—
SUM6 SP SC	1.94	0.84	2	0	6	69	0.72	4.68
WSUM6 SP SC	4.84	1.79	4	0	15	69	0.57	2.16
AG	1.03	0.78	1	0	4	88	0.39	5.11
CONFAB	0	—	0	0	0	0	—	—
CP	0.01	0.02	0	0	1	2	0.02	34.16
MOR	1.05	0.81	1	0	4	99	0.18	5.24
PER	0.94	0.69	1	0	5	93	−0.16	4.80
PSV	0.31	0.18	0	0	2	19	0.17	14.83

Table J   (Continued)

Variable	Mean	SD	Age 16 − N = 150 Mode	Min	Max	Freq	SK	KU
R	22.28	5.19	21	12	34	150	1.26	0.26
P	6.22	1.61	6	2	11	150	0.41	−0.06
W	8.89	3.37	9	3	15	150	−0.36	1.19
D	11.34	3.18	11	5	24	150	−0.73	−0.67
Dd	2.09	0.84	1	0	7	118	2.74	4.93
S	0.94	0.69	1	0	5	124	2.01	6.21
DQ+	6.33	2.14	6	1	13	150	1.79	−0.13
DQv/+	0.76	0.66	0	0	4	79	2.45	3.21
DQo	13.75	3.91	14	9	29	150	1.30	0.97
DQv	1.44	0.85	1	0	7	112	−0.61	2.99
FQ+	0.69	0.39	0	0	4	44	3.77	8.21
FQo	17.36	4.49	17	12	29	150	−1.06	−0.22
FQu	3.13	1.23	3	0	10	146	0.79	0.99
FQ−	1.01	0.61	1	0	6	83	1.89	6.92
M	3.23	1.09	3	1	9	150	1.27	4.73
M^a	2.12	0.92	2	0	9	148	0.79	3.19
M^p	1.11	0.58	1	0	5	92	−0.19	4.51
M−	0.38	0.21	0	0	2	21	2.61	6.98
FM	3.43	1.31	3	1	9	150	0.89	0.68
m	0.33	0.24	0	0	4	41	2.89	5.48
a	4.67	1.09	5	1	11	150	−0.84	1.69
p	2.26	0.79	2	0	7	108	1.02	1.55
FC	2.24	0.87	2	1	7	150	0.59	2.03
CF	2.02	0.84	2	0	4	141	0.88	2.13
C+Cn	0.13	0.14	0	0	1	13	1.01	16.26
Wgt Sum C	3.34	1.26	2.5	0.5	7.0	150	−0.04	−0.02
FC'+C'F+C'	0.71	0.52	0	0	8	61	2.38	8.96
FT+TF+T	1.01	0.73	1	0	3	133	0.36	7.94
FV+VF+V	0.24	0.18	0	0	1	28	4.16	16.49
FY+YF+Y	0.38	0.56	0	0	3	43	2.89	20.02
Sum Shad'g	2.08	0.86	2	0	8	131	1.24	3.85
Fr+rF	0.34	0.28	0	0	1	40	2.24	26.11
(2)	8.94	2.21	8	3	22	150	0.24	0.28
FD	0.68	0.44	1	0	2	106	−0.49	9.11
F	10.13	3.39	11	4	27	150	−0.08	−0.61

Table J (Continued—Age 16)

Variable	Mean	SD	Mode	Min	Max	Freq	SK	KU
Zf	11.87	3.14	10	3	17	150	2.31	1.67
Zd	0.36	2.49	0	−5.5	6	150	0.27	0.78
EA	6.57	2.38	7	1.5	12	150	−0.13	0.26
es	5.85	3.03	6	2	17	150	2.46	1.94
D Score	0.22	1.41	0	−3	3	150	0.57	1.16
ADJ D	0.41	1.27	0	−3	3	150	0.71	1.03
Afr	0.72	0.11	0.65	0.12	0.90	150	0.57	−0.23
3r+(2)/R	0.44	0.10	0.40	0.13	0.95	150	0.09	0.93
Lambda	0.83	0.14	0.72	0.22	1.85	150	0.46	1.24
Blends	4.18	1.78	4	1	8	150	0.85	2.07
Col-Sh B1	0.63	0.51	0	0	3	62	1.86	3.39
X+%	0.81	0.09	0.78	0.35	1.00	150	0.39	1.26
F+%	0.83	0.12	0.67	0.33	1.00	150	0.54	1.59
X−%	0.07	0.04	0.05	0	0.22	83	0.49	3.24
A%	0.45	0.11	0.38	0.15	0.80	150	0.85	1.35
Prim Cont	7.28	1.95	7	3	12	150	0.92	0.42
Pure H	2.71	1.57	3	0	5	139	−0.17	2.30
All H Cont	4.80	1.64	5	0	9	149	−0.79	0.67
S-Constell	3.16	1.86	3	0	7	119	0.74	2.64
(Adult)								
SCZI	0.62	0.48	0	0	4	53	1.32	2.99
DEPI	1.17	1.23	1	0	4	102	0.73	2.06
DV	0.21	0.26	0	0	2	19	0.81	6.80
DR	0.14	0.18	0	0	1	13	0.14	9.27
INCOM	0.63	0.34	0	0	2	69	0.60	7.23
FABCOM	0.31	0.34	0	0	2	29	0.39	7.05
ALOG	0.29	0.24	0	0	2	41	0.67	5.83
CONTAM	0	—	0	0	0	0	—	—
SUM6 SP SC	1.78	1.03	2	0	7	99	1.03	3.90
WSUM6 SP SC	4.36	1.71	4	0	18	99	0.82	2.30
AG	0.98	0.88	1	0	2	81	0.36	3.41
CONFAB	0	—	0	0	0	0	—	—
CP	0.01	0.04	0	0	1	3	0.06	18.28
MOR	1.08	0.89	1	0	4	123	0.46	3.96
PER	0.74	0.83	1	0	3	96	1.04	3.22
PSV	0.31	0.14	0	0	1	36	0.71	8.03

Table K. Frequencies and Percentages Concerning Directionality for 18 Structural Variables for 1580 Nonpatients by Age Group from 5 Through 16

Variable	Age 5 N = 110 Freq	%	Age 6 N = 105 Freq	%	Age 7 N = 145 Freq	%	Age 8 N = 140 Freq	%	Age 9 N = 150 Freq	%	Age 10 N = 130 Freq	%
EB Style												
$M - WSUM\ C \geq 2$	5	4%	7	7%	14	10%	21	15%	39	26%	38	29%
$M - WSUM\ C = +1.5$ to -1.5	49	46%	25	24%	45	31%	53	38%	33	22%	45	35%
$WSUM\ C - M \geq 2$	66	60%	72	68%	86	59%	66	47%	78	52%	47	36%
EA − es Differences												
D Score < 0	81	74%	69	66%	79	54%	82	59%	34	23%	23	18%
ADJ D Score < 0	77	70%	62	59%	74	51%	76	54%	31	21%	20	15%
Zd Score $> +3.0$	16	15%	15	14%	27	19%	31	22%	46	31%	41	32%
Zd Score < -3.0	46	42%	31	30%	38	26%	36	26%	29	19%	27	21%
Form Quality Deviations												
X+% $< .70$	17	15%	18	17%	22	15%	29	21%	47	31%	29	22%
F+% $< .70$	18	16%	18	17%	30	21%	17	12%	25	17%	25	19%
X−% $> .15$	7	6%	8	8%	19	13%	9	6%	8	5%	7	5%
S-Constellation ≥ 7	0	—	1	1%	3	2%	3	2%	6	4%	5	4%
SCZI ≥ 4	4	4%	3	3%	6	4%	4	3%	11	7%	3	2%
DEPI ≥ 4	9	8%	2	2%	8	6%	2	1%	14	9%	8	6%
Miscellaneous												
FM+m $<$ Sum Shading	14	12%	4	3%	11	8%	18	13%	13	9%	13	10%
$a < p$	3	3%	2	2%	9	6%	13	9%	15	10%	22	17%
$M^a < m^p$	2	2%	3	3%	8	6%	10	7%	9	6%	8	6%
3r+(2)/R $< -1\ SD$	20	18%	9	9%	20	14%	19	14%	19	13%	20	15%
Afr $< -1\ SD$	21	19%	10	10%	21	15%	17	12%	17	11%	16	12%
Lambda ≥ 1.5	23	21%	19	18%	33	23%	16	11%	18	12%	16	12%
Pure H < 2	34	31%	39	37%	38	26%	16	11%	17	11%	23	18%
Isolat Index $> \frac{1}{4} R$	13	12%	14	13%	29	20%	20	14%	18	12%	19	15%

Table K (Continued)

Variable	Age 11 N = 150 Freq	%	Age 12 N = 140 Freq	%	Age 13 N = 125 Freq	%	Age 14 N = 115 Freq	%	Age 15 N = 120 Freq	%	Age 16 N = 150 Freq	%
EB Style												
$M - WSUM\ C \geq 2$	46	31%	38	27%	36	29%	38	33%	46	38%	56	37%
$M - WSUM\ C = +1.5$ to -1.5	45	30%	51	36%	47	38%	33	29%	22	18%	28	19%
$WSUM\ C - M \geq 2$	59	39%	51	36%	42	34%	44	38%	52	43%	66	44%
EA − es Differences												
$D\ Score < 0$	29	19%	30	21%	24	19%	26	23%	29	24%	16	11%
$ADJ\ D\ Score < 0$	24	16%	26	19%	20	16%	21	18%	23	19%	12	8%
$Zd\ Score > +3.0$	46	31%	36	26%	23	18%	22	19%	27	23%	33	22%
$Zd\ Score < -3.0$	23	15%	28	20%	15	12%	17	15%	18	15%	15	10%
Form Quality Deviations												
$X+\% < .70$	29	19%	14	10%	24	19%	21	18%	24	20%	28	19%
$F+\% < .70$	41	27%	33	24%	28	22%	17	15%	16	13%	20	13%
$X-\% > .15$	9	6%	6	4%	7	6%	5	4%	7	6%	10	7%
$S\text{-}Constellation \geq 7$	8	5%	8	6%	12	10%	10	9%	12	10%	3	2%
$SCZI \geq 4$	5	3%	2	1%	3	2%	0	—	0	—	1	1%
$DEPI \geq 4$	11	7%	9	6%	8	6%	6	5%	9	8%	13	9%
Miscellaneous												
$FM+m < Sum\ Shading$	16	11%	29	21%	17	14%	19	17%	23	19%	19	13%
$a < p$	19	13%	23	16%	19	15%	13	11%	12	10%	16	11%
$M^a < M^p$	11	7%	13	9%	9	7%	6	5%	4	3%	7	5%
$3r+(2)/R < -1\ SD$	19	13%	12	9%	15	12%	18	16%	12	10%	19	13%
$Afr < -1\ SD$	27	18%	22	16%	24	19%	21	18%	14	12%	28	19%
$Lambda \geq 1.5$	13	9%	14	10%	11	9%	9	8%	9	8%	11	7%
$Pure\ H < 2$	21	14%	19	14%	13	10%	11	10%	16	13%	14	9%
$Isolation\ Index \geq \frac{1}{4}\ R$	23	15%	22	16%	19	15%	16	14%	18	15%	18	12%

THE PSYCHIATRIC REFERENCE GROUPS

As noted earlier, the data presented for the three psychiatric groups included here are random selections of approximately 25% of the total samples available in the protocol pool at the Rorschach Research Foundation. All meet the criteria for these designations as listed in DSM-III, and approximately 75% of the schizophrenics and 65% of the depressives are cases in which the *Research Diagnostic Criteria* (Spitzer, Endicott, & Robbins, 1978) has also been applied to establish diagnostic categories. They should *not* be considered in the context of normative samples because they are not stratified against any particular baseline data such as age, sex, educational level, socioeconomic level, and so on. They have been included to provide a frame of reference concerning the frequencies and distributions of Rorschach variables, and especially to illustrate that the ranges for many variables, like those for the nonpatient sample, are often quite extensive even though the data for some variables cluster in a considerably different way than those for the nonpatients.

The Schizophrenic Sample   This group consists of 179 females and 141 males, ranging in age from 19 to 48, with an average of 27.3 ($SD = 5.9$); 248 are white and 72 are black or Hispanic. The records were collected at 26 facilities in 17 states, with 196 from federal, state, county, or city hospitals, and 124 from private hospitals. The average number of years of completed education is 11.78 ($SD = 4.83$), with a range from 8 to 20 years. The majority, 203, are first admissions, although nearly all have some previous outpatient psychiatric history; 188 are single, separated, or divorced. Socioeconomic levels range from SES 3 through SES 9.

Table L.   Descriptive Statistics for 69 Rorschach Variables for 320 Inpatient Schizophrenics

Variable	Mean	SD	Mode	Min	Max	Freq	SK	KU
R	20.01	8.49	12	10	55	320	12.13	2.15
P	4.21	1.89	4	1	9	320	0.43	−0.44
W	8.45	4.78	8	0	23	318	4.71	0.80
D	7.91	6.02	4	0	28	306	7.25	1.43
Dd	3.62	3.91	1	0	25	272	9.77	8.58
S	2.28	2.02	1	0	9	252	1.94	0.66
DQ+	5.65	3.79	4	0	16	304	2.74	−0.04
DQv/+	0.15	0.50	0	0	3	32	1.91	14.93
DQo	12.20	7.08	8	3	45	320	13.63	4.52
DQv	1.92	1.97	1	0	10	244	3.16	2.86
FQ+	0.26	0.77	0	0	7	52	3.91	35.69
FQo	10.09	4.57	7	2	27	320	3.38	0.76
FQu	2.52	2.21	1	0	12	288	3.98	4.14
FQ−	6.45	4.22	5	0	27	314	5.92	3.47
M	4.39	3.29	3	0	16	292	3.46	1.26
M^a	2.69	2.36	2	0	12	264	2.92	1.76
M^p	1.69	1.82	0	0	8	220	2.37	1.35
M−	1.53	1.67	0	0	9	214	2.82	4.17
FM	2.59	2.51	2	0	15	254	3.88	3.38
m	1.24	1.35	0	0	7	204	1.90	2.46
a	5.14	3.84	2	0	16	298	3.33	0.26
p	2.97	2.54	1	0	11	264	2.14	0.09
FC	1.22	1.48	0	0	7	192	2.42	2.57
CF	1.55	1.51	0	0	8	228	1.75	1.57

Table L (Continued)

Variable	Mean	SD	Mode	Min	Max	Freq	SK	KU
C+Cn	0.62	0.87	0	0	4	134	1.26	1.94
Wgt Sum C	2.97	2.27	0	0	11	282	1.68	0.21
FC'+C'F+C'	1.31	1.47	0	0	8	196	2.11	2.59
FT+TF+T	0.49	1.15	0	0	9	96	5.38	27.87
FV+VF+V	0.63	1.34	0	0	10	104	5.11	18.74
FY+YF+Y	1.56	2.00	0	0	11	190	3.41	3.14
Sum Shad'g	3.99	4.09	1	0	25	272	8.47	5.84
Fr+rF	0.19	0.55	0	0	3	40	1.77	10.27
(2)	6.84	4.62	8	0	29	306	6.62	3.63
FD	0.86	1.07	0	0	4	166	1.37	1.01
F	8.06	5.63	6	1	30	320	9.15	3.04
Zf	10.88	4.81	9	2	26	320	3.68	0.51
Zd	1.04	4.42	−3.5	−12.5	9.5	320	−1.35	−0.28
EA	7.36	4.46	6	0	23	318	4.00	0.61
es	7.82	5.87	4	0	28	298	6.15	0.87
D Score	−0.16	1.64	0	−7	5	320	−1.19	3.66
ADJ D	0.27	1.32	0	−4	5	320	0.74	2.45
Afr	0.49	0.19	0.50	0.19	1.38	320	0.32	4.62
3r+(2)/R	0.37	0.18	0.50	0	1.08	308	0.05	0.45
Lambda	1.23	2.64	1.00	0.07	29	320	20.90	75.53
Blends	3.88	3.27	1	0	19	276	4.16	2.69
Col-Sh B1	0.60	0.99	0	0	6	122	2.38	7.62
X+%	0.53	0.17	0.50	0.14	0.93	320	0.02	−0.32
F+%	0.55	0.25	0.50	0	1.00	308	0.02	−0.31
X−%	0.31	0.15	0.33	0	0.70	314	0.03	−0.38
A%	0.44	0.15	0.42	0.07	0.86	320	0.05	−0.19
Prim Cont	5.38	2.05	4	2	12	320	1.47	0.03
Pure H	2.28	2.01	1	0	9	256	1.65	−0.02
All H Cont	5.41	3.40	6	0	19	314	4.09	2.37
S-Constell	4.73	1.89	5	1	10	320	0.49	−0.31
SCZI	3.96	1.02	4	0	5	318	−0.91	−0.37
DEPI	1.34	1.10	1	0	5	242	0.77	0.26
DV	1.37	1.69	0	0	10	169	2.64	2.07
DR	1.21	1.58	0	0	11	148	3.18	2.08
INCOM	1.51	1.71	0	0	10	212	3.15	4.68
FABCOM	1.59	1.63	0	0	7	249	2.05	1.15
ALOG	0.86	1.26	0	0	6	174	1.86	3.78
CONTAM	0.18	0.50	0	0	3	59	1.54	10.79
SUM6 SP SC	6.58	5.13	5	0	29	304	6.61	3.23
WSUM6 SP SC	16.88	10.24	12	0	68	304	4.41	3.53
AG	0.74	1.10	0	0	8	168	2.64	8.36
CONFAB	0	—	0	0	0	0	—	—
CP	0.02	0.14	0	0	1	11	0.96	28.03
MOR	0.94	1.64	0	0	10	169	3.36	5.19
PER	1.11	2.38	0	0	12	140	7.24	10.44
PSV	0.16	0.45	0	0	3	44	1.44	12.29

Table M.   Frequencies and Percentages Concerning Directionality for 18 Structural Variables for 320 Inpatient Schizophrenics

Variable	Freq	%
EB Style		
$M - $ WSUM $C \geqslant 2$ (Introversive)	144	45.0
$M - $ WSUM $C = +1.5$ to -1.5 (Ambient)	134	41.9
WSUM $C - M \geqslant 2$ (Extratensive)	42	13.1
EA $-$ es Differences: Overload		
D Score < 0	86	26.9
ADJ D Score < 0	52	16.3
Zd Score $> +3.0$ (Overincorporator)	98	30.6
Zd Score < -3.0 (Underincorporator)	66	20.6
Form Quality Deviations		
$X+\% < .70$	270	84.4
$F+\% < .70$	236	73.8
$X-\% > .15$	272	85.0
S-Constellation $\geqslant 8$	26	8.1
Schizophrenia Index		
$SCZI = 5$	104	32.5
$SCZI = 4$	142	44.4
Depression Index		
$DEPI = 5$	4	1.3
$DEPI = 4$	4	1.3
Miscellaneous Variables		
$FM+m < $ SUM SHADING	118	36.9
$a < p$	68	21.3
$M^a < M^p$	84	26.3
$3r+(2)/R < .30$	124	38.8
$Afr < .55$	198	61.8
Lambda $\geqslant 1.5$	58	18.1
Pure H < 2	154	48.1
Isolation Index $> \frac{1}{4}R$	24	7.5

The Depression Sample   This group consists of 111 males and 99 females. They range in age from 19 to 61 years, with an average of 37.13 ($SD = 14.05$); 172 are white and 38 are black or Hispanic. The records were collected at 22 facilities in 13 states, with 88 from federal, state, county, or city hospitals, and 132 from private hospitals. The average number of years of completed education is 11.92 ($SD = 4.83$), with a range of 9 to 21 years. All are first admissions, and 101 are single, separated, or divorced. Socioeconomic levels range from SES 2 through SES 8.

Table N.   Descriptive Statistics for 69 Rorschach Variables for 210 Inpatient Depressives

Variable	Mean	SD	Mode	Min	Max	Freq	SK	KU
R	19.50	7.95	12	10	55	210	13.25	3.85
P	5.25	2.01	4	1	11	210	0.38	0.19
W	8.08	4.00	7	0	21	208	2.91	0.58
D	8.57	5.97	4	0	34	208	9.66	3.62
Dd	2.86	3.15	1	0	19	182	8.80	9.83
S	2.21	1.95	0	0	11	166	2.51	2.71

Table N (Continued)

Variable	Mean	SD	Mode	Min	Max	Freq	SK	KU
DQ+	5.44	3.50	7	0	18	206	3.62	1.31
DQv/+	0.83	0.67	0	0	4	56	0.94	8.72
DQo	11.66	6.87	9	2	44	210	11.22	4.59
DQv	2.17	1.69	1	0	9	176	1.90	0.64
FQ+	0.36	0.76	0	0	6	46	3.37	24.66
FQo	12.80	5.26	9	5	32	210	5.18	1.05
FQu	2.69	2.09	1	0	9	196	2.45	0.99
FQ−	3.00	2.83	2	0	24	192	9.47	11.57
M	3.34	2.42	4	0	11	186	1.58	0.06
M^a	2.05	1.93	0	0	9	158	2.02	0.91
M^p	1.30	1.48	0	0	6	124	1.57	0.37
M−	0.33	0.67	0	0	3	50	1.43	4.05
FM	2.63	2.18	2	0	13	188	3.56	4.08
m	1.44	1.71	0	0	12	142	4.55	12.31
a	4.65	3.18	4	0	13	196	1.95	−0.31
p	2.78	2.46	1	0	11	178	2.52	0.56
FC	1.49	1.78	0	0	6	122	2.01	0.14
CF	1.55	1.48	1	0	6	152	1.43	0.28
C+Cn	0.56	0.93	0	0	4	77	1.56	2.07
Wgt Sum C	3.10	2.31	0	0	10	178	1.61	0.32
FC'+C'F+C'	2.99	1.71	2	0	8	188	1.05	0.14
FT+TF+T	0.93	1.42	0	0	7	122	3.31	6.23
FV+VF+V	1.25	1.27	1	0	7	169	1.65	2.66
FY+YF+Y	1.31	1.32	0	0	7	142	1.64	2.14
Sum Shad'g	6.48	3.74	3	0	19	207	4.30	1.43
Fr+rF	0.14	0.40	0	0	2	26	1.15	7.89
(2)	6.51	3.67	7	1	19	210	3.13	1.48
FD	1.14	1.26	0	0	5	138	1.49	0.82
F	7.19	4.92	3	1	33	210	8.99	6.15
Zf	11.48	4.17	10	3	21	210	3.02	0.12
Zd	0.34	4.14	3.5	−13	12.5	210	−1.28	0.44
EA	6.44	3.92	5	0	18	202	2.91	0.47
es	9.55	5.42	8	1	24	210	3.81	0.02
D Score	−0.99	1.56	0	−6	3	210	−1.02	0.59
ADJ D	−0.52	1.43	0	−6	3	210	−0.88	1.96
Afr	0.47	0.16	0.50	0.10	1.00	210	0.10	0.73
3r+(2)/R	0.32	0.16	0.17	0.08	1.00	210	0.12	0.69
Lambda	0.81	1.13	0.50	0.08	10.0	210	6.41	22.15
Blends	4.28	3.18	3	0	15	186	2.50	0.38
Col-Sh B1	0.90	1.12	1	0	5	149	0.59	1.02
X+%	0.68	0.12	0.63	0.33	0.95	210	−0.02	−0.11
F+%	0.69	0.23	1.00	0	1.00	206	−0.14	0.26
X−%	0.15	0.10	0.16	0	0.44	192	0.06	0.18
A%	0.47	0.14	0.33	0.21	0.82	210	0.06	−0.44
Prim Cont	5.72	2.17	6	3	12	210	2.11	0.70
Pure H	1.90	1.41	1	0	6	182	1.28	0.26
All H Cont	4.16	2.63	4	0	12	202	2.04	0.45
S-Constell	5.65	2.04	5	0	10	210	−0.38	−0.28
SCZI	1.91	1.29	1	0	5	210	0.62	−0.26
DEPI	3.57	1.23	4	0	5	199	0.08	−0.73
DV	0.63	0.72	0	0	3	126	3.69	4.31
DR	0.63	0.93	1	0	3	182	3.03	0.75
INCOM	0.91	1.14	0	0	7	116	2.29	6.54
FABCOM	0.54	0.85	0	0	4	78	1.50	2.88

Table N (Continued)

Variable	Mean	SD	Mode	Min	Max	Freq	SK	KU
ALOG	0.21	0.49	0	0	3	36	1.04	3.94
CONTAM	0	—	0	0	0	0	—	—
SUM6 SP SC	3.12	2.76	2	0	11	192	2.86	2.09
WSUM6 SP SC	6.98	5.96	0	0	26	192	7.29	3.09
AG	0.63	0.75	0	0	5	78	2.45	11.77
CONFAB	0	—	0	0	0	0	—	—
CP	0.16	0.37	0	0	2	10	0.84	24.72
MOR	3.47	2.09	2	0	12	203	2.49	0.78
PER	1.10	1.78	1	0	5	106	1.93	1.46
PSV	0.18	0.43	0	0	2	34	1.01	4.81

Table O.   Frequencies and Percentages Concerning Directionality for 18 Structural Variables for 210 Inpatient Depressives

Variable	Freq	%
EB Style		
$M - \text{WSUM } C \geq 2$ (Introversive)	62	29.5
$M - \text{WSUM } C = +1.5 \text{ to } -1.5$ (Ambitent)	110	52.4
$\text{WSUM } C - M \geq 2$ (Extratensive)	38	18.1
EA − es Differences: Overload		
D Score < 0	116	55.2
ADJ D Score < 0	88	41.9
Zd Score $> +3.0$ (Overincorporator)	62	29.5
Zd Score < -3.0 (Underincorporator)	38	18.1
Form Quality Deviations		
$X+\% < .70$	116	55.2
$F+\% < .70$	100	47.6
$X-\% > .15$	96	45.7
S-Constellation ≥ 8	27	12.4
Schizophrenia Index		
$SCZI = 5$	10	4.8
$SCZI = 4$	14	6.7
Depression Index		
$DEPI = 5$	26	12.4
$DEPI = 4$	78	37.2
Miscellaneous Variables		
$FM+m < \text{Sum Shading}$	122	58.1
$a < p$	50	23.8
$M^a < M^p$	52	24.8
$3r+(2)/R < .30$	82	39.0
$Afr < .55$	146	69.5
Lambda ≥ 1.5	24	11.4
Pure H < 2	108	51.4
Isolation Index $> \frac{1}{4}R$	10	4.8

The Character Problem Sample   This group consists of 121 males and 79 females. They range in age from 18 to 47, with an average of 23.61 (*SD* = 5.14); 139 are white and 61 are black or Hispanic. Most of the records (164) were collected at 29 outpatient units in 10 states, and the remaining 36 were contributed by private practitioners. The majority of subjects (124) have histories that include drug and/or alcohol abuse, and 113 have been involved at least once in legal disputes. Twenty-two have records of psychiatric hospitalization, but none longer than 10 days; 109 are single, separated, or divorced. Socioeconomic levels range from SES 4 through SES 9.

Table P.   Descriptive Statistics for 69 Rorschach Variables for 200 Outpatient Character Problems

Variable	Mean	SD	Mode	Min	Max	Freq	SK	KU
R	17.95	5.41	17	10	34	200	5.65	0.54
P	5.12	1.90	5	0	9	194	−0.47	−0.37
W	7.35	3.84	6	1	23	200	5.23	3.39
D	8.02	4.81	4	0	21	196	2.86	−0.18
Dd	2.59	2.37	0	0	9	154	1.92	−0.25
S	1.92	1.60	1	0	7	156	1.62	0.85
DQ+	3.94	2.45	1	0	12	194	1.30	−0.12
DQv/+	0.91	0.67	0	0	4	76	1.72	4.86
DQo	11.63	5.71	10	3	27	200	5.45	0.52
DQv	1.80	1.52	1	0	7	157	1.01	−0.44
FQ+	0.22	0.76	0	0	5	22	3.26	20.28
FQo	12.17	3.92	13	5	23	200	2.66	0.01
FQu	2.75	1.55	2	0	7	188	1.32	0.59
FQ−	2.31	2.22	3	0	11	180	3.27	2.57
M	2.33	1.91	2	0	9	175	2.49	1.81
M^a	1.48	1.57	0	0	8	138	2.41	3.01
M^p	0.84	0.95	0	0	4	114	1.16	1.25
M−	0.18	0.52	0	0	3	26	1.67	10.87
FM	2.26	1.63	1	0	7	176	1.07	−0.08
m	1.03	1.11	0	0	5	134	1.29	0.99
a	3.41	2.54	2	0	12	181	2.49	0.76
p	2.22	1.65	1	0	7	178	1.21	−0.22
FC	0.97	1.33	0	0	5	96	1.97	1.56
CF	0.99	1.23	1	0	6	141	1.75	1.79
C+Cn	0.64	0.83	0	0	3	86	1.37	2.10
Wgt Sum C	2.60	1.70	2	0	6.5	165	1.31	−0.56
FC'+C'F+C'	0.78	1.12	0	0	5	101	1.51	1.39
FT+TF+T	0.44	0.67	0	0	3	70	0.95	1.45
FV+VF+V	0.25	0.59	0	0	3	34	1.45	5.68
FY+YF+Y	1.13	1.31	0	0	7	126	2.09	3.26
Sum Shad'g	2.61	1.93	2	0	9	177	2.11	0.35
Fr+rF	0.41	0.54	0	0	4	63	1.51	8.14
(2)	6.59	2.43	6	0	21	198	4.18	2.38
FD	0.69	1.13	0	0	7	73	3.07	10.10
F	9.52	5.17	10	0	25	199	4.34	0.86
Zf	9.10	4.15	6	1	24	200	3.62	1.43
Zd	−0.26	4.01	−0.5	−14	8.5	200	−2.02	0.74
EA	4.44	2.85	2	0	14.5	196	2.71	0.92
es	6.88	3.66	4	0	18	198	3.93	0.79
D Score	−0.68	1.09	0	−4	2	200	−0.99	1.04
ADJ D	−0.14	0.86	0	−2	2	200	0.07	0.96
Afr	0.51	0.18	0.33	0.21	1.13	200	0.31	1.97

Table P (Continued)

Variable	Mean	SD	Mode	Min	Max	Freq	SK	KU
$3r+(2)/R$	0.42	0.17	0.39	0	0.95	198	0.07	0.42
Lambda	1.51	1.43	1.00	0	11	200	4.83	14.78
Blends	2.54	2.39	0	0	12	151	3.00	2.13
Col-Sh $B1$	0.41	0.81	0	0	3	58	1.42	2.19
$X+\%$	0.70	0.13	0.75	0.36	1.00	200	0.01	-0.03
$F+\%$	0.71	0.19	1.00	0	1.00	200	-0.12	1.04
$X-\%$	0.15	0.09	0	0	0.47	180	0.06	0.36
$A\%$	0.55	0.13	0.56	0.10	0.82	200	-0.04	0.51
Prim Cont	5.11	1.52	5	2	8	200	-0.14	-0.53
Pure H	1.71	1.41	1	0	6	169	1.64	1.02
All *H* Cont	3.72	2.55	2	0	12	191	3.33	2.39
S-Constell	4.08	1.85	4	0	8	195	-0.37	-0.57
SCZI	1.75	1.09	2	0	5	178	0.61	0.38
DEPRI	0.90	0.98	0	0	3	111	0.77	-0.51
DV	0.74	1.86	0	0	5	98	2.16	0.69
DR	0.90	1.29	0	0	4	83	1.96	1.07
INCOM	0.98	1.29	0	0	6	99	1.99	2.66
FABCOM	0.54	0.90	0	0	6	74	2.48	11.80
ALOG	0.09	0.29	0	0	1	29	0.81	5.57
CONTAM	0.04	0.20	0	0	1	7	0.92	19.81
SUM6 SP SC	3.29	2.98	2	0	20	174	5.85	7.84
WSUM6 SP SC	6.52	4.65	3	0	48	174	13.13	10.28
AG	1.06	1.07	1	0	8	156	2.10	5.45
CONFAB	0	—	0	0	0	0	—	—
CP	0	—	0	0	0	0	—	—
MOR	0.99	1.26	0	0	5	114	1.79	1.57
PER	0.86	1.57	0	0	11	93	5.15	12.26
PSV	0.25	0.46	0	0	2	48	0.67	5.90

Table Q.   Frequencies and Percentages Concerning Directionality for 18 Structural Variables for 200 Character Problems

Variable	Freq	%
EB Style		
$M - $ WSUM $C \geq 2$ (Introversive)	49	24.5
$M - $ WSUM $C = +1.5$ to -1.5 (Ambitent)	112	56.0
WSUM $C - M \geq 2$ (Extratensive)	39	19.5
EA $-$ es Differences: Overload		
D Score < 0	68	34.0
ADJ D Score < 0	51	25.5
Zd Score $> +3.0$ (Overincorporator)	38	19.0
Zd Score < -3.0 (Underincorporator)	38	19.0
Form Quality Deviations		
$X+\% < .70$	93	46.5
$F+\% < .70$	90	45.0
$X-\% > .15$	86	43.0
S-Constellation ≥ 8	4	2.0
Schizophrenia Index		
$SCZI = 5$	4	2.0
$SCZI = 4$	8	4.0
Depression Index		
$DEPI = 5$	0	—
$DEPI = 4$	0	—
Miscellaneous Variables		
$FM+m < $ Sum Shading	54	27.0
$a < p$	60	30.0
$M^a < M^p$	51	25.5
$3r+(2)/R < .30$	51	25.5
$Afr < .55$	151	75.5
Lambda ≥ 1.5	83	41.5
Pure H < 2	111	55.5
Isolation Index $> \frac{1}{4}R$	18	9.0

PART IV

Interpretation

CHAPTER 13

Introduction

The interpretation of Rorschach data is complex, but not nearly as complex as often is implied. It requires, as does the interpretation of any psychological test, training, skill, and experience. The fundamental requirements for interpretation include a reasonably good knowledge of personality and behavioral theories, an expertise in psychopathology, and a knowledge of the test itself. This composite background affords the core of information that is necessary to develop and review interpretive postulates in the context of the broad framework of human behaviors. Obviously, access to normative and reference data is also important to the formation and acceptance or rejection of interpretive hypotheses.

Magical thinking or crystal ball operations have no place in Rorschach interpretation. Quite the contrary, the process involves analysis and synthesis, drawing intelligently from the quantitative and qualitative material in the record. Many can learn to administer and code or score the Rorschach, but the training required for interpretation goes well beyond that level. A well-trained clerk can become a good examiner, but rarely, if ever, a qualified interpreter. A valid interpretation is the product of a well-administered and accurately scored test, plus the variety of skills reflected in the good clinician; that is, the knowledge, skills, and experience that are important to the translation of the myriad of Rorschach scores and words into a meaningful understanding of the person. In other words, the response is a composite of a perceptual procedure and a projective process. The idiography of the Rorschach data frequently represents projection at its most exquisite level, but such projection almost always, except for the most extremely disoriented subjects, is combined with a perceptual component. When interpreters approach the Rorschach data, they must recognize that some of their interpretations will be based on the perceptual elements of the responses, and they will gauge this against nomothetic data available to them, such as reference norms. Concurrently, they will be alert to the projective features of the responses which will often add the "flesh" to the nomothetic skeleton. Both kinds of data are Rorschach data, and together they constitute that which is to be interpreted.

THE INTERPRETIVE PROCESS

Rorschach (1921) was very cautious about what kinds of conclusions might be drawn from the test data. He indicated that he did not know how to differentiate manifest from latent symptoms, and questioned the value of the test for studying "unconscious" characteristics of thinking. Although it seems plausible that Rorschach would have accepted Frank's projective hypothesis as applicable to the test, Rorschach himself gave no indication that he considered such a process in the test. He was especially forceful in emphasizing that the test does not provoke a continuing "stream" of thought, but rather is one requiring adaptation to external stimuli.

As the Rorschach has "matured," so too has the process of Rorschach interpretation. Each of the authorities of the test has gone well beyond Rorschach's original position concerning interpretation. Almost all have used the bulk of Rorschach's interpretive postulates as the nucleus of their own interpretive frameworks. Most of those postulates have ultimately gained solid empirical support. But Rorschach was far less concerned with the validity of specific test factors as applied to interpretation, as he was with stressing the necessity of approaching the test data in its totality. He very accurately perceived that similar test signs or features, such as a given number of M responses, would, in different test configurations, be interpreted differently. For example, a preponderance of M answers in a protocol might indicate the existence of a strong tendency to use the inner life for gratification. Assuming that statement to be valid, it provides, at best, only a very limited understanding of the person. Important questions concerning the degree of adaptivity afforded by that inner life, or the extent to which the tendency to the inner life impairs interaction with the environment, cannot be answered simply by studying the number of M's in the protocol. In fact, if there is also a preponderance of color responses in the record, the statement itself *would not be valid*. Similarly, many other Rorschach features could alter, or negate, any statement taken from a single "sign."

Each of the Rorschach systematizers, although differing in their own approaches, has solidly agreed with Rorschach's recommendation that the totality of the test must be considered in interpretation. This has generally been referred to in the literature as the "global" approach and, in effect, it requires that *all* Rorschach data be considered in the interpretive process in a manner which is concerned with the configuration of data, as opposed to the interpretation of pieces of data in isolation. This process is essentially the same as occurs in any clinical interpretation, whether that interpretation be of data drawn from interviews, tests, or therapy sessions. Levy (1963) offers an excellent work on the subject of psychological interpretation which identifies the components of the process in more detail than is necessary here; however, extrapolating from Levy, Rorschach interpretation might best be described as a two-stage procedure. The first stage is a propositional one, whereas the second stage is one of integration.

THE PROPOSITIONAL STAGE

The onset of Rorschach intepretation begins with a careful review of each of the test components. These include the Structural Summary, with all of its frequencies, ratios, and percentages, the specific scorings of responses and their sequence of occurrence, the verbalizations given during the Free Association and, finally, the verbalizations given during the Inquiry. As the various component parts of each of these Rorschach units are surveyed, propositions or hypotheses are formulated. At this point it is important that no reasonable hypothesis be rejected simply because it does not seem compatible with other propositions generated from the review. It is also quite important that all of the components are studied, not simply those that are unusual or dramatic. It is true that the unusual or dramatic are probably more distinctly representative of the idiography of the subject, but the usual or commonplace are equally important in "getting at" the entire person.

The propositions are usually generated through a cross-checking of several features within a unit or across units. For example, it might be noted in the Structural Summary that a subject has given a below average number of responses, has an absence of color responses, and has a proportionally high frequency of Popular responses, and that most of the responses given are of good form quality. The composite of these features leads to at least one and possibly two hypotheses. First, because of the low R and absence of color, the possibility of constriction and/or defensiveness must be entertained. Second, the high frequency of P and the fact that most of the responses are of good form quality suggest a capacity and/or willingness to approach the blots in a conventional or conforming manner. Numerous questions and additional hypotheses can be generated from these two propositions. For instance, does the tendency toward conventionality in percepts represent a defensive style? In a more serious context, does the absence of color plus the tendency toward giving conventional answers represent a defensive containment of emotion as is often found in the depressed person? Neither of these questions could be answered from the four bits of data given here, but the existence of these data does establish a propositional framework against which other data will be reviewed.

Although the absolute use of single signs to form postulates is generally unwarranted, there are occasional exceptions. These are generally instances where the datum is very striking and unique. A response, such as "the remnants of a decayed penis," cannot help but warrant some hypothesizing by the interpreter. Similarly, the complete absence of good form quality leads to obvious speculation about the failures of reality contact. It is important to stress, however, that even when these strikingly unique single features do occur in a protocol, the interpreter should not neglect the remainder of the data on the assumption that "the case is solved." It is not uncommon to find protocols that contain an extremely unique or even bizzare component, the interpretive significance of which will be tempered substantially by other data in the record.

The actual number of propositions that might be generated from a given protocol will vary with the "richness" of the protocol plus the deductive skills of the interpreter. The Rorschach is a *wideband procedure,* that is, one that may yield information relevant to many different decisions. Cronbach and Gleser (1957), in their discussion of decision theory, point to the fact that the wideband technique, although often condemned on the basis of validation research, renders information from which numerous hypotheses can be formulated, some of which, when they are confirmed, have great practical importance. They indicate that, although any single hypothesis may be questionable or undependable, the sequential accumulation of hypotheses will often draw attention to information which might otherwise be missed by the interpreter.

Each of the four major units of the protocol, the Structual Summary, the Sequence of Scores, the Associations, and the Inquiry, contain data from which propositions are formulated. Ordinarily, the interpreter will begin with the Structural Summary in his or her review and proceed through the sequence analysis to the verbalizations. This procedure keeps the interpreter from "getting caught up" in the unique or sometimes dramatic verbalizations prematurely. Those kinds of verbalizations may be quite important in the interpretive process; however, they can also be very misleading, especially to the novice interpreter. As propositions accumulate throughout the procedure, the interpreter finds many that are related either directly or indirectly to each other. No terminal decisions are made prior to reviewing all data in the record. The ultimate weight given any Rorschach feature is determined during the second stage of interpretation, that of integration.

THE INTEGRATION STAGE

After the numerous propositions have been formulated by reviewing each of the four major units of the Rorschach data, the interpreter comes to the point of creating a meaningful description of the subject. This description is the product of a logical integration of the various postulates that have been formed. It is not simply a process of adding statements together, but instead involves the clinical conceptualization of the psychology of a person. Some of the propositions previously formulated may be rejected, although more commonly they are modified or clarified by other propositions. It is here that their clinicians go beyond specific data, using their propositional statements as a base and adding to that base their own deductive logic and knowledge of human behavior and psychopathology. This is the output of the Rorschach clinician. The yield is essentially descriptive, designed to aid in understanding the subject. It is predicated on a matrix of data which has led to propositions and conceptions. It is not necessarily *predictive* at this point, nor does it ultimately need to be predictive. Predictions and recommendations, although clearly a function for the psychodiagnostician, accumulate from the total information available to the clinician regarding the subject. Rorschach interpretation may be only one element of that information. For example, a Rorschach description may include information to the effect that a subject is "quick" to display emotion under stressful conditions. Assuming that statement to be valid, it provides only a limited understanding of the person and the manner in which he or she handles emotion. A major unanswered question is whether this proclivity is used adaptively, or whether it is a liability. Other Rorschach data may add some clarification to the issue. It may be determined that contact with reality is reasonably effective, that sufficient interest in people exists so as not to avoid them, that he or she is able to perceive things conventionally, and that the person apparently does not experience overwhelming feelings of tension or anxiety. All of these factors might lead the interpreter to "predict" that the subject probably handles emotions effectively, and that there is no need for concern that he or she will be dominated by these affective experiences. Such a recommendation or prediction, however, is not based on the Rorschach data, but on an intelligent hunch of the interpreter. If the same interpreter already knew that the subject had a history of temper outbursts plus some incidents of assaultiveness, it is highly unlikely that the same recommendations or predictions would be made. But that added information would not change the Rorschach-derived conclusions. The description that the subject is quick to show emotion under stress, that reality contact is reasonably effective, that he or she maintains a normal or average interest in people, and is able to perceive things conventionally remains true. The added behavioral information simply clarifies how the emotion is displayed. Naturally, this added clarification is critically important to the clinician who may be asked to speculate concerning future emotional displays and exemplifies how inputs from many sources, including the Rorschach, contribute to the process of making recommendations or predictions. The focus of the integration stage, however, is not oriented toward prediction, except that it includes information which may ultimately contribute to predictions and/or recommendations. Sarbin (1941) has suggested that any diagnostic statement is meaningful only when it has reference to the future; that is, when it is predictive. Unfortunately, Sarbin's position tends to neglect the scientifically diagnostic importance of simply understanding a person. This position has been well defended by Holt (1970), and it is in the context of the Holt premise that the integrative stage of Rorschach interpretation renders its greatest yield.

Blind Interpretation   The matters of prediction and recommendation raise the specter of blind analysis or interpretation of the Rorschach data. This has been a controversial issue for the Rorschach, and one that has often been confusingly distorted. Blind interpretation implies that the interpreter works only with the test data, possibly also knowing the age, sex, and marital status of the subject. At times, the interpreter may also have a useful referral question which poses a specific question, but more commonly these questions are vague and/or overinclusive.

There has been considerable divergence among Rorschachers, especially among those who have researched the test, regarding the value and appropriateness of the blind method. Rorschach had suggested that the method would be useful to validate the test, and used it himself, apparently developing several of his more important postulates by keeping himself completely naive concerning the subject. He did not endorse the usefulness of blind interpretation, and there has been considerable disagreement regarding how material developed through blind interpretation should be used. Beck (1960) and Piotrowski (1957, 1964) have been the most staunch supporters of blind interpretation. Each contends that the test should be interpreted completely before other information concerning the subject is available, and then that interpretation integrated with data from other tests and social history information, *without changing the Rorschach interpretation.* Beck's 1960 work demonstrates very neatly how this may be accomplished, and Piotrowski's entire approach to a computerized Rorschach interpretation has been based on the validity of this premise.

The Rapaport-Schafer approach offers only partial agreement with the position of Beck and Piotrowski. They are oriented toward the concept of the test battery and argue that all data should be interpreted blindly, but in totality, so that postulates derived from Rorschach data might be altered by the total data pattern. The Klopfer position concerning blind analysis, which once strongly advocated this approach, changed gradually as his experience with the test increased. Klopfer et al. (1954) recommend that interpretation should always begin with the Rorschach, and essentially in the blind, but cautions that some Rorschach-derived conclusions may be modified or omitted if other data sources provide clearly different conclusions. The Hertz approach to the matter of blind interpretation probably differs most extensively from Beck and Piotrowski. Although endorsing the blind approach for teaching purposes, Hertz advocates an "interactionist" approach to the clinical interpretation of the test. This method of interpretation calls for Rorschach interpretation to occur in conjunction with, and regard for, all other test data plus the complete socioeducational-developmental history. Hertz defends this approach on the premise that the varieties of data contribute to a more realistic and meaningful interpretation of any given data.

The issue of blind interpretation has probably been given more notoriety than may have been warranted. This was especially true for the period from 1935 to 1955 when the question of Rorschach validity was so frequently challenged and defended. Numerous studies using a blind methodology to evaluate the validity of the test were reported during this period. They generally fall into three design categories: (1) those using a blind interpretation to generate a *personality description* which was then compared for congruence with personality descriptions created by "expert" judges using methods other than the Rorschach, (2) those using blind analysis to derive a *diagnostic impression* versus diagnostic impressions rendered by "expert" judges, and (3) those using blind analysis versus some previously *established criteria.* A summary of 24 of these studies is shown in Table 30. It will be noted from examination of Table 30 that the results are generally mixed, although a substantial majority do provide support for the Rorschach.

The issue of blind interpretation, as has been recommended by several of the Rorschach systematizers, and the approach to the issue of the test validity using blind interpretation, *are not the same issues.* The systematizers conceptualize blind interpretation as a clinical method designed to keep the interpreter free of any sets or biases. Beck, Klopfer, and Piotrowski all maintain that the best way to approach the test is free of any set. None suggests that the process of clinical interpretation or diagnosis necessarily ends with the Rorschach summary developed in the "blind," although each has demonstrated a phenomenal skill in being able to produce a thorough and highly accurate personality

Table 30. Summary of Blind Analysis Studies Concerning the Rorschach

Author	N	Design	Conclusions
Abel (1942)	1	Blind analysis versus case study	Agreement with case study by Margaret Mead
Bailick and Hamlin (1954)	25	Blind estimate of I.Q. versus Wechsler scores	Four judges made valid estimates of I.Q. showing correlations of .61, .64, .69, and .73
Benjamin and Brosin (1938)	36	Accuracy of Blind analyses versus extensive case analyses	The blind analyses were as "accurate" as the extensive case analyses
Benjamin and Ebaugh (1938)	55	Blind analysis versus final clinical diagnosis	84.7% correct
Chambers and Hamlin (1957)		Twenty clinicians were asked to identify each of five protocols according to five diagnostic groupings	Selections were correct in 58 of 100 attempts
Clapp (1938)	1	Blind analysis versus clinical case data	"High agreement"
Cummings (1954)	10	Blind analysis versus established diagnoses of 10 patients in five diagnostic groups using a single Rorschach card	"Analysis significant"
Grant, Ives, and Razoni (1952)	146	Blind ratings on a 4 point scale of normal subjects by three Rorschach "experts" and two inexperienced judges	Rorschach judges placed from between 61 and 71% of subjects on the maladjusted end of the continuum with a high correlation between judges
Hamlin and Newton (1938)	2	Blind ratings of adjustment versus established evaluation	Ratings were "reasonably accurate"
Hertz and Rubenstein (1938)	1	Blind analysis versus data collected in 14 interviews	"High agreement"
Kluckhohn and Rosenzweig (1949)	2	Blind analysis versus anthropological data	"High agreement"
Krugman (1942)	20	Comparisons by three blind judges in matching interpretations by two experienced examiners for 20 subjects	The three judges made a "perfect" score in matching the pairs of interpretations to the subjects
Lisansky (1956)	40	Blind judges versus judges using life history data	Rorschach judges did not show significantly better agreement than did the life history judges
Little and Shneidman (1959)	12	Blind analyses compared to previously existing assessment and with each other	Diagnostic agreement better than chance although wide variations occurred in the assignment of diagnostic categories
Monroe (1945)	1	Blind analysis versus teacher observations	"Satisfactory agreement"
Newton (1954)	5	Blind analysis versus comprehensive case material and psychiatric evaluation	Rorschach judgements correlate significantly teria
Oberholzer (1944)	37	Blind analysis versus data collected by ethnologist	"Considerable" congruency
Palmer (1949)	28	Blind analyses to be selected by patient's therapist	In 39% of the cases the selection of the therapist was correct

304

Table 30 (Continued)

Author	N	Design	Conclusions
Schachtel (1942)	3	Blind analysis versus anthropological findings	"Close convergence"
Siegel (1948)	26	Blind analysis versus psychiatric evaluations	88.5% agreement
Silverman (1959)	10	Blind analysis versus evaluations of psychotherapists using 30 blind judges each analyzing protocols for seven variables	Blind analysis agreed with therapists judgements greater than chance although validity coefficients ranged from low to moderate
Swift (1944)	26	Blind analysis versus psychiatrist evaluations	88% agreement
Symonds (1955)	1	Blind analysis by seven judges versus comprehensive case study	65% agreement
Vernon (1936)	45	Blind analysis versus personality sketches by two psychologists	Correlation of .83

description from nothing other than a blind Rorschach interpretation. Even with this skill, however, all have remained clinical realists, recognizing the limitations of the Rorschach and the importance of other kinds of data. Each conceives of the Rorschach interpretation as a nuclear understanding of the subject, which is added to by inputs from other sources, thus providing a complete clinical evaluation. They differ only in terms of *how* additional data should be used, not *whether* they should be used.

The researchers have attempted to use the method of blind interpretation as a test of the test, as Rorschach himself had suggested. Although these have been generally legitimate designs, the goal of the researcher in using the method is different than that of the clinician using the method. The researcher uses the blind interpretation as an end in itself, which becomes compared with other criteria. The interpretation is not extended or clarified by other inputs, as is the case in the clinical setting. Unfortunately, critics of the Rorschach have frequently cited the sometimes limited findings derived from the blind interpretation research works as both a criticism of the test and of the procedure as useful with the test. Such a position, of course, neglects the manner in which blind interpretation is commonly used, that is, as a beginning rather than an end.

It is in keeping with the recommendations of Beck, Klopfer, and Piotrowski that interpreters of the Comprehensive System are encouraged to begin their interpretation *in the blind*. This means developing propositions only from the Rorschach data, and ultimately integrating these postulates into a meaningful description of the subject. This is a difficult challenge for many Rorschachers, because the interpreter is often the one responsible for administering the test, and will naturally be influenced to some extent by that event, and by the cursory review of the verbalizations which occurs during the process of scoring the test. The astute clinician is aware of this, and makes attempts to restrict interpretive logic only to the Rorschach data. If the interpreter has already developed subjective impressions, either positive or negative, concerning the subject, he or she should not create premature sets that could influence the interpretation or cause the neglect of any data. Sometimes, even data from a brief history can cause such sets, as has been illustrated quite well by Levy (1970) who found that simple demographic information, such as socioeconomic status, can have an impact on diagnostic conclusions.

It should be obvious to any well-trained clinician that the injection of feelings, prejudice, bias, or sets into the interpretation of any data converts the interpretive process from science to an art form. When that occurs, a considerable risk is created that personality descriptions, diagnoses, and recommendations for intervention and/or disposition will be different than if an empirically based approach had been employed. Assuming a lawfulness to the behaviors of humans, anyone with a thorough grasp of the test and a reasonably good understanding of people should be able to render valid and useful interpretations from Rorschach data.

COOKBOOKS AND COMPUTERS

Ideally, the final interpretive yield from the Rorschach will represent an intermingling of empirically based findings, that is, those conservative interpretations that are based on research, with a conceptual framework in which links are drawn between the test data and aspects of personality functioning. Such an approach extends well beyond a simplistic "cookbook" effort at data translation, which sometimes can be overly simplistic or concrete, and even quite misleading. Many years ago, Meehl (1956) made an intelligent and intriguing appeal for a "cookbook" approach to diagnostics, which would simplify the task and provide more time for clinicians to perform other important tasks. Although Meehl's position was reasonable, particularly for the task of "hanging" diagnostic labels, it is not very applicable to Rorschach interpretation. There is no simple checklist of Rorschach signs that automatically can be translated as representative of aspects of personality or behavior. Unfortunately, the novice interpreter often believes that such simple equations do exist, and searches for them quite diligently. This tendency has often been encouraged by some Rorschach authors who have conveyed the impression that simplistic translations of scores, or classes of response contents, are useful procedures in interpretation. That supposition is *pure nonsense,* and the unwitting interpreter who is bound to that procedure would do better to avoid the use of the Rorschach in assessment work. The test is far too complex for a simplistic sign approach, and the validity of the interpretation will depend largely on the extent to which the interpreter achieves the full measure of data integration in forming the description of the subject.

The cookbook approach to test interpretation is probably best illustrated by the several elaborate computer programs that have been developed to translate psychological test scores into an interpretive narrative. Many have been well received in the professional community, especially some of those written for *MMPI* interpretation, and evidence is building to support their usefulness (Moreland, 1984). Nonetheless, computers do only as they are instructed or programmed, and it is highly unlikely that any computer program has been written for a complex psychological test that will consider the multitude of possibilities regarding the relationships among test variables or between test variables and the history of the subject. In other words, the computer program scans variables and combinations of variables *as instructed,* but has no capacity for deviating from those instructions. As a consequence, the empirically based computer scan of test data may be very accurate in generating some important descriptive and/or diagnostic information; however, it does not integrate that information with other *nonprogrammed* variables, nor does it conceptualize. Thus anyone using a computer "cookbook" program properly for a complex psychological test will usually go well beyond the computer print or narrative in forming final descriptive, diagnostic, or recommendation statements. Failure to do so creates a high risk that some important data will not be integrated in a meaningful way, and/or that some data, relevant to final judgments or conclusions, may be neglected completely.

Matarazzo (1983) has summarized the potential hazards of computerized psychological testing quite well, and those same hazards apply to any interpretive procedure, whether human or mechanistic, that is based on the naive assumption that a checklist of signs can be translated directly into information regarding features of personality or behaviors. However, it is erroneous to conclude that the sophisticated cookbook approach, as represented in *some* computer interpretation programs, has little or no value in assessment. Any program that insures a thorough scanning of a large number of variables and combinations of variables can provide a useful assist to interpretation because of speed and reliability. Some of the *MMPI* programs illustrate this and the same principles can be applied to some, *but not all,* of the data of the Rorschach. For example, a computer assist program has been developed at the Rorschach Research Foundation that scans 29 clusters of variables, derived from 313 structural features of the test (Exner, 1983, 1984). It is a large program that requires a great deal of storage space to permit the thousands of operations which are involved. Most, but not all of the scanning involves a search for unusual data, and each time such data are discovered a numbered statement is printed. In most cases, between 15 and 30 statements result, *none of which are based on single signs or data points.* If triggered, a statement indicates the presence of several findings, the composite of which is sufficient to warrant an interpretive postulate.

In effect, the computer search of the Rorschach structural data follows the same procedures that typically are used by the well-trained Rorschach interpreter. Although it has the advantage of consistency and speed, it has the disadvantages previously mentioned; that is, it fails to integrate findings beyond points for which it is programmed. It does follow logical, decision-tree rules—that is, if datum *A* is positive, search datum *B,* and so on; but even though it follows this logical progression search, it still does not encompass all of the data available in the Rorschach. As such, it becomes a useful tool, but cannot possibly capture the full uniqueness of the subject as represented by the total test.

LOGICAL PROGRESSION IN INTERPRETATION

Earlier, it was noted that interpretation should begin with the development of hypotheses, or propositions, which ultimately become integrated into more conclusive statements. The procedures for doing this are relatively straightforward in Rorschach work. The cardinal rule is to begin with those data that have the greatest empirically based sturdiness, exploiting them fully, and then working through data that require more clinical, or subjective, skill to be used appropriately. This means that the interpreter will begin with the data of the *Structural Summary,* which includes the frequencies for each of the codes, plus the numerous ratios, percentages, and derivations that are obtained from those frequencies. These are the data that have the greatest reliability, and these are the data for which much validation data have accumulated. The *Structural Summary* contains more than 100 variables, and it is these variables that the computer program is designed to search.

Generally, 15 to 30 well-based hypotheses or propositions will be developed from the Structural Summary. Next, the interpreter proceeds to the *Sequence of Scores,* which affords a picture of the coding for the answers in the order in which they occurred. Sometimes the Sequence of Scores will provide important information about clusterings of codes and also about the manner in which the subject has approached the blots. For instance, some subjects will always use the whole blot for their first response to each blot, whereas others may frequently select an uncommon detail area for their first answer. Some subjects may give all of their minus answers only to blots containing chromatic color, whereas others may always give minus answers as their first response to a blot. Any such patterns or clusters can add important information to postulates developed from the Structural Summary.

The final step in the interpretive procedure is a careful review of the words that have been used. Obviously, this is a search for the projected material. Many words, as noted in Chapter 2, simply reflect the way in which the subject has classified the stimulus, but some of the verbal material may go well beyond the level of classification and, as such, they present a challenge for the interpreter. They are not words related to simple classification of the stimulus. Instead, they are embellishments that go beyond the features of the stimulus field. As projected material, they reflect some of the idiography of the subject and can be very important in enhancing previously developed propositions. The interpretive usefulness of this material depends greatly on the clinical skills of the interpreter. Some of the material may have obvious ramifications, but much may be more subtle and remain a mystery even when explored fully in light of other available data. Some may be symbolic, allowing several possible postulates but, unfortunately, often of a nature that is impossible to cross-validate. Each response represents something concerning the psychological operations of the person, motives, sets, attitudes, experience, and so on, and the interpretive challenge is to sort out as many of these features as possible. It is not an easy task, and there is always the possibility that an interpreter will be unduly influenced by a premature set in attempting to work with the data. The most conservative approach is to rely on frequency data. When a substantial accumulation of response features occurs, whether scores or words, the data become pregnant by reason of reason and their translation is made easier.

As the interpretive procedure moves from one data set to another—that is, from the Structural Summary, through the Sequence of Scores, and finally to the verbal material— a psychological picture of the subject gradually unfolds. Each finding is like a piece of a puzzle to be fitted neatly in place. In most records the picture begins to form quickly as the Structural data are reviewed, and usually the portrait is extensive before the Sequence or verbal material are considered. Most of it is based on nomothetic considerations, but even the Structural data will often provide much idiographic information because of the mixture of features that is discovered. The review of the Sequence and of the verbal material helps to flesh out the picture by adding more elements of uniqueness.

Logical integration of findings is important *at each step* in the procedure. Sometimes, findings may appear discordant or even contradictory. When that occurs, one *is not* discarded in favor of the other. Instead, more data are searched until reconciliation is achieved. This involves the logical process of inductive and deductive reasoning and, quite often, knowledge about personality and behavior becomes crucial to the resolution. If the Rorschach is viewed as a reliably recorded and accurately coded sampling of behaviors, then each behavior, in some way, contributes to the understanding of the person. None *taken separately* will provide the full portrait and must be viewed as inconclusive representations. Collectively, however, each compliments the others in some way, and the composite should afford a portrayal of a person which can be used effectively to understand his or her functioning.

REFERENCES

Abel, T. M. (1948) The Rorschach test in a study of culture. *Journal of Projective Techniques* **12,** 1–15.

Bailick, I., and Hamlin, R. (1954) The clinician as judge: Details of procedure in judging projective material. *Journal of Consulting Psychology,* **18,** 239–242.

Beck, S. J. (1960) *The Rorschach Experiment: Ventures in Blind Diagnosis.* New York: Grune & Stratton.

Benjamin, J. D., and Brosin, H. W. (1938) The reliability and validity of the Rorschach Test. In Benjamin, J. D. and Ebaugh, F. G., *The diagnostic validity of the Rorschach Test. American Journal of Psychiatry,* **94,** 1163–1168.

Benjamin, J. D., and Ebaugh, F. G. (1938) The diagnostic validity of the Rorschach test. *American Journal of Psychiatry,* **94,** 1163–1168.

Chambers, G. S., and Hamlin, R. (1957) The validity of judgments based on "blind" Rorschach records. *Journal of Consulting Psychology,* **21,** 105–109.

Clapp, H., Kaplan, A. H., and Miale, F. R. Clinical validation of Rorschach interpretations. *Rorschach Research Exchange,* **2,** 153–163.

Cronbach, L. J., and Gleser, G. C. (1957) *Psychological Tests and Personnel Decisions.* Urbana: University of Illinois Press.

Cummings, S. T. (1954) The clinician as judge: Judgments of adjustment from Rorschach single-card performance. *Journal of Consulting Psychology,* **18,** 243–247.

Exner, J. E. (1983) *A computer program to assist in Rorschach interpretation.* Bayville, N.Y.: Rorschach Workshops.

Exner, J. E. (1984) *A computer program to assist in Rorschach interpretation.* (Revised) Bayville, N.Y.: Rorschach Workshops.

Frank, L. K. (1939) Projective methods for the study of personality. *Journal of Psychology,* **8,** 389–413.

Grant, M. Q., Ives, V., and Razoni, J. H. (1952) Reliability and validity of judges' ratings of adjustment on the Rorschach. *Psychological Monographs,* **66,** No. 234.

Hamlin, R., and Newton, R. (1952) Comparisons of a schizophrenic and a normal subject, both rated by clinicians as well adjusted on the basis of "blind analysis." *Eastern Psychological Association.* Atlantic City, N. J.

Hertz, M. R., and Rubenstein, B. B. (1949) A comparison of three blind Rorschach cases. *American Journal of Orthopsychiatry,* **19,** 295–313.

Holt, R. R. (1970) Yet another look at clinical and statistical prediction: Or, is clinical psychology worthwhile. *American Psychologist,* **25,** 337–349.

Klopfer, B., Ainsworth, M. D., Klopfer, W., and Holt, R. (1954) *Developments in the Rorschach Technique.* Vol. 1. Yonkers-on-Hudson, N.Y.: World Book.

Kluckhohn, S., and Rosenzweig, S. (1949) Two Navajo children over a five year period. *American Journal of Orthopsychiatry,* **19,** 266–278.

Krugman, J. (1942) A clinical validation of the Rorschach with problem children. *Rorschach Research Exchange,* **5,** 61–70.

Levy, L. (1963) *Psychological Interpretation.* New York: Holt, Rinehart and Winston.

Levy, M. R., (1970) Issues in the personality assessment of lower class patients. *Journal of Projective Techniques,* **34,** 6–9.

Lisansky, E. S. (1956) The inter-examiner reliability of the Rorschach test. *Journal of Projective Techniques,* **20,** 310–317.

Little, K. B., and Shneidman, E. S. (1959) Congruencies among interpretations of psychological test and anamnestic data. *Psychological Monographs,* **27,** No. 476.

Matarazzo, J. M. (1983) Computerized psychological testing. *Science,* **221,** 323.

Meehl, P. E. (1956) Wanted—A good cookbook. *American Psychologist,* **11,** 263–272.

Monroe, R. L. (1945) Three diagnostic methods applied to Sally. *Journal of Abnormal Psychology,* **40,** 215–227.

Moreland, K. L. (1984) Some ruminations on the validation of automated psychological reports. National Computer Systems: Minneapolis.

Newton, R. (1954) The clinician as judge: Total Rorschach and clinical case material. *Journal of Consulting Psychology,* **18,** 248–250.

Oberholzer, E. (1944) Blind analysis of the people of Alor. In DuBois, C. *The People of Alor.* Minneapolis: University of Minnesota Press.

Palmer, J. O. (1949) Two approaches to Rorschach validation. *American Psychologist,* **4,** 270–271.

Piotrowski, Z. (1957) *Perceptanalysis.* New York: Macmillan.

Piotrowski, Z. (1964) Digital computer interpretation of ink-blot test data. *Psychiatric Quarterly,* **38,** 1–26.

Rorschach, H. (1921) *Psychodiagnostics.* Bern: Bircher.

Sarbin, T. R. (1941) Clinical psychology—Art or science. *Psychometrika,* **6,** 391–400.

Schachtel, A. H. (1942) Blind interpretation of six Pilaga Indian children. *American Journal of Orthopsychiatry,* **12,** 679–712.

Siegel, M. (1948) The diagnostic and prognostic validity of the Rorschach test in child guidance clinics. *American Journal of Orthopsychiatry,* **18,** 119–133.

Silverman, L. H. (1959) A Q-Sort study of evaluations made from projective techniques. *Psychological Monographs,* **27,** No. 477.

Swift, J. W. (1944) Matchings of teacher's descriptions and Rorschach analysis of pre-school children. *Child Development,* **15,** 217–244.

Symonds, P. M. (1955) A contribution to our knowledge of the validity of the Rorschach. *Journal of Projective Techniques,* **19,** 152–162.

Vernon, P. H. (1936) The evaluation of the matching method. *Journal of Educational Psychology,* **27,** 1–17.

CHAPTER 14

Structural Data I—
Validity, Controls,
and Coping Styles

The structural data should be approached systematically, moving in a logical progression from point to point, with the objective of formulating postulates when the accumulation of findings warrants, or ruling out the presence of some characteristics when that is appropriate. The Structural Summary page of the *Structural Summary Blank* has been organized to facilitate the procedure by clustering variables that are, or may be related to similar issues, such as stress tolerance, capacity for control, the use of affect, and so on. But before addressing any issues concerning diagnosis or the descriptive aspects of personality functioning, the length of the record must be considered. This is *always* the first datum to be reviewed.

NUMBER OF RESPONSES (*R*)

There are two important reasons to begin with a review of *R*. First, to insure that the protocol is of sufficient length to be regarded as interpretively useful. Responses are representative samples of processing and decision operations, and many interpretive postulates and/or conclusions are derived from data concerning the frequency with which different kinds of operations occur. If the overall sample is too sparse, some issues cannot be addressed at all, and propositions concerning other issues will be much more tenuous than is useful to quality assessment. Second, *R* is also used to determine if extrapolation may be required in the application of some of the normative data.

The *R* will naturally vary from subject to subject. Most adult subjects give between 17 and 27*R* under the instructions of the Comprehensive System. Deviations from this range are *not* indicative of psychopathology, but they should be carefully considered. In some instances the examiner may provoke the longer or shorter record; however, this is the exception rather than the rule. A test of this postulate was completed using 16 student examiners, none of whom had prior Rorschach training. After three 2-hour training sessions in the mechanics of administration, including a demonstration plus role-playing, each collected two "familiarization" protocols which were discarded. Subsequently, each tested five subjects drawn randomly from a pool containing both psychiatric and nonpsychiatric subjects. Fifty-nine of the 80 protocols collected were of the expected length (17 to 27*R*), whereas the 21 records with *R*'s above or below the expected range were reasonably distributed across examiners, so that in only three cases did an examiner obtain more than one record the length of which deviated from the expected range. In those three instances, one examiner obtained four out of five records containing less than 17*R*, and in another instance, one examiner obtained four or five protocols containing more than 27R. Observation of these two examiners, each taking a sixth protocol, revealed that both were deviating from standard procedure, one manifesting rather abrupt tactics whereas the second used considerable reinforcement, both verbal and nonverbal. These data seem especially useful in studying the expected length of records because none of the examiners were informed, until after the study was completed, of the purpose of the study, nor were they given any specific information concerning expected length.

Adult records that are less than 17 responses, or those from children that are less than 15 responses, usually signal some defensiveness or resistance. Briefer records are also more commonplace among those who are intellectually limited, neurologically impaired, or markedly depressed. When R is low, the interpreter must be alert to the fact that some of the proportions and percentages can be altered considerably by one or two answers. This caution becomes especially important for records in which R is 13 or less. Longer records pose a similar issue. If R exceeds 32, it is likely that the subject has exhausted most of the W possibilities, and thus a proportionally higher number of D and/or Dd answers can be expected and the number of Popular answers will probably exceed the average. In either instance some logical extrapolation of normative data will be important to the final interpretation.

R, LAMBDA, AND QUESTIONS OF VALIDITY

Although the issue of extrapolation of normative data is obviously important, the number of responses is much more critical to the issue of the validity of the record. As noted earlier, each response reflects a sample of cognitive behavior, and if the number of samples available is too few, the behavior is probably not representative. *Any record of less than 10 answers should be discarded as invalid.* In some cases the few responses that have been delivered may be clinically useful, but the structural data are too sparse to be used meaningfully. If R falls between 10 and 12, the *possibility that the record does not contain sufficient data to be interpretively useful is substantial.* An R of 10, 11, or 12 does not automatically mean that a record is invalid, for many of this length provide important data. If R is less than 12, however, the hypothesis that the record is of questionable validity will be correct for more than 90% of all protocols from clients older than 7. The key to the decision about whether a brief record is valid is the *Lambda (L).*

L represents the proportion of pure F responses in the protocol, and pure F answers do correlate with a kind of psychological economy operation. Whenever L is disproportionately high, that is, greater than 1.2 for adults, or greater than 1.5 for children who are older than 7, it signals that most of the responses which have been selected to deliver are generally simplistic, pure F answers. They are responses that ignore or neglect the complexities of the stimulus field. They are developed by using only the contours of the blot, thereby excluding other stimuli in the field. Brief records of 10, 11, or 12 answers that consist mainly of pure F responses, that is, those in which L is inordinately high, indicate that the subject has "refused" to process and/or mediate the stimuli as requested. This may be the result of a defensive intent to avoid the task, or it may represent the product of a more basic coping style. In either case the low R, high L records reflect a subtle form of rejection or nonparticipation in the task presented. As such they must be considered as being of *questionable validity,* and any interpretive conclusions drawn from them should be applied very cautiously. This should not be interpreted to suggest that pure F answers are undesirable; that is not the case. Almost all subjects deliver some pure *F* answers, and the failure to do so can signify a serious problem.

Lambda and the Pure Form Response *(F)*   Rorschach (1921) was the first to note the importance of the pure *F* answer. He suggested that it was related to the attention-concentration features of the subject's thinking. Both Beck (1945) and Klopfer et al. (1954) have implied that pure *F* relates to a form of "affect delay," agreeing to some extent with Rapaport et al.'s (1946) notion that decisions related to the pure *F* response involve formal reasoning. All three suggest that the stimulus properties of the blots may create some affective and/or conflict state, and that the decision to select a pure *F* answer indicates some form of defensiveness. Rapaport suggested a parallel between Hartmann's notion of a conflict-free sphere of ego functioning and the decision to deliver the pure *F*. Neither Beck nor Klopfer accepted this position. Instead, they argued that affect and/or conflict may be present during the decision process, but that it is somehow controlled by the more deliberate and probably conscious operations.

There are a variety of empirical data that support the Beck-Klopfer position concerning pure *F*. In the developmental studies of Ames et al. (1952, 1971), the normative data of Exner and Weiner (1982), and the longitudinal study of Exner, Thomas, and Mason (1985), a relatively high proportion of pure *F* answers are found in the records of children and adolescents, with that proportion decreasing as age increases. Klopfer interpreted this as a form of rigidity, reflecting the inability of the child to exhibit emotion and/or conflict without fear or reprisal. Beck (1944), Paulsen (1941), and Swift (1945) have all reported that the proportion of pure *F* has a significant relation to intelligence; that is, the more retarded children give significantly lower frequencies of pure *F*. Significantly lower proportions of pure *F* have also been noted among epileptics (Arluck, 1940). Rabin et al. (1954) reports that the proportion of pure *F* increases under intoxication but the quality of the responses decreases. Buhler and LeFever (1947) report that alcoholics generally give a proportionally higher frequency of pure *F* answers than do "psychopaths." Henry and Rotter (1956) found that more pure *F* responses are produced by subjects who have a knowledge of the purpose of the test. Hafner (1958) reports that when subjects are instructed to respond as quickly as possible, a significantly lower proportion of pure *F* answers occur. The composite of these data appear to indicate that when the subject is in the more defensive position, he or she is prone to increase the number of pure Form answers. The data also suggest that when the subject is unable to promote the necessary delays required for the formulation of the pure *F* answer (as in the organic or characterological style prone toward impulse display), the proportion of pure *F* answers will be proportionally lowered.

These findings also gain some support from the studies of the more severe psychopathologies. Sherman (1955), for example, notes that the incidence of pure *F* is relatively lower among the acute schizophrenics, a phenomenon which he interprets as experiencing much stress as well as struggling for some solution to the crisis state. Kelley, Margulies, and Barrera (1941) have reported a significant increase of the pure *F* frequency after one ECT treatment. Rapaport et al. (1946) have noted a significantly greater proportion of pure *F* answers among paranoid schizophrenics than other types of schizophrenia. Goldman (1960) has found that recovering schizophrenics tend to give significantly higher proportions of pure *F* than occurred prior to remission. A significantly higher pure *F* is found among the 53 schizophrenics studied by Exner and Murillo (1973) at discharge than at admission. In another study completed for this work, 109 patients, approximately half of whom had been diagnosed as schizophrenic, were evaluated at admission and again 8 to 10 weeks after discharge of hospitalization. A significant increase in the proportion of pure F is found after discharge. Exner and Murillo (1977) have also found that schizophrenics who remain out-of-hospital for a period of 1 to 3 years have a significantly higher Lambda than do schizophrenics who are readmitted during the first year after discharge.

Whereas adult nonpatients tend to give about 30 to 35% of pure F responses in their records, the proportions of pure F are considerably higher among those subjects who have histories of asocial or antisocial behaviors. For example, the average Lambda for the reference sample of subjects with character problems is 1.51 ($SD = 1.43$). Nearly 42% of those 200 subjects have Lambda's greater than 1.5 and more than one-half of the total sample has been involved at least once in legal action. In effect, the high Lambda in a record of average length or greater indicates that the avoidance and/or simplification operations that are represented in the high frequency of pure F answers is probably *stylistic*. It denotes the type of person who approaches the environment in an overly simplistic or overly economical manner, and as a result these persons often find themselves in confrontational situations. This is not necessarily because they deliberately violate rules or ignore the expectations of others. Instead, they have a psychological set, or response style that orients them to avoid, ignore, or reject stimulus complexity as much as possible. Thus they often find themselves at odds with the expectations or demands of the world. Subjects with this form of coping style will often have a lower than average $X + \%$ and tend to give fewer *Popular* responses, mainly because they view the environment more uniquely than do most people. Usually the histories of these subjects will include information concerning their avoidant or overly economical style. If the history is contradictory to this postulate, the high L in a record of average length or longer should be interpreted in the situational context; that is, the subject has apparently responded to the stress of the ambiguous task demand by being ultraconservative.

When the frequency of pure F answers is significantly lower than average, leading to a low Lambda, a much different picture is indicated. As noted earlier, most subjects will give some pure F responses. These answers, when not used excessively, can be viewed as a healthy backing away from complexity, as if psychologically resting and using a simpler approach to the task. The failure to do this raises three interpretive possibilities. First, some people have difficulty identifying the most economical ways of handling task demand. Frequently, they are victims of their unfulfilled needs, conflicts, and emotions. As a result they do not always use their resources effectively. Their preoccupations and/or apprehensions often interfere with concentration or logical reasoning, and thus they often fail to perceive easier or economical solutions, which leads to an overinvolvement with stimuli around them. It is not a deliberate involvement, but rather an inability to back away. When this is the cause of the low L, there will be many other features of the record that signal turmoil.

Two other conditions can also produce a low Lambda. Both can be viewed somewhat more positively than the circumstance of psychological turmoil, one more so than the other. Some achievement-oriented people have the advantage of being flexible and able to adapt easily to situations. If these persons view the test as a challenge to their coping skills, they will often sacrifice economy to gain a sense of accomplishment. Therefore they frequently reject the simpler responses and strive to deal effectively with the complexity of the stimuli. When the low Lambda is created by this striving, many features of the record will convey a picture of control, flexibility, adaptibility, and psychological sturdiness. The $X + \%$ and the number of *Popular* responses are usually well within the average range, the *Zf* and number of *W* and *DQ+* answers are usually elevated, and typically, the *Zd* score is in the normal range.

The third condition that often produces a low Lambda is also related to an orientation to accomplishment, but it is created less from the sense of challenge and more from the need to avoid error or failure. It is identified by an elevated *Zd* score. If the *Zd* score is greater than +3.0, it indicates that the subject tends to invest more effort in organizing the stimulus field than is typical or necessary. It is a kind of cognitive inefficiency that can be either an asset or liability, depending on the circumstance in which it occurs. This characteristic is called *overincorporation,* and is described in more detail in the section concerning *Zf* and *Zd.* There is a significant, positive correlation between overincorporation and a low Lambda, with the overincorporative style usually being the causal element. When both are noted in a protocol, other data concerning stability, reality testing, clarity of thinking, stress tolerance, and control will be the decisive elements in determining whether the low Lambda is cause for concern, or merely a by-product of a more firmly entrenched cognitive style.

STRESS TOLERANCE AND CONTROL

After reviewing *R,* and Lambda if necessary to establish that the protocol is valid for purposes of interpretation, a cluster of six variables provides the first data set from which to begin developing a description of the subject. Four of the six have been labeled as the *Four Square* (Exner, 1978). They are the *EB* (Erlebnistypus), *EA* (Experience Actual), *eb* (Experience Base), and *es* (Experienced Stimulation). Each can provide useful interpretive information, but collectively they present a much broader picture about several important psychological features. The remaining two variables in the cluster are the *D Score,* and the *Adjusted D Score,* both of which are calculated from the data of the Four Square.

THE *D* SCORE

The *D* score is the first point in the data cluster to be reviewed. As noted in Chapter 10, it is a scaled difference score that is derived from the *EA-es* raw score. It provides information concerning the relationship among resources that are available for use and stimulus demands that are being made on the individual (Exner, 1978; Weiner-Levy & Exner, 1981; Exner, 1983). As such, it can be used to address the issues of control and stress tolerance. The majority of adult subjects, both patients and nonpatients, will have a *D* score of 0. This indicates that, *under most circumstances,* sufficient resources are available to be able to initiate and direct behavior in a deliberate and meaningful way, and that stimulus demands being experienced generally do not exceed the capacities of the subject for being able to control behavior. This does *not mean* that behaviors selected and implemented will necessarily be effective, adaptive, or even logical. It simply means that the person has sufficient resources accessible to be able to form and direct behavior. Subjects with a *D* score of 0 usually have an adequate tolerance for the stresses of everyday living, and it is only under conditions of intense, prolonged, and/or unexpected stress that their controls falter significantly.

If the *D* score exceeds 0, such as +1, +2, and so on, it signifies greater capability for control and greater tolerance for stress because the resources available for use are well in excess of the demands for responses. Apparently, people with D scores greater than 0 have been able to identify and organize their resources in ways that make them readily available. This creates an increase in the capacity for control, and as a by-product the tolerance for stress (even prolonged, intense, and/or unexpected stresses) is improved considerably. As the magnitude of the positive D score increases, so too do the capacities for control and greater stress tolerance. At first glance this feature may appear to be a very desirable characteristic of the personality structure, and for some people that can be the case. However, it is important to emphasize that the D *score has little to do with adjustment or adaptive behavior.*

For instance, 29% of the subjects in the schizophrenia reference sample have D scores greater than 0 as contrasted with 28% of the adult nonpatient normative sample. Patients who have D scores greater than 0 have sturdy controls and are not easily disorganized by stress situations, in spite of their pathology. Patients with D scores of $+1$ or greater are frequently more difficult to treat because they tend to use their resources to avoid direct confrontations with the experiences of frailty and/or helplessness that often serve to promote motivation for growth or change. If the elements that lead to very sturdy control, as represented by the elevated D score, have been organized prematurely in the developmental cycle, the result can be a form of rigidity that produces an excessive distancing from many experiences that have value in extending or broadening sensitivity to, and awareness of, the environment. Thus if a pathological element becomes pervasive in the personality structure, as in schizophrenia or even in less serious conditions, the possibilities for change are reduced substantially.

On the other hand, subjects with D scores in the minus range, -1, -2, and so on, are more limited in available resources as contrasted to the demands made on them. As a consequence they are vulnerable to becoming overwhelmed by stimulus demands, and this creates a state of *stimulus overload.* This is a condition in which the frequency and/or intensity of stimulus demands exceeds the range of responses that can be formulated or implemented effectively. Thus some behaviors are not well formulated and others may not have sufficient follow-through in their implementation to cope effectively with the demand situation. Some people, especially those who fall into the $D-2$, $D-3$ or lower categories, are in an almost continuous state of overload. They are beset with more experienced demands for responses than they can handle easily. The result is that many of their behaviors are insufficient or even inappropriate, and when new demands occur, their lives can become marked by disorganization or even chaos. This is commonplace among children, but far less so for the adult. If the subject experiencing overload is prone to manifest thinking and feelings in overt behavior, he or she will often appear distraught and/or disorganized, even to the casual observer. Conversely, those who are more prone to internalize thoughts and feelings will often experience bouts of anxiety, apprehension, helplessness, tension, or depression.

Whereas the overload state is not uncommon among children, it can be an extremely detrimental situation for the older person. The sometimes disorganized and chaotic child is usually regarded more favorably than is the disorganized or chaotic adult. The disorganized child is typically judged as being the product of limited development and the resulting lack of maturity. The same features are much less acceptable in the adult, even though the causes may be the same. An overload condition, as reflected in the minus D score, *can be* the result of a perpetuated developmental failure. These are the more immature people whose lives seem to be marked by one chaotic event after another, or whose general pattern of activity will be marked by an excessive frequency of ineffective and/or maladaptive behaviors. However, *it is unrealistic to presume that minus D scores only reflect a form of immaturity*. Some people are besieged with pathology later in life, and as a result are gradually pushed into an overload state. As stimulus demands increase in breadth and frequency because of the pathology, resources may become overtaxed and spread too thin. This creates an increasing vulnerability to becoming disorganized and this can become a chronic state.

Obviously, it is very important to distinguish those overload conditions that are chronic from those that have been created by situational circumstances. All people have tolerance limits, so that even the individual who is ordinarily a $D+1$ or $+2$ can be thrust into overload by intense or prolonged stress. The key in determining whether the D score represents a chronic condition or a situationally related state is provided by another of the six variables in the data set.

THE ADJUSTED *D* SCORE

As noted in Chapter 10, the *Adjusted D Score* is calculated by subtracting the sum m except 1, and the sum for the Y variables except 1, from the *es* raw score, and then recalculating *EA-es* and applying the result to the D Score Conversion Table. This adjustment is necessary because the m and Y variables apparently are related to situational phenomena.

The *m* and *Y* Variables   The m and Y variables (FY, YF, Y) are quite unstable. In every retest study, whether short term or long term for both adults and children, the resulting retest correlations rarely exceed .50, and in most instances fall between 0 and .30 (Exner, 1978, 1983; Exner, Armbruster, & Viglione, 1978; Exner, Thomas, & Mason, 1985; Exner & Weiner, 1982). In spite of the lack of temporal stability, there are considerable data indicating that both are interpretively significant when the frequencies for either are elevated. The means for both range from slightly less than 1.0 to slightly more than 1.0 for various adult groups, both patient and nonpatient, and they are consistently less than 0.5 for nonpatient children. It is because the means for nonpatient adults are approximately 1.0 for both variables that the adjusted *EA-es* raw score includes one m and/or one Y if either has occurred in the protocol.

Research concerning m was rather sparse prior to the 1970s. It was included as a coding variable in the Klopfer, Hertz, and Piotrowski Systems, and generally posited to represent the thoughts or drives that are not well integrated into the cognitive framework. Klopfer, Hertz, and Piotrowski have suggested that m is probably associated with the experience of frustration, especially regarding interpersonal relations. McArthur and King (1954) found that a combination of m plus a preponderance of chromatic color responses differentiated unsuccessful college students, whereas Majumber and Roy (1962) reported a significant elevation in m among juvenile delinquents. Neel (1960), using models of motoric and ideational inhibition, found that either condition causes an elevation in m as compared with control subjects. She interpreted her findings as evidence for tension and/or conflict created by the inability to integrate needs with behavior. Piotrowski and Schreiber (1952) found that m responses tend to disappear in the posttreatment records of patients who are judged as responding successfully to treatment.

Shalit (1965) was the first to report definitive findings concerning the relation of m to situational stress. He was able to collect retest Rorschachs from 20 Israeli seamen under the natural stress conditions of being on a relatively small ship during a severe storm condition. All had been tested previously, about 1 year earlier, when they entered the Israeli Navy. Shalit found that the retest frequencies for M and FM remained essentially the same, but the frequencies for m increased significantly. He interpreted this finding as related to the stressful condition created by the storm, postulating that the elevations in m reflect a sense of disruption and fear of disintegration of controls. The Shalit finding posed an obvious challenge for research concerning m; that is, if m does correlate with the sense of disruption of controls under stress, the issue of helplessness or lack of control should be an important independent variable in any study designed to test the validity of his findings.

Exner and Walker (1973) retested 20 inpatient depressives 1 day before their first ECT. Fourteen of the 20 had at least one m in their first protocol, which had been collected within the period of 5 to 7 days after admission ($M = 1.26$, $SD = 0.83$). The retest protocols included 16 that contained m, with a significant increase in the mean ($M = 2.57$, $SD = 1.09$, $p < .05$). A second retest of those subjects was administered when they were discharged, and only six of the 20 contained m responses ($M = 0.39$, $SD = 0.88$), even though the records were generally longer than either of the first two tests.

Armbruster, Miller, and Exner (1974) tested 20 Army paratroop trainees on one of their first 3 days of training and retested them the evening before their first parachute jump. Three of the 20 subjects had m responses in their first test ($M = 0.16$, $SD = 0.48$), whereas 12 produced at least one m in the retest ($M = 1.68$, $SD = 0.73$). In another natural stress study, 25 elective surgery patients were tested several weeks before surgery, and then retested the day before or morning of the surgery (Exner, Armbruster, Walker, & Cooper, 1975). The baseline records, collected 25 to 63 days prior to surgery, included 10 with a total of 16 m answers. Nineteen of the retest records contained m responses, for a total of 41 ($p < .02$). In addition, 13 of the baseline records contained a total of 20 Y determinants, whereas 21 of the retest records contained at least one Y variable, for a total of 56 ($p < .01$). A second retest was administered during an interval of 60 to 70 days after discharge. Fourteen m responses appeared in eight of the 25 records, and only 16 Y determinants occurred among 10 of the protocols.

Exner (1978) found that patients in long-term psychotherapy average nearly two m and about one Y at the beginning of treatment. After approximately nine months, those averages are nearly double, with the increases appearing mainly in the protocols of patients judged by their therapists to be encountering significant struggles and experiencing considerable distress. Campo (1977) studied 72 patients, each of whom had at least three m answers in their Rorschachs and concluded that elevations in m do not coincide with the severity of disturbance, but do correlate with severe distress experiences.

The pre-1970s literature concerning the Y variable is more extensive than for m, but also is more contradictory. Some of the contradiction was created by the fact that each of the systematizers used different criteria and symbols for the coding of diffuse shading. Binder (1932) was the first to offer a detailed approach to the coding of achromatic and shading answers. Following his lead, each of the systematizers included a variety of scores to denote different types of achromatic and shading responses, but failed to agree on the criteria for most of them, including diffuse shading, although each considered it to be an important determinant in the test. Although most of the systematizers postulated that diffuse shading answers have some relation to anxiety, they have differed concerning its form and impact. Beck (1945) suggested that diffuse shading responses reveal a painful "absence of action." Later, Beck and Molish (1967) extended this explanation, postulating that diffuse shading signals a sense of paralysis. They speculated that when the answer is form dominated, as in FY, the experience might be regarded more favorably, because it serves as a stimulus to action. Conversely, they argued that the *YF* and *Y* type of responses are indicative of an inability to respond. Rapaport et al. (1946) hypothesized that diffuse shading responses represent a form of anxiety of a magnitude that often supersedes other need states in forcing and/or directing behavior. Klopfer et al. (1954) postulated that diffuse shading answers represent a form of free-floating anxiety. Both positions—that is, Beck's diffuse shading-passivity hypothesis and the Rapaport diffuse shading-anxiety hypothesis—have been studied in many investigations and some support is available for each.

Buhler and LeFever (1947) were among the earliest to test the shading-anxiety postulate in their study of alcoholics. They assumed that alcoholics were more anxious than were nonalcoholics. They report a significantly greater use of diffuse shading among alcoholics. Eichler (1951) and Cox and Sarason (1954) both note significant increases in the use of diffuse shading under an experimentally induced stress situation. Similarly, Levitt and Grosz (1960) obtained significantly more *Y* responses after anxiety had been induced hypnotically. Lebo et al. (1960) treated 12 of 24 high anxiety subjects with CO_2 and found a significant decrease in *Y* answers as compared with the untreated group. Although these studies tend to support the shading-anxiety hypothesis, numerous works contradict the hypothesis. Several studies have found no relationship between scores on the Taylor Manifest Anxiety Scale and diffuse shading answers (Goodstein, 1954; Holtzman et al., 1954; Goodstein & Goldberger, 1955; Levitt, 1957; and Waller, 1960). Schwartz and Kates (1957) used an experimentally induced stress model and found that stressed subjects gave significantly fewer *Y* variant answers than did controls. Berger (1953), Fisher (1958), and Schon and Bard (1958) each used designs in which the Rorschach was administered under "real life" stress situations and found no evidence that the *Y* variants were associated with the stressful situation. Neuringer has suggested that anxiety manifestations are probably better judged by a constellation of variables rather than by one variable such as the *Y*-type answers. A similar position is implied by Goldfried, Stricker, and Weiner (1971) in their review of Elizur's Rorschach scoring for anxiety which focuses mainly on verbalizations in the test. The data concerning shading and anxiety are obviously equivocal, and at best, may be interpreted to indicate that *Y* answers represent *some types of anxiety at times,* but *cannot be routinely taken as a direct index of anxiety.*

Studies concerning the diffuse shading-passivity hypothesis are less numerous than those dealing with the anxiety issue, but the findings are clearly more consistent in favoring the Beck postulate. Klebanoff (1946) found that flyers experiencing "operational fatigue" give significantly greater numbers of *Y* variants. He also noted a tendency of these subjects toward withdrawal and passivity. Elstein (1965) found the *Y* variants significantly related to passivity toward the environment. He noted that "high *Y*" subjects are more inhibited and resigned to their situation, and suggests that they attempt to seal themselves off from the world. Salmon et al. (1972) report the use of a factorial model to study various determinants. Unfortunately, they grouped all responses to gray-black features as "shading," but did find a striking correlation between "shading" and emotion and intellectual control, the composite of which could equal withdrawal behaviors.

Unfortunately, most of these studies failed to differentiate types of anxiety, levels of stress tolerance, or degrees of helplessness. In other words, the issue of control, or the potential for loss of control, may confound the correct interpretation of some findings. For instance, Viglione (1980) used an unsolvable anagram design to produce frustration among a randomly selected half of a group of volunteer college students. He was able to demonstrate a significant elevation in state anxiety among the subjects in his experimental group, but the Rorschachs of those subjects did not differ significantly from those of his nonfrustrated control subjects, and neither group showed elevations for m or Y, or the sum of the achromatic and shading variables. In studies such as these, although well designed and with effective independent variables, subjects remain largely in control even though they may experience some frustration. Under more natural stress conditions, that option is not available. For instance, Ridgeway and Exner (1980) administered the Rorschach and the McClelland Need Achievement Scale to first-year medical students shortly after they began their training. Both tests were readministered either 2 or 3 days before the subjects took their first major examination in anatomy. Significant elevations were found for both m and Y in the retest records.

In another study, Exner, Thomas, Cohen, Ridgeway, and Cooper (1981) tested 54 medical inpatients 1 or 2 days prior to discharge. One group was comprised of 27 males who had been hospitalized 13 to 17 days earlier because of a myocardial infarction. Although recovered from the incident, these men would remain at some risk for at least a 90-day postdischarge interval. The control group consisted of 27 males recovering from orthopedic surgery. Their average length of hospitalization was 19 days. Although most remained in casts, no significant risk factor existed concerning their recovery or future health. Both groups were retested during an interval of 93 to 118 days after discharge. Frequency data concerning the m and Y variables in both tests are presented for each group in Table 31. The cardiac group, continuing at risk at the time of the first test, gave more than twice as many m ($M = 2.15$, $SD = 1.01$) and Y ($M = 2.56$, $SD = 0.84$) responses than did the orthopedic group, yet 8 to 10 weeks later, when the risk factor had declined substantially, the two groups did not differ significantly and both had frequencies for m and Y that are similar to the nonpatient normative data.

Table 31.   Frequency Data for m and Y for Two Tests of Two Groups of Male Medical Patients

Variable	Cardiac Group $N = 27$		Orthopedic Group $N = 27$		
	Test 1	Test 2	Test 1	Test 2	p
m (Total)	58[a]	22	26	21	.01
No. of Protocols	24	19	20	17	ns
Y (Total)	69[a]	25	29	21	.01
No. of Protocols	25	20	19	18	ns

[a] Significantly more than all other groups.

The means and frequencies for both m and Y are generally much higher among situational crisis patients than for any other psychiatric groups. For example, the mean m for 62 first-admission patients diagnosed as Acute Post-traumatic Stress Disorder is 2.74 ($SD = 1.21$) and the mean Y for this group is 2.87 ($SD = 1.29$). Retest data, collected 14 to 19 days after the first test, for 41 of those subjects, all judged to have improved sufficiently to be discharged, show a very significant reduction in the mean values for both variables ($m = 1.14$, $SD = 1.02$; $Y = 1.29$, $SD = 0.93$).

In the L. S. protocol, included in Chapter 10 to illustrate coding and calculations, the D score is -2, indicating a marked overload state. However, the *Adjusted D Score* is zero, indicating that the overload state has a situational relationship. It is reasonable to assume that, under different conditions, the subject has relatively adequate tolerance for stress and sufficient resources available to formulate and implement most required behaviors. However, the current overload creates many more impingements and demands than the subject can contend with easily, thereby markedly limiting his or her capacities for dealing with new stimuli, especially those that are stressful. This increases the likelihood that some of the subject's decisions may not be well formulated, and some behaviors may not be adequately implemented. A reduction of this overload state would be an obvious early objective in any treatment plan. The importance of the two *D* scores may be appreciated more fully by a review of the components included in their calculation—that is, the variables of the *Four Square, EA, EB, es,* and *eb*.

THE EXPERIENCE ACTUAL *(EA)*

Beck (1960) conceptualized the *EA*, working in part from a suggestion of Rorschach, but mainly from data for subjects who had completed psychotherapy. He postulated that by summing the two sides of the *EB*, that is, the human movement answers *(M)*, and the weighted values for the chromatic color responses *(FC, CF, C)*, the result would provide an index of the extent to which resources are organized in a manner that makes them accessible. He noted that subjects completing treatment successfully usually have retest *EB*'s which show the same directionality as in their pretreatment protocols, but the numbers in the ratio tend to be considerably larger *even though the posttreatment records were not significantly longer.* Beck argued that the increases in human movement and chromatic color answers represented the development of more inner life and affective experiences, thereby constituting a broadening of available resources. An obvious assumption underpinning Beck's hypothesis is that both human movement and chromatic color answers are related to use of resources.

Findings by Bash (1955) and Piotrowski and Schreiber (1952) lend support to Beck's concept although neither conceptualized the process. Bash administered Card IX to 28 subjects 200 times in succession, using a 5-second exposure and a 15-second interval. He found that the *M : C* ratio for 18 of these subjects gradually became nearly equal; that is, a numerical decline of one component and an increase in the other component occurred. Although a change in this experimental *EB* was noted, the numerical values comprising the *EB* remained essentially stable. Piotrowski and Shreiber studied 13 patients before and after prolonged psychoanalytic treatment. They report that both sides of the *EB* ratio increased significantly after treatment although the directions of the ratio generally remained constant, a finding comparable with that reported by Beck. One other study (Erginel, 1972) appears to lend some support to the *EA* concept. Erginel used data from an earlier study (Kemalof, 1952) in which six series of inkblots, similar to the Rorschach, had been administered to 12 subjects on six consecutive days. Erginel illustrates that the *M* + Sum *C* does fluctuate on a daily basis and interprets this as a function of mood shifts. Interestingly, the *EB*'s generally appear to maintain a relatively constant direction, and the *EA*'s fluctuate 4.0 or less in 50 (70%) of the 72 observations. Beck (1972) has suggested that the *EA* permits an evaluation of the *EB* which goes beyond response style.

Exner (1974) reported findings that also appear to lend some support to the Beck postulate concerning *EA*. In one study, 30 patients and 30 nonpatients were retested after an 18-month interval. The mean *EA* for the nonpatients was 6.25 at the first test and 6.75

at the second test. The patient group was subdivided into two groups on the basis of independent ratings of improvement provided by both professionals and relatives. The mean *EA*'s for the unimproved group were 3.50 at pretreatment and 4.25 at the second test, whereas for the group rated as significantly improved the mean *EA* at pretreatment was 3.75 versus a mean of 7.25 in the second test ($p < .02$). In a second study, two groups of 12 patients each were tested prior to, and at the termination of treatment. One group had been in long-term psychotherapy, averaging 131 sessions during an average interval of 20.2 months. The second group was treated using supportive and directive methods, averaging 47.4 sessions, extending over an average period of 10.3 months. Both groups received medication as deemed appropriate, but the medication was not considered as a primary treatment method. The pretreatment mean *EA*'s were very similar for both groups, 4.51 for the long-term group and 4.76 for the supportive group. The posttreatment mean *EA*'s were quite different, 5.51 for the supportive group versus 8.26 for the long-term group ($p < .05$).

The *EA* retest reliability is very substantial among nonpatient adults, regardless of whether the retest is administered after a brief interval or a much longer period. The data in Table 4 (Chapter 2) include *EA* retest correlations of .83 after 1 year and .85 after 3 years. Conversely, the *EA* retest correlation for a group of 30 patients retested after only six months of intensive psychotherapy is .70, and for the same group retested after 18 months is .58 (Exner, 1978). Similarly, the *EA* retest correlations for children, although ranging from .80 upward when retested after brief intervals, are very modest and often not significant when the retest is administered after a period of nine months or longer, ranging from .19 to .45 (Exner & Weiner, 1982; Exner, Thomas & Mason, 1985). The data in Table J (Chapter 12) show that the mean values for *EA* among nonpatient children increase each year from ages five through 13, but rarely more than by 0.5 in any one year. These data suggest a relationship between *EA* and some of the elements of development, however, if there is an interpretive usefulness to the absolute value of *EA* it has remained elusive. Exner, Viglione, and Gillespie (1984) have reported a consistently positive significant correlation between *EA* and *Zf*. *Zf* has a modest positive significant correlation with intelligence and also with the need for achievement; thus either of these elements may be integral to *EA*. However, *EA* is not significantly correlated with intelligence when the range of IQ's used falls on a normal distribution from 80 to 120 ($r = .12$). On the other hand, if the IQ range is restricted from 110 to 140, the correlation is positive and significant ($r = .38$). Possibly the most conservative explanation for this finding is that more intelligent people are able to identify and organize resources in ways that make them more easily accessible.

The most crucial assumption relevant to an understanding of *EA* and its relation to the two *D* scores is that the two variables involved in its calculation, *M* and the weighted *Sum C*, are manifestations of the use of resource, or stated differently, are related to *deliberately* initiated psychological behaviors. The data supporting this assumption are mainly of an inferential variety, but substantial in quantity. Some have evolved from studies focusing specifically on *M* or the Chromatic Color responses, but much has generated from studies concerning the *EB*.

THE ERLEBNISTYPUS (*EB*)

Rorschach (1921) considered the *EB* as one of the most important characteristics of the test. He proposed that it reflects the underlying preferential response style of the individual. The *EB* represents the ratio of the Sum of the *M* answers to the Sum of the *weighted* chromatic color responses, using weights of 0.5 for *FC,* 1.0 for *CF,* and 1.5 for Pure *C* and *Cn.* The reason for this particular scheme of weights is not completely clear; however, it appears as though Rorschach noted that chromatic color answers occur with a greater frequency than *M* responses and believed the weights should represent some equalization of those average frequencies, and at the same time include appropriate emphasis for the color answers that minimize or exclude the use of form.

Rorschach hypothesized that when the ratio is distinctly weighed in the *M* direction, the person is more prone to use his or her inner life for basic gratifications. He termed this introversiveness but was careful to note that it is not the same as the Jungian concept of introversion. Whereas the Jungian introvert is generally conceptualized as being distanciated from people and frequently perceived as isolated or withdrawn into himself, Rorschach's notion of introversiveness focuses on the manner in which the resources of the person are used, *but* does not necessarily imply direct overt behavioral correlates. Thus the introversive person may be regarded by others as outgoing in his social relationships, but internally, he is prone to use his inner life for the satisfaction of his important needs. At the opposite pole is the extratensive person, whose *EB* is markedly weighed on the color side of the ratio. The extratensive is prone to use the interactions between himself and his world for gratification of his more basic needs. It is the *depth* of affective exchange that often marks the extratensive person; that is, he manifests affect to *his world* more routinely than does the introversive. Rorschach also defined the ambient, that is, one whose *EB* contains equal, or nearly equal values on each side of the ratio. He postulated (erroneously, as it turns out) that the ambient may be the most flexible of the three types or styles with regard to the use of resources for obtaining gratification.

Rorschach perceived the *EB* as illustrating a constitutionally predisposed response tendency, emphasizing that the introversive and extratensive features are not opposites, but simply psychological styles or preferences. He believed that the style is a relatively stable psychological feature of the individual, but also noted that various conditions could alter the response preference, either temporarily or permanently. For instance, unusual or prolonged stress conditions might elicit a transient alteration in the style, whereas some treatment effects might create a more permanent change. He also postulated that when the *EB* displays very low frequencies, such as 0:1 or 1:0, a coarctation has occurred in the development or functioning of the style, or in instances of psychopathology, may reflect a rigid defensive effort in which an almost complete paralysis of affect forms the basis of the effort. The literature concerning the *EB* is varied and sometimes confusing because of a tendency by some to equate the notions of the introversive or extratensive styles with the behavioral expectations implied in the Jungian model of introversion-extraversion, even though Rorschach specifically disclaimed any such relationship (Bash, 1955; Klopfer, 1954; Mindness, 1955). Most investigations have focused on the two basic styles, introversive and extratensive.

Goldfarb (1945, 1949) found that children raised from very early life under impersonal institution conditions show marked extratensive features. Rabinovitch, Kennard, and Fister (1955) report significant EEG differences between extreme *EB* styles and suggest that introversive subjects show greater indices of "cortical harmony." Singer and Spohn (1954) and Singer and Herman (1954) report evidence for a relation between styles and the frequency of motor activity during a waiting period. Singer (1960), in a literature review concerning *EB,* suggests that support clearly exists for the postulate that two dimensions of constitutional temperament are represented in the ratio, one representing a capacity for internal experience and the second reflecting activity or motility. Molish

(1967) suggests, in his literature review, that the elements illustrated in the *EB* have critical directing effect on most all nuances of personality and their related correlates of behavior. Both Singer and Molish cite studies demonstrating that introversives respond differently than extratensives in a variety of behavioral situations, such as problem solving, stress situations, and environmental responsiveness.

The directionality of the *EB* appears to be remarkably stable for the adult. Exner, Armbruster, and Viglione (1978) found that 77 of the 100 nonpatient adult subjects participating in their three-year retest study were either introversive or extratensive in both tests. They used a two point or greater difference between *M* and *Sum C* as the criterion for differentiation. In the retest, only two of those 77 subjects had changed directionality. Similarly, 39 of the 50 nonpatient adults participating in the one-year retest shown in Table 4 (Chapter 2) had *EB*'s in the first test in which one side of the ratio was 2 or more points greater than the other side. After one year, 38 of the 39 continued to show a difference of at least 2 points in the ratio and none changed directionality.

The directionality of the *EB* is far less stable in children over long intervals. As will be noted from examination of the data in Table K, the majority of children ages 5 through 7 show an extratensive style, whereas 10% or less show an introversive style. Also, the percentage of children who fall into the ambient range is significantly larger through age 14 than for the nonpatient adult group. Exner and Weiner (1982) found that only 12 of 26 8-year-olds showing an extratensive style continued to be extratensive at age 14, whereas seven of nine eight-year-olds who showed an introversive style continued to manifest that style at age 14. Exner, Thomas, and Mason (1985) found a considerable variability in the *EB* style for 57 subjects who were tested five times at intervals of 2 years, beginning at age eight. The composite of normative, reliability, and longitudinal data suggest that *if* the preferential features of introversiveness or extratensiveness become enduring characteristics of the personality, the stabilization will probably occur prior to early adulthood, and for most people during early to mid-adolescence.

The normative data indicate that slightly more than three-fourths of nonpatient adults are either introversive or extratensive and that the proportions of each are about the same. This distribution is quite different than found among patient groups. For instance, the schizophrenic reference group includes 45% who are introversive, 13% who are extratensive, and about 42% who are ambient. The reference group of depressives reveals that about 30% are introversive, 18% extratensive, and 52% are ambient, and among the reference group of character problems about 25% are introversive, 20% extratensive, and 56% are ambients. These data are consistent with those previously reported for nonpatient and psychiatric groups (Exner, 1974; Exner, 1978) and support the postulate that, contrary to Rorschach's notion, the ambient is *not* the more flexible or adaptive of the three styles. On the contrary, the ambient appears to be much more vulnerable to intra- or interpersonal problems. Findings from several other studies also support this position. For instance, when the retest reliabilities of the 100 nonpatients retested after three years (Exner, Armbruster, & Viglione, 1978) were reviewed by *EB* style, the 20 ambients in the group show consistently lower retest correlations for most variables than do either of the other groups (Exner, 1978). This finding suggests less consistency in coping behaviors.

In a problem-solving study involving 15 introversives, 15 extratensives, and 15 ambients (Exner, 1978), the introversives were found to perform the fewest operations before reaching the solutions. The extratensives performed more operations but were able to achieve solutions to the problems in about the same amount of time as the introversives.

The ambitents performed more operations than the extratensives, required significantly more time to achieve solutions than either the extratensives or introversives, and repeated more operations and made significantly more errors in the operations. These data indicate that it is impossible to distinguish whether the introversive or extratensive styles might be the more preferable or efficient, but it is clear that the ambitents are the least efficient and least consistent in their behavior patterns. These findings are consistent with those reported by Rosenthal (1954). He also concluded that although the introversive and extratensive styles of problem solving are clearly different, both are equally proficient in terms of achieving solutions.

Exner and Murillo (1975) studied 148 inpatients for a period of 1 year after their discharge from hospitalization. The Rorschach was administered at discharge and the patients subdivided into cells on the basis of the *EB* and for whether *EA* was greater than *es*. Forty-one of the patients were rehospitalized within the first 12 months, of whom 49% were ambitents, and nearly 70% had values for *es* that were higher than *EA*. Exner (1978) also followed 279 outpatients from the beginning of their treatment through a period of 28 months to evaluate changes as a function of different types of intervention. Seven modes of intervention were involved, ranging from dynamic psychotherapy to biofeedback. Evaluations concerning progress were collected at 90-day intervals from the patients, therapists, and significant others, and each patient was retested each nine months, regardless of whether he or she had terminated treatment. The lowest mean ratings concerning progress or improvement occurred for the ambitent subjects at *each* 90-day interval during the first 12 months, *irrespective of type of treatment*. Subsequent data indicate that significantly more patients continued in or reentered treatment if they had *EB*'s showing an ambitent status at termination, or at the 18-month retest.

These data strongly suggest that the ambitent is much more vulnerable to difficulty in coping situations than either the introversive or extratensive. Their failure to develop a consistent preference or style in their coping behaviors seems to lead to less efficiency and more vacillation. Because they usually require more time to complete tasks, it is logical to assume that they invest more energy in the process. In contrast, the preferential consistency that marks the introversive and extratensive styles leads to greater efficiency because the psychological routines involved are more stabilized. Consequently, people with either of those styles are apparently less vulnerable to difficulty during coping behaviors.

As noted earlier, the two styles are quite different from each other. Introversive subjects prefer to delay final decisions until they can mentally review alternatives and potential results. They rely heavily on their own ideation for decisions and direction, and apparently, as suggested by Rorschach, are able to derive gratification from their inner life more easily than do others. Although there is no evidence to suggest that the introversive person dislikes or avoids emotions, there are data to indicate that the introversive attempts to exert greater control of feelings during ideational operations. Blatt and Feirstein (1977) found that introversive subjects show greater cardiac variability during problem solving. Exner, Thomas, and Martin (1980) used a six-channel physiograph to record cardiac and respiratory rates and GSR, taken at the scalp, of two groups of 15 subjects each during a problem-solving task similar to that used in the Blatt and Feirstein study. Fifteen of the subjects were clearly introversive ($M > Sum\ C$ by 4 or more points) and 15 were clearly extratensive ($Sum\ C > M$ by 4 or more points). All had *D scores* of 0 or $+1$. A baseline recording was taken during a 5-minute resting period following the attachment of electrodes. The subject was given instruction concerning the problems and permitted to work for up to 10 minutes on a trial problem for purposes of adaptation. The target recordings were then taken for the next 30 minutes, during which the subject worked on two problems of increasing difficulty. The findings for the cardiac activity are similar to those of Blatt and Feirstein; that is, subjects in the introversive group showed more variability, *with a general tendency for the rate to reduce.* During a three-minute rest period between problems there was significantly less variability, and the rate tended to increase.

A similar pattern toward decrease was found for the respiratory rate of the introversives, which reversed during the 3-minute rest interval, and the GSR values also tended to become lower throughout the entire 30-minute session. The extratensive group showed significantly less cardiac and respiratory variability during the activity phase, with *both tending to increase* shortly after beginning the task and remaining at a significantly higher level than baseline. During the 3-minute rest interval the cardiac rate showed more variability than for the introversive group and tended to become lower, as did the respiratory rate. The GSR values for the extratensives tended to increase gradually during the first 10 minutes of the task, and remained significantly higher than the baseline throughout the 30-minute interval.

Chu and Exner (1981) studied 20 introversive and 20 extratensive subjects, all with *D scores of 0,* for speed and accuracy in adding columns of four-digit numbers under two conditions. All of the subjects were juniors or seniors in college, majoring in Business Administration, and the groups were comparable for cumulative grade point average. In one condition subjects worked in a quiet room, whereas in the second they worked in a room with interference conditions created by random noises and flashing strobe lights. The groups did not differ for the number of columns completed or for number of calculation errors under the quiet condition; however, the introversive group completed significantly more columns and made significantly fewer calculational errors than the extratensive group under the interference condition. Some added understanding of the introversive style can be gleaned by a review of some of the research published concerning *M*.

THE HUMAN MOVEMENT RESPONSE (*M*)

It is important to caution that, although *M* has probably been the subject of more investigations than any other Rorschach determinant, many investigations have neglected some or all of the problems inherent in efforts to study a very complex variable in isolation. Although there does appear to be a common psychological element for all *M* responses, there are also many variations on that element which create some risk in generalizing from studies in which all *M*'s are ordered into a single category. The common element lies in the fact that *all movement responses, human and nonhuman, involve some form of projection.* The blots do not move. Thus the formation of a movement answer must include features that are mentally created by the subject and attributed to the stimulus field. This is why the specific content of the *M* answer takes on a special importance in the qualitative interpretation of a protocol. This factor creates a problem for the study in which all *M*'s are combined into a single category, disregarding whether they involve real or unreal figures, single or multiple figures, are aggressive or cooperative, active or passive, or are given to a tiny *Dd* area rather than to a *W* or *D*.

For instance, Piotrowski (1957) and Exner (1974) have demonstrated that differences in the characteristics of *M* do relate to differences in behavioral and interpersonal effectiveness. Subjects who give more cooperative *M*'s are generally oriented toward more socially effective behaviors. Subjects who give significantly large numbers of passive *M* are more prone to avoid decision responsibility and prefer to be more dependent on others for direction. Exner (1983) found that subjects with high frequencies of aggressive *M* answers show higher frequencies of verbal and nonverbal aggressive behaviors, and are also prone to view interpersonal relationships as being commonly marked by aggressiveness. Witkin et al. (1962) found a high positive correlation between assertive *M*'s and Field Independence. Wagner and Hoover (1971, 1972) report that drama students, drum majorettes, and cheerleaders tend to give more "exhibitionistic" *M* responses. Findings such as these indicate the need for caution in generalizing results of studies in which all *M* responses are treated in the same way. Nonetheless, the quantity of research concerning *M* does tend to blend together to help us gain some understanding of the process related to the formation of these types of answers.

Several studies suggest a positive relationship between *M* and intellectual operations. Most have involved the use of I.Q. or some other direct measure of intelligence and the frequency and/or quality of *M* responses (Paulsen, 1941; Abrams, 1955; Altus, 1958; Sommer & Sommer, 1958; Tanaka, 1958; Ogdon & Allee, 1959). Schulman (1953) reports that *M* is positively correlated with abstract thinking and has demonstrated that the activity in both functions requires some delaying operations. Levine, Glass, and Meltzoff (1957) have also demonstrated that *M* and the higher levels of intellectual operation require delaying activity. Conversely, Mason and Exner (1984) failed to find significant correlations between *M* and any of the WAIS subtests for a group of 179 nonpatient adults. However, Exner, Viglione, and Gillespie (1984) did find a significant positive correlation between *M* and *Zf*. Kallstedt (1952) noted significantly fewer *M* in the protocols of adolescents than in those of adults. Ames et al. (1971) and Exner and Weiner (1982) found the mean for *M* to be significantly lower in young children as contrasted with older children or adults. A gradual increase occurs in the mean for *M* at each year from age 5 through age 13. Ames (1960) has reported that the frequency of *M* responses tends to decline in the elderly.

The *M* has frequently been identified as an index of creativity; however, the empirical findings on this issue are somewhat equivocal. The different criteria that have been used for creativity appear to have clouded the problem considerably (Dana, 1968). Hersh (1962) has found a significant relationship between *M* and artistic talent. Richter and Winter (1966) report a positive relation between "intuition and perception" scores and *M*. Dudek (1968) has found that subjects giving a large number of *M*'s show greater ease in expressing themselves "creatively" in TAT stories and Lowenfield Mosaic Designs. By most other criteria, however, *M* and creativity appear unrelated.

The results of work concerning *M* and fantasy have been much more definitive. Page (1957) reports a direct relationship between *M* and daydreaming. Loveland and Singer (1959), Palmer (1963), and Lerner (1966) have noted that increased *M* is related to sleep and/or dream deprivation. Orlinsky (1966) has also shown a significant relation between *M* and dream recall and total dream time. Dana (1968) has also demonstrated a positive relation between *M* and fantasy. He suggests that *M* answers can represent any/or all of six different psychologic actions, including fantasy, time sense, intellect, creativeness, delay, and some aspects of interpersonal relations. Cocking, Dana, and Dana (1969) report findings that appear to confirm the relationship between *M* and fantasy, time estimation, and intellect.

The relationship between *M* and motor inhibition has been the subject of numerous investigations, essentially because Rorschach postulated the occurrence of kinesthetic activity when *M* answers are formed. Singer, Meltzoff, and Goldman (1952) found that *M* increased after subjects were instructed to "freeze" in awkward positions. Similarly, an increased *M* has been noted after an enforced period of delay (Singer & Herman, 1954; Singer & Spohn, 1954). Bendick and Klopfer (1964) report a significant increase in both *M* and *FM* answers under conditions of motor inhibition, and significant increases in *M*, *FM*, and *m* under conditions of experimentally induced sensory deprivation. In an earlier work, Klein and Schlesinger (1951) presented data to suggest that a relationship may exist between motor inhibition and a variety of Rorschach responses, including movement answers. In a similar context, Steele and Kahn (1969) failed to find significant increases in muscle potential with the production of movement answers. They did note, however, a tendency of subjects who produced many *M*'s to show increases in muscle potential. Possibly of greater interest is the fact that increases in muscle potential were noted accompanying almost all aggressive content answers, regardless of whether movement was involved. Motor expression has also been noted as precipitating an increase in the frequency of movement answers by Cooper and Caston (1970). They used two sets of Holtzman Ink Blots given before and after a 5-minute period of physical exercise. In general, the issue of kinesthetic activity in movement answers is, at best, only an indirect approach to the study of the psychological activity associated with their formulation, and the contribution of these works to interpretation of *M* answers is still an open issue. Possibly, studies concerning the relationship between *M* and the delay of behavior have a more direct relevance to the interpretation of this kind of response.

Frankle (1953) and Mirin (1955) have both demonstrated that subjects who produce greater numbers of *M* tend to longer motor delays in their social adjustments. Beri and Blacker (1956) have found that mean reaction times to the blots are significantly longer for subjects giving more *M* than Color responses. Levine and Spivack (1962) report a significant correlation between the productivity of *M* and an independent index of repression. Earlier, Hertzman, Orlansky, and Seitz (1944) noted that high *M* producers showed a greater tolerance for anorexia due to simulated high altitude conditions (18,500 feet) than did subjects giving low frequencies of *M*.

Some of the important data concerning the interpretation of *M* are derived from studies of various psychopathological groups. Guirdham (1936) noted that depressives tend to give lower frequencies of *M*. Schmidt and Fonda (1954) report a high occurrence of *M* among manic patients. Gibby et al. (1955) found that hallucinatory patients give significantly more *M* than do delusional nonhallucinatory patients. Thomas (1955) offers similar findings. King (1960) has shown that paranoid schizophrenics who have interpersonal delusions produce significantly more *M* than do paranoid schizophrenics with somatic delusions.

Rorschach suggested that when the form quality of *M* is poor, the likelihood of psychopathology appears to be greater. That postulate has been supported by many findings (Beck, 1945, 1965; Rapaport, Gill, & Schafer, 1946; Phillips & Smith, 1953; Molish, 1965; Weiner, 1966; Exner, 1974, 1978). Weiner (1966) has suggested that the *M*-response is probably related to deficient social skills and poor interpersonal relationships. Exner (1978) and Exner and Weiner (1982) have included the *M*-answer as one of the critical criteria for the differentiation of schizophrenia. Brain-injured subjects tend to give fewer *M*'s in their records (Piotrowski 1937, 1940; Evans & Marmorston, 1964). The presence of good quality *M*'s has been regarded as a positive prognostic indicator, especially for the seriously disturbed subject. This factor is weighed heavily in both the Rorschach Prognostic Rating Scale (Klopfer, Kirkner, Wisham, & Baker, 1951) and the Piotrowski Prognostic Index (Piotrowski & Briklin, 1958, 1961). Rees and Jones (1951) and Lipton, Tamerin, and Lotesta (1951) report that good quality *M*'s significantly differentiate schizophrenics who respond favorably to somatic treatments. Piotrowski (1939), Halpern (1940), and Stotsky (1952) have all reported significant increases in the frequency of *M* among patients who show improvement versus those who do not. Exner (1974) compared the admission and discharge records of 71 schizophrenics followed in a relapse study and did not find a significant increase in *M* in the second test; however, 19 of the 71 patients who relapsed during the first year after discharge did have significantly fewer *M*'s in both of their tests as compared with the records of the 52 nonrelapsers.

Any attempt to summarize the full psychological meaning of *M* responses will probably fall short of describing the extremely complex activities to which they relate. Clearly, *M* involves the elements of reasoning, imagination, and a higher form of conceptualization. It is also contingent on a form of delay from yielding to more spontaneous translations of, or responses to a stimulus field, during which time an active and deliberate form of ideation occurs. This deliberate directing of one's inner life breeds images and/or fantasies that become the basis of decision making concerning the selection of responses for a given constellation of stimuli. Response tendencies may be thwarted and/or displaced into continuing ideational activity, or they may be externalized, either directly or indirectly, into behaviors. *M*-related activity does not appear to be a conscious process, although some of the reasoning involved probably does include a conscious focusing of attention. In effect, the presence of *M* indicates the use of a delaying tactic through which the stimulus field, and potential responses to it, are sorted more extensively than might otherwise be the case.

Obviously, the presence of *M* and/or the frequency of *M* cannot be interpreted accurately without giving consideration to several other test variables. Almost all subjects have some *M* in their records. The adult nonpatient normative data reveal that 597 of the 600 subjects in the sample have at least one *M*. Similarly, the normative data for 9-year-olds indicate that 146 of the 150 subjects in that sample give at least one *M* answer. However, the introversive subject with a record containing five *M* responses will be prone to use the delaying tactic much more frequently in decision operations than will the extratensive subject who also has five *M*'s in his or her record. This is why the data of the *EB* have such an interpretive importance.

As noted earlier, those with extratensive styles approach problem solving quite differently than do introversives. They make many more operations even though their times to decisions or solutions are not significantly different from introversives. They appear to be trial-and-error oriented, willing to make errors as a trade-off for the information they receive. Logically, it appears that they rely more on external feedback than do introversives in decision operations; however, the data supporting that assumption are sparse and indirect, and some data suggest that the postulate is incomplete, oversimplified, or erroneous. For instance, even though the extratensives use more operations in problem-solving activities, a variety of studies have failed to establish a relationship between *EB* style and various measures of Field Dependence and Field Independence. Similarly, frequency data concerning internal versus external Locus of Control are about the same for nonpatient introversives and extratensives. An extension of the hypothesis concerning the use of external stimuli by extratensives (which does have some support) is that they are more prone to invest affect into their decision operations and, as a consequence, are more likely to use interaction with the world as a source of information and/or gratification. In other words, they are more oriented to seek and/or respond to external stimuli when formulating coping responses.

To illustrate, Exner and Thomas (1982) videotaped structured 7-minute interviews of

15 extratensive and 15 introversive nonpatient college students who were volunteers participating in another study. The interviews were all conducted by the same person and followed a questionnaire format concerning attitudes about academic requirements. The tapes, replayed without sound, were rated for postural-gestural behaviors, such as leaning forward, chair turning, arm movements, hand gestures, and such, by three raters who had no familiarity with the nature of the study. The mean rating for the extratensive subjects was 15.64 (SD = 4.61) versus a mean of 8.22 (SD = 4.07) for the introversive group (p < .02).

As noted earlier, introversive or extratensive styles that are indicated in the records of children under 13 are unlikely to persist over lengthy time periods; however, substantial proportions of the nonpatient subjects in each age group between 5 and 10 show an extratensive style, whereas very few manifest an introversive style. In fact, the proportion of introversive subjects at each age level, from 5 through 16, is consistently less than the proportion of extratensives. Interestingly, the adult nonpatient sample includes slightly more introversive than extratensive subjects. Most psychiatric groups include a substantial proportion of ambients, but the remaining subjects do not tend to divide evenly between the introversive and extratensive styles. For example, the reference samples for schizophrenics and depressives include relatively small proportions of extratensives. Conversely, a review of data for 100 outpatients who have hysteroid features reveals that 54 have an extratensive style, whereas only 11 have an introversive style. Some added understanding of the extratensive style can be derived by reviewing some of the research concerning chromatic color answers.

CHROMATIC COLOR RESPONSES *(FC, CF, C)*

Rorschach (1921) proposed that responses involving the chromatic colors of the blots relate to affect. He argued that they provide some index of emotional excitability, and the extent to which the use of color is merged with form can be viewed as representing "degrees of stabilization" of affective urges. In this context, *FC* answers supposedly illustrate more modulation or control of affective displays, whereas *CF* and *C* responses are related to instances of discharge in which the emotion is considerably more pronounced and dominating. Rorschach speculated that the *CF* responses are related to actions in which far less cognitive adaptation occurs, as in circumstances when emotions such as irritation, suggestiveness, sensitivity, or empathy dominate the formation and direction of behaviors. He postulated that the pure *C* responses relate to actions marked by little or no adaptation, as in instances of impulsiveness or lability. He pointed out that the ratio of *FC* to *CF* + *C* responses might be an index of the extent to which control is present in the affective state of the individual.

Although data do support some of Rorschach's postulates, he may have been overly simplistic in suggesting the fine discriminations between the three variables, and especially concerning the differentiation between *CF* and *C,* because both have considerably less temporal stability than does the combination of the two. For example, the long-term retest studies in Chapter 2 reveal retest correlations for the combination of *CF* + *C* of about .80, whereas the correlations for either variable, taken separately, range from .51 to .66. Similarly, the short-term retest studies presented in Chapter 2 show correlations for the composite of *CF* + *C* ranging from .83 to .92, whereas the correlations for the variables taken separately range from .59 to .76. This does not mean that a *C* response should be regarded as equivalent to *CF*. *C* does seem related to a more intense, less well-controlled form of affective discharge; however, *it is erroneous to assume that the more limited control is a trait-like feature, such as an impulsive style.* The elements of control and/or proneness to impulsiveness are much more directly related to the *D* scores. The types of chromatic color responses do reflect the aspects of modulation, or lack thereof, of emotional displays, but they *do not necessarily* relate directly to elements of control. In this framework, the *FC:CF + C* ratio does have interpretive value, as does the *Weighted Sum C* entered in the *EB,* and both can provide important information concerning affective adaptability.

Chromatic color responses appear to vary considerably in terms of how much or how little cognitive effort and complexity is involved. Schachtel (1943) was among the first to argue that the perception of color involves minimal activity and defined color responses as reflecting a passive process. Rickers-Ovsiankina (1943) reviewed a significant number of research works concerning perception, and also concluded that color perception is a more immediate process than form perception, requiring less cognitive activity in the mediation of the stimulus input. Rapaport (1946) suggested that the *CF* and *C* answers represent a short-circuiting of delay functions. Shapiro (1956, 1960) reviewed a broad variety of clinical and experimental literature to define a ''mode of perception'' associated with the color experience. He argued that some color responses do involve more perceptual passivity, in which the cognitive functions necessary for affective delay are relaxed, and that the impact of the discharge on behavior will be proportional to the degree of relaxation that has occurred. Piotrowski (1957) has hypothesized that *FC* responses involve much more cognitive complexity, because they require delay in merging contour and color in precise ways. He has agreed that the *CF* and *C* responses represent situations in which the cognitive elements are overly relaxed, or even possibly overwhelmed by affective states.

The theory linking chromatic color responses to affective activity has often been a point of controversy. Unfortunately, much of that controversy has not focused on correlates of color responses, but rather on the concept of ''color-shock,'' which was introduced by Rorschach and defined as a startle reaction to the chromatically colored figures. Extensive listings of indices of color-shock were developed between 1932 and 1950, including such elements as long reaction times, disruption of sequence, failure to give Popular answers, lower *R,* and so on. Much Rorschach literature of the 1940s and 1950s was marked by attempts to validate the various listings, but none was successful by contemporary research standards. Keehn (1954) reviewed many of those studies and concluded that few, if any, of the signs were actually precipitated by the color features of the blots. Crumpton (1956) noted that color-shock signs will occur as often to achromatic versions of the chromatic blots.

It is unfortunate that much research effort was devoted to studies on color-shock and then the negative findings were translated as being directly applicable to the color-affect theory. The studies that have approached the issue more directly have generally been supportive of the concept. Klatskin (1952) found that subjects giving responses in which both color and texture are present are more susceptible to stress. Wallen (1948) found that the ''affective quality'' of the chromatic colors has a facilitating effect on responses.

Grayson (1956) has reported that the composite of color and form rather than color alone influences productivity. Crumpton (1956) has found that color cards tend to elicit more undesirable affect and more aggressive and passive contents than do achromatic cards. Forsyth (1959) reports that the color cards facilitate an anxiety score. Exner (1959) has found that both *R* and content scores are altered significantly when Card I is presented in a variety of chromatic colors as contrasted with the standard gray-black version. One of the most frequently cited studies, generally used to support arguments against the color-affect hypothesis, is that of Baughman (1959). He used eight groups of subjects, administering one the standard Rorschach series, a second an achromatic series, a third the standard Rorschach series with a modified inquiry, and the remaining five groups each one set of modified Rorschach cards. Although the Baughman analysis of data was quite thorough, he neglected a specific comparison of the standard and achromatic Rorschach groups for R to the chromatically colored cards (II, III, VIII, IX, and X). A review of his data suggests that the group responding to the standard series gave nearly 200 more answers than did those responding to the achromatic series, the majority of which were to Cards II, III, VIII, IX, and X.

Another controversial approach to the color-affect hypothesis is shown in studies concerning the proportional number of answers to Cards VIII, IX, and X of the test. Both Klopfer and Kelley (1942) and Beck et al. (1961) have postulated that the number of responses to the last three cards, as contrasted with the R to the remaining cards, gives some index of the "affective" responsiveness to one's world. Even though they have disagreed on the method for calculating this proportion (Klopfer using 8-9-10%, and Beck using the Affective Ratio), they have agreed on this basic principle. When the proportion of R to Cards VIII, IX, and X is high, the subject is regarded as affectively responsive, and conversely, when the proportion is low, the subject is viewed as affectively guarded and/or withdrawn from affective stimulation. Several studies have investigated this postulate but have generally reported negative findings (Sapenfield & Buker, 1949; Dubrovner et al., 1950; Allen et al., 1951; Perlman, 1951; and Meyer, 1951). Unfortunately, most of these works are marked by flaws in experimental design, such as using either a group administration technique, or a test-retest method. Exner (1962) used a matched groups design, administering one group the standard Rorschach series and the second group an achromatic version. The results clearly demonstrate that the colored cards of the standard series stimulate a greater productivity to each of the three cards. Reaction times were also generally longer to the standard chromatic series than to the achromatic versions. Although these data lend no direct support to either the color-affect, or 8-9-10% hypotheses, they do indicate that color, as a stimulus, has a substantial impact on the formulation of answers.

The developmental Rorschach literature also lends some support to the color-affect hypothesis. Many investigators have reported that the C response is predominant in the very young child (Halpern, 1940; Klopfer & Margolies, 1941; Ford, 1946; Rabin & Beck, 1950; Ames et al., 1952, 1971). Ames also found that CF responses become more dominant after year two, and remain so through year 16, although a gradual increase in FC answers is noted at each year level. Her findings are generally consistent with the normative data for children included in Chapter 12, although the Chapter 12 data indicate that FC answers have slightly higher means than the means for CF beginning at age 15.

Brennen and Richard (1943) reported that subjects with high *Weighted Sum C* (WSumC) are more easily hypnotized than those with low WSumC. Similarly, Steisel (1952) and Linton (1954) have noted that subjects with high WSumC are more likely to alter their judgments in accord with the suggestions of a confederate examiner. Mann (1956) found a significant relationship between the number of words related to the environment and the WSumC. Exner and Armbruster (1979) found a significant correlation (rho = .48) between the WSumC and the total score on the Zuckerman (1971) Sensation Seeking Scale among 30 assembly line workers at a manufacturing plant. Weigel and

Exner (1981) had 54 nonpatient office workers give preferential ratings for a series of 60 slides using a 5-point scale, with the highest value assigned for the most preferred. The group included 21 extratensives, 14 ambitents, and 19 introversives. Thirty of the slides were nature scenes or photos of buildings, and 30 involved interactions among people, or between a person and an animal, such as a boy playing with a dog. When the subjects were divided into two groups of 27 each, based on a median split of the distribution of WSumC scores, *no* significant difference occurred between the groups; when the 14 ambitents were discarded from the distribution, however, the remaining 20 subjects in the upper half showed significantly higher mean preference values for *both sets of slides* than did the 20 subjects in the lower half of the distribution. As might be expected, 14 of the 20 subjects in the upper half of the WSumC distribution are extratensive.

The interpretive value of data concerning the frequencies and types of chromatic color responses is derived mainly from the *FC:CF + C* ratio; *however,* those data only can be integrated accurately into the interpretation when studied in relation to the *D* scores, and all of the data of the Four Square. Thus further elaboration concerning the *FC:CF + C* ratio must be deferred until the next chapter.

THE EXPERIENCE BASE *(eb)*

The *eb* is a derivation of a ratio suggested by Klopfer (1954). He offered the faulty postulate that it was useful in identifying response tendencies "that are not fully accepted by, or available to the subject" at a given time. He postulated that *FM* and *m* answers relate to introversive features and that achromatic and shading answers relate to extratensive tendencies, a premise held by many Rorschachers involved in the early development of the test. The flaw in that postulate was created by the logical assumption that the process related to *M* is also related to the variables *FM* and *m,* and that the process related to chromatic color responses is also related to the achromatic color and shading variables. The variety of validity studies concerning these variables, plus intercorrelational studies, offer no support for that assumption. For instance, intercorrelations between *M* and *FM* range from .11 to .19, and between .10 and .20 for *M* and *FM + m*. Similarly, the intercorrelations between Sum of Achromatic and Shading (*SH*) and WSumC range from .22 to .24, between *SH* and *FC* range from − .14 to − .19, and between *SH* and *CF + C* from .23 to .37 (Exner, 1983; Exner, Viglione, & Gillespie, 1984). Only the latter, .37, is statistically significant. It was found in only one sample of nonpatient adults and has not replicated in other samples.

As noted in Chapter 10, the *eb* is entered as the Sum of *FM + m* on the left side, and the Sum of all achromatic color and shading variables (*SH*) on the right. The distinction of the two groupings of variables is important because, although there are no demonstrable process relationships between the variables in the *eb* and those in the *EB,* they do share some common features. As with *M,* the *FM* and *m* answers involve some form of projection, because the movement features do not exist in the stimulus field, but more important, all three also appear to relate to forms of ideation. Whereas the *M* answers concern deliberately formulated and directed ideation, the *FM* and *m* answers apparently relate to mental activity that is provoked, but not necessarily directed, by demand stimuli. Similarly, chromatic color and the *SH* responses all relate to affect. Whereas the chromatic color answers relate to the deliberate discharge of affect, the *SH* variables relate to the experience of affect that is created by demand stimuli. Thus the *eb* is organized to provide information about the experiences of stimulus demand.

The *FM* and *m* Variables   As mentioned earlier, both of these variables seem related to the presence of mental activity that is provoked by demand states. In that context, they are similar, yet they are also very different. The research concerning *m* has already been described. It is an unstable, state-related variable that appears to be induced by situational stress. The mental activity to which it relates seems to involve a sense of helplessness and/or loss of control. It is reasonable to hypothesize that when this activity is present, the subject will experience some difficulties in attention and concentration, and that efforts at reasoning can be interrupted or diverted easily.

The *FM* variable appears to relate to a different process, possibly one that has more altering and fewer disruptive features. *FM* is reasonably stable over time. The retest data for *FM* in Chapter 2 are quite intriguing in that they show correlations ranging from the lower to upper .70's, *regardless* of whether the retest is done after a brief 3-week period or a lengthy 3-year interval. Most other Rorschach variables that have retest correlations in the .70's for long intervals will have retest correlations in the .80's, or even into the .90's over brief periods of time. The consistency of these retest correlations for *FM* suggests that, although it is reasonably stable, situational variables may also influence the process to which it relates.

Rorschach did not include a coding for animal movement in his research and, later, both Beck and Rapaport decided to follow his decision. Klopfer devised the *FM* coding and Hertz and Piotrowski adopted it into their approaches. All three, operating under the false premise that a relationship existed between *M* and *FM,* assumed that it represented a more primitive form of thinking, which is not necessarily true. However, all three also suggested that it has a relation to some awareness of impulses that are striving for gratification, which does seem to be true.

FM has been researched less than many other Rorschach variables, possibly because it did not appear in all of the earlier approaches to the test. Nonetheless, the data that have accumulated offer several consistent findings from which some seemingly valid judgments concerning the process can be made. First, *FM* has been shown to increase under diminished states of consciousness, such as those produced by alcohol (Piotrowski & Abrahamsen, 1952) and sodium amytal (Warshaw, Leiser, Izner, & Sterne, 1954). Exner, Zalis, and Schumacher (1976) studied the records of 15 chronic amphetamine users, all of whom were between the ages of 17 and 22. They note a substantially high frequency of *FM* as contrasted with a control group of 15 chronic marijuana users in the same age range. There were, of course, other differences between the two groups. The amphetamine subjects showed many of the features of the acute schizophrenic, whereas the marijuana users did not illustrate psychotic features. Nonetheless, the *FM* frequency was much higher for the first group. This finding prompted an examination of the protocols of 190 female subjects, half of whom are prostitutes. The prostitute subjects had been classified by intraoccupational socioeconomic level criteria, ranging from the very "high-priced" call girl to the addicted part-time streetwalker (Exner, Wylie, Leura, & Parrill, 1977). The streetwalkers, identified in the study as the Class V Group, consisted of only 10 subjects, all of whom were heroin addicted. They were matched, on the basis of marital status, intelligence, birth order, and educational level, with 10 controls who were not prostitutes. There were many features in the protocols of the two groups that differentiated one from another, but one major difference occurred in the frequency of *FM* answers. The 10 addicted prostitutes gave almost twice as many *FM* answers as did the controls.

Much of the data concerning *FM* suggests that the ideational process correlated with this variable is provoked by unmet need states. In theory, these would be the unprovoked thoughts that occur most often when a person is not deliberating focusing attention on a coping issue. For instance, the kinds of mental activity that keep the intended sleeper awake may be *FM*-related actions. Findings of several studies seem to offer support for this postulate.

Exner, Cooper, and Walker (1975) studied the Rorschach changes of nine *very* over-weight males during a 10-day medically supervised dietary program. Each of the subjects began the program with at least 50 pounds of excess weight, and the procedure for the diet involved hospitalization, during which only the intake of fluid was permitted. The "fluid only" phase of the program was the first segment of a more extended weight control regimen. Rorschachs were administered the day before hospitalization, and again on the 10th day of hospitalization. The average weight loss during this period was 18.4 pounds, and at least psychologically, all nine subjects were "very hungry" on the 10th hospital day. The average number of *FM* answers given in the prediet protocols was 3.77, which is very similar to the nonpatient norm. The retest records showed a mean *FM* of 4.96, which is not significantly different from the prediet mean; however, the variation *within* the sample was striking. Two subjects produced considerably fewer *FM* answers at the second testing, one moving from three to zero, and a second from four to one. One additional subject remained essentially at the same point, giving three *FM*'s at the first record and four in the second. The other seven subjects increased substantially for *FM* at the second test, the smallest increase being from two *FM*'s at the first test to four at the second. Thus although the data are not statistically defensible, the majority of subjects did move upward for *FM,* most showing a considerable change.

The second study in this series involved the testing of 15 juvenile offenders (Exner, Bryant, & Miller, 1975). All were tested at entry to a juvenile detention center and again at the 60th day of detention. All 15 had been sentenced to an "indeterminant period" of detention for offenses ranging from auto theft to assault, an act typically marking a series of antisocial acts in the history of the subject. Most such subjects are released from detention after 75 to 90 days, but others are detained for a considerably longer period. Thus at the 60-day interval, none of the subjects knew the probable date of release. The average number of *FM* responses at the first testing was 4.27 ($SD = 1.3$), whereas at the second testing, the mean *FM* had increased to 6.89 ($SD = 1.9$). A test for differences between the means yields a *t* of 4.68 ($p < .05$).

In the Ridgeway and Exner (1980) study, in which first-year medical school students were tested twice, the subjects were also administered the McClelland (1953) Need Achievement Scale, and Rank Order Correlations calculated for several Rorschach varia-bles and *NAch*. None was significant for the first test, but a rho $= .41$ *($p < .01$)* was discovered between *FM* and *NAch* in the second test, which was administered 2 or 3 days before their first major anatomy examination, a situation that logically should give rise to the achievement need.

Exner (1979) paid 15 male volunteers to participate in a physical restraint study. Each was tested 1 week prior to the laboratory restraint to establish baseline data. Subjects were paid in relation to the amount of time they elected to remain in restraint. The subjects were restrained in a large wooden chair using 32 leather straps, so that when all were secured the subject could do little more than move fingertips, toes, and eyes. Subjects were able to terminate the restraint by signaling the experimenter, using a button attached to one arm of the chair that caused a bell to ring. Prior to being released, however, the subject was administered a second Rorschach, with the examiner holding the cards. The mean *FM* for the group in the baseline data was 3.26 (*SD* = 1.64), whereas the mean *FM* in the retest was 5.42 (*SD* = 2.02), $p < .02$.

The means for *FM* are relatively consistent across age groups in the normative data. They do increase slightly between years 5 to 8, but then tend to hover between 3.0 and 3.5 through age 16, and are also at about 3.5 for adults. These findings seem to cast some doubt on the postulate that *FM* is related to a more primitive form of ideation. It seems more likely that it relates to a process that is not deliberately initiated, and less well controlled or directed.

Haan (1964) reported that when *FM* exceeds *M*, there is a high correlation with several measures of defensiveness, including intellectualization, rationalization, regression, and substitution. She suggests that *FM* may reflect either an overt expression of impulse, or an internalization of behavior, oriented toward containment of the impulse. However, this defensiveness is apparently not very effective if relapse is used as a criterion. Exner, Murillo, and Cannovo (1973) followed 105 nonschizophrenic patients for 1 year following discharge from hospitalization. Twenty-four were rehospitalized during the first 12 months and 17 had more *FM* than *M* in their discharge records, as contrasted with only nine of 81 nonrelapsers. Exner (1978) has also noted that withdrawn children tend to have more *M* than *FM*.

There are a number of studies that suggest *FM* is related to behavioral dysfunction. Piotrowski and Abrahamsen (1952) report that subjects who give more *FMs* tend to be much more aggressive under states of diminished consciousness, such as under the influence of alcohol or drugs. Earlier, Thompson (1948) found that *FM* is significantly correlated with MMPI measures of irresponsibility, aggressiveness, and distractability. Sommer and Sommer (1958) found a significant correlation between *FM* and assaultive behavior, and Altus (1958) reported that students scoring high on the MMPI Schizophrenia Scale give significantly more *FM* than do students scoring low on that scale. Berryman (1961) found that *FM* is related to the level of productivity in creative artists. Piotrowski and Schreiber (1952) found that the quality of *FMs* tends to change during treatment, generally becoming more assertive and less passive. They note that these changes correspond to behavioral changes in which successfully treated subjects demonstrate more "vitality and liveliness" in their actions. Exner (1978) found that a group of 480 adolescents, classified as behavior or conduct disorders, have a slightly, but not significantly, higher mean for *FM* as contrasted with nonpatient adolescents, averaging nearly four per record.

The entry on the left side of the *eb* offers some indication about mental activity that is being prompted by demand experiences. The demands may be stress related or need related or, as is most often the case, by the composite of both. This activity appears to serve a stimulating or alerting function, like an ideational signal system, that tends to prompt a person into action. In that context, it can be regarded as a positive compliment to coping resources. On the other hand, if the activity is extremely diverse and/or excessive, it can become a disruptive force. This is probably what happens in cases of insomnia, or to people who complain about "racing thoughts," or "having too many things on my mind."

The value on the left side of the *eb* is *always* expected to be higher than the value on the right side. This is true for about 90% of nonpatient children between the ages of five and 10, 85% of nonpatient children between ages 11 and 16, and more than 80% of the nonpatient adults. This is also true of most patient groups, although the proportions of subjects with a higher left side value tend to be less than for nonpatient groups. For instance, the reference sample of character disorders has 73% with a higher left side *eb*, and the schizophrenic sample has only 63% higher on the left side. The reference sample of seriously depressed subjects includes 58% who have a higher value in the *right side of the eb*. This is not a surprising finding, because each of the four variables included in the right side value of the *eb* is related to irritating affective experiences that are created by demand situations.

The Achromatic and Shading Variables *(SH)*   The symbol *SH* has often been used to represent a composite value of the four variables, *C', T, V,* and *Y;* however, it can be somewhat misleading to those not thoroughly familiar with the Rorschach. It can be misinterpreted to imply that each of the four variables share many common features, a presumption that is *not* really true. It is true, as noted earlier, that all four are related to impinging or irritating affects, but beyond that common element they are quite different from each other. One of the four, *Y,* is highly unstable, two others, *T* and *V,* are very stable for their presence or absence, and the fourth, *C',* usually has retest correlations ranging from the middle .60's to the middle .70's, but rarely higher or lower. Like *FM* it seems to have some trait like stability, but is also influenced by state conditions. The composite does have use as the right side value of the *eb* by providing a crude index of subjectively felt distress. Usually the value will range between 1 and 3 among nonpatients, but can often be higher for subjects in that group, and in patient groups. The absolute value, taken alone, has little interpretive significance unless it is inordinately higher, such as greater than 5, *or if it exceeds the value in the left side of the eb.* Either of those circumstances signals the presence of distress. Obviously, the frequencies for each of the four variables comprising *SH* should be reviewed carefully in any record, but when the *SH* composite indicates the presence of distress, that process of review becomes more urgent, because it provides information concerning the features of the distress and its implications in relation to the *D* scores, especially the *Adjusted D Score.* The data from two records may illustrate this best:

CASE 1

$EB = 4:1.5$ $EA = 5.5$
$$D = -1$$
$$AdjD = 0$$
$eb = 4:6$ $es = 10$
$FM = 2, m = 2, T = 2, C' = 0, V = 0,$
$Y = 4$

CASE 2

$EB = 4:1.5$ $EA = 5.5$
$$D = -1$$
$$AdjD = 0$$
$eb = 4:6$ $es = 10$
$FM = 2, m = 2, T = 0, C' = 3, V = 1, Y = 2$

In these cases, the *D* scores and the data of the Four Square are identical. Both subjects show an introversive *EB,* both *D* scores indicate an overload state, and when adjusted for situationally related stress, both *Adj D* scores are zero. However, they differ for the variables comprising the *SH* value. Case 1 is a rather clear illustration of some form of reactive distress. Six of the 10 variables in the *eb* (two *m*'s and four *Y)* are related to some situational experience, and the remaining segment of the *SH* composite consists of two texture responses. Elevations in texture are often related to experiences of emotional loss, and thus it is reasonable to speculate about a loss-stress relationship in Case 1. Case 2 also has an elevation in the situational related variables (two *m*'s and two *Y*'s), but the remaining elements in the right side *eb* value consist of one vista and three achromatic color variables. Because these are more stable variables, it is likely that much of the experienced distress is more chronic, and although the *Adj D Score* is zero, the presence of some enduring distress is more likely to create a predisposition to being thrown into overload by added stress, even though the additional stresses might be modest. Thus Case 2 is more likely to be a person in some situation related difficulties that are overlaying a more chronic distress state. Although firm conclusions concerning either case are contingent on completed interpretations of the records, these findings suggest that treatment planning for the two subjects will have different objectives. A more thorough review of the variables comprising *SH* should clarify this.

As noted earlier, the *Y* variables appear related to emotional experiences that are fomented by situations of helplessness, loss of control, and/or concerns about the possibility of being unable to respond effectively. Apparently, the affect associated with *Y* can take a variety of forms, such as anxiety, apprehensiveness, tension, or simply a state of uneasiness. Slightly less than half of nonpatient adults give at least one *Y* response ($M = 0.98$), as contrasted with 59% of the Schizophrenic reference group ($M = 1.56$), 63% of the Character Problems ($M = 1.13$), and 68% of the Depressives ($M = 1.31$).

Texture answers appear most consistently among the records of nonpatients, both adults and children. Ninety percent of all subjects in the nonpatient normative sample give at least one texture response, and most give *only* one ($M = 1.16$). Patients give texture answers far less frequently than do nonpatients and thus the absense of *T*, as well as elevations in *T*, are interpretively important. Klopfer (1938) was the first to recognize the importance of a separate coding for texture answers, and later Klopfer et al. (1954) suggested that it is related to needs for affection and dependency. McFate and Orr (1949) have noted that *TF* and *T* answers occur more frequently among young adolescents than in older adolescents or adults. Kallstedt (1952) has suggested that this is because young adolescents are more socially and sexually insecure. Montalto (1952) found that 6- and 7-year-old children whose mothers were more restrictive gave significantly more texture answers than do those of the same ages who have democratic mothers. Breecher (1956) found more texture responses among patients who had been maternally overprotected as contrasted with those who had been maternally rejected. She suggested that maternal rejection causes a reduction in the "need to be liked."

Hertz (1948) reported that texture responses reflect a cautious sensitivity, related to a willingness to be more open with the environment. Brown et al. (1950) found that psychosomatic patients give significantly fewer texture answers than do patients being treated for other complaints. Steiner (1947) reported that unsuccessful workers give significantly more texture answers than do successful workers. Allerhand (1954) noted that texture responses correlate with an index of anxiety in an experimental induced conflict situation, although Waller (1960) was unable to find a relation between texture and scores on the Welsh or Taylor anxiety scales, but did find texture related to an overall "impression" of anxiety. Potanin (1959) found that individuals who "acknowledge" dependency features prefer geometric designs with textural details significantly more than do people who describe themselves as independent. Coan (1956) studied Rorschach variables factorially, and concluded that the blends containing *M* and a texture variable relate to inner sensitivity or empathy. Exner (1978) demonstrated that when patients do articulate texture, they tend to do so with a substantially greater frequency than do nonpatients.

Exner and Bryant (1974) found that 30 recently separated or divorced subjects averaged 3.57 texture responses ($SD = 1.21$) and that none had *T-less* protocols, whereas demographically matched controls averaged 1.31 texture answers ($SD = 0.96$). Twenty-one of the 30 separated or divorced subjects were retested after 6 months, at which time 14 reported having reconstituted or replaced the lost relationship. Those 21 subjects had averaged 3.49 texture answers in the first test, as compared with 2.64 in the second test. Exner and Leura (1975) found an average of 2.87 texture answers ($SD = 1.12$) in a group of 23 children, ages 8 to 12, who had been placed in foster homes for the first time within the preceding 60 days because of the loss of one or both parents. Exner, Leventrosser, and Mason (1980) found that 36 of 50 first admission depressed patients who had at least one texture response also reported having a transitional object as a young child, such as a teddy bear, favorite blanket, and so on. Conversely, only 10 of 50 first admission depressed patients who had *T-less* records reported having a transitional object. Those data are similar to findings of Exner and Chu (1981) concerning nonpatient adults.

Subjects who have *T*-less protocols appear to have several psychological characteristics that are quite different from those who deliver texture answers. The first hint of this was noted by Leura and Exner (1976), who tested 32 foster-home children aged 7 to 11 who had had no placement lasting longer than 14 months, and a control group of 32 children of about the same intellectual level who had lived with their true parents since birth. The mean *T* for the foster-home group was 0.457 ($SD = 0.26$), *and 20 subjects produced T-less records*. The mean *T* for the 32 control subjects was 1.47 ($SD = 0.52$), and only three of those gave *T*-less protocols. A retest after four months of 16 of the 20 *T*-less foster home subjects showed that 15 of the 16 remained *T*-less. This marked difference cannot be attributed to the "failure of articulation" element. In the first testing, the 20 subjects averaged 1.4 gray-black or shading answers, with 16 of the 20 delivering such responses. Most involved *C'* or *Y*. In the retest, the 15 *T*-less subjects averaged 1.7 gray-black, shading answers with at least one in every record. These data appear to support the premise that, for some subjects, the affective experience of emotional or dependency needs may become "neutralized," and if this experience occurs, it takes on a durable characteristic. Pierce (1978) reported a similar finding in the protocols of 52 children who had experienced an absent parent prior to age eight. In that sample, *T* appeared in only seven protocols.

Exner (1978) also found that therapists tend to rate *T*-less patients lower in motivation for treatment during the first three months of contact than they do patients who have *T* in their pretreatment records. Exner, Martin, and Thomas (1983) found that *T*-less subjects tend to select seats in a waiting room that are more distant from a collaborator who was seated diagonally from the entry door than did subjects who gave *T* in their records. In fact, subjects who had elevations in *T* in their protocols tended to sit as close to the collaborator as possible, and frequently spoke to the collaborator, whereas the *T*-less subjects rarely spoke during the 10-minute waiting period.

The data concerning *T* are quite compelling. Most nonpatients give one *T* response, usually an *FT* answer to Card VI. People who elevate for *T* have greater needs for closeness, and the elevation gives some indication of those needs. They apparently experience loneliness or stronger than usual needs to be dependent on others. On the other hand, people who do not give *T* in their records appear to be more guarded and/or distant in interpersonal contacts. They also appear to be more concerned with issues of personal space than are most people. Interestingly, *T*-less subjects usually will give at least one texture answer in records that are taken after 6 to 9 months of treatment, regardless of the type of intervention (Exner, 1978).

Achromatic Color responses show a higher mean among nonpatients (1.31) than the texture responses; however, they are given by a smaller proportion of subjects. Whereas T responses are given by about 90% of the normative sample, the C' variables appear in only 75% of those records. They appear in 90% of the records of depressed patients, 61% of the Schizophrenic reference sample, and in 51% of the records of the reference sample of Character Problems. Klopfer (1938) was the first to provide a specific coding for responses in which the white, gray, or black features of the blots are used as color. He postulated that these answers correlate with a tendency to tone down affect, but cautioned that the specific process involved would be defined by the presence or absence of other test features. For instance, he hypothesized that C' answers, involving the use of white space as color, might relate to a euphoric characteristic *if* the record is also marked by a substantial number of chromatic color responses. Later, Klopfer hypothesized that the C' answers might be related to depressive features (Klopfer & Spiegelman, 1956). Rapaport et al., (1946) suggested that the process related to the C' types of response might be more conscious and defensive against direct affective expression. Piotrowski (1957) also postulated that the C' responses are related to depressive feelings, but emphasized that the euphoric element is likely to be present if the responses involve white or light-gray areas of the blots, citing the findings of Weber (1937) that alcoholics give significantly more C' answers involving the white and light-gray areas.

Exner (1974) found that C' responses are given about twice as frequently by psychosomatics, obsessives, and schizoids as by nonpatients, and about three times as frequently as given by patients diagnosed as passive-aggressive or psychopathic. Exner (1974) also reviewed the pretreatment protocols of 64 first admission affective disorders who had been placed on a "suicide watch" at the time of admission. Sixteen of the 64 made suicide gestures within 55 days of admission, and only five of those 16 records (31%) contained C' responses as contrasted with 34 of the 48 (71%) of the patients who did not make a gesture. These findings tend to support the postulate that a relationship does exist between affective constraint and C'. Exner and Leura (1977) found that the records of 20 adolescents, being evaluated for disposition recommendations related to "acting out" offenses, contained *significantly more* C' answers ($M = 2.77$; $SD = 1.03$) than did the records of 20 nonpatient adolescents ($M = 1.12$; $SD = 0.79$) used as controls for the study, $p <$ .01. Both groups were retested after 8 weeks, at which time all disposition decisions concerning the acting out subjects had been made and implemented. The control subjects gave about as many C' answers in the retest as they had in the first test ($M = 1.07, SD = 0.87$), whereas the acting out group gave significantly fewer C' responses than they had in the first test ($M = 1.11$; $SD = 0.94$). These data offer some support for Rapaport's suggestion that the process related to C' may be defensive. The findings also coincide with retest correlational data mentioned earlier, indicating that although C' is relatively stable, it is apparently subject to fluctuation under some state influences.

Some of the most compelling data concerning C' responses come from the normative and reference samples. As noted previously, 90% of the depressives give at least one C' answer, and the mean for the group is 2.99, as compared with means of 1.31 for both nonpatients and schizophrenics, and 0.78 for the Character Disorder group. Exner (1978) has noted that inpatient depressives, retested at discharge when the clinical manifestations of depression have abated, usually give fewer than half the number of C' responses that were present in the pretreatment records, even though the retest records tend to be significantly longer. An elevation in C' responses has been found to be one of five variables useful in the identification of some serious depressive disturbances (Exner, 1983).

Assuming that the C' answer does relate to a form of affective constraint, it is important for the interpreter to evaluate the use of form in those responses. When form is dominant, as in the *FC'* response, the operations involved in the constraint are probably more cognitively controlled than when the reverse is true. The process of constraint should not be confused with anxiety, although anxiety may sometimes accompany the experience. Rather, it is like a psychological "biting of one's tongue," whereby the emotion is internalized and consequently creates some irritation. It is the irritation that is represented by the *C"* variable, which, experientially, can probably take any of several forms, ranging from a vague uneasiness or discomfort to a much more marked experience of tension.

Vista responses were first identified by Rorschach (1923) in a passing reference to answers containing dimensional features. Klopfer and Kelley (1942) and Beck (1944) both created separate codings to account for the dimensional answers based on the shading features of the blots. Both suggested that they are related to a form of introspection. Klopfer posited that they represent efforts at taking distance to handle anxiety, whereas Beck perceived them as related to a more morose feeling tone created by depression and/or feelings of inferiority. Vista responses are the least frequently given type of shading response, occurring in only 27% of the adult nonpatient normative sample records ($M = 0.48$), 17% of the Character Disorder protocols ($M = 0.25$), and 33% of the Schizophrenic records ($M = 0.63$). It is extremely rare among young nonpatient children, appearing in only 28 of 930 records of youngsters between the ages of 5 and 11 in the normative sample. The frequency of *V* responses is greater among adolescents. It increases significantly at the 12-year level and approaches the mean and proportional frequency for nonpatient adults in each of the adolescent years. Vista responses appear more frequently in the records of seriously depressed subjects. The reference sample of depressed inpatients shows that 80% contain at least one *V* answer ($M = 1.25$). Klopfer (1946) and Light and Amick (1956) found very low frequencies of vista responses among the elderly.

Meltzer (1944) has shown that vista answers occur with a significantly greater frequency among stutterers than nonstutterers. Bradway et al. (1946) reported that vista responses are related to "treatability" in delinquent adolescent females. Buhler and LeFever (1947) found that alcoholics give significantly more vista answers than do psychopathic personalities. They interpret this to indicate that alcoholics are more self-critical. Rabinovitch (1954) has shown that vista answers are significantly correlated with the greater GSR deflections and perceptual thresholds, and interprets this as reflecting an attempt to avoid unpleasant stimuli. Fiske and Baughman (1953) have noted that the incidence of vista answers tends to increase among outpatients with the length of the record.

Exner (1974) found that vista answers occur more frequently among subjects who make suicidal gestures within 60 days after being tested. Exner and Wylie (1977) found that an elevation in vista responses is significantly correlated with effected suicides that occur within 60 days after being tested, and included that finding as one variable in the Suicide Constellation. Exner, Martin, and Mason (1984) have cross-validated the efficacy of the Suicide Constellation using a sample of 101 subjects who effected their own death within 60 days of being tested. They found that the vista variable remains as a highly important variable in the Constellation. Exner (1974, 1978) has reported that vista answers tend to increase in records of patients who have been in uncovering forms of psychotherapy for at least 6 months as contrasted with pretreatment records. Exner (1974) has also found that patients in group psychotherapy who have vista answers in their pretreatment records tend to give more self-focusing statements during the group sessions.

The data concerning vista answers appear to support the Klopfer-Beck positions that it is related to a "taking distance," introspective process; however, it is doubtful that the relation is direct. Instead, it seems to be related to a negative emotional experience that is generated by the self-focusing behavior. Obviously, the very low frequency with which the vista answer appears makes its presence in any record interpretively important. Unlike the texture answer that is expected to appear in a record, the vista response *is not*. Its absence is generally a more favorable sign than its presence. When *V* is present, it signals the presence of discomfort, and possibly even pain, that is being produced by a kind of ruminative self-inspection which is focusing on *perceived* negative features of the self. Although the presence of a single *FV* response in an average length record might be considered positively in the context of prognosis for early treatment motivation, the self-defacing aspects of the process that give rise to the negative feelings can be a marked obstacle to early treatment gains. Probably the only time that the presence of vista answers can be viewed positively is when the subject has been in some form of uncovering or developmental intervention for several months. In that circumstance, the intervention process is designed to promote self-inspection, much of which will focus on negative features and thus can be expected to generate the experiences of pain and/or irritation. However, vista answers are not expected to appear in the records of patients who are nearing termination. Although the process of self-inspection will undoubtedly continue after treatment, irritation and/or pain should not be a routine product of the process. This is usually indicated by the presence of another Rorschach variable that is also related to taking distance and self-inspecting, but which is apparently *not* related to affective experience.

THE FORM DIMENSION RESPONSE *(FD)*

The *FD* was first identified by a separate coding in the early development of the Comprehensive System (Exner, 1974). Klopfer and Kelley (1942) had included them, idiomatically, in the vista category. Beck (1944) coded some of them for vista, but only those for which the unarticulated use of shading seemed probable. The impetus for considering a separate coding was provoked by the previously mentioned study of 64 inpatients who had been placed on a suicide watch. Those records averaged more than three *FD* responses as contrasted with about one *FD* in the records of nonpatients. Thus at first glance it appeared that *FD* might be related to depressive features common in the subject preoccupied with self-destruction. However, the records of psychiatric outpatients also contained significantly more *FD* responses than the nonpatient sample, averaging more than two. Those findings led to the postulate that *FD* might relate to introspection, the logic being that outpatients, in the therapeutic routine, are encouraged to be self-examining. Subsequently, three studies were completed, the results of which appear to support this postulate.

In the first, it was found that introversive subjects, both patients and nonpatients, average significantly more *FD* responses ($M = 2.42$; $SD = 0.94$) than do extratensives ($M = 0.93$; $SD = 0.91$), $p < .01$. This finding suggested that *FD* is related to delay and/or internalization. In the second study 40 subjects were selected from a waiting list at a mental health facility and randomly assigned, 10 each to four "holding" groups. They were informed that, while waiting for the assignment of individual therapists, they could participate 2 hours each week in group sessions designed to focus on treatment plans and objectives. The group sessions were videotaped and the audio material on the tapes for the first three sessions was scored by three raters who had no knowledge of the nature of the study. They used a two-dimensional grid to record whether the verbal material was self- or other-directed, and whether the content referred to the past, present, or future. The 40 subjects were divided into two groups of 20 each for the purposes of data analysis, using a median split of the distribution of *FD* frequencies. The mean *FD* for the upper half was 2.83, and for the lower half was 1.34. The ratings of the audio material revealed that the subjects in the upper half of the distribution gave significantly more self-directed statements than did the subjects in the lower half. In addition, the subjects in the upper half had significantly more statements focusing on the past and present than did those in the lower half. The two groups did not differ on two measures of egocentricity, and thus it seems reasonable to conclude that the more self-focusing statements were not simply a manifestation of self-centeredness.

In the third study, 15 outpatients, entering dynamically oriented psychotherapy, were tested a few days prior to their first therapy session and retested after the tenth session. It was hypothesized that *FD* should increase at the retest, assuming that the patients would become more involved in the introspective process. Subjective ratings of "self-awareness" were also collected from each patient's therapist after the first, fifth, and tenth sessions. The results show a mean *FD* of 2.06 *(SD* = 1.03) with a range of 0 to 4 in the pretreatment records. In the second test the mean increased to 3.11 *(SD* = 0.89), $p < .05$, and the range increased to 1 to 6. The therapist ratings of self-awareness were on a 5-point scale. The correlation between *FD* and the ratings after the first session were not significant $(r = .13)$; however, the correlation between *FD* and the ratings done after the tenth session were significant $(r = .37, p < .02)$. These data seemed to offer added support to the proposition that *FD* is related to a psychological activity involving self-inspection, or at least self-awareness, and consequently the *FD* category was added into the System.

Data that have accumulated since 1974 have also provided support for the basic hypothesis concerning *FD*. Exner, Wylie, and Kline (1977) tested 279 outpatients prior to their first session, and retested them three times, at intervals of 9, 18, and 27 months after the onset of treatment. The patients were unequally distributed across seven treatment modalities, ranging from biofeedback $(N = 28)$ to psychoanalytic psychotherapy $(N = 56)$. Many of the patients involved in the briefer forms of treatment, such as biofeedback, assertiveness training, and systematic desensitization, had terminated prior to the first retest, and only 54 of the 279 remained in treatment at the 27th month. The mean *pretreatment FD* for the entire group is 1.52 *(SD* = 1.03), as contrasted with a mean *FD* of 2.71 *(SD* = 1.18) at the first retest, $p < .01$. Interestingly, the mean for *vista* also increased significantly, nearly doubling from 0.89 in the pretreatment records to 1.68 in the protocols of the first retest. The 18-month retest showed a slight but not significant reduction in the mean *FD* as compared with the nine-month retest, to 2.39 *(SD* = 1.18); however, when the group was subdivided into terminated $(N = 157)$, and continuing in treatment $(N = 122)$ differences were discovered. The mean *FD* for the terminated group was 1.67 *(SD* = 1.02) which is similar to the pretreatment data. The mean *FD* for the group continuing in treatment was 3.49 *(SD* = 1.29) which *is* significantly higher than the mean for the second test. More important, when the nine-month retest data were reanalyzed using the 18-month subgroups, the means for *FD* *did not show a significant difference* (terminated = 2.51 versus continuing = 2.92).

A second important finding in the 18-month retest data is that the mean for *vista* decreased significantly for the total group, from 1.68 at nine months to 0.78, and when the subgroups were reviewed, both show relatively low mean values for vista (terminated =

0.63 versus continuing = 0.94). Thus it would appear that the introspective process is facilitated by a variety of intervention methods, and that during the early phases of intervention, some of that process evokes the sorts of affective irritation associated with vista answers. Apparently the irritation is lessened considerably as the intervention is extended or terminated; however, if intervention continues, the process of self-inspection, as reflected in the *FD* answers, remains at a higher than average level.

FD answers occur most frequently in the records of nonpatients. The adult normative sample shows that 75% gave at least one *FD* response. The frequency and mean gradually increase with age among children. About 21% of nonpatient children, ages five to seven, give an *FD* answer. The proportion increases to 54% among children, ages eight to 10, and about 75% among children 11 to 16. People voluntarily seeking outpatient treatment average nearly two *FD* answers. Conversely, the schizophrenic reference group shows that only 52% gave at least one *FD* response ($M = 0.86$), and the character disorder group has *FD* in only 37% of the records ($M = 0.69$). The inpatient depressive reference group shows a mean *FD* of 1.14, which is essentially the same as for nonpatient adults. However, *FD* appears in only 66% of the protocols in that sample. The presence of one or two *FD*'s in a record of an adolescent or adult probably indicates that the self-inspecting process, important for growth and/or change, is present. An elevation in *FD* may signal that the process is being abused. For instance, the Suicide Constellation includes the item $FV + VF + V + FD > 2$. In other words, it is not only the irritating affect generated by introspection, as represented by vista answers, which is a valid predictor, but any indication of an exaggerated involvement with self-examination, as can be indicated by an elevation in *FD*. On the other hand, the absence of *FD* in the record of an adolescent or adult may suggest the avoidance of self-awareness and/or examination. Obviously, this might not portend well for the early phases of intervention.

THE EXPERIENCED STIMULATION *(es)*

The preceding discourse concerning the *Experience Base* and *FD* should have clarified the importance of creating a crude index that relates to impinging or demanding stimulus experiences. The *es* is designed for that purpose and, when studied in relation to the *EA*, and adjusted for the probability of metric variance, it does afford some important data concerning control and stress tolerance that is represented in the *D* scores. Collectively, the data of the *D* scores and the Four Square provide a rich point of beginning the interpretation of a Rorschach protocol. They fall far short of providing an elaborate picture of the subject, but they also create the cornerstone of information on which the remaining interpretive postulates are built. A neglect of these data means that the interpretation of the Rorschach will be incomplete and probably erroneous, but if they are included as the basis from which the interpretation develops, the many other indices regarding psychological styles and operations that are available in the Structural data of the test will become much more meaningful.

REFERENCES

Abrams, E. W. (1955) Predictions of intelligence from certain Rorschach factors. *Journal of Clinical Psychology*, **11**, 81–84.

Allen, R. M., Manne, S. H., and Stiff, M. (1951) The role of color in Rorschach's Test: A preliminary normative report on a college student population. *Journal of Projective Techniques,* **15,** 235–242.

Allerhand, M. E. (1954) Chiaroscuro determinants of the Rorschach Test as an indicator of manifest anxiety. *Journal of Projective Techniques,* **18,** 407–413.

Altus, W. D. (1958) Group Rorschach and Q-L discrepancies on the ACE. *Psychological Reports,* **4,** 469.

Ames, L. B. (1960) Constancy of content in Rorschach responses. *Journal of Genetic Psychology,* **96,** 145–164.

Ames, L. B. Learned, J., Metraux, R., and Walker, R. N. (1952) *Child Rorschach Responses.* New York: Harper & Row.

Ames, L. B., Metraux, R. W., and Walker, R. N. (1971) *Adolescent Rorschach Responses.* New York: Brunner/Mazel.

Arluck, E. W., (1940) A study of some personality differences between epileptics and normals. *Rorschach Research Exchange,* **4,** 154–156.

Armbruster, G. L., Miller, A. S., and Exner, J. E. (1974) Rorschach responses of parachute trainees at the beginning of training and shortly before their first jump. Workshops Study No. 201 (unpublished). Rorschach Workshops.

Bash, K. W. (1955) Einstellungstypus and Erlebnistypus: C. G. Jung and Herman Rorschach. *Journal of Projective Techniques,* **19,** 236–242.

Baughman, E. E. (1958) An experimental analysis of the relationship between stimulus structure and behavior in the Rorschach. *Journal of Projective Techniques,* **23,** 134–183.

Beck, S. J. (1944) *Rorschach's Test. I: Basic Processes.* New York: Grune & Stratton.

Beck, S. J. (1945) *Rorschach's Test. II: A Variety of Personality Pictures.* New York: Grune & Stratton.

Beck, S.J. (1960) *The Rorschach Experiment: Ventures in Blind Diagnosis.* New York: Grune & Stratton.

Beck, S. J. (1972) Personal Communication.

Beck, S. J., Beck, A., Levitt, E. E., and Molish, H. B. (1961) *Rorschach's Test. I: Basic Processes.* (3rd ed.) New York: Grune & Stratton.

Beck, S. J. and Molish, H. B. (1967) *Rorschach's Test. II: A Variety of Personality Pictures.* (2nd Ed.) New York: Grune & Stratton.

Bendick, M. R., and Klopfer, W. G. (1964). The effects of sensory deprivation and motor inhibition on Rorschach movement responses. *Journal of Projective Techniques,* **28,** 261–264.

Berger, D. (1953) The Rorschach as a measure of real life stress. *Journal of Consulting Psychology,* **17,** 355–358.

Beri, J., and Blacker, E. (1956) External and internal stimulus factors in Rorschach performance. *Journal of Consulting Psychology,* **20,** 1–7.

Berryman, E. (1961) Poet's responses to the Rorschach. *Journal of General Psychology,* **64,** 349–358.

Binder, H. (1932) *Die Helldunkeldeutungen im psychodiagnostischem experiment von Rorschach.* Zurich: Urell Fussli.

Blatt, S. J., and Feirstein, A. (1977) Cardiac response and personality organization. *Journal of Consulting and Clinical Psychology,* **45,** 111–123.

Bradway, K., Lion, E., and Corrigan, H. (1946) The use of the Rorschach in a psychiatric study of promiscuous girls. *Rorschach Research Exchange,* **9,** 105–110.

Breecher, S. (1956) The Rorschach reaction patterns of maternally overprotected and rejected schizophrenics. *Journal of Nervous and Mental Disorders,* **123,** 41–52.

Brennen, M., and Richard, S. (1943) Use of the Rorschach Test in predicting hypnotizability, *Bulletin of the Menninger Clinic,* **7,** 183–187.

Brown, M., Bresnoban, T. J., Chakie, F. R., Peters, B., Poser, E. G., and Tougas, R. V. (1950) Personality factors in duodenal ulcer: A Rorschach study. *Psychosomatic Medicine,* **12,** 1–5.

Buhler, C., and LeFever, D. (1977) A Rorschach study on the psychological characteristics of alcoholics. *Quarterly Journal of Studies on Alcoholism.* **8,** 197–260.

Campo, V. (1977) On the meaning of the inaminate movement response. Ninth International Rorschach Congress, Fribourg. Switzerland.

Chu, A. Y., and Exner, J. E. (1981) EB style as related to distractibility in a calculation task. Workshops Study No. 280 (unpublished), Rorschach Workshops.

Coan, R. (1956) A factor analysis of Rorschach determinants. *Journal of Projective Techniques,* **20,** 280–287.

Cocking, R. R., Dana, J. M., and Dana, R. H. (1969) Six constructs to define Rorschach M: A response. *Journal of Projective Techniques and Personality Assessment,* **33,** 322–323.

Cooper, L., and Caston, J. (1970) Physical activity and increases in M response. *Journal of Projective Techniques and Personality Assessment,* **34,** 295–301.

Cox, F. N., and Sarason, S. B. (1954) Test anxiety and Rorschach performance. *Journal of Abnormal and Social Psychology,* **49,** 371–377.

Crumpton, E. (1956) The influence of color on the Rorschach Test. *Journal of Projective Techniques,* **20,** 150–158.

Dana, R. H. (1968) Six constructs to define Rorschach M. *Journal of Projective Techniques and Personality Assessment,* **32,** 138–145.

Dubrovner, R. J., Von Lackum, W. J., and Jost, H. A. (1950) A study of the effect of color on productivity and reaction time in the Rorschach Test. *Journal of Clinical Psychology,* **6,** 331–336.

Dudek, S. Z. (1968) M an active energy system correlating Rorschach M with ease of creative expression. *Journal of Projective Techniques and Personality Assessment.* **32,** 453–461.

Eichler, R. M. (1951) Experimental stress and alleged Rorschach indices of anxiety. *Journal of Abnormal and Social Psychology,* **46,** 344–356.

Elstein, A. S. (1956) Behavioral correlates of the Rorschach shading determinant. *Journal of Consulting Psychology,* **29,** 231–236.

Erginel, A. (1972) On the test-retest reliability of the Rorschach. *Journal of Personality Assessment,* **36,** 203–212.

Evans, R. B., and Mormorston, J. (1964) Rorschach signs of brain damage in cerebral thrombosis. *Perceptual Motor Skills,* **18,** 977–988.

Exner, J. E. (1959) The influence of chromatic and achromatic color in the Rorschach. *Journal of Projective Techniques,* **23,** 418–425.

Exner, J. E. (1962) The effect of color on productivity in Cards VIII, IX, X of the Rorschach. *Journal of Projective Techniques,* **26,** 30–33.

Exner, J. E. (1974) *The Rorschach: A Comprehensive System. Volume 1.* New York: Wiley.

Exner, J. E. (1978) *The Rorschach: A Comprehensive System. Volume 2. Current research and advanced interpretation.* New York: Wiley.

Exner, J. E. (1979) The effects of voluntary restraint on Rorschach retests. Workshops Study No. 258 (unpublished), Rorschach Workshops.

Exner, J. E. (1983) Rorschach assessment. In I. B. Weiner (Ed.) *Clinical Methods in Psychology* (2nd Ed.). New York: Wiley.

Exner, J. E., and Armbruster, G. L. (1979) Correlations between some Rorschach variables and Zuckerman sensation seeking scores. Workshops Study No. 252 (unpublished), Rorschach Workshops.

Exner, J. E., Armbruster, G. L., and Viglione, D. (1978) The temporal stability of some Rorschach features. *Journal of Personality Assessment,* **42,** 474–482.

Exner, J. E., Armbruster, G. L., Walker, E. J. and Cooper, W. H. (1975) Anticipation of elective surgery as manifest in Rorschach records. Workshops Study No. 213 (unpublished), Rorschach Workshops.

Exner, J. E., and Bryant, E. L. (1974) Rorschach responses of subjects recently divorced or separated. Workshops Study No. 206 (unpublished), Rorschach Workshops.

Exner, J. E., Bryant, E. L., and Miller, A. S. (1975) Rorschach responses of some juvenile offenders. Workshops Study No. 214 (unpublished). Rorschach Workshops.

Exner, J. E. and Chu, A. Y. (1981) Reports of transitional objects among nonpatient adults as related to the presence or absence of T in the Rorschach. Workshops Study No. 277 (unpublished), Rorschach Workshops.

Exner, J. E., Cooper, W. H., and Walker, E. J. (1975) Retest of overweight males on a strict dietary regimen. Workshops Study No. 210 (unpublished), Rorschach Workshops.

Exner, J. E. and Leura, A. V. (1975) Rorschach responses of recently foster placed children. Workshops Study No. 196 (unpublished), Rorschach Workshops.

Exner, J. E., and Leura, A. V. (1977) Rorschach performances of volunteer and nonvolunteer adolescents. Workshops Study No. 238 (unpublished), Rorschach Workshops.

Exner, J. E., Levantrosser, C., and Mason, B. (1980) Reports of transitional objects among first admission depressives as related to the presence or absence of T in the Rorschach. Workshops Study No. 266 (unpublished), Rorschach Workshops.

Exner, J. E., Martin, L. S. and Mason, B. (1984) A review of the Suicide Constellation. 11th International Rorschach Congress, Barcelona.

Exner, J. E., Martin, L. S. and Thomas, E. A. (1983) Preference for waiting room seating among subjects with elevations or absence of *T* in the Rorschach. Workshops Study No. 282 (unpublished), Rorschach Workshops.

Exner, J. E., and Murillo, L. G. (1973) Effectiveness of regressive ECT with process schizophrenics. *Diseases of the Nervous System,* **34,** 44–48.

Exner, J. E., and Murillo, L. G. (1975) Early prediction of posthospitalization relapse. *Journal of Psychiatric Research,* **12,** 231–237.

Exner, J. E., and Murillo, L. G. (1977) A long-term follow up of schizophrenics treated with regressive ECT. *Diseases of the Nervous System,* **38,** 162–168.

Exner, J. E., Murillo, L. G., and Cannavo, F. (1973) Disagreement between ex-patient and relative behavioral reports as related to relapse in non-schizophrenic patients. Eastern Psychological Association, Washington, D.C.

Exner, J. E., and Thomas, E. E. (1982) Postural–gestural behaviors among introversives and extratensives during a structured inteview. Workshops Study No. 292 (unpublished) Rorschach Workshops.

Exner, J. E., Thomas, E. A., Cohen, J. B., Ridgeway, E. M., and Cooper, W. H. (1981) Stress indices in the Rorschachs of patients recovering from myocardial infarctions. Workshops Study No. 286 (unpublished), Rorschach Workshops.

Exner, J. E., Thomas, E. A. and Martin, L. S. (1980) Alterations in GSR and cardiac and respiratory rates in Introversives and Extratensives during problem solving. Workshops Study No. 272 (unpublished), Rorschach Workshops.

Exner, J. E., Thomas, E. A. and Mason, B. (1985) Children's Rorschach's: Description and prediction. *Journal of Personality Assessment,* **49,** 13–20.

Exner, J. E., Viglione, D. J. and Gillespie, R. (1984) Relationships between Rorschach variables as relevant to the interpretation of structural data. *Journal of Personality Assessment,* **48,** 65–70.

Exner, J. E., and Walker, E. J. (1973) Rorschach responses of depressed patients prior to ECT. Workshops Study No. 197 (unpublished), Rorschach Workshops.

Exner, J. E., and Weiner, I. B. (1982) *The Rorschach: A Comprehensive System. Volume 3, Assessment of children and adolescents.* New York: Wiley.

Exner, J. E., and Wylie, J. (1977) Some Rorschach data concerning suicide. *Journal of Personality Assessment,* **41,** 339–348.

Exner, J. E., Wylie, J. R., and Kline, J. R. (1977) Variations in Rorschach performance during a 28 month interval as related to seven intervention modalities. Workshops Study No. 240 (unpublished), Rorschach Workshops.

Exner, J. E., Wylie, J. R., Leura, A. V., and Parrill, T. (1977) Some psychological characteristics of prostitutes. *Journal of Personality Assessment,* **41,** 474–485.

Exner, J. E., Zalis, T., and Schumacher, J. (1976) Rorschach protocols of chronic amphetamine users. Workshops Study No. 233 (unpublished), Rorschach Workshops.

Fisher, R. L. (1958) The effects of a disturbing situation upon the stability of various projective tests. *Psychological Monographs,* **72** 1–23.

Fiske, D. W., and Baughman, E. E. (1953) The relationship between Rorschach scoring categories and the total number of responses. *Journal of Abnormal and Social Psychology,* **48** 25–30.

Ford, M. (1946) The application of the Rorschach Test to young children. *University of Minnesota Child Welfare Monographs, No. 23.*

Forsyth, R. P. (1959) The influence of color, shading and Welsh anxiety level on Elizur Rorschach content analysis of anxiety and hostility. *Journal of Projective Techniques,* **23,** 207–213.

Frankle, A. H. (1953) Rorschach human movement and human content responses as indices of the adequacy of interpersonal relationships of social work students. Unpublished doctoral dissertation, University of Chicago.

Gibby, R. G., Stotsky, B. A., Harrington, R. L., and Thomas, R. W. (1955) Rorschach determinant shift among hallucinatory and delusional patients. *Journal of Consulting Psychology,* **19,** 44–46.

Goldfarb, W. (1945) Psychological privation in infancy and subsequent adjustment. *American Journal of Orthopsychiatry,* **15,** 249–254.

Goldfarb, W. (1949) Rorschach test differences between family reared, institution reared, and schizophrenic children. *American Journal of Orthopsychiatry,* **19,** 624–633.

Goldfried, M. R., Stricker, G., and Weiner, I. B. (1971) *Rorschach Handbook of Clinical and Research Applications.* Englewood Cliffs, N.J.: Prentice-Hall.

Goldman, R. (1960) Changes in Rorschach performance and clinical improvement in schizophrenia. *Journal of Consulting Psychology,* **24,** 403–407.

Goodstein, L. D. (1954) Interrelationships among several measures of anxiety and hostility. *Journal of Consulting Psychology,* **18,** 35–39.

Goodstein, L. D., and Goldberger, L. (1955) Manifest anxiety and Rorschach performance in a chronic patient population. *Journal of Consulting Psychology,* **19,** 339–344.

Grayson, H. M. (1956) Rorschach productivity and card preferences as influenced by experimental variation of color and shading. *Journal of Projective Techniques,* **20,** 288–296.

Guirdham, A. (1936) The diagnosis of depression by the Rorschach Test. *British Journal of Medical Psychology,* **16,** 130–145.

Hafner, A. J. (1958) Response time and Rorschach behavior. *Journal of Clinical Psychology,* **14,** 154–155.

Haan, N. (1964) An investigation of the relationships of Rorschach scores, patterns and behaviors to coping and defense mechanisms. *Journal of Projective Techniques and Personality Assessment,* **28,** 429–441.

Halpern, F. (1940) Rorschach interpretation of the personality structure of schizophrenics who benefit from insulin therapy. *Psychiatric Quarterly,* **14,** 826–833.

Henry, E. M., and Rotter, J. B. (1956) Situational influences on Rorschach responses. *Journal of Consulting Psychology,* **20,** 457–462.

Hersh, C. (1962) The cognitive functioning of the creative person: A developmental analysis. *Journal of Projective Techniques,* **26,** 193–200.

Hertz, M. R. (1948) Suicidal configurations in Rorschach records. *Rorschach Research Exchange,* **12,** 3–58.

Hertzman, M., Orlansky, D., and Seitz, C. P. (1944) Personality organization and anoxia tolerance. *Psychosomatic Medicine,* **6,** 317–331.

Holtzman, W. H., Iscoe, I., and Calvin, A. D. (1954) Rorschach color responses and manifest anxiety in college women. *Journal of Consulting Psychology,* **18,** 317–324.

Kallstedt, F. E. (1952) A Rorschach study of 66 adolescents. *Journal of Clinical Psychology,* **8,** 129–132.

Keehn, J. D. (1954) The response to color and ego functions: A critique in light of recent experimental evidence. *Psychological Bulletin,* **51,** 65–67.

Kelley, D., Margulies, H., and Barrera, S. (1944) The stability of the Rorschach method as demonstrated in electric convulsive therapy cases. *Rorschach Research Exchange,* **5,** 44–48.

Kemalof, S. (1952) The effect of practice in the Rorschach Test. In Peters, W. (Ed.), *Studies in Psychology and Pedagogy.* Instanbul: University of Istanbul Press.

King, G. F. (1960) Rorschach human movement and delusional content. *Journal of Projective Techniques,* **24,** 161–163.

Klatskin, E. H. (1952) An analysis of the effect of the test situation upon the Rorschach record: Formal scoring characteristics. *Journal of Projective Techniques,* **16,** 193–199.

Klein, G. S., and Schlesinger, H. G. (1951) Perceptual attitudes toward instability: Prediction of apparent movement experiences from Rorschach responses. *Journal of Personality,* **19,** 289–302.

Klebanoff, S. A. (1946) Rorschach study of operational fatigue in Army Air Force Combat Personnel. *Rorschach Research Exchange,* **9,** 115–120.

Klopfer, B. (1938) The shading resonses. *Rorschach Research Exchange,* **2,** 76–79.

Klopfer, B., Ainsworth, M., Klopfer, W., and Holt, R. (1954) *Developments in the Rorschach Technique.* Vol. 1. Yonkers-on-Hudson, N.Y.: World Book.

Klopfer, B., and Kelley, D. (1942) *The Rorschach Technique.* Yonkers-on-Hudson, N.Y.: World Book Company.

Klopfer, B., Kirkner, F., Wisham, W., and Baker, G. (1951) Rorschach prognostic rating scale. *Journal of Projective Techniques,* **15,** 425–428.

Klopfer, B., and Margulies, H. (1941) Rorschach reactions in early childhood. *Rorschach Research Exchange,* **5,** 1–23.

Klopfer, B., and Spiegelman, M. (1956) Differential diagnosis. In Klopfer, B. et al. (Eds.), *Developments in the Rorschach Technique. II: Fields of Application.* Yonkers-on-Hudson, N.Y.: World Book.

Klopfer, W. (1946) Rorschach patterns of old age. *Rorschach Research Exchange,* **10,** 145–166.

Lebo, D., Toal, R., and Brick, H. (1960) Rorschach performances in the amelioration and continuation of observable anxiety. *Journal of General Psychology,* **63,** 75–80.

Lerner, B. (1966) Rorschach movement and dreams. A validation study using drug-induced deprivation. *Journal of Abnormal Psychology,* **71,** 75–87.

Leura, A. V., and Exner, J. E. (1976) Rorschach performances of children with a multiple foster home history. Workshops Study No. 220 (unpublished), Rorschach Workshops.

Levine, M., Glass, H. and Meltzoff, J. (1957) The inhibition process. Rorschach human movement response and intelligence. *Journal of Consulting Psychology,* **21,** 45–49.

Levine, M., and Spivack, G. (1962) Human movement responses and verbal expression in the Rorschach Test. *Journal of Projective Techniques,* **26**, 299–304.

Levitt, E. E. (1957) Alleged Rorschach anxiety indices in children. *Journal of Projective Techniques,* **21**, 261–264.

Levitt, E. E., and Grosz, H. J. (1960) A comparison of quantifiable Rorschach anxiety indicators in hypnotically induced anxiety and normal states. *Journal of Consulting Psychology,* **24**, 31–34.

Light, B. H., and Amick, J. (1956) Rorschach responses of normal aged. *Journal of Projective Techniques,* **20**, 185–195.

Linton, H. B. (1954) Rorschach correlates of response to suggestion. *Journal of Abnormal and Social Psychology,* **49**, 75–83.

Lipton, M. B., Tamarin, S., and Latesta, P. (1951) Test evidence of personality change and prognosis by means of the Rorschach and Wechsler-Bellevue tests on 17 insulin treated paranoid schizophrenics. *Psychiatric Quarterly,* **25**, 434–444.

Loveland, N. T., and Singer, M. T. (1959) Projective test assessment of the effects of sleep deprivation. *Journal of Projective Techniques,* **23**, 323–334.

Majumber, A. K, and Roy, A. B. (1962) Latent personality content of juvenile delinquents. *Journal of Psychological Research,* **1**, 4–8.

Mann, L. (1956) The relation of Rorschach indices of extratension and introversion to a measure of responsiveness to the immediate environment. *Journal of Consulting Psychology,* **20,** 114–118.

Mason, B. and Exner, J. E. (1984) Correlations between WAIS subtests and nonpatient adult Rorschach data. Workshops Study No. 289 (unpublished), Rorschach Workshops.

McArthur, C. C., and King, S. (1954) Rorschach configurations associated with college achievement. *Journal of Educational Psychology,* **45**, 492–498.

McClelland, D. C., Atkinson, J. W., Clark, R. W., and Lowell, E. L. (1953) *The Achievement Motive.* New York: Appleton-Century-Crofts.

McFate, M. Q., and Orr, F. G. (1949) Through adolescence with the Rorschach. *Rorschach Research Exchange,* **13**, 302–319.

Meltzer, H. (1944) Personality differences between stuttering and nonstuttering children as indicated by the Rorschach Test. *Journal of Psychology,* **17**, 39–59.

Meyer, B. T. (1951) An investigation of color shock in the Rorschach Test. *Journal of Clinical Psychology,* **7**, 367–370.

Mindness, H. (1955) Analytic psychology and the Rorschach test. *Journal of Projective Techniques,* **19,** 243–252.

Mirin, B. (1955) The Rorschach human movement response and role taking behavior. *Journal of Nervous and Mental Disorders,* **122**, 270–275.

Molish, H. B. (1965) Psychological structure in four groups of children. In Beck, S. J. (Ed.), *Psychological Processes in the Schizophrenic Adaptation.* New York: Grune & Stratton.

Molish, H. B. (1967) Critique and problems of the Rorschach. A survey. In Beck, S. J. and Molish, H. B. *Rorschach's Test. II: A Variety of Personality Pictures.* (2nd Ed.) New York: Grune & Stratton.

Montalto, F. D. (1952) Maternal behavior and child personality: A Rorschach study. *Journal of Projective Techniques,* **16**, 151–178.

Neel, F. A. (1960) Inhibition and perception of movement on the Rorschach. *Journal of Consulting Psychology,* **24**, 224–229.

Ogdon, D. P., and Allee, R. (1959) Rorschach relationships with intelligence among familial mental defectives. *American Journal of Mental Deficiency,* **63**, 889–896.

Orlinski, D. E. (1966) Rorschach test correlates of dreaming and dream recall. *Journal of Projective Techniques and Personality Assessment,* **30**, 250–253.

Page, H. A (1957) Studies in fantasy-daydreaming frequency and Rorschach scoring categories. *Journal of Consulting Psychology*, **21**, 111–114.

Palmer, J. O. (1963) Alterations in Rorschach's experience balance under conditions of food and sleep deprivation: A construct validation study. *Journal of Projective Techniques*, **27**, 208–213.

Paulsen, A. (1941) Rorschachs of school beginners. *Rorschach Research Exchange*, **5**, 24–29.

Perlman, J. A. (1951) Color and the validity of the Rorschach 8-9-10 per cent. *Journal of Consulting Psychology*, **15**, 122–126.

Phillips, L., and Smith, J. G. (1953) *Rorschach Interpretation: Advanced Technique*. New York: Grune & Stratton.

Pierce, G. E. (1978) The absent parent and the Rorschach "T" response. In E. J. Hunter and D. S. Nice (Eds.) *Children of military families*. Washington, D. C.: U.S. Government Printing Office.

Piotrowski, Z. (1937) The Rorschach ink-blot method in organic disturbances of the central nervous system. *Journal of Nervous and Mental Disorders*, **86**, 525–537.

Piotrowski, Z. (1939) Rorschach manifestations of improvement in insulin treated schizophrenics. *Psychosomatic Medicine*, **1**, 508–526.

Piotrowski, Z. (1940) Positive and negative Rorschach organic reactions. *Rorschach Research Exchange*, **4**, 147–151.

Piotrowski, Z. (1957) *Perceptanalysis*. New York: Macmillan.

Piotrowski, Z., and Abrahamsen, D. (1952) Sexual crime, alcohol, and the Rorschach Test. *Psychiatric Quarterly Supplement*, **26**, 248–260.

Piotrowski, Z., and Bricklin, B. (1958) A long-term prognostic criterion for schizophrenics based on Rorschach data. *Psychiatric Quarterly Supplement*, **32**, 315–329.

Piotrowski, Z., and Bricklin, B. A second validation of a long-term Rorschach prognostic index for schizophrenic patients. *Journal of Consulting Psychology*, **25**, 123–128.

Piotrowski, Z., and Schreiber, M. (1952) Rorschach perceptanalytic measurement of personality changes during and after intensive psychoanalytically oriented psychotherapy. In Bychowski, G., and Despert, J. L. (Eds), *Specialized Techniques in Psychotherapy*. New York: Basic Books.

Potanin, N. (1959) Perceptual preferences as a function of personality variables under normal and stressful conditions. *Journal of Abnormal and Social Psychology*, **55**, 108–113.

Rabin, A. I., and Beck, S. J. (1950) Genetic aspects of some Rorschach factors. *American Journal of Orthopsychiatry*, **20**, 595–599.

Rabin, A., Papania, N., and McMichael, A. (1954) Some effects of alcohol on Rorschach performance. *Journal of Clinical Psychology*, **10**, 252–255.

Rabinovitch, S. (1954) Physiological response, perceptual threshold, and Rorschach Test anxiety indices. *Journal of Projective Techniques*, **18**, 379–386.

Rabinovitch, M. S., Kennard, M. A., and Fister, W. P. (1955) Personality correlates of electroencephalographic findings. *Canadian Journal of Psychology*, **9**, 29–41.

Rapaport, D., Gill, M., and Schafer, R. (1946) *Psychological Diagnostic Testing*. Vol. 2. Chicago: Yearbook Publishers.

Rees, W. L., and Jones, A. M. (1951) An evaluation of the Rorschach Test as a prognostic aid in the treatment of schizophrenics by insulin coma therapy, electronarcosis, electroconvulsive therapy, and leucotomy. *Journal of Mental Science*, **97**, 681–689.

Richter, R. H., and Winter, W. D. (1966) Holtzman ink-blot correlates of creative potential. *Journal of Projective Techniques and Personality Assessment*, **30**, 62–67.

Rickers-Ovsiankina, M. (1943) Some theoretical considerations regarding the Rorschach method. *Rorschach Research Exchange*, **7**, 14–53.

Ridgeway, E. M., and Exner, J. E. (1980) Rorschach correlates of achievement needs in medical students under an arousal state. Workshops Study No. 274 (unpublished), Rorschach Workshops.

Rorschach, H. (1921) *Psychodiagnostics*. Bern: Bircher (Transl. Hans Huber Verlag, 1942).

Rorschach, H. (1923) The application of the form interpretation test. In *Zeitschrift fur die gesamte Neurologie und Psychiatrie*.

Rosenthal, M. (1954) Some behavioral correlates of the Rorschach experience balance. Unpublished doctoral dissertation. Boston University.

Salmon, P., Arnold, J. M., and Collyer, Y. M. (1972) What do the determinants determine: The internal validity of the Rorschach. *Journal of Personality Assessment*, **36**, 33–38.

Sapenfield, B., and Buker, S. L. (1949) Validity of the Rorschach 8–9–10 per cent as an indicator of responsiveness to color. *Journal of Consulting Psychology*, **13**, 268–271.

Schachtel, E. G. (1943) On color and affect. *Psychiatry*, **6**, 393–409.

Schmidt, H., and Fonda, C. (1954) Rorschach scores in the manic states. *Journal of Psychology*, **38**, 427–437.

Schon, M., and Bard, M. (1958) The effects of hypophysectomy on personality in women with metastastic breast cancer as revealed by the Rorschach Test. *Journal of Projective Techniques*, **22**, 440–445.

Schulman, I. (1953) The relation between perception of movement on the Rorschach Test and levels of conceptualization. Unpublished doctoral dissertation, New York University.

Schwartz, F., and Kates, S. L. (1957) Rorschach performance, anxiety level and stress. *Journal of Projective Techniques*, **21**, 154–160.

Shalit, B. (1965) Effects of environmental stimulation on the M, FM, and m responses in the Rorschach. *Journal of Projective Techniques and Personality Assessment*, **29**, 228–231.

Shapiro, D. (1956) Color-response and perceptual passivity. *Journal of Projective Techniques*, **20**, 52–69.

Shapiro, D. (1960) A perceptual understanding of color response. In Rickers-Ovsiankina, M. (Ed.), *Rorschach Psychology*. New York: Wiley.

Sherman, M. H. (1955) A psychoanalytic definition of Rorschach determinants. *Psychoanalysis*, **3**, 68–76.

Singer, J. L., and Herman, J. (1954) Motor and fantasy correlates of Rorschach human movement responses. *Journal of Consulting Psychology*, **16**, 325–331.

Singer, J. L. (1960) The experience type: Some behavioral correlates and theoretical implications. In Rickers-Ovsiankina, M. (Ed.), *Rorschach Psychology*. New York: Wiley.

Singer, J. L., and Herman, J. (1954) Motor and fantasy correlates of Rorschach human movement responses. *Journal of Consulting Psychology*, **18**, 325–331.

Singer, J. L., Meltzoff, J., and Goldman, G. D. (1952) Rorschach movement responses following motor inhibition and hyperactivity. *Journal of Consulting Psychology*, **16**, 359–364.

Singer, J. L., and Spohn, H. (1954) Some behavioral correlates of Rorschach's experience-type. *Journal of Consulting Psychology*, **18**, 1–9.

Sommer, R., and Sommer, D. T. (1958) Assaultiveness and two types of Rorschach color responses. *Journal of Consulting Psychology*, **22**, 57–62.

Steele, N. M., and Kahn, M. W. (1969) Kinesthesis and the Rorschach M response. *Journal of Projective Techniques and Personality Assessment*, **33**, 5–10.

Steiner, M. E. (1947) The use of the Rorschach method in industry. *Rorschach Research Exchange*, **11**, 46–52.

Steisel, I. M. (1952) The Rorschach Test and suggestibility. *Journal of Abnormal and Social Psychology*, **47**, 607–614.

Stotsky, B. A. (1952) A comparison of remitting and nonremitting schizophrenics on psychological tests. *Journal of Abnormal and Social Psychology*, **47,** 489–496.

Swift, J. W. (1945) Rorschach responses of eighty-two pre-school children. *Rorschach Research Exchange*, **7,** 74–84.

Tanaka, F. (1958) Rorschach movement responses in relation to intelligence. *Japanese Journal of Educational Psychology*, **6,** 85–91.

Thomas, H. F. (1955) The relationship of movement responses on the Rorschach Test to the defense mechanism of projection. *Journal of Abnormal and Social Psychology*, **50,** 41–44.

Thompson, G. M. (1948) MMPI correlates of movement responses on the Rorschach. *American Psychologist*, **3,** 348–349.

Viglione, D. J. (1980) A study of the effect of stress and state anxiety on Rorschach performance. Doctoral dissertation, Long Island University.

Wagner, E. E., and Hoover, T. O. (1971) Exhibitionistic *M* in drum majors: A validation. *Perceptual Motor Skills*, **32,** 125–126.

Wagner, E. E., and Hoover, T. O. (1972) Behavioral implications of Rorschach's human movement response. Further validation based on exhibitionistic *M*'s. *Perceptual Motor Skills*, **35,** 27–30.

Wallen, R. (1948) The nature of color shock. *Journal of Abnormal and Social Psychology*, **43,** 346–356.

Waller, P. F. (1960) The relationship between the Rorschach shading response and other indices of anxiety. *Journal of Projective Techniques*, **24,** 211–216.

Warshaw, L., Leiser, R., Izner, S. M., and Sterne, S. B. (1954) The clinical significance and theory of sodium amytal Rorschach Testing. *Journal of Projective Techniques*, **18,** 248–251.

Weber, A. (1937) Delirium tremens und alkoholhalluzinose in Rorschachschen Formdeutversuch. *Zeitschrift fur die gesamte Neurologie und Psychiatrie*, **159.**

Weigel, R. B., and Exner, J. E. (1981) *EB* style and preference for interpersonal and impersonal slides among nonpatient adults. Workshop Study No. 291 (unpublished), Rorschach Workshops.

Weiner, I. B. (1966) *Psychodiagnosis in Schizophrenia*. New York: Wiley.

Wetherhorn. M. (1956) Flexor-extensor movement on the Rorschach. *Journal of Consulting Psychology*, **20,** 204.

Wiener-Levy, D., and Exner, J. E. (1981) The Rorschach *EA-ep* variable as related to persistence in a task frustration situation under feedback conditions. *Journal of Personality Assessment*, **45,** 118–124.

Witkin, H. A., Dyk, R. B., Faterson, H. F., Goodenough, D. R., and Karp, S. A. (1962) *Psychological Differentiation: Studies of Development*. New York: Wiley.

Zuckerman, M. (1971) Dimensions in sensation seeking. *Journal of Consulting and Clinical Psychology*, **36,** 45–52.

CHAPTER 15

Structural Data II—
Cognition, Ideation, and Affect

The beginning description of the subject is broadened by adding information from a myriad of issues, such as quality of cognitive operations, perceptual accuracy, flexibility of ideation and attitudes, modulation of affect, goal orientation, self-concept, interest in people, and so on. Issues such as these must be addressed if the final interpretation is to be meaningful. Each is approached by reviewing clusters of interrelated variables. The progression of the review may vary depending on the initial findings yielded by Lambda, the *D* scores, and the Four Square; whatever progression is selected, however, all variables ultimately must be scanned in the process. For instance, if Lambda is not elevated, the Adjusted *D* score is at least zero, and the *EB* indicates an extratensive coping style, so the next logical points of focus might concern issues of affective processing and control, because the extratensive style suggests that affect may be a more important element in the daily activities of the subject than might be the case if the *EB* indicated an introversive coping style. On the other hand, if Lambda is elevated, data concerning perceptual accuracy, conventionality, and cognitive processing might be the next logical foci for review, because the elevation in Lambda raises questions about a tendency to oversimplify and/or neglect stimulus elements in the environment. Thus the order in which variables are presented here is not necessarily the most appropriate order for the review of some records. Generally, it follows the format of the Structural Summary and represents a progression that can be used in most cases, and may be a useful sequence for the novice to follow to insure that data are not neglected.

COGNITIVE INITIATIVE AND COMPLEXITY *(Zf, DQ,* Location, *Zd)*

Quite often, information concerning capacities for control and coping style preference can be enhanced by data regarding the level and quality of the cognitive operations that have been manifested in the selection and delivery of answers in the test. This requires a review of four data points in the Structural Summary. Each offers some information about the cognitive operations, but collectively, as with the data of the Four Square, they serve to render a much richer picture about some of the cognitive functioning of the subject.

Organizing Activity *(Zf)* The frequency of organizing activity *(Zf)* provides an indication about the extent to which the subject has approached the task, using cognitive tactics that typically are more demanding than some other mediational approaches. Answers that include a *Z* score, with the possible exception of *Wo* responses to Card V, require considerably more mediational effort than is required in forming a more simplistic *D* answer that avoids any blot integration. Although some basic intellectual talent is required for *Z*, the

354

actual frequency and type of Z are influenced by many other features. Most subjects, both adults and children, patients and nonpatients, have some type of Z in about 40 to 50% of their answers. Obviously, high Lambda subjects tend to have lower Z frequencies. When the Zf is low, it may indicate an intellectual limitation, but more likely it denotes a reluctance to tackle the complexity of the stimulus field. A high Zf may be the product of intellectual striving or a need to deal with the stimulus field in a more careful and precise manner. The reliability data for Zf are substantial for both brief and lengthy retest intervals. The data in Chapter 2 show retest correlations ranging from .89 to .92 for brief intervals, and .83 to .85 for much longer periods of time. Although the Zf provides information about the initiative of the subject to approach the task with more effort than might be required, taken alone it can be misleading, because the levels of effort vary, and the quality of the organized product can be distributed along a continuum ranging from mediocre to very sophisticated.

For instance, younger clients tend to have about the same proportion of Z in their records as do adults. At the same time, younger clients usually have a smaller proportion of $DQ+$ responses than adults. In other words, there are fewer responses in the records of younger clients that involve an organization of adjacent or distant details, and more that are based on Wo or integrated S responses. This probably reflects the "devil may care" approach that frequently characterizes the way in which the child takes on a task, but it also reflects the more simplistic level of cognition that is commonplace among children. As a consequence, the ZSums of children are usually lower than for adults. Obviously, the DQ distribution is also an important data set from which information concerning the quality of the organizing efforts can be gleaned, as well as providing other important data about the level and quality of cognitive operations.

DQ Distribution   The coding for developmental quality (DQ) appears to be related to the willingness and capacity to analyze and synthesize the stimulus field in a meaningful way. Generally, a higher frequency of $DQ+$ answers is found among brighter and psychologically more complex subjects, whereas the lower-level DQv responses occur most frequently among children and intellectually limited and/or neurologically impaired subjects. Children under the age of 10 can be expected to give between 3 and 5 DQv answers, but from the age of 10 upward the frequencies decline substantially so that by age 16 a frequency of more than 2 is somewhat unusual. Adult groups, both patient and nonpatient, usually have a mode of 1 for DQv, although most patient groups have slightly higher means for the variable than does the nonpatient normative sample. As noted in Chapter 5, an earlier version of the DQ coding included a minus code that was linked directly to minus Form Quality (Exner, 1974). Like the DQv, the $DQ-$ was also considered as indicative of a lower level of cognitive functioning and frequently appeared in the records of seriously disturbed subjects. The combined frequency of DQv and $DQ-$ did differentiate the more severe disturbances (Friedman, 1952; Becker, 1956; Wilensky, 1959); however, it would appear that most of the variance contributing to the differentiation can be accounted for by the $DQ-$. In other words, the discrimination was generated mainly by data concerning perceptual inaccuracy rather than the level of cognitive maturity and complexity. A hint of this was noted by Siegel (1953) who noted that paranoid schizophrenics manifest a high frequency of lower-level DQ responses even though they tend to function at a much higher cognitive level than do other schizophrenics.

The $DQv/+$ is the least frequent of the four types of answers. It appears more frequently in the records of children and adolescents than adults. It is most notable in the records of youngsters between the ages of 9 and 15. In the younger subject, it is probably a more positive sign, indicating an orientation toward a higher level of cognitive activity; however, frequencies of 2 or more in the records of adults suggest that the orientation toward a more sophisticated cognitive level is somehow aborted by problems that are apparently related to form commitment.

The DQo is the most frequently given answer and represents a kind of cognitive economy that does not sacrifice the quality of operations as does the DQv. Whereas DQv answers reflect a concrete, overly simplistic, and diffuse form of cognitive functioning, the DQo represents a more conservative, but committed, processing effort. In some ways, the DQo can be considered similar to pure F responses in that both relate to a cognitive action that avoids complexity and instead involves a straightforward definition of the stimulus field or part of it. It is for this reason that Z scores assigned to Wo responses are generally lower for the more solid blots than for $D+$ responses to the same blots.

The correlation between Zf and the composite of $DQ+$ and $DQv/+$ answers, derived from the nonpatient adult sample, is quite significant, $r = .417$ ($p < .01$). Therefore if Zf is elevated in the record of an adult or a subject in mid-adolescence, the frequencies of $DQ+$ and $DQv/+$ are expected to be at least average or above. If this is not the case, it signals that the effort is present, but the cognitive activity is less sophisticated and/or complex than might be expected. Obviously, if Zf is elevated and the frequency of $DQ+$ responses is substantial, it indicates that the subject is not only working hard at the task, but doing so with a complex and sophisticated cognitive effort.

It is very important to avoid the erroneous assumption that complex and sophisticated cognitive activity is somehow synonomous with efficiency or effective adjustment. *That is not true*. The process may be very complex, but not necessarily grounded in reality or oriented toward effective adjustment. Many symptom patterns evolve from very elaborate cognitive operations. Among the best illustrations of this are the systematized delusional systems that are usually built through an intricate but unrealistic network of very complex cognitive activity.

Location Distribution   The distribution of location selections is another data set that provides some information about cognitive activity. The data offer some clues about how the subject approaches the environment, especially those aspects of it that require forms of coping activity. They do not reveal why the approach has been employed, but simply that it has been used. Most of this information is derived by reviewing the proportions of each of the three location codes. For example, someone who gives a high frequency of Dd answers is very likely to have a different approach to problem solving than the person who gives W responses almost exclusively. Both may be effective, or even creative, or conversely, both may be handicapped by an excessive commitment to a single approach. One thing is almost certain: either will be limited by their own psychological approach to the extent that they cannot function easily in the approach mode of the other. Most nonpatients older than age 9 tend to give more D answers than W answers and give a very low frequency of Dd responses. Younger children also tend to give very few Dd responses, but they usually will give more W than D responses.

1. The W Response: Rorschach (1921) postulated that W has a relation to intellectual operations, suggesting that it denotes the ability to organize the components of one's environment into a meaningful concept. Beck (1932) did find a positive correlation between W and intellectual operations; however, the literature on this issue has been somewhat contradictory. Abrams (1955) reported a correlation of nearly .40 between W and

I.Q., but a substantially lower correlation was reported by Armitage et al. (1955) for the same variables. Previously, McCandless (1949) reported no significant findings in studying the *W* answer as related to academic achievement, and Wittenborn (1950) found no relationship between *W* and several measures of mental ability. Lotsoff (1953) reported that *W* is related to verbal fluency but not necessarily to intelligence per se. Holzberg and Belmont (1952) and Wishner (1948) failed to find any significant relationship between *W* and the Similarities subtest of the Wechsler-Bellevue Scale. Mason and Exner (1984) found low but statistically significant correlations between *W* and the Comprehension (.20), Similarities (.24), Digit Symbol (.20), and Object Assembly (.19) subtests of the WAIS, using a sample of 171 nonpatient adults; however, no significant relationships were discovered between *W* and Verbal, Performance, or Full Scale I.Q.s. Developmental data are somewhat contradictory to the premise that a relationship exists between the frequency of *W* and intelligence. Ames et al. (1971) found that the greatest proportion of *W* answers occurs in the records of 3- and 4-year-olds, with a gradual decline in the proportion through adolescence until it approximates the general adult proportion, which is between 30 and 40% of the record.

When the location frequencies, including the *W* responses, are studied for *DQ,* the findings are much more consistent, and definitive relationships are found with different kinds of intellectual operations. Friedman (1952) found that nonpatient adults give significantly more *W+* answers than do schizophrenics or children. Frank (1952) has shown the same to be true when nonpatients and neurotics are compared. Blatt and Allison (1963) reported a significant positive relationship between higher *DQ W*'s and problem-solving ability. Ames et al. (1971) also found that the quality of *W* responses increases through adolescence, and a similar finding is reported by Exner and Weiner (1982). In general then, although *W* can be taken as some index of motivation to deal with the entire stimulus field, its relation to more sophisticated and/or complex cognitive operations must be derived from a review of the *DQ* codes that have been included in the response.

There is still another issue that must be considered in the interpretation of *W* answers. Beck (1945) reported that *W*'s occur with the greatest frequency to Cards V, I, IV, and VI. He suggested that this is because they are the most solid of the 10 figures and consequently do not require as much synthesizing to form a *W* response. This is why the *Z* values for *W* responses differ considerably across the 10 blots. Beck's findings were reaffirmed by Exner (1974), using a sample of 200 adult nonpatient records. A review of the 600 records in the adult nonpatient normative sample reveals that *W* occurs more frequently than *D* on Cards I and V, whereas *D* is the more frequent response to the remaining eight blots. As might be expected, *W* occurs with the lowest frequency to Cards III and X, which are the most broken figures.

Obviously, the absolute frequency of *W* answers adds little to the overall interpretive yield when taken alone. Although the data concerning *Zf* and the *DQ* distribution shed some light on its relevance, there are also two other reference points that help to make the *W* frequency more interpretively meaningful. The first is the relation of *W* to *M,* and the second is the relationship between *W* and *D.* Both can be quite important to the interpretation, especially if the *W* frequency is higher or lower than expected.

2. *W:M* **Ratio.** Whenever *W* is elevated it signals the investment of more effort than might be necessary for the task. However, this should not automatically be considered as a negative finding. If the resources of the subject are considerable, the extra effort being generated in the overselection of *W*'s may, in fact, have a very modest psychological cost to the subject. In that *M* responses relate to reasoning and higher forms of conceptualization, as well as the process of giving deliberate direction to ideational focusing, the frequency of M responses can be regarded as a crude index of some of the functional capabilities that are necessary for achievement oriented activities. Adults, both patient and nonpatient, average about twice as many W responses as M responses, and approximately 70% will have a $W:M$ ratio that falls in the range of 1.5:1 to 2.5:1. In this context, if the frequency of W answers is substantially greater than the number of M responses—that is, if the ratio exceeds 3:1—it may indicate that the subject is striving to accomplish more than is reasonable in light of current functional capacities. This postulate is strengthened in cases where the DQ distribution shows a low frequency of $DQ+$ responses. It suggests that if this tendency occurs in everyday behaviors, the probability of failure to achieve objectives is increased, and the consequent impact of those failures can often include the experience of frustration.

Although this is an unusual and possibly important finding in the record of an adult, it is relatively commonplace among children. For instance, 5- and 6-year-olds will frequently have a $W:M$ ratio of 8:1 or even greater, and 9- and 10-year olds often have $W:M$ ratios of 4:1 or greater. Youngsters are notorious for overestimating their capacities and setting inordinately high goals. Fortunately, they are also notorious for placing little value on most of those goals, and thus are usually able to deal with the consequences of failure in a more casual way so that any impact of frustration is relatively brief.

When the frequency of W responses is disproportionately low in relation to the M frequency (i.e., 1:1 or lower), it suggests that the subject is very cautious, and possibly overly conservative in defining objectives for achievement. However, this postulate may not be valid if the Zf and frequency of $DQ+$ responses are at least average. If both Zf and $DQ+$ are average or above average in a record in which the $W:M$ ratio is disproportionately low, the issue of underestimating capabilities and/or conservative goal setting must be reviewed in the context of a possible orientation toward being overly economical. This requires a review of the D and Dd frequencies and the $W:D$ ratio.

3. The D Response. Rorschach (1921) hypothesized that D answers represent the ability to perceive and react to the obvious characteristics of the environment. This assumption appears logical in that the majority of responses in most records are D selections. Whereas the subject who gives multiple W responses to the same blot must retranslate or reclassify the figure, the presence of several relatively discrete detail segments in each blot lends itself to the easier formulation of multiple potential answers. Thus when selecting answers to be delivered, it seems quite probable that many more D answers are available. In that context, the selection of the D response is compatible with the natural orientation of most subjects to accomplish the task efficiently and economically. This is why a $W:D$ ratio has been included in the Structural Summary.

4. $W:D$ Ratio. The relationship of W to D must be considered in the context of R. If R is less than 17, it is likely that the frequency of W will be nearly equal to, or possibly even greater than D. When the record is of average length or longer, D is always expected to exceed W, typically with a ratio of about 1.5:1 to 2:1. If D exceeds W by more than 2:1, it signals that there may be an overemphasis on being economical or, stated differently, a tendency to back away from the more demanding efforts that may be required to form a W response. If the record is of at least average length and W is equal to or greater than D, it indicates that the subject is sacrificing economy for some other purpose. This is not necessarily a negative finding, depending on the extent and quality of resources available to the subject; however, in some instances it may suggest that the subject is not using his or her resources in the most efficient manner.

For example, subjects in the two inpatient reference samples, schizophrenic and depressive, give lower proportions of *D* answers than do outpatients or nonpatients. Interestingly, both give significantly more *Dd* responses than do the nonpatients. This may be because sets and/or disorganization created by their pathology tend to overshadow identification of more economical solutions, or that preoccupations orient them toward different searching patterns of the blots. Friedman (1952) has reported that severely disturbed subjects tend to give significantly higher proportions of *D* responses that have a lower-level *DQ*. Exner and Murillo (1973) and Murillo and Exner (1973) noted a significant increase in the proportions of *D* in the records of schizophrenics after a remission of major symptoms occurred. They noted that this increase corresponded to other findings indicating that the patients were more cautious, conservative, and oriented toward making more socially acceptable behaviors than had been true in their pretreatment evaluations.

Whereas the *W+* response to a broken or semibroken blot can be considered as reflecting a substantial cognitive involvement, *D+* answers to the more solid blots represent a similar cognitive effort. This is also noted in the higher *Z* values assigned to responses that involve adjacent or distant detail use in the solid blots. Thus although the frequency of *D* is generally regarded as indicating a tendency to economize, an abundant number of *D+* answers requires a qualification to that conclusion. For instance, a *W:D* ratio of 5:15 will usually be translated as suggesting a very conservative, possibly overly economical approach to the coping task. But if at least half of the 15 *D* answers are *DQ+*, it would be reasonable to assume that the conservative approach is not designed mainly to economize. Instead, it probably relates to a concern about preciseness, and could even reflect a perfectionistic orientation. If the latter is true, it is likely that the record will also be marked by an elevation in *Dd* responses.

5. The *Dd* Response. *Dd* answers occur with a significantly lower frequency that either *W* or *D*. Frequencies of one to three *Dd* answers are not uncommon in records of average length, but more than three is an unusual finding and requires careful review. In many cases, an elevation in *Dd* answers signals a markedly atypical, and usually obsessive approach to the world; however, elevations in *Dd* can be caused by other elements. An elevated *Dd* frequency can be caused by an excessive number of space responses. This is not uncommon among children and adolescents. Elevations in *Dd* can also be a form of avoidance through which the subject tries to create a more narrow environment that is easier to manage. Klebanoff (1949) found that male paretics give significantly more *Dd* than do nonpatients. Schachter and Cotte (1948) reported a substantial elevation of *Dd* in the protocols of prostitutes taken shortly after their arrest. Kadinsky (1952) concluded that the relationship between *Dd* and external adjustment is negative, but between *Dd* and internal adjustment is positive. Rabin et al. (1954), using a retest method, found that *Dd* increases significantly after the ingestion of substantial quantities of alcohol.

In general, *Dd* can be interpreted as representing a form of respite from the ambiguities of the blot areas. When the proportion of *Dd* is within the average range of one to three, it is probably a positive sign, showing both the initiative and capacity to back away temporarily. If the frequency is disproportionate, it can indicate a form of perfectionism or a tendency to flee from routine coping demands. *Dd* answers that include a movement determinant can be especially important because they involve projection to an unusual area. Thus they should be studied carefully for any indications of impairment to the ideational process.

Organizational Efficiency *(Zd)* Although the integration of findings from *Zf, DQ,* and Location provides useful information concerning some of the cognitive operations, another data point, the Zd score, can often broaden the yield. Whereas the Zf relates to the effort to organize the stimulus field and DQ offers information about the quality of the effort, the Zd score provides data related to the efficiency involved in processing the stimuli. Approximately 70% of nonpatient adolescents and adults have Zd scores that fall within the range of $+3.0$ to -3.0. The mean Zd for most groups older than age 10 hovers around zero. Younger children tend to have a greater incidence of Zd scores that are less than zero, and substantial numbers of five-, six, and 7-year-olds will have Zd scores less than -3.0. When the Comprehensive System was first formulated, information concerning the interpretive use of the score was very sparse. It was included in the System because, as noted in Chapter 7, deviations from the $+3.0$ to -3.0 range occurred much more frequently among psychiatric subjects than nonpatients, and this suggested the possibility of some problems in cognitive processing. Subsequent research has shed considerable light on that original speculation.

Exner and Leura (1974) found that children with Zd scores of less than -3.0 made signicantly more errors in a "Simon Says" game than did children with Zd scores in the $+3.0$ to -3.0 range. They also found that children with Zd scores greater than $+3.0$ made significantly fewer errors in the game than did children with scores in the average range. Leura and Exner (1977) found Zd scores of less than -3.0 in the protocols of 14 of 15 children who had been diagnosed as "hyperactive" and who had abnormal EEG's. Exner (1978) reported that Zd scores exceeding $+3.0$ appear more frequently in the protocols of subjects who have obsessive or perfectionistic personality features, whereas Zd scores of less than -3.0 appear more frequently in the records of subjects who manifest more impulsive-like decision operations in problem-solving behaviors. Based on the composite of findings, Exner (1978) concluded that subjects with Zd scores less than -3.0 have a tendency to be negligent in processing information, and this creates the probability that some of their responses will be formulated before a stimulus field is fully mediated. He defined this process as *underincorporation*. On the opposite side of the average range are subjects with Zd scores greater than $+3.0$, who appear to invest more effort in their processing activities. They are prone to approach each new stimulus field with caution and thoroughness. This characteristic has been labeled as *overincorporation*.

The distinction between underincorporation and overincorporation, as contrasted with those with Zd scores in the average range, has been confirmed by several other findings. Exner and Caraway (1974) found that overincorporators are much more reluctant than underincorporators to makes guesses about movie and book titles, and proverbs, when only parts of words are displayed. Bryant and Exner (1974) tested over- and underincorporators, using the Minnesota Paper Form Board. Half of each group took the test under a 10-minute time limit and the other half took the test with no time limit. They found that the underincorporators completed almost twice as many problems as the overincorporators when working under the time limit, *but* they also made about twice as many errors. Thus the scores of the two groups were not significantly different. Under the no time limit condition, overincorporators attempted significantly more items and achieved significantly more correct solutions. Exner and Bryant (1975) found that underincorporators performed better in a serial learning task after 10 training trials; however, when the number of training trials was doubled, the accurate recall of the overincorporators was far superior to the underincorporators. Bryant, Kline, and Exner (1978) found that overincorporators averaged significantly longer times to complete the Trails B test in the Halstead-Reitan than subjects with Zd scores in the average range.

Exner, Bryant, and Armbruster (1979) studied the eye scanning patterns of 12 adolescents in a matching familiar figures task. Four of the subjects were overincorporators, four were underincorporators, and four had *Zd* scores in the average range. The task involved the exposure of six target faces, each for 750 milliseconds, and each exposure was followed by the exposure of a field of nine faces for an interval of 750 milliseconds. Subjects were instructed to indicate which of the field faces was the same as the target face by using a light pointer. Eye activity was recorded for the 750 millisecond intervals, during which the target faces were exposed. The overincorporators averaged more than twice as many scan paths (crossing a previously viewed space again) as did the underincorporators, and significantly more than those with *Zd* scores in the average range. Overincorporators and subjects with average *Zd* scores had significantly more horizontal sweeps of the target than underincorporators, and the overincorporators also showed a greater tendency to complete vertical sweeping scans than did either of the other groups. The average number of correct identifications was slightly but not significantly greater for the average group—4.9 (overincorporators = 4.3; underincorporators = 4.3).

Sixty-three of the 279 outpatients (23%) followed for 27 months by Exner (1978) had *Zd* scores of −3.5 or less at the beginning of treatment. In the first retest, after 9 months, only 17 of the 63 continued to have *Zd* scores in the underincorporator range, and only four other subjects, all of whom had *Zd* scores between 0 and −3.0 in the first test, had *Zd* scores of −.3.5 or less at the first retest. The 18-month retest data show that 26 of the 279 had *Zd* scores of −3.5 or less, including 20 who had similar scores in the pretreatment test. These data suggest that underincorporation is corrected somewhat easily by most forms of intervention. The data concerning overincorporation for this group is quite different. Forty-seven of the 279 patients (17%) had *Zd* scores of +3.5 or greater in the pretreatment test. At the first retest, 71 subjects, including 42 of the original 47, had scores in the overincorporative range. The 18-month retest data show that the frequency had increased to 89 and included 69 who had been overincorporative in the first retest, and 44 of the 47 who had scores in that range in the pretreatment test. The 27-month retest data are most striking, because 102 of the 279 (37%) had *Zd* scores greater than +3.0, including 42 of the original 47 and 86 of the 89 from the second retest. A closer inspection of the data revealed that all but three of the 24 subjects who moved into the overincorporator range in the first retest were continuing in treatment, as were all subjects who moved into that range at the second retest and all 14 subjects who moved into the range at the 27-month retest. Thus unlike underincorporation, which appears to be altered easily, overincorporation does not appear to change as a function of intervention. To the contrary, it appears to be provoked by long-term intervention. This is probably because intervention, as a process, promotes a greater attentiveness to, and searching through, of stimuli.

Underincorporation appears to be a clear liability, except for the young child, because of stimulus neglect. Conversely, overincorporation can be advantageous in a variety of situations, especially those in which careful processing of information is important. Apparently, overincorporation becomes a liability when the subject has the experience that time available for processing is insufficient. Exner and Stanley (1979) used four subjects from each of the three categories in a time estimation pilot study. Subjects were seated in a totally darkened room and asked to estimate time intervals of 2, 6, and 15 minutes. The four overincorporators each underestimated the actual amount of elapsed time for each of the intervals. Subjects in the average range tended to overestimate elapsed time for 15 minutes, but not for either of the other intervals. The underincorporators had a mixed performance, with two underestimating the two-minute intervals, but overestimating the five- and 15-minute intervals, and the remaining two overestimating all three intervals.

Although overincorporation does appear frequently among people who are more ob-sessive or perfectionistic, it should not be misconstrued as a good "diagnostic" indicator for that feature or for psychopathology in general. Nearly 18% of the adult nonpatient normative sample have *Zd* scores in the overincorporative range. A review of the records of 100 obsessive and 100 hysteroid outpatients, drawn randomly from the protocol pool at the Rorschach Research Foundation, reveals that 51 of the obsessives and 23 of the hys-teroids have *Zd* scores greater than + 3.0. Similarly, 31% of the protocols in the schizo-phrenic reference sample, 30% of the records in the sample of depressives, and 19% of the character disorder group have this same characteristic. In addition, nearly 25% of the nonpatient children between the ages of 10 and 16 have *Zd* scores greater than + 3.0. Underincorporation is most common among younger children. Nearly 28% of nonpatient children between the ages of five and nine have *Zd* scores of less than − 3.0, as contrasted with only 7% of the adult nonpatient group. The schizophrenic sample shows that 21% are underincorporators, as are 18% of the depressives and 19% of the character problems. Whereas overincorporation is probably not a viable treatment objective, underincorpora-tion should be considered as a high priority target for change when discovered in the record of an adolescent or adult because its presence, as a cognitive tactic, can be very disruptive to other operations, especially those involving complex decision making. The data suggest that it can be altered most easily by the creation of delaying tactics, using procedures such as those described by Meichenbaum (1974).

COGNITIVE RIGIDITY AND DYSFUNCTION *(PSV, CONFAB)*

It has been noted earlier that the Rorschach has, at best, only limited value as an index of intelligence or providing information about discrete cognitive operations such as atten-tion-concentration, memory operations, and such. Nonetheless, there are instances in which unusual responses or response patterns occur which provide a strong hint that some cognitive operations are limited or impaired. These involve the responses for which the Special Scores *PSV* (Perseveration) or *CONFAB* (Confabulation) have been assigned. The criteria for coding these unusual responses, described in Chapter 9, should leave no doubt that they signify some sort of cognitive problem.

Perseverations are the more frequent of these two types of answers, but even so, they are uncommon, especially among adults. Approximately 5% of the subjects in the adult nonpatient sample gave *PSV* responses, but never more than one each. They appear signif-icantly more often among the three adult psychiatric reference samples with approxi-mately 15% of the schizophrenics and depressives giving at least one and as many as three, and the character problem group containing 24% who gave at least one and as many as two. *PSV*'s occur much more frequently among younger children. For instance, the sample of five-year-old nonpatients includes 50% who gave at least one and as many as four *PSV* answers. Similarly, 44% of the subjects in the eight-year-old group gave at least one *PSV*, and as many as three. The upper limit of the range does not decrease to one until after age 11 and even then the younger teenage nonpatient groups include as many as 23%, each giving one *PSV*.

Patients with *severe* neurological impairments tend to give a higher frequency of *PSV* answers; however, they are typically of the "mechanistic" variety, that is, repeating the same answer on each of several consecutive cards. Neurologically involved patients who are only mildly or moderately impaired show no greater frequency of *PSV* answers than do psychiatric patients.

The overwhelming majority of *PSV* answers (86%) are "within card perseverations." In effect, the subject delivers almost the same response as the next answer to the blot as was given previously. When this occurs, it appears to signal a failure of cognitive shifting, and the implication is that the subject has some problem with cognitive inflexibility or *rigidity* as related to information processing or decision making. Obviously, many elements such as neurological impairment, intellectual deficit, or a kind of psychological paralysis can create such a condition. The high frequency with which it occurs among younger children suggests that, in some instances, the cognitive operations have not developed to a more adult-like level. If this is true, intelligence test data may provide important clues in sorting through this finding.

If the *PSV* occurs only once in a record, it probably indicates that the subject was momentarily rigid in decision or selection operations, an event that can occur in many people. If the *PSV* frequency is 2, a careful review of non-Rorschach data related to cognitive operations is clearly in order, even if the subject shows clear and unequivocal features of a major disturbance. Whenever the *PSV* value exceeds 2, there is no question that the cognitive functioning of the subject, other than a young child, should be thoroughly evaluated as might be done by some form of neuropsychological screening.

If the *PSV* responses, regardless of frequency, are "across card perseverations," such as the subject reporting the *same* two people fighting, or the *same* butterfly, on two or three different cards, a different kind of shift failure is implied, and is probably not related to cognitive limitations. Instead, these kinds of answers signal a marked preoccupation, usually provoked by a psychopathological state, and occurring most commonly among seriously disturbed psychiatric subjects. When "across card" perseverations occur, the interpreter should make a decision about whether and/or how best to pursue the implications of the responses. For example, if the content has an interpersonal feature such as people fighting, TAT stories might provide some very enlightening information. On the other hand, a carefully developed history is often the best source from which information concerning preoccupations is derived.

Confabulations (*CONFAB*) are much more rare than the *PSV*. They do not occur among nonpatient adults or any of the adult psychiatric reference samples. They do appear once among the samples of nonpatient children for the age groups 5, 6, 7, 9, and 12, and twice in the eight-year-old group. Rorschach hypothesized that they represent a form of impaired perception such as might be found among intellectually limited, organic, or schizophrenic subjects. Obviously, it is a highly unique form of response in which some of the more important cognitive controls fail, or are lacking. As might be expected, research concerning the *CONFAB* is sparse. Most Rorschach examiners will never take a record that contains a *CONFAB* response unless they deal frequently with very young children or people who have notable intellectual deficits. The protocol pool at the Rorschach Research Foundation includes 17 records collected from severely retarded young adults who have Full Scale WAIS I.Q.s of less than 65, a population for which the Rorschach is usually not applicable. Although the records are very brief and barren, seven of the 17 do contain legitimate *CONFAB* answers. *CONFAB* responses should not be confused with autistic or bizarre responses such as are commonplace among schizophrenic or psychotic subjects. Those are coded with other Special Scores. The *CONFAB* involves a blatant overgeneralization that often disregards the natural contours of the blot. It seems to reflect a serious form of intellectual dysfunction or alogical cognitive operation, neither of which is characteristic of common psychopathological states. Obviously, if one does occur, other forms of cognitive evaluation are required.

CONVENTIONALITY AND PERCEPTUAL ACCURACY *(P, X + %, F + %, X − %)*

One of the most important issues in describing personality functioning is whether the subject is oriented toward making conventional or acceptable responses. One person can be ultraconventional, or another can be overly idiosyncratic. Either of these orientations toward reality can be a liability to effective adaptation. At the extreme, a person may be prone to distort perceptual inputs, and this can be a very serious impediment to efforts at maintaining effective adjustment in the environment. Six data sources exist in the Structural Summary, the composite of which provides considerable information about these features.

Popular Responses *(P)*   The common or Popular response was originally regarded by Rorschach as reflecting the ability to perceive and respond to the commonplace features of the blots. The high frequency with which these answers occur, at least once in every three records, seems to support that contention. Baughman (1954) found that *P* was one of the most stable features in the test, and least subject to any undue sets created by examiners. His findings are supported in the variety of retest studies reported here and elsewhere (Exner, 1978, 1983; Exner, Armbruster, & Viglione, 1978; Exner & Weiner, 1982) in which the short-term reliabilities range from .84 to .88, and over longer intervals from .79 to .86. Bourguinon and Nett (1955) and Hallowell (1956) have demonstrated that the listing of Populars holds well for other cultural groups, a finding also supported in work presented here. Leighton and Kluckhorn (1947), Honigmann (1948), Joseph and Murray (1951), and Fried (1977) have all demonstrated that some responses are uniquely Popular for specific cultures; however, they are usually added Populars rather than replacements for the basic listing. Beck (1932), Kerr (1934), and Hertz (1940) all reported a low incidence of *P* among intellectually retarded subjects. Ames et al. (1971) has reported that a gradual increase in the frequency of Popular answers occurs among children as they become older, a finding similar to that found in the nonpatient sample presented here.

In that *P* has a finite limit of 13, as opposed to other Rorschach variables, it is relatively easy to identify deviant frequencies. Nonpatient adults average nearly seven with a mode of 6, schizophrenics average about four with a mode of 4 (which is significantly lower than for nonpatients, $p < .02$). Depressives have an average of slightly more than five, but with a mode of 4, and the character disorders group averages about five, with a mode of 5. The skewness and kurtosis values of the curves for each group suggest that the distribution follows a relatively normal curve. Thus it would be expected that most adult subjects should render between five and eight Popular responses. When this is not the case, the data become interpretively important.

A low frequency of Popular responses in the record of an adult, four or less, reflects either an inability *or* unwillingness of the subject to deliver that which may be the most obvious possible answer. *It does not necessarily signify poor reality testing,* but simply that, for some reason, the subject offered responses which were less typical than expected.

Interestingly, the correlation between the frequency of P answers and the $X+\%$ is negligible, $-.02$ for 100 nonpatient adults (Exner, Viglione, & Gillespie, 1984). Thus it does not necessarily hold true that the person oriented to giving commonplace answers will also yield a considerable frequency of Popular responses. According to these findings, the $X+\%$ can be quite substantial and yet a relatively low number of Popular answers might be included in the record. Low P, as noted above, simply indicates that a subject has not responded in the most economical or conventional manner possible in light of the requirements of the task. It may signal serious pathology, but it also may signal a more unique personality who does not violate reality, but instead tends to deal with it in a common, but not highly conventional manner. The basic key to sorting through this issue will rest with the data of the $X+\%$.

It is also useful to review the Sequence of Scores to identify those cards to which Popular responses were not given. Table 24 in Chapter 8 includes the percentages of nonpatients and nonschizophrenic patients used in developing the Form Quality Table, who gave Popular responses to the blots. As noted there, the range is considerable. More than 90% of the subjects gave the Popular response to Card VIII, whereas only about 35% gave the Popular response to Card II. Thus if P is low, it is expected that the few Populars given will involve the blots to which high percentages of Populars occur—namely, VIII, V, I, and III. If P is consistently absent to these Cards, the interpreter is likely to find other evidence indicating the presence of severe pathology, or an intense form of nonconformity.

On the other end of the continuum, some subjects give an overabundance of Popular answers. If Lambda is high, greater than 1.5, this may simply reflect the effort to economize described in Chapter 14. Conversely, if Lambda is not high, the elevation in Popular answers probably indicates an orientation toward the more simplistic and correct, and can hint of a commitment to conventionality that is well beyond that which might be expected. Subjects who give many Popular responses usually have a high $X+\%$, and this is the next point in the composite data cluster to be reviewed.

Form Quality *(X+%, F+%, X−%)*   One of the most important elements among the structural data of the Rorschach is the form quality. Form is a basic ingredient to almost all Rorschach answers. Baughman (1959), in his classic work on the stimulus features of the blots, clearly demonstrated the dominant role that form plays in the formulation of most answers. His work, and that of Exner (1959), can be viewed as offering clear evidence for the important role of this determinant. In both works the color and shading properties of the blots were altered, sometimes causing major variations in the frequencies for the use of different determinants and/or response contents. *In both studies,* however, the proportion of responses that include form remained relatively stable. Mason, Cohen, and Exner (1985) have reported on a series of factor analyses of Rorschach data for groups of nonpatients, schizophrenics, and depressives. Although the overall factor structures were different for each group, form was consistently a dominant element in the first factor for each group.

Rorschach noted that a substantial portion of responses are pure F, and that almost all of the remaining responses will be marked by some inclusion of contour features. He postulated that the manner and quality in which form is applied in creating the response represents the subject's ability to perceive things conventionally, or realistically. In that context, he devised a scheme of differentiating the form quality of answers into + (good) or $-$ (poor), and created the $F + \%$ to reflect the percentage of good *Pure* form responses in the record, arguing that when that percentage is low, it equates with limited perceptual accuracy and possibly poor reality testing.

Generally, the inclusion of form in a response has been considered as an "ego" or thinking operation. Rapaport et al. (1946), for example, drawing from the concepts of ego psychology, argue that the use of form denotes a process of formal reasoning in which the mediation of the stimulus calls attention to the contours. Implicit in the operation is the direction of attention, forms of control, and making discriminating judgments with regard to the standards of the environment. Korchin (1960) has discussed the process in the conceptual framework of perceptual organizing activity. Beck (1945) postulated that when the quality of the form use is good, the subject demonstrates a respect for reality, whereas the frequent use of poor form indicates a disregard for this element. The bulk of research concerning form quality that was published during the first 50 years after Rorschach's death focused on the $F + \%$, and gained considerable support for his contentions about it.

Form Quality-Form *(F + %)*   As Molish (1967) has noted, the $F + \%$ tends to vary with both intellect and the affective state of the subject. Much early Rorschach research concerned its relation to intellect. Beck (1930, 1932) reported relatively high correlations between the low $F + \%$ and limited intellectual endowment. Similar findings were reported later by Klopfer and Kelley (1942) and Sloan (1947). However, studies concerning the relationship between the $F + \%$ and nonretarded subjects have yielded more contradictory findings. Several (Paulsen, 1941; Holzberg & Belmont, 1952; Abrams, 1955; Armitage et al., 1955) reported significant correlations between $F + \%$ and I.Q. or M.A., but others (Wishner, 1948; Gibby, 1951; Taulbee, 1955) have reported that no single Rorschach variable, or grouping of variables, shows consistently significant correlations with intelligence. Those findings are consistent with the report of Mason and Exner (1985). Ames et al. (1971) found that the $F + \%$ is generally low for very young children, but that it typically exceeds 80% by the sixth year.

A review of studies concerning brain-injured subjects (Molish, 1959) indicates that substantial variations exist for form quality, a finding that Molish interpreted to represent differences in the type of damage experienced and the consequent impairment to adaptive functioning. The data concerning $F + \%$ among geriatric subjects are also somewhat mixed. Klopfer (1946), Davidson and Kruglov (1952), Ames et al. (1954), and Caldwell (1954) all noted a decline in the mean $F + \%$ in older subjects; however, Prados and Fried (1943) and Chesrow et al. (1949) reported that older subjects maintain a relatively high $F + \%$.

The most striking data concerning the $F + \%$ have generated from the studies of more severely disturbed psychiatric patients, and especially schizophrenics. Weiner (1966) pointed out: "Virtually all studies of $F + \%$ in schizophrenia and control groups have replicated the findings presented by Beck and Rickers-Ovsiankina in their historically significant 1938 contributions." In each of those studies schizophrenics showed a mean $F + \%$ in the 60s, whereas controls yielded significantly higher means, 87.3 for the Rickers group, and 83.9 for the Beck group. Similar findings have been reported by Friedman (1952), Berkowitz and Levine (1953), Knopf (1956), and Molish and Beck (1958). Sherman (1952) divided a group of 71 nonpatients and 66 schizophrenics into high and low responder groups. He found that the $F + \%$ differentiated the nonpatients from the schizophrenics regardless of record length. These accumulated findings led Beck to suggest that whenever the $F + \%$ equals 60% or lower, it is indicative of serious psychopathology, or representative of marked intellectual limitations or brain dysfunction. That suggestion coincides well with the data for the adult nonpatient normative sample, which shows a mean of 76 with a standard deviation of 17.

Goldberger (1961) used an isolation design and found that subjects with higher $F + \%$'s were more capable of handling the "primary process intrusions of sensory deprivation." Baker and Harris (1949) came to similar conclusions from a design using "speed quality" under stress. Several authors report a significant increase in the $F + \%$ as the result of therapeutic change (Piotrowski, 1939; Kisker, 1942; Beck, 1948); however, Zamansky and Goldman (1960) reported on a well-designed study of 96 hospitalized patients and found no significant increase in $F + \%$ following intervention, although a "global" analysis of the pre- and posttreatment records was significantly differentiating. Exner and Murillo (1973) found that the $F + \%$'s of 53 schizophrenic subjects increased approximately 10 percentage points (which is not statistically significant) at discharge from hospitalization as contrasted with their admission records.

Although the $F + \%$ can often provide a valuable input to the interpretation of a record, it does have marked limitations. As Weiner (1966) has pointed out, it often represents only a small proportion of the total responses and, as such, may offer only a glimpse of how appropriately form has been used. Its value is probably limited to records in which at least eight Pure F responses occur, or when Lambda is greater than .70. When neither of those criteria are met, it signals that the $F + \%$ will be based on a very small number of responses, and thus the percentage can shift dramatically as a function of the FQ coding of one or two answers. It was for this reason that Weiner (1966) recommended the use of the Extended $F + \%$, a calculation first described by Rapaport, et al. (1946) and elaborated on by Schafer (1954). It included all responses in which F was the primary feature in the determinant, such as Pure F, FC, FC', FT, and so on. Weiner correctly pointed out that this variable might be a more reliable measure of perceptual accuracy because it represents a larger number of answers in most protocols.

Feldman et al. (1954) reported a correlation of approximately .80 between the $F + \%$ and the Extended $F + \%$, although Cass and McReynolds (1951) had previously reported that the Extended $F + \%$ is generally higher than the $F + \%$ for nonpatient adults. Exner (1974) reported correlations of .78 between $F + \%$ and the Extended $F + \%$ among nonpatients, .73 among schizophrenics, and .62 among inpatient nonschizophrenics. That series of studies also revealed that nearly 35% of all $FQ -$ codings occur to responses in which the form feature is *not* the dominant characteristic, such as CF, YF, and so on. Those findings led to the decision to test a calculation that would include the form quality for all responses in the record.

Extended Form Quality *(X + %)*   Early studies on the $X + \%$ illustrate that is does discriminate quite well among nonpatient and the more seriously disturbed psychiatric groups (Exner, 1974, 1978). The mean $X + \%$ for nonpatients, both children and adults, tends to hover around 80%. Standard deviations are typically around 10%. Standard deviations for patient groups tend to be slightly, but not significantly, higher, indicating a somewhat greater dispersion of the scores. Similarly, means for patient groups tend to be somewhat lower than for nonpatients, but usually not significantly lower unless the patient group consists of seriously disturbed subjects. For instance, the mean $X + \%$ for schizophrenics is 53%, and as will be noted in Table M, 85% of the schizophrenics in the reference sample have $X + \%$'s lower than 70%, as contrasted with only 10% of the nonpatient normative sample. Retest reliabilities for the $X+\%$ are consistently high, over both brief and lengthy intervals, usually ranging from the mid .80's to low .90's, and it is the *only* variable that shows a consistently high retest reliability when studied longitudinally from age 8 through age 16 (Exner, Thomas, & Mason, 1985). It has proven to be an important variable in the Suicide Constellation (Exner & Wylie, 1977), and a critical variable in the identification of schizophrenia (Exner, 1978, 1983; Exner & Weiner, 1982).

Interpretively, the $X+\%$ provides data that relate to the use of the form features of the blots in a commonplace, reality-oriented manner. Although some aspects of perceptual accuracy are related to it, it is probably more of a measure of perceptual and/or mediational conventionality, because the calculation is based on the proportion of answers that are defined as commonplace by frequency criteria. Thus when the $X+\%$ is high—that is, greater than 90%—it suggests that the subject may be overly conventional in translating stimulus inputs, and possibly sacrificing individuality to do so. If this is true, it will usually be confirmed by an elevation in Popular responses and, in the instance of the perfection-oriented person, also by the presence of an elevation in the frequency of Dd answers.

When the $X+\%$ is low—that is, less than 70%—it signifies that the subject tends to translate stimulus fields in ways that are more atypical. A low $X+\%$ may be caused by any or a combination of three features, perceptual-mediational distortion, overcommitment to individuality, or failures in modulating affective experiences. The determination of which of those features exist requires a review of three other data points, the $X-\%$, and the frequency distributions of the form quality coding for the entire record (FQx) and for the pure F responses (FQf).

Perceptual-Mediational Distortion $(X-\%)$ The $X-\%$ represents the proportion of uncommon responses in the record that disregard the appropriate use of the contours of the blots. These are the answers in which the objects specified are, at best, very difficult to see, and in many instances impossible to find. In effect, they are violations of reality. Minus responses are not uncommon, but usually occur in low frequencies. For example, nearly 80% of the adults in the nonpatient normative sample gave at least one minus answer, and the mean $X-\%$ for the group is 6%. Nonschizophrenic patient groups tend to give slightly but not significantly more minus answers. The depressive reference sample shows that 91% of those subjects gave at least one minus response. The mode for the group is 2, and the mean $X-\%$ is 15%. Higher frequencies of minus responses are common among schizophrenic subjects. The reference sample of schizophrenics shows a mean for $FQ-$ of more than 6, a mode of 5, and a mean $X-\%$ of 31%.

When the $X-\%$ is elevated, that is, greater than 15%, it should be cause for concern. It indicates that the subject is having some difficulty in translating perceptual inputs appropriately or accurately. It is important to try to distinguish whether the impairment is specific or diffuse. In many cases, impairments that are created by preoccupations may be revealed by a clustering of the minus responses in a specific class of contents or determinants. This is most common in protocols that have elevations in the $X-\%$, but with $X+\%$ in the average range. For instance, a review of 60 records of elective surgery patients shows the $X-\%$ to be elevated in 37 cases, but only 11 have $X+\%$'s lower than 70%. Approximately 65% of their minus responses include contents of anatomy or x-ray. Similarly, many subjects who have problems in emotional control give most of their minus form quality in answers that include chromatic color determinants. If no clustering of the minus answers is detected, it should be assumed that the impairment has a more diffuse impact.

Obviously, if the $X+\%$ is low *and* the $X-\%$ is elevated, it is reasonable to conclude that the magnitude of the impairment is considerable, and interfering significantly with the capacity of the subject to make appropriate responses. As the $X-\%$ increases, the greater the probability of inappropriate behavior, and whenever it exceeds 20%, the likelihood of major impairment is substantial.

Form Quality Frequencies *(FQx, FQf)*   In many cases the low $X+\%$ is not created by an abundance of minus answers. Instead, it is the product of a high frequency of unusual (u) responses. As noted earlier, these are low frequency answers that can be seen easily, because they do not violate the appropriate use of the blot contours. They reflect a less common way of translating the stimulus field that still abides by the demands of reality. In effect, they typify those instances in which the subject exerts some of the features of his or her individuality. When they occur in low frequencies, they are probably a healthy sign, but when they occur in excessive numbers, to the point of reducing the $X+\%$ beyond the lower limit of the average range, they can signal an excessive commitment to the self, and an unwillingness to adhere to the standards of conventionality. The difference between low $X+\%$'s based on $FQ-$ responses versus those created by FQu responses have been shown to discriminate ''process and reactive'' schizophrenics (Zukowsky, 1961), improvement among schizophrenics (Saretsky, 1963), and legally sane from legally insane murders (Kahn, 1967).

High frequencies of FQu responses occur in the records of those who, for any of a variety of reasons, feel less committed to conventionality. If the environment makes few demands on this sort of person for conformity to behavioral expectations, the consequence of the low $X+\%$ may be negligible; however, in instances when the environment is less accepting of this unconventional orientation, the likelihood of frequent confrontations is considerable. As might be expected, many subjects who run afoul of social rules and regulations have records in which the $X+\%$ is low because of an elevation in FQu answers, and many also have low P and/or a higher than average Lambda.

Another variable that is itemized in the FQx distribution is the frequency of responses in which form is not used at all, such as *Pure C, T, C'*, and so on. In rare cases the $X+\%$ can be reduced because of a high frequency of these *no form* answers. They represent instances in which the subject was unable or unwilling to inject some aspect of control and/or direction to the affective experience. As such, they also reflect a detachment from, or disregard for, reality and conventionality. If the $X+\%$ is low because the subject is easily overwhelmed by affect, the basic D score will probably be in the minus range. This is most commonly found in the records of very young children, or older subjects who are less mature or experiencing intense distress. These people may be quite aware of conventionality but simply unable to modulate their feelings in ways that permit them to engage in conventional behaviors. Conversely, if the basic D score is zero or greater, it suggests that the low $X+\%$, high no form subject is more prone to give way to feelings rather than attempt to invest more effort required for control.

CHARACTERISTICS OF IDEATION *(a:p, M^a:M^p, M Quality,* SUM6 *Sp Sc)*

Four sets of data in the Structural Summary can often add useful information concerning some of the characteristics of ideation. These include the two active-passive ratios, the form quality distribution of the *M* responses, and the frequency and WSum6 data concerning the Special Scores, *DV, INCOM, DR, FABCOM, ALOG,* and *CONTAM*. When studied collectively, they sometimes create an important yield concerning flexibility in changing sets, tendencies toward passivity, abuses of fantasy, and/or problems in thinking and logic.

The *a:p* Ratio   Rorschach suspected that differences in the type of movement answers could be used to discriminate features of personality. He described them as being marked by *flexion* or *extension,* the former being defined as those in which the action is toward the center of the blot, the latter for those in which the action pulled away from the center axis of the blot. He argued that extensor movement answers reflect assertiveness, whereas flexor answers indicate submissiveness or compliance. Hammer and Jacks (1955) found that aggressive sex offenders give significantly more extensor *M*'s, whereas the more passive offenders, such as exhibitionists, tend to give more flexor *M*'s. Mirin (1955) found that schizophrenics giving predominantly extensor *M*'s were resistive to contradictions in a memory task, whereas those giving more flexor *M*'s were more willing to give in to the contradictions. Wetherhorn (1956) used a special series of blots designed to provoke more movement answers and found no relationships between the extensor-flexor *M*'s and measures of ascendancy-submissiveness, or masculinity-femininity.

Both Beck et al. (1961) and Piotrowski (1960) warned about the limitations of approaching movement answers using Rorschach's flexor-extensor concept. Beck correctly pointed out that many movement answers do not meet either of those criteria, because they are "static," such as a person standing, or sleeping, or looking. Piotrowski classified *M*'s as favorable versus unfavorable using features such as cooperativeness, lack of restraint, confident postures, and such, and was able to differentiate effective and nonadaptive parole conduct of released army prisoners. He also evaluated successful and unsuccessful business executives and found that the successful group gave more self-assertive and confident *M* answers. Exner (1974) found that first admission acute schizophrenics and forensic subjects gave significantly more hostile *M* and *FM* answers than other psychiatric groups or nonpatients. He also found that when all movement answers were coded as *active* or *passive,* following a suggestion by Piotrowski, active movement responses occurred significantly more in the records of the acute schizophrenics, subjects with a history of assaultiveness (regardless of diagnosis), and a group of character disorders, whereas passive movement answers occurred more frequently in the records of long-term inpatient schizophrenics, depressives, and outpatient neurotics. He also noted that a proportional difference score, comparing the frequencies of active and passive movement answers, differentiated patients from nonpatients. Those findings suggested that a more consistent form of thinking or inner experience is common among people experiencing difficulties in adjustment; that is, less shifting occurs from the forms of ideation characterized by the active or passive designations. In other words, ideational sets that are formed are more difficult to interrupt or alter.

The results of several investigations seem to support this postulate, and suggest that the data of the *a:p* ratio relate to the features of cognitive flexibility versus narrowness or constriction. Exner (1974) found that significantly larger proportional difference scores between *a* and *p* existed among unimproved patients as contrasted with improved patients, although both groups had considerable discrepancies between the values for *a* and *p* at the onset of treatment. Similarly, Exner and Wylie (1974) found that therapist ratings concerning responsiveness of patients in two treatment sessions were significantly higher for those who entered treatment with the values in the *a:p* ratio less than proportions of 3:1 than those entering treatment with *a:p* proportions of more than 3:1. Exner and Bryant (1974) asked two groups, each consisting of 15 high school students, to write as many uses as they could formulate for each of eight items, such as a key, a toothpick, a golf tee, and so on, considered separately or in combinations. Subjects in one group all had values of five or more in one side of the *a:p* ratio, and zero in the other side. Subjects in the second group all had *a:p* ratios in which the value in one side exceeded the other by two or less. The groups did not differ for the number of uses for the items considered separately; however, the group with *a:p* values close together recorded more than twice as many uses for the items taken in various combinations.

The reliability correlations for active and passive movement are generally quite high for both brief and lengthy intervals. They range from the mid .80's to low .90's for active movement, and from the upper .70's to mid .80's for passive movement. The cognitive operations with which they correlate also seem pervasive in other ideational activities. For instance, Exner (1974) paid 34 female subjects to induce a 10-minute period of daydreaming on each of 25 consecutive days, and to record those daydreams in a diary. The activity of the central figure in the daydream was scored as being active or passive, and for whether a shift from one characteristic to the other occurred. Those scores were then compared with the data from the *a:p* ratios in the Rorschachs of the subjects that had been collected prior to the onset of the daydream routine. Twenty of the 34 subjects had *a:p* ratios in which one value was more than three times that of the other, whereas 14 had *a:p* ratios in which neither value was more than twice the other. The results showed that subjects who give a large majority of Rorschach movement responses in a single direction also have the majority of daydream scores in the same direction, and have relatively few shifts in the activity of the central figure of the daydream. The opposite is true for the subjects who have less discrepant values for active and passive movement answers in their Rorschachs. They reported daydreams in which an almost equal mixture of active and passive characteristics are assigned to the central figure, and showed shifts from one characteristic to the other in a significant number of their daydreams.

This collection of findings suggests that, as the numbers in the ratio become more discrepant from each other, ideational sets tend to be more well fixed and difficult to alter. Conversely, as the numbers in the ratio tend to approximate each other, greater flexibility in ideational or cognitive approach to issues seems to exist. The notion of flexibility-inflexibility should not be taken to identify pathology automatically, or even a proneness to pathology, for that is not the case. Some people are less flexible than others in their ability to take a different perspective in attitudes, ideas, or values, but this does not necessarily predispose pathology. Individual differences are rampant for this feature among most any population. Thus the data of the *a:p* ratio bring some focus concerning the psychological proneness of the subject to experience, consider, or think about events or relationships between events, in more varied ways as contrasted to a more narrow and well-fixed set of conclusions. Clearly, the presence of cognitive or ideational inflexibility is often important in understanding the persistence of seemingly maladaptive symptoms or habits, and can be a major element of concern in planning forms of intervention. Practically every therapist has encountered the patient who, in one session, seems to grasp reflections or interpretations quite profoundly, but in the very next session reacts to the same sort of material as if the previous experience never occurred. Many therapists tend to interpret this phenomenon as a form of resistance or defensiveness, but it is more likely that a characteristic of inflexibility exists, tending to inhibit a full processing and/or integration of the previous material.

Although assaultive subjects, acute schizophrenics, and some subjects with character problems do tend to give significantly more active movement than other psychiatric groups, research seeking specific behavioral correlates with active movement has yielded negative findings. In other words, a high frequency of active movement responses *does not* equate with an unusual frequency of active behaviors, or with any special class of behaviors. This is apparently because most people give more active than passive movement responses. Adult nonpatients give nearly twice as many active movement answers as passive responses, and that ratio is relatively consistent for most groups, including nonpatient children. Only 3% of nonpatient adults give more passive than active movement responses, and the proportions of nonpatient children giving more passive than active movement answers range from 2 to 12%, depending on the age group.

Some patient groups have higher proportions of subjects who give more passive than active movement. For example, this occurs for 21% of the subjects in the schizophrenic reference sample, 24% in the sample of depressives, and 30% in the character disorder reference group. Exner (1978) devised an index of behavioral passivity using 20 items in the Katz Adjustment Scale. The entire KAS was completed for 279 outpatients by a significant other of the patient, 9 months after treatment had been initiated. All subjects were volunteers in a long-term treatment effects study, the design of which required psychological testing and behavioral evaluations at 9-month intervals for at least 3 years, regardless of whether treatment had terminated. Examination of the Rorschachs collected at the 9-month interval revealed that 83 of the 279 subjects had *a:p* ratios in which *p* exceeded *a* by more than 1. Their mean score for the passivity index was 11.6 (*SD* = 4.2). A comparison group of 83 other patients was randomly drawn from the remaining 196 subjects. The mean passivity score for that group was 5.3 (*SD* = 3.3), yielding a highly significant difference between the groups (*p* < .001).

In a related study (Exner & Kazaoka, 1978) videotapes were recorded for the first two sessions of two groups of eight subjects each participating in assertiveness training. Rorschachs were administered prior to the training, and revealed that seven of the 16 trainees had *a:p* ratios in which *p* exceeded *a* by more than 1. The videotapes were scored for the frequencies of verbal and nonverbal dependency gestures by subject, by two groups of three raters each. One group of raters scored only the audio segment of the tapes, whereas the second group scored using both the audio and visual data. The seven subjects who began the training with the *passive a:p* ratios were scored for nearly twice as many verbal dependency statements and approximately the same number of nonverbal dependency gestures during the two sessions as were the other 11 subjects.

The findings of these studies seem to indicate that when people give significantly more passive movement responses—that is, when *p* exceeds *a* by more than 1—a tendency toward more passive and possibly dependent behaviors exists. The tendency toward dependency appears to be even more marked if the record includes at least one food response. Schafer (1954) had postulated that *Fd* responses are related to oral dependency characteristics. In the Exner and Kazaoka study the four assertiveness training subjects who scored highest for dependency gestures had at least one *Fd* response in their records. Those findings provoked another videotape study, involving a class of 24 sixth-grade students. The class was recorded twice during one week, in both instances during art instruction. The students were learning to paint with acrylics and often had reason to request aid from the teacher. The tapes were scored for (1) requests for assistance from the teacher and (2) follow-up questions to the teacher. Contrary to expectations, the six students who had Rorschach $a:p$ ratios in which p exceeds a by more than 1 did not make more requests for assistance than did the other 18 students, but seven students, including three who had passive $a:p$ ratios, with at least one Fd response, made nearly twice as many requests for help, and nearly four times as many follow-up questions after the help was provided than did the other students. A review of the protocols of 36 inpatients, diagnosed according to the DSM-III criteria as being "Passive-Dependent," included 21 with Fd responses, as contrasted with only five of 36 randomly selected nonpatient records, two of 36 schizophrenic records drawn randomly, and eight of 36 records of depressive patients drawn randomly from the protocol pool.

The M^a:M^p Ratio The findings concerning the $a:p$ ratio suggested that a closer examination of the M^a:M^p ratio might also reveal useful data concerning some of the ideational characteristics of subjects. A review of the daydream ratings of active and passive (Exner, 1974) for 34 female subjects showed that seven of the 34 had 15 or more daydreams that were rated as passive, whereas none of the remaining subjects had more than nine passive daydreams. Of additonal interest was the finding that only 11 of the 123 passive daydreams given by those seven subjects contained shifts in the role of the central character, that is, moving from a passive to active role or vice versa. Four of the seven subjects had passive $a:p$ ratios, but *all* seven had M^a:M^p ratios in which the value for passive M was greater than active M. Only one of the remaining 27 records contained more passive M than active M.

Exner, Armbruster, and Wylie (1976) recruited 24 nonpatient adults who had been administered Rorschachs for the normative sample. Each had given at least six M responses, and 12 had given more M active than M passive, whereas the remaining 12 had given more M^p than M^a. They were asked to write endings for each of six TAT stories that had been created to present dilemma situations. For example, the figure in Card 3BM was featured as having lost a job, the boy in 13B was described as having wandered away from a picnic and was lost, and so on. The story endings were scored for (1) positive or negative outcome, (2) outcomes involving new people injected into the story, and (3) outcomes initiated by the central figure of the story versus those contingent on the actions of someone else. The overwhelming majority of the outcomes were positive (88%) and did not differentiate the two groups. The 12 subjects with higher M^p added new people to 38 of the 72 endings (53%), whereas the higher M^a subjects added new people to only 17 of their endings (24%, $p < .05$). The most striking difference concerned the initiation of outcomes. Forty-nine of the 72 outcomes given by the higher M^p group (68%) were initiated by someone other than the central figure of the story. The higher M^a group did this in only 21 (29%) of their endings ($p < .01$).

Additional data contributing to an understanding of the M^a:M^p ratio has been gleaned from therapist ratings. Fourteen therapists completed ratings for 56 patients after the third, sixth, and ninth treatment sessions (Exner, 1978). All had entered dynamically oriented psychotherapy. The ratings concerned a variety of treatment issues and observations, such as promptness, estimates about motivation for treatment, ease of sharing concerns, and such. Among the items included were ones concerning requests for direction, lengthy intervals of silence during the session, and impressions of a general sense of helplessness. Fifteen of the 56 patients gave pretreatment Rorschachs in which M^p was greater than M^a. The therapist ratings for that group were significantly higher for requests for direction and impressions of a general sense of helplessness when compared with those for the other 41 patients.

Exner (1978) has suggested that when M^p is greater than M^a, it indicates that the ideation of the subject, especially fantasies, will be marked much more than is common by a "Snow White" feature—that is, being more likely to take flight into passive forms of fantasy as a defensive maneuver, and also being less likely to initiate decisions or behaviors if the alternative that others will do so is available. Approximately 11% of the nonpatient adults in the normative sample have this characteristic as contrasted with 26% of the schizophrenic reference sample and 25% of the depressives and character disorders. Interestingly, the percentages are much lower for nonpatient children, ranging from 2 to 9%, depending on the age group.

The Snow White feature is probably much more of a liability for the introversive than for extratensives, because introversives are more prone to rely on the workings of their inner life. It is probably an even greater liability for the schizophrenic. The composite of disturbed thinking and fantasy abuse can only portend poorly for appropriate decision making. This is not relevant only to schizophrenia. Any person who engages in unusual patterns of thinking is more likely to emit poorly organized or implemented decisions. Evidence for the presence of problems in thinking is often revealed in two other data sets in the Structural Summary.

The M Quality   The M Quality distribution consists of a listing of the form quality frequencies for the human movement responses in the record. Because the frequency of M is usually low, ranging from 3 to 10 for the subjects in the adult nonpatient sample, most or all of these are expected to include an appropriate use of form. As noted in Chapter 14, M responses appear to reflect the deliberate directing of thinking and, as such, the more they deviate from the realities of the stimulus field, the more likely the thinking activity will be marked by deviation. M's also include projections that, in some ways, represent some of the inner qualities of the subject. Only three subjects of the 600 in the adult nonpatient sample did not give M responses, and of the 597 who did give at least one M, only 38 (6%) gave $M-$ responses. This is in contrast to 15% of the reference sample of character problems who gave at least one M, 27% of the depressives who had M's in their record, and 73% of the schizophrenics who gave M responses.

The presence of one $M-$ response is sufficient to raise concern about peculiarity in ideation. If the frequency is greater than 1, the likelihood of a marked thinking problem is increased considerably. Two $M-$ responses is an unusual finding, and if more than two occur, the presence of active, disoriented, psychotic-like thinking is practically certain. If some or all of the $M-$ answers are passive, it increases the probability that characteristics are present from which delusional operations evolve. It is also very important to study the contents of $M-$ answers carefully to determine if they have homogeneous features. This is frequently the case in reactive psychoses or in severe disturbances that include a well-fixed delusional system.

A second kind of M response that often signifies disturbed thinking is the one in which there is no form use. These are abstract or symbolic responses, such as "This represents madness," or "It is the depth of depression," or "It smells delicious." They represent a form of detachment from, or marked disregard for, the stimulus field, and may have features which are quite similar to a hallucinatory-like operation. M no form responses are quite rare and when they occur, they should be interpreted in the same context as if a significant elevation in $M-$ responses exists.

Whereas the *M* − and *M* no form responses indicate the probability of serious problems in thinking, *M*u responses represent an idiographic, but not necessarily peculiar form of ideation. One or two *M*u answers can be taken as a positive sign, *if* the record also contains other *M*'s in which the form features are used in a more conventional manner. If the record contains several *M*'s, most or all of which are *M*u, it may indicate that the thinking of the subject is overly unique and/or eccentric, but not necessarily maladaptive. The extent to which this may or may not be a liability must be judged in light of other personality characteristics that are indicated in the record, and especially whether there is other evidence of considerable cognitive slippage. If so, this will usually be revealed by an elevation in the number and variety of the six Critical Special Scores.

Six Critical Special Scores & *WSUM6* The six Critical Special Scores—*DV, INCOM, DR, FABCOM, ALOG,* and *CONTAM*—are used to identify events in which some difficulty occurred in cognitive processing. None of these events, with the possible exception of the *CONTAM*, are necessarily cause for concern, *provided* that they occur with very low frequencies. Nearly 75% of the subjects in the nonpatient sample gave at least one response for which one of these six Special Scores was assigned, and the mean for the group is closer to 2 than to 1. Nonpatient children tend to give more. For example, 7-year-olds average more than 5, and 10-year-olds average nearly 4. Collectively, they represent a crude continuum regarding cognitive mismanagement or dysfunction, with the *DV* near one end and signifying modest cognitive slippage, and the *CONTAM* near the other end, representing considerable cognitive dysfunction. The *FABCOM* answers probably fall slightly to the right of the midpoint of the continuum. Generally, nonpatient adults give more of the Special Scores that are on the left side of the continuum, that is, the *DV, INCOM,* and *DR* responses. Twenty-three percent of the 449 nonpatient records that contain any of the six Special Scores include a *DV* response, 58% contain an *INCOM* response, and 46% a *DR* response. Conversely, only 16% of the records containing these Special Scores have a *FABCOM,* 10% an *ALOG,* and only three records in the entire sample contain *CONTAM*'s. At the other extreme, the 320 subject schizophrenic reference samples average more than six Special Scores, and include 304 records (95%) that have at least one. In that group, 56% contain at least one *DV,* 70% at least one *INCOM,* 49% at least one *DR,* 82% one or more *FABCOM*'s, 57% at least one *ALOG,* and nearly 20% contain at least one *CONTAM.*

The *DV* appears to involve brief instances of cognitive mismanagement. Distorted language use or idiosyncratic modes of expression impede the subject's ability to communicate clearly. They appear most commonly among the records of children who have yet to develop the language skills necessary to convey an impression easily. Although not uncommon among adults, they are not expected in the record of a bright person, and when they occur, the content of the *DV* may carry considerable importance. Taken alone, two or three *DV* responses have little importance, but if they occur with a much higher frequency in the adult record, some sort of cognitive problem exists.

INCOM's are the most common of the six Special Scores in the records of nonpatient adults and also appear frequently in the records of children. They signify unusual condensations of blot details in a single object and, as such, apparently indicate a form of discrimination failure, and reflect a kind of concrete reasoning. As with the *DV* responses, one or two *INCOM*'s, as the only Critical Special Scores in the record, usually will not be cause for concern.

DR responses usually represent a more serious form of dysfunction than in either the

DV or *INCOM*. Although they occur in about one-third of the adult nonpatient records and about half of the schizophrenic records, they are most common among subjects with affective problems. For instance, they appear in nearly 90% of the records of the depressive reference sample. They illustrate a peculiarity in the verbiage of the subject that may be the product of poor judgment, but more likely illustrate poor control over ideational impulses. Most *DR* responses are detachments from the task and often consist of circumstantial-like ramblings. The presence of even one *DR* should be weighed carefully, because it could offer a clue to potential ideational instability. Larger numbers of *DR* answers suggest that patterns of disjointed thinking may exist which can interfere significantly with effective decision making.

FABCOM answers typically are more serious than any of the first three because they involve an irrational synthesizing action. They are not uncommon among younger children but, as Weiner and Exner (1978) have noted, the frequency of *FABCOM*'s becomes markedly lower during adolescence. They appear most frequently in the records of schizophrenics, and reflect the very loose associations that often occur in thinking which is inconsistent, disorganized, and primitive. As with the *DR*, the presence of a single *FABCOM* should be weighed carefully, and elevations should be regarded as a very negative sign.

ALOG answers also occur with a considerable frequency among younger children, but that frequency falls markedly during adolescence. They appear in between 10 to 15% of the records for most adult groups, but usually with very low frequencies of one or two. They are much more common in the protocols of severely disturbed subjects, especially schizophrenics. They represent forms of strained reasoning in which faulty cause-and-effect relationships are simplistically created and maintained. They are a mark of poor logic and flawed judgment, either of which can have substantial effects on decision operations and the formation of behaviors.

CONTAM responses illustrate the most severe form of cognitive disorganization that is detected in the Rorschach. They involve a completely unrealistic merging of experience. It may be that some form of perceptual merging also occurs, but this has never been established. It is clear that there is a fluidity of thinking which also involves strained reasoning. The process creates a product that is the antithesis of adaptive behavior.

Ideally, a record will contain none of the six Critical Special Scores but, as has been noted earlier, the majority of subjects from almost most every group manifest one or more of these forms of slippage as they take the test. One, two, or three, especially of the less serious, is not an uncommon finding among nonpatient adults, and even more occur among nonpatient children. However, when the sum exceeds four in the record of an adult, or more than one standard deviation above the age mean for a younger client, the data are too compelling to avoid concluding that some disturbance in thinking exists. In many cases, the sum of the weightings for each of the scores can offer ready information concerning the extent to which impairment may exist (WSUM6).

Nonpatient adults have a mean WSUM6 of nearly four and a standard deviation indicating that six, or even seven may not be uncommon. If a more liberal application of two standard deviations above the mean is applied, a WSUM6 greater than nine reflects less than 8% of the nonpatient sample. However, the interpretation of data concerning the six Critical Special Scores should not be approached concretely. Obviously, the presence of a combination of three *DV*'s and three *INCOM*'s can be regarded more favorably than if the combination consists of two *DR*, two *FABCOM*, and two *ALOG* responses. The first combination yields a WSUM6 of nine, whereas the second yields a WSUM6 of 24. The second combination offers reasonably clear evidence of disturbed thinking, whereas the first falls along a border of maybe or maybe not. But there are other ways to approach the data. It is faulty to assume that all responses falling into the same category represent the same magnitude of slippage or disarray. For example, "A bat with his hands out" is an *INCOM* as is, "A 12-legged fox." Both involve some sort of cognitive dysfunction, but the latter is much more bizarre than the former. Similarly, "Two dogs playing patty-cake," and "Two women tearing apart the propeller of an ocean liner" are both *FAB-COM* answers, but again, the latter is much more bizarre and suggests a greater magnitude of dysfunction. Thus in addition to a review of the frequency data for each category, the interpreter must also consider the characteristics of the specific responses.

It is also important to review whether the Special Scores cluster in any particular way, such as all, or almost all, involving the same determinants or contents. If clustering does occur, it may provide some clarification about the features of the thinking problem. For example, a review of 70 protocols of inpatients diagnosed as paranoid schizophrenic by DSM-III criteria reveals that nearly two-thirds of their Critical Special Scores appear in responses involving human content, even though human content responses constitute only about 25% of the total *R* in their records. This is not too surprising, because paranoid ideation often focuses on elements related to interpersonal relations. In a similar pattern, subjects in the depressive reference sample gave more than 60% of their six Critical Special Scores in responses that also have achromatic or chromatic color determinants, even though those answers represent less than one-third of the responses that they delivered. It seems logical to postulate that this probably reflects some of the impact of their affective difficulties on their thinking.

CHARACTERISTICS OF AFFECT *(FC:CF + C, Afr, S, CP, Blends)*

It has been noted in the preceding chapter that the variables included in the right side of the *eb* provide some information about irritating affective stimulation that is being experienced by the subject, but they do not address some other important issues concerning the affective experience of the subject. These concern the extent to which affective displays are modulated, interest and/or willingness for affective exchange, complexity of affect, and the like. Five variables in the Structural Summary often serve to flesh out useful information concerning some of the ways in which the subject uses and/or responds to affect.

The *FC:CF + C* Ratio   This ratio provides an index of the extent to which emotional discharges are modulated. The data of the ratio are most meaningful when studied in relation to the data of the *EB* and the *D* scores. Although the issue of modulation is important for any person, it becomes even more so for the extratensive, who is prone to approach coping demands with a more affectively oriented, trial-and-error style. In a similar vein, if either or both the *D* scores fall into the minus range, controls will be much more limited, and the capacities for modulation of affect will be more vulnerable to interference by even modest, but unexpected stress experiences.

As indicated earlier, less cognitive effort is required to identify colors than forms. Thus color responses can involve a more passive process, but when specific form demands are injected into the translation of color stimuli, it suggests that more cognitive control has been inserted into the process. It is for this reason that *FC* responses equate more with a passive affective experience that has been controlled and/or directed by cognitive elements. On the other hand, *CF* and *C* responses illustrate instances in which the subject has been more prone to give way to the affective stimulus, and inject less cognitive modulation into the translation of the stimulus field.

The stability of the directionality shown in the ratio is considerable. Exner, Armbruster, and Viglione (1978) found, in their data concerning 100 nonpatient adults retested after 3 years, that if the value in one side of the ratio exceeded the other by at least 1 point in the first test, the same directionality existed in the second test. The same stability has been found in retest studies for both patients and nonpatients when the retest is administered after a briefer interval.

Adult nonpatients give about 1½ to 2½ times more *FC* responses than *CF* + *C*. Children do the opposite, giving significantly more *CF* + *C* than *FC* at every age through age 12, and even into the midadolescent years, the values for *FC* are usually not much greater than for *CF* + *C*. Patient groups tend to have *FC:CF* + *C* ratios that are much more like those of younger clients—that is, being 1:1 or with the greater number on the right side of the ratio. This is probably because most patients experience problems in emotional control more so than is common among nonpatients. There are important exceptions. For instance, analysis of the protocols of 48 outpatients, all being treated for psychosomatic problems, indicates that 27 have *FC:CF* + *C* ratios of 4:1 or greater, and only four have *FC:CF* + *C* ratios in which the value of *FC* is less than 1½ times that of *CF* + *C*. Thus when the ratio exceeds 3:1, it appears to indicate that the subject exerts considerably more effort at modulation of affect discharges than is typical, and when the ratio contains a value on the right side that is equal to or greater than that on the left, it suggests that the subject is less willing or less able to modulate affective displays to the same extent that is commonplace among adults.

A higher right-side value in the ratio should not automatically be translated as signaling *lack* of control, because that issue is probably more contingent on the elements reflected in the *D* score, form quality, and stability of ideation. However, it does suggest that the emotional behaviors will be marked more often by characteristics of intensity or even impulsiveness. For instance, Gill (1966) found that subjects who delay responses in a problem-solving task gave significantly more *FC* than *CF* + *C* answers, whereas those who did not manifest delay in forming their responses gave significantly more *CF* + *C*. There have also been several studies in which a higher frequency of *CF* + *C* responses has been found to correlate with impulsive or aggressive behaviors (Gardner, 1951; Storment & Finney, 1953; Finney, 1955; Sommer & Sommer, 1958; Townsend, 1967).

Stotsky (1952) reported that treatment success is achieved more frequently among schizophrenics whose pretreatment protocols show more *FC* than *CF* + *C*. Exner, Murillo, and Cannavo (1973) found significant shifts from more *CF* + *C* to more *FC* when comparing the pre- and posttreatment records of 105 nonschizophrenic inpatients. Exner and Murillo (1975) found a significantly greater proportion of higher right-side *FC:CF* + *C* ratios in the discharge Rorschachs of patients who relapsed within 12 months following discharge as contrasted with nonrelapsers. Exner (1978) found that 116 of 199 outpatients, who were subsequently rated as improved by significant others, had more *CF* + *C* than *FC* in their pretreatment protocols, but only 61 continued to have more *CF* + *C* in protocols that were collected 28 months after the onset of treatment.

As indicated in Chapter 14, *CF* and *C* responses have considerably lower retest reliabilities than does the combination *CF* + *C*. Nonetheless, the presence of a Pure *C* answer in the *FC:CF* + *C* ratio should not be regarded lightly, except in the records of children for whom such findings are common. Any formless response signifies a failure to modulate an impulse. It may indicate lability—that is, when the person is unable to intercede cognitively because the affective experience is so intense—but it can also signal an instance in which some decision has been made to give way to the impulse rather than exert the effort necessary to intercede. In either instance, the Pure *C* response is commensurate with emotional behaviors that essentially are void of control. If the *FC:CF + C* ratio is marked by multiple Pure *C* answers, the likelihood that at least one will occur in a retest record is substantial. A review of retest data for 300 patient and nonpatient adults reveals that when only one Pure *C* occurred in a first test, the probability of it reoccurring in a second test is no greater than .65, but if two or more Pure *C*'s occurred in the first test, the probability of at least one occurring in the second test exceeds .90. Therefore if multiple Pure *C* responses appear, it is very likely that some behaviors of the subject will be featured by very intense emotional characteristics. Although this may not be disabling, the tendency creates a potential for interference with effective adjustment patterns in the adult.

The Affective Ratio *(Afr)*   Another datum providing information about the responsiveness of a person to emotional stimulation is the index derived from the proportion of answers to the last three blots, the *Afr*. It is one of the more intriguing variables in the test because it is difficult to establish a sound conceptual linkage that easily explains why the empirical data concerning it fall as they do. The retest correlations for the *Afr* are remarkably high. They range from the mid .80's to low .90's for both nonpatient children and adults retested after brief intervals, *and the same range* is found for adults when the retest is administered after a lengthy interval. For instance, Exner, Armbruster, and Viglione (1978) found a retest correlation of .90 for the *Afr* for their 100 nonpatient adults retested after 3 years. Findings such as these make it difficult to discount the notion that some form of style is involved.

Much of the conceptual intrigue concerning the *Afr* generates from the fact that Cards VIII, IX, and X are the only totally chromatic blots in the series. As cited in Chapter 14, the Baughman (1959) data revealed that subjects gave substantially more responses to the standard Rorschach than to a totally achromatic version, and the bulk of the difference was created by more answers to the five blots containing chromatic color. Exner (1962) also found that subjects gave significantly more responses to the last three blots when they were presented in their natural chromatic form than when they were presented in achromatic versions. The obvious conclusion is that chromatically colored stimuli tend to provoke more answers, but that offers no support of substance for the premise that a link exists between responses to chromatically colored stimuli and emotion. There are, however, some data that support that premise.

Exner (1978) subdivided the 100 nonpatient adults retested in the Exner, Armbruster, and Viglione study, using the data of the *EB,* to determine if the high long-term reliability of the *Afr* is consistent by style. The division yielded 37 introversives, 43 extratensives, and 20 ambitents, and the retest correlations were consistently high for all three groups, but the *mean Afr*'s for the groups were quite different from each other. The mean *Afr* for the ambitents actually falls between the means for the other two groups, *which are significantly different from each other* (Introversive = .62, *SD* = .13; Ambitent = .67, *SD* = .11; Extratensive = .79, *SD* = .14, *p* <.05). Thus each group is relatively consistent within itself, but the two extreme groups differ considerably in terms of the proportional average number of responses to the last three cards. This is an intriguing finding, because it coincides with the fact that extratensives tend to become more involved with affect in coping situations. The distributions of *Afr* for the introversives and extratensives overlap considerably, with introversives ranging from .42 to .97, and extratensives ranging from .53 to 1.17. Some introversives have values for *Afr* that exceed either end of the average range of about .50 to .80, *but none of the extratensives have Afr's falling below the average range.*

These findings prompted a review of the records of outpatients participating in the long-term treatment effects study. The 279 subjects, divided on the basis of the *EB* of their pretreatment Rorschachs, include 51 ambients, 99 extratensives, and 128 introversives, with *Afr* means of .73, .69, and .67, respectively; however, the *Afr* distributions for the introversive and extratensive subjects *are almost bimodal.* The introversive sample includes 36 subjects with *Afr's* of less than .40, and another 31 subjects with *Afr's* above .80. Similarly, the extratensive group includes 27 subjects with *Afr's* below .50, and 33 with *Afr's* greater than .90. These findings suggest that although patients, as a group, or as subgroups, do not differ substantially for the mean *Afr,* they do show markedly different distributions of *Afr* values than is found among nonpatients. In other words, patients tend to fall at the upper and lower extremes more often. This group of patients was retested at approximately 9-month intervals, regardless of whether they had terminated or were continuing in treatment. At the end of the 27th month, 199 of the 279 subjects were rated as significantly improved by significant others. A review of their third retest Rorschachs, collected during the 27th or 28th month of the study, showed that 172 remained relatively consistent for *EB* directionality, with 10 still in the ambient range, 92 being introversive, and 69 extratensive. A review of the distribution of *Afr* values for the introversive and extratensive subjects reveals means of .63 and .71, respectively, with the values being *normally distributed for each group.* The bimodality that was evident in the first testing was not apparent at the third retest. Conversely, the distribution of *Afr* values for the 80 subjects who were *not* rated as being improved continued to show considerable bimodality, with 27 subjects with *Afr's* lower than .50, and 24 with *Afr's* higher than .80. One of the more fascinating findings is that 38 of those 51 subjects also had *FC:CF + C* ratios in which *CF + C* is greater than *FC,* but there is *no difference* among subjects falling in the extremes for *EB* style. About as many at each end of the distribution are introversive as are extratensive. Interestingly, 19 of the 27 subjects with low *Afr's* have Adjusted *D* scores of zero or in the plus range, whereas 17 of the 21 subjects with high *Afr's* have Adjusted *D* scores in the minus range.

Data processing completed for this work, following from earlier findings (Exner, 1978), included a random draw of 300 subjects, disregarding patient or nonpatient status, who gave Rorschachs containing at least three achromatic color responses, and 300 subjects who gave no *C'* responses. The mean *Afr* for the group with elevations in *C'* answers is .79 (*SD* = .14), whereas the mean *Afr* for the group giving no achromatic color responses is .55 (*SD* = .16), yielding a significant difference (*p* <.01). These findings appear quite important because they indicate that subjects who have difficulty expressing affect tend to respond to stimuli that seem to have affective properties more frequently than do subjects who do not tend to inhibit or internalize feelings. This finding is even more important when the groups are studied for *EB* style and the frequencies and weighted sum of chromatic color answers. The *C'* positive group included 121 extratensives, 107 introversives, and 72 ambients, with a mean WSUMC of 4.94 (*SD* = 1.87). The *C'* negative group included 103 extratensives, 118 introversives, and 79 ambients, with a WSUMC mean of 4.56 (*SD* = 1.93). In effect, the two samples did not differ significantly for *EB* styles or the WSUMC.

Some of the developmental data also appear to support the notion of a linkage between the *Afr* and receptivity to emotionally toned stimuli. The mean *Afr* for children between the ages of 5 and 8 drops from 1.07 to .81. It hovers in the upper .70's to low .80's through age 12 and then drops gradually again to .72 for the 16-year-old group. The standard deviations at each age fall within .02 to .03 of .15, and the other descriptive statistics concerning the shape of the distributions indicate that most are very close to normality. These data seem to coincide well with what is known about the easy excitability of younger children, and how that feature gradually becomes more subdued or modulated with age.

Thus the style or operation represented by the Affective Ratio seems to involve a psychological receptiveness to emotionally provoking stimuli. It apparently reflects the proneness to invest effort in the cognitive processing of those stimuli,*and the level of processing itself becomes a form of response, which in turn serves as a stimulus to other responses.* It does not relate directly to the issue of affective control, but can have an indirect relationship. For example, elevations signify a tendency toward overresponsiveness, whereas low *Afr*'s signify avoidance tendencies. Overresponsiveness can increase the likelihood for more affective exchanges, which can create an overload on resources and produce more limited controls. Conversely, an awareness of overresponsiveness might cause some to attempt to be more constrained in exchanges to avoid overload, and overcontrol can be a consequence. Similarly, an avoidance of emotionally provocative stimuli could be the product of concerns about control. Obviously, any combination of over- or under-control, and under- or overresponsiveness can create a potential for affective disarray.

The Space Response *(S)*   Data concerning answers that include the use of white space can often add information concerning some of the affective characteristics of the subject. Rorschach postulated that the use of white space in responses represents a form of opposition or negativism, arguing that it requires an alteration in the figure-ground relationship. Beck (1945) and Rapaport et al. (1946) have endorsed this hypothesis, but have also cautioned that it may simply indicate a form of contrariness that may serve to accent the idiographic features of the person. Klopfer et al. (1954) had added to this by suggesting that it can be interpreted as a form of constructive self-assertiveness, whereas Piotrowski (1957) has argued that it can represent a striving for independence. All have emphasized that when it occurs with considerable frequency, it can illustrate some impingement to reality contact.

The literature offers at least partial support for this general position. Counts and Mensh (1950) used a retest model and found a significant increase in *S* after hypnotically inducing conflict. Fonda (1951) and Bandura (1954) both found a significant positive relation between *S* and oppositional tendencies. Rosen (1952) reported a significant correlation between the frequency of *S* and high *Pd* scores on the MMPI, but did not find a relationship between *S* and the diagnosis of psychopathy. Rapaport et al. (1946) found the highest incidence of *S* among paranoid schizophrenics and Molish (1955) has posited that when *S* appears in schizophrenic records, it represents a process through which a passive resistance to the environment is maintained. Fonda (1960) reviewed the literature concerning *S* and concluded that the proportion of *S* in the record gives some indication of the effort being devoted to the defense of autonomy.

The data for *S* fall on a clear J-curve for most groups. About 90% of adult nonpatients give at least one *S* answer, and the mean for that group approaches 2, although the mode is 1. Nearly 80% of all patients give at least one *S* response, and most groups have means for

S of about 2 and modes of 1. The exceptions to the neat J-curve distribution occur among depressives who show a mean of more than 2, but a mode of zero, and hysteroids who have a mean of nearly three but a mode of zero. Those groups appear to divide, with many giving no *S* answers, and many giving considerably more than is reflected in the mean. Surprisingly, nonpatient adolescents have somewhat lower means for *S* than do nonpatient adults, and several age groups have modes of zero. Children between the ages of 6 and 12 have means and modes for *S* that are more similar to those of nonpatient adults.

The most common *S* responses occur to Cards I (variations of a face), and II (rocket), and least frequently to Cards IV, V, VI, and VIII. Rorschach probably was only partially correct in his assumption that all *S* answers involve some alteration in the figure and ground relation. This does not seem to be the case for Card I, to which nearly 20% of nonpatient adults and nearly 30% of nonpatient children give some sort of face response, usually the face of a cat, a mask, or a Halloween pumpkin. That kind of answer continues to be given with about the same frequency if the white areas are colored either light or dark gray—that is, still maintaining the contrast effect for the contours. However, if the contours are eliminated by coloring the white areas a gray-black—that is, homogeneous with the immediate surroundings—the frequency of face responses is reduced to zero. It is possible that some other internal space areas are perceived as part of figure rather than ground, but most space responses do appear to involve some sort of reversal effect.

The reliability data for *S* suggest that all space responses do not necessarily correlate with the same psychological operations, because they are quite variable. Retest correlations range from .59 to .73 for brief intervals, and from .72 to .79 for lengthy intervals. The fact that lower retest correlations are found for brief intervals provoked a decision to subdivide 165 pairs of brief interval retest protocols, from both patients and nonpatients and including adults and children, in which at least one *S* response appeared in the first record, into three groups: (1) those containing only *WS* and/or *DS* answers, (2) those containing only *DdS* answers, and (3) those containing a combination of *WS* and/or *DS* plus *DdS* responses.

Subsequently, a fourth group was created containing records in which all *S* answers appeared in Card I, or a combination of Cards I and II in the first test. The retest correlation for the group ($N = 38$) in which only *WS* and/or *DS* response appear is .63. The correlation for the group containing only *DdS* answers ($N = 33$) is .71, but the retest correlation for the group containing a mixture of *WS* and/or *DS* plus *DdS* ($N = 94$) is .86. As might be suspected, the latter group has a mean for *S* (3.97, $SD = 1.1$) that is significantly greater than either of the other two groups, 1.23 and 1.41, respectively ($p < .05$). In other words, as *S* elevates well beyond the mean, it reflects a more stable characteristic. The retest correlation for the group of records in which all *S* answers occurred to Card I, or the combination of Cards I and II ($N = 28$) is only .32, which suggests that these responses are more situationally related, and probably are a product of resistance to taking the test.

A computer search, by diagnostic groups, of protocols in the pool at the Rorschach Research Foundation containing four or more *S* responses yielded five groups in which that criterion was positive for at least 15% of the subjects. They are inpatient depressives (17%), borderline personality disorders (21%), paranoid schizophrenics (23%), adolescent conduct disorders (19%), and neurologically impaired children with marked learning disabilities (15%). Earlier (Exner & Wylie, 1977), it had been discovered that a frequency of four or more *S* responses loaded positively as a variable in the Suicide Constellation. Although the personality characteristics of each group are generally quite different than in the other groups, a common thread of dissatisfaction and difficulty handling anger tends to exist among all. Thus these findings seem to offer some support for the general proposition that elevations in *S* suggest more negativism, and possibly the existence of anger that is provoked by intense and/or prolonged experiences of dissatisfaction.

It is also of interest to note that when the records of the high *S* subjects were studied, by groups, for other characteristics of affect, the groups of depressives and impaired children included a disproportionate number with *Afr*'s less than .45 and *FC:CF + C* ratios in which *CF + C* is the greater value. The group of schizophrenics also included a disproportionate number of records with a very low *Afr*, but those records contained *FC:CF + C* ratios in which *FC* was usually the greater value. The records of the borderlines and conduct disorders included a disproportionate number with *Afr*'s greater than .80 and more than 75% of those also had more *CF + C* than *FC*.

Although the data concerning *S* remain somewhat sparse, it seems reasonable to conclude that the presence of one or two *S* responses in an average length record is probably a positive sign in which the oppositional features are provoked by the need to remain somewhat independent in relation to task demands. If the *S* responses occur very early in the sequence of answers, it suggests that the oppositionality is more directly related to the test situation. On the other hand, as *S* is elevated, and especially if it exceeds 3, the oppositionality is probably more pervasive as a trait-like feature of the personality and, as such, can easily give rise to hostility or anger when autonomy is threatened. In that context it can reflect a potentially serious impediment to other operations and relations.

Color Projection *(CP)*   The Special Score *CP* can also provide some data concerning how the subject responds to affective experience. It was first suggested by Piotrowski (1957) to account for instances in which a subject identified achromatic blot areas as being chromatic. He postulated that it represents an ingenuine emotion, that is, an attempt to deal with a feeling of helplessness by substituting a rather transparent and unrealistic positive emotional tone. That premise has been difficult to test because the incidence of *CP* responses is infrequent in most groups of subjects. *CP*'s appear in only seven of the 600 protocols in the adult nonpatient normative sample (1%), and only 42 of the 1580 records of nonpatient children (3%). It appears in about 3% of the records in the schizophrenic reference sample, but *none* of the protocols for the sample of character problems. Among inpatients, it occurs with the greatest frequency among depressives, about 5%.

A review of 430 records of outpatients who originally volunteered to participate in the long-term treatment effects study revealed considerably higher proportions of *CP* responses in several diagnostic groups. This group was targeted because therapist evaluations of the patients had been collected after each of several sessions early into treatment, and additional evaluations were obtained after more lengthy intervals. Nearly 12% of the records contained at least one *CP* answer, and some contained as many as three *CP*'s. They appeared in higher than expected proportion of protocols of patients whose primary symptom patterns were described as psychosomatic (17%), hysteroid-like problems in dealing with affect (17%), depression (9%), and obsessive-like features (9%). Collectively, these groups included 369 of the 430 subjects in the study, with 46 giving at least one *CP* answer. The protocols of the remaining 61 subjects included five, each of which contained one *CP* answer. The therapist evaluations included a section pertaining to tactics of defense, and if this was discernible, as many as three were to be listed, such as fantasy, displacement, denial, intellectualization, and so on. Forty-two of the 51 subjects who gave at least one *CP* response were described in the evaluations as having marked tendencies to use denial as a defensive tactic. Three comparison groups of 51 patients each were randomly drawn from the remaining 379 patients in the study. In the first, 17 of the 51 were described as using denial as a defensive tactic; in the second, 14 of the 51, and in the third, 18 of the 51 were described as having this feature. Each of the three chi-squares is statistically significant ($p < .02$).

Although these findings result from only one study, they seemed sufficiently compelling to include the *CP* Special Score in the System (Exner, 1978). Interpretively, it does appear to relate to an abuse of denial as a tactic to deal with unwanted emotions. Interestingly, the 51 subjects who gave *CP* responses had, as a group, a significantly higher mean for *C'* answers (4.92, *SD* = 1.39) than did any of the three randomly selected comparison groups (2.47 to 2.93, *SD*'s = 1.94 to 2.23, $p < .05$). The very low frequency with which this kind of answer occurs makes its presence even more significant, and emphasizes the necessity of carefully weaving this finding into other data concerning emotional features.

Blend Responses   When more than one determinant is present in a response, it indicates that the activity occurring in the formation and delivery of the answer was more complex than might have been expected or required. In some respects the blend response can be regarded as representing the extreme opposite of the pure *F* response. Whereas pure *F* denotes a simple, straightforward classification, the blend is the product of activity in which considerable analysis and synthesis of stimulus elements occurs. Slightly more than one-fifth of the responses given by nonpatient adults are blends, and all 600 subjects in the normative sample gave at least one. Nonpatient children and adolescents tend to give proportionally fewer blend answers, although most give at least one. Eighty-five to 90% of most patient groups give at least one blend, although they appear in only about 75% of the protocols of the character disorder reference sample. Exner (1974) reported that more records with no blends are found among subjects with I.Q.s of less than 90, but Mason and Exner (1984) found only very low, nonsignificant correlations between Verbal I.Q. ($r = 4mi.03$) and Performance I.Q. ($r = .02$) and the frequency of blends. As might be suspected, they also found a significant negative correlation between Lambda and blends ($r = .28$).

The interpretation of blends should be based on both the quantity and substance. The absence of blends in the record of an adolescent or adult is a negative sign, indicating a form of psychological narrowness or constriction. It probably also indicates less sensitivity to oneself and the environment. At the other extreme, a significant elevation in the number of blends—that is, eight or more in an average length record—signals much more complexity than is customary. If the subject has an abundance of resource readily accessible, the complexity might be viewed as an asset to functioning, because it suggests a greater sensitivity to stimuli. If the resources are more limited, however, an excess of blends indicates that the subject is overly involved in processing, and this can create a difficult if not impossible psychological burden for the subject.

All determinants, with the exception of pure *F,* are related to operations that have some affective properties. Although the movement and *FD* determinants are more directly related to ideational activities, those activities often involve, or give rise to affect. Approximately 70% of all blends have at least one movement determinant, but less than 2% consist exclusively of movement determinants, such as *M,FM, M.m,* or *FM.m.* About 7% of all blends consist exclusively of one of the movement determinants plus *FD.* More than 90% of all blends include at least one determinant that is related directly to affective experience—that is, chromatic or achromatic color, or one of the shading determinants. In many instances, the substance of the blend provides some clue about how the affective elements are working in the psychological operations of the subject. For instance, a blend of $M^a.FC$ will generally be regarded much more positively than $CF.FM^p$. In the former, the delay factor is dominant and the affect apparently well modulated. In the latter, less well-modulated affect is dominant and merged with a need-related component that has a passive quality. Similarly, a blend of $M^p.FC'$ suggests a form of passive affective constraint, which may not be regarded very favorably, yet it is much more positive than a blend such as $m^p.YF$, which reeks of a sense of paralysis. As the number of determinants in a blend increases, so too does the complexity of operations that has been involved. About 20% of all blends involve more than two determinants, and about 5% involve more than three determinants. These typically are elaborate responses and often have very revealing contents.

There are two types of blends that are of special importance to the review of affective features. They are the *Shading Blend* and the *Color Shading Blend.* The shading blend is the response in which at least two of the achromatic and/or shading determinants are present, such as *FT.FY, FV.FC', C'F.YF,* and so on. These are very unusual responses, occurring only twice in the 600 records of nonpatient adults, not at all among the character disorder reference group, and in only seven of the schizophrenic protocols. They are much more frequent in the records of the depressive reference sample, appearing in 24 of the 210 protocols (11%). They also appear in 11 of the 161 records of outpatients whose primary symptom pattern is depression (7%), and in eight of 68 records of first admission inpatient drug abusers who were tested after approximately 1 week of detoxfication (12%). Because all four of the achromatic and shading variables relate to irritating or painful affective experience, the presence of two or more in a single answer probably indicates a more tormented experience. The substance of the shading blend is also important. If it contains only two of the critical variables, and one of the two is a *Y* variable, it is likely that the experience is more situationally related. On the other hand, if the critical variables do not include *Y,* the intense distress is probably much more chronic.

The Color Shading Blend occurs much more frequently than the Shading Blend. These are responses in which a chromatic color determinant and at least one of the four achromatic or shading determinants is present. At least one Color Shading Blend appears in 254 of the 600 adult nonpatient protocols (42%). They appear in between 15 and 25% of the records of young nonpatient children, ages 5 to 8, and in more than half of the records of nonpatient youngsters between the ages of 11 and 13. In fact, approximately 70% of the 13-year-old group gave at least one. That is the only nonpatient group having a mode greater than zero for this variable. Color Shading Blends appear most frequently in the records of depressives. More than 70% of the records in the depressive reference sample, and nearly 70% of the records of outpatient depressives in the long-term treatment effects study, contain at least one, and nearly one-fourth of the records in both groups have three or more. In contrast, they appear in nearly 40% of schizophrenic records, slightly more than 40% of nondepressed outpatients, and about 30% of the character problem group.

Bcck (1949) was the first to elaborate on the Color Shading Blend, suggesting that it represents a form of simultaneous pleasure and pain. Applebaum and Holzman (1962) found that color shading blends appear more frequently in the records of subjects prone to suicide. Exner and Wylie (1977) also found that it does correlate significantly with effected suicide ($r = .34, p < .01$), but because of the high frequency with which it appears in other groups, it is not an effective discriminator when taken alone. Nonetheless, it does load positively into the Suicide Constellation. Applebaum and Colson (1968) have suggested that it reflects an aborted form of emotional experience. Exner (1978) has postulated that it represents more of a mixed or confused emotional experience which, at times, can indicate the presence of ambivalence.

The retest reliabilities for *all* color shading blends are relatively modest, ranging from .48 to .57 for lengthy retest intervals, and .55 to .67 for retests administered during a period of 30 days or less. However, as Castles (1984) has suggested, those correlations are somewhat misleading because of the Y variable. Approximately 60% of the color shading blends given by nonpatients, and nearly 40% of those given by patients contain a Y variable, suggesting that a situational factor has contributed to the formation of the blend answer. When the retest reliabilities were calculated for 150 adult nonpatients retested after lengthy intervals, and divided into two groups based on whether the color shading blends contained a Y variable, the correlations for those including Y ranged from .28 to .41; for those not including the Y variable they ranged from .68 to .79. When the retest records of 130 nonpatient adults and children who took the second test within 30 days were divided in the same way, the retest correlations for those containing a Y variable ranged from .16 to .34, whereas the correlations for the group in which the blends did not contain a Y variable ranged from .73 to .82. These findings suggest that, as with the shading blends, the characteristic may be situationally related, even being provoked by the test-taking situation, or it may be of a more chronic nature. If chronic, the element of ambivalence is much more likely to exist as a trait-like feature. In either instance, the presence of a Color Shading Blend signals some difficulty with affect that should be noted in the context of other findings concerning affective characteristics. A confusion in feelings can mark many events, and if the mixed feelings are related to a specific situation, it does not necessarily predispose faulty or ineffective adjustment to other emotional situations. Conversely, ambivalence, as a trait-like feature, creates many more potential hazards to the maintenance of consistency in affective reactions to various classes of emotional stimulation and, as such, can greatly affect a variety of relationships in the environment.

REFERENCES

Abrams, E. W. (1955) Predictions of intelligence from certain Rorschach factors. *Journal of Clinical Psychology,* **11,** 81–84.

Ames, L. B., Learned, J., Metraux, R. W., and Walker, R. N. (1954) *Rorschach Responses in Old Age.* New York: Harper & Row.

Ames, L. B., Metraux, R. W., and Walker, R. N. (1971) *Adolescent Rorschach Responses.* New York: Brunner/Mazel.

Applebaum, S. A., and Colson, D. B. (1968) A reexamination of the color-shading Rorschach Test response. *Journal of Projective Techniques and Personality Assessment,* **32,** 160–164.

Applebaum, S. A., and Holtzman, P. S. (1962) The color-shading response and suicide. *Journal of Projective Techniques,* **26,** 155–11.

Armitage, S. G., Greenberg, T. D., Pearl, D., Berger, D. G., and Daston, P. G. (1955) Predicting intelligence from the Rorschach. *Journal of Consulting Psychology,* **19,** 321–329.

Baker, L. M. and Harris, J. G. (1949) The validation of Rorschach test result against laboratory behavior. *Journal of Clinical Psychology,* **5,** 161–164.

Bandura, A. (1954) The Rorschach white space response and oppositional behavior. *Journal of Consulting Psychology,* **18,** 17–21.

Baughman, E. E. (1954) A comparative analysis of Rorschach forms with altered stimulus characteristics. *Journal of Projective Techniques,* **18,** 151–164.

Baughman, E. E. (1959) An experimental analysis of the relationship between stimulus structure and behavior in the Rorschach. *Journal of Projective Techniques, 23,* 134–183.

Beck, S. J. (1930) The Rorschach Test and personality diagnosis: The feeble minded. *American Journal of Psychiatry,* **10,** 19–52.

Beck, S. J. (1932) The Rorschach Test as applied to a feeble-minded group. *Archives of Psychology,* **84,** 136.

Beck, S. J. (1945) *Rorschach's Test. II. A Variety of Personality Pictures.* New York: Grune & Stratton.

Beck, S. J. (1949) *Rorschach's Test. I: Basic Processes.* (2nd Ed.) New York: Grune & Stratton.

Beck, S. J. (1948) Rorschach F Plus and the Ego in treatment. *American Journal of Orthopsychiatry,* **18,** 395–401.

Beck, S. J., Beck, A., Levitt, E. and Molish, H. B. (1961) *Rorschach's Test. I: Basic Processes.* (3rd Ed.) New York: Grune & Stratton.

Becker, W. C. (1956) A genetic approach to the interpretation and evaluation of the process-reactive distinction in schizophrenia. *Journal of Abnormal and Social Psychology, 53,* 229–236.

Berkowitz, M., and Levine J. (1953) Rorschach scoring categories as diagnostic "signs." *Journal of Consulting Psychology,* **17,** 110–112.

Blatt, S. J., and Allison, J. (1963) Methodological considerations in Rorschach research: The *W* response as an expression of abstractive and integrated strivings. *Journal of Projective Techniques, 27,* 269–278.

Bourguinon, E. E., and Nett, E. W. (1955) Rorschach Populars in a sample of Haitian protocols. *Journal of Projective Techniques,* **19,** 117–124.

Bryant, E. L., and Exner, J. E. (1974) Performance on the Revised Minnesota Paper Form Board Test by under and overincorporators under timed and nontimed conditions. Workshops Study No. 188 (unpublished), Rorschach Workshops.

Bryant, E. L., Kline, J. R., and Exner, J. E. (1978) Trails A and B performance as related to the *Zd* score. Workshops Study No. 259 (Unpublished), Rorschach Workshops.

Caldwell, B. M. (1954) The use of the Rorschach in personality research with the aged. *Journal of Gerontology,* **9,** 316–323.

Cass, W. A., and McReynolds, P. (1951) A contribution to the Rorschach norms. *Journal of Consulting Psychology,* **15,** 178–184.

Castles, J. (1984) Personal Communication. Alumni Workshop, Nassau.

Chesrow, E. J. Woiska, P. H., and Reinitz, A. H. (1949) A psychometric evaluation of aged white males. *Geriatrics,* **4,** 169–177.

Counts, R. M., and Mensh, I. N. (1950) Personality characteristics in hypnotically induced hostility. *Journal of Clinical Psychology,* **6,** 325–330.

Davidson, H. H., and Kruglov, L. (1952) Personality characteristics of the institutionalized aged. *Journal of Consulting Psychology,* **16,** 5–12.

Exner, J. E. (1959) The influence of chromatic and achromatic color in the Rorschach. *Journal of Projective Techniques, 23,* 418–425.

Exner, J. E. (1962) The effect of color on productivity in Cards VIII, IX, X of the Rorschach. *Journal of Projective Techniques,* **26,** 30–33.

Exner, J. E. (1974) *The Rorschach: A Comprehensive System. Volume 1.* New York: Wiley.

Exner, J. E. (1978) *The Rorschach: A Comprehensive System. Volume 2: Current research and advanced interpretation.* New York: Wiley.

Exner, J. E. (1983) Rorschach Assessment. In I. B. Weiner (Ed.) *Clinical Methods in Psychology*, (2nd Ed.). New York: Wiley.

Exner, J. E., Armbruster, G. L., and Viglione, D. (1978) The temporal stability of some Rorschach features. *Journal of Personality Assessment*, **42**, 474–482.

Exner, J. E., Armbruster, G. L., and Wylie, J. R. (1976) TAT stories and the $M^a:M^p$ ratio. Workshops Study No. 225 (unpublished), Rorschach Workshops.

Exner, J. E., and Bryant, E. L. (1974) Flexibility in creative efforts as related to three Rorschach variables. Workshops Study No. 187 (unpublished), Rorschach Workshops.

Exner, J. E., and Bryant, E. L. (1975) Serial learning by over and underincorporators with limited and unlimited numbers of training trials. Workshops Study No. 194 (unpublished), Rorschach Workshops.

Exner, J. E., Bryant, E. L. and Armbruster, G. L. (1979) Eye activity in a matching familiar figures task of 12 adolescents selected on the basis of *Zd* scores. Workshops Study No. 263 (unpublished), Rorschach Workshops.

Exner, J. E., and Caraway, E. W. (1974) Identification of incomplete stimuli by high positive *Zd* and high negative *Zd* subjects. Workshops Study No. 186 (unpublished), Rorschach Workshops.

Exner, J. E., and Kazaoka, K. (1978) Dependency gestures of 16 assertiveness trainees as related to Rorschach movement responses. Workshops Study No. 261 (unpublished), Rorschach Workshops.

Exner, J. E., and Leura, A. V. (1974) "Simon says" errors and the *Zd* score in young children. Workshops Study No. 204 (unpublished), Rorschach Workshops.

Exner, J. E., and Leura, A. V. (1977) Rorschach performances of volunteer and nonvolunteer adolescents. Workshops Study No. 238 (unpublished), Rorschach Workshops.

Exner, J. E., and Murillo, L. G. (1973) Effectiveness of regressive ECT with process schizophrenia. *Diseases of the Nervous System*, **34**, 44–48.

Exner, J. E., and Murillo, L. G. (1975) Early prediction of posthospitalization relapse. *Journal of Psychiatric Research*, **12**, 231–237.

Exner, J. E., Murillo, L. G., and Cannavo, F. (1973) Disagreement between patient and relative behavioral reports as related to relapse in nonschizophrenic patients. Eastern Psychological Association, Washington, D.C.

Exner, J. E., and Stanley, F. B. (1979) Time estimates for three intervals by 12 subjects selected on the basis of *Zd* scores. Workshops Study No. 268 (unpublished), Rorschach Workshops.

Exner, J. E., Thomas, E. A., and Mason, B. (1985) Children's Rorschachs: Description and prediction. *Journal of Personality Assessment*, **49**, 13–20.

Exner, J. E., Viglione, D. J., and Gillespie, R. (1984) Relationships between Rorschach variables as relevant to the interpretation of structural data. *Journal of Personality Assessment*, **48**, 65–70.

Exner, J. E., and Weiner, I. B. (1982) *The Rorschach: A Comprehensive System. Volume 3: Assessment of children and adolescents*. New York: Wiley.

Exner, J. E., and Wylie, J. R. (1974) Therapist ratings of patient "insight" in an uncovering form of psychotherapy. Workshops Study No. 192 (unpublished), Rorschach Workshops.

Exner, J. E. and Wylie, J. R. (1977) Some Rorschach data concerning suicide. *Journal of Personality Assessment*, **41**, 339–348.

Feldman, M. J., Gurrslin, C., Kaplan, M. L., and Sharlock, N. (1954) A preliminary study to develop a more discriminating F + ratio. *Journal of Clinical Psychology*, **10**, 47–51.

Finney, P. C. (1955) Rorschach Test correlates of assaultive behavior. *Journal of Projective Techniques*, **19**, 6–16.

Fonda, C. P. (1951) The nature and meaning of the Rorschach white space response. *Journal of Abnormal and Social Psychology,* **46,** 367–377.

Fonda, C. P. (1960) The white space response. In Rickers-Ovsiankina, M. (Ed.), *Rorschach Psychology.* New York: Wiley.

Frank, I. H. (1952) A genetic evaluation of perceptual structuralization in certain psychoneurotic disorders by means of the Rorschach Technique. Unpublished doctoral dissertation, Boston University.

Fried, R. (1977) Christmas elves on the Rorschach: a popular Finnish response and its cultural significance. IXth International Congress of Rorschach and other projective techniques. Fribourg, Switzerlnd.

Friedman, H. (1952) Perceptual regression in schizophrenia: An hypothesis suggested byuse of the Rorschach Test. *Journal of Genetic Psychology.* **81,** 63–98.

Gardner, R. W. (1951) Impulsivity as indicated by Rorschach Test factors. *Journal of Consulting Psychology,* **15,** 464–468.

Gibby, R. G. (1951) The stability of certain Rorschach variables under conditions of experimentally induced sets: The intellectual variables. *Journal of Projective Techniques,* **3,** 3–25.

Gill, H. S. (1966) Delay of response and reaction to color on the Rorschach. *Journal of Projective Techniques and Personality Assessment,* **30,** 545–552.

Goldberger, L. (1961) Reactions to perceptual isolation and Rorschach manifestations of the primary process. *Journal of Projective Techniques,* **25,** 287–302.

Hallowell, A. I. (1956) The Rorschach Technique in personality and culture studies. In Klopfer, B. et al. (Eds.), *Developments in the Rorshach Technique.* Vol. 2. Yonkers-on-Hudson, N.Y.: World Book.

Hammer, E. F., and Jacks, I. (1955) A study of Rorschach flexor and extensor human movement responses. *Journal of Clinical Psychology,* **11,** 63–67.

Hertz, M. R. (1940) The shading response in the Rorschach inkblot test: A review of its scoring and interpretation. *Journal of General Psychology,* **23,** 123–167.

Holtzberg, J. D., and Belmont, L. (1952) The relationship between factors on the Wechsler Bellevue and Rorschach having common psychological rationale. *Journal of Consulting Psychology,* **16,** 23–30.

Honigmann, J. J. (1949) *Culture and Ethos of Kaska Society.* Yale University Publications in Anthropology, No. 40.

Joseph, A., and Murray, V. F. (1951) *Chamorros and Carolinians of Saipan: Personality Studies.* Howard University Press.

Kadinsky, D. (1952) Significance of depth psychology of apperceptive tendencies in the Rorschach Test. *Rorschachiana,* **4,** 36–37.

Kahn, M. W. (1967) Correlates of Rorschach reality adherence in the assessment of murderers who plead insanity. *Journal of Projective Techniques,* **31,** 44–47.

Kerr, M. (1934) The Rorschach Test applied to children. *British Journal of Psychology,* **25,** 170–185.

Kisker, G. W. (1942) A projective approach to personality patterns during insulin shock and metrazol convulsive therapy. *Journal of Abnormal and Social Psychology,* **37,** 120–124.

Klebanoff, S. G. (1949) The Rorschach Test in an analysis of personality in general paresis. *Journal of Personality,* **17,** 261–272.

Klopfer, W. (1946) Rorschach patterns of old age. *Rorschach Research Exchange,* **10,** 145–166.

Klopfer, B., Ainsworth, M. D., Klopfer, W. G., and Holt, R. R. (1954) *Developments in the Rorschach Technique. I: Theory and Technique.* Yonkers-on-Hudson, N.Y.: World Book.

Klopfer, B., and Kelley, D. (1942) *The Rorschach Technique*. Yonkers-on-Hudson, N.Y.: World Book.

Knopf, I. J. (1956) Rorschach summary scores and differential diagnosis. *Journal of Consulting Psychology,* **20,** 99–104.

Korchin, S. J. (1960) Form perception and ego functioning. In Rickers-Ovsiankina, M. (Ed.), *Rorschach Psychology*. New York: Wiley.

Leighton, D., and Kluckholm, C. (1947) *Children of the People: The Navaho Individual and His Development*. Harvard University Press.

Lotsoff, E. (1953) Intelligence, verbal fluency and the Rorschach Test. *Journal of Consulting Psychology,* **17,** 21–24.

McCandless, B. B. (1949) The Rorschach as a predictor of academic success. *Journal of Applied Psychology,* **33,** 43–50.

Mason, B. J., Cohen, J. B., and Exner, J. E. (1985) Schizophrenic, depressive, and nonpatient personality organizations described by Rorschach factor structures. *Journal of Personality Assessment,* **49,** 295–305.

Mason, B. J., and Exner, J. E. (1984) Correlations between WAIS subtests and nonpatient adult Rorschach data. Workshops Study 289 (unpublished), Rorschach Workshops.

Meichanbaum, D. H. (1974) *Cognitive Behavior Modification*. Morristown, N.J.: General Learning Press.

Mirin, B. (1955) The Rorschach human movement response and role taking behavior. *Journal of Nervous and Mental Disorders,* **122,** 270–275.

Molish, H. B. (1955) Schizophrenic reaction types in a Naval hospital population as evaluated by the Rorschach Test. Bureau of Medicine and Surgery, Navy Department, Washington, D.C.

Molish, H. B. (1959) Contributions of projective tests to psychological diagnosis in organic brain damage. In Beck, S. J., and Molish, H. B. (Eds.), *Reflexes to Intelligence*. Glencoe, Ill.: The Free Press.

Molish, H. B. (1967) Critique and Problems of Research. In Beck, S. J., and Molish, H. B. *Rorschach's Test. II: A Variety of Personality Pictures*. (2nd Ed.) New York: Grune & Stratton.

Molish, H. B., and Beck, S. J. (1958) Further exploration of the six schizophrenias: Type S-3. *American Journal of Orthopsychiatry,* **28,** 483–505, 807–827.

Murillo, L. G., and Exner, J. E. (1973) The effects of regressive ECT with process schizophrenics. *American Journal of Psychiatry,* **130,** 269–273.

Paulsen, A. (1941) Rorschachs of school beginners. *Rorschach Research Exchange,* **5,** 24–29.

Piotrowski, Z. (1939) Rorschach manifestations of improvement in insulin treated schizophrenics. *Psychosomatic Medicine,* **1,** 508–526.

Piotrowksi, Z. (1957) *Perceptanalysis*. New York: Macmillan.

Piotrowski, Z. (1960) The movement score. In Rickers-Ovsiankina, M. (Ed.), *Rorschach Psychology*. New York: Wiley.

Prados, M., and Fried, E. (1943) Personality structure of the older aged groups. *Journal of Clinical Psychology,* **3,** 113–120.

Rabin, A., Papania, N., and McMichael, A. (1954) Some effects of alcohol on Rorschach performance. *Journal of Clinical Psychology,* **10,** 252–255.

Rapaport, D., Gill, M., and Schafer, R. (1946) *Psychological Diagnostic Testing*. Vol. 2. Chicago: Yearbook Publishers.

Rorschach, H. (1921) *Psychodiagnostics*. Bern: Bircher (Transl. Hans Huber Verlag, 1942).

Rosen, E. (1952) MMPI and Rorschach correlates of the Rorschach white space response. *Journal of Clinical Psychology,* **8,** 283–288.

Saretsky, T. (1963) The effect of chlorapromazine on primary process thought maifestations. Unpublished doctoral dissertation, New York University.

Schachter, W., and Cotte, S. (1948) Prostitution and the Rorschach Test. *Archives of Neurology,* **67,** 123–138.

Schafer, R. (1954) *Psychoanalytic Interpretation in Rorschach Testing.* New York: Grune & Stratton.

Sherman, M. H. (1952) A comparison of formal and content factors in the diagnostic testing of schizophrenia. *Genetic Psychology Monographs,* **46,** 183–234.

Siegel, E. L. (1953) Genetic parallels of perceptual structuralization in paranoid schizophrenia: An analysis by means of the Rorschach Technique. *Journal of Projective Techniques,* **17,** 151–161.

Sloan, W. (1947) Mental deficiency as a symptom of personality disturbance. *American Journal of Mental Deficiency,* **52,** 31–36.

Sommer, R., and Sommer, D. (1958) Assaultiveness and two types of Rorschach color responses. *Journal of Consulting Psychology,* **22,** 57–62.

Storment, C. T., and Finney, B. C. (1953) Projection and behavior: A Rorschach study of assaultive mental hospital patients. *Journal of Projective Techniques,* **17,** 349–360.

Stotsky, B. A. (1952) A comparison of remitting and non-remitting schizophrenics on psychological tests. *Journal of Abnormal and Social Psychology,* **47,** 489–496.

Taulbee, E. S. (1955) The use of the Rorschach Test in evaluating the intellectual levels of functioning in schizophrenia. *Journal of Projective Techniques,* **19,** 163–169.

Townsend, J. K. (1967) The relation between Rorschach signs of aggression and behavioral aggression in emotionally disturbed boys. *Journal of Projective Techniques and Personality Assessment,* **31,** 13–21.

Weiner, I. B. (1966) *Psychodiagnosis in Schizophrenia.* New York: Wiley.

Weiner, I. B., and Exner, J. E. (1978) Rorschach indices of disordered thinking in patient and nonpatient adolescents and adults. *Journal of Personality Assessment,* **42,** 339–343.

Wetherhorn, M. (1956) Flexor-extensor movement on the Rorschach. *Journal of Consulting Psychology,* **20,** 204.

Wilensky, H. (1959) Rorschach developmental level and social participation of chronic schizophrenics. *Journal of Projective Techniques,* **23,** 87–92.

Wishner, J. (1948) Rorschach intellectual indicators in neurotics. *American Journal of Orthopsychiatry,* **18,** 265–279.

Wittenborn, J. R. (1950) Statistical tests of certain Rorschach assumptions: The internal consistency of scoring categories. *Journal of Consulting Psychology,* **14,** 1–19.

Zamansky, H. J., and Goldman, A. E. (1960) A comparison of two methods of analyzing Rorschach data in assessing therapeutic change. *Journal of Projective Techniques,* **24,** 75–82.

Zukowsky, E. (1961) Measuring primary and secondary process thinking in schizophrenics and normals by means of the Rorschach. Unpublished doctoral dissertation, Michigan State University.

CHAPTER 16

Structural Data III—
Self-Image and Interpersonal Attitudes

Some other issues that are important to personality description, diagnoses, and treatment planning include self-perception and views of, or attitudes toward others. Both can be relevant to the formulation of a wide variety of decisions and behaviors, especially those involving interactions with others. As with the features related to cognition, ideation, and affect, there is no single Rorschach variable that can provide unequivocal information concerning these features. There are, however, some clusters of structural variables that sometimes can be useful in addressing these issues.

CHARACTERISTICS OF SELF-IMAGE *(3r + (2)/R, MOR, PER, Ab + Art, An + Xy)*

The notion of self-image or self-concept generally embraces some very broad parameters. No tactic of evaluating self-image has been totally successful, although a multitude of instruments and procedures have been devised for that purpose (Wylie, 1974, 1979). The Rorschach is no exception, especially because it focuses much more on the intrapersonal rather than the interpersonal characteristics of the subject. Consequently, hypotheses concerning interpersonal relationships are drawn much more inferentially, by piecing together findings concerning views of the self and others.

The Egocentricity Index *(3r + (2)/R)* The separate codings for reflections *(Fr, rF)* and pairs (2) evolved somewhat fortuitously from a study comparing four groups of 20 subjects each: inpatient depressives who had made a recent suicide gesture, inpatient male homosexuals, imprisoned character disorders who had been diagnosed as antisocial personalities, and adult nonpatients drawn mainly from a college population (Exner, 1969). Frequency data revealed that reflections appeared in more than 75% of the records of the homosexual and antisocial groups, but not at all among the depressives and in only three nonpatient records. Because the reflection answers were all based on the symmetry of the blots, it was decided to tally the frequency with which the symmetry of the blots was used to report identical pairs of objects. The tally revealed that the homosexual group gave significantly more pairs than did the other groups, and that the depressives gave significantly fewer pairs than the other groups.

Raychaudhuri and Mukerji (1971) used four groups of 15 subjects each, from a prison population, to study reflections and pairs. The groups were comprised of active homosexuals, passive homosexuals, sociopaths, and controls. They found that both homosexual groups gave significantly more reflections than either of the other two groups, and that sociopaths gave significantly more reflections than the controls. They found the number of pair answers to be significantly high in both homosexual groups, *and* among controls when contrasted with the sociopathic group.

These findings provoked a hypothesis that reflection and pair answers might, in some way, be related to overinvolvement with the self. To test that postulate, a sentence completion blank was constructed following a format similar to one used by Watson in her study of narcissism (1965). An original blank of 50 stems was reduced to 30, most of which contain the personal pronouns *I, me,* or *my,* and administered to 750 nonpatient adults. Responses were scored for whether the answer focused on the self (S), such as, *I worry:* about my future, or focused on others (0), such as, *I worry:* about the homeless people of the world. Eighty subjects, 40 with the highest number of S responses, and 40 with the highest number of 0 responses, were administered the Rorschach by 14 examiners. Reflection answers appeared in the records of 37 of the 40 high S subjects as contrasted with only two records of the high 0 subjects. The high S group also gave nearly 2½ times the number of pair responses as the high 0 group. The blank, entitled the *Self Focus Sentence Completion* (SFSC), was then standardized on a population of more than 2500 subjects (Exner, 1973). The 30 subjects from each extreme of the resulting distribution were administered the Rorschach by 16 examiners. Reflection and pair responses appeared more than twice as often among the 30 high S subjects as among the records of the high 0 group.

These findings stimulated a decision to combine the reflection and pair responses into a single variable that would also account for the number of responses in a record. This procedure involved the SFSC scores and Rorschach data for 325 nonpatient adults. The decision to weigh reflections with a value of 3 in the Egocentricity Index resulted from a discriminant functions analysis designed to differentiate the strength of each of the two Rorschach variables, and the frequency for each, to identify the quintile on the SFSC distribution into which a subject would fall. The results indicated that reflections have a geometric property to identify those subjects falling in the upper two quintiles, and the weighting of 3 represents a conservative averaging of that property.

The first validation study concerning the usefulness of the Egocentricity Index focused on a behavioral index of self-centeredness. Twenty-one male candidates for an engineering position were administered several psychological tests, including the Rorschach, by examiners naive about the nature of the study. Subsequently, they were interviewed by a member of the personnel staff of the corporation to which they were applying for employment. The interviews were conducted in a 12 by 17 foot office, which had an 8 by 8 foot one-way vision mirror on one wall. Each candidate was escorted to the office by a receptionist and invited to be seated next to a desk to await the interviewer. The mirrored wall was to the left of the subject. Interviewers arrived no earlier than 10 minutes after the candidate, and during that waiting period a video camera was used to film the candidate. The tapes were subsequently replayed, and the amount of time each candidate spent viewing himself in the mirror was tallied. The range of mirror viewing time for the group was from 6 to 104 seconds, with a median of 49 seconds.

The group was divided on the basis of these data, using a median split and eliminating the candidate at the midpoint. The average mirror viewing time for the upper half was 68.5″, and 27.1″ for the lower half ($p < .01$). The 10 protocols of subjects in the upper half contained six with reflections and 103 pair responses, whereas the 10 of subjects in the lower half contained no reflections and 68 pair responses. The groups are significantly different for both variables, and for the Egocentricity Index (Upper $10 = .476$, $SD = .13$; Lower $10 = .298$, $SD = .14$, $p < .01$). The first 10 minutes of the interviews were audio recorded, and then scored for the number of times the candidate used the personal pronouns, *I, me,* or *my* during that segment. The scores ranged from 57 to 148. A rank order correlation compairing that distribution with the distribution of values for the Egocentricity Index yielded a *rho* correlation of .67, $p <.01$.

Exner (1974) used ratings on the Inpatient Multidimensional Psychiatric Scale (IMPS) completed during the first week of hospitalization, and again by different raters six to eight weeks after discharge, to differentiate 180 patients into groups of "improved" and "unimproved." Rorschachs were administered at about the same times the ratings were done. The admission Rorschachs for the patients who did not have depression as a major symptom ($N = 106$) showed a mean Egocentricity Index of .474 ($SD = .11$), which is significantly higher than the mean for a nonpatient control group, .35 ($SD = .07$). The patients who did have depression as a major symptom ($N = 74$) had a mean Egocentricity Index that was significantly lower than the other patient group, .278 ($SD = .12$). The data from the post-discharge Rorschachs for the subjects rated as unimproved were very similar to the admission data (Nondepressed $M = .493, SD = .13$; Depressed $M = .272, SD = .10$). The data for the patients rated as improved showed a shift toward the mean for nonpatient controls (Nondepressed $M = .385, SD = .09$; Depressed $M = .324, SD = .10$). The improved groups are not significantly different from each other or from the control group.

The temporal consistency for the Egocentricity Index is quite substantial, with correlations ranging from the mid .80's to low .90's for both brief and long-term retests. Long-term retest correlations are considerably lower for children through age 14, after which it appears to have the same stability as for adults. The mean for the Index is generally in the mid to upper .30's for nonpatient adults, with a relatively modest standard deviation. Thus cut off points of .31 to .42 appear to provide the best estimate of an average range. The curves for the distribution of Index values usually have some skewness to the left, but with somewhat higher peaks than a normal curve. For instance, the nonpatient adult normative sample shows a mean of .39 and SD of .11; however, the mode is .32, and although the skewness is almost perfect (.01), the kurtosis is 2.91, reflecting the large number of values falling slightly to the left of the mean. Distributions for patient groups tend to be more skewed to the left but with lower kurtosis values. For example, the mean for the schizophrenic reference sample is .37, but the mode is .50, and 39% of that sample have values *less than* .30. Similarly, the data for the character disorder group shows a mean of .42, a mode of .39, and 25% of the sample with values of less than .30. In other words, elements of bimodality tend to mark both samples. This is much more the case among depressives. The reference sample of depressives has a mean of .32, but a mode of .17, with 82 of the 200 subjects (39%) with values of less than .30.

The data for younger clients also provide some indirect support for the notion that the Index relates to self-involvement. Children are generally quite self-centered, especially during the earlier developmental years. This trait seems to be well illustrated in the gradual decline that occurs in the means for the Index from ages 5 through 16. At 5, the nonpatient children show a mean of .61, with a mode of .56. By age 8, the mean drops to .56 with a mode of .50. At age 11, the mean is .50 and the mode .48, and by age 16 the mean is .44, with a mode of .40. Similar declines have been shown by age for children with behavior problems and withdrawn children, although the means for the former typically are higher than for nonpatients, and for the latter typically are lower than nonpatients (Exner, 1978). A similar pattern of decline for the frequencies of reflection responses appears among all groups of children, with younger children tending to give more, and mid-adolescents having about the same frequencies as adults.

Exner, Wylie, and Bryant (1974) collected peer nominations from 37 group psychotherapy patients, distributed across four groups, after the fourth month of treatment. A 30-item form was used, with the responses given anonymously, with two entries (most and least) for each item. The items ranged over a variety of interpersonal preferences and behaviors, such as most and least trusted, attending a party with, seeking advice from, loaning a car to, sensitive to others, and so on. Ten of the 37 subjects had produced reflections in their Rorschach administered prior to treatment. Seven of the 10 were consistently ranked *least* for 11 of the 30 items, and all 10 were ranked *least* for the "seeking advice from," and "telling problems to" items. Interestingly, the mean Egocentricity Index for these 10 subjects, .57, did not differ significantly from the mean Index for the 10 other subjects who received the most positive nominations (.47). Another interesting finding is that the subjects who were mentioned least frequently tended to have substantially lower indices than others in the groups. Exner et al. (1975) were unable to establish any significant relationships between the Egocentricity Index and either the Field Dependence-Independence Phenomenon as measured by the rod and frame, or Locus of Control as measured by the I-E Scale.

Data from the 27-month interval of the long-term treatment effects study (Exner, 1978) indicate that a change from a too high or too low Egocentricity Index to the average range occurred significantly more often among patients who were rated as improved at the 27th month as contrasted with those who were rated as unimproved. Exner and Murillo (1977) were able to follow the post-hospitalization adjustment of 44 schizophrenics for 36 months. They were from a group of 70 multiple admission schizophrenics who had participated in a treatment effects study and had sustained enough improvement to remain out of the hospital. The 3-year behavioral evaluations indicated that almost all were able to function with reasonable effectiveness in their environments. About half had been treated with ECT plus psychotherapy and the other half with phenothiazines and psychotherapy. The mean pretreatment Egocentricity indices for both groups were significantly higher than average—.53 and .51, respectively. At intervals of both one and three years postdischarge, the mean Index for the ECT plus psychotherapy group was in the mid .30's—.37 and .35—whereas the mean for the group treated with drugs plus psychotherapy remained consistently high—.51 and .53. In this instance, the much higher Egocentricity Index of the drug-treated group does not appear to have created a significant handicap. It seems likely that the overly self-centered person is less prone to malfunction provided that he or she exists in an environment where self-centeredness is accepted or even encouraged. For instance, Winter and Exner (1973) tested 18 subjects who were successful performing artists with no psychiatric history. The Index for this group averaged .48, with a range of .40 to .62, and seven of the records contained reflection answers. Similarly, Exner et al. (1979) obtained the protocols of 39 successful theatrical dancers, none of whom have any admitted psychiatric history. The mean Egocentricity Index for the group is .47, with a range from .28 to .77, and 14 of the records contain at least one reflection answer.

Although a high Egocentricity Index probably becomes a liability for subjects in some situations, a lower than average Index appears to portend far more adjustment hazards. Exner and Murillo (1975) found that 16 of 22 relapsing nonschizophrenics had Egocentricity indices of less than .30 at discharge, whereas only four of the 55 nonrelapsers from this group had an Index of less than .30. Low Egocentricity indices tend to appear with a much greater frequency among the protocols of subjects with obsessive styles, such as obsessive-compulsives, depressives, phobics, and psychosomatics. A lower than average Index is very common in the records of effected adult suicides, and loaded positively into the original Suicide Constellation (Exner & Wylie, 1977). This was reaffirmed in a cross-validation of the Suicide Constellation; however, it was also found that higher than average indices also have a discriminant function (Exner, Martin, & Mason, 1984).

Thomas, Exner, and Baker (1982) used the Gough Adjective Checklist with 225 college students. Each student responded to the ACL twice during the same session, in a counterbalanced design, once with the instruction to "describe yourself," and once with the instruction to "describe yourself as you would like to be." A difference score was calculated for each subject, and the 20 subjects falling at each extreme were recruited to take the Rorschach. The average difference score for students in the upper extreme was 9.4 and in the lower extreme was 38.9, the latter showing the greatest discrepancy between the "real" and "ideal." The mean Egocentricity Index for the upper extreme group is 48.9 (SD = .09), and 11 of the records contained 16 reflection answers. The mean Index for the group in the lower extreme is .31 (SD = .12), and none of the records contained reflection responses (p < .01).

Interpretively, the Egocentricity Index should be approached as a measure of psychological self-focusing or self-concern. An excess of self-concern *or* a lack of self-concern both can be potential liabilities. In other words, egocentricity is a natural phenomenon that probably functions as an asset unless overdone or underdeveloped. An excess of self-centeredness, as illustrated by a high Index, does not necessarily equate with a positive self-image, but does represent the likelihood of more involvement with the self at the expense of a lesser, or more superficial involvement with others. If the Index includes a reflection response, it suggests that the self-involvement will be marked by a more juvenile, narcissistic-like tendency to overestimate personal worth. A low Egocentricity Index appears to signal negative self-esteem, that is, placing a low value on personal worth, probably because of a sense of failure to meet desires and/or expectations for oneself. It seems reasonably clear that a low Index is a precursor to an increase in the frequency and/or intensity of depressive experiences.

Morbid Content *(MOR)*   The Special Score *MOR* evolved from efforts to study depression in children. Some previous efforts to use morbid content as a suicide indicator had been reported to have achieved some modest success (White & Schreiber, 1952; Sakheim, 1955; Fleischer, 1957; Thomas, Ross, Brown, & Duszynski, 1973). Extrapolating from those works, plus some of the criteria listed for the Fisher and Cleveland (1958) Penetration scoring, a listing of possible criteria for *MOR* was submitted to five judges who worked independently. Subsequently, those definitions that were selected by all five judges as reflecting some aspect of morbidity were integrated, and the resulting criteria tested for interscorer reliability, which yielded a 95% agreement among 10 scorers and 15 records that contained a total of 57 *MOR* answers (Exner & McCoy, 1981).

The retest reliability of *MOR* among nonpatient adults ranges from .66 to .71 for long-term retests, to .78 to .88 when the retest is administered during a period of 30 days or less. The reliability of *MOR* among nonpatient children, over brief intervals, is slightly higher than for adults, ranging from .84 to .94. This is probably because children tend to have a greater proportion of records in which *one MOR* appears. Only 47% of nonpatient adults have at least one *MOR* in their records as compared to between 82% and 94% of the records of younger nonpatients. The mean for nonpatient adults is 0.7, with a mode of zero, whereas the means for all age groups of children and adolescents, except 14-year-olds, is slightly more than 1.0, and all but the 16-year-olds have modes of 1. This is apparently because younger clients give a greater frequency of the "flattened" animal response to Card VI, a response which is, by far, the most frequently given *MOR* by both children and adults.

Schizophrenics, character problems, and nondepressed outpatients average about one *MOR* answer, and they appear in slightly more than half of the protocols of those groups. The mean for the depressive reference sample is 3.47, which is significantly higher than for any other groups. The mode for depressives is 2, and 203 of the 210 subjects (97%) in that group have at least one *MOR* in their records. Exner and Weiner (1982) found that inpatient children with a primary symptom of depression average nearly three *MOR* responses as compared with about one for other inpatient children. They were also able to retest 22 depressed inpatient children after approximately 8 months of treatment and found that the mean for that group had declined from 2.94 in the first test to 1.01 in the second test.

There is a significant negative correlation ($r = -.41$, $p < .01$) between *MOR* and the Egocentricity Index; that is, as *MOR* is elevated, the Index tends to be lower. A considerable elevation in *MOR,* greater than three, was found in 72 of 101 (71%) protocols collected within 60 days prior to an effected suicide. This is the group of records used to cross-validate the original Suicide Constellation discovered by Exner and Wylie (1977). A discriminant functions analysis reveals that *MOR* > 3 does contribute to the differentiation of the suicide group from various control groups and, as such, it has been added as a twelfth variable to the revised Suicide Constellation (Exner, Martin, & Mason, 1984).

The pretreatment records of the 430 outpatients who volunteered to participate in the long-term treatment effects study (Exner, 1978) were coded for *MOR,* and any containing three or more *MOR* responses were used to create a separate group, disregarding presenting symptom patterns ($N = 76$). The therapist ratings for these patients, completed early into treatment, were reviewed and compared with the ratings of 76 other patients, drawn randomly from the remaining 354 subjects in the study. There was no *single* markedly consistent difference between the groups; however, a composite of nine items concerning attitudes toward the self, the presenting problem, and expectations for the future were rated significantly lower, that is, more negatively for the high *MOR* group.

MOR responses involve some form of projection as they embellish the classification of the stimulus field by attributing features to the object that are not obvious in the field. In that context, this composite of findings suggests that elevations in *MOR* signify either or both of two features. First, that the self-image is conceptualized by the subject to include more negative, and possibly damaged features than is commonplace and, second, that the orientation toward the self, and probably toward the environment, is marked by considerable pessimism. Obviously, either can predispose problems in adaptation, and either can foment a tendency toward anger, dissatisfaction, and/or depression. A variety of other features might mix with an elevation in *MOR* responses that can become a significant precursor to dysfunction. For instance, the composite of an elevation in *MOR,* a low Egocentricity Index, an elevation in *S,* and a low *X + %,* which is reduced mainly by *u* answers, sets the psychological stage for some types of asocial behaviors that can be inordinately detrimental to the long-term adjustment of the subject.

The *An + Xy* Contents Another data set that can often provide information about problems in self-image or self-concern is the *An + Xy* content frequencies. Anatomy responses occur with a significantly greater frequency than do x-ray answers, but both appear related to issues of body concern. The *An* response, because of its more substantial frequency, has been studied in more detail than *Xy* answers, but in the overall picture they are correlated with similar features. Beck (1945) speculated that they are related to issues of body concern. Shatin (1952) found a significantly greater frequency of *An* answers among psychosomatics than is the case for "neurotics." Zolliker (1943) earlier had found a substantially high incidence of *An* answers in the records of women suffering psychiatric complications due to pregnancy. Rapaport et al. (1946) found a high incidence of these responses among "neurasthenics." Weiss and Winnik (1963) have postulated that matters of physical health may not be relevant to the interpretation of *An* answers, arguing that these answers can indicate a vicarious preoccupation with body concern without directly experiencing physiological discomfort. However, that argument seems tenuous at best. Exner et al. (1975) found elevations in *An* responses in both elective surgery patients and overweight patients beginning a stringently controlled dietary routine. In fact, the records of 331 medical outpatients and inpatients reveal a mean for *An* of slightly more than two. Draguns, Haley, and Philips (1967) concluded from a literature review that *An* responses signal a form of self-absorption that can be the product of either autism or physiological changes such as those created by pregnancy, pubescence, or physical illness.

Nonpatient adults average about 0.6 *An* responses, and nonpatient children, through age 11, average about 0.9. Young adolescents, ages 12 to 15, average slightly more than 1.0 *An* answers. Patients, both adults and children, have larger proportions of records in which *An* answers occur, and have higher means for the variable, ranging from 1.2 for outpatient adults to 1.7 for inpatient depressives. About one-third of the *An* responses given by patients are *FQ−*, whereas less than 10% of the *An* responses given by nonpatients are minus answers. X-ray responses occur much less frequently among nonpatients than among patients. Only five of the 600 adult nonpatients in the normative sample gave an *Xy* answer, as did only 17 of the 1580 nonpatient children. Among psychiatric patients, they occur most frequently among schizophrenics and depressed patients with problems in body functioning. Exner, Murillo, and Sternklar (1979) found an average of 2.2 *Xy* answers among 21 inpatient schizophrenics who manifest body delusions, and an average of 1.7 *Xy* answers among 17 depressed inpatients who had problems in body functioning, as contrasted with a mean of 0.3 among other schizophrenics and depressives.

Thus any elevation in the composite of *An + Xy* should be taken as an indication of body concern. If no obvious medical cause for the concern is evident in the history of the subject, it is likely to have a psychogenic origin, and probably relates in some way to the overall conception of the self. If the composite includes *Xy* answers, the concern is probably marked by more distressful feelings, because they usually involve the achromatic or shading determinants, whereas the *An* responses that are not pure *F* answers are more likely to involve chromatic color.

The Personal Response *(PER)*   Another way to gain information concerning self-concept involves the array and frequency of tactics used as manuevers of defense. In the preceding chapter it was noted that elevations in *Mp* responses indicate a tendency to abuse fantasy, and that the presence of the Special Score *CP* apparently denotes an overuse of denial. Another aspect of protecting the self seems evident when *PER* responses occur with an above average frequency.

The initial interest in this Special Score evolved during the collection of normative samples for children. Many examiners questioned whether these verbalizations should be coded as *DR,* because they often seem to be irrelevant to the response. The normative data reveal that the largest average number of *PER* answers is given by 5-year-olds, 4.4, and that at least one appears in 93 of the 110 records in that sample. A gradual and consistent decline in *PER* occurs as age increases, to 3.5 for 8-year-olds, 2.3 for 10-year-olds, 1.4 for 13's, and slightly less than 1.0 for the 15- and 16-year-old groups, which is about the same as the mean of 1.06 for nonpatient adults. Although the means for *PER* beyond age 10 are quite low, the proportion of protocols in which at least one *PER* appears is substantial for all nonpatient groups. For example, one or more *PER* answers appear in about 75% of the records given by 12-year-olds, 77% of the 15-year-olds, and 68% of the nonpatient adults.

Like the *MOR* response, the distributions for nonpatients fall on a neat J-curve which has a very limited range, usually 0 to 5, but as narrow as 0 to 3 for some age groups, and a mode of 1. The distribution of *PER* in the depressive reference sample is about the same as for nonpatient adults, and the range is also 0 to 5; however, the distributions for other patient groups are somewhat different. For example, less than half of the subjects in the schizophrenic and character disorder reference samples gave at least one *PER*. The mode for both groups is zero, but the means are about the same as for nonpatients. This is because the ranges for both groups are more than twice as extensive as for nonpatients. More than one-third of the schizophrenics who gave a *PER* response gave at least three, and the same is true for more than 40% of the character disorders who gave *PER* answers. Thus although most of the subjects in both groups give no *PER,* a substantial number have elevations in *PER*.

A computer search of outpatient samples yielded two groups in which the mean for *PER* exceeded three. The first consists of 65 clearly obsessive adults ($M = 3.76$, $SD = 1.4$), and the second is a sample of 45 male adolescents in treatment because of problems in handling displays of anger ($M = 3.69$, $SD = 1.2$). Only six of the obsessive patients and seven of the adolescents had records in which no *PER* occurred. The modes for both groups are 3, and the ranges in each extending to 10. The data from the Thomas, Exner, and Baker (1982) study, in which 225 college students were administered the Gough Adjective Check List, revealed that the 20 subjects who had the least discrepancy between their "real and ideal" scores averaged 2.69 *PER* answers, whereas the 20 subjects from the opposite extreme of the ACL distribution average 0.7. Exner and Weiner (1982) used six assistants to record various behaviors that occurred among three fourth- and fifth-grade classes during interactive tasks assigned by teachers. Each class was observed by two raters for two 1-hour periods on each of five consecutive days. Among behaviors recorded were denial responses such as, "It's not my fault, he told me to do it," or "We would have finished if she hadn't fouled up," and so on. Subsequently, the five students with the highest frequency of denial behaviors, plus five others randomly selected from the remaining students, were administered the Rorschach by one of six examiners who were not familiar with the study. The five target students averaged 3.9 *PER* answers as contrasted with 2.16 for the control sample.

A computer search of the pretreatment protocols of the 430 outpatients who volunteered for the long-term treatment effects study (Exner, 1978) identified 82 (19%) in which *PER* appeared at least four times ($M = 5.73$, $SD = 1.6$). A review of the therapist ratings of those patients, for the early sessions of treatment, reveals that more than two-thirds (57) were rated as resistive, or having questionable motivation for treatment, as compared with less than 25% of a second group of 82 patients randomly selected from the remaining 348 subjects in the study ($M = 1.12$, $SD = 2.09$, $p < .01$).

The findings concerning the *PER* responses suggest that subjects giving significantly higher frequencies have some need to be overly precise in defending their self-image. On the surface, it may appear that some *PER* answers are more an indication of an openness or willingness to share information about oneself. That element may exist in some kinds of *PER* responses, such as the child who reports a butterfly, and then adds, ''I caught one like this, it was really pretty.'' But at a different level, the *PER* provides more sturdiness to the percept, and consequently to the self. The personal commentary serves to provide reassurance, as if psychologically saying, ''I know that I am right because I am drawing from direct experience,'' and in doing so, the subject feels able to fend off any potential challenge from the examiner.

The *Ab + Art* Contents   Another maneuver that is sometimes used to ward off threats to the self is intellectualization. Schafer (1954) postulated that this tactic often might be represented in Rorschach answers that contain symbolic or abstract features. The therapist ratings completed for the early treatment sessions, for the 430 outpatients who had volunteered to participate in the long-term treatment effects study, were computer subdivided on the basis of defensive tactics, to conduct a retrospective study of this hypothesis. In all, 104 patients (24%) were evaluated by the therapists as having marked tendencies to employ an intellectual approach to emotional issues. Two samples, one of 104 patients randomly selected from the remaining 324 subjects, and a second sample of 104 drawn randomly from the adult nonpatient protocol pool, were created as control groups. The target sample included 71 records (68%) in which at least one *Ab* appeared as a primary or secondary content, and the average for the sample is 0.94 ($SD = 0.71$), as compared with a mean of 0.58 ($SD = 0.61$) for the patient controls ($p > .20$, ns), and 0.38 ($SD = 0.44$) for the nonpatient controls ($p < .05$). However, *Ab* primary or secondary contents appeared in only 46 (44%) of the patient control protocols and in 27 (26) of the nonpatient records.

In light of the fact that the mean for *Ab* contents did not discriminate between the two patient groups, although the proportions of records in which *Ab* answers appears are considerable, a computer search was conducted to determine whether the combination of *Ab* and one or more other contents might provide a significant differentiation. It calculated all possible dyad and triad combinations that would include *Ab,* using both primary and secondary contents. The results identified the combination of *Ab + Art* as having the greatest strength to discriminate the two patient groups from each other, and from the nonpatient group. The mean *Ab + Art* for the target sample is 3.49 ($SD = 1.23$), with a mode of 3 and a range from 0 to 11. Either or both contents appear in 100 of the 104 records (96%). Interestingly, this group includes 43 of the 65 obsessives who have more than three *PER* responses. The mean for the patient control group is 1.29 ($SD = 0.99$, $p < .02$). The mode is 1, with a range from 0 to 4, and either or both contents appear in 68 of the protocols (65%). The mean for the nonpatient control group is 0.97 ($SD = 0.92$, $p < .01$). The mode is 0, with a range of 0 to 4, and either or both contents appear in only 48 of the records (46%).

Exner and Hillman (1984) reviewed the records of 76 paranoid schizophrenics, following the speculation that they are often more prone to intellectualize, and found that the mean for the *Ab + Art* variable was 3.22 ($SD = 1.1$). A randomly drawn sample of 76 nonparanoid schizophrenics, used for comparison, shows a mean for *Ab + Art* of 1.33 ($SD = 1.0$, $p < .05$). The mean and distribution for this latter group are very similar to the mean of 1.14 ($SD = 0.89$) for the adult nonpatient normative sample. Children between the ages of 5 and 13 give very few *Ab* answers, but do average slightly more than 1.0 *Art* response. Adolescents between the ages of 14 and 16 average 0.35 *Ab* answers and 1.1 *Art* responses.

Although the consistency of these findings seems sufficient to add the *Ab + Art* variable into the Structural Summary, the interpretation of the data must be approached conservatively, because the findings have been developed retrospectively. A combined frequency of 3, which does exceed one *SD* above the mean for adults, is probably not very indicative of an excessive use of intellectualization in an average length record. On the other hand, as the frequency increases beyond 3, and especially in protocols that include *Ab* contents, it seems impossible to avoid the postulate that intellectualization is an important feature in defending the self.

INTERPERSONAL PERCEPTIONS *(H, Hd, Isolate:R, AG)*

Rorschach data concerning interpersonal interests and views of others are also very inferential, and must be pieced together very carefully before formulating any hypotheses. Most but not all of these postulates will be derived from the responses containing human contents, especially the human movement responses, but because the latter often occur with low to modest frequencies, other data also become important to the fleshing out of a meaningful picture.

Human Contents *(H, Hd, (H), (Hd))*   Ames et al, (1971) found that human contents tend to increase gradually through each of the early developmental years to about age 10, after which the proportion remains relatively stable through adolescence. Those findings are consistent with the normative data for younger clients (Exner & Weiner, 1982). When *all* human contents are considered, the data for ages 12 through 16 are not unlike those for nonpatient adults. Each of those age groups has a mean that falls between 4 and 5, and a mode of 5. The mean for the adult nonpatients is slightly more than 5, but with a mode of 4.

Most patient groups also have means for human content that fall between more than 4 to slightly more than 6. For instance, the mean for the depressive reference sample is slightly more than 4, with a mode of 4. The schizophrenic reference sample has a mean of more than five human contents, and a mode of 6. A randomly selected group of 250 outpatients shows a mean of 6.03, with a mode of 5.

The absence of human content is an unusual finding, even in the records of younger children. The five-year-old nonpatient sample includes 86% of the protocols that contain at least one human content, and that proportion increases to nearly 90% for the six-year-olds. From age seven through age 12, the proportion ranges from 94 to 96%, and after age 12 into adulthood, 99 or 100% of the samples contain at least one human content. The absence of human content appears to signal a marked lack of interest in and/or detachment from people which, except for the very young child, probably has some psychopathological features, and will almost always indicate problems in identity and/or self-image (Exner, 1978).

Lower than average frequencies of human content are more common among subjects who do not appear to identify closely with typical social values. A significantly lower than average frequency of human contents has been noted by Walters (1953) in the records of criminals, and by Ray (1963) and Richardson (1963) among adjudicated delinquents. Exner, Bryant, and Miller (1975) found that the protocols of 15 adolescents, awaiting sentencing for serious assault crimes, included six with no human content and five others in which the frequency of human contents was 1 or 2. The reference sample of character disorders has a mean of less than 4 and a mode of 2. Several studies (Halpern, 1940; Morris, 1943; Stotsky, 1952; Goldman, 1960; Piotrowski & Bricklin, 1961) have found positive relationships between the frequency of human contents and treatment effectiveness. Draguns, Haley, and Phillips (1967) have suggested that the frequency of human content varies with cognitive development and the potential for social relations. Their review of literature suggests that low frequencies of human contents may be an effective index from which to differentiate those who have withdrawn from social contacts. The data for the 430 outpatients in the long-term treatment effects study seems to support this postulate. The 50 subjects who were rated by therapists as being the most isolated interpersonally had, on the average, very low frequencies of human contents ($M = 1.84$, $SD = 1.21$), and also had very low Affective Ratios ($M = .374$, $SD = .11$).

Although the frequency of human contents is important, because it provides some indications about interest in people, and possibly the extent to which a person identifies with the social environment, the frequency of *Pure H* responses adds very important information concerning views of, and attitudes toward the social environment as they involve real figures. The proportion of human contents that is *Pure H* usually ranges from one-third to one-half among nonpatient children, ages 8 through 13. After age 13, and into adulthood, the proportion of *Pure H* increases significantly, to between one-half and two-thirds of all human contents. The mean for *Pure H* among nonpatient adults is about 3, with a mode of 2. Among older nonpatient adolescents the mean is greater than 2, and the mode is 3.

Patient groups tend to have lower means and modes for *Pure H*. For instance, the means for both the schizophrenic and depressive reference samples are about 2, and the modes for both groups are 1. The mean for the character disorder group is less than 2 and the mode is 1. Slightly less than 80% of the schizophrenic group gave at least one *Pure H*, as contrasted with 85% of the character disorders, 87% of the depressives, and 96% of the nonpatient adults. Moreover, 38% of the adult nonpatient records that contain human contents are *exclusively Pure H*. This occurred in only 9% of the protocols of depressives, 3% of the schizophrenic records, and 7% of the character disorder group. As the proportion of *Pure H* increases it seems to indicate that interests in and views of the social environment are probably based more in the context of real experience, regardless of whether those experiences have been favorable or unfavorable.

At the opposite extreme are records in which the frequency of human contents is near or above average, but the frequency of *Pure H* is 1 or zero. In these cases, most or all of the human responses consist of *Hd,* or the parenthesized human contents, *(H)* and *(Hd)*. Protocols such as these occur most frequently among psychiatric subjects and very young children. One-hundred eighteen of the 600 adult nonpatient records (19%) have this characteristic, as do between 9% and 18% of the records of younger nonpatients, ages 10 to 16. Conversely, 154 of the 320 schizophrenic reference sample protocols have this feature (48%), as do 108 of the 210 depressive records (47%), and 111 of the 200 records of the character disorder group (55%).

Beck (1945) suggested that an emphasis on *Hd* answers occurs in people who feel constricted in their world. Klopfer et al. (1954) felt that *Hd* answers signal a form of compulsiveness and/or intellectual approach. Sherman (1952) and Vinson (1960) found significantly more *Hd* in the records of schizophrenics than among nonpatients. Molish (1967) has suggested that as the balance of human contents shifts in favor of *Hd*, it is indicative of a constrictive form of defense. The sample of nonpatient adults contains 3.86 *Pure H* for every one *Hd* answer. When the parenthesized human contents *(H)* and *(Hd)* are included, the ratio shifts slightly to 3.19 $H + (H)$ for each 1 $Hd + (Hd)$. Most psychiatric groups have a higher proportion of Hd to H than nonpatients; however, when the parenthesized human contents are added to the ratio, the proportion of $H + (H):Hd + (Hd)$ is about 3:1. The most marked exception to this is found in a combined sample of 76 paranoid schizophrenics and 43 inpatients described as having a ''paranoid style.'' The ratio of $H + (H):Hd + (Hd)$ for these 119 protocols is 1.62:1, and they include 81 (68%) in which the ratio is essentially 1:1, or in which the value for $Hd + (Hd)$ is greater (Exner & Hillman, 1984).

The frequency of the parenthesized human contents typically is quite low among nonpatient adults ($M = 0.64$, SD $= 0.77$), but is almost twice as large for nonpatient children between the ages of 5 and 9 ($M = 1.24$, $SD = 0.83$). Patients with marked paranoid features average nearly four ($M = 3.79$) parenthesized human contents. Elevations are also common among schizophrenics and character disorders, although less so among depressed patients. Molish (1967) has pointed out that these answers may indicate forms of denial as related to the social environment. They clearly seem to indicate a detachment from the real world, and probably signal an investment in fantasy.

The Structural Summary includes four data points that are helpful in identifying those instances in which the distribution of human contents deviates from the expected. The first is the ratio of $H + (H):Hd + (Hd)$, which should always be at least 3:1, if not greater, such as 4:1, 5:1, and so on. Any elevation in Hd answers should be some cause for concern, because it probably signifies an overly pedantic and possibly distorted view of others. The second is the frequency of *Pure H* responses, and this is expected to include at least half of the total human contents. When the frequency falls below half of the human contents, it suggests that impressions of people are probably formulated more from nonreal than real experiences. The third is the ratio of $H + A:Hd + Ad$. It is included to focus on the frequency of Hd and Ad answers that occur in the record. As has already been noted, Hd answers are much more common among people who are more guarded and suspicious in their views of the social environment. Sometimes, however, subjects with this feature give a very low frequency of human contents, and if only those data are considered, the presence of this characteristic might be neglected. Rorschach noted that animal contents reflect the largest single class of response. A variety of studies have confirmed that impression (Beck et al., 1950; Cass & McReynolds, 1951; Brockway et al. 1954; Neff & Glaser, 1954; Wedemeyer, 1954). Ames et al. (1971) note that about half of the responses of children and slightly less than half of those given by adolescence are of animals, and Beck et al. (1961) found an average of about 45% of responses in adult records include animal contents. The normatve samples for nonpatient adults and younger subjects are consistent with those findings. Apparently, animal responses occur most frequently because this class of contents involves a very broad array of shapes, thereby increasing the probability that at least one will have some congruence with the contours of a blot or blot areas. But just as Hd responses occur infrequently, so too do Ad answers. Thus the $H + A:Hd + Ad$ ratio should always have a much larger value on the left side, at least 4:1. If the value on the right side is greater than one-fourth that of the left, it suggests that views of the social environment may be somewhat unusual. The Exner and Hillman (1984) review of 119 protocols of patients with marked paranoid features shows that 93 (78%) have $H + A:Hd + Ad$ ratios in which the right side value equals 50% or more of the left side value. The fourth ratio, $(H) + (A):(Hd) + (Ad)$, is designed to call attention to the frequencies of responses in which some detachment from reality exists. If any such responses occur, the value is expected to appear in the left side of the ratio, and low frequencies such as 1:0 or 2:1 are commonplace, especially among younger subjects. If the combined values exceed 3, or if the higher value is on the right side of the ratio, consideration should be afforded to the possibility that the social environment is often misinterpreted.

The Aggressive Movement Response *(AG)*   The frequency of *AG* responses may also provide some information concerning views of, and reactions to, the social environment. The notion of a Special Score for aggressive movement answers was derived from some of the work of Piotrowski (1957). He has argued that the characteristics of *M* responses often translate directly into impressions about people and responses to them. Kazaoka, Sloane, and Exner (1978) rated videotapes of the occupational and recreational therapy activities of seven inpatient groups for verbal and nonverbal aggressiveness. Each group, containing 10 patients, was taped for two 20-minute segments, once during occupational therapy in which the patients were encouraged to do clay construction, and once during recreational therapy in which each group was divided into two teams of five each to play basketball. The tapes were scored independently by each of three raters using the Fels Institute Aggression Scale. Rorschachs were administered to the 70 patients by seven examiners, each giving 10, who had no knowledge of the nature of the study.

The 70 subjects were divided into two equal groups twice, once by a median split of the distribution of the scores for verbal aggressiveness, and once by a median split of the distribution of scores for physical aggressiveness. The groups did not differ significantly for *AG* scores when divided on the basis of verbal aggressiveness (Upper Half = 3.07, *SD* = 1.98; Lower Half = 1.71, *SD* = 1.57, *p* >.20, ns). When the 15 subjects at each extreme of the verbal aggressiveness distribution were compared, however, they did differ significantly for *AG* (Upper 15 = 4.21, *SD* = 2.03; Lower 15 = 0.94, *SD* = 1.09, *p* <.01). When the division was based on the distribution of physical aggressiveness scores, the difference was more substantial (Upper Half = 3.57, *SD* = 1.81; Lower Half = 1.06, *SD* = 1.13, *p* <.05), and when the 15 subjects at each extreme of the distribution were compared, the magnitude of the difference was much greater (Upper 15 = 4.16, *SD* = 1.94; Lower 15 = 0.78, *SD* = 1.08, *p* <.01). Interestingly, when the scores for verbal and physical aggressiveness were combined and the distribution split at the median again, the two groups did not differ significantly (Upper = 4.06, *SD* = 1.83; Lower = 2.79; *SD* = 1.74, *p*. >.20, ns), but the 15 subjects in each extreme did differ significantly (Upper 15 = 5.39; *SD* = 2.01; Lower 15 = 1.88, *SD* = 1.2, *p* <.02).

In another study 33 sixth grade children, who had been administered the Rorschach 2 to 3 weeks earlier, were videotaped during two 30-minute free periods in their classroom (Exner, Kazaoka, & Morris, 1979). The tapes were scored independently by two raters, using the Fels Aggression Scale, for verbal and nonverbal aggressiveness. The group was divided twice, using a median split of the distributions for verbal and nonverbal aggression, and discarding the middle subject. The mean *AG* scores for the upper half were significantly greater than for the lower half in both instances (Upper Verbal = 3.86, *SD* = 1.1; Lower Verbal = 1.2, *SD* = 0.87, *p* <.05; Upper Physical = 3.99, *SD* = 1.3; Lower Physical = 0.96, *SD* = 0.89, *p* <.02), although an analysis of the group split on the basis of the combined scores was not significant (*p* >.10).

The records of the 430 outpatients who began the long-term treatment effects study include 82 (19%) that contain at least three *AG* answers. Therapist ratings for the early treatment sessions did not include any items specifically relating to a history of aggressive activity, but ratings were requested for manifestations of hostility during the sessions, and a second group of items concerned attitudes toward people. A comparison group of 82 subjects was randomly drawn from the remaining 348 subjects. Forty-one of the 82 subjects were rated as manifesting significant hostility during at least two of the three sessions, as contrasted with 15 subjects from the comparison group ($p <.01$), and 51 of the 82 were rated as being markedly hostile in their attitudes toward people, as contrasted with 22 subjects from the comparison group ($p <.05$).

This composite of studies appears to support the notion that elevations in *AG* signify an increased likelihood for aggressive behaviors, either verbal or nonverbal, and that they also indicate attitudes toward others that are more negative and/or hostile than is customary. Quite likely, people with elevations in *AG* see the social environment as marked by aggressiveness, and they have incorporated that attitude or set, so that it has become a feature of their own personality, and consequently a feature that marks some of their behavior. It seems likely that the manifestations of aggressiveness will vary considerably, being influenced by other characteristics, such as reality testing, affective controls, and stress tolerance. Thus the high *AG* subject who has reasonably adequate controls (*D* score of zero or greater), prefers to avoid emotionally toned stimuli (low Affective ratio), modulates emotion effectively (more *FC* than *CF + C*), and forms most responses with regard to convention (average or higher $X + \%$ and number of Populars), will manifest the features of aggressiveness in ways that are more in keeping with socially accepted behaviors. On the other hand, the high *AG* person who has more limited controls (*D* score of less than zero), does not modulate emotional discharges very well (more *CF + C* than *FC*), is less concerned with conventional behaviors (low $X + \%$ and/or number of Populars), and is very oppositional (elevated *S*), is probably much more likely to express his or her set toward aggressiveness in ways that are much more directly observable.

The Isolation Index *(Isolate:R)* Another datum that will sometimes provide information concerning one's views and reactions to the social environment is the Isolation Index. It evolved through a series of computer search investigations concerning content categories. Throughout Rorschach history it has seemed logical to assume that an elevation in the frequency for any content category has some interpretive significance. This is because the frequencies for most categories are very low, with the exception of the Animal and Human contents. None average more than two for most groups, except Botany, which has a mean of 2.03 (*SD* = 1.1) for nonpatient adults. Many authors (Beck, 1945; Klopfer & Kelley, 1942; Rapaport, Gill, & Schafer, 1946; Piotrowski, 1957; Draguns, Haley, & Phillips, 1967; Exner, 1974) have postulated that elevations in a single category indicate some form of conflict or preoccupation; with the exception of the *An + Xy* composite, however, no empirical data support this proposition. In that context, the computer searches were designed to study individual content categories plus various combinations of categories as they might relate to other data available concerning subjects.

The first hint that the combination of Botany, Clouds, Geography, Landscape, and Nature categories might relate to social isolation or withdrawal occurred by studying the contents in the first protocols of the 430 outpatients who volunteered to participate in the long-term treatment effects study. Therapist ratings for the early sessions contained items about social behaviors, such as frequency of social contacts outside the immediate family, feelings of social alienation or isolation, and so on. The correlation between a composite of these ratings and the combination of the five content categories is $r = .26$ for the entire group ($p <.01$); however, when the 100 subjects from each extreme of the distribution of therapist ratings were analyzed separately, the results are quite striking. For the 100 evaluated as having the most active and positive social relations, the correlation with the combined frequencies of the five contents is $-.22$ ($p < .05$), but for the 100 evaluated as being the least active and/or having the most negative social relations, the correlation with the combined frequencies for the five contents is .47 ($p < .001$).

An examination of the frequency data for the five combined contents revealed that 73 of the 100 subjects rated positively had scores of 4 or less ($M = 2.87$, $SD = 2.02$), whereas 67 of the 100 subjects rated negatively had scores of 5 or more ($M = 5.68$, $SD = 2.29$, $p > .15$, ns). Although the means for the two groups are not significantly different when compared for absolute values, they are significantly different when the scores are analyzed in relation to R. The protocols of 77 of the 100 subjects rated negatively for social relations have combined content scores that exceed one-fourth of R, and in 48 of those cases the score exceeds one-third of R. Conversely, only 14 of the records for the 100 subjects rated positively have scores for the combined contents that exceed one-fourth of R, and only two exceed one-third of R.

These findings appeared to indicate that a proportionally high frequency of the combined five contents signals some difficulties in the interpersonal sphere; however, other findings suggested that this proposition was far too encompassing, and possibly erroneous. As will be noted from the tables in Chapter 11, only 8% of the schizophrenia reference sample, 5% of the depressive sample, and 9% of the character disorder group have a sum of the five contents that exceeds one-fourth of R. Yet all three of those psychiatric groups are well known for problems in interpersonal relationships. On the other hand, 14% of the adult nonpatients and between 12% and 20% of the nonpatient children and adolescent samples meet this critical criterion. At first glance, these data suggest that proportional elevations in the sum of the five contents is more favorable.

The next clue to the significance of the *Isolate:R* Index was revealed by a review of data for other psychiatric samples. Two groups surfaced in this process, both of which have substantial percentages of protocols in which the sum of the five contents exceeds one-fourth of R. The first is a combined group of 505 children and adolescents who have teacher ratings, or psychologist evaluations, indicating that they are markedly withdrawn from social contact (Exner, 1978). Of those 505 records, 394 (78%) have a sum of the five contents that exceeds one-fourth of R, and 209 (41%) have a score that exceeds one-third of R. The second group consists of 146 outpatient adults diagnosed as "schizoid," or "schizotypal personality disorder." Of the 146 records, 107 (74%) contain a sum of the five content categories that exceeds one-fourth of R, and 54 of those (37%) have a score that exceeds one-third of R. These data, combined with earlier findings, appear to indicate that, rather than interpersonal difficulties, proportional elevations in the sum of the five contents signify some sort of social isolation. Two studies have been completed to test this postulate.

Farber, Exner, and Thomas (1982) used a peer nomination design with 139 high school sophomores and juniors in an effort to identify subjects having the most limited social contact with others in their classes. The nominations included 15 items, all of which related to interpersonal preferences or behaviors, such as most popular, best dancer, most friendly, most humorous, most helpful, best listener, most sensitive to others, most fun to be with, most responsible, most trustworthy, and so on. All of the items focused on positive rather than negative features. Eighteen students received no nominations, and they, plus 18 other students selected randomly as controls from the remaining 120, were recruited to take the Rorschach. Each subject received a $10 payment for volunteering. The target sample shows a mean sum of the five contents of 6.13 ($SD = 2.3$), whereas the control group has a mean of 3.78 ($SD = 1.54$, $p > .15$, ns). The target sample has a mean

R of 19.87 (SD = 4.1), and the control group a mean R of 20.47 (SD = 3.8). However, 13 of the 18 subjects in the target sample (72%) have a *Isolate:R* in which the value in the left exceeds one-fourth of the value on the right, as contrasted with only three (17%) of the 18 controls ($p < .05$).

In the second study, a 30-item peer nomination inventory was used with 64 female college students, all of whom lived in the same dormitory at a small residential college (Exner & Farber, 1983). They had volunteered to participate in a psychological study concerning stresses of campus living in exchange for a donation toward new furnishings for one of the study rooms in the dormitory. All were administered several psychological tests and completed several questionnaires including the one concerning peer nominations. The 30 items included the 15 used in the previous study, plus 15 negative items, such as least friendly, most disruptive, most insensitive to others, most outspoken, most irritating, least responsible, most argumentative, and *least interested in being with people*. All subjects received at least two nominations, and 14 were nominated at least once as being least interested in being with people; however, nine of the 14 received at least 20 such nominations as compared with fewer than six for the remaining five subjects. Those nine subjects averaged 7.33 for the sum of the five *Isolate* contents with a mean R of 21.6. *All* had *Isolate:R* ratios in which the left value exceeded one-fourth of the right side value. For comparison, five randomly selected groups of nine subjects each were drawn from the remaining 55 students. In one group, three subjects had *Isolate:R* ratios in which the left value exceeded one-fourth of the right value ($p > .15$, ns), but in the other four groups only one or zero had ratios in which the left side was of this magnitude ($p < .05$).

Collectively, the data concerning the *Isolate:R* seem to support the premise that when the left side value is greater than one-fourth the right side value, a marked tendency toward social isolation exists; however, the ratio should be used cautiously. The prospective findings are based on two relatively small samples of nonpatient students, and the retrospective data, although consistent, leave unanswered the question of why significantly smaller proportions of inpatients have this feature in their records than do nonpatients. Possibly most have not been socially isolated, and their social difficulties have contributed to their difficulties. But that is quite speculative. In most instances, an elevated *Isolate:R* ratio will occur in records in which other variables also signal some form of disinterest or withdrawal from others, such as a very low Affective Ratio, or a very low number of human contents, or the absence of *Pure H*. Also, in most cases of social isolation, other non-Rorschach data such as personal reports, reports of significant others, observations, and such, will provide the main source of social isolation information. There are obvious exceptions, especially among adolescents who claim many friendships, but the claim proves to be an overgeneralization based on the knowledge of names of classmates. Thus an elevation in the Isolation Index should be regarded as a signal to explore the breadth and depth of social relations. The five contents contributing to the Index are all nonhuman, nonsocial, inanimate, and usually static objects. Very possibly, the subject who identifies more with those characteristics will, in fact, be the more detached and isolated individual.

REFERENCES

Ames, L. B., Metraux, R. W., and Walker, R. N. (1971) *Adolescent Rorschach Responses*. New York: Brunner/Mazel.

Beck, S. J. (1945) *Rorschach's Test. II: A Variety of Personality Pictures.* New York: Grune & Stratton.

Beck, S. J., Beck, A., Levitt, E., and Molish, H. B. (1961) *Rorschach's Test. I: Basic Processes.* (3rd Ed.) New York: Grune & Stratton.

Beck, S. J., Rabin, A. I, Thiesen, W. G., Molish, H. B. and Thetford, W. N. (1950) The normal personality as projected in the Rorschach Test. *Journal of Psychology,* **30,** 241–298.

Brockway, A. L., Gleser, G. C., and Utlett, G. A. (1954) Rorschach concepts of normality. *Journal of Consulting Psychology,* **18,** 259–265.

Cass, W. A., and McReynolds, P. A. (1951) A contribution to Rorschach norms. *Journal of Consulting Psychology,* **15,** 178–183.

Draguns, J. G., Haley, E. M., and Phillips, L. (1967) Studies of Rorschach content: A review of the research literature. Part 1: Traditional content categories. *Journal of Projective Techniques and Personality Assessment,* **31,** 3–32.

Exner, J. E. (1969) Rorschach responses as an index of narcissism. *Journal of Projective Techniques and Personality Assessment,* **33,** 324–330.

Exner, J. E. (1973) The Self Focus Sentence Completion: A Study of Egocentricity. *Journal of Personality Assessment,* **37,** 437–455.

Exner, J. E. (1974) *The Rorschach: A Comprehensive System. Volume 1.* New York: Wiley.

Exner, J. E. (1978) *The Rorschach: A Comprehensive System. Volume 2: Current research and advanced interpretation.* New York: Wiley.

Exner, J. E., Armbruster, G. L., Walker, E. J., and Cooper, W. H. (1975) Anticipation of elective surgery as manifest in Rorschach records. Workshops Study No. 213 (unpublished), Rorschach Workshops.

Exner, J. E., Bryant, E. L., and Miller, A. S. (1975) Rorschach responses of some juvenile offenders. Workshops Study No. 214 (unpublished), Rorschach Workshops.

Exner, J. E., and Farber, J. G. (1983) Peer nominations among female college students living in a dormitory setting. Workshops Study No. 290 (unpublished), Rorschach Workshops.

Exner, J. E., and Hillman, L. (1984) A comparison of content distributions for the records of 76 paranoid schizophrenics and 76 nonparanoid schizophrenics. Workshops Study No. 293 (unpublished), Rorschach Workshops.

Exner, J. E., Kazaoka, K., and Morris, H. M. (1979) Verbal and nonverbal aggression among sixth grade students during free periods as related to a Rorschach Special Score for aggression. Workshops Study No. 255 (unpublished), Rorschach Workshops.

Exner, J. E., Kuhn, B., Schumacher, J., and Fishman, R. (1975) The relation of Field Dependence and Locus of Control to the Rorschach index of egocentricity. Workshops Study No. 189 (unpublished), Rorschach Workshops.

Exner, J. E., Martin, L. S., and Mason, B. (1984) A review of the Rorschach Suicide Constellation. 11th International Congress of Rorschach and Projective Techniques. Barcelona, Spain.

Exner, J. E., and McCoy, R. (1981) An experimental score for morbid content (MOR). Workshops Study No. 260 (unpublished), Rorschach Workshops.

Exner, J. E., and Murillo, L. G. (1975) Early prediction of posthospitalization relapse. *Journal of Psychiatric Research,* **12,** 231–237.

Exner, J. E., and Murillo, L. G. (1977) A long term followup of schizophrenics treated with regressive ECT. *Diseases of the Nervous System,* **38,** 162–168.

Exner, J. E., Murillo, L. G., and Sternklar, S. (1979) Anatomy and x-ray responses among patients with body delusions or body problems. Workshops Study No. 257 (unpublished), Rorschach Workshops.

Exner, J. E., and Weiner, I. B. (1982) *The Rorschach: A Comprehensive System. Volume 3: Assessment of children and adolescents.* New York: Wiley.

Exner, J. E., Weiss, L. J., Coleman, M., and Rose, R. B. (1979) Rorschach variables for a group of occupationally successful dancers. Workshops Study No. 250 (unpublished), Rorschach Workshops.

Exner, J. E., and Wylie, J. R. (1977) Some Rorschach data concerning suicide. *Journal of Personality Assessment*, **41**, 339–348.

Exner, J. E., Wylie, J. R., and Bryant, E. L. (1974) Peer preference nominations among outpatients in four psychotherapy groups. Workshops Study No. 199 (unpublished), Rorschach Workshops.

Farber, J. L., Exner, J. E., and Thomas, E. E. (1982) Peer nominations among 139 high school students as related to the Isolation Index. Workshops Study No. 288 (unpublished), Rorschach Workshops.

Fisher, S., and Cleveland, S.E. (1958) *Body Image and Personality*, New York: Van Nostrand Reinhold.

Fleischer, M. S. (1957) Differential Rorschach configurations of suicidal patients: a psychological study of threatened, attempted, and successful suicides. Unpublished doctoral dissertation, Yeshiva University.

Goldman, R. Changes in Rorschach performance and clinical improvement in schizophrenia. *Journal of Consulting Psychology*, **24**, 403–407.

Halpern, F. (1940) Rorschach interpretation of the personality structure of schizophrenics who benefit from insulin therapy. *Psychiatric Quarterly*, **14**, 826–833.

Kazaoka, K., Sloane, K., and Exner, J. E. (1978) Verbal and nonverbal aggressive behaviors among 70 inpatients during occupational and recreational therapy. Workshops Study No. 254 (unpublished), Rorschach Workshops.

Klopfer, B., Ainsworth, M., Klopfer, W., and Holt, R. (1954) *Developments in the Rorschach Technique. I: Technique and Theory.* Yonkers-on-Hudson, N.Y.: World Book.

Klopfer, B., and Kelley, D. (1942) *The Rorschach Technique.* Yonkers-on-Hudson, N.Y.: World Book.

Molish, H. B. (1967) Critique and problems of the Rorschach. A survey. In Beck, S. J. and Molish, H. B. *Rorschach's Test. II: A Variety of Personality Pictures.* (2nd Ed.) New York: Grune & Stratton.

Morris, W. W. (1943) Prognostic possibilities of the Rorschach method in metrazol therapy. *American Journal of Psychiatry*, **100**, 222–230.

Neff, W. S., and Glaser, N. M. (1954) Normative data on the Rorschach. *Journal of Psychology*, **37**, 95–104.

Piotrowski, Z. (1957) *Perceptanalysis.* New York: Macmillan.

Piotrowski, Z. A., and Bricklin, B. (1961) A second validation of a long term prognostic index for schizophrenic patients. *Journal of Consulting Psychology*, **25**, 123–128.

Rapaport, D., Gill, M., and Schafer, R. (1946) *Diagnostic Psychological Testing.* Vol. 2, Chicago: Yearbook Publishers.

Ray, A. B. (1963) Juvenile delinquency by Rorschach inkblots. *Psychologia*, **6**, 190–192.

Raychaudhuri, M., and Mukerji, K. (1971) Homosexual-narcissistic "reflections" in the Rorschach: An examination of Exner's diagnostic Rorschach signs. *Rorschachiana Japonica*, **12**, 119–126.

Richardson, H. (1963) Rorschachs of adolescent approved school girls, compared with Ames normal adolescents. *Rorschach Newsletter*, **8**, 3–8.

Sakheim, G. A. (1953) Suicidal responses on the Rorschach Test: A validation study. *Journal of Nervous and Mental Disease*, **122**, 332–344.

Schafer, R. (1954) *Psychoanalytic Interpretation in Rorschach Testing.* New York: Grune & Stratton.

Shatin, L. (1952) Psychoneurosis and psychosomatic reaction. A Rorschach study. *Journal of Consulting Psychology,* **16,** 220–223.

Sherman, M. (1952) A comparison of formal and content factors in the diagnostic testing of schizophrenia. *Genetic Psychology Monographs,* **46,** 183–234.

Stotsky, B. A. (1952) A comparison of remitting and non-remitting schizophrenics on psychological tests. *Journal of Abnormal and Social Psychology,* **47,** 489–496.

Thomas, C. B., Ross, D. C., Brown, B. S., and Duszynski, K. R. (1973) A prospective study of the Rorschachs of suicides: The predictive potential of pathological content. *The Johns Hopkins Medical Journal,* **132,** 334–360.

Thomas, E. E., Exner, J. E., and Baker, W. (1982) Ratings of real versus ideal self among 225 college students. Workshops Study No. 287 (unpublished), Rorschach Workshops.

Vinson, D. B. (1960) Responses to the Rorschach Test that identify thinking, feelings, and behavior. *Journal of Clinical and Experimental Psychopathology,* **21,** 34–40.

Walters, R. H. (1953) A preliminary analysis of the Rorschach records of fifty prison inmates. *Journal of Projective Techniques,* **17,** 436–446.

Watson, A. (1965) Objects and objectivity: A study in the relationship between narcissism and intellectual subjectivity. Unpublished doctoral dissertation, University of Chicago.

Wedemeyer, B. (1954) Rorschach statistics on a group of 136 normal men. *Journal of Psychology,* **37,** 51–58.

Weiss, A. A., and Winnik, H. Z. (1963) A contribution to the meaning of anatomy responses on the Rorschach Test. *Israel Annual of Psychiatry,* **1,** 265–276.

White, M. A., and Schreiber, H. (1952) Diagnosing "suicidal risks" on the Rorschach. *Psychiatric Quarterly Supplement,* **26,** 161–189.

Winter, L. B., and Exner, J. E. (1973) Some psychological characteristics of successful theatrical artists. Workshops Study No. 183 (unpublished), Rorschach Workshops.

Wylie, R. C. (1974) *The Self Concept. Volume 1: A review of methodological considerations and measuring instruments.* Lincoln: University of Nebraska Press.

Wylie, R. C. (1979) *The Self Concept. Volume 2: Theory and research on selected topics.* Lincoln: University of Nebraska Press.

Zolliker, A. (1943) Schwangerschaftsdepression and Rorschach'scher formdeutversuch. *Schweiz Archeives Neurologie und Psychiatrie,* **53,** 62–78.

CHAPTER 17

Structural Data IV—
Special Indices

There are three other data points in the Structural Summary that have special importance and, ordinarily, they should be reviewed after the record has been checked for validity, but before the descriptive interpretation begins. They are included to provide an early warning about the possibility of major problems. One concerns the possibility of suicide potential *(S-CON)*, the second is an index that can alert to the possibility of schizophrenia *(SCZI)*, and the third may signal the presence of a major affective problem *(DEPI)*. When any of the three exceed critical cut-off points, the interpreter must divert from the customary routine of scanning structural data and pursue the issue raised by the elevated score. Obviously, if the findings are positive for any of these problems, the descriptive interpretation will be formulated in that context and, in some instances, an awareness of the presence of one of these problems can be valuable in clarifying findings concerning other psychological characteristics. Although all three are based on reasonably sturdy empirical data, none of the three are infallible, and any interpreter would be foolhardy to assume that any of these issues can be ruled out simply by reviewing these indices.

THE SUICIDE CONSTELLATION *(S-CON)*

The early identification of the potential for self-destructive behavior is a persistent challenge for the clinician. The classic works of Shneidman and Farberow (1957) and Farberow and Shneidman (1961) have demonstrated clear relationships between demographic and/or behavioral variables and effected suicide, and it is unlikely that any test data, taken alone, will provide a greater discrimination of suicidal risk. Nonetheless, those data often are not available, thus when test data can provide clues concerning this risk, they should be taken seriously as a warning to conduct a more extensive evaluation of the issue.

Any review of the research literature concerning suicide reveals a host of methodological and interpretive problems. Criterion variables often differ considerably, and data from suicidal subjects are often collected too long before, or too long after, the critical event. Possibly even more important is the matter of *intent*, which is extremely difficult, if not impossible, to judge at a very precise level. Some suicides are effected by means that ordinarily are not expected to produce death, such as taking 12 or 15 aspirin, but such deaths do occur. On the other hand, there are people who survive self-inflicted gunshot wounds to the head. It seems unlikely that the intent to die was greater for the aspirin-taker than for the gunshot victim, yet on a purely demographic basis, the former is recorded as an effected suicide, whereas the latter is recorded as merely an attempt. Although some of these problems are potentially solvable, research concerning suicide is confounded by the scientific issue of prediction. Studies concerning suicide are really postdictive or retrospective, usually based on data collected from subjects who have been identified by other sources as suicidal (most commonly by reason of a prior attempt) or, in fewer instances, are based on data collected before the attempted or effected suicide. Thus even if a potential predictor is discovered, moral commitment to prevention clearly takes precedence over the scientific fantasy to test the predictor by letting events run their full course.

The complexity of features that promotes self-destruction is such that no single variable (or small group of variables) can be expected to be accurate in identifying suicide potential. This point is made quite well in a thorough review of the pre-1970 literature concerning Rorschach data and the suicidal subject (Goldfried, Stricker, & Weiner, 1971). They note that research has focused on single signs, such as the color-shading response (Applebaum & Holzman, 1962); multi-sign approaches (Piotrowski, 1950; Martin, 1951; Sakheim, 1955; Fleischer, 1957); content indicators (Lindner, 1946, White & Schreiber, 1952; Thomas et al., 1973); symbolic content (Sapolsky, 1963); and the use of signs and content combined (Hertz, 1948, 1949). Although many of these studies have demonstrated statistically significant differences between suicidal and nonsuicidal subjects, the actual number of *true positive cases* identified is often less than two-thirds, whereas the number of *false positive cases* often exceeds one-third. Thus although the findings from such studies are important, their clinical utility is often quite limited.

During the first 5 years after the Rorschach Research Foundation was created, 41 protocols became available that had been administered within 60 days prior to an effected suicide. That sample was increased to 59 in 1975 by the response to a solicitation letter that was sent to 108 clinical installations throughout North America, requesting the records of subjects meeting this criterion. The structural data were computer searched for all possible combinations of variables, and variable frequencies, to detect those appearing in at least 30 of the 59 records. The records were also subdivided using the method by which death was invoked as a crude index of intent or lethality, in an attempt to determine if that issue might be confounding to any findings. Class I suicides were defined as those in which the act employed a tactic that is almost certain to produce death, and for which essentially *no* rescue time is available after the act is initiated (explosives, jumping from great heights, cutting vital organs, etc.). Class II suicides involve an act that also has a very high probability of producing death, but some rescue time is available after the act is initiated (hanging, ingestion of most poisons, drowning, etc.). Class III suicides were defined as those in which the act has a very low probability of invoking death, and considerable rescue time is available after it is initiated (inhaling gases, cutting nonvital organs, ingesting analgesics or soporifics, etc.).

Whenever a cluster of six or more items appeared in 30 or more records of the target group, the computer would randomly draw three control groups of 50 subjects each, one consisting of schizophrenics, one of inpatient depressives, and one of nonpatients. The control groups were searched for the same constellation of items found in the target group, and chi-squares were calculated to determine whether the frequencies for the target group were significantly different from the controls. In the course of these analyses several constellations of variables were discovered in more than 30 of the target protocols; however, only three differentiated that group from *all* three control groups at a statistically significant level, and one of those had considerably greater discriminatory power. Consequently, that group of 11 variables was incorporated into the format of the Comprehensive System and identified as the Suicide Constellation (Exner & Wylie, 1977). An expectancy table revealed that, *using a cut-off of eight or more variables positive*, it correctly identified 44 of the 59 suicide cases (75%), while identifying 10 of the 50 depressives (20%), six of the schizophrenics (12%), and none of the nonpatients as *false positives*. When reviewed by Class of act, it correctly identified 14 of 19 Class I subjects (74%), 20 of 24 Class II subjects (83%), and 10 of 16 Class III cases (63%). If the cut-off is lowered to 7, it correctly identifies more than 80% of the target sample; *however,* the number of false positives from the control groups also increases substantially, and includes 58% of the depressive sample, 38% of the schizophrenics, and even 8% of the nonpatients as false positives. Thus the cut-off of eight has been employed as the critical point at which the data appear sufficient to warrant concern.

During the period from 1977 to 1984, additional protocols, meeting the criterion of having been administered within 60 days prior to an effected suicide, accumulated in the data pool of the Rorschach Research Foundation. Most were contributed by alumni of Rorschach Workshops, the continuing education section of the Foundation. By 1984, the number of new records had reached 101, and provided a reasonable sample against which to test the validity of the original finding. The new protocols include 41 males and 60 females, ranging in age from 19 to 55 years, with an average of approximately 30 years. They were also subdivided into Class of act, using the same criteria as in the original study, to provide some index of intent. Three groups of 101 subjects each, one consisting of inpatient depressives, one of schizophrenics, and one of nonpatients, were randomly drawn from the protocol pool to use as controls. Frequency distributions for each of the 11 variables in the *S-CON* were generated for each of the four groups, plus the three subgroups in the target sample. Variables were ranked within each group and subgroup from 1 (most frequent) to 11 (least frequent). A stepwise discriminant functions analysis was also used to evaluate the respective power of each variable to discriminate within each group, and to establish classification weights. Five other variables were also tested for discriminant power because they occurred with substantial frequencies among the target subjects. They included $MOR > 3$, $AG > 2$, $An + Bl > 2$, $Afr < .40$, and $T = 0$.

The first series of analyses indicate that the original 11 variable constellation did identify 75 of the 101 suicide cases correctly (74%), while misidentifying as false positives only 12 of the 101 depressives (12%), six of the 101 schizophrenics (6%), and none of the nonpatients, *if the cut-off of eight positive variables is applied.* As in the original study, a cut-off of seven increased the "correct" rate by about 10%, but also inflated the number of false positives from the two psychiatric groups to unacceptable levels (depressives = 31%; schizophrenics = 19%). The additional analyses yielded some other important findings. First, when four of the five other variables were added into the constellation, both separately and collectively, the number of correct identifications in the target sample did not improve. They are $AG > 2$, $An + Bl > 2$, $Afr < .40$, and $T = 0$. However, the addition of the fifth variable, $MOR > 3$, improved the discriminating power of the *S-CON* significantly. When added to the original constellation, and continuing to use the cut-off of eight positive variables, the correct identification of the suicide group was increased to nearly 80%, whereas the number of false positives among the three control groups does not increase.

A second yield from the added analyses, and especially from the discriminant functions analysis with $MOR > 3$ added, concerned the Egocentricity Index. In the original constellation it was defined as positive when having a value of less than .30. In the 1977 sample, it was the third most powerful contributing variable, and did correlate significantly, independent of other variables, with effected suicide ($r = .32$). In the 1984 sample, when defined as positive by a value of less than .30, the weighted rank dropped to eight in relation to all 12 variables and, taken alone, it failed to correlate significantly with effected suicide ($r = .20$). A further examination of the data revealed that a somewhat bimodal feature existed in the distribution of scores for the Index in the target sample. In the 1977 sample, 40 of the 59 subjects had Egocentricity Index scores of less than .30, whereas nine others had scores higher than .40. When the upper group was added in an experimental trial to define the variable as positive, no improvement in the discrimination occurred, and thus the possibility of using upper and lower cut-offs to define the variable as positive was discarded. In the 1984 sample, however, only 61 of the 101 subjects had scores of less than .31, *and 27 others had scores greater than .44.* On the other hand, most subjects in the schizophrenia and nonpatient control groups had Egocentricity Indices falling between .31 and .44, and the sample of depressives had scores generally falling between .20 and .36. Thus by altering the criterion for the Index as a positive variable in the *S-CON* to the bimodal cut-offs of less than .31 or greater than .44, a refinement of the discriminatory power of the constellation is realized, without significantly increasing the false positive rate among controls. The discriminatory power of the revised 12 variable *S-CON* is shown in Table 32.

It will be noted that if the cut-off of eight positive variables is applied, 83% of the target group are identified correctly, including more than 90% of the Class I subjects, 76% of the Class II subjects, and nearly 80% of the Class III subjects, while misidentifying only 12% of the depressive controls, 6% of the schizophrenic controls, and none of the nonpatients. As with the 1977 sample, a cut-off of seven improves the target identifications by more than 10%, but also more than doubles the proportion of false positives among the two psychiatric control groups, and includes the false positive identification of one nonpatient subject.

It is important to stress that, although the *S-CON* seems quite useful for the identification of some subjects who seem at high risk for self-destruction, or a preoccupation with self-destruction, a *false negative rate* of more than 15% exists within the target sample when the cut-off of eight is applied, and a *false positive rate* of more than 10% exists among depressive controls. These data confirm the earlier caution that the *S-CON* is by no means infallible. If eight or more variables are positive, it should be taken as a warning, and further exploration of the possibility of self-destructive features should be pursued expeditiously. Conversely, if the *S-CON* contains fewer than eight positive variables, it should *not be misinterpreted* as signifying that no suicidal risk element is present.

The *S-CON* and Younger Clients   The *S-CON* was developed on an adult population. The youngest subject in the 1977 sample was 18, and the youngest in the 1984 sample was 19. Nonetheless, it probably does have some applicability as a warning indicator when used with 15- and 16-year-old subjects, because most of the normative data for those ages are quite similar to those for adults. *It is probably not* useful for subjects who are younger than 15 because many of the variables are expected to be positive among children and younger adolescents, even nonpatients, such as a lower R, some elevation in S, $CF + C > FC$, $es > EA$, and *Pure H* less than two. Exner (1978) has reported on an attempt to devise an *S-CON* for younger clients, using the same methodology as for the adult version; however, the effort has been fraught with problems, the major one being a lack of data. An eight-variable constellation was developed, using fewer than 40 protocols that had been collected from subjects between the ages of 8 and 16, who effected *or* attempted suicide within 60 days after taking the test. The obvious broad age range, plus the fact that the records included a mixture of attempted and effected suicides, could hardly be expected to yield more than mediocre results. The computer search indicated that if seven of

Table 32. Frequency of Cases Identified by Number of Positive Variables in a 12-Item Constellation, from an Effected Suicide Group, Subdivided by Classification of Method Employed, Plus Three Control Groups

									Number of Positive Variables							
	12		11		10		9		8		7		6		5 or less	
Group	N	%	N	%	N	%	N	%	N	%	N	%	N	%	N	%
Effected Suicides																
Combined N = 101	1	1%	14	14%	19	19%	49	49%	84	83%	95	95%	99	98%	101	100%
Class I N = 36	0	—	8	22%	11	31%	18	50%	33	92%	35	97%	36	100%	36	100%
Class II N = 46	1	2%	6	13%	7	15%	21	46%	35	76%	42	91%	45	98%	46	100%
Class III N = 19	0	—	2	11%	2	11%	9	47%	15	79%	16	84%	16	84%	19	100%
Control Groups																
Inpatient Depressed N = 101	0	—	0	—	0	—	2	2%	12	12%	26	26%	44	44%	101	100%
Schizophrenic N = 101	0	—	0	—	1	1%	3	3%	6	6%	16	16%	33	33%	101	100%
Nonpatients N = 101	0	—	0	—	0	—	0	—	0	—	1	1%	2	3%	101	100%

415

the eight variables were positive, nearly 75% of the target sample was correctly identified; however, the false positive rate among psychiatric children exceeds 25%, and even about 5% of nonpatient children are misidentified as having characteristics common among suicidal youngsters. Thus the results reflect an interesting exercise in futility that will probably persist until a sufficient number of protocols are available from younger clients who effect death, or attempt to effect death, within a relatively brief period following the administration of the test.

THE SCHIZOPHRENIA INDEX (SCZI)

The issue of identifying schizophrenia has been both complex and controversial for many decades. Although most formats for the diagnosis of schizophrenia begin with the general agreement that schizophrenia involves some form of thought disorder, there is much less agreement about the way in which the disturbance is manifest, and about which added features, taken from the many that seem to characterize schizophrenia, are truly differentiating. In part, the difficulties posed in the identification of schizophrenia stem from the basic conceptualizations about schizophrenia. Khouri (1977) has pointed out the sharp differences that exist among those who purport a continuum concept of schizophrenia, and those who identify schizophrenia as a discretely different entity from all other mental dysfunctions. Moreover, conceptualizations of schizophrenia frequently differ considerably regarding the major etiological factors. Some stress the importance of a potential genetic element, whereas others afford major emphasis to environmental factors. Possibly, the diversity of opinions concerning schizophrenia is best portrayed in a series of articles, in the *Schizophrenia Bulletin,* that attempt to address the question, ''What is schizophrenia?'' (Meltzer & Liberman, 1982; Snyder, Kety, & Goldstein, 1982; Strauss & Carpenter, 1983; Zubin & Ludwig, 1983; Bowers & Wing, 1983; Bleuler, 1984).

Diagnostic manifestations of schizophrenia have also been at issue, except for the common agreement that thinking problems will be evident. For example, Satorius, Shapiro, and Jablensky (1974) have used frequency distributions of the presence of 12 behavioral variables, observed in a large cross-cultural group, to illustrate the schizophrenic condition. They note that 97% of the schizophrenics manifest a lack of insight, about 70% have some form of hallucination, two-thirds show signs of delusions, and about half have some form of thinking alienation. In a similar context, Carpenter, Strauss, and Bartko (1973) used a computer analysis of 360 items and 55 combinations of items to differentiate schizophrenics from nonschizophrenics. They reported that the 12 most discriminating signs include restricted affect, poor insight, thinking aloud, failure to awaken early, poor interpersonal relations, widespread delusions, incoherent speech, bizarre delusions, nihilistic delusions, lack of elation, lack of depressed facies, and unreliable information. They find that if a combination of six or more is present, two-thirds of the schizophrenics are correctly identified, whereas only 4% of the nonschizophrenics are misidentified.

Some of the difficulties in differentiating schizophrenia from nonschizophrenia arise because of attempts to refine the diagnosis—that is, differentiating categories, such as paranoid, catatonic, and such—or to delineate degrees of involvement, as in borderline or incipient schizophrenia. For example, Kety et al. (1968) and Kety et al. (1975) have suggested the notion of a spectrum of schizophrenias. Their conceptualization is based mainly on a series of investigations that have involved elaborate record keeping about adopted children, a design that permits some separation of the genetic element from environmental influences. The spectrum concept is not markedly different from the older notion of a family of schizophrenias (Bleuler, 1911) and is directed at a group of disorders that varies in severity, but all of which appear to be genetically related. In the ''hard'' or ''firm'' area of the spectrum lie disorders labeled chronic schizophrenia, borderline states, and some acute schizophrenic disturbances. In the less firm or ''soft'' area of the spectrum appear some of the acute schizophrenic reactions, the schizotypal personality, and the schizoid style. Although the notion of the spectrum is primarily a research classification, its relation to previously developed conceptualizations of schizophrenia requires attention in any Rorschach related research involving the differentiation of the condition.

Whatever the approach to classification, it is clear that the diagnostician, regardless of the technique employed, confronts a substantial task in attempting to differentiate schizophrenia. Haier (1980) has reviewed a variety of approaches to diagnostic decisions concerning schizophrenia, and points out that not everyone uses the same criteria for the diagnosis, and many criteria are unreliable. Haier has also noted that when methods designed essentially for research purposes are compared, such as the *Research Diagnostic Criteria* (Spitzer, Endicott, & Robbins, 1978), *New Haven Schizophrenia Index* (Astrachan et al., 1972), *Carpenter and Strauss Flexible Criterion* (Carpenter, Strauss, & Bartko, 1973), the *St. Louis Criterion* (Feighner et al., 1972), and the *Taylor and Abrams Criteria* (Taylor & Abrams, 1975), the agreement among the sets about who is schizophrenic differs considerably and, on the average, agreement is moderate to low. Because the DSM-III criteria for schizophrenia is derived mainly from the Research Diagnostic Criteria *(RDC)*, it will probably form the basis for most diagnostic decisions concerning schizophrenia in the immediate future. As Haier has noted, it tends to narrow the concept of schizophrenia away from the spectrum concept so that the notion of a unitary disease is also diminished. At the same time the increasing emphasis on biological factors may ultimately lead to a more precise definition of subtypes.

Accurate diagnosis of schizophrenia is important, mainly because of the intervention consequences. The bulk of recent research on the treatment of schizophrenia indicates that the response to intervention is generally much more positive if the treatment includes a somatic core, predominantly some form of antipsychotic medication (May, 1968; Hogarty et al. 1974; May, Tuma, & Dixon, 1976; Exner & Murillo, 1977). There are findings that suggest some kinds of schizophrenic subjects may not respond favorably to drug treatment (Klein, Rosen, & Oaks, 1973; Rappaport et al., 1976), and although the data may be somewhat equivocal, they highlight the importance of a thorough description of the patient before intervention planning is finalized. As Keith et al. (1976) have emphasized, a description focusing on data from the assessment of cognitive functioning and social interests, plus interpersonal skills, can be especially important in determining an intervention model. The results of the Boston Psychotherapy Study with schizophrenics (Stanton et al., 1984; Gunderson et al., 1984) also appear to suggest that accurate diagnosis of schizophrenia *plus* a meaningful description of assets and liabilities may be critical to the ultimate determination of the intervention plan.

Rorschach Manifestations of Schizophrenia There have been many attempts to identify Rorschach variables that will afford a valid differentiation of schizophrenia (Rapaport et al., 1946; Piotrowski & Lewis, 1950; Theisen, 1952; Watkins & Stauffacher, 1952; Beck, 1965; Weiner, 1966). All have achieved some success, but with less than consistent uniformity. Diversity in results has often been the result of heterogeneity of samples, and because of varying emphasis on different subcategories in the overall scheme of classification. Weiner, (1966, 1971) has offered a compelling argument that the most accurate use of the Rorschach for identifying schizophrenia will be one in which the test variables will be conceptually linked to the entity. In other words, as features of the condition are identified and clarified, Rorschach data can be approached in terms of which variables best reflect those features. It has been essentially this approach that has been used in the study of Rorschach manifestations of schizophrenia.

Although listings of features of schizophrenia sometimes differ sharply in length and/or content, almost all include reference to four basic characteristics—*inaccurate perception, disordered thinking, inadequate controls,* and *interpersonal ineptness.* There are several Rorschach variables that relate to these features, either directly or indirectly. However, none of these variables is exclusive to schizophrenia. For instance, many psychiatric groups have inadequate controls, such as some histrionics, borderline personalities, impulsive styles, inadequate personalities, and so on. Similarly, several psychiatric groups, such as schizoids, immature personalities, and some character disorders, tend to be inept in social relationships. *But no group, other than schizophrenia, has been defined or conceptualized as having both the problems of disordered thinking and inaccurate perception.* It is because of this that data concerning these two features have been the focus in studying Rorschach manifestations of schizophrenia, and those findings have formed the basis from which the Schizophrenia Index has evolved.

Inaccurate Perception   Schizophrenics typically have some difficulty perceiving their world and themselves accurately. Their perceptual distortions are often reflected in poor or inappropriate judgment. They have difficulty in assessing their own experience realistically and, as a consequence, tend to act in odd or strange ways, say things that are out of place, and harbor farfetched ideas. In the most extreme form, perceptual distortions create the basis for hallucinatory experience; that is, the more a person distorts the reality of what is seen, heard, smelled, and so on, the greater the probability that they will experience sensory impressions for which there is no realistic external stimuli.

As noted in Chapter 15, four Rorschach variables, P, $X+\%$, $F+\%$, and $X-\%$, relate to the issues of conventionality and perceptual accuracy. Two of these, the $X+\%$ and the $X-\%$, are especially important in detecting problems in perceptual accuracy. The first identifies the proportion of instances in which the translation of the stimulus field is atypical, whereas the second indicates the proportion of those atypical translations that involve perceptual-mediational distortion. The mean $X+\%$ for nonpatients, both adults and children, is about 80%, with a standard deviation of 10% or less. It is the *only* variable that has consistently high long-term retest reliability during the developmental years (Exner, Thomas, & Mason, 1985). Thus if the $X+\%$ falls below 70%, it signals a tendency to translate the world in an unconventional manner. If it falls below 60%, that tendency is very marked, and probably impairing effective adjustment. The mean $X-\%$ for nonpatient adults and children falls between 4 and 8%, with standard deviations between 4 and 6%. When it exceeds 15%, considerable distortion is indicated, and if it exceeds 20%, the distortion is probably of a disabling magnitude. The inpatient depressive reference sample has a mean $X+\%$ of 69% and a mean $X-\%$ of 15%. The character disorders group has a mean $X+\%$ of 70% and a mean $X-\%$ of 15%. The schizophrenic reference sample has a mean $X+\%$ of 53%, and a mean $X-\%$ of 31%, both of which are significantly different from either of the other two psychiatric groups.

The 1974 finding that schizophrenics, as a group, have a significantly lower average

$X + \%$ than other groups was not surprising in light of earlier work concerning the $F + \%$ (Exner, 1974). Taken alone, however, the $X + \%$ does not differentiate schizophrenics from nonschizophrenics at a substantial level. For instance, 116 of the 210 subjects in the depressive reference sample (55%) have $X + \%$'s lower than 70%, and 54 of those (26%) have $X + \%$'s lower than 60%. Similarly, 93 of the 200 character disorder subjects (46%) have $X + \%$'s of less than 70%, and 51 (26%) are lower than 60%. In the schizophrenic sample 270 of the 320 subjects have an $X + \%$ of less than 70% (85%), which is a significantly greater proportion than either of the other groups, and 199 are lower than 60% (62%). But if either value is selected as a critical cut-off for purposes of differentiation, the number of false positives from both the depressive and character disorders groups would be substantial. On the other hand, if a composite of $X + \% < 70\%$ *and* $X - \% > 20\%$ is applied, a much different picture unfolds. Although 46% of the subjects in the depressive sample do have $X - \%$'s greater than 15%, only 23 (11%) have an $X + \%$ lower than 70% *and* $X - \%$ greater than 15%, and only 14 (7%) have an $X + \%$ lower than 70% and $X - \%$ greater than 20%. The frequencies are even lower among the character disorders group, and only four subjects from the adult nonpatient sample meet this criterion. Conversely, 267 of the 320 subjects in the schizophrenic sample have both of these features (83%). In fact, if records of less than 15 answers are excluded, slightly more than 94% of the schizophrenics have both an $X + \%$ lower than 70%, and an $X - \%$ greater than 20%. This is why these two variables have been included in the Schizophrenia Index.

It is important to caution that when both are positive, it does not necessarily signal schizophrenia, but simply indicates that a form of perceptual inaccuracy exists such as is common in schizophrenia. But similar problems in perceptual accuracy are not uncommon among neurologically disabled subjects, reactive psychotics, some types of learning disability, and some subjects with more severe affective disorders. However, when this combination of variables relating to problems in perceptual accuracy is linked to other variables concerning disordered thought, a more discrete differentiation of schizophrenia becomes possible.

Disordered Thinking   This is probably the most clinically obvious feature among schizophrenics. Incoherent or disordered thought can take many forms. In some instances it may manifest as a disruption in the sequence of thoughts. In other instances it will be noted by a predominance of unreasonable conclusions concerning cause-and-effect relationships, or in bewildering abstract preoccupations, or in very idiosyncratic symbolism, or by persistent and very marked overgeneralizations. The *inappropriate M* responses (i.e., $M -$ and *M no form* answers) and the six Critical Special Scores appear to capture many of these forms of disarray when they occur in the Rorschach.

$M -$ responses occur with a relatively low frequency among most groups, except schizophrenics. They appear in only 38 of the 600 adult nonpatient records (6%), 26 of the 200 character disorders records (13%), and 50 of the 210 depressive protocols (25%), as contrasted with 214 of the 320 schizophrenic records (67%). If $M -$ does appear in the record of a nonschizophrenic, the probability is that the frequency will be 1. Only five adult nonpatients, five character disorder subjects, and nine depressives gave more than one $M -$, so that the means for those groups of .03, .18, and .33, respectively, are quite low. Conversely, 139 of the 214 schizophrenic records contain more than one $M -$, and the mean for the group is 1.5. M responses that have no form are much more rare. They do not appear in any of the records of nonpatient adults or character disorders and in only seven depressive records, as compared with 22 of the schizophrenic protocols. As noted in

Chapter 15, the presence of either $M-$ or M *no form* is sufficient to warrant concern about the presence of strange or disordered thinking, and an elevation in frequency seems to be a clear signal that problems in ideation exist.

Similarly, the frequency of the Sum of the six Critical Special Scores tends to be significantly lower among most all groups as compared with schizophrenics. For example, although about 75% of the nonpatient adults do have at least one of these Special Scores in their record, the mean for the group is 1.6, and the mode is 1. Approximately 87% of the character disorders protocols contain at least one of these Special Scores, and the mean for the group is 3.29, with a mode of 2. More than 90% of the depressive records have at least one Critical Special Score and the mean for the group is 3.12, with a mode of 2. Only 16 of the 320 schizophrenic records (95%) contain none of the Critical Special Scores, and all 16 records have fewer than 13 answers. The mean for the group, 6.58, is significantly greater than any of the other groups, as is the mode of 5. Moreover, if the severity of the scores is considered by examination of the sum of their weighted values (*WSUM6*), the mean for the schizophrenic group is 16.88 (mode $=$ 12), as contrasted with 3.96 for nonpatients, 6.52 for the character disorders, and 6.98 for the depressives. This illustrates that the schizophrenics not only give more of the Critical Special Scores, but they also tend to give more of those with higher weighted values. Thus as noted in Chapter 15, whenever the number of Critical Special Scores exceeds four, and/or the *WSUM6* is greater than 11, *in the record of an adult,* the likelihood that significant cognitive slippage exists is considerable and, of course, as the numbers increase, a greater magnitude of the disordered thinking is indicated. If the protocol is from a child, the critical cut-off points will be defined by using the scores that exceed one standard deviation above the mean for the appropriate age group.

As with the issue of perceptual inaccuracy, evidence of disordered thinking, taken alone, does not indicate schizophrenia. It merely indicates that a thinking problem is present that may be similar to that found in schizophrenia. Several other groups, such as some drug-related conditions, schizotypal personality disorders, and some forms of affective disturbance, commonly manifest some problems in thinking and often have significant elevations in either or both the Sum of the six Critical Special Scores, or the *WSUM6*. It is for this reason that the *SZCI* includes data concerning *both* perceptual inaccuracy and disordered thinking.

When the Comprehensive System was published in 1974, it did not include any of the Special Scores, or the $X-\%$. Thus early attempts to identify structural data that might differentiate schizophrenia were doomed at the start. The data yield was both compelling and frustrating. For instance, the first sample of schizophrenics contained 125 cases that were obtained from four psychiatric hospitals. The mean $X+\%$ for that group was 58%, and 112 (89%) had $X+\%$'s lower than 70%. In addition, it was found that 109 (87%) contained more $FQ-$ answers than FQu responses. A third important finding was that 92 contained at least one $M-$ response. When the criterion of all three of those variables being positive was applied to the sample, it did correctly identify 89 of the 125 subjects (71%), but when also applied to a randomly selected sample of 125 inpatient depressives, 49 (39%) were misidentified as being schizophrenic. Obviously, the substantial number of false negatives and false positives forewarned of little potential clinical utility.

Five of the six Critical Special Scores were added to the System in 1976 (Exner, Weiner, & Schuyler, 1976), but were not weighted at that time. By that time, the schizophrenia sample had increased to 210 cases. That sample was screened using the original three variables, $(X+\% < .70, FQ- > FQu, M- > 0)$, plus a fourth which was defined as positive if the Sum of the five Special Scores exceeded 4 (Exner, 1978). The data revealed that 153 (68%) of the 225 schizophrenic records were positive for *all four variables.* A random sample of 225 nonschizophrenic inpatient cases was drawn from the protocol pool and also screened for the four variables. Although 92 (41%) were positive for various combinations of three variables, only 24 (11%) were positive for all four.

These findings suggested that the four variables could be used as the nucleus of a cluster that might have considerable utility for screening structural data for the possible presence of schizophrenia. Consequently, several other variables were added to the cluster, separately and in combinations, to determine whether the true positive rate could be improved, and the false positive rate decreased. Most of these were variables concerning limited emotional modulation and interersonal interests. Unfortunately, none improved the discriminatory power of the cluster; however, further searching of the schizophrenic records revealed that the distribution of Special Scores generally had frequencies in which the combination of the more serious ones—*FABCOM, ALOG,* and *CONTAM*—was equal to or greater than the sum of the *DV* and *INCOM* answers. The reverse was generally true among the records of control patients. This finding was defined as a fifth variable, and the two groups rescreened. The results indicated that 179 (80%) of the schizophrenic cases had at least four of the five variables positive, and 101 (45%) were positive *for all five.* In the control group, 29 (13%) had at least four of the five variables positive, but only 11 cases (5%) were positive for all five variables. Thus the addition of the fifth variable increased the true positive rate considerably, but did not increase the false positive rate significantly. In that context, the five-variable cluster seemed ready to be tested prospectively, as an experimental Schizophrenia Index (Exner, 1978).

At about the same time that the experimental Index was defined, The Research Diagnostic Criteria (RDC) became available for use to identify schizophrenia (Spitzer, Endicott, & Robins, 1977, 1978). Prior to that time, the schizophrenia sample at the Rorschach Research Foundation had been selected using the Inpatient Multidimensional Psychiatric Scale (IMPS), plus the reports of significant others as recorded in the Katz Adjustment Scale (KAS). A composite score had been employed, using the "Schizophrenia Disorganization" Score of the IMPS, and a symptom score derived from the KAS. The RDC appeared to be well standardized, with high interrater reliability, and obviously would be the forerunner of the classification decisions for the pending DSM-III. Thus it was selected to be the validating criterion against which the experimental Index would be tested. During the next 17 months, 85 protocols were collected from first admission patients at seven psychiatric hospitals. Two are in the East, two in the Southeast, one in the Southwest, one in the Midwest, and one in the Far West. Five are public facilities involved in psychiatric training, and two are privately controlled. All of the patients presented symptoms of bizarreness or psychotic-like ideation on admission, and the issue of schizophrenia was raised by the admitting physician. RDC data were collected for all patients.

The results of the RDC indicated that 46 of the 85 subjects met the criteria for schizophrenia, whereas the remaining 39 did not. Most of the 39 were affective disorders, but several were drug-induced psychoses or reactive psychoses. The computer search of the protocols for the five variables in the experimental Index was set to require that the $X + \%$ be less than 70%. This was done because of the very high percentage of schizophrenics who meet this criterion. Thus if the $X + \%$ was less than 70%, the computer would test for each of the remaining four variables. If the $X + \%$ was 70% or higher, the computer would automatically place the subject in the "nonschizophrenic" category. The program was also set for two selections, one requiring that all of the remaining four variables be positive, and the second requiring that only three of the remaining four variables be positive. The results indicated that when the composite of $X + \%$ <70% and any three of the remaining four variables are positive was applied, the selection correctly identified 40 of the 46 schizophrenics (87%), but identified five nonschizophrenics as false positives. The more stringent criterion of all five variables being positive correctly identified 35 of the 46 schizophrenics (76%), *and identified no false positives* (Exner, 1981, 1983).

As a second step in validating the usefulness of the experimental Index, the records of 43 inpatient children, for whom the RDC had also been completed, were subjected to the same computer search. The RDC findings identified 20 of the children as schizophrenic and 23 as not schizophrenic. The composite of $X + \%$ <70% plus any three of the remaining four variables being positive correctly identified 16 of the 20 schizophrenic children *and selected no false positives*. When all five variables being positive was required, 13 of the 20 were correctly identified (Exner & Weiner, 1982). At about the same time 90 schizophrenic cases became available from Spain that had been identified using either the RDC or the DSM-III criteria. The computer search of that group yielded about the same true positive rate. Twenty-eight of the 90 (31%) were positive for all five variables, and 39 others (43%) contained four positive variables (Vives, 1983).

The next step in refining the Index involved a review of the false negative cases from each of the schizophrenia groups to determine whether there was a consistency among them. Three elements were detected. First, many had very low $X + \%$'s, and with the frequency of minus answers greater than four, *but not greater than the number of u responses*. This provoked the creation of the $X - \%$ as a substitute for the variable $FQ - >$ *FQu*. Second, more than 75% contained no *M* answers. Thus at most, only four variables could be positive. Third, more than two-thirds were relatively brief protocols, having fewer than 13 answers. In most of those cases, the Sum of the Special Scores exceeded 4, however, the majority of the Special Scores were *DV* or *INCOM* responses. Subsequently, the *DV* answers from 200 schizophrenic records and 200 nonschizophrenic records were reviewed. The original *DV* coding included three subcategories. The results indicated that one subcategory—that for peculiar or circumstantial responses—occurred much more frequently among the schizophrenics than among the nonschizophrenics. Thus it was separated out as the sixth Critical Special Score, *DR,* and experimental weights were assigned for each of the six Special Scores to determine if a weighted sum might be more discriminating than the variable $FABCOM + ALOG + CONTAM > DV + INCOM$. In addition, another computer search was completed, using 300 cases that had been diagnosed as schizophrenic by DSM-III criteria, to determine whether a greater weighting should be afforded in the Index if the record contained more than one $M -$ answer. As a result of these procedures the current Schizophrenic Index evolved (Exner, 1984).

The potential efficacy of the *SCZI* is probably best illustrated by the results of a repeated random selection procedure. This involves a "Monte Carlo" type random draw of 100 subjects each, from five groups in the total data pool, for which at least 400 cases are available in each group. Each draw included: (1) 100 DSM-III diagnosed schizophrenics drawn from a pool of more than 900, (2) 100 nonschizophrenic outpatients drawn from a pool of more than 400, (3) 100 nonschizophrenic inpatients drawn from a pool of more than 600, (4) 100 inpatient affective disorders drawn from a pool of more than 800, and (5) 100 nonpatient adults drawn from a pool of more than 1200. The results of each draw are shown in Table 33.

None of the schizophrenic samples have fewer than 72 correctly identified subjects,

Table 33.   Frequency of *SCZI* Identifications, Using Four or Five Variables Positive for Six Random Selections of 100 Subjects from Each of Five Groups

	Schizophrenic	Nonschizophrenic Outpatient	Nonschizophrenic Inpatient	Affective Disorders	Nonpatient
	N	*N*	*N*	*N*	*N*
DRAW #1					
SCZI = 4	46	3	4	3	2
SCZI = 5	26	1	1	2	0
DRAW #2					
SCZI # 4	39	6	6	9	0
SCZI = 5	37	0	1	0	0
DRAW #3					
SCZI = 4	51	4	7	8	4
SCZI = 5	32	1	0	2	0
DRAW #4					
SCZI = 4	43	5	5	6	0
SCZI = 5	36	3	2	4	0
DRAW #5					
SCZI = 4	48	9	6	10	3
SCZI = 5	33	0	2	2	0
DRAW #6					
SCZI = 4	56	6	8	7	2
SCZI = 5	31	0	0	2	0

and three of the six have more than 80, if *either* four or five positive variables are the accepted criterion. The proportion is substantially lower in each draw if the criterion is restricted only to cases in which all five variables are positive. The data for the four comparison groups indicate that the false positive rate is consistently lower than 10%, if either criteria are applied, except for three of the six affective disorders samples in which 10 or 12 misidentifications occurred. These findings are consistent with the data for nonpatients and the three reference samples provided in Chapter 12. The schizophrenic reference sample includes 104 of the 320 cases (33%) in which all five variables are positive, and 142 others (44%) have four positive variables. The depressive sample contains 10 of the 210 cases (5%) in which the *SCZI* equals 5, and 14 (7%) in which the *SCZI* is 4. Only four (2%) of the 200 character disorder cases have an *SCZI* of 5, and eight (4%) others have four variables positive. The adult nonpatient sample contains six cases (1%) in which four variables are positive and *none* with an *SCZI* of 5.

Obviously, the *SCZI* should be used cautiously. If five variables are positive, the likelihood of schizophrenia is considerable, and the likelihood of a false positive is quite low. On the other hand, when only four variables are positive, the probability of schizophrenia being present is substantial, but the possibility of a false positive cannot be ignored. For instance, Weiner (1964) and Exner (1978) have both reported that Rorschachs taken within 30 days after an amphetamine-induced psychosis are likely to include the basic features of schizophrenia. This does not appear to be the case for other types of drug abuse, but the issue has not been studied extensively. Exner (1978) did not find evidence of schizophrenia in small samples of heroine or cocaine abusers. Gordon (1980) has reported on both polydrug abusers and sedative-hypnotic drug abusers. Neither group included the characteristics of *both* perceptual inaccuracy and disordered thinking with a significant frequency; however, a positive finding for one of the two features was commonplace.

Another group that may have a higher frequency of false positives is the schizoaffective disorder. Prior to DSM-III this condition was considered as a type of schizophrenia because of the marked peculiarity in thinking, and was included as part of the "hard" spectrum concept. The protocol pool of the Rorschach Research Foundation includes only 58 cases which, by DSM-III standards, are unequivocal for the diagnosis of schizoaffective disturbance. Seven of the 58 have an *SCZI* of 5, and 15 others have four positive variables. However, they do tend to differentiate from the schizophrenic subjects by *also* having elevations on the Depression Index.

THE DEPRESSION INDEX *(DEPI)*

Although the search for indices of depressive features has met with considerable success, the search for a cluster of variables that might be useful in identifying those cases in which depression is included in the diagnostic label has been far less successful. The problem seems to be twofold. First, depression as a complaint or symptom is very common among psychiatric subjects. Depression is a more socially acceptable symptom than strange thinking, poor reality contact, or sexual dysfunctioning, and thus it is not uncommon for patients readily to concede to the experience. As an unfortunate consequence, many patients are admitted to hospitals, or to outpatient care, with the naively decided diagnosis of depression, and the initial focus of treatment centers on this feature. Second, unlike the marked features of schizophrenia, depression may in fact, be a major element in a variety of syndromes, ranging from reactive distress to the schizoaffective disturbance. As a consequence, the search for a data cluster that will discriminate the markedly depressed person from those who are dissatisfied, unhappy, or distressed has required the screening of different groups. These include dysthymics (neurotic depression), unipolar depressives, bipolar depressives, and the schizoaffective disturbance. The protocol pool of the Foundation does include more than 800 such cases, but the overwhelming majority are of the dysthymic or unipolar variety. A computer search program was designed following the same format used in the development of the *SCZI;* that is, testing variables that are empirically and/or conceptually linked to depressive features, plus any others that appeared in more than 50% of the records of 680 dysthymic or unipolar subjects.

The first computer search identified seven variables as having some discriminatory function $(FV + VF + V > 0$, $MOR > 3$, $3r + (2)/R < .30$, Color-Shading Blend > 0, $FC' + C'F + C' > 3$, $Afr < .45$, $FM > m$). The results of a pilot test of the cluster, involving the differentiation of 80 first admission patients into the categories of Major Depressive Disorder versus Other seemed encouraging. Programmed to sort using the criterion of any five variables positive, the computer did correctly identify 35 of 43 depressives (81%), while misidentifying, as false positives, nine of 37 (24%) "other" patients (Exner, 1983). *But,* when the cluster was retested, using a randomly drawn sample of 200 dysthymic and unipolar subjects, plus three randomly selected control groups, 100 schizophrenics, 100 nondepressed inpatients, and 100 nonpatient adults, two of the seven were not discriminatory (*Afr* <.45, *FM* > *m*), and deleted from the cluster. The five remaining variables that comprise the *DEPI* do discriminate quite effectively between depressive groups and the three control groups, but the issue of a cut-off score for the cluster has been difficult to address. In that context, the *DEPI* must still be considered experimental. The yield is far from spectacular, as may be best illustrated from a search of the entire data pool of affective disordered subjects, and using three randomly selected groups of 200 each, schizophrenics, nondepressed inpatients, and nonpatients, for comparison.

If the criterion of three positive variables is employed, it does detect 476 (70%) of the 680 subjects from the dysthymic and unipolar groups, and 98 (74%) of the 132 subjects in the combined smaller samples of bipolar and schizoaffective cases. Unfortunately, the incidence of false positives among the control groups is considerable, ranging from 30% of the nondepressed inpatients, to nearly 10% of the nonpatient sample. If the cut-off score is increased to 4, the number of true positives falls sharply. Only 367 (51%) of the 680 dysthymic and unipolar subjects have four or more variables positive, and only 82 (12%) have a *DEPI* of 5. Similarly, only 73 (56%) of the 132 dysthymic and unipolar cases contain four positive variables, and only 17 (13%) have all five variables positive. On the other hand, using a cut-off of 4 also reduces the number of false positives quite markedly. Eight of the 200 records in the nondepressed inpatient sample, six of the schizophrenic cases, and two nonpatient protocols contain four positive variables. *None* of the nonpatient or nondepressed inpatient cases, and only six of the schizophrenic records have five positive variables.

At this point, it seems that three general rules are appropriate to the use of the *DEPI*. First, if three variables are positive, the subject probably has some features that are commensurate with the frequent experience of depression; *however,* depression may not be a major issue in the diagnostic decision or intervention formulation. Conversely, if the record contains four positive variables, the presence of depression, or the proclivity for frequent experiences of depression is considerable, and any intervention plan should not neglect this characteristic. Finally, if the *DEPI* equals 5, the conclusion should be obvious, because the probability of a false positive is almost nonexistent. It is important to stress that, as with the *S-CON* and the *SCZI*, if the number of positive variables is less than three, *depression, as a major issue, is not ruled out.*

REFERENCES

Applebaum, S. A., and Holtzman, P. S. (1962) The color-shading response and suicide. *Journal of Projective Techniques,* **26,** 155–161.

Astrachan, B. M., Harrow, M., Adler, D., Bauer, L., Schwartz, A., Schwartz, C., and Tucker, G. A. (1972) A checklist for the diagnosis of schizophrenia. *British Journal of Psychiatry,* **121,** 529–539.

Beck, S. J.(1965) *Psychological Process in the Schizophrenic Adaptation.* New York: Grune & Stratton.

Bleuler, E. (1950) *Dementia Praecox or the Group of Schizophrenias* (1911). New York: International Universities Press.

Bleuler, M. (1984) What is schizophrenia? *Schizophrenia Bulletin,* **10,** 8–10.

Bowers, M. B., and Wing, J. K. (1983) What is schizophrenia? *Schizophrenia Bulletin,* **9,** 495–499.

Carpenter, W. T., Strauss, J. S., and Bartko, J. J. (1973) Flexible system for the diagnosis of schizophrenia: Report from the WHO International pilot study of schizophrenia. *Science,* **182,** 1275–1278.

Exner, J. E. (1981) The response process and diagnostic efficacy. 10th International Rorschach Congress, Washington, D.C.

Exner, J. E. (1974) *The Rorschach: A Comprehensive System. Volume 1.* New York: Wiley.

Exner, J. E. (1978) *The Rorschach: A Comprehensive System. Volume 2: Current research and advanced interpretation.* New York: Wiley.

Exner, J. E. (1983) Rorschach assessment. In I. B. Weiner (Ed.), *Clinical Methods in Psychology* (2nd Ed.). New York: Wiley.

Exner, J. E. (1984) The Schizophrenia Index. *Alumni Newsletter.* Bayville, N.Y.: Rorschach Workshops.

Exner, J. E., and Murillo, L. G. (1977) A long term follow-up of schizophrenic treated with regressive ECT. *Diseases of the Nervous System,* **38,** 162–168.

Exner, J. E., Thomas, E. A., and Mason, B. (1985) Children's Rorschachs: Description and prediction. *Journal of Personality Assessment,* **49,** 13–20.

Exner, J. E., and Weiner, I. B. (1982) *The Rorschach: A Comprehensive System. Volume 3: Assessment of children and adolescents.* New York: Wiley.

Exner, J. E., Weiner, I. B., and Schuyler, W. (1976) *A Rorschach Workbook for the Comprehensive System.* Bayville, N.Y.: Rorschach Workshops.

Exner, J. E., and Wylie, J. R. (1977) Some Rorschach data concerning suicide. *Journal of Personality Assessment,* **41,** 339–348.

Farberow, N. L., and Shneidman, E. S. (1961) (Eds.) *The Cry for Help.* New York: McGraw-Hill.

Feighner, J. P., Robins, E., Guze, S. B., Woodruff, R. A., Winokur, G., and Munoz, R. (1972) Diagnostic criteria for use in psychiatric research. *Archives of General Psychiatry,* **26,** 57–63.

Fleischer, M. S. (1957) Differential Rorschach configurations of suicidal patients: a psychological study of threatened, attempted, and successful suicides. Unpublished doctoral dissertation. Yeshiva University.

Goldfried, M., Stricker, G., and Weiner, I. B. (1971) *Rorschach Handbook of Clinical and Research Applications.* Englewood Cliffs, N.J.: Prentice Hall.

Gordon, L. B. (1980) Preferential drug abuse: Defenses and behavioral correlates. *Journal of Personality Assessment,* **44,** 345–350.

Gunderson, J. G., Frank, A. F., Katz, H. M., Vannicelli, M. L., Frosch, J. P., and Knapp, P. H. (1984) Effects of psychotherapy in schizophrenia: II. Comparative outcome of two forms of treatment. *Schizophrenia Bulletin,* **10,** 564–598.

Haier, R. J. (1980) The diagnosis of schizophrenia: A review of recent developments. *Schizophrenia Bulletin,* **6,** 417–428.

Hertz, M. R. (1948) Suicidal configurations in Rorschach records. *Rorschach Research Exchange and Journal of Projective Techniques,* **12,** 3–58.

Hertz, M. R. (1949) Further study of "suicidal" configurations in Rorschach records. *Rorschach Research Exchange and Journal of Projective Techniques,* **13,** 44–73.

Hogarty, G. E., Goldberg, S. C., Schooler, N. R., and Ulrich, R. F. (1974) The collaborative study group: Drug and sociotherapy in the aftercare of schizophrenic patients II. Two year relapse rates. *Archives of General Psychiatry,* **31,** 603–608.

Keith, S. J., Gunderson, J.G., Reifman, A., Buchsbaum, S., and Mosher, L. R. (1976) Special report: Schizophrenia, 1976. *Schizophrenia Bulletin,* **2,** 510–565.

Kety, S. S., Rosenthal, D., Wender, P. H., and Schulsinger, F. (1968) The types and prevalence of mental illness in the biological and adoptive families of adoptive schizophrenics. In Rosenthal, D., and Kety, S. S. (Eds.), *The Transmission of Schizophrenia.* Oxford: Pergamon Press.

Kety, S. S., Rosenthal, D., Wender, P. H., Schulsinger, F., and Jacobsen, B. (1975) Mental illness in the biological and adoptive families of adopted individuals who have become schizophrenic: A preliminary report based on psychiatric interviews. In Fieve, R. R., Rosenthal, D., and Brill, II. (Eds.), *Genetic Research in Psychiatry.* Baltimore: Johns Hopkins University Press.

Khouri, P. (1977) Continuum versus dichotomy in theories of schizophrenia. *Schizophrenia Bulletin, 3,* 262–267.

Klein, D. F., Rosen, B., and Oaks, G. (1973) Premorbid asocial adjustment and response to phenothiazine treatment among schizophrenic patients. *Archives of General Psychiatry, 29,* 480–484.

Lindner, R. M. (1946) Content analysis in Rorschach work. *Rorschach Research Exchange, 10,* 121–129.

Martin, H. (1951) A Rorschach study of suicide. Unpublished doctoral dissertation. University of Kentucky.

May, P. R. A. (1968) *Treatment of Schizophrenia.* New York: Science House.

May, P. R. A., Tuma, A. H., and Dixon, W. J. (1976) Schizophrenia—A follow-up study of results of treatment: I. Design and other problems. *Archives of General Psychiatry, 33,* 474–478.

Meltzer, H. Y., and Liberman, R. P. (1982) What is schizophrenia? *Schizophrenia Bulletin, 8,* 433–437.

Piotrowski, Z. (1950) *A Rorschach Compendium: Revised and enlarged, Psychiatric Quarterly, 24,* 543–596.

Piotrowski, Z., and Lewis, N. D. C. (1950) An experimental Rorschach diagnostic aid for some forms of schizophrenia. *American Journal of Psychiatry, 107,* 360–366.

Rapaport, D., Gill, M., and Schafer, R. (1946) *Psychological Diagnostic Testing. Volume II.* Chicago: Yearbook Publishers.

Rappaport, M., Hopkins, H. K., Hall, K., Belleza, T., and Silverman, J. (1976) Acute schizophrenia and phenothiazine utilization. I. Clinical outcome. Final Report, National Institute of Mental Health, NIMH Grant 16445.

Sakheim, G. A. (1955) Suicidal responses on the Rorschach test. *Journal of Nervous and Mental Disease, 122,* 332–344.

Sapolsky, A. (1963) An indicator of suicidal ideation of the Rorschach test. *Journal of Projective Techniques and Personality Assessment, 27,* 332–335.

Satorious, N., Shapiro, R., and Jablensky. A. (1974) The international pilot study of schizophrenia. *Schizophrenia Bulletin, 1,* 21–34.

Shneidman, E. S., and Farberow, N. L. (1957) *Clues to Suicide,* New York: McGraw-Hill.

Snyder, S. H., Kety, S. S., and Goldstein, M. J. (1982) What is schizophrenia? *Schizophrenia Bulletin, 8,* 595–602.

Spitzer, R. L., Endicott, J., and Robins, E. (1977) *Research Diagnostic Criteria* (RDC) for a selected group of functional disorders. New York State Psychiatric Institute.

Spitzer, R. L., Endicott, J. E., and Robins, E. (1978) *Research Diagnostic Criteria for a Selected Group of Functional Disorders.* (3rd Ed.) New York: New York State Psychiatric Institute.

Stanton, A. H., Gunderson, J. G., Knapp, P. H., Frank, A. F., Vannicelli, M. L., Schnitzer, R., and Rosenthal, R. (1984) Effects of psychotherapy in schizophrenia: I. Design and implementation of a controlled study. *Schizophrenia Bulletin, 10,* 520–563.

Strauss, J. S., and Carpenter, W. T. (1983) What is schizophrenia? *Schizophrenia Bulletin, 9,* 7–10.

Taylor, M. A., and Abrams, R. (1975) A critique of the St. Louis psychiatric research criteria for schizophrenia. *American Journal of Psychiatry,* **132,** 1276–1280.

Thiesen, J. W. (1952) A pattern analysis of structural characteristics of the Rorschach test in schizophrenia. *Journal of Consulting Psychology,* **16,** 365–370.

Thomas, C. B., Ross, D. C., Brown, B. S., and Duszynski, K. R. (1973) A prospective study of the Rorschachs of suicides: The predictive potential of pathological content. *The Johns Hopkins Medical Journal,* **132,** 334–360.

Vives, M. (1983) Analysis of Rorschach data from acute and chronic Spanish schizophrenics. Workshops Study No. 291 (unpublished), Rorschach Workshops.

Watkins, J. G., and Stauffacher, J. C. (1952) An index of pathological thinking in the Rorschach. *Journal of Projective Techniques,* **16,** 276–286.

White, M. A., and Schreiber, H. (1952) Diagnosing "suicidal risks" on the Rorschach. *Psychiatric Quarterly Supplement,* **26,** 161–189.

Weiner, I. B. (1964) Differential diagnosis in amphetamine psychosis. *Psychiatric Quarterly,* **38,** 707–716.

Weiner, I. B. (1966) *Psychodiagnosis in Schizophrenia.* New York: Wiley.

Weiner, I. B. (1977) Rorschach indices of disordered thinking in patient and nonpatient adolescents. IX International Rorschach Congress, Fribourg, Switzerland.

Zubin, J., and Ludwig, A. M. (1983) What is schizophrenia? *Schizophrenia Bulletin,* **9,** 331–335.

CHAPTER 18

The Finished Interpretation

The material in the four preceding chapters has focused on the many structural variables of the test. They represent the nuclear data of the test; that is, they are reliable and valid as indicators of many features of personality. As such, they form the basis from which the interpretation begins. Taken separately, or in clusters, they reveal much about the Rorschach subject. Nevertheless, they do not represent the total Rorschach yield, nor could they be used exclusively as the basis for a final test report. Analysis of the *Sequence of Scores,* and the *Verbalizations,* will often add extensively to the fleshing out of the total picture. Consequently, the finished interpretation requires a careful blending of findings from each of these three sources. It is not a lengthy task, requiring days of rumination, but it is one that requires thoroughness, logic and, most of all, a knowledge of people.

Possibly the most important caution to be exercised in Rorschach interpretation concerns the interpreter rather than the test data. Most subjects who are administered the Rorschach have some presenting problem, and the focus of interpretation is often oriented toward gaining some better understanding of the problem, in terms of cause, characteristic, and correction. It is because of this that many interpretations tend to emphasize the dysfunction and, unfortunately, can be very misleading because they neglect adequate concern for the more positive or salient characteristics of the subject. The finished interpretation should capture the uniqueness of the person, including *both* assets and liabilities. It should be a *descriptive* interpretation from which the intelligent professional, within cautious guidelines, can draw some logical conclusions and, when required, make some logical predictions. The Rorschach, however, is often not at its best when used predictively, for the data reflect the present more than either the past or the future. Thus statements about the past or the future must be of a more speculative nature. For instance, one of the greatest values of the Rorschach is for its use in planning intervention. This is not because any particular Rorschach variable equates directly with a particular form of treatment, but rather because the Rorschach will reflect the liabilities of the subject. These can be conceptualized in terms of targets for intervention. The issue hinges on what features of the Rorschach will hopefully be altered as a result of treatment. At this point, the interpreter must review his or her knowledge of the variety of intervention modalities as they relate to each of the relevant targets, addressing the issue of which may be most likely to effect the desired changes.

ANALYSIS OF THE SEQUENCE AND VERBALIZATIONS

It is important to emphasize that propositions formulated from the review of the Sequence of Scores, or from the verbal material, will be more subjective than those developed from the structural data. This is not to suggest that they are less valuable, because that is not the case. *It does signal the need for conservatism.* It is often tempting to form speculations from these data, especially from the verbal material, but it is vital that those speculations are couched in the framework of the findings from the structural data. They should be used mainly as clarifying and/or enriching material. If the analyses of the Sequence and Verbalizations are approached in this way, they can be expected to enrich the previously developed material.

The Sequence of Scores   There is no special step-by-step procedure that is used in reviewing the Sequence of Scores, but it is important that several issues be addressed in the review. First, is there a consistency of approach? Did the subject always, or almost always, give the same pattern of location selections, such as starting with a *W* and moving to *D,* or vice versa, or was the approach more inconsistent? Generally, evidence of a consistent approach can be generalized to many areas of coping or problem solving. Inconsistent approaches are found much more frequently in the records of ambitents than either the introversive or extratensive subjects.

Second, is there any clustering of minus or *u* answers? They may all occur at the beginning of the test, or at the end, or all to chromatic blots, and so on. Similarly, is there any clustering of blend responses? When clusters occur, they can often add information to issues such as conventionality versus unconventionality, or complexity versus economy.

Third, if minus responses have occurred, are they followed *in the same card* by a more appropriate response? If this is the case, it may signal some awareness of, or resiliency from, the poorer selection, a much more favorable finding than if the subject returns the card after delivering the inappropriate response. Conversely, do minus answers always occur as the first response to a blot? If this occurs, it may signal that problems in perceptual accuracy may be a function of hasty decision operations. This seems especially the case if most or all of the minus answers are followed by more appropriate responses.

Fourth, where do the Popular answers occur? Are they among those given most frequently, such as on Cards VIII, V, and I? Many times the absence of the *P (P* failure) can be as interpretively revealing as the presence of *P.* For instance, if a record is *T-less,* did the *P* still occur to Card VI? If so, it probably strengthens the postulate concerning the absence of *T.*

Fifth, is the organizational activity consistent throughout the protocol, or does it tend to cluster in segments of the record? If the organizing effort does not appear to be very consistent, it may shed some added light on information developed from the Lambda, *W:D, W:M,* and/or *Zd* data.

Sixth, do the *S* responses cluster at the beginning of the record? If they do, it signals situational resistance, and even if *S* is elevated in the record, it should *not* be translated as a trait-like feature of oppositionality. On the other hand, if several *S* answers are spread throughout the record, the oppositional characteristic is probably trait-like.

Seventh, is there any pattern to the delivery of Special Scores? For instance, do they all occur to the achromatic cards, or to the chromatic cards? For example, some subjects with a low *Afr* will give all, or most all, of their Special Scores to blots containing chromatic features, suggesting that emotionally toned stimuli tend to provoke some forms of disarray.

Obviously, these seven issues do not encompass all possibilities, but they can be used as a beginning in the search through the Sequence of Scores. The challenge is to detect any unusual features or patterns, and merge those findings with information that has been developed from the structural data.

Analysis of the Verbal Material   Rorschach (1921) was very cautious in his estimate of the interpretive yield from the verbal material. He pointed to the fact that the test does not provoke a ''free flow'' of ideation but states that if unconscious or subconscious ideation did occur in the test, it would be manifest in the content. It does seem highly plausible, in light of Rorschach's training and orientation, that he would have accepted Franks' *Projective Hypothesis* (1939) as relevant to the interpretation of the test.

Lindner (1943, 1944, 1946, 1947) was among the first to make a formal argument encouraging a greater emphasis on ''content analysis'' than had been the case previously. He cited instances in which the scoring configurations did not provide an accurate ''diagnostic'' picture of psychopaths but where sequence analysis of the verbalizations was successful. He also presented a series of classes of answers to different areas of the blots which could be interpreted as symbolically representative of different types of psychopathological ideation. Following from Lindner's lead, many works have focused on the analysis of content as related to diagnostic types, personality traits, and the ''meaning'' of specific classes of verbalizations. Some of these, especially those dealing with traits, have evolved special scorings for particular classes of contents (Elizur—anxiety, 1949; Elizur—hostility, 1949; Walker—aggression, 1951; Stone—aggression, 1953; Wheeler—homosexuality, 1949; Smith & Coleman—tension, 1956; Fisher & Cleveland—body image boundary, 1958; Holt—defense effectiveness, 1960, 1966). Unfortunately, with the possible exception of the Holt index of defense effectiveness, these scoring approaches have yielded equivocal findings. This does not negate the usefulness of verbalization analysis, but instead emphasizes the problems involved in attempting to ''formalize'' these data into specific categories. For example, a review of the research concerning the Wheeler 20 signs of homosexuality suggests that six of the 20 signs are ''unquestionably poor,'' six other hold up ''fairly well under empirical test,'' and the remaining 12 are ambiguous (Goldfried, Stricker, & Weiner, 1971). Studies attempting to equate specific classes of content with a *specific* ''symbolic'' meaning have been equally limited in success. Goldfarb (1945) and Golfried (1963) both emphasize that animal contents are not universal in their symbolic meaning. Several studies (Bochner & Halpern, 1945; Meer & Singer, 1950; Rosen, 1951; Phillips & Smith, 1953; Hirschstein & Rabin, 1955; Levy, 1958; Zelin & Sechrest, 1963) have explored the postulate that Cards IV and VII represent ''father and mother,'' respectively. Findings that have been positive are equivocal, and not supported by more sophisticated research designs (Wallach, 1983).

The same negative findings have evolved concerning the significance of other blot stimuli, such as Cards III or X representing interpersonal connotations, or that Card VI represents sexuality. It is *very dangerous* for an interpreter to operate under these faulty assumptions. As noted earlier, sexual contents usually signify some form of preoccupation, and Pascal et al. (1950) have presented evidence to indicate that genital contents do have some universal meaning. Molish (1967) has pointed out that sexual contents are useful to interpretation because they are much more direct than symbolic. Prandoni et al. (1973) did find a greater frequency of sexual contents in the records of sex offenders but, like Molish, cautions that these types of answers have little meaning when interpreted in isolation.

One of the most common approaches to the analysis of the verbal material is based on the logical grouping of responses that appears to have a common theme, or very common characteristics. Schafer (1954) has presented one of the most comprehensive approaches to the verbal material using this method. He cites 14 broad ranging categories, using psychoanalytic constructs, which include dependency, aggressiveness, conflicts, fears, and such, and provides illustrations of how different contents may relate to the same theme. Although some of these examples are useful only if applied in the psychoanalytic framework, such as the response of ''mud'' reflecting an ''anal'' orientation, most serve to represent a consistency of themes that can be useful regardless of theoretical orientation. For instance, Schafer suggests that answers which include references to God, police, Ku Klux Klan figures, family crests, castles, and riches may all be related to an authority orientation. Similarly, a clustering of answers involving jellyfish, badly skinned animals, a straw man, weak branches, and such can relate to feelings of inadequacy and/or impotency. Schafer's work is a classic of this kind and can be of use by an interpreter, regardless of orientation, because it tends to give emphasis to the "obvious" classes of response that might "fit together" to convey idiographic needs, preoccupations, and such. Schafer also points to the importance of studying the emotional tone that is often conveyed by the wording of a subject.

Obviously, some of this is conveyed in Special Scores, such as *MOR,* or *AG,* but in many cases the repetitious use or a word or tone in describing objects can add new information. For example, a subject may consistently begin an answer by saying, "Boy, this is another loser," or "I'm just no good at this," either of which might suggest a sense of insecurity or inadequacy.

Historically, most interpreters have attempted to derive some information from each response, proceeding in a methodical but often concrete response-by-response approach to the record. Although this is an admirable objective, the approach can be naive and very misleading. It is appropriate if the interpreter wants to insure that no important information is neglected, *but it is erroneous to assume that all responses will yield some new or enhancing information.*

Most of the useful information that can be gleaned from the analysis of the verbalizations comes mainly from the *projected material.* These are the movement responses, the answers which contain material that goes well beyond the stimulus field, or the answers in which the objects reported are embellished. In some records, every answer will have one or more of these features; in most protocols, however, this is not the case, and the interpreter should avoid becoming burdened by trying to determine why a specific object was reported, or if there is symbolic significance in the selection of a response. As with the structural data, people tend to be redundant in their verbal behaviors *if* those behaviors are manifestations of needs or attitudes or conflicts. For example, if a thrice married and now separated woman gives responses such as, "A vulgar man displaying his thing," "The ugly neckbone of a person like men have," "A vandal with a fire in his gut," and "An evil man peering into a window," it takes little more than common sense to develop the postulate that she does not care for males, and probably feels threatened and/or victimized by them. These are all rich responses that involve movement or embellishments.

At the other extreme, a subject might give a sequence of answers to Cards I through IV such as "A bat," "The face of a cat," "Two dogs," "A hole in the ground," "A butterfly," "Some blood," "Two people," "A furry gorilla," and "A willow tree." This sequence of nine responses to the first four blots contains *no* movement, and there are *no* embellishments, but they are not all *Pure F* answers. The hole could involve *vista* or *FD,* the blood and possibly the butterfly can include chromatic color, and the gorilla response almost certainly will include texture. *Yet, none includes any clear projected features.* They are essentially classification answers and, as such, contribute little or nothing to the analysis of the verbal material.

There are two other pitfalls that can occur in analyzing verbal material about which caution should be exercised. First, some interpreters are prone to read the material in the response *and* the Inquiry together, as if a single stream of ideation is represented. *This is not the case,* because the verbal material in the original response is delivered much earlier, *and under a different set of conditions than the material in the Inquiry.* When giving the original answers, the subject is operating under a fairly ambiguous set of instructions, and usually he or she will be naive to the blots. Thus projected material that occurs is issued somewhat freely, and because of that it has considerable interpretive value. The task of the Inquiry is much more structured. The subject is encouraged to more verbiage and, under this circumstance, embellishments are much more commonplace. They must be addressed with great caution, and used only if there is good reason to believe that they are not provoked by the instructions of the Inquiry. Thus the analysis of the verbalizations should *always* begin by reading *vertically,* through the original responses, and ignoring the verbal material of the Inquiry while doing so. This process should generate most of the postulates that will be derived from the verbal material. Naturally, the Inquiry should not be ignored. If used conservatively, and *after* completing the review of the original responses, some of the elaborations in the Inquiry can often be quite useful in clarifying or supporting other material. But just as new information that is developed in the Inquiry is usually not included in the coding of an answer, new information developed in the Inquiry ordinarily should not be used to develop a new series of hypothesis. A second problem that the interpreter must avoid when dealing with the verbal material is the development of premature sets. It is sometimes very easy to become caught up in a single answer or two. The result can be a misleading and/or erroneous postulate that is afforded considerable weight and, in turn, other data that might support alternative or contradictory positions are ignored.

If propositions developed from the Sequence and/or Verbalizations are inconsistent with the postulates developed from the structural data, it is usually better to opt in favor of the structure, if reconciliation is impossible. These are usually rare instances, because in most cases seeming discrepancies can be logically resolved. For example, the structural data of a 20 response protocol might include four minus and three u answers, yielding an $X+\%$ of 65%, and an $X-\%$ of 20%. This composite gives rise to the proposition that problems in perceptual accuracy exist. However, the Sequence of Scores could reveal that the minus answers all appear within the first two cards, and that all are S responses, whereas no other S answers occurred later in the record, and the u responses are scattered in the remaining responses. This finding may appear inconsistent with the hypothesis concerning perceptual inaccuracy developed from the structure, but it is not. However, the original postulate does require considerable modification. The new findings suggest that the subject was apparently quite resistive to taking the test, and that resistance caused the subject to disregard and/or distort the stimulus field until a sense of adaptation to the task occurred. In other words, the subject probably does have some problems in perceptual accuracy *under conditions of threat or irritating demand,* but it would be misleading to suggest that this problem tends to be all-pervasive.

Similarly, a record might have an *SCZI* of 4, strongly suggesting the possibility of schizophrenia. The protocol might include six Critical Special Scores, consisting of two *DV*'s, three *INCOM*'s, and one *FABCOM,* yielding a *WSUM6* of 12. However, a reading of the responses that include the Special Scores could reveal that the *DV*'s are rather simple misuses of words; that the *INCOM*'s are all instances in which the subject has assigned hands to animals in a child-like and not bizarre way; and that the *FABCOM* is also of a more immature variety, such as "Two ants trying to lift a post." Thus the verbal analysis argues against the presence of seriously disordered thought and, consequently, against the diagnosis of schizophrenia. But the data are not necessarily contradictory. The *SCZI* indicated the presence of perceptual problems and cognitive slippage. The analysis of the verbalizations confirms that some cognitive slippage does appear to exist, and although not of the magnitude common to schizophrenia, it must be cause for further consideration, possibly operating on the newly developed premise that the cognitive operations are marked by considerable developmental lag.

The complete or finished interpretation must involve all of the components of the test, weaving together each set of findings with the others, to develop a psychological portrait that does justice to the subject by capturing and displaying as many descriptive statements concerning the array of assets, liabilities, and potential behaviors as is possible. The process can be exemplified by reviewing the protocol that was included in Chapter 10 to aid in illustrating the calculations for the Structural Summary.

THE L.S. PROTOCOL

L.S. (26-year-old male, married, one child (male one-year-old), high school teacher) is a self-referral to a community counseling center, complaining that he feels very tense, anxious, and suffers from insomnia. He notes that during the past six months he has been having some difficulties preparing his daily lesson plans, and is worried by the fact that he will be among a group of teachers to be evaluated during the next two months concerning contract renewal. He attributes the onset of his problem to a variety of factors. He had intended to begin part-time graduate study about a year ago, but deferred the decision to do so because his wife had endured a difficult pregnancy and he felt obligated to assist with their newborn son. The child had some respiratory problems during his first year and was rehospitalized once at age four months for a three-week period. Apparently those problems have been corrected, but the subject continues to express concern for his health. He also reports that his relationship with his wife has become more distant since the birth of the child, suggesting that because each has been preoccupied with the infant, they have had little time for each other. He admits that they have quarreled about the possibility of having more children—she would prefer to, he would not. Originally they had agreed on two children, and on the assumption that she would work as a substitute teacher during their early developmental years. He now feels that was an unrealistic assumption.

He is the oldest of three male siblings, all of whom are college graduates. His brother, age 24, is a chemist and his brother, age 21, has recently entered law school. Both parents are living. The father, age 59, is a skilled blue-collar worker, and the mother, age 57, a housewife. Both are high school graduates and take considerable pride in the fact that all three sons are college graduates. His wife, age 25, is also a college graduate, having majored in elementary education and taught third grade for three years before becoming pregnant. During the second trimester of her pregnancy she began having fluid problems and resigned her position on her doctor's advice.

He reports that he enjoys playing tennis, but that he has not found much time to do so since the birth of his son, and because he continually is behind in his class preparation. He says that he enjoys teaching some of his classes, but admits that he sometimes has discipline problems with his students. He feels that he would probably do better in a junior college position, but recognizes that is impossible to obtain unless he completes an advanced degree. The Structural Summary for the L. S. protocol is shown in Table 34.

Structural Interpretation   There is no reason to question the interpretive usefulness of the record as 25 responses were given. The scores in the Special Indices all fall well below the critical cut-offs (*S-CON* = 2, *SCZI* = 0, *DEPI* = 1), and thus it is appropriate to move to the other structural data.

The basic D score of -2 provides the first confirmation of the difficulty reported by the

Table 34. Structural Summary—L.S. Protocol

```
===============================================================================
 R = 25    Zf = 13    ZSum = 39.5    P =  8    (2) =  7    Fr+rF =  O

LOCATION            DETERMINANTS              CONTENTS      S-CONSTELLATION
FEATURES            BLENDS        SINGLE                      (ADULT)
                                              H   =  4, O   NO..FV+VF+V+FD>?
W  =  8            m.CF          M  =  3     (H) =  O, O   NO..Col-Shd Bl>O
  (Wv  =   O)      FM.FT.FD      FM =  3     Hd  =  2, O   YES..Ego<.31,>.44
D  = 16           m.FY          m  =  O     (Hd)=  O, O   NO..MOR > 3
Dd = 1            FM.FD         C  =  O     A   =  8, O   NO..Zd > +- 3.5
S  = 1            M.m           Cn =  O     (A) =  O, 1   YES..es > EA
                                CF =  O     Ad  =  2, O   NO..CF+C+Cn > FC
   DQ                           FC =  3     (Ad)=  O, O   NO..X+ < .70
........(FQ-)                    C' =  O     Ab  =  O, O   NO..S > 3
                                C'F=  O     Al  =  O, O   NO..P < 3 or > 8
 +  =  9 ( O)                    FC'=  O     An  =  O, O   NO..Pure H < 2
v/+ =  O ( O)                    T  =  O     Art =  1, O   NO..R < 17
 o  = 16 ( O)                    TF =  O     Ay  =  1, O     2.....TOTAL
 v  =  O ( O)                    FT =  1     Bl  =  O, O
                                V  =  O     Bt  =  2, 1   SPECIAL SCORINGS
                                VF =  O     Cg  =  1, O     DV    =  O
                                FV =  O     Cl  =  O, O     INCOM =  O
                                Y  =  O     Ex  =  O, O     DR    =  O
                                YF =  O     Fi  =  O, 1     FABCOM =  O
        FORM QUALITY            FY =  1     Fd  =  O, O     ALOG  =  O
                                rF =  O     Ge  =  O, O     CONTAM =  O
  FQx      FQf      M Qual.     Fr =  O     Hh  =  1, O     --- WSUM6 =  O
                                FD =  O     La  =  O, O     AG    =  O
 +  =  2   +  = O   +  =  1     F  =  9     Na  =  O, O     CONFAB =  O
 o  = 22   o  = 9   o  =  3                 Sc  =  2, O     CP    =  O
 u  =  1   u  = O   u  =  O                 Sx  =  O, O     MOR   =  1
 -  =  O   -  = O   -  =  O                 Xy  =  O, O     PER   =  1
none=  O            none=  O               Idio=  1, 2     PSV   =  O
===============================================================================
              RATIOS, PERCENTAGES, AND DERIVATIONS

ZSum-Zest =  39.5 - 41.5       FC:CF+C  =  3: 1    W:M      =  8: 4
                                 (Pure C =  O)
Zd        =  -2.0                                  W:D      =  8:16
                               Afr      =  0.56
.---------------------------.                      Isolate:R =  3:25
:EB  =  4: 2.5   EA =  6.5:     3r+(2)/R =  0.28
:                  >D= -2                          Ab+Art   =  1
:eb  =  8: 4     es = 12  :     L        =  0.56
'---------------------------'                      An+Xy    =  O
(FM= 5 " C'= O T= 2) (Adj D=  O) Blends:R =  5:25
(m = 3 " V = O Y= 2)                               H(H):Hd(Hd)=  4: 2
                               X+%      =  0.96       (Pure H =  4)
                                (F+%    =  1.00)   (HHd):(AAd) =  O: O
a:p       =  7: 5              X-%      =  0.00
                                                  H+A:Hd+Ad  = 12: 4
Ma:Mp     =  4: O
-------------------------------------------------------------------------------
         SCZI = O             DEPI = 1            S-CON = 2
===============================================================================
(C)1976,1983 BY JOHN E. EXNER, JR.
```

subject. He is in considerable stimulus overload, experiencing many more demands than he is capable of responding to easily. Consequently, his tolerance for stress is quite limited, and many of his decisions and/or behaviors may not be well formulated or implemented. This is most likely to be the case when he is confronted with new or unexpected situations that exceed the parameters of his everyday routines. The fact that the *Adjusted D* score is 0 indicates that the overload condition is mainly situational; that is, he is experiencing some form of situational stress which is creating a marked sense of helplessness and/or loss of control. This is readily apparent when the elements of the *eb* are examined. It contains three *m* and two *Y* responses, values considerably greater than expected, and highlighting the intensity of the precarious state he is experiencing. Obviously, the pending work evaluation may be contributing to this, especially as it grows nearer; however, the *eb* also contains two *T* responses, indicating that some of the irritation is being generated by strong needs for affection, and probably the experience of loneliness. Thus his strained or difficult relationship with his wife may also be a contributing stressor.

There are two other datum in the Four Square that are important. The first is the *EB* of 4:2.5, indicating that he is an ambient. As such, he is not very efficient in his coping habits. Instead, he apparently vacillates between efforts at delay and the more intuitive trial-and-error approach. Because neither approach is well developed, neither will be used efficiently. Therefore he can be expected to require more time for coping activity, and is likely to make more errors, and repeat more errors, before coming to closure on an issue. This may be a contributing factor to the difficulties that he reports in keeping ahead on his lesson plans, and may also be related to some of the problems he reports in maintaining discipline in his classes. His own lack of consistency makes him less predictable to others, and as a result, students may be more prone to test him. The second element in the Four Square worth noting is the value of the *EA*, 6.5. Although it falls within the average range for nonpatient adults, it seems a bit modest for the bright college graduate. *If* this speculation is valid, it suggests that he does not have as many resources readily available for use as should be the case, and could indicate less maturity than might be expected.

His cognitive operations appear to be reasonably sophisticated. He gave nine *DQ* + responses, has a *Zf* of 13, and the *Zd* score of − 2.0 is within the average range, as is the *W:M* of 8:4. The *W:D* ratio of 1:2 suggests considerable, but not necessarily excessive, economizing in his cognitive activities. The one negative element in the cognitive array is the elevated *X* + % of 94%, with two superior-overelaborated *FQ* + answers. There are no minus answers, and only one *u* response, and the number of *P* responses falls on the high side of the average range. This indicates that he is the type of person who is overly committed to conventionality, and may be sacrificing some of his own uniqueness as a result.

There is no evidence to suggest problems in thinking. The form use in his *M* answers is appropriate, the record contains no Critical Special Scores, the $M^a:M^p$ ratio is appropriately higher on the left side, and the *a:p* ratio shows a reasonable mixture, thereby suggesting some flexibility in thinking and attitudes. An interesting finding that has no empirical correlate is that all five passive movement answers are nonhuman. Typically, if passive movement answers occur with any substantial frequency, they appear in a mixture of human and nonhuman responses. Because that did not occur, in spite of the sizable number involved, they will warrant special attention in the analysis of the verbalizations.

There is no marked evidence of any serious problems with affect, other than those already noted in relation to the overload state. The record includes only one *S* response and the *Afr* of .56 is in the average range. The *FC:CF* + *C* of 3:1 is within acceptable limits, but may signal a slight tendency toward overcontrol of affective displays. If true, that is not unexpected in light of the overcommitment to conventionality.

Another significant liability appears when the data concerning self-concept are reviewed. The Egocentricity Index of .28 is quite low, signaling that his self-esteem is more negative than positive. This is a liability for anyone, but probably even more so for the person who is strongly committed to convention and social acceptance. There are also two *FD* responses, suggesting that he is somewhat more introspective than most adults. Although this is generally a favorable sign, it might also indicate a tendency to focus more on his negative self-value. Fortunately, there is only one *MOR* in the record, and no evidence from the composite of *PER* and *Ab + Art* that he is overly defensive. This may portend well for intervention, especially because he is a self-referral. He is clearly interested in people, as indicated from the six human contents, and the fact that four of the six are *Pure H* suggests that his conceptualizations about people are generally based in experience.

Thus as a beginning, a psychological picture is unfolding of a reasonably bright, cognitively competent person, who may be slightly less mature in terms of resource development than would be expected. He is in serious overload that is apparently being provoked by situationally related stresses. Although his ideation seems clear, and his thinking and attitudes reasonably flexible, he is also overly committed to conventionality and apparently sacrificing some of his own uniqueness because of it. One of the consequences of this may be a tendency to overcontrol his emotional displays. Although very interested in people, he is experiencing considerably more loneliness than should be the case. He is quite introspective, but also doubts his own personal worth, and this composite could breed greater future problems if not corrected. Possibly some of the data in the Sequence of Scores, which is presented as Table 35, will aid in broadening the picture.

Table 35.   Scoring Sequence—L.S. Protocol

CARD	NO.	LOC.	#	DETERMINANT(S)	(2)	CONTENT(S)	POP	Z	SPECIAL SCORES
I	1	Wo	1	FMpo		A	P	1.0	
	2	W+	1	Mao	2	H,(A)		4.0	
	3	Ddo	24	Fo		Id			
II	4	D+	1	FMpo	2	Ad	P	3.0	
	5	DS+	5	ma.CFo		Sc,Fi		4.5	
III	6	D+	1	Mao	2	H	P	3.0	
	7	Do	3	FCo		Cg			
IV	8	W+	1	FMp.FT.FDo		A,Bt		4.0	
	9	Do	3	FYo		Bt			PER
V	10	Wo	1	Fo		A	P	1.0	
VI	11	Wo	1	FTo		Ad	P	2.5	MOR
	12	Do	4	mp.FY+		Sc			
	13	Do	3	Fo		Ay			
VII	14	D+	1	Fo	2	Hd,Id	P	1.0	
	15	Do	2	Fo		A			
	16	W+	1	Mao	2	H		3.0	
VIII	17	Wo	1	FCo		Art		4.5	
	18	Do	1	Fo	2	A	P		
	19	Do	4	FMa.FDu		A			
IX	20	Do	4	Fo		Hd			
	21	Do	8	Fo		Hh			
	22	D+	1	Ma.mp+		H,Id		2.5	
X	23	Do	1	Fo	2	A	P		
	24	Do	7	FMao		A			
	25	W+	1	FCo		Bt		5.5	

(C)1976, 1983 BY JOHN E. EXNER, JR.
    ABBREVIATIONS USED ABOVE:
        FOR DQ: "/" = "v/+"; FOR CONTENTS: "Id" = "IDIOGRAPHIC CONTENT"
        SPECIAL SCORES: "INC" = "INCOM", "FAB" = "FABCOM", "CON" = "CONTAM"
                        "CFB" = "CONFAB"

Interpretation of the Scoring Sequence   His sequence is marked by evidence of both effort and conservatism. The effort can be noted in the fact that he gives three answers to each of six cards, *including the last five*. In other words, even after having "learned" that two answers would be acceptable by his performance on Cards II, III, and IV, he goes beyond that. Similarly, all but one of his first responses are marked by an organizing effort. These are important findings because they relate to the question of a tendency toward excessive economizing raised from the structural data. On the other hand, his location approach is more mixed and economical. He does give a *W,* as a first answer to five cards, but they are the more solid blots to which *W* answers are easier to formulate. Similarly, seven of his first 10 answers are Popular responses; that is, he enters on a very conservative note. Also, although he gives 15 answers to the last five blots, only three are *W* answers. His five blend answers are scattered, so that no unusual complexity appears in the record. Overall there is nothing dramatic in the sequence, although the data support some of the findings from the structure; namely, that he does strive to do well, but that his striving is also marked by a cautiousness. The former might be a product of his commitment to convention, whereas the latter may reflect his proneness to place a low value on his own worth.

Analysis of the Content   Although it has been noted earlier that a response-by-response review of the content is often a concrete and simplistic approach, it seems appropriate here for purposes of illustration.

CARD I   1. Looks like a bat gliding along
           2. It could also be a modern dance of some sort, with a woman in the center with her hands in the air and two creatures dancing around her.
           3. Say, this lower part could be a bell

The first, or *signature,* response can often convey quite a bit about the way in which the subject generally approaches new coping situations. It has been selected from many available and, as such, probably represents something about the decision of the subject regarding how to approach the task. His first answer has two interesting features. The passive movement reflected in the word *gliding* is of considerable interest, especially because it coincides in an almost predictable way with previously developed hypotheses about him. It is probably more notable because bats usually are not noted for gliding. They are much more active, so that this is an almost incongruous use of the word. His second response is also striking for its content. It also affords an illustration of how some interpreters can become trapped into misleading speculation. The central figure is a woman, and some may attempt to deal with that very literally, suggesting that it may represent his wife, or some aspect of his own "feminine" identity, and so on. *However, in this instance the sex of the figure must be ignored.* It is very rare that the *D*4 area is ever identified as a man or a child. The figure probably does represent the subject, but it is the movement that conveys the projection, *not* the sex of the figure. The hands are "in the air," which seems like a passive, possibly helpless, or signaling gesture. Creatures are dancing around. They might be playful, or celebrating, but because they are *creatures,* they are possibly threatening. If the latter is true, the response seems to be a good representation of his helplessness and the threats that he is experiencing. His third answer, a bell, should be taken as a classification answer under most circumstances; however, it does occur to a *Dd* area and may have some significance. It does seem quite interesting to note that it is an alerting instrument, following a response that can easily be translated as a plea for help.

CARD II   4. It could be a couple of dogs touching noses

5. The center could be a rocket ship taking off and the red could be the exhaust fire

The movement in the first answer is tentative and exploratory. It involves domestic animals, in a cautious, nonaggressive activity. It is followed by a "flight" response. The rocket is *taking off*. It is intriguing to question whether this is a typical response in his interpersonal world.

CARD III   6. A couple of men bending over to lift something up

7. The center red area could be a bow tie

The movement in response 6 is cooperative, but also tentative. They are bending over to lift, but the lifting has yet to occur. The bow tie must be taken as a classification response. If it has any useful meaning it is not clear, except possibly that it is an object used as a form of social attire.

CARD IV   8. It could be a gorilla sitting on a stump

9. A delicate flower

The classification of Card IV as a gorilla is very commonplace, thus the type of animal should not be given any special emphasis. Again, it is the movement that is important. It is passive. To this point in the record, all of the movement, with the exception of the rocket response, has been passive or cautious. The next answer seems important because of the embellishment *delicate*. It conveys a sense of fragility.

CARD V   10. It could be a bat or a butterfly, I think more a butterfly now that I look at it because I said bat before.

The specific content adds little because it is so common; however, the vacillation noted early in the response may be important because it also ties together well with previously developed hypotheses.

CARD VI   11. Would you believe an animal skin?

12. This could be a submarine cruising along in the darkness

13. You know, that could be a totem pole too

The animal skin answer is also very common and not very revealing for its content. The way in which the response was delivered, however, seems unusual, "Would you believe . . . ?" It conveys a sense of challenge to his own credibility, and may reflect his insecurity. The second answer is much more intriguing. Submarines are weapons that can hide easily. This one is "cruising," which may suggest cautiously searching, ". . . along in the darkness." The answer not only raises questions about his needs to protect and conceal himself, but on a more symbolic level, raises an issue about his aggressive and sexual urges, and how he may attempt to handle them. The third answer might also have some relation, an object of worship, but because it is a common classification answer, such speculation is probably inappropriate.

CARD VII   14. A couple of kids

15. This way it looks like a scotty dog

16. This way it looks like a couple of women doing the can-can

The first two responses add little, because they are classification responses that have not been embellished. The third answer is clearly the most active form of movement in the record thus far. It is a form of exhibitionistic movement, involving an historically "naughty" routine that carries sexual connotations. It may signal a desire to be more open and active in his sexuality. If so, it is easy to understand how the desire would be difficult to manifest in light of other data in the record.

CARD VIII   17. The whole thing could be an emblem
            18. This thing on the side could be animals of some sort
            19. You know, this top part looks like a sand crab, like it was leaping forward, going away from you

The first two answers should be addressed as classification responses and afforded little weight, but it is interesting to note that emblems, badges, and such are often found among records of subjects with status needs. The third answer offers more. Like the submarine, it is also hard-shelled, but most important, like the rocket it is a flight response, ". . . going away from you." This seems to add fuel to the issue of whether some of his previously noted strong needs for closeness are not the result of his own overly cautious and possibly avoidant behaviors in his interpersonal world.

CARD IX   20. This looks like Teddy Roosevelt's head
           21. This center part could be a vase
           22. You know, this way it looks like a person on a motorcycle or a bike

Again, the first two responses must be taken as classification responses, although it is interesting to note that Mr. Roosevelt gained considerable status in his time. For the third time in a row, it is the third answer that has the greatest yield, and it is difficult to avoid the speculation that he retains the blot until some message is formed. It is a person *on* a motorcycle, an object often associated with a more reckless life-style, *or* a bike, the self-propelled, more conventional object. This may signify some conflict about how best to express needs and affects.

CARD X   23. These blue things look like crabs
          24. This brown could be a deer jumping
          25. This way, it looks like a floral scene, with a huge flower in the center and smaller flowers around it

The first answer, a Popular, must be taken as a classification response. If it has value, it is because it adds to several answers, the rocket, the submarine, the crab on Card VIII, and possibly the vase on Card IX, representing a composite of objects with firm exteriors. Fisher and Cleveland would note that these answers reflect a "barrier," or defensiveness to intrusion. The second answer, a deer jumping, is more revealing. The movement is more avoidant, which is not inconsistent with many of his previous answers. The last answer, although also a classification response, is interesting because it is a *display,* possibly similar to those of the modern dance on Card I, the can-can dancers on Card VII, or the emblem on Card VIII. It has a *huge* flower *in the center*—that is, the point of attraction. At the same time the content, flowers, like the answer on Card IV, a delicate flower, may convey a sense of wanting to be attractive, but in a gentle manner, or at least one that acknowledges his own sense of fragility.

Overall, the analysis of the responses seems to indicate that he is a cautious, conservative fellow, possibly fearful of being open in his interpersonal world, tentative about his affective displays, yet wanting to be more open about his affect, and probably his sexuality. He seems uncertain about his own life-style and, unfortunately, will often take flight easily from more appealing but less conventional behaviors because of his strong sense of inadequacy and/or insecurity. As a result he cannot deal with many of his needs easily, if at all, especially his strong needs for closeness or his needs for status.

As noted earlier, the material in the Inquiry ordinarily should not be given the same weight as the responses, and it must be used very cautiously for purposes of clarification. A search of the Inquiry in the L. S. record does add information. The bat, in the first answer, is described as having "small feet," the woman in the second answer is described as having her hands raised, ". . . in sort of supplication . . . ," and the creatures ". . . represent something symbolic of whatever she's doing." Supplication is a humble request, and the symbolic relation of the creatures seems to confirm the postulate about being overwhelmed by internal threat. His elaboration to response 7 on Card III is worth noting, because he describes the tie as, ". . . those big red bow ties that clowns sometimes wear." This hints at the possibility that he may often feel awkward, or even the possible object of humor when he is affective, *or,* that some of his affective displays are false and concealing. He personalizes his ninth answer about the delicate flower, ". . . my wife grows them . . . ," again raising many interesting questions about their relationship. The dancers that he reports on Card VII are, ". . . dancing on one leg . . . ," appropriate for the scene, but nonetheless precarious. The emblem on Card VIII is elaborated as, ". . . a family crest . . . ," not surprising in light of the pride that his parents take in the achievements of their sons.

SUMMARY

Any summary of the L. S. record must begin by emphasizing the serious overload state, because this has definite implications for intervention. This is not a patient who can be treated casually on a once per week basis. The current stresses must be defined and appropriate supports provided to the point that he feels some relief in being able to contend with them. Once that occurs, some of the more chronic liabilities can be addressed. It seems obvious that beneath the surface of the hard-working, conscientious husband and father, lies a very insecure personality structure that is not fully developed. He has been unable to find ways of being consistent in coping, and apparently feels much more fragile and/or vulnerable than he conveys. He has tried to adopt a role of being a responsible adult, but he has interpreted this as being much more conventional than most people, often sacrificing his own needs and/or feelings as a result. He would like to be much closer to others than is the case, but he seems confused, or at least uncertain, about what role to adopt to accomplish this. His relationship with his wife may be much more precarious than he concedes, and it must be explored thoroughly in the course of intervention planning, and possibly even at the onset of treatment, because it could be contributing significantly to his current stress state.

Long-term intervention should focus on development, that is, aiding him to define and develop many of his potentially rich resources. He is bright, cognitively competent, and apparently there is enough flexibility in his thinking and attitudes to make him amenable to new tactics of thinking and behavior. He is the type of person who, if aided through his current stresses so that his tolerance for new events is improved, should be able to profit considerably from any of a variety of longer-term intervention strategies, especially those focusing on growth and dealing with day-to-day issues. If the marital relationship is precarious, marital therapy would be an obvious option, and over a longer period of time some other group experience could be useful in aiding in the development of interpersonal tactics, which will be more in accord with his needs and objectives. The goal of intervention should be to help him identify his own unique features, and to be able to use them effectively without feeling that he is violating the expectations of others.

REFERENCES

Bochner, R., and Halpern, F. (1945) *The Clinical Application of the Rorschach Test*. New York: Grune & Stratton.

Elizur, A. (1949) Content analysis of the Rorschach with regard to anxiety and hostility. *Journal of Projective Techniques*, **13**, 247–284.

Exner, J., and Exner, D. (1972) How clinicians use the Rorschach. *Journal of Personality Assessment*, **36**, 403–408.

Fisher, S., and Cleveland, S. (1958) *Body Image and Personality*. New York: Van Nostrand Reinhold.

Frank, L. K. (1939) Projective methods for the study of personality. *Journal of Personality*, **8**, 389–413.

Goldfarb, W. (1945) The animal symbol in the Rorschach Test and animal association test. *Rorschach Research Exchange*, **9**, 8–22.

Goldfried, M. (1963) The connotative meanings of some animals for college students. *Journal of Projective Techniques*, **27**, 60–67.

Goldfried, M., Stricker, G., and Weiner, I. (1971) *Rorschach Handbook of Clinical and Research Applications*. Englewood Cliffs, N.J.: Prentice-Hall.

Hirschstein, R., and Rabin, A. I. (1955) Reactions to Rorschach cards IV and VII as a function of parental availability in childhood. *Journal of Consulting Psychology*, **19**, 473–474.

Holt, R. R. (1960) Cognitive controls and primary processes. *Journal of Psychoanalytic Research*, **4**, 105–112.

Holt, R. R. (1966) Measuring libidinal and aggressive motives and their controls by means of the Rorschach Test. In Levine, D. (Ed.), *Nebraska Symposium on Motivation*. Lincoln: University of Nebraska Press.

Levy, E. (1958) Stimulus values of Rorschach cards for children. *Journal of Projective Techniques*, **22**, 293–295.

Lindner, R. M. (1943) The Rorschach Test and the diagnosis of psychopathic personality. *Journal of Criminal Psychopathology*, **1**, 69.

Lindner, R. M. (1944) Some significant Rorschach responses. *Journal of Criminal Psycholopathology*, **4**, 775.

Lindner, R. M. (1946) Content analysis in Rorschach work. *Rorschach Research Exchange*, **10**, 121–129.

Lindner, R. M. (1947) Analysis of Rorschach's Test by content. *Journal of Clinical Psychopathology*, **8**, 707–719.

Meer, B., and Singer J. (1950) A note of the "father" and "mother" cards in the Rorschach inkblots, *Journal of Consulting Psychology*, **14**, 482–484.

Molish, H. B. (1967) Critique and problems of research: A survey. In Beck, S. J., and Molish, H. B. *Rorschach's Test. II: A Variety of Personality Pictures*. (2nd Ed.) New York: Grune & Stratton.

Pascal, G., Ruesch, H. Devine, D., and Suttell, B. (1950) A study of genital symbols on the Rorschach Test: Presentation of method and results. *Journal of Abnormal and Social Psychology*, **45**, 285–289.

Phillips, L., and Smith, J. G. (1953) *Rorschach Interpretation: Advanced Technique*. New York: Grune & Stratton.

Prandoni, J., Matranga, J., Jensen, D., and Waison, M. (1973) Selected Rorschach characteristics of sex offenders. *Journal of Personality Assessment, 37,* 334–336.

Rorschach, H. (1921) *Psychodiagnostics*. Bern: Bircher (Transl. Hans Huber Verlag, 1942).

Rosen, E. (1951) Symbolic meanings in the Rorschach cards: A statistical study. *Journal of Clinical Psychology, 7,* 239–244.

Schafer, R. (1954) *Psychoanalytic Interpretation in Rorschach Testing*. New York: Grune & Stratton.

Smith, J., and Coleman, J. (1956) The relationship between manifestation of hostility in projective techniques and overt behavior. *Journal of Projective Techniques, 20,* 326–334.

Stone, H. (1953) Relationship of hostile aggressive behavior to aggressive content of the Rorschach and Thematic Apperception Test. Unpublished doctoral dissertation, University of California at Los Angeles.

Walker, R. G. (1951) A comparison of clinical manifestations of hostility with Rorschach and MAPS performance. *Journal of Projective Techniques, 15,* 444–460.

Wallach, J. D. (1983) Affective-symbolic connotations of the Rorschach inkblots: Fact or fantasy. *Perceptual and Motor Skills, 56,* 287–295.

Wheeler, W. M. (1949) An analysis of Rorschach indices of male homosexuality. *Journal of Projective Techniques, 13,* 97–126.

Zelin, M., and Sechrest, L. (1963) The validity of the ''mother'' and ''father'' cards of the Rorschach. *Journal of Projective Techniques and Personality Assessment, 27,* 114–121.

PART V

Clinical Applications

CHAPTER 19

Some Assessment Issues

This chapter contains five clinical cases. They are neither simple nor complex, but rather, represent some of the most common assessment issues that are often posed to those responsible for the assessment of the majority of patients for whom the Rorschach might be an appropriate assessment tactic. They have been selected to provide an illustration of what the Rorschach, used properly, can and cannot reveal concerning issues of diagnosis, describing personality, and the formulation of recommendations concerning intervention and/or disposition. They have also been selected because they portray the manner in which the logical progression of interpretation might deviate from the methodical approach to the test data as was illustrated in the L. S. protocol described in Chapter 18.

In some instances, the data in the Special Indices may precipitate a review of some variables earlier than described in the more standard format. In other instances, findings from a review of the *D* scores and/or the Four Square might provoke an earlier review of other data sets than would occur if the more methodical approach is employed. Either approach to interpretation should yield the same findings; however, as has been noted earlier, each significant finding should generate new questions for the interpreter. If the questions are pursued logically at the time that they arise, the quest for the most comprehensive description of the subject, and answers to the assessment issues that have been posed, will probably unfold more readily, and with greater ease. For instance, if the *SCZI* is elevated to or beyond the critical cut-off score of 4, it is illogical to proceed to the data of the Four Square without first attempting to confirm or reject the implication that schizophrenia may be present. If the finding of the *SCZI* is confirmed, it will have far different consequences in developing the personality description and treatment recommendations, than if it is rejected. Similarly, if the data of the Four Square reveal an extratensive style for a subject referred because of impulsive-like activity, it seems illogical to study issues concerning cognition before addressing the issues of affective control. If the data concerning emotional control indicate limited modulation, the finding will dictate a somewhat different basis for the unfolding description than if an opposite finding occurred.

PROTOCOL 1: A QUESTION CONCERNING TENSION AND DEPRESSION

Referral   C. F. was referred by a psychologist who had seen her previously for about 5 months supportively, shortly after the "break-up" of her first marriage. He had not had any contact with her for approximately 2 years, during which time she had remarried and given birth to a daughter. He had treated her, during their earlier contact with supportive methods, believing that her symptoms at that time, "nervousness and depression," were related to the divorce action. He now wonders if he may have been "remiss" in terminating her and states in the referral, "She currently complains again of tension and depression, plus occasional spells during which she loses her sense of time and place and feels overwhelmed by her emotions. She has not actually had lapses in memory but is very vague for events that occur during these periods. I would appreciate an independent evaluation of her personality and any guidance you may offer about the most appropriate treatment plans.''

History   C. F. was born and raised in a large metropolitan area. She graduated from high school with honors and completed 1 year of college in a local liberal arts school, on scholarship, before she married for the first time. She is a reasonably attractive, 25-year-old blonde, slight in build, but conscientious in dress so as to maximize her physical assets. She is the oldest of four children, having three younger brothers, the oldest of whom is a recent college graduate, and the younger two who are still in high school. Both parents are living, the father, age 51, is an industrial salesman, the mother, age 50, a housewife. The parents expressed disappointment at C. F.'s early marriage; she was 19 at the time, and had just completed her first year at college. Her marriage lasted approximately 3 years and according to her statement, her husband, who was her own age, ''just didn't want much from life. We were incompatible and I doubt that we would have married if I hadn't gotten all caught up in him being a football hero.'' She indicates that he demanded ''too much of my time and didn't give me any freedom to do the things that I wanted.'' Shortly after her marriage C. F. began working as a receptionist in a law firm while her husband continued in college. She states, ''There were always guys after me, you know, on the prowl, and I always felt funny about it cause some were really nice.'' Ultimately, she did have two extramarital affairs, the second of which precipitated the divorce. She remarried about 5 months after her divorce, during which time she had liaisons with several men, including her present husband who is a law clerk. She became pregnant approximately 4 months after her remarriage, ''it was a wonderful experience.'' Delivery was normal and ''my husband has been a brick through the whole thing.'' She notes that her husband is extremely helpful with her daughter, who is now 20-months old. ''I don't know what I'd do without him, they get along so well together.'' She says of her marriage, ''We are really close, a real family, and it will be even better when I get over whatever is wrong. But right now I know there are some things that aren't right and it just keeps me on edge all of the time.'' She reports feelings of being confined, ''Sometimes I just have to get out of the house 'cause it feels like its closing in on me. I'm just on edge all of the time, and sometimes I just cry for no reason at all.'' She has been taking a variety of mild, antianxiety tranquilizers prescribed by her physician, but reports that they have not helped very much, ''Some days I feel really great, but then the next day I'm all uptight again.'' She says that her sexual relationship with her husband is, ''just like always, you know, it's o.k.,'' but also admits that she does not experience orgasm at each event, ''. . . but I think that will get better.'' Her contact with her parents is infrequent, ''because they never wanted me to marry in the first place and were really upset when I did it again'' but writes frequently to her two oldest brothers. She suggests that her feelings of discomfort are created by ''some unknown thing in my body, like some physical thing,'' but admits that several physicians have not detected any physiological problems. She is especially ''tired'' in the mornings, ''I always wake up with a backache or something like that, like I couldn't sleep right,'' and yet she also has trouble going to sleep, ''I lie awake some nights until two or three o'clock.'' Her menstrual cycle is normal although she does complain of ''severe cramps, like a knife cutting into me'' during the first day or two of menstruation. She does not want any more children ''immediately,'' but speculates that she might have four or five more ''if I can get myself straight.''

Protocol #1. 25-Year-Old, Married, One Child, Housewife

Card	Response	Inquiry	Scoring
I	1. Oh gee; it ll a bf	E: (Rpts S's resp) S: The W thg ll that bec of the way the outside is w the wgs	Wo Fo A P 1.0
	S: Do u want more? E: Take your time, you'll probably find something else too.		
	2. Well it cb, a cats face too, hissing	E: (Rpts S's resp) S: These r the ears & the eyes & mouth r the white parts, it has puffy cheeks too lik it was hissing lik cats do	WSo FMªo Ad 3.5 AG
	3. This cntr prt c.b. the body of a wm w.o. a head	E: (Rpts S's resp) S: I can c the body part here (points), c these r the legs & the breasts but there's no head	Do Fo Hd Mor
II	4. Wow, look at the color, it ll blood on these dogs, or mayb its paint, yes that's it they have been playing in the paint & got it all over them	E: (Rpts S's resp) S: I don't kno why I said bld at first cause it doesn't ll that but it does ll paint that these dogs, c thyr playg, touchg their noses & thyv got paint on their legs	D+ FMª.CFo (2) A, Art P 3.0
	5. Ths top red paint might be a part of the body, lik inside, maybe a kidney, there's one on each side	E: (Rpts S's resp) S: Well it ll a kidney, the way its shaped E: I'm not sure I c it as u do S: Kidneys just ll that, the roundness like that	Do F− (2) An
III	6. It ll 2 cannibals & theyr carrying a pot up to this fire, its red, like fire, like a bonfire	E: (Rpts S's resp) S: The fire is back here & they r carrying ths pot E: I'm not sure I c the cannibals S: Rite here, c, 2 black men, lik cannibals, they tall & lanky lik cannibals	D+ Mª.FC'.CF.FD (2) H,Fi P 4.0

Protocol #1 (Continued)

Card	Response		Inquiry	Scoring
V 7.	If u turn it ths way the dark part ll an ugly bug	E: S:	(Rpts S's resp) Well it might be a spider with the big eyes, sort of the bulging kind & the legs here	Do F− A
IV 8	I'd have to say a monster man of s.s., all covered w fur, see all those lines, like fur	E: S:	(Rpts S's resp) It's a great big monster lik in science fiction, all furry w big legs & a head that almost isn't even there, just a littl thing & a big tail too	Wo FTo (H) P 2.0
V 9.	Oh, a child dressed in a rabbit suit, standing to get her picture taken, it looks furry (Rubs Card)	E: S:	(Rpts S's resp) Its lik a littl girl going to a party lik for halloween, she has a bunny hat & this fur suit like a bunny, ths other stuff doesn't count	Do Mp.FTo (H)
10.	It cld b another bf too	E: S:	(Rpts S's resp) It has the wgs here & the bunny hat wld b the feelers	Wo Fo A P 1.0
11.	There r 2 legs too, one on each side	E: S:	(Rpts S's resp) They just ll legs, lik u c in a stocking ad or s.t.	Do Fo (2) Hd
VI 12.	I'm not sure what ths top c.b. but the rest ll a piece of fur, (rubs card) you can almost feel it	E: S:	(Rpts S's resp) It's lik an unfinished coat or fur jacket or s.t., it really hasn't taken shape yet altho these c.b. arm parts here, its just a piece of fur	Do TFo Cg
V 13.	If u turn it ths way ths part ll 2 birds in a nest, waiting to be fed, u just c the heads stickg up	E: S:	(Rpts S's resp) Its their heads (points) & this is the nest & they r just lik waiting for the mother bird	Dd+ FMpo (2) Ad, Na 2.5

VII	14.	Ths is a littl girl who just had her hair fixed & she's lookg at herslf in the mirror	D+ Mp.Fro Hd P 3.0
		E: (Rpts S's resp) S: She has a pony tail that's probably held up w a comb or pins, she's really cute. I don't kno what the lower part is, it doesn't count	
	15.	It c.b. rain clds too	Wv C'Fo Cl
		E: (Rpts S's resp) S: Oh, I d.k. why I said that, they just look all black lik rain clouds, there r 4 of them or mayb 6 I guess	
VIII	16.	Oh, ths is pretty, its like a candy house	WS+ CF.C'Fu Fd 4.5
		S: Well its all different kinds of candy put togthr to ll a house lik in fairy tales, the diffrmt colors r diffrnt candies & the white parts r frosting E: I'm not sure I c it as u do S: Here is the roof & the windows & the door, its not supposed to ll a real hous, but lik a fairy tale house	
	< 17.	If u turn it ths way it ll a beaver stepping over some stones & thgs seeing himself reflected in the water	W+ FM^a.Fr.FCo A, Ls P 4.5
		E: (Rpts S's resp) S: Its an A lik a beaver or s.t. but its funny all pink lik that, mayb it's a reflect fr the sun that gives that color Its lik in the forest, very colorful, & he's just walkg along, lik a crossing of the stream or pool of water	
	18.	There c.b. a skeleton in there too, lik a rib cage	DSo Fo An 4.0
		E: (Rpts S's resp) S: Rite here (points) u can see the spaces in it, it just ll s. bodies ribs	
IX	19.	My God, more colors, I can c a waterfall in a canyon	D+ m^p.CF.FDo Na, Ls 2.5
		E: (Rpts S's resp) S: Its in the cntr, u can c the water falling, its set back in the jungle, all this green stuff, the pink part doesn't count tho, there is a cliff in front of it all colored by the sun & the waterfall in back in the distance	
	20.	There are 2 unborn children here in the pink	DO FCo (2) (H)
		E: (Rpts S's resp) S: I said unborn bec they r pink thy hav the big heads & the littl bodies, lik twins	

Card	Response	Inquiry	Scoring
21.	This thg in the cntr ll s.t. I hav on my desk to put papers on, its a sharp spike	E: (Rpts S's resp) S: I brought it home when I quit working, it is s.t. u just poke the hole thru the paper & the pink wld b the base tht holds it	Do Fo Id Per
22.	Wow, it ll s.b. thru paint all over the place, a mess	E: (Rpts S's resp) S: It just ll paint spattered all over when I first lookd at it, mayb its an artist's palate	Wv C Art
23.	Ths c.b. spiders here	E: (Rpts S's resp) S: They hav all those legs that ll a spider to me, don't thy ll that to u?	Do Fo (2) A P
24.	These c.b. fried eggs 2 of 'em	E: (Rpts S's resp) S: Lik they were fried in butter cause thy'r yellow, ths is the yoke part & ths is the white only its yellow bec of the butter	Do FCo (2) Fd
25.	Ths other yellow parts c.b. rose buds	E: (Rpts S's resp) S: Thyr pretty lik littl roses waiting to open, just the buds & the littl stem, like yellow rosebuds	Do FCo (2) Bt

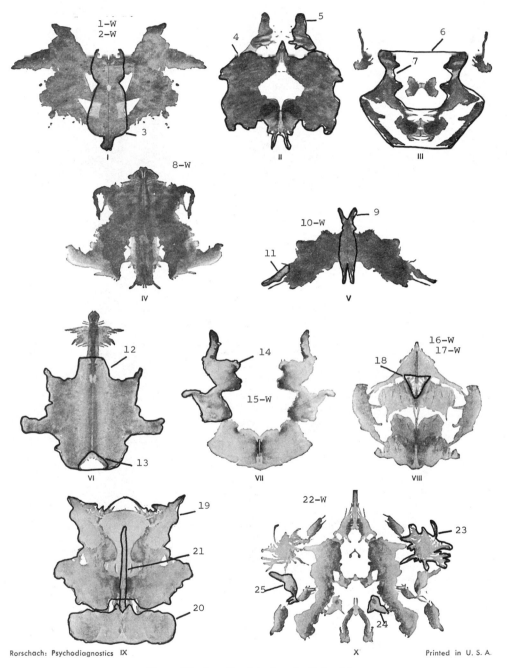

Figure 17. Location Selections for Protocol 1.

Table 36. Structural Summary—Protocol #1

```
================================================================================
  R = 25      Zf = 12     ZSum = 35.5     P = 8      (2) = 9     Fr+rF = 2

 LOCATION            DETERMINANTS               CONTENTS     S-CONSTELLATION
 FEATURES             BLENDS          SINGLE                    (ADULT)
                                                 H   = 1, O    NO..FV+VF+V+FD>2
 W   =  8      FM.CF            M   = O          (H) = 3, O    YES..Col-Shd Bl>0
  (Wv  =  2)   M.FC'.CF.FD      FM  = 2          Hd  = 3, O    YES..Ego<.31,>.44
 D   = 16      M.FT             m   = O          (Hd)= 0, O    NO..MOR > 3
 Dd  =  1      M.Fr             C   = 1          A   = 6, O    NO..Zd > +- 3.5
 S   =  3      CF.C'F           Cn  = O          (A) = 0, O    YES..es > EA
               FM.Fr.FC         CF  = O          Ad  = 2, O    YES..CF+C+Cn > FC
    DQ         m.CF.FD          FC  = 3          (Ad)= 0, O    NO..X+ < .70
.........(FQ-)                  C'  = O          Ab  = 0, O    NO..S > 3
                                C'F = 1          Al  = 0, O    NO..P < 3 or > 8
    +  =  7 ( O)                FC' = O          An  = 2, O    YES..Pure H < 2
  v/+ =  0 ( O)                 T   = O          Art = 1, 1    NO..R < 17
    o  = 16 ( 2)                TF  = 1          Ay  = 0, 0     5.....TOTAL
    v  =  2 ( O)                FT  = 1          Bl  = 0, O
                                V   = O          Bt  = 1, O    SPECIAL SCORINGS
                                VF  = O          Cg  = 1, O      DV    = O
                                FV  = O          Cl  = 1, O      INCOM = O
                                Y   = O          Ex  = 0, O      DR    = O
                                YF  = O          Fi  = 0, 1      FABCOM = O
              FORM QUALITY      FY  = O          Fd  = 1, O      ALOG  = O
                                rF  = O          Ge  = 0, O      CONTAM = O
   FQx        FQf      M Qual.  Fr  = O          Hh  = 0, O      --- WSUM6 = O
                                FD  = O          Ls  = 0, 2      AG    = 1
    +  =  O    +  = O    +  = O F   = 9          Na  = 1, 1      CONFAB = O
    o  = 21    o  = 7    o  = 3                  Sc  = 0, 0      CP    = O
    u  =  1    u  = O    u  = O                  Sx  = 0, 0      MOR   = 1
    -  =  2    -  = 2    -  = O                  Xy  = 0, 0      PER   = 1
 none=  1    none= O   none= O                   Idio= 2, 0      PSV   = O
================================================================================

              RATIOS, PERCENTAGES, AND DERIVATIONS

 ZSum-Zest =  35.5 - 38.0      FC:CF+C = 4: 5    W:M      = 8: 3
                                 (Pure C =  1)
 Zd        = -2.5                                W:D      = 8:16
                               Afr     = 0.67
.---------------------------.                    Isolate:R =  6:25
 :EB =  3: 7.5   EA = 10.5:    3r+(2)/R = 0.60
 :            >D=  0                             Ab+Art   = 2
 :eb =  5: 6     es = 11  :    L       = 0.56
 '---------------------------'                   An+Xy    = 2
 (FM= 4 " C'= 3 T= 3) (Adj D=  O)  Blends:R = 7:25
 (m = 1 " V = O Y= O)                            H(H):Hd(Hd)=  4: 3
                               X+%     = 0.84      (Pure H =  1)
 a:p      = 4: 4               (F+%    = 0.78) (HHd):(AAd) = 3: O
                               X-%     = 0.08
 Ma:Mp    = 1: 2                                 H+A:Hd+Ad = 10: 5
 ---------------------------------------------------------------------------
          SCZI = 1           DEPI = 2           S-CON = 5
================================================================================
(C)1976,1983 BY JOHN E. EXNER, JR.
```

454

Table 37. Scoring Sequence—Protocol #1

===
```
CARD NO. LOC.  #      DETERMINANT(S)    (2) CONTENT(S) POP   Z    SPECIAL SCORES
```
===
```
 I    1 Wo    1 Fo                         A         P   1.0
      2 WSo   1 FMao                       Ad            3.5  AG
      3 Do    4 Fo                         Hd                      MOR

 II   4 D+    1 FMa.CFo             2 A,Art           P   3.0
      5 Do    2 F-                  2 An

III   6 D+    1 Ma.FC'.CF.FDo       2 H,Fi           P   4.0
      7 Do    1 F-                     A

 IV   8 Wo    1 FTo                    (H)            P   2.0

 V    9 Do    7 Mp.FTo                 (H)
     10 Wo    1 Fo                     A             P   1.0
     11 Do    1 Fo                  2 Hd

 VI  12 Do    1 TFo                    Cg
     13 Dd+  33 FMpo                2 Ad,Na              2.5

VII  14 D+    2 Mp.Fro                 Hd             P   3.0
     15 Wv    1 C'Fo                   Cl

VIII 16 WS+   1 CF.C'Fu                Id                 4.5
     17 W+    1 FMa.Fr.FCo             A,Ls           P   4.5
     18 DSo   3 Fo                     An                 4.0

 IX  19 D+    2 mp.CF.FDo              Na,Ls              2.5
     20 Do    6 FCo                 2 (H)
     21 Do    9 Fo                     Id                      PER

 X   22 Wv    1 C                      Art
     23 Do    1 Fo                  2 A              P
     24 Do    2 FCo                 2 Fd
     25 Do   15 FCo                 2 Bt
```
===
```
(C)1976, 1983 BY JOHN E. EXNER, JR.
   ABBREVIATIONS USED ABOVE:
   FOR DQ: "/" = "v/+"; FOR CONTENTS: "Id" = "IDIOGRAPHIC CONTENT"
   SPECIAL SCORES: "INC" = "INCOM", "FAB" = "FABCOM", "CON" = "CONTAM"
                   "CFB" = "CONFAB"
```

STRUCTURAL INTERPRETATION

R is 25, thus there is no reason to question the interpretive usefulness of the record. A scan of the Special Indices shows no unusual elevations. Both *D* scores are 0, indicating that, ordinarily, she has sufficient resource available from which to formulate and implement decisions, and that her tolerance for everyday stress is reasonably good. This seems particularly important because the value of *es,* 11, is considerable, suggesting that she is able to handle considerable stimulus demand. The *eb* has a higher value on the right side, confirming the experience of distress about which she complains. The record includes three *C'* responses, indicating that some of the distress is being created by a tendency to internalize feelings that she would prefer to externalize, a procedure which would be more consistent with the extratensive style noted by the *EB* of 3:7.5. The presence of the extratensive style suggests that she is the type of person who usually invests affect into her decision operations, and that she approaches most coping situations using a trial-and-error method. People like this are prone to derive most of their gratifications through emotional exchange, thus when she inhibits affective displays by turning feelings inward, it runs counter to her more natural psychological orientation.

A more striking finding is the presence of three T responses, signaling that some of the distress is being generated by strong needs for affective closeness. Usually, when T is elevated to this magnitude, feelings of loneliness are experienced and readily apparent. In most cases they are the product of some recent emotional loss. According to the history she provides, however, there is no *obvious* recent loss. This poses a question about whether the affective needs are more long-standing and chronically ungratified, *or* if a sense of loss has been created more recently by elements that are not readily apparent. Some information regarding this issue can be generated from a review of the variables related to the self and interpersonal attitudes. Her Egocentricity Index is very elevated, .60, indicating an excess of self-focusing activity, probably at the expense of adequate involvement with her world. Moreover, there are two reflection answers, revealing that her marked self-centeredness is characterized by tendencies to overglorify her personal worth in ways that are probably narcissistic-like. This feature will often interfere with the development and/or maintenance of deep and/or mature interpersonal relations. The presence of seven human contents indicates that she is interested in people, but only *one* of the seven is a *Pure H,* suggesting that her conceptualizations of people are not well developed or based on real experience. In fact, the presence of three parenthesized human contents strongly suggests that many of her impressions of others, and possibly of herself, are derived more from fantasy than reality. This hypothesis is afforded support by some of the data related to the characteristics of her ideation. The record contains only three M responses, but two of the three are M^p. This signifies the Snow White feature—that is, the tendency to take flight into fantasy in a way that becomes an abusive use of her deliberate thinking. Among the more significant characteristics of this type of person is an orientation away from responsibility and a preference to be more dependent on the direction of others. This dependency element is also indicated by the presence of an Fd content.

The other characteristics of her ideation are unremarkable. There are no Critical Special Scores and all three of her M responses show a conventional use of form. The $a:p$ ratio is evenly balanced, suggesting that her thinking can be flexible, and that she is not overly rigid in her values. Her cognitive operations appear to be appropriately economical ($W:D = 8:16$), and she oftens makes an effort to organize her world in a meaningful way ($Zf = 12; DQ = 7$). She is quite attuned to conventionality ($X+\% = 84\%; P = 8$) and, generally, she does no more distorting of perceptual inputs than most people ($X-\% = 8\%$).

Another potentially significant liability is represented in the $FC:CF+C$ ratio of 4:5. It indicates that when she discharges affect, which is a common event in her coping activities, many of those experiences will be marked by less modulation than is customary for adults. This failure to modulate increases the intensity of the emotion, and as a result the feelings become strongly, and sometimes overly influential in her thinking, her decisions, and her behaviors. It is important that this feature *not* be misinterpreted as an inability to control emotions. The Adjusted D score indicates that adequate controls are present most of the time. It signifies a failure to commit resources in ways that are necessary to modulate emotional displays effectively. In fact, the presence of one *Pure C* response suggests that, at times, she passively gives way to her feelings, allowing them to direct, or even command her actions. The tactic of limiting modulation of emotions should not automatically be translated as a significant liability. It is commonplace among children and adolescents, and not uncommon among some adults who are sufficiently mature, to be able to create and maintain smooth interpersonal relations. They often give the appearance of being intense, but still competent and likable. However, it is a disadvantage to the adult who is not able to create deep, mature relationships, and who is overly wrapped up in oneself, and prone to excessive dependency on others.

The postulate that it is a significant liability for her seems supported by two other elements in the record that concern emotion. First, she gave two Color-Shading Blend responses, indicating that her feelings may often be marked by confusion and/or ambivalence, which can only serve to exacerbate the problems created by her failures in control. Also, there are three S responses in the record, suggesting that some of her feelings will be marked by oppositional, negative, or possibly even hostile features. When added to the composite of other personality characteristics indicated by the structural data, this finding suggests that some of her behaviors may have passive-aggressive characteristics.

The slight elevation in $An + Xy$ indicates more body concern than is common for adults, and probably relates to her proposition that some of her feelings of discomfort are created by ". . . some unknown thing in my body, like some physical thing." A more positive finding is that the record contains two FD responses, signaling that she does make an effort to take distance and engage in self-examination. This can be an especially favorable finding if some form of psychotherapy is undertaken.

ANALYSIS OF THE SCORING SEQUENCE

Her approach is generally unremarkable, being oriented to large detail areas most of the time. In most instances the W answer occurs first in the card, if it is to occur. Five of her seven blend responses appear to color cards, again offering evidence that she is attracted to, but also confused by affectively toned stimuli. She has Popular answers on every card and shows organizational activity on all but Card X, to which she gives her only "formless" and most labile response. Her *Pure F* answers, with the exception of the first response in the test, appear consistently after more complex determinants have been used. This may indicate an awareness of her tendencies to "overrespond" to ambiguity, and an attempt to constrain this responsiveness. This possibly relates to the large number of P answers, suggesting that her awareness of convention does prompt her to attempt more "restrained" behaviors.

There are two specific propositions that can be developed from the sequence of scores:

1. She becomes ambivalent under the pressures of emotionally toned stimuli, prompted to make an affective response but also prompted to constrained her affect.

2. Her displays of affect are usually followed by noticeable efforts for delay and containment, although her most creative activity ordinarily occurs under affectively charged conditions.

ANALYSIS OF THE RESPONSES

The responses are reasonably rich in idiographic comments. Her use of "Oh gee, . . . , wow, oh, my God" all serve to illustrate one of the ways that her affect is displayed. They are ineffectual delays, signifying her own feelings and generally convey the notion of threat from the external world. She seeks guidance from others, "Do you want more?," but becomes defensively hostile, "hissing" when encouraged to go beyond that for which she is prepared. Her third answer in Card I, "a woman without a head," may suggest her own lack of cognitive control. The impact of the colors is obvious throughout the protocol by her comments and by the manner in which it is often the focal point of her answer. Her constant struggle to inhibit these affective responses is exemplified in Card II where she quickly identifies the red as blood, but then in a counterphobic move, alters the identification to paint and the dogs as playing. Many of her percepts seem juvenile, or even infantile, "monster man . . . child dressed in a rabbit suit, standing to get her picture taken . . . a piece of fur . . . two birds waiting to be fed . . . a little girl looking at herself in the mirror . . . a candy house . . . unborn children." These illustrate her immature ideation and suggest a regressive orientation. She prefers to be "a child" or at least sees herself as one, and if her affective displays are a good index of her behaviors, she apparently acts "childishly" much of the time. The birds waiting in the nest to be fed reflects her dependency wants. Her egocentricity is conveyed very directly by such responses as, the little girl waiting to have her picture taken, and the one who is looking in the mirror. The candy house and the fried eggs reveal an "oral" emphasis, giving further support for the notion of her immaturity. The "rain clouds" answer, following the mirror response on Card VIII, seems to indicate some feelings of pain and the prospect of "bad weather ahead" as a result of her excessive concern with herself. It might be speculated that this sort of preoccupation led to the end of her first marriage and may be jeopardizing her current marriage. The "unborn children" may reflect either her own regressive features *or* her fears of giving birth to other children. The "spindle" response on Card IX is probably quite idiographic and can have many meanings, probably all of which relate to some expression of aggression; that is, she has a "sharp spike" to put papers on. The paint responses are generally considered "anal" in nature by the analytic school, suggesting a willingness to display affect "all over the place" in this instance. She consistently identifies with "feminine" contents throughout the record.

ANALYSIS OF THE INQUIRY

The verbalizations in the Inquiry add considerable support to the previously generated propositions. Her comment, "I don't know why I saw blood," to Card II typifies her attempts to minimize her more aggressive affective responses. Similarly, she suggests that the cannibals are "like you see on TV" rather than real figures. The monster is a "science fiction" character, and the "spattered paint" becomes an artist's palate. The egocentric answers are equally striking, "a little girl going to a party . . . she's really cute," both indicating an intense self-focus. The candy house is "like in fairy tales . . . it's not supposed to be a real house," illustrating the world of fantasy and denial that she is most aligned with. The jacket that "hasn't really taken shape" reflects her own lack of growth, as do the birds "just like waiting for the mother bird." Her emphasis on various body parts, "puffy cheeks . . . breasts . . . kidneys . . . ribs . . . bodies . . . a stocking ad . . . legs" and so on, suggests a reasonably strong preoccupation with her own body and may illustrate some of her own somatic complaints. A less direct but possibly more omnipotent form of egocentric ideation is hinted at in her references to things "colored by the sun" on Cards VIII and IX. Her attempts at form accuracy in the Inquiry frequently falter to a reliance on the coloring of the blots, giving more evidence of her limited capability to detach herself from emotion in her ideation and/or behaviors.

SUMMARY OF PROTOCOL 1

The psychological picture that has unfolded is strongly indicative of a person who is heavily committed to the experience and use of emotion as a way of living. Unfortunately, she seems very immature, and apparently has never learned to value the importance of modulating her feelings. As a result, she often does not exert the control of her own discharges with sufficient frequency, and this permits her emotions to become overly intense and/or influential on her much more often than should be the case. Many of her feelings are confusing to her, and some are marked by considerable negativism or hostility. Thus although her thinking is clear, and her perceptual accuracy is well within acceptable limits, many of her behaviors are quite likely to be inefficient or even maladaptive. In part, her failure to inject effective modulation into her emotional displays may be the product of her inordinate, child-like self-centeredness, which causes her to attend much more to herself and much less to the world around her than should be the case. Her lack of development has perpetuated a tendency to be excessively dependent, and possibly demanding on others for decisions and direction, and apparently she often takes flight into fantasy for the specific purpose of avoiding responsibility and/or confrontations. Her attitudes toward, and awareness of others are not well founded in real experience and, as a consequence, her interpersonal world lacks both depth and maturity. It seems likely that her first marriage probably failed because she made excessive demands on her husband, and her current marriage may be marked by more difficulties than initially meet the eye. She has very strong needs for closeness, and their presence, plus her overall immaturity, cannot help to make the caring for a newborn a tast that is difficult if not threatening. It seems impossible to avoid the speculation that some of her apparent sense of loneliness may result from the fact that her husband is devoting time to the care of their child and, consequently, less time to her.

Currently, she is experiencing considerable distress. In part, this appears to be occurring because she is attempting to conceal and internalize some of her intense feelings, but much of it could result from an anticipated sense of abandonment or rejection. In effect, she portrays a very immature, histrionic personality, caught up in a centrifuge of often confusing and/or conflicting intense feelings, attempting to cope with them, as well as with everyday responsibilities, in her persistently immature, denying, and sometimes impulsive manner. She often wants to do what is correct and appropriate, but she is often hindered from this objective by her own immaturity. Some of the product is a form of passive-aggressive behavior that can only serve further to impair her interpersonal relationships.

It seems quite likely that her therapist was remiss in attributing many of her first presenting characteristics to the stresses of the breakup of her first marriage. Possibly, if he had continued to see her, some of her current long-standing problems would have been more apparent. In any event, she is now in another difficult time. He could elect some form of supportive treatment, but the magnitude of her development liabilities plus the intensity of her pleas of helplessness seem to make this a poor choice for intervention. Even if the support were to bring some relief, the likelihood of a reoccurrence of symptoms is considerable. Thus it seems reasonable to make two recommendations. First, it is appropriate and necessary to evaluate the status of her marriage more thoroughly than is possible from the history she provides. It is possible that the undercurrents of her problems have not yet interfered significantly with her relationship with her husband, but that seems unlikely. If this postulate is true, a form of marital therapy, as a support, could be in order. Second, and regardless of the first, she should be in a form of developmental therapy.

There are several approaches that could be useful, ranging from some of the long-term cognitive approaches to the more psychodynamically insight-oriented approach. It also seems appropriate to recommend consideration of a female therapist, especially if the evaluation of the marriage indicates signs of weakness or open conflict. She now sees herself as a child, or at least assumes a role that is much more typical of the dependent child than the adult woman. She has also been rejected by at least one male in her life, and that could cause her to be overly cautious and/or denying with a male therapist. Conversely, working with a female therapist might offer her a new opportunity to explore her identity from a different perspective, and in a situation that avoids many of the hazards that could be created by her earlier experiences with males, including her previous therapeutic experience.

PROTOCOL 2: A QUESTION OF ADOLESCENT WITHDRAWAL

Referral   This 17-year-old male was admitted voluntarily to a private psychiatric hospital on the encouragement of his parents and after one interview with a consulting psychiatrist. The parents have been increasingly concerned about him for approximately a year and one-half, during which he has become more withdrawn from them, his siblings, and from friendships that he had developed during his earlier school years. They have been informed by some of his teachers that he seems detached and uninterested and, as a result, his grades have dropped from A's and B's during his first year in high school, to C's and D's during his recently completed third year. He has attributed this to a lack of interest, and has responded to their efforts to encourage him by more withdrawal. For the past several months he has isolated himself from his family by remaining in his room, except for meals, listening to music, or by taking long rides on his prized 10-speed bicycle. Shortly before his admission, he had been repairing a tire on his bicycle and suddenly took a sledgehammer to it, ruining it completely. It was this event that precipitated the psychiatric consult, and the recommendation by the psychiatrist that he be hospitalized for evaluation. After 8 days of hospitalization, the staff consensus favored a tentative diagnosis of "Borderline Personality Disorder," with a recommendation for long-term outpatient care. At that time, psychological evaluation was requested to assist in identifying treatment objectives.

History   The subject is the third child, and oldest son in a family of five children. His older sisters are ages 22 and 20, the older being married and living out of the home, and the second a college junior still living at home. His younger siblings are ages 8 and 6. The considerable disparity between his age and that of his next younger sibling is created by the fact that his mother, now age 44, suffered from vascular problems following his birth and was encouraged to avoid further pregnancies. Once the condition cleared, after several years of medical care, she and her husband agreed to have "one more" child. The youngest child was, according to the mother, "very unexpected but very welcome." The father, age 48, owns a small construction firm. There is no psychiatric history in the immediate family, but the mother does report that two of her close relatives, an uncle and a cousin, have both been hospitalized for long periods because of "nervous breakdowns." The subject has been hospitalized shortly after beginning his senior year in high school. He expresses some confusion about the destruction of the bicycle, suggesting that he lost his temper because one of the bolts that was disconnected could not be refitted in place. He argues that it was "a dumb thing to do," but when pressed on the issue he notes that the bike, "was getting old anyhow and sometimes it wouldn't do the things I wanted it to." He discounts his poor school performance during the past two years as unimportant and the result of "lousy teachers who are only in it for the money." He says that he has promised himself to do better in the current year, "and when I get back I'll really show them what I can do." He admits to some experiences of depression, but suggests that is common for "people struggling to grow up." He says that the concern of his parents about his lost friendships is "unimportant," because most of the young people with whom he associated in the past are "too out of it." He accuses them of being "just into dope a lot," and implies that he has tried several drugs but finds them offensive. He claims that he has "dated" frequently, but his parents feel this is not true. He indicates that he has not had any "real" sexual experience, "but I've fooled around a little." He feels that his current problems with his parents are "just a misunderstanding, they're great and we'll work it all out, really we will." He admits that he does not get along well with his siblings, but then adds, "they're really o.k. too, and we can get along better." He feels very apprehensive about being in the hospital, but suggests that "it'll maybe get some people off my back while I sort things out. It could be a good thing, maybe." He denies any strangeness in his thinking or hallucinatory experiences. His parents report a relatively normal developmental history and no serious medical illnesses, and indicate that, until the episode with the bike, they have not observed any loss of temper since his preschool years.

Protocol #2. V.M., 17 Years Old.

Card	Response	Inquiry	Scoring				
I	1. A face w 4 eyes	*E:* (Rpts *S*'s resp) *S:* Ther's the top 2 eyes & thes r the bttm 2 eyes & ths is the nose. The way the bttm eyes get lighter ll a smile too. Ths r the ears & cheeks (points), its lik a face tht wld b carvd in a pumpkin	*WSo*	*Fyo*	*(Hd)*	3.5	*INC*
	E: Most peopl c mor thn 1 thg 2. They do? Well, it ll s.k. of flying object	*E:* (Rpts *S*'s resp) *S:* I can't defin wht kind, but here r its wings & it ll its in flt. Its not wrkg too hard at it since its wgs r'nt fully spread. It mite b a bat *E:* I'm not sure I c it lik u do *S:* How can u tell if someone is sick or not from these, c its the *W* thg	*Wo*	*FMᵃo*	*A*	*P* 1.0	
II	3. It ll a face & a wide open mouth	*E:* (Rpts *S*'s resp) *S:* Hr r the eyes & ths r the eyebrows. The mouth is here & leads into the nose here. *E:* U mentioned a face *S:* Like s.o. is screaming & spitting up bld rite here r the spots	*WS+*	*Mᵃ.CF−*	*Hd, Bl*	4.5	*MOR*
	4. It also ll a grave w a cross at the tombstne, a blk cross on top of the white tombstn	*E:* (Rpts *S*'s resp) *S:* Ths prt here (white) is the dirt like u r lookg at it from a distance. Ths is the grave hr & up here is the cross. Ths line here (points) cuts the grave from the tombstn	*DS+*	*FC'.FD−Id*	4.5		*MOR*

462

		No.	Response	Inquiry	Location & DQ	Determinants & FQ	(2)	Content	Pop	Z	Special Scores
III		5.	Ths ll to me lik 2 girls pulling on s.o.'s face	E: (Rpts S's resp) S: Ths is the girl, her head, breast & legs. Ths ll the face thyr pulling on, the eyes, nose & mouth. Its in the proc of being torn apart by ths 2 girls. The eyes r bulging out of the guy's face. The girls r pulling him w their arms	D+	M^a.FD–	(2)	H,Hd	P	3.0	FAB, AG, MOR
		6.	Ths 2 thg here r broken guitars	E: (Rpts S's resp) S: On either side here, it ll s.o. has smashed them fr a side angle so the neck is hanging off, & the bttm is bent lik a boot, lik its guts r hanging out, lik the wire & other stuff, thts rite here (points)	Do	Fu	(2)	Id			MOR
IV	10″	7.	Tht ll, uh, ll one of thos guys from a "Keep on trucking" poster. Coming out of his body is a dragon	E: (Rpts S's resp) S: Its taken fr a vantage, horizon type drawing. Thes r his feet & hr r his arms & thy r a little deformed. His head has little shape but its ther. That's the dragon comg fr betwn his legs, or sk of monster E: I'm not clear abt the vantage, horizon type drawing S: Lik if u keep lookg at it, it gets thinner & thinner so tht u don't c it anymore.	W+	FDu	(H),(A)		P	4.0	FAB, MOR, DV
V		8.	Tht ll a bf	E: (Rpts S's resp) S: Hr r its antlers & wgs & there r the legs or whatevr u want to call them	Wo	Fo		A	P	1.0	INC

463

Protocol #2 (Continued)

Card	Response	Inquiry	Scoring
9.	It also ll it cb a man w wgs & antlers. He's got a line running rite dwn the middle of him	E: (Rpts S's resp) S: Yeah, her's his head & antlers & legs. Ths drk line running dwn him is from where they made the inkblot	Do Fo (H) INC
VI 10.	It ll s.k. of machine & its speared half the sun	E: (Rpts S's resp) S: Yeah, ths is the machine, ths prt here. Ths line running dwn the middle is what u'd get in the machin to run it. Its s.k. of drill & its got half the sun. Thr r flames coming fr the sun so its got half the sun	W+ m^au Sc, Na 2.5 FAB
11.	Its also a plain inkblot	E: (Rpts S's resp) S: It ll s.b. put ink on a pc of paper & folded it togthr. Thy prob fooled around a littl by pushg the ink around to get the shades, then they opned it up & said "wow, I've made s.t." but there's no real shape to it.	Wv Y Art
VII 12.	It ll 2 Egyptian girls doing an Egyptial dance	E: (Rpts S's resp) S: Yeah, here's their heads w their hair up. It comes over their forehead. Here's the chin, u can't c the mouth well. Thes r their arms out lik that, u can c them fr the head to the waist, ths dwn here is nothing	D+ M^ao (2) Hd P 3.0 DV
13.	Or it c.b. 2 gals on rockng chairs	E: (Rpts S's resp) S: Thes r rockg chairs balanced on the corner, mayb rockers lik blks of wood w a rounded bttm. The girls r the same as before & they just kinda rock on it.	W+ m^pu (2) H,Hh P 2.5

Card	Time	No.	Response	Inquiry	Loc.	Determinant	(2)	Content	Z	Special
VIII	6″	14.	Ths ll 2 bears clmbg either side of a mt, 2 pink bears, or red, whtevr tht is	E: (Rpts S's resp) S: Here r the bears & thyr in motion, going up the side of the mt. Thy r on opposite sides of the mt.	W+	$FM^a.FCo$	(2)	A,Ls	F 4.5	INC
		15.	In the mt is a face of an Eskimo, or Indian type ruler or god. It ll the bears hav their paws on his hair	E: (Rpts S's resp) S: Yeah, here r his eyes & his nose here. Ths green area is his mouth & he's got all the lines of his face, he's even got a littl paint on his face, lik littl green bits of paint on it here. Ths is his hair, its long hair, the bears hav opposite paws on his hair	D+	$FMp.FC-$	(2)	Hd,A	3.0	FAB
IX	23″	16.	It ll 2 profiles of Alfred Hitchcock	E: (Rpts S's resp) S: 2 bad profiles, rt here is the forehead & ths white part is his eye, ths is his nose & mouth is ths littl indentatn, he's got a pimple on his chin	DSo	Fu	(2)	Hd	5.0	
		17.	Or, the head of a pig thy killed in Lord of the Flies	E: (Rpts S's resp) S: The same prt again, lik a profile of tht pig thy stuck on the stake & its drippg bld down here but evaporating up here E: Evaporating? S: Lik all the juice inside is evap up into the air	W+	$mp.CF-$		(Ad),Bl	5.5	MOR, INC
X	4″	18.	Ths is just all kinds of bugs, yeah thts wht it is	E: Yeah, all kinds of bugs. Ths 2 blue ones r bugs & up hre ths 2 ll crawly brwn bugs. E.t. in the pic. gives more life to the bugs, u can detect their presence easier	W+	FCo	(2)	A	5.5	DR
		19.	It's also got a face in it	E: (RPTS S's resp) S: Hr r the eyes & the nose w a moustache like parts of the face & if u turn it upsid dwn get exactly the same, c'?. here r the nose, eyes & moustache again	DdSo	F-		Hd	6.0	

465

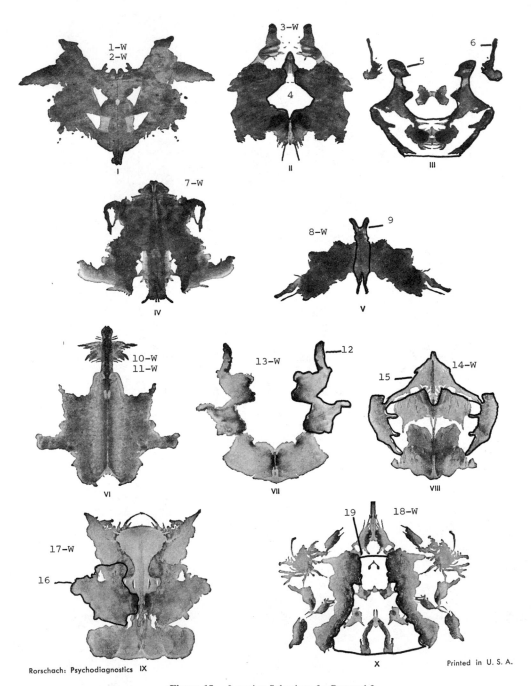

Figure 18. Location Selections for Protocol 2.

Table 38. Structural Summary—Protocol #2

```
=========================================================================
  R = 19    Zf = 16     ZSum = 59.0     P = 8      (2) = 8    Fr+rF = 0
```

LOCATION FEATURES	DETERMINANTS BLENDS	SINGLE	CONTENTS	S-CONSTELLATION (ADULT)

```
LOCATION            DETERMINANTS            CONTENTS     S-CONSTELLATION
FEATURES              BLENDS      SINGLE                      (ADULT)
                                           H   = 2, 0   YES..FV+VF+V+FD>2
W   = 11            M.CF         M  = 2    (H) = 2, 0   NO...Col-Shd Bl>0
  (Wv =  1)         FC'.FD       FM = 1    Hd  = 5, 1   NO...Ego<.31,>.44
D   =  7            M.FD         m  = 1    (Hd)= 1, 0   YES..MOR > 3
Dd  =  1            FM.FC        C  = 0    A   = 4, 1   YES..Zd > +- 3.5
S   =  5            FM.FC        Cn = 0    (A) = 0, 1   YES..es > EA
                    m.CF         CF = 0    Ad  = 0, 0   NO...CF+C+Cn > FC
  DQ                             FC = 1    (Ad)= 1, 0   YES..X+ < .70
.........(FQ-)                   C'  = 0   Ab  = 0, 0   YES..S > 3
                                 C'F = 0   Al  = 0, 0   NO...P < 3 or > 8
  +  = 11 ( 5)                   FC' = 0   An  = 0, 0   NO...Pure H < 2
v/+  =  0 ( 0)                   T   = 0   Art = 1, 0   NO...R < 17
 o   =  7 ( 1)                   TF  = 0   Ay  = 0, 0    6.....TOTAL
 v   =  1 ( 0)                   FT  = 0   Bl  = 0, 2
                                 V   = 0   Bt  = 0, 0   SPECIAL SCORINGS
                                 VF  = 0   Cg  = 0, 0      DV    = 2
                                 FV  = 0   Cl  = 0, 0      INCOM = 5
                                 Y   = 1   Ex  = 0, 0      DR    = 1
              FORM QUALITY       YF  = 0   Fi  = 0, 0      FABCOM= 4
                                 FY  = 1   Fd  = 0, 0      ALOG  = 0
   FQx       FQf      M Qual.    rF  = 0   Ge  = 0, 0      CONTAM= 0
                                 Fr  = 0   Hh  = 0, 1    --- WSUM6 =31
                                 FD  = 1   Ls  = 0, 1      AG    = 1
  +  =  0    + = 0    +  = 0     F   = 5   Na  = 0, 1      CONFAB= 0
  o  =  7    o = 2    o  = 1               Sc  = 1, 0      CP    = 0
  u  =  5    u = 2    u  = 1               Sx  = 0, 0      MOR   = 6
  -  =  6    - = 1    -  = 2               Xy  = 0, 0      PER   = 0
none=  1             none= 0               Idio= 2, 0      PSV   = 0
=========================================================================
```

RATIOS, PERCENTAGES, AND DERIVATIONS

```
ZSum-Zest = 59.0 - 52.5        FC:CF+C = 3: 2    W:M      = 11: 4
                                 (Pure C =  0)
Zd       =  6.5                                  W:D      = 11: 7
                               Afr     = 0.46
.----------------------------.                   Isolate:R =  2:19
:EB  = 4: 3.5   EA = 7.5:     3r+(2)/R = 0.42
:                    >D=  0                       Ab+Art   =  1
:eb  = 5: 3     ea = 8 :      L       = 0.36
'----------------------------'                   An+Xy    =  0
(FM= 3 " C'= 1 T= 0) (Adj D=  0)  Blends:R = 6:19
(m = 2 " V = 0 Y= 2)                              H(H):Hd(Hd)=  4: 6
                               X+%     = 0.37       (Pure H =  2)
a:p      = 6: 3                (F+%    = 0.40)  (HHd):(AAd) =  3: 1
Ma:Mp    = 3: 1                X-%     = 0.32    H+A:Hd+Ad =  8: 7
-------------------------------------------------------------------------
          SCZI = 5            DEPI = 1              S-CON = 6
=========================================================================
```

(C)1976,1983 BY JOHN E. EXNER, JR.

Table 39. Scoring Sequence—Protocol #2

```
=================================================================
CARD NO. LOC. #    DETERMINANT(S)    (2) CONTENT(S) POP  Z   SPECIAL SCORES
=================================================================
  I    1 WSo   1 FYo                    (Hd)              3.5 INC
       2 Wo    1 FMao                   A            P    1.0

 II    3 WS+   1 Ma.CF-                 Hd,Bl             4.5 MOR
       4 DS+   5 FC'.FD-                Id                4.5 MOR

III    5 D+    1 Ma.FD-               2 H,Hd         P    3.0 FAB,AG,MOR
       6 Do    2 Fu                   2 Id                    MOR

 IV    7 W+    1 FDu                    (H),(A)      P    4.0 FAB,MOR,DV

  V    8 Wo    1 Fo                     A            P    1.0 INC
       9 Do    7 Fo                     (H)                  INC

 VI   10 W+    1 mau                    Sc,Na             2.5 FAB
      11 Wv    1 Y                      Art

VII   12 D+    2 Mao                  2 Hd           P    3.0 DV
      13 W+    1 Mpu                  2 H,Hh         P    2.5

VIII  14 W+    1 FMa.FCo             2 A,Ls         P    4.5 INC
      15 D+    1 FMp.FC-             2 Hd,A         P    3.0 FAB

 IX   16 DSo   1 Fu                  2 Hd                5.0
      17 W+    1 mp.CF-                (Ad),Bl            5.5 MOR,INC

  X   18 W+    1 FCo                 2 A                 5.5 DR
      19 DdSo 30 F-                    Hd                6.0
=================================================================
```
(C)1976, 1983 BY JOHN E. EXNER, JR.
    ABBREVIATIONS USED ABOVE:
      FOR DQ: "/" = "v/+"; FOR CONTENTS: "Id" = "IDIOGRAPHIC CONTENT"
      SPECIAL SCORES: "INC" = "INCOM", "FAB" = "FABCOM", "CON" = "CONTAM"
                      "CFB" = "CONFAB"

STRUCTURAL INTERPRETATION

He gave 19 responses, suggesting that the record is interpretatively useful. An inspection of the Special Indices reveals that the *SCZI* is 5, warning of the possibility of schizophrenia. As noted in Chapter 17, when the *SCZI* is 5, regardless of whether the subject is an adult or child, the likelihood of schizophrenia is considerable, and the probability of a false positive is quite remote. There are some conditions that could produce a schizophrenic-like record, including extensive drug abuse, especially if amphetamines have been involved, but the subject denies any extensive drug history. Obviously, a recommendation to be included in the report should call for a careful drug screen, in spite of the subject's denial of drug use. A closer inspection of the variables contributing to the elevation of the *SCZI* reveals that almost all possibilities are positive. The $X+\%$ of 37% is very low, there are more minus than u responses, and the $X-\%$ is 32%. These data support the contention that he manifests considerable perceptual distortion, such as is commonly found among schizophrenics. His 19 answers include 12 Critical Special Scores, with a WSUM6 of 31, which is inordinately high. In addition, there are two $M-$ responses in the record. Collectively, these data indicate the presence of seriously disordered thought, which may be similar to that found among schizophrenics. None of the positive variables are marginal. The $X+\%$ is very low and the $X-\%$ quite high. The number of Critical Special Scores is three times the cut-off of 4, and the weighted Sum is nearly three times the critical cut-off of 11, and there are two $M-$ answers. The magnitude of each substantially reduces the likelihood that the *SCZI* may be identifying schizophrenia erroneously.

In spite of this, it is appropriate to review some of the responses in the record at this point, to determine whether elements or bizarreness are obvious. As noted in Chapter 15, it is naive to assume that all of the responses falling into one category represent equal degrees of slippage or dysfunction. Some obviously reflect more ideational disruption than others, even though they may be in the same category. In most cases when schizophrenia is present, the element of strange or bizarre thinking is very striking in some of the responses. They are not simply unusual, but tend to stand out like a beacon in the way that they reflect the disordered thought. Usually, it is best to begin by reviewing the answers to which the most serious of the Special Scores have been assigned, such as the *FABCOM, ALOG,* and *CONTAM* responses, plus those answers containing the $M-$ element.

His first *FABCOM* occurs to Card III, response 5, which is two girls pulling on someone's face, which is also one of his $M-$ answers. The second is to Card IV, response 7, which is a poster of a guy with a dragon coming out of his body. The third, to Card VI, response 10, is a machine that has speared half the sun, and the last is to Card VIII, response 15, a face and bears having their paws on his hair. The other $M-$ answer was given to Card II, response 3, a face. Although that answer might not be judged as a seriously disordered and bizarre sort of response, *all* of the *FABCOM* responses are marked by considerable bizarreness and, as such, serve to confirm the presence of seriously disordered thinking. Thus the diagnosis of schizophrenia seems certain unless evidence of serious toxicity is discovered from drug screen data. In view of this finding, the description that is developed from the other data of the test must be framed with regard to the fact that a serious disturbance, probably schizophrenia, exists.

Both D scores are 0, denoting that he has reasonably good capacities for control, and ordinarily will have sufficient resources accessible from which to formulate and implement responses. At first glance, this finding may seem incompatible with the presence of schizophrenia, but it is not. The capacity for control has little to do with the direction or quality of thinking, or the accuracy of perception. It simply indicates that, under most circumstances, he is not overwhelmed by the features of his disturbance. The history is commensurate with this finding. The bicycle incident is the only strikingly bizarre event reported, and during 8 days of hospitalization few, if any, indicators of a serious disturbance have appeared. In other words, if he can avoid intense and/or prolonged stress experiences, the issue of behavioral control is not a significant problem for him. This can be viewed as both an asset and a liability. It is an asset because it does permit him to avoid being thrown into frequent psychotic episodes, but it is a liability because it also provides the capacity to conceal, from himself and others, the magnitude of his disorder. One consequence of this is that it may create some obstacles to effective treatment. For example, during the past several months he had attempted to isolate himself from others, and has done so with some degree of success. This may indicate that he has some awareness of his plight, and especially of the need to avoid stress. It illustrates how his capacity for control permits him to avoid being overwhelmed, albeit that his tactic of doing so has only limited effectiveness, and over longer periods of time is maladaptive.

The data of the Four Square reveal three important characteristics, one of which suggests that his capacity for control may be diminishing. Although the D score is 0, there are two *m* and two *Y* responses, indicating that he is experiencing situationally related stress, probably as a result of being hospitalized. He *is* feeling some loss of control and a sense of being unable to make responses. This suggests that if he is impinged upon by more stress experiences, such as might result from more prolonged hospitalization, or conversely, by discharge into a threatening environment, his controls could be overwhelmed. Thus although his controls are currently sufficient, they may be more marginal when viewed in the context of future stress levels he can be expected to experience as the result of being carefully scrutinized. Second, the datum of the *EB* indicate that he is an ambitent. He is not consistent or predictable in his coping behaviors and, as a result, is less efficient and more time-consuming in his problem-solving activities. This can be a significant liability if complex demands are forced on him. Third, the data of the Four Square indicate that the record contains no *T* responses. Apparently he does not experience his needs for closeness in ways that are similar to most people. One result of this is that he tends to be more distant and/or guarded in his interpersonal relationships, and more concerned about issues of personal space than should be the case. This finding raises questions about his perceptions of himself and others.

The Egocentricity Index, .42, is within average limits, suggesting that his self-focusing activity is no greater or less than would be expected for an adult. However, there are six *MOR* responses, indicating that his self-image is marked by many negative features and that he may perceive himself as damaged in some way. In addition, his thinking and attitudes will often be marked by more pessimism than should be the case. He is quite interested in people, as revealed by the presence of 10 human contents, but only two of those are *Pure H*. This signals that his conceptions of people are not well developed, and often based more on imagined than real experience. The $H + A:Hd + Ad$ ratio of 8:7 shows a disproportionate number of *Hd* and *Ad* contents. This provokes questions about whether he may be unduly guarded and overly suspicious about his interpersonal world. People with these paranoid-like features usually give Rorschachs in which *T* is absent, significantly high or significantly low frequencies of human contents appear, and $Hd + Ad$ is disproportionate to $H + A$. This composite indicates a preoccupation about people common to the overly suspicious individual.

In addition to evidence of a preoccupation with people, records of subjects with paranoid-like features typically have an above average *Zf*, a *Zd* score indicating overincorporation, and the *S* frequency is often elevated. The high *Zf* and *Zd* reveal the extensive effort that is committed to organizing carefully each new stimulus situation. It reflects the psychological vigilance that is common to the paranoid style. The high *S* relates to the sense of negativism or hostility that often characterizes the thinking and attitudes of the overly suspicious person. His record is positive for all of these features. In addition to the *T-less* finding, the large number of *H* contents, and the elevated $Hd + Ad$, the *Zf* is 16, the *Zd* is $+6.5$, and there are five *S* responses. Therefore it seems reasonable to conclude that the disturbance is marked by many paranoid features which may also create some obstacles to treatment, especially in the early stages. Often, records of paranoid people contain an unusually large number of answers that include an overemphasis on profiles, eyes, teeth, and/or other sense organs. Seven of his 19 answers (1, 2, 5, 15, 16, 17, 19) include these features.

Although the *S* answers indicate considerable negativism, there is no unusual elevation in *AG* answers, which is a positive finding. Also, the $FC:CF + C$ ratio of 3:2 indicates that he is capable of modulating his affective displays relatively well. The *Afr* is lower than average, suggesting that he prefers to avoid situations that include emotional stimulation. This is probably to his advantage in light of the tendency to misinterpret stimuli and become confused in his thinking. Interestingly, although he does engage in considerable distortion when translating stimuli, he also gave eight *Popular* answers. This is a very positive finding, because it indicates that he can and does translate very obvious stimuli in a conventional manner. Another positive finding is the presence of three *FD* answers, which signals that he is already engaged in more self-inspection than is common for adults, and much more than is typical of the seriously disturbed patient. This can be an asset to the early phases of intervention, once the barriers created by his strong sense of guardedness are lowered. Another potential asset to treatment is reflected in the *a:p* ratio of 6:3, which suggests that there is no unusual rigidity in his thinking or values. The presence of 11 *DQ+* responses indicates that much of his cognitive processing activity is characterized by reasonably sophisticated operations, and the *W:M* ratio of 11:4 implies that he is not setting inordinately high goals. The *W:D* ratio of 11:7, and the low Lambda of .36 both signify that he is not very economical in his cognitive efforts, but this is to be expected when overincorporation is present, and especially when combined with a hyper-vigilant paranoid style.

ANALYSIS OF THE SCORING SEQUENCE

His general approach is *W* oriented. He gives a *W* response to all of the blots except Card III, and his first answer to seven of the 10 cards is *W*. This is not surprising in light of his overincorporative and defensive styles. An important finding in the sequence is that all of his minus answers, and all of his blend responses were given to blots that contain chromatic colors. This suggests that the affective stimuli that he attempts to avoid may be much more disruptive than had been implied by the structural data. Obviously, any treatment plan should include tactics designed to aid him in identifying ways to deal with affective stimuli more effectively. Another important finding from the sequence is that his Popular responses are given to those blots which have the highest frequency of *P* answers. This seems to confirm the postulate that he can identify very obvious stimuli in a conventional manner. The fact that a Special Score, an *INCOM,* occurs in his very first response signals some of the intense problems that mark his thinking. It was selected from many potential answers available and, as such, illustrates some of the faulty judgment that will be displayed in his everyday behaviors. Similarly, he does not recover well when perceptual distortions occur. Not one of his minus responses is followed by an ordinary response to the same card. In fact, he leaves the test by giving a minus answer as his last response. This suggests a serious naiveté about his behavior. He is not very aware of the inappropriateness of some of his actions and, as a consequence, is prone to repeat inappropriate responses much more often than is desirable. This is a finding which adds to the likelihood that he will be very resistive to any acknowledgment that he may have serious problems, and strengthens the prediction that the early phases of any treatment program will be met by withdrawal and denial unless he is afforded obvious and convincing evidence of the fact. Unfortunately, he gives the impression of the type of patient that may abide by the obvious rules of any environment unless they become too stressful. As such, he will often appear much healthier than is truly the case.

ANALYSIS OF THE RESPONSES

Many of his associations appear to illustrate his unique form of ideation. His first answer, "a face with four eyes," offers a clue to his "supersuspicious" style of functioning. The face and wide-open mouth on Card II add support to this notion and may reflect a strong oral component. The "grave" response, also on Card II may represent his own feeling of impending doom, and shed some light on his reported experience of depression. In Card III, he offers a Popular *M* answer, but then tends to spoil it by perceiving part of the blot as someone's face being pulled apart. His second answer to Card III could be illustrative of the product of the "pulling," "broken guitars," which are used as instruments of affective exchange. The dragon, coming from the human form on Card IV, appears to reveal a sense of fear and confusion concerning his own sexuality, and the phrase "keep on trucking" might hint of feelings of impotency. The confusion of thinking is also represented in his description of a man with wings and antlers on Card V. His first response to Card VI is possibly the most symbolic and most revealing in the record, a "machine and it's speared half the sun." Again, he concentrates on a phallic-like area, defining it as a machine, and identifies "half the sun" as its target. The implication here may be that his own sexuality, or at least his conceptualization of sexuality, is interfering with his role image, that of the "sun." It is also tempting to translate this response as reflecting his struggle between childhood and becoming an adult. Interestingly, his next answer is the most passively oriented in the record, using a crude form of denial as the base. His responses to Card VII vacillate from active to passive movement, possibly indicating more about his ideational struggles. His first answer to Card VIII is conventional and well organized, but his lack of cognitive control is evidenced in the fabulization that he offers next in a response involving a "ruler or god." Both responses to Card IX include heads, offering more evidence regarding the "seat" of his problem, that is, in his thinking. The second of these, that of a dead pig, provides an indication of his own self-image and, again, hints of a feeling of impending doom. His last response is quite unconventional and suggests his negative paranoidlike guardedness.

ANALYSIS OF THE INQUIRY

In several of his responses, he begins his description of human or animal contents by emphasizing the eyes and other facial features. His response to Card I, "It's not working too hard at it since its wings aren't fully spread," is probably indicative of his helplessness plus his feelings of not being "fully grown" yet. His characterization of the face on Card II as someone "screaming and spitting up blood" seems to dramatize his own agony and tenuous affective control. The elaboration that he gives to both responses on Card III offers some indication of his own "tattered" self-image and provides added support for the notion that conflicts about masculinity and sexuality have led to his disarray. This is also evidenced in his reaffirmation of the "dragon coming from between his legs or some kind of monster" on Card IV. His unique and confused form of thinking is illustrated again by his answers to responses 10, 11, 15, 16, and 17, all of which contain very idiographic comments. The midline represents "what you'd get in the machine to run it," the profile has a "pimple on his chin," and "all the juice inside is evaporating up into the air." These sorts of comments illustrate a naive, almost childlike elaboration of form and color, and no doubt have special meaning in his distorted ideation. For instance, the "juice evaporating" might represent some strange feelings of depersonalization or loss of sensation or diminution in affect. It would be precarious, however, to draw such specific conclusions without additional evidence. At best, this material can be taken as indicative of his disorganization, helplessness, and limited contact with reality.

SUMMARY OF PROTOCOL 2

It seems very apparent that this young man is quite disturbed. His thinking is confused and disordered, and he is very prone to distort reality rather severely. He seems inordinately affected by emotionally toned stimuli. Emotions seem to torment him and exacerbate his confused identity. He has become extraordinarily guarded in perceiving and dealing with people, and resorts to a form of psychological isolation as a way of defending himself from the threats posed by a world that he cannot contend with easily. He is obviously bright, and has learned to draw on his resources in ways that permit him to maintain a facade of a withdrawn eccentric, but not severely disturbed person. Beneath that facade, which tends to work well when he is not under unusually intense stress, is a very fragile and frightened person who is overly guarded about people, and very confused about his own role in his environment. It seems quite probable that the prospect of assuming an adult role in life is becoming overwhelming to him. He has struggled to retain controls, but that battle has a considerable cost and he is gradually losing in his fight for stability. The overall psychological picture is one of gradual deterioration, with an increasing probability that he will manifest overt characteristics of psychosis soon unless he is relieved of pressures to engage in a ''normal'' pattern of social interaction. It seems clear that this cannot be the case, and the predictable consequences are a major disruption to his current form of cautious adaptation to his world. His hypervigilant state cannot help but ultimately reduce his tolerance for new stress, because it requires a major commitment of many of his resources. Intervention in a case such as this requires careful planning, plus a very tactful entry to the process. He is probably very unwilling to admit to any major problems, and apparently was admitted only for evaluation. The ''news'' that he has a major disturbance may be met with considerable resistance, and any efforts to involve him into an active treatment program can be expected to be received with similar results. His statement at admission that his hospitalization will, ''. . . maybe get some people off my back while I sort things out,'' forewarns of some of the difficulties that may be encountered by those who seek to help.

PROTOCOL 3: A QUESTION OF PSYCHOSOMATIC INVOLVEMENT

Referral   This 23-year-old female was referred for evaluation by her physician after reviewing the results of a neurological examination that he had requested. The neurological referral was made after her fifth visit to him during a four-month period. Her initial complaint had been feelings of fatigue, but during each of the last two visits she also reported an increasing frequency of headaches. The neurological examination included an EEG and a CT-Scan, plus a neuropsychological examination. All results were negative and the consulting neurologist recommended a psychiatric evaluation, suggesting that the headaches are probably psychosomatic. The data from the neuropsychological evaluation yielded a WAIS Verbal I.Q. of 136, with Scaled Scores ranging from 14 on Digit Span to 18 on Information, and a Performance I.Q. of 131, with Scaled Scores ranging from 11 on Picture Arrangement to 17 on Object Assembly. Her Wechsler Memory Quotient is 123. She made no errors on the Aphasia Screening Test and her performances on the various tests of the Halstead-Reitan are all within normal limits.

History   The subject is the oldest of three children, having a sister, age 19, who is in her second year of college, and a brother, age 17, who is in his third year in high school. Both parents are living. Her father, age 47, is a journalist. Her mother, age 44, is a housewife. According to the subject, there is no psychiatric history in the immediate family. The developmental history she provides is unremarkable. She ranked second in her high school graduating class and went on to obtain a Bachelors Degree in Sociology from a prestigious university, graduating magna cum laude at age 21. Shortly thereafter she obtained employment with an advertising firm for which she continues to work. Currently, she is the leader of a six-member team responsible for designing and constructing layouts for TV and magazine advertising. She was promoted to her current position approximately 10 months prior to the evaluation. She states that she enjoys her work and feels that she has made several close friendships with her co-workers.

She maintains her own apartment and reports a history of varied social-emotional relationships. She notes that, as a high school student she dated frequently but had no sustained emotional ties. During college she also dated frequently and did have one "prolonged" relationship during her sophomore year. Her first sexual experience was at age 18, during her first year at college, and since that time has engaged in intercourse with a variable frequency, ". . . depending on how much I get involved with the guy." She notes that she has manifested some poor judgment about sex, having become pregnant during the summer following her junior year in college. She learned of her pregnancy shortly before her senior year began and struggled with the idea of having an abortion. She decided against this, and withdrew after completing the first semester of her senior year, at the onset of her third trimester of pregnancy, to live in a home for unwed expectant mothers. She was supported in this decision by her parents, whom she describes as being ". . . terrifically understanding about the whole mess." Early into her pregnancy she had considered retaining custody of the child, but ultimately decided to place the child, a female born during the spring, for adoption. She describes her decision as, "I know in my heart that I did the right thing. I don't believe that I could have given her everything that she needed and then both of our lives would have gotten worse. I know that she's in a good home because they are very careful about placement." She went on to add that she would like to have information about her daughter from time to time, but realizes that is impossible. She returned to the university during the summer following the birth and graduated in August.

She discounts the possibility that her headaches are related to the decision to relinquish custody of her daughter: "If they are really psychological, they are because I'm not happy with myself now." She freely admits to having several disappointments in her more recent emotional life, noting that most of the men with whom she becomes involved do not meet her standards, "I don't think that I expect too much, but they all seem so immature, and I want more than that in a relationship." None of the relationships that she has established with men since her graduation have lasted longer than 6 months, and she has consistently refused propositions to "live in." She does want to marry and looks forward to having children. She notes that she had headaches during high school and college, ". . . usually when I felt the pressure of exams," but argues that they were "different" than the ones she now experiences. She describes them as being "more dull," in contrast to the current, which she characterizes as having a rapid onset and one-sided, ". . . usually on the left, but not always." She says that now they occur with a much greater frequency, often four to six times per week. She says that the pain is, "very sharp," and admits that her physician has chided her because she tends to abuse antipain medication that he has prescribed.

Protocol #3. A 23-Year-Old-Female

Card	Response	Inquiry	Scoring
I	1. Ugh, ths re me of a witch burning of s.s., lik in Salem E: Take your time, u'll probably find somethg else too	E: (Rpts S's resp) S: The witch is in the cntr w her arms up in the air, its a vague outline bec of all the smoke rising all around her. The fire isn't obvious but the smok is billowing all around her, all dark	W+ $MP.m^a.YFu$ (H), Fi 4.0 *MOR*
	2. I suppose it c.b a bf too but is all ruined w holes in it	E: (Rpts S's resp) S: These c.b. wgs (points) but thy r pretty ragged, its dead I suppose bec of the holes in the wgs	WS+ Fo A P 3.5 *MOR*
II	3. This is grotesque, I thk it c.b. 2 people fiting & both are badly injured	E: (Rpts S's resp) S: Thy 11 twins bec thy'r the same on each side, thy r surely hurtg e.o. bec of the bld on their heads & all over their lowr prts, it c.b. prehistoric men in a death struggle, bent in agony, neither wants to lose in spite of those wounds	W+ $M^a.CFo$ 2 (H) BL 4.5 *MOR, AG*
	The cntr c.b. water in a pit or puddle	E: (Rpts S's resp) S: I thk of the white prt as the water & its down in this pit, the sides around it seem to go in E: Go in? S: The different colors give it a sense of depth	DdSv/+ VFo Na 4.5
III	5. My God, ths 11 2 ghouls, thy r tugging at a baskt of bones	E: (Rpts S's resp) S: It struck me rite away lik that, 2 indescribable creatures, lik in sc fict having torn some poor A apart & now thy'r fiting over the bones	D+ M^ao 2 (H), An P 3.0 *MOR, AG*

475

Protocol #3 (Continued)

Card	Response	Inquiry	Scoring
IV	6. Some creature lying down, lik from sc fict all cvrd w moss or s.t., mayb fur, yes mayb fur or moss, a vague hulk w the feet towd u	E: (Rpts S's resp) S: The feet r so big he must be lying dwn w the ft toward u & it ll moss all over him, its not real, just a sc fict creature lying there, lik a martian	Wo Mp.FT.FDo (H) Bt P 2.0
V	7. Well, the most I can mak of it is a bat swooping dwn lik to get s.t.	E: (Rpts S's resp) S: The wgs wide sprd & its all dark black, lik it was at nite, it has claws out here (points)	Wo FM^a.FC'o A P 1.0
	8. Ths thg c.b. roots	E: (Rpts S's resp) S: It was almost an afterthot, thy just ll roots of a bush or tree	Do Fo BT
VI	9. My first impression was of a totem pole, lik the Indians worship	E: (Rpts S's resp) S: I supp thy don't really worship the pole but what it stands for E: I'm not sure how u c it S: It has wgs & ths (points is the pole)	Do Fo Ay
VII	10. It ll fried food to me, not really chicken or shrimp, mayb shrimp, u can c the roundedness of the pieces, mayb scallops	E: Yes, probably scallops, thy'r breaded, several pieces, just up here (points), the way thy r painted on here makes them ll thy'r dimensional	Do FVu Fd
VIII	11. Ths ll s.t. from an Anat book, an illustration of different parts of the human insides	E: (Rpts S's resp) S: The rib cage is there, c the spaces in betwn the ribs (points) & the pink c.b. lungs or kidneys & the lowr part the stomach, its all colorful the way an Anat illustr is in the bio. texts	WS+ FCo An, Art 4.5
	12. The lowr part c.b. ice cream too, orange & strawberry mixed in a bunch	E: (Rpts S's resp) S: Just a scoop of mixed ice cream as if it were made that way, I'v never seen it lik this tho	Dv CF.YFo Fd

IX

v 13. Ths way its an explosion, lik
an atomic explosion with the
flames & smoke shooting out
all over

E: (Rpts S's resp)
S: Well it has the mushroom cloud &
there is fire (orange) & smoke (green)
all over, the different colors of the
green give the impr of the layers of
smoke

W+ m^a.CF.VFo Ex,F 5.5 AG

X

14. A maple seed has landed in a
puddle of water

E: (Rpts S's resp)
S: It's rite here (points) & the white is
the puddle of water, its just laying
there with no place to root

DdS+ m^po Bt,Na 6.● MOR

15. A crab has caught a bug

E: (Rpts S's resp)
S: Ths blue prt is the crab & the little grn
prt is the bug, the crab has caught it &
will eat it I suppose, it has no chance
to get away bec of all the legs of the
crab

D+ FM^ao A P 4.0 MOR, AG

16. A cocker spaniel, 2 of thm,
waiting for s.t. to happen, just
sitting there

E: (Rpts S's resp)
S: It ll one on each side, as if thy were
just sitting & waiting, c this is the frnt
leg

Do FM^po 2 A

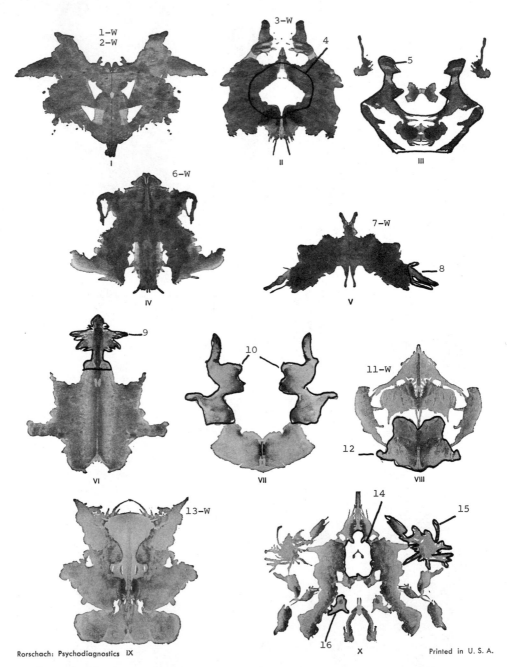

Figure 19. Location Selections for Protocol 3.

Table 40. Structural Summary—Protocol #3

```
================================================================================
  R = 16      Zf = 11      ZSum = 42.5      P = 5      (2) = 3      Fr+rF = 0

LOCATION             DETERMINANTS              CONTENTS        S-CONSTELLATION
FEATURES                BLENDS        SINGLE                       (ADULT)
                                                H  = 0, 0      YES..FV+VF+V+FD>2
W    = 7           M.m.YF          M   = 1      (H) = 4, 0     YES..Col-Shd Bl>0
  (Wv  =  0)       M.CF            FM  = 2      Hd  = 0, 0     YES..Ego<.31,>.44
D    = 7           M.FT.FD         m   = 1      (Hd)= 0, 0     YES..MOR > 3
Dd   = 2           FM.FC'          C   = 0      A   = 4, 0     YES..Zd > +- 3.5
S    = 4           CF.YF           Cn  = 0      (A) = 0, 0     YES..es > EA
                   m.CF.VF         CF  = 0      Ad  = 0, 0     YES..CF+C+Cn > FC
    DQ                             FC  = 1      (Ad)= 0, 0     NO..X+ < .70
........(FQ-)                      C'  = 0      Ab  = 0, 0     YES..S > 3
                                   C'F = 0      Al  = 0, 0     NO..P < 3 or > 8
   +  = 8 ( 0)                     FC' = 0      An  = 1, 1     YES..Pure H < 2
  v/+ = 1 ( 0)                     T   = 0      Art = 0, 1     YES..R < 17
   o  = 6 ( 0)                     TF  = 0      Ay  = 1, 0     10.....TOTAL
   v  = 1 ( 0)                     FT  = 0      Bl  = 0, 1
                                   V   = 0      Bt  = 2, 1     SPECIAL SCORINGS
                                   VF  = 1      Cg  = 0, 0        DV    = 0
                                   FV  = 1      Cl  = 0, 0       INCOM  = 0
                                   Y   = 0      Ex  = 1, 0        DR    = 0
          FORM QUALITY             YF  = 0      Fi  = 0, 2      FABCOM  = 0
                                   FY  = 0      Fd  = 2, 0       ALOG   = 0
                                   rF  = 0      Ge  = 0, 0      CONTAM  = 0
   FQx        FQf      M Qual.     Fr  = 0      Hh  = 0, 0      --- WSUM6 = 0
                                   FD  = 0      Ls  = 0, 0        AG    = 4
  +  = 0    +  = 0    +  = 0       F   = 3      Na  = 1, 1      CONFAB  = 0
  o  = 14   o  = 3    o  = 3                    Sc  = 0, 0        CP    = 0
  u  = 2    u  = 0    u  = 1                    Sx  = 0, 0       MOR    = 6
  -  = 0    -  = 0    -  = 0                    Xy  = 0, 0       PER    = 0
none = 0             none = 0                   Idio= 0, 0       PSV    = 0
================================================================================
```

```
                  RATIOS, PERCENTAGES, AND DERIVATIONS

ZSum-Zest = 42.5 - 34.5      FC:CF+C  = 1: 3      W:M      = 7: 4
                                (Pure C = 0)
Zd        = 8.0                                   W:D      = 7: 7
                             Afr      = 0.60
.-------------------------.                       Isolate:R = 5:16
:EB = 4: 3.5    EA = 7.5:    3r+(2)/R = 0.19
:                   >D= -2                         Ab+Art   = 1
:eb = 6: 7    es = 13  :     L        = 0.23
'-------------------------'                        An+Xy    = 2
(FM = 3 " C'= 1 T= 1) (Adj D= 0)  Blends:R = 6:16
(m = 3 " V = 3 Y= 2)                              H(H):Hd(Hd)= 4: 0
                             X+%      = 0.88         (Pure H = 0)
a:p      = 6: 4               (F+%     = 1.00)   (HHd):(AAd)  = 4: 0
                             X-%      = 0.00
Ma:Mp    = 2: 2                                  H+A:Hd+Ad  = 8: 0
-----------------------------------------------------------------------
             SCZI = 0        DEPI = 4            S-CON =10
================================================================================
```

Table 41.   Scoring Sequence—Protocol #3

```
=============================================================================
CARD NO. LOC. #     DETERMINANT(S)   (2) CONTENT(S) POP  Z    SPECIAL SCORES
=============================================================================
  I    1 W+     1 Mp.ma.YFu           (H),Fi             4.0  MOR
       2 WS+    1 Fo                   A             P   3.5  MOR

 II    3 W+     1 Ma.CFo           2   (H),Bl            4.5  MOR,AG
       4 DdS/  99 VFo                  Na                4.5

III    5 D+     1 Mao             2   (H),An         P   3.0  MOR,AG

 IV    6 Wo     1 Mp.FT.FDo            (H),Bt        P   2.0

  V    7 Wo     1 FMa.FC'o             A             P   1.0
       8 Do    10 Fo                   Bt

 VI    9 Do     3 Fo                   Ay

VII   10 Do     2 FVu                  Fd

VIII  11 WS+    1 FCo                  An,Art            4.5
      12 Dv     2 CF.YFo               Fd

 IX   13 W+     1 ma.CF.VFo            Ex,Fi             5.5  AG

  X   14 DdS+  29 mpo                  Bt,Na             6.0  MOR
      15 D+     1 FMao                 A             P   4.0  MOR,AG
      16 Do     2 FMpo            2    A
=============================================================================
(C)1976, 1983 BY JOHN E. EXNER, JR.
   ABBREVIATIONS USED ABOVE:
   FOR DQ: "/" = "v/+"; FOR CONTENTS: "Id" = "IDIOGRAPHIC CONTENT"
   SPECIAL SCORES: "INC" = "INCOM", "FAB" = "FABCOM", "CON" = "CONTAM"
                       "CFB" = "CONFAB"
```

STRUCTURAL INTERPRETATION

Two of the three Special Indices are at or beyond critical cutoff points. The Suicide Constellation contains 10 positive variables. This is a very notable finding and cause for immediate concern, especially because she is an outpatient and has given no hint about any preoccupation with, or inclination toward, self-destructive behavior. *Whenever the Suicide Constellation exceeds 7, it should provoke a rapid response to ascertain the validity of a self-destructive possibility.* There is always the possibility that the Constellation has identified a false positive, particularly if substantial depression is present; however, it would be foolhardy to ignore the finding. Usually, a brief interview, conducted by a skilled professional and focusing on the issue, will uncover inclinations toward self-destruction, even if information developed in earlier interviews has failed to do so.

It seems reasonably clear that considerable depression is present. The Depression Index of 4 suggests the likelihood of a major affective involvement. As noted in Chapter 17, the Depression Index tends to misidentify, as false negatives, a significant proportion of subjects who are seriously depressed or prone to frequent experiences of intense depression. On the other hand, the probability of identifying as false positives those who are not depressed is quite remote. Therefore whenever four or five variables in the Index are positive, it is almost certain that the personality structure of the subject will include several characteristics that are commensurate with the presence of, or potential for severe depression. An examination of this record for the variables that are positive in the Index reveals that she has three Vista responses, six *MOR* answers, two Color-Shading Blends, and a substantially low Egocentricity Index of .19.

The elevation in Vista answers signifies that she is engaging in considerable self-examining behavior, and apparently focusing mainly on features that she regards as liabilities. The result is negative, irritating affect. This is evidenced when only one Vista answer is present, and when the frequency is as high as three or more, it is likely that the negative feelings are quite tormenting. One of the two Color-Shading Blends contains a *Y* variable that might not be stable over time and, as such, could reflect some form of transient confusion about her feelings. However, the second contains one of the Vista answers, which is much more stable, suggesting that the confusion she has concerning emotion is probably more long-standing and could represent considerable ambivalence. The six *MOR* responses indicate that her self-image is much more negative than positive and that she probably conceptualizes herself as damaged in some way. As a result, her thinking and attitudes are prone to be marked by considerable pessimism. Her very low Egocentricity Index denotes a low sense of personal worth or self-esteem. Collectively, these are ingredients from which feelings of depression evolve quite easily, and because all are relatively stable, it seems apparent that she has been experiencing considerable depression for quite some time.

The condition is made more complex by the presence of some reasonably intense situational stress. The *D* score is −2, but when adjusted, becomes 0. The record contains three *m* and two *Y* responses, signaling that she is experiencing problems in control and the corresponding feelings of helplessness often produced by such problems. The magnitude of the stimulus overload state is so extensive that it is very likely she often experiences demands to which she is unable to make well-organized responses. In some instances, her decisions may not be formulated fully, or her efforts to implement responses may be marked by some disorganization. Her tolerance for stress in this state is very limited and easily exceeded. She is especially vulnerable to dysfunctioning in new or unexpected situations that go beyond the easily recognized structure of daily routines. It might be speculated that the increase in the frequency and intensity of her headaches is the product of the situationally related condition. However, the situational condition could, itself, be the result of an increasing awareness of frequent intense depressive episodes and her inability to contend effectively with them. The *eb* of 6:7 has the higher value unexpectedly on the right side of the ratio. This is a sign of considerable distress and serves as more confirmation of the substantial affective disarray that is occurring. The intensity of the condition, plus the concerns for some self-destructive potential argue against outpatient care. She is in crisis and requires more than most outpatient forms of treatment can provide easily.

The *EB* of 4:3.5 reflects the ambitent, who has yet to develop a consistent coping style. This means that she will often invest more energy than might be required to achieve solutions, and that much of her behavior will be less efficient and more unpredictable than if a consistent style were present. The question might be raised about how she has been able to achieve success in her work when impaired by all of these liabilities. The answer seems to lie in a review of her cognitive operations. The intelligence test data reveal that she is very bright, possibly much more so than the requirements of her job demand. The location distribution shows that she does economize reasonably well. She gives seven *W* answers in her 16 responses. The *Zf* of 11 might be considered slightly high for a short record, and signifies some of the effort that she makes to insure that each new stimulus event is meaningful. The *DQ* distribution shows that eight of her answers are synthesized, reflecting considerable cognitive sophistication and not at all surprising in light of her very substantial I.Q. In addition, the *Zd* score of $+8.0$ shows that she overincorporates in her organizing efforts. In other words, she works much harder than is necessary when processing information, probably striving for a form of perfectionism. The *W:M* of 7:4 reveals that she is relatively conservative about setting goals. Thus it would seem that she has selected an occupation in which the likelihood of success is very considerable for one who is as intellectually talented as she, in spite of some of her liabilities. The five *Popular* responses indicate that she is able to make commonplace translations of new stimuli, but possibly more important is the fact that the $X+\%$ is 88% and the record contains *no* minus answers. She is quite attuned to convention, and seeks to make sure that most of her behaviors will fall into that framework. The *a:p* ratio of 6:4 suggests that there is no unusual inflexibility to her thinking or attitudes, and the form quality of her *M* responses shows that her thinking is not marked by unusual characteristics. This seems confirmed by the fact that there are none of the six Critical Special Scores in the record.

Issues of affective control, and her interpersonal perceptions are another matter. The *Afr* of .60 is well within normal limits, indicating that, like most people, she is interested in emotional stimulation. However, the $FC:CF+C$ of 1:3 suggests that in many instances when emotional displays occur, she does not modulate well. Her feelings become overly intense and intrusive to her thinking, her decisions, and her behaviors. This finding is made more important by the fact that the record contains four *S* responses and four *AG* responses. The elevated *S* suggests a very negative, oppositional, and possibly hostile orientation toward the world. The *AG* responses indicate that she perceives the interpersonal world as being marked by considerable aggressiveness, and has probably adopted that role as part of her own model for interacting with people. These findings portend poorly for her interpersonal relationships, and when the human contents are reviewed, more potential for trouble is uncovered. She does have four *H* contents; however, all four are *(H)*. Thus although she may have as much interest in people as do most adults, her concepts about people are drawn mainly from imagined or fantasized experience. In effect, she does not understand people very well. and this may contribute to her negative conceptions about herself. It does seem clear that she would like to be close to others. There is the expected *T* in the record, suggesting that she experiences needs for closeness in ways that are common. Moreover, there are two *Fd* contents, strongly suggesting that she would prefer to be in dependent relationships with others. This characteristic may be a key to the fact that her emotional contacts with men are short-lived. She may be too demanding on them, and if those demands are expressed in aggressive ways, it is easy to hypothesize why they might shy away, or why the relationship would become more tenuous. The Isolation Index, 5:16, exceeds the critical level, and suggests that she is probably much more socially isolated than she readily admits. The slight elevation in $An+Xy$ is to be expected in light of her presenting symptoms.

ANALYSIS OF THE SCORING SEQUENCE

Her approach is somewhat variable. She tends to give *W* answers to those blots that are more solid, and *D*'s to those that are more broken. This is generally consistent with her ability to economize when necessary. Her blends are scattered, and with one exception occur as her first answer to a blot. A more puzzling finding is the fact that her four *M* answers appear as first responses to each of the first four cards and are included in the sequence of her first six answers. It seems possible that her capacity to delay, as is reflected in *M* answers, somehow became impaired, and as a result she tended to be much more influenced in the selection of her last 10 answers by the impingements of demanding stimuli. If this is true, it may signify the ease with which the overload state causes disruptive, and more affective behavior. It is also interesting to note that four of her six *MOR* answers appear in the same sequence. This may indicate that her very negative self-image contributed significantly to the apparent dysfunction that occurred. The finding also gives rise to the speculation that, under different conditions, her preferred style may be more introversive, but that the marked affective disarray has interfered with that tendency. In any event, the last half of the record is substantially different than the first half, including the fact that she does not give Popular answers to any of the blots VI through IX, and has proportionally far fewer organized responses.

ANALYSIS OF THE RESPONSES

The record is very rich in projected material. She enters the test with a morbid and negative response, a witch burning, that probably reflects both her feelings of negativism about herself and her sense of helplessness about it. The sense of damage is conveyed rather clearly in the second answer, a ruined butterfly, and again in the third answer, people fighting and both are *badly* injured. The fourth answer, water in a puddle, also may convey her feelings of being helpless and trapped. The negativism persists in the fifth answer, two ghouls, and the struggle that was indicated in the third answer appears again. The ghouls are tugging at a basket of bones. Her sixth response, a creature lying down, is striking because of the elaboration, covered with fur or moss. Whereas fur has a protective and desirable feature, moss has no protective property and is prone to grow in dank places. To this point the record is very marked by negativism, pessimism, and conflict. Subsequently, the characteristics of the answers change considerably. Her seventh answer, a bat swooping down like to get something, has a subtle aggressive quality. The next two answers, roots and a totem pole, are more simplistic classification answers. Both are *D* responses and may indicate her need to back away from the very complex operations that have been invoked earlier. But her effort to do this seems to result in a much different performance. The tenth response, fried food, is unusual because of its content, and important because of two elements. It reflects considerable indecisiveness, and it seems more juvenile than might be expected from such a bright and seemingly accomplished person. This answer marks the beginning of another sequence that is very different in quality than represented by her first six responses.

As noted earlier, food responses tend to relate to a dependency orientation, and are much more common among youngsters. The next two answers have similar qualities. The first is an illustration of anatomy, and the second is another food response. The anatomy illustration may indicate her sense of being exposed, whereas the food response is a much less sophisticated and more child-like answer, ". . . mixed in a bunch." It is the first of her Color-Shading Blends and followed by another, an explosion, ". . . with smoke and flames shooting out all over," suggesting the sense of psychological disorganization that she is experiencing. The last three answers all convey a strong sense of helplessness and paralysis. A maple seed has landed in a puddle, a crab has caught a bug, and she leaves the test by reporting two cocker spaniels waiting for something to happen. Thus the latter half of the record, which contains no human contents, is characterized by much more juvenile sorts of answers, and with contents and embellishments that portray a sense of confusion, exposure, and helplessness. There is no real sense of sturdiness, or even struggle. Instead, this part of the sequence seems to illustrate a form of more passive resignation. The marked difference between this sequence of answers, and those to the first four blots is suggestive of some regressive features and serves as an added warning concerning her very precarious state.

ANALYSIS OF THE INQUIRY

Much of her elaboration in the Inquiry simply adds to previous postulates about her tormented and disorganized state. The witch in response 1 is described as having her arms in the air and smoke billowing all around her. The butterfly in answer 2 is dead, and the people in response 3 are described as "in a death struggle, bent in agony . . ." The ghouls in answer 5 are "indescribable" and have torn some poor creature apart. The creature in Card IV is clarified as having "moss all over him." Her comment to Card VI, response 9, is particularly intriguing—"I suppose they don't really worship the pole, but what it stands for." It seems quite symbolic although the meaning is not fully clear. On a simplistic level it may raise numerous questions about her perceptions of sex and sexuality. Viewed differently, however, it could relate to some confusion about status. The helplessness that she experiences is clearly reaffirmed in her comments about the last three responses. The seed is "just laying there with no place to root." The bug has "no chance to get away . . . ," and the dogs are "just sitting and waiting . . . ."

SUMMARY OF PROTOCOL 3

This is a very seriously depressed woman who seems to be hanging onto her world by her psychological fingertips. Although very intelligent, and still able to use some of her more sophisticated cognitive operations effectively, she is continually battered by a very negative self-image and the consequences of a prolonged struggle with herself. She is in considerable pain, but apparently some threads of need to present herself in ways that do not threaten her integrity further inhibit her from sharing the torment that is present. Instead, she has resorted to a previous symptom pattern, headaches, to seek attention and probably support. Her current state of substantial stimulus overload creates continual hazards to her efforts at effective functioning, and although she often makes a strong effort to contend with her pain, it ultimately becomes overwhelming and causes her to drift into less mature forms of passive resignation concerning her plight. She harbors considerable hostility and sees the world and interpersonal relationships as being marked by aggression, and apparently will often manifest aggressiveness in her contacts with others. This tactic, when added to the fact that she has never developed a reality based conception of people, only serves to insure that her interpersonal relations will be superficial and short-lived.

Her failure to experience the close relationships that she would prefer only exacerbates her needs to be dependent. The cyclical experiences of interpersonal failure serve to reinforce her negative self-image and further reduce the value she places on her personal worth. It seems clear that the depression she experiences has been present in a serious form for quite some time, and is increasing in both frequency and intensity. Although she denies that her decision to relinquish custody of her daughter plays any role in her current state, that issue should not be overlooked as an important predisposition to her current plight. Now, the impact of the depression has become even more disruptive because of some situationally experienced stress. The cause of the latter is not clear. It could relate to some new interpersonal disappointment, or it could also be the product of an increasing awareness about many of her own deficiencies. It could also be the product of the accumulated experiences of frustration that she has encountered. In any event, it has placed her on the brink of major disorganization. It also seems clear that the suicide potential is quite real, and this should be the first focus of intervention. Obviously, her precarious state, plus the suicide potential, are both factors that argue strongly against initiating efforts at intervention without providing considerable structure and continual support for her. In that context, it seems appropriate to recommend hospitalization, at least for a brief period, until she can be eased into a recognized pattern of intervention supports that will include well-defined preliminary objectives which she can clearly understand and accept in her quest for reconstitution.

PROTOCOL 4: A QUESTION OF IMPULSIVENESS

Referral   This is a court referral, the subject having been indicted on one count of aggravated assault and one count of attempted homicide. The consulting psychologist was asked to act as an *amicus curiae* to the court in a pretrial hearing, during which the defense intends to offer a plea of "not guilty," based on the premise that the subject acted during a state of diminished capacity that was created either by a neurological or psychiatric condition. The subject claims to have no memory for the event, and also claims a history of similar behaviors, some of which resulted in a psychiatric discharge from military service. A specific question posed by the court is whether evidence exists that would favor a decision by the court for commitment to hospitalization rather than routine trial action.

History   L. H. is an impressive-looking individual of medium height and weight. He stands out as well groomed and neat. He has a husky voice and a ready smile that seems to have "cooperativeness" written all over it. He picks his words carefully, and after a short while in the interview, it becomes obvious that he wants to make a good impression. Prior to psychological evaluation, he had a complete neurological examination that yielded negative findings. He is the third child, and oldest son, in a family of four. His father was an accountant and the mother a housewife. His older sisters, now ages 38 and 40, both married shortly after completing high school. Both parents are deceased, the father at age 58 of a coronary, the mother at age 59 from cancer. He does not know the whereabouts of his younger brother, age 29. L. H. is a high school graduate and has taken "a few" college courses "here and there." He has marked memory lapses for his various jobs but estimates that he has held "at least a dozen," all of which fall into the "blue collar" category except one as a salesman in an appliance store. He currently works as a fork lift operator in a storage warehouse, but claims to also make "a lot of extra money" gambling and "things like that." He describes his sex history with some rather grandiose claims of conquest: "I'd never get married with all the available women around. . . . Women just seem to want to fall into bed with me. . . . No kidding doc, I haven't paid my own rent in two years. . . . I guess I'm lucky to have the natural talent that women go for." He claims his first sexual experience occurred at age 11 when he was seduced by "an older girl." He says that he may have fathered "a kid or two," but has no definite knowledge of any of his past loves giving birth. Most of his jobs have lasted less than one year, and he admits to being fired twice for fighting with supervisors. He freely admits to the attempted strangulation of the girl friend with whom he had been living for about 8 months, "I don't know what happened, one minute we were o.k. and the next minute I was like a wild man, I went crazy." He claims that similar events have happened at least twice, both times leading to some assault on females. He openly admits to problems with his temper and says that, "It got really bad when I was in the Army. I lasted only four months after they drafted me." Military records indicate that he was discharged with a diagnosis of "Schizoid Personality with epileptoid features." He says that he does drink frequently, "Mostly beer," and that he has used drugs as a trial but did not like the effects. He claims that each time he has a "severe" temper control problem, he has no memory for the event. He expresses remorse concerning the attempted strangulation of his girl friend. He states, "It's about time that I got some help because this temper is really bad and I don't want to hurt anyone, not really."

Protocol #4   32 Year Old Male

Card	Response	Inquiry	Scoring
I	1. Holy Christ: I d.k. what ths is, mayb its a naked wm in the cntr w her hands up, like a model	E: (Rpts S's resp) S: Yeah, the more I look at it the more it ll that. Here's her hips & it ll the hands in the air, as if she's modeling s.t., but if she naked what's she modeling? That's a thought isn't it. E: Can u show me a bit more so that I c it the way u do? S: Well, c here is the outline, u can't c her head, mayb its back lik she was laughing, she looks pretty sexy to me doc.	Do M^ao H
	E: (Most people c more than 1 thg) S: Gee, I don't c nothg else.		
II	2. Oh u'r really kidding me aren't u? Am I supposed to tell u wht ths really ll to me? (E: Yes) Well doc ths is a good one, ths bttm prt ll some a-a- well I was gonna say pussy, but I'll say vagina to make it a littl better, how's that?	E: (Rpts S's resp) S: I heard somewhere if u c tht stuff u'r preoccup'd w it, is that right? E: Can u show me how u c it? S: Well it has the fuzzy look to it lik there was hair & u can c the slit, I'm tryg to b honest about it cause I hav a big responsibility to try & get bettr	Do FTo S×
	3. Ths top prt ll a bldy thumb	E: (Rpts S's resp) S: Well it's all red lik bld, & its shaped lik a thumb, mite hav had an accident, there's really 2 of them, 1 on each side	Do CF⁻ (2) Hd, Bl MOR
III	4. The ll 2 wm doing s. t. in ths pot, no wait a minute, its lik	E: (Rpts S's resp) S: Yeah, lik she's makin bad apples in her	W+ M^a.Fro (H), Hh, Art P 5.5

487

Protocol #4 (Continued)

Card	Response	Inquiry	Scoring
	a witch, lik in snow white & she's doing s.t., brewing s.t. in the pot & lookin in the mirror	den & thes red thgs r lik decorations, sort of symbols of her cult, lik trophies or s.t. E: Decorations? S: Just thgs on the wall, I d.k. what.	
IV	V5. Ths is some old tattered & torn hide, mayb it was a jacket once but now its all ruined from being weathered	E: (Rpts S's resp) S: The W thg ll tht, altho the arms r gone I guess, it ll its all greasy & beat up E: Greasy & beat up? S: Yeah, c the drk splotches on it c.b. grease & its all ragged around the edges	Wv YFu Cg MOR
V	6. Ths ll a bat bearing down on a target w his feelrs stretch'd out ready to strike	E: (Rpts S's resp) S: It apparently sightd its prey & now its about to gobble it up E: Can u show me how u c it? S: Sure, c the wgs (points) & the body, it looks stiff, lik it's ready to strike	Wo FMao A P 1.0 AG
VI	7. Well, I said I'd b honest, u'll prob lock me up & throw away the key, but ths top prt ll a man's—well—his sex organ, penis that is	E: (Rpts S's resp) S: Its ths top thg, I hav to admit these side thgs don't fit, at least I never saw one w feathers altho it wld b popular as hell I'll bet E: Can u tell me what maks it ll tht? S: Hell, if u don't c it u'd bettr lock me up & thro away the key, it just ll that 2 me damn it (Throws card down).	Do Fo Sx
VII	8. ll a cpl of pieces of fried chicken to me	E: (Rpts S's resp) S: Well, thy'r sort of drumsticks altho the shape isn't really right, thy hav lik breading on them lik u get in chkn in a basket. E: Where is it that u c them?	Do TFu (2) Fd

488

VIII

S: Ths bttm prt isn't included, altho I guess u can c it as anothr piece

E: U mentioned breading

S: Thy look ruff & drk lik breadg, lik u kno, breadg is that way

V9. If u turn it ths way it ll a cpl of can-can dancers going at it

E: (Rpts S's resp)

S: Thy hav thyr heads touchg lik thy were in a chorus line or s.s. of specialty dance, c the legs r kicking outward so u can't c it, u can c only one on each — W+ M^a o (2) H 2.5

V10. Ths prt ll sherbet, its got a glassy look to it, differnt from real ice cream

E: (Rpts S' resp)

S: Yeah, its all colord like sherbet, orange & raspberry I guess & its kind of grainy lik sherbet — Dv C.T Fa

<11. ll a wolf, ready to spring at s.t., he's being reflected in a river or pond

E: (Rpts S's resp)

S: C the legs here & the body & the wolf head, there's no tail tho, he's ready to spring, standg on some rocks or s.t. being reflectd dwn here I d.k. what ths (points to front prt) mite b, mayb a stump or s.t. — W+ FM^a.Fro A,Ls P 4.5 MOR, AG

IX

V12. ll the whole damn world is blowing up, u get the feelg of a lot of force

E: (Rpts S's resp)

S: Lots of force, lik an atomic blast but it has so much color that it has 2 b the world or at least part of it, c all the fire here—I guess we'd b bettr off if it happened — Wv m^a.CFo Ex.Fi AG, MOR, ALOG

13. If u turn it ths way the pink ll cotton candy, no stick but a couple of 'em, c one on each side, sticky like candy

E: (Rpts S's resp)

S: Well they'r pink & fluffy lookg, fuzzy lik cotton candy, u can't c the stick tho, just the round ball of cotton candy lik is on the stick like at a fair — Dv CF.TFo 2) Fd

E: u said they were sticky like?

S: Thy ll if u pick them up, Thy'll stick to ur fingers

Protocol #4 (Continued)

Card	Response		Inquiry	Scoring
I	14. Well a cpl lady bugs at the top eatin on a weed	E: S:	(Rpts S's resp) They hav legs & antennae, c (points) they look pretty good lik lady bugs	$D+$ $FM^a o$ (2) A, Bt 4.0
	15. The pink ll bld stains	E: S:	(Rpts S's resp) Yeah, they ll bld stains to me, prob dried up cause the red isn't as dark as fresh bld, just a blob of dried bld	Dv C Bl MOR
	16. Ths up here ll a spider tht has caught a bug in its claws & is going to devour it	E: S:	(Rpts S's resp) It has a lot of legs, I don't kno wht the grn thg is, s.k. of bug I guess, the ole spider has really got it tho	$D+$ $FM^a o$ A P 4.0 AG
	17. Mayb a cpl dogs down here lik they were baying at the moon or s.t.	E: S:	(Rpts S's resp) C here thy r, 1 on each side, the heads are tilted up lik thy were baying like dogs do	Do $FM^a o$ (2) A
	18. Ths blue thgs ll some sex thgs lik a cpl of ovaries or s.t., if there were a—penis there they cld b testicles but there isn't any so thy must b ovaries	E: S:	(Rpts S's resp) They just rem me of that, I d.k. exactly why, I guess bec of the way they r formed there, I d.k. what that is between them tho, mayb a clitoris but that isn't where it's supposed to be	Do $F-$ (2) Sx $ALOG$

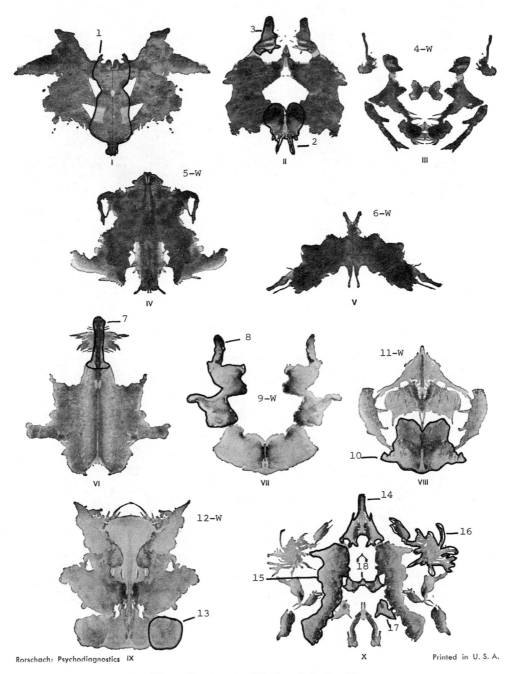

Rorschach: Psychodiagnostics IX

Printed in U. S. A.

Figure 20. Location Selections for Protocol 4.

Table 42. Structural Summary—Protocol #4

```
=========================================================================
 R = 18      Zf = 6      ZSum = 21.5      P = 4      (2) = 7    Fr+rF = 2

 LOCATION            DETERMINANTS            CONTENTS     S-CONSTELLATION
 FEATURES        BLENDS                                       (ADULT)
                              SINGLE
                                         H   = 2, 0    NO..FV+VF+V+FD>2
 W   = 6         M.Fr        M   = 2     (H) = 1, 0    YES..Col-Shd Bl>0
   (Wv = 2)      C.T         FM  = 4     Hd  = 1, 0    YES..Ego<.31,>.44
 D   = 12        FM.Fr       m   = 0     (Hd)= 0, 0    YES..MOR > 3
 Dd  = 0         m.CF        C   = 1     A   = 5, 0    YES..Zd > +- 3.5
 S   = 0         CF.TF       Cn  = 0     (A) = 0, 0    YES..es > EA
                             CF  = 1     Ad  = 0, 0    YES..CF+C+Cn > FC
      DQ                     FC  = 0     (Ad)= 0, 0    YES..X+ < .70
 .........(FQ-)               C'  = 0     Ab  = 0, 0    NO..S > 3
                             C'F = 0     Al  = 0, 0    NO..P < 3 or > 8
   +  = 5 ( 0)               FC'= 0      An  = 0, 0    NO..Pure H < 2
 v/+  = 0 ( 0)               T   = 0     Art = 0, 1    NO..R < 17
   o  = 8 ( 2)               TF  = 1     Ay  = 0, 0     7.....TOTAL
   v  = 5 ( 0)               FT  = 1     Bl  = 1, 1
                             V   = 0     Bt  = 0, 1    SPECIAL SCORINGS
                             VF  = 0     Cg  = 1, 0       DV   = 0
                             FV  = 0     Cl  = 0, 0      INCOM  = 0
                             Y   = 0     Ex  = 1, 0       DR   = 0
                             YF  = 1     Fi  = 0, 1     FABCOM  = 0
      FORM QUALITY           FY  = 0     Fd  = 3, 0      ALOG   = 2
                             rF  = 0     Ge  = 0, 0     CONTAM  = 0
   FQx        FQf    M Qual. Fr  = 0     Hh  = 0, 1     --- WSUM6 =10
                             FD  = 0     Ls  = 0, 1      AG   = 4
   +  = 0    + = 0    + = 0  F   = 2     Na  = 0, 0     CONFAB  = 0
   o  = 12   o = 1    o = 3              Sc  = 0, 0      CP   = 0
   u  = 2    u = 0    u = 0              Sx  = 3, 0      MOR  = 5
   -  = 2    - = 1    - = 0              Xy  = 0, 0      PER  = 0
 none= 2           none= 0              Idio= 0, 0      PSV  = 0
=========================================================================
```

RATIOS, PERCENTAGES, AND DERIVATIONS

```
ZSum-Zest = 21.5 - 17.0      FC:CF+C = 0: 5    W:M     = 6: 3
                              (Pure C = 2)
Zd        =   4.5                              W:D     = 6:12
                             Afr     = 1.00
.------------------------.                     Isolate:R = 2:18
:EB = 3: 6.0    EA = 9.0:    3r+(2)/R = 0.72
:                   >D= 0                       Ab+Art    = 1
:eb = 6: 5    es = 11 :      L      = 0.13
'------------------------'                      An+Xy     = 0
(FM= 5 " C'= 0 T= 4) (Adj D= 0)  Blends:R = 5:18
(m = 1 " V = 0 Y= 1)                            H(H):Hd(Hd)= 3: 1
                             X+%  = 0.67          (Pure H = 2)
a:p     = 9: 0               (F+% = 0.50)   (HHd):(AAd) = 1: 0
                             X-%  = 0.11
Ma:Mp   = 3: 0                                  H+A:Hd+Ad = 8: 1
--------------------------------------------------------------------
          SCZI = 3          DEPI = 2          S-CON = 7
=========================================================================
```
(C)1976,1983 BY JOHN E. EXNER, JR.

492

Table 43.   Scoring Sequence—Protocol #4

```
=================================================================
CARD NO. LOC.  #   DETERMINANT(S)   (2) CONTENT(S) POP  Z   SPECIAL SCORES
=================================================================
  I    1 Do   4 Mao                    H
  II   2 Do   3 FTo                    Sx
       3 Do,  2 CF-                   2 Hd,Bl               MOR
 III   4 W+   1 Ma.Fro                 (H),Hh,Art P  5.5
  IV   5 Wv   1 YFu                    Cg                   MOR
   V   6 Wo   1 FMao                   A          P  1.0 AG
  VI   7 Do   6 Fo                     Sx
 VII   8 Do   2 TFu                   2 Fd
       9 W+   1 Mao                   2 H            2.5
VIII  10 Dv   2 C.T                    Fd
      11 W+   1 FMa.Fro                A,Ls       P  4.5 MOR,AG
  IX  12 Wv   1 ma.CFo                 Ex,Fi            AG,MOR,ALOG
      13 Dv   4 CF.TFo               2 Fd
   X  14 D+  11 FMao                  2 A,Bt         4.0
      15 Dv   9 C                      Bl                   MOR
      16 D+   1 FMao                   A          P  4.0 AG
      17 Do   2 FMao                  2 A
      18 Do   6 F-                    2 Sx                  ALOG
=================================================================
(C)1976, 1983 BY JOHN E. EXNER, JR.
   ABBREVIATIONS USED ABOVE:
   FOR DQ: "/" = "v/+"; FOR CONTENTS: "Id" = "IDIOGRAPHIC CONTENT"
   SPECIAL SCORES: "INC" = "INCOM", "FAB" = "FABCOM", "CON" = "CONTAM"
                   "CFB" = "CONFAB"
```

STRUCTURAL INTERPRETATION

None of the Special Indices has scores that are at or above the critical cut-offs. Both *D* scores are 0, indicating that, ordinarily, he has enough resource available from which to formulate and direct behaviors as he experiences demands for them. This finding does not rule out the possibility of being overwhelmed by unexpected and/or severe stress; however, it does place some doubt on the likelihood of dissociative-like outbursts of rage, or other forms of intense emotional display that might result from frequent losses of control, *unless* they are provoked by some relatively intense stress experience. At the same time, the presence of an Adjusted *D* score of 0 does not address the issue of diminished states of consciousness. It implies that, under ordinary circumstances his capacities for control seem sufficient. On the other hand, it is impossible to predict, from Rorschach data, how this capacity might be altered in states of intoxication, or in other conditions, such as might be seizure provoked.

The *EB* of 3:6.0 reveals the presence of an extratensive coping preference. Thus in most situations, he will approach stimulus demands by releasing affect and it will usually mark his thinking, his attitudes, his decisions, and his behaviors. This preferential style is also characterized by trial-and-error approaches to problem solving, and a tendency to seek gratification of his own needs through emotional exchange. The presence of a reasonably well-established coping style is a favorable finding; however, a review of other variables that are related to affect raises some serious concerns. The *FC:CF + C* ratio of

0:5 signifies that, much of the time, he *fails to use* his capacities for control to modulate his affective displays in ways that are common to adults. Instead, his failure to do so permits his emotions to become much more intense, and the fact that two of his responses are *Pure C* strongly suggests that he is the type of person who *passively gives way* to his feelings. In those situations, his emotions will often reach such levels of intensity that they often direct or command the nature of his thinking and behaviors. These findings make it highly likely that some of his behaviors will be marked by impulsive-like characteristics; however, it is important to distinguish those behaviors from ones that are the true product of lability, that is, when controls *are* insufficient and the person easily becomes over-whelmed by the intensity of feeling. His behaviors, even though appearing impulsive, are *not* the product of loss of control, but rather result from a failure to direct available resources in ways that will invoke modulation. This finding seems even more important in light of the well above average *Afr* of 1.0 that signals a very strong interest in and recep-tiveness to processing emotionally toned stimuli. Strong interests in being in or around emotional situations is not in itself a liability; however, it does suggest that he may be the type of person who searches out emotional stimulus situations, possibly in concert with his orientation to gratify needs through emotional exchange. If this hypothesis is valid, it reveals that he tends to immerse himself psychologically in situations in which affective exchange demands or expectations are commonplace. Under such circumstances, his proneness to release affect in less controlled ways cannot help but become a significant liability, because the displays will often be too intense.

A review of the *eb* reveals that the major element contributing to his experience of stimulus demand stems from very strong needs for emotional closeness. The presence of four *T* responses is quite unusual and, ordinarily, frequencies of this magnitude will occur only when the subject has recently experienced a significant emotional loss. It is possible that the flight of his girl friend, following his attack, could provoke this substantial sense of loss; however, it seems important to note that his interview statements make no men-tion of a desire for reconciliation and, in fact, he conveyed the impression that his attrac-tiveness to women makes any broken relation easy to replace. Thus the magnitude of the texture answers could signify a much more long-standing experience of affective depriva-tion, which could account for the Don Juan-like behaviors. If this postulate is valid, it may signify that he is the type of person whose unmet needs for closeness are so strong that few "normal" adult relationships could be sufficiently fulfilling. If this proves to be the case, the failure to modulate emotional displays could easily give rise to behaviors that are much more juvenile and demanding. The record also contains three *Fd* contents, indicat-ing very strong dependency needs that are more common among young children than adults. In this context, the data concerning self-image and the perceptions of others are very relevant.

His Egocentricity Index of .72 is well above the average range, suggesting that he is highly self-centered. The presence of two reflection answers reveals that the self-centered-ness includes a very strong element of overglorification of self-value, which includes some of the characteristics of narcissism. This feature suggests that many of his behaviors will focus on the necessity to gratify his own needs, irrespective of the expense to others. The record does contain four human contents, including two *Pure H* responses. This suggests that he is interested in people, and that some of his conceptions about them are based in his own experiences. The characteristics of the two *Pure H* answers may shed added light on this issue. Whether or not that proves the case, there are two other datum that argue in favor of a hypothesis that his interpersonal world is fraught with problems.

These are the five *MOR* and four *AG* responses. The elevation in *MOR* reveals a very damaged self-image that is much more negative than positive. It also suggests that much of his thinking will be marked by considerable pessimism, which will tend to be pervasive in his relations with others. At first glance, this seems contradictory to the findings from the elevated Egocentricity Index, and especially with the presence of narcissistic-like features, but this need not be the case.

The narcissistic features are probably very long-standing, having developed during the early developmental years, and perpetuated by a failure to discover many of the positive realities of the interpersonal world. In the Piagetian model, it signals a failure of decentration. At the same time his experiences with people apparently have been far less satisfying than he may have anticipated or desired. Thus an internal conflict concerning self-image has evolved. He has a strong, almost infantile-like need to perceive himself as important to the world, yet, he has experienced many disappointments in his development that have created some acknowledgment of being a battered or damaged person. Apparently, his tactic of attempting to resolve this conflict is best illustrated by the several *AG* answers that he has delivered in the test. He has come to perceive people as aggressive, and has identified with that model of exchange as the basis for some of his own interpersonal behaviors. This composite might have resulted in many roles that could have permitted him to avoid his current plight, such as the demanding teacher, the punitive minister, the overly enthusiastic law enforcement officer, or the political keeper of the morality of the world. Unfortunately for him, his immaturity, lack of intellect, and inability to profit from experience make any of those roles unlikely, if not impossible. When the issues of his conflicted self-image and distorted interpersonal world are merged with his affective style and failure to modulate his emotional displays, the potential consequences must include a very high probability for inappropriate, maladaptive social behaviors, some of which will be characterized by his aggressive orientation.

This picture becomes even more negative when some of the characteristics of his cognitive operations are reviewed. First, the *Zd* score of $+4.5$ indicates the presence of an overincorporative style; that is, when he organizes new stimuli, he devotes considerably more effort than is necessary, apparently to insure that he is not negligent. This could be an asset for him but, unfortunately, he does not do this enough. The *ZF* of 6 indicates only a limited initiative to organize. The *W:D* of 6:12 reveals that he tends to be quite economical, and the *W:M* of 6:3 suggests that he does not overextend himself when setting goals. These are probably both favorable findings, and the five *DQ+* answers seem respectable in this context. A much more negative finding is the fact that he delivered 5 *DQv* responses, signifying that many of his cognitive operations are overly concrete and simplistic. In addition, the record contains two *ALOG* responses, suggesting that his judgment or reasoning may often be more strained or illogical than should be the case.

The importance of these findings is increased when the data concerning perception are reviewed. The $X+\%$ of 67% is lower than desirable, although the $X-\%$ is not significantly elevated. There are only four *Popular* responses, which is lower than average for the adult. These findings indicate that he tends to translate many aspects of his world in ways that are less conventional, and in some cases may even be negligent of the obvious. The *FQx* distribution, which contains two minus, two *u,* and two *no form* responses, reveals that in some instances he will distort inputs, whereas in other instances he will simply translate them idiographically or ignore them in favor of his own feelings. Although none of these features is necessarily unusual for many people, collectively they create a significant potential for unconventional responses that can only serve to increase the overall proclivity for maladaptive behaviors. Moreover, the *a:p* ratio of 9:0 indicates that much of his thinking and attitudes will be marked by considerable inflexibility. It will not be easy for him to view things differently or alter many of the values that he has adopted. In this context, it is important to note that the record contains three *Sx* responses, signaling the presence of a preoccupation. The rigidity of his thinking will probably make it very difficult to approach or alter that preoccupation which, on a more speculative level, is probably related to the Don Juan attitude toward women that he manifested in the interview.

ANALYSIS OF THE SCORING SEQUENCE

His approach is somewhat mixed and generally economical. He enters the solid blots with *W* answers, and the more complex blots, with the exception of III, with *D*'s. In spite of the fact that the record contains four *T* responses, he did not give the *Popular* texture answer to Card VI. One of the four, to Card II, has a sex content, and the remaining three all have *Fd* contents. This seems to support an earlier postulate that his needs for closeness are long-standing, and apparently quite primitive. His five Blend responses all occur to blots containing chromatic color, which seems to confirm the hypothesis that the presence of emotionally toned stimuli does give rise to greater complexity in his psychological operations. Both of his minus answers also occur to chromatically color blots, and there is no recovery after either. There is no special clustering of organized answers, and the earlier notation that his cognitive efforts are often overly concrete or simplistic is well illustrated by the fact that three of his first answers, and both responses given to Card IX, are *DQv*.

ANALYSIS OF THE RESPONSES

The responses contain much rich material, some because of the contents, but many because of his comments and embellishments. Several reflect his concreteness and poor judgment as he apparently tries to defend himself by manipulation, whereas several others provide good illustrations of the consequences of his failure to delay or modulate feelings, so that the answers include many impulsive-like characteristics. His very first comment, "Holy Christ . . . a naked woman . . ." sets the tone for the record, and his response to the encouragement of the examiner conveys some of the nonconformity hypothesized earlier. The comment preceding his second response hints at his defensive attempts to be manipulative, "Oh, you're really kidding me aren't you . . . Well doc, this is a good one . . . I was gonna say pussy, but I'll say vagina to make it a little better, how's that?" The fact that he says what he said he would not say reflects how he fails to delay. Interestingly, the response also illustrates that he is often aware of inappropriateness, but does little to alter his approach. The third answer, a bloody thumb, could be translated to raise questions about the presence of feelings of inadequacy concerning masculinity. Response 4 contains his second human content, a witch, which is one of his reflection answers, and suggesting the possibility of a magical or grandiose quality in some of his thinking. His fifth response, and second *MOR*, "old tattered and torn . . . ruined . . ." conveys his negative self-image quite well, and also raises questions about feelings of adequacy in his role model. The sixth answer, a bat bearing down on his target, is probably a good representation of how aggressiveness will appear in his behaviors, that is, following some awareness of damage or inadequacy. The naiveté in his judgment is also reflected quite well in his preface to answer 7, "Well I said I'd be honest, you'll probably lock me up and throw away the key . . . ." None of his food responses are form dominant—fried chicken, sherbet, and cotton candy—which probably illustrates the intensity and influence of his dependency orientation. His aggressive responses are all quite intense. The bat is bearing down, the wolf is ready to spring, the "whole damn" world is being blown up, and the spider is going to devour the bug. His last answer, a minus, provides a very strong suggestion about the cause for his sexual preoccupation and concerns with adequacy, ". . . if there were a penis there they could be testicles, but there isn't any so they must be ovaries." Both of his *Pure H* answers, a model, and can-can dancers, are exhibitionistic, another feature that probably is quite important to the role he attempts to play to conceal his very pronounced sense of inadequacy.

ANALYSIS OF THE INQUIRY

Much of the Inquiry material reflects the superficiality of his facade, which he often attempts to conceal by attempting to use a naive and somewhat dramatic approach when he is confronted with challenges. The magnitude of his sexual preoccupation is also confirmed in several of his answers, such as ". . . but if she's naked what's she modeling? . . . like there was the hair and you can see the slit . . . I have to admit these side things don't fit, at least I never saw one with feathers although it would be popular as hell I'll bet . . . I don't know what that is between them though, maybe a clitoris, but that isn't where it's supposed to be." His manipulative attempts seem overly obvious at times: "I'm trying to be honest about it cause I have a big responsibility to try and get better. . . . Hell, if you don't see it you'd better lock me up and throw away the key." A less direct view of his own self-image and valuation of his actions may be found in his description of the response to Card III, "like she's making bad apples in her den and these red things are . . . sort of symbols of her cult, like trophies. . . ." This seems to indicate that he is aware of the negative features of his behaviors but also gains reinforcement from them.

SUMMARY OF PROTOCOL 4

It seems reasonably clear that there is no significant psychiatric disability from which to build a case that could be used to mitigate the circumstances concerning the assault on his girl friend. He is a very primitive person, but not one who could be described as being easily victimized by irresistible impulses or frequent diminished states of consciousness, unless the latter is self-induced, as could be the case by the abuse of drugs or alcohol. He is not without the capacity for control, but rather, one who has not learned the social values of control, or one who is unwilling to invest the effort necessary to initiate controls when he engages in emotional discharge. He is far too self-centered to restrain himself from the prospects of immediate relief from stress, or immediate gratification of his own needs, and far too insecure in his own identity to have developed much sensitivity to others. In fact, it is likely that most of his interpersonal relations are perceived by him as sources from which to fulfill his strong unmet needs for closeness and dependency. In other words, he tries to take as much as possible from the relationship while giving as little as possible to it. Exhibitionism and aggressiveness have become important features in the facade with which he tries to conceal his own sense of inadequacy and damage, and sustain his more infantile tendency to self-glorification. Sexual activity appears to have become a highly valued behavior, probably because it serves to counteract many of the underlying concerns that he has about masculinity. In effect, it would not be unrealistic to describe him as a psychopathic personality, easily prone to give way to his feelings as his wants dictate, and with little or no regard for the future consequences of his behaviors. Even if this were not a forensic case, and the subject were seeking some form of treatment, it is unlikely that he would persist in any intervention routine, other than one which would be supportive and reinforcing, because the threats to him that would arise during other forms of treatment would quickly be weighed as being far greater than any gains that he might perceive possible. In that context, it seems difficult, if not impossible, to make any recommendations to the court that might be beneficial to him in his current situation.

PROTOCOL 5: A QUESTION OF CHRONIC ANXIETY

Referral   This 28-year-old female was referred because of frequent bouts of intense anxiety. She has reported episodes of intense anxiety from time to time for approximately 4 years. Historically, both her physician and psychiatrist attributed them to the problems that she experienced with a duodenal ulcer that first appeared at about age 24. She was described at that time as a tense, somewhat anxious, and very achievement oriented person. She was treated with a variety of medications and dietary regimens for approximately 3 years, and also participated in an intervention program of systematic desensitization for about 1 year. During that time the ulcer seemed well under control and dissipating. The ulcer flared again about 1 year prior to this evaluation and required surgery, after which she reentered systematic desensitization for a 4-month period. During a period of 5 months following her termination from that program she has been symptom free; however, during the past 60 days, she has had reoccurring episodes of intense anxiety and apprehension which she describes as, "panic attacks." There has been no reappearance of physical symptoms, but she complains of serious interference to concentration, and some sleep difficulties. The psychiatrist is requesting the evaluation before deciding on another course of intervention.

History   She is an attractive, short, dark-haired registered nurse who currently has supervisory responsibility for six other nurses and a supporting staff of 13 health care providers on a 44-bed general medical ward. She holds a B.S. degree in Nursing from a well-known university, and has worked at the same hospital for 7 years. Her work history is excellent. She manifests good patient relationships, accomplishes her own duties thoroughly and efficiently, and since being promoted to a "Head Nurse" position slightly more than 2 years ago, has set "commendable" standards for herself and those who work with her. She lives alone in a hospital apartment, dating irregularly. She was engaged during college to a resident physician, but "our interests didn't coincide, and so we called it off." She implies virginity but politely refuses to speak of sexual matters: "That is a personal matter that I'm not prepared to talk about now." She is the oldest of two daughters of parents who emigrated from a middle European country shortly after they married. Her family was poor during her developmental years, living in a "cold-water flat" in a large eastern city until she entered high school. By that time, her father had been able to establish himself as a skilled tradesman and purchased a small "duplex" house where the family still lives. She entered college on a nursing scholarship and maintained a "Dean's list" average throughout her 4 years there. She dated frequently in high school and in college but "never for very long with one person." She is very thrifty in her spending habits, preferring to "save my money for a rainy day, or in the event that my parents ever need it." She attends a Protestant church each Sunday, "more to set an example than because I have a belief. In fact, I'm probably an agnostic although I don't go around telling everybody." Her younger sister, age 25, is now married to a businessman, after having completed 2 years of college, and is currently pregnant. She describes both of her parents as the "salt of the earth." She indicates that both are very hard working, conservative, and "vigorously sincere." She says that she feels closer to her father than her mother but is uncomfortable in making any distinction between them. She verbalizes a feeling of contempt for many of her colleagues, "who work their eight to five and get out as quickly as they can. They just don't have much concern for those who they are suppose to be serving." She has great faith in "most doctors," but admits that she has seen some who she feels would fare better in other professions. She says that she sleeps well, has no appetite problems, exercises daily, likes horseback riding, tennis, and an occasional movie.

Protocol #5   28-Year-Old Female

Card	Response		Inquiry	Scoring
I	1. Two wm, prob witches dancing @ a fig. in the cntr, it seems to b a person, quite helpless, its a wm too bec u can c her breasts and hip & she has her hands up	E: S:	(Rpts S's resp) Well, the witches r on each side, the hav big dark cloaks on & they'r doing a dance, I can't really tell if its a ritual or if theyr burng her at the stake. She is just there in the cntr w her hands up	W+ $M^{a-p}.FC'o$ (2) H, (H) 4.0 AG, MOR *(The scoring of a-p is used as both features of M appear. Both are counted in the a:p ratio)*
	2. It cld b an x-ray of a pelvis too	E: S:	(Rpts S's resp) Yes, the *W* thg ll one, its dark lik an x-ray & it has the general structure of a pelvic area, u c, u get the slant of the pelvic arch here	Wo FYo Xy 1.0
II	3. At the top it ll 2 hens preparing to fite w e.o., these red areas	E: S:	(Rpts S's resp) It ll 2 hens primping for a fite u can c the heads & feet & legs	D+ $FM^a u$ (2) A 5.5 AG
	4. The cntr ll a temple of worship w a tower of silver or platinum	E: S:	(Rpts S's resp) Ths cntr white area is the temple & ths ll the tower, it clearly has the form of a towr & its colord like silver or platinum or some other valuable metal wld b colord, its the metal part that really attracts people to the temple bec its so valuable	DS+ FC'o Id 4.5
III	5. 2 wm fiting over s.t. valuable, it ll a basket that theyr fitg over, they must b angry the way theyr tugging so hard	E: S:	(Rpts S's resp) Oh yes, these r the wm, u c the breast outline & the hi-heels, & theyr thin like wm & this is the basket, it must b full of goodies bec each wants it for her own, but neither seems able to get it	D+ $M^a o$ (2) H, Id P 3.0 AG

			Location/Determinant scoring

IV

V6.   Well, ths c.b. an x-ray too, I'm not sure of what, possbly a pelvic arch again & the sacral area of the cord

E: (Rpts S's resp)
S: It's ths *W* thg, its kind of dark & it has a shape that conceivably cld b the pelvic area if u stretch u'r immag a littl. Ths prt wld b the part of the cord, & the rest the pelvis, it definitely has that kind of darkness to it like an x-ray

Wo   FYo   Xy   2   0

V

7.   2 peopl leang against s.t., lying down w thr backs against ths thg in the cntr. I thnk thy'r wm, almost but not quite rstg back to back w thr legs stretchd out like thy wer relxg like they wrkd hard at s.t. & now theyr takg a break

S: Oh I rem ths one, I've sat lik that many times during the war when we'v had a surgery break. I use to hav a good friend who was killed in Seoul & most of the time when we couldn't rest for a long time we'd prop up like ths, u c her r the legs extendg outward

W+   MPo   (2)   H   2.5   PER

VI

8.   A weapon, here at the top, lik an arrow that u would thrust at someone in battle, it has a spear type tip, s.t. u wld use to hurt or maim or kill

E: (Rpts S's resp)
S: Yes, just ths top, it has a kind of dull tip lik it cld really do damage if it were misused, it just has the general characteristics of a weapon

Do   Fu   Sc

9.   U kno, ths cntr prt cld be a rivr or a road, far away, as if u were stdg on a mt or s.t. lookg down at it

S: Well, u hav to stretch u'r immag to c the next one, r u ready?
E: Go rite ahead
S: Well, it's just a straight line, as a road or river but its so small u'd hav to be far away to c it lik ths, c rite here (points)

Do   FDo   Ls

VII

10.   2 wm arguing @ s.t. w e.o., u just c their heads, it ll thy r disagreeg @ s.t.

E: (Rpts S's resp)
S: Yes, just the head parts, mayb thy r the one's I saw earlier who were fitg ovr the basket of precious stuff, u

D+   M^{a}o   (2)   Hd   P   3.0   AG, PSV

Protocol #5 (Continued)

Card	Free Association	Inquiry	Scoring
	<11. If u turn it ths way it cld b a scottie dog w his flat snout & stubby legs here	can c the facial features rather distinctly, especially the lips here, & ths wld b a hair piece of s.s. E: (Rpts S's resp) S: Its a good liknss to one, ths is the tail & the snout & the funny littl legs	Do Fo A
VIII	12. There's a rib cage here, at the cntr	E: (Rpts S's resp) S: Its here (points), it has a pretty good formation lik a rib cage has	Do Fo An
	13. The W thg seems to be s.s. of anatomy chart but I can't identify the specific prts, oh!, bettr still, it cld b internal viscera & ths bttm prt cld b s.s. of internal wound, it has a bloody mass effect there	E: (Rpts S's resp) S: Well not really a chart of An, it looks much more like the visceral organs & ths orag-pink prt here ll a wound, the organs r not clerly delineatd but it could b, the colorg is so strkg parr ticulry the effect of the wound but the other parts r also colord much like the visceral organs might b	Wv CFo An, Bl MOR
IX	14. The orange ll 2 witches hovrg ovr a cauldron lik they r argug @ wht to mix in it, thy hav peakd hats on	E: (Rpts S's resp) S: Rite here (points) thy r pointg to the cauldron here in the middle, I can't say what's goig on but thy r apparrently arguing about what mixture shld go in it	Dd+ Maₒ (2) (H), Id,Cg 2.5 AG
	15. U kno, ths cntr prt cld b a glass candl holder w a candle in it, lik u can c thru it	E: (Rpts S's resp) S: Well its rite here where the cauldron is except that it goes down further than the cauldron & u can c the candle inside it, u see thgs lik that in res-	DS+ mP.FVo Id 5.0

X

X

16. 2 A's tryg to do s.t. to ths pole lik thg, mayb thyr tryg to capture it or mayb thyr tryg to climb up it or mayb thyr not sure what to do w it

turants some times, it has a milky colrg about it as if the candle was givg off lite

E: (Rpts S's resp)

S: Thy just look confused @ ths thg, thy r unknwn creatures w little legs & antennae, almst no legs at all, I can't decide what ths is, mayb its s.s. of food & thy r arguing about when to eat it, its difficult to decide

D+ FMᵃₒ (2) (A) 4.0

17. Ths cld b a seed fr a tree, a maple tree I believe, I'm not sure but there is s.s. of tree that has seeds shaped like ths & they turn brown after thy fall

S: The seed is easier to decrib, u c it is rite here (points) & its brwn as if it were ready for plantg or whatever when they fall so as to start a new tree

Do FCo Bt MOR

503

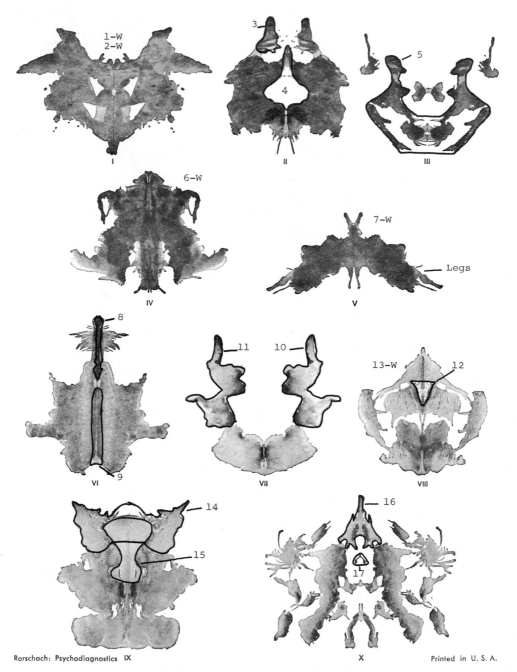

Figure 21. Location Selections for Protocol 5.

504

Table 44. Structural Summary—Protocol #5

```
===============================================================================
R = 17      Zf = 11     ZSum = 37.0     P = 3      (2) = 7     Fr+rF = 0
```

LOCATION FEATURES	DETERMINANTS		CONTENTS	S-CONSTELLATION (ADULT)

LOCATION FEATURES	BLENDS	SINGLE	CONTENTS	S-CONSTELLATION (ADULT)
			H = 3, 0	NO..FV+VF+V+FD>2
W = 5	M.FC'	M = 4	(H) = 1, 1	NO..Col-Shd Bl>0
(Wv = 1)	m.FV	FM = 2	Hd = 1, 0	NO..Ego<.31,>.44
D = 11		m = 0	(Hd)= 0, 0	NO..MOR > 3
Dd = 1		C = 0	A = 2, 0	NO..Zd > +- 3.5
S = 2		Cn = 0	(A) = 1, 0	YES..es > EA
		CF = 1	Ad = 0, 0	NO..CF+C+Cn > FC
DQ		FC = 1	(Ad)= 0, 0	NO..X+ < .70
........(FQ-)		C' = 0	Ab = 0, 0	NO..S > 3
		C'F = 0	Al = 0, 0	NO..P < 3 or > 8
+ = 9 (0)		FC'= 1	An = 2, 0	NO..Pure H < 2
v/+ = 0 (0)		T = 0	Art = 0, 0	NO..R < 17
o = 7 (0)		TF = 0	Ay = 0, 0	1.....TOTAL
v = 1 (0)		FT = 0	Bl = 0, 1	
		V = 0	Bt = 1, 0	SPECIAL SCORINGS
		VF = 0	Cg = 0, 1	DV = 0
		FV = 0	Cl = 0, 0	INCOM = 0
		Y = 0	Ex = 0, 0	DR = 0
		YF = 0	Fi = 0, 0	FABCOM = 0
FORM QUALITY		FY = 2	Fd = 0, 0	ALOG = 0
		rF = 0	Ge = 0, 0	CONTAM = 0
FQx FQf M Qual.		Fr = 0	Hh = 0, 0	--- WSUM6 = 0
		FD = 1	Ls = 1, 0	AG = 5
+ = 0 + = 0 + = 0		F = 3	Na = 0, 0	CONFAB = 0
o = 15 o = 2 o = 5			Sc = 1, 0	CP = 0
u = 2 u = 1 u = 0			Sx = 0, 0	MOR = 3
- = 0 - = 0 - = 0			Xy = 2, 0	PER = 1
none= 0 none= 0			Idio= 2, 2	PSV = 1

```
===============================================================================
```

RATIOS, PERCENTAGES, AND DERIVATIONS

```
ZSum-Zest = 37.0 - 34.5       FC:CF+C  = 1: 1    W:M       = 5: 5
                                 (Pure C =  0)
Zd        =   2.5                                W:D       = 5:11
                              Afr      = 0.55
.----------------------.                         Isolate:R =  2:17
:EB =  5: 1.5   EA = 6.5:     3r+(2)/R = 0.41
:                   >D=  0                        Ab+Art    =  0
:eb =  3: 5     es = 8  :     L        = 0.21
'----------------------'                          An+Xy     =  4
(FM= 2 " C'= 2 T= 0) (Adj D=  0)  Blends:R =  2:17
(m = 1 " V = 1 Y= 2)                              H(H):Hd(Hd)=  4: 1
                              X+%      = 0.88        (Pure H =  3)
a:p       =  6: 2               (F+%    = 0.67)   (HHd):(AAd) =  1: 1
                              X-%      = 0.00
Ma:Mp     =  4: 1                                H+A:Hd+Ad =  7: 1
-------------------------------------------------------------------------------
        SCZI = 0          DEPI = 1             S-CON = 1
===============================================================================
(C)1976,1983 BY JOHN E. EXNER, JR.
```

505

Table 45.   Scoring Sequence—Protocol #5

```
================================================================================
CARD NO. LOC.  #     DETERMINANT(S)   (2) CONTENT(S) POP  Z    SPECIAL SCORES
================================================================================
  I    1 W+    1 Ma.FC'o          2 H,(H)           4.0  AG,MOR
       2 Wo    1 FYo                Xy              1.0
 II    3 D+    2 FMau             2 A               5.5  AG
       4 DS+   5 FC'o               Id              4.5
III    5 D+    1 Mao              2 H,Id         P  3.0  AG
 IV    6 Wo    1 FYo                Xy              2.0
  V    7 W+    1 Mpo              2 H               2.5  PER
 VI    8 Do    2 Fu                 Sc
       9 Do   12 FDo                Ls
VII   10 D+    2 Mao              2 Hd           P  3.0  AG,PSV
      11 Do    2 Fo                 A
VIII  12 Do    3 Fo                 An
      13 Wv    1 CFo                An,Bl              MOR
 IX   14 Dd+  99 Mao              2 (H),Id,Cg    P  2.5  AG
      15 DS+   8 mp.FVo             Id              5.0
  X   16 D+   11 FMao             2 (A)             4.0
      17 Do    3 FCo                Bt                 MOR
================================================================================
```
(C)1976, 1983 BY JOHN E. EXNER, JR.
   ABBREVIATIONS USED ABOVE:
      FOR DQ: "/" = "v/+"; FOR CONTENTS: "Id" = "IDIOGRAPHIC CONTENT"
      SPECIAL SCORES: "INC" = "INCOM", "FAB" = "FABCOM", "CON" = "CONTAM"
              "CFB" = "CONFAB"

STRUCTURAL INTERPRETATION

None of the Special Indices contains elevated scores. Both *D* scores are 0, indicating that, ordinarily, she has sufficient resources available to draw on in forming and directing behaviors when demands for coping occur. Her tolerance for stress should be reasonably good, and ill-formed, or impulsive-like activities are not likely to occur unless she is in unusual stress situations. The higher right side value in the *eb* does indicate that she is in some form of distress, probably signaling some of the anxiety and/or apprehension that she is reporting. Interestingly, however, the sum of the achromatic and shading variables, 5, is not inordinately high. The record does contain two *Y* responses, suggesting some situationally related irritation, and two *C'* answers, indicating that some of the distress is being provoked by the internalization of feelings, but this does not necessarily seem excessive. There is also 1 Vista response. It is possible that the psychological process related to the Vista answer is creating much of the irritation. It signals the presence of some painful focusing on liabilities. This finding argues in favor of a review of data concerning the self and others before continuing with a more standard scan of other structural features.

The Egocentricity Index of .41 is within normal limits and gives no hint that she may be focusing to excess either on herself or her world. Conversely, there are three *MOR* answers in the record, indicating that her self-image may be more negative than positive, that it may include some sense of damage, and that some of her thinking will be marked by more pessimism than should be the case. There is also a substantial elevation in the $An + Xy$ cluster, which indicates a very substantial body concern. It is possible that this could be a by-product of her long ulcer history; however, because she has been free of physical symptoms for a considerable period, alternative postulates must also be considered. Usually, when elevations in $An + Xy$ appear in the records of subjects who do not have obvious physical problems, it signifies an unusual preoccupation which can have some properties that are obsessive, or even delusional. It would be premature to draw that conclusion at this point, but it is an important consideration as other data are brought into focus. The record is *T-less,* indicating that she does not experience her own needs for closeness in ways that are common and, as a result, she tends to be somewhat more guarded and distant in her interpersonal relations, and more concerned than most people about issues of personal space. There are five human contents in the protocol, which is about average for an adult, and three of the five are *Pure H*. Thus she seems quite interested in people, and apparently her conceptions of them are based in experience.

On the other hand, there are five *AG* responses, suggesting that she perceives relations between people as often marked by aggression, and that she has incorporated some of these features as a part of her own interpersonal style. The composite of her somewhat aggressive orientation in relating to others, plus her more guarded approach to them, could easily lead people to maintain more superficial contacts with her, or even avoid contact when possible. If this postulate is valid, it leads to the speculation that she may have become more negatively introspective because of the lack of a satisfying, or at least conventional social life. The data concerning her perceptual operations can add more to this.

Her $X + \%$ of 88% is substantial, but still within normal limits. There are no minus responses in the record, and *only* three *Popular* responses. This suggests that most of her behaviors are quite conventional, but that in some instances, when responses should seem obvious, she tends to take a different approach. The data concerning her other cognitive operations are not very remarkable, but do suggest that she may be an overly conservative person. The *Zf* reveals that she organizes 11 of her 17 answers, and the *Zd* score of $+2.5$ indicates that she does so efficiently. The *W:D* ratio of 5:11 shows that she is reasonably economical, even though the low *Lambda* of .21 indicates that she does not back away from complexity and, in fact, is probably overly involved with it. There are nine *DQ +* responses, pointing to a relatively sophisticated effort; however, the *W:M* of 5:5 reveals that she does not set high goals for herself in light of her functional capabilities. To the contrary, she appears very conservative in this respect.

The *EB* of 5:1.5 portrays an introversive style. She prefers to delay before making responses to afford time to think about the variety of alternative responses that might be available in a situation. The form quality distribution of her *M* answers shows that they are all conventional, and there are no Critical Special Scores. Thus the likelihood of a delusional system is extremely remote, but this does not rule out the possibility of an obsessive-like preoccupation. The *a:p* ratio of 6:2 suggests some inflexibility in her thinking and attitudes, but nothing approaching a pathological magnitude. The *FC:CF + C* ratio of 1:1 indicates that she does not always modulate affective displays carefully, but when studied in terms of the low numbers in the ratio, plus the fact that she is introversive, this does not seem to be a significant finding. The *Afr* of .55 signals that she is open to emotional stimuli, and as willing to process them as most people. The record also contains a *PSV* response. If it is a Within Card *PSV*, it could be an important finding, because it might indicate a problem in shifting sets. That finding seems unlikely in light of the sophisticated level of cognition that is apparent. Conversely, if it is an Across Card *PSV,* it may be revealing of some preoccupation.

ANALYSIS OF THE SCORING SEQUENCE

She uses a *D* approach except to three of the solid blots—I, IV, and V—to which she gives only *W* answers. This illustrates her economical and conservative approach to goal setting. At the same time, she enters seven of the 10 cards by giving a synthesis response, showing that, in spite of her conservatism, her cognitive operations remain quite sophisticated. This is also reflected by the fact that she actively organizes in eight of the 10 cards. Her *Popular* responses all involve human contents, and all three involve *M* determinants that include aggressive characteristics. Thus although the object reported involves a very conventional identification, a human, the projections concerning those objects are quite atypical. The *P* failures also may be important. Usually, if a subject gives a low frequency of *Popular* answers, they do give those that have the highest frequency of occurrence, that is, including VIII and V, and either I or VI. She did not give any of those, even though she gave two answers to three of those four blots. This seems to reaffirm the postulate that, although she does translate perceptual inputs in ways that are conventional, she often avoids the obvious in favor of some more idiographic decision. This may be especially important concerning Card VIII, to which she gave two answers, both involving anatomy contents, while failing to identify the Popular animals. The *PSV* answer is the first response to Card VII; thus it must be an Across Card *PSV,* and could be revealing of a preoccupation.

ANALYSIS OF THE RESPONSES

The responses are very rich in idiographic descriptions. Many are unusually long, involving almost meticulous elaborations or embellishments, and obviously containing considerable projected material. Several clearly involve conflict, such as is illustrated in the very first answer, "Two women, probably witches, dancing around . . . a person, quite helpless . . ." This seems to convey a value conflict, witches typically being magical and possibly evil, dancing around the helpless women. It is followed by the first of her two *Xy* responses, an x-ray of a pelvis. It is important to raise the question of whether the undue emphasis on *An* and *Xy* responses could be occupation related. Usually, this is *not* the case. Nonpatient physicians, nurses, and other medical workers do not give significantly more of these kinds of answers, especially x-ray responses. An x-ray is an exposure that permits the viewer to see through and often can imply a sense of vulnerability. Her second x-ray response, and her only answer to Card IV is also of the pelvic area, making it impossible to avoid speculation about sexual concerns, or at least sex role identity. Her first anatomy response to Card VIII is of a rib cage, and does not appear to have an obvious relation to the x-ray answers; however, the second anatomy answer to the same blot seems quite revealing if a symbolic translation is valid. She begins by describing an anatomy chart, but then alters the answer, ". . . oh! Better still, it could be internal viscera and this bottom part could be some sort of internal wound, it has a bloody mass effect there." The uniqueness of the answer and the way it developed seem also to offer a strong hint about sexual issues.

Her first response to Card II, hens preparing to fight, is also followed by an answer that is symbolically tempting, a temple of worship with a tower of silver or platinum. The internal conflict is again represented by her response to Card III, two women fighting over something valuable. Her answer to Card V, two women leaning against something, is intriguing because of the elaboration "I think they are women, almost but not quite resting back to back . . . . ." Close relationships are usually not back to back. It is an avoidant position that seems emphasized by her comment, *almost but not quite*. Her first response to Card VI can also be addressed symbolically because of the embellishment. The first is a weapon, described as something, "you would thrust at someone . . . something you would use to hurt or maim, or kill." It is followed by an answer in which she distances herself from the object, a river or road, "as if you were standing on a mountain or something looking down at it." Her first answer to Card VII is the *PSV* answer, two women arguing, whom she later identifies in the Inquiry as the same ones that she reported on Card III are fighting over something valuable. This theme seems repeated by her first answer to Card IX, two witches arguing about what to mix in a cauldron, which is followed by another answer, her Vista response, that may have considerable significance. It is a glass candle holder with a candle in it. Similar to the x-ray and anatomy answers it is a "see through" response, suggesting exposure and vulnerability. Also, the possible symbolism of the objects cannot be ignored easily. Her first answer to Card X is also embellished, "two animals trying to do something to this pole like thing, maybe they are trying to capture it . . ." Her last answer, a maple seed, is intriguing because of the underlying suggestion, ". . . they turn brown after they fall," implying that they either die or take root.

ANALYSIS OF THE INQUIRY

The Inquiry material is also quite rich in elaboration, and reemphasizes much of the conflict noted earlier. In the first answer she notes, "I can't tell if it's a ritual or if they are burning her at the stake. . . ." In the seemingly symbolic response 4, she says, "it's the metal part that really attracts people to the temple because it's so valuable." In answer 5 she adds, "it must be full of goodies because each wants it for her own, but neither seems able to get it." She defends against elaboration of her answer to Card V, people leaning against something, by personalizing the explanation. The first answer to Card VI is also elaborated in an intriguing way, ". . . it could really do damage if it were misused . . ." In response 13 she stresses the coloring, "particularly the effect of the wound . . . ." The animals in response 16 are described as, "They just looked confused about this thing . . . maybe it's some sort of food and they are arguing about when to eat it . . . ." Her last answer may be one of the most important. As implied in the original response, the seed might live or die, which she seems to reaffirm "as if it were ready for planting or whatever . . . ."

SUMMARY OF PROTOCOL 5

It is unfortunate that she was reluctant to offer a more detailed history about her interpersonal relationships, and especially her sex history in the pretest interview, because that information is crucial to any attempts to bring closure to the findings from the test. There is no question that she is in distress, and that much of that distress seems to have evolved from her perception of herself and her relationships in the world. Her capacity for control seems adequate and her tolerance for stress sufficient to meet most of the demands of everyday living. She appears to have a well-developed coping preference with which she will usually delay responses until she can give consideration to alternatives. Her thinking is clear and somewhat flexible, although she does have a marked preoccupation that probably has to do with sexuality. Her perceptual accuracy is very conventional; however, it would be erroneous to describe her as committed to conformity. Often she also seems to express uniqueness by avoiding obvious conforming situations. Her cognitive operations are quite sophisticated, although she may be too economical at times, and probably overly conservative in setting goals. She seems to be able to handle her affect appropriately, and is as willing to process emotionally toned stimuli as most adults.

The key to her problem appears to lie in her perception of herself and her relations with people. Her self-image is much more negative than should be the case, and it seems clear that she often approaches interpersonal exchange with more aggressiveness than is common for most adults. She perceives the world as an aggressive and confusing place, and obviously is raising many questions about her role in it. Those questions appear to have evolved because she is preoccupied with her own identity. She seems to have some unresolved intrigue with sexuality that continues to pose conflicts for her. Her vagueness in the interview about her sexual history raises more questions than can be answered here. She may be sensing the fact that her emotional isolation is atypical and, as such, disconcerting. She may have experienced a series of disappointments in her social-emotional relationships. She may be a virgin who is struggling about that issue, or she may find herself dissatisfied with the conventional feminine role that she has attempted to play. A much more detailed history is required before any of these can be answered. It is reasonable to speculate that her ulcer was related to one or more of these issues, and that resolution of that problem may have, in some way, removed a defense on which she often relied. The panic attacks that she describes are quite real, and can be expected to continue and probably increase in frequency until the issues of intrapersonal and interpersonal roles can be addressed through some uncovering form of intervention.

Author Index

Abel, T.M., 303, 309
Abrahamsen, D., 336
Abrams, E., 327, 344, 356, 366, 368
Abrams, R., 417, 428
Abramson, L.S., 30, 53, 334, 351
Adler, D., 425
Ainsworth, M.D., 12, 25, 89, 135, 152, 349, 389, 409
Alinsky, D., 46, 56
Allee, R., 327, 350
Allen, R.M., 332, 345
Allerhand, M.E., 338, 345
Allison, J., 357, 387
Altus, W.D., 327, 336, 345
Ames, L.B., 30, 53, 313, 327, 332, 345, 357, 364, 366, 386, 401, 407
Amick, J., 341, 350
Applebaum, S., 385, 386, 412, 425
Arluck, E., 313, 345
Armbruster, G.L., 31, 41, 45, 50, 53, 54, 317, 318, 324, 332, 345, 346, 347, 360, 364, 373, 378, 379, 388, 408
Arnold, J., 352
Astrachan, B., 425
Atkinson, J., 350

Baileck, I., 303, 309
Baker, G., 328, 349
Baker, L., 367, 386
Baker, W., 396, 399, 410
Bandura, A., 381, 386
Bard, M., 319, 352
Barrera, S., 313, 349
Bartko, J.J., 416, 417, 426
Bash, K.W., 321, 323, 345
Bauer, L., 425
Baughman, E.E., 64, 73, 78, 79, 122, 134, 332, 341, 345, 348, 364, 379, 387
Beck, A.G., 30, 53, 345, 387, 408
Beck, S.J., 11, 12, 18, 24, 29, 30, 54, 62, 79, 82, 84, 89, 93, 95, 98, 103, 106, 119, 134, 137, 138, 141, 142, 146, 151, 153, 154, 157, 160, 303, 309, 313, 318, 321, 328, 332, 341, 342, 345, 351, 356, 357, 364, 366, 367, 370, 381, 385, 387, 390, 398, 402, 403, 405, 408, 417, 425

Becker, W.C., 355, 387
Belleza, T., 427
Belmont, L., 357, 366, 389
Bendick, M.R., 328, 345
Benjamin, J.D., 303, 309
Berger, D., 319, 345, 386
Beri, J., 328, 345
Berkowitz, M., 366, 387
Berryman, E., 366, 387
Binder, H., 7, 10, 24, 116, 119, 134, 318, 345
Binet, A., 3, 24
Blacker, E., 328, 345
Blake, R., 142, 152
Blatt, S.J., 141, 151, 325, 345, 357, 387, 417, 425
Bleuler, E., 417, 425
Bleuler, M., 416, 425
Bloom, B.S., 61, 81, 157, 160
Bochner, R., 431, 442
Bourguinon, E.E., 364, 387
Bowers, M., 416, 425
Bradway, K., 341, 345
Brawer, F., 12, 25
Breecher, S., 338, 345
Brennan, M., 332, 346
Bresnoban, T.J., 346
Brick, H., 349
Bricklin, B., 328, 351, 402, 409
Brockway, A.L., 403, 408
Brosin, H.W., 303, 309
Brown, B.S., 396, 410, 428
Brown, M., 338, 346
Browne, C.G., 15, 25
Brubaker, R., 146, 151
Bryant, E.L., 50, 54, 335, 338, 347, 360, 371, 387, 388, 394, 401, 408, 409
Buchsmaum, S., 426
Buhler, C., 313, 319, 341, 346
Buker, 322, 352

Caldwell, B.L., 366, 387
Calvin, A.D., 349
Campo, V., 116, 120, 135, 318, 346
Cannavo, F., 336, 347, 378, 388
Caraway, E.W., 360, 388
Carp, A.L., 64, 79

Carpenter, W.T., 416, 417, 426, 427
Cass, W.A., 367, 387, 403, 408
Caston, J., 328, 346
Cattell, R.B., 28, 53
Chakie, F.R., 346
Chambers, J.S., 303, 309
Chesrow, E.J., 366, 387
Chu, A.Y., 326, 339, 346, 347
Clapp, H., 303, 309
Clark, R., 350
Cleveland, S.E., 396, 409, 431, 442
Clore, J.L., 17, 26
Coan, R., 338, 346
Cocking, R.R., 327, 346
Coffin, T.E., 30, 54, 63, 79
Cohen, J.B., 30, 45, 5,1, 54, 320, 347, 365, 390
Coleman, J., 431, 443
Coleman, M., 409
Colligan, S.C., 39, 54
Collyer, Y.M., 352
Colson, D.B., 386
Cooper, L., 328, 346
Cooper, W.H., 50, 54, 318, 320, 335, 347, 408
Corrigan, H., 345
Cotte, S., 359, 391
Counts, R.M., 381, 387
Cox, F.M., 64, 79, 319, 346
Cronbach, L.J., 83, 89, 301, 309
Crumpton, E.E., 331, 346
Cummings, S.T., 304, 309

Dahlstrom, L.E., 41, 54
Dahlstrom, W.G., 41, 54
Dana, J.M., 327, 346
Dana, R.H., 327, 346
Daston, P.G., 386
Davidson, H.H., 146, 152, 153, 160, 366, 387
Dearborn, G., 4, 24
de de Santos, D.R., 116, 120, 135
Devine, D., 27, 56, 442
Dinoff, M., 31, 54
Dixon, W.J., 417, 427
Draguns, J.G., 398, 402, 405, 408
Dubrovner, R.J., 30, 54, 332, 346
Dudek, S.Z., 327, 346
Duszynski, K.R., 396, 410, 428

Ebaugh, F.G., 303, 309
Eichler, R.M., 319, 346
Elizur, A., 431, 442
Ellenberger, H., 4, 6, 24, 118, 135
Elstein, A.S., 319, 346
Endicott, J.E., 417, 421, 427
Erginel, A., 321, 346
Eron, L., 3, 26, 89
Evans, R.B., 328, 346
Exner, D.E., 20, 24, 92, 98, 442

Exner, J.E., 14, 18, 20, 24, 29–31, 35, 37–39,
    41–43, 45–47, 50, 51, 54–56, 61, 62, 64, 66,
    69, 73, 79, 82, 89, 91, 95, 98, 101, 106, 122,
    129, 131, 135, 142, 150, 161, 168, 169, 307,
    309, 313–315, 317, 318, 320–329, 331–336,
    338–348, 350, 352, 353, 355, 357, 359–361,
    364–368, 370–374, 376, 378–380, 382,
    384–388, 390–401, 403–410, 412, 414,
    417–424, 426, 442

Farber, J., 406, 407, 408, 409
Farberow, N., 411, 426, 427
Faterson, H.F., 353
Feighner, J., 417, 426
Feirstein, A., 325, 345
Feldman, M.J., 367, 388
Finney, B.C., 378, 388, 391
Fisher, D.F., 35, 55
Fisher, R.L., 319, 348
Fisher, S., 396, 409, 431, 442
Fishman, R., 408
Fiske, D.W., 60, 80, 341, 348
Fister, W.P., 322, 351
Fleischer, M.S., 396, 409, 412, 426
Fonda, C., 142, 152, 328, 352, 381, 389
Ford, M., 44, 55, 332, 348
Forsyth, R.P., 331, 348
Fosberg, I.A., 64, 79
Foster, J.M., 65, 80
Frank, A., 426, 427
Frank, I.H., 357, 389
Frank, L.K., 15, 24, 55, 309, 431, 442
Frankle, A.H., 328, 348
Freud, S., 15, 24
Fried, E., 366, 390
Fried, R., 159, 160, 364, 389
Friedman, H., 84, 89, 95, 98, 355, 357, 359, 366,
    389
Frosch, J., 426

Gage, N.L., 60, 79
Gardner, R.W., 378, 389
George, L.M., 64, 79
Gibby, R.G., 30, 55, 64, 73, 79, 328, 348, 366,
    389
Giedt, F.H., 60, 80
Gill, H.S., 328, 351, 378, 389
Gill, M., 26, 60, 80, 89, 99, 135, 152, 160, 390,
    405, 409, 427
Gillespie, R., 322, 327, 333, 347, 365, 388
Glaser, N.M., 403, 409
Glass, H., 327, 349
Gleser, G.C., 301, 309, 408
Goetcheus, G., 30, 55
Goldberg, S.C., 426
Goldberger, L., 319, 348, 367, 389
Goldfarb, W., 322, 348, 431, 442

Goldfried, M.R., 160, 319, 348, 411, 426, 431, 442
Goldman, A.E., 367, 391
Goldman, G.D., 328, 352
Goldman, R., 313, 348, 402, 409
Goldstein, K., 319
Goldstein, M., 416, 427
Goodenough, D.R., 353
Goodman, N.L., 42, 55, 65, 80
Goodstein, L.D., 348
Gordon, L.B., 424, 426
Gough, H.G., 17, 24
Grant, M.Q., 304, 309
Grayson, H.M., 331, 348
Greaves, S.T., 31, 55
Greenberg, T.D., 386
Grisso, J.T., 61, 80
Gross, L., 31, 55
Grosz, H.J., 319, 350
Guirdham, A., 328, 348
Gunderson, J.G., 417, 426, 427
Gurrslin, C., 388
Guze, S., 426

Haan, N., 336, 348
Hafner, A.J., 313, 348
Haier, R., 417, 426
Haley, E.M., 398, 402, 405, 408
Hall, K., 427
Haller, N., 50, 55, 64, 80
Hallowell, A.I., 364, 389
Halpern, F., 27, 55, 329, 332, 348, 402, 409, 431, 442
Hamlin, R.M., 303, 304, 309
Hammer, E.F., 370, 389
Hark, L.J., 61, 62, 79
Harrington, R.L., 348
Harris, J.G., 367, 386
Harrow, M., 425
Harrower, M.R., 29, 56, 60, 80
Henri, V., 3, 24
Henry, E.M., 313, 349
Herman, J., 322, 328, 252
Herron, E.W., 83, 89
Hersen, M., 31, 55
Hersh, C., 327, 349
Hertz, M.R., 12, 24, 25, 44, 55, 62, 80, 82, 84, 89, 91, 98, 103, 119, 135, 141, 142, 146, 151, 154, 160, 304, 309, 338, 349, 364, 389, 412, 426
Hertzman, M., 328, 349
Hillman, L.B., 51, 54, 400, 403, 408
Hirschstein, R., 431, 442
Hochberg, J., 35, 55
Hogarty, G.E., 417, 426
Holt, R.R., 12, 17, 18, 25, 61, 80, 89, 135, 152, 302, 309, 349, 389, 409, 431, 442
Holtzman, P.S., 385, 386, 412, 425

Holtzman, W.H., 83, 89, 319, 349
Holzberg, J.D., 45, 47, 55, 357, 366, 389
Honigmann, J.J., 364, 389
Hoover, T.O., 327, 353
Hopkins, H.K., 427
Horiuchi, H., 38, 55
Hutt, M., 30, 55

Ingram, R., 146, 151
Iscoe, I., 349
Ives, V., 304, 309
Izner, S.M., 334, 353

Jablensky, A., 416, 427
Jacks, I., 370, 389
Jackson, C.W., 20, 25
Jacobsen, B., 427
Jensen, A.R., 325
Jensen, D., 443
Jolles, I., 142, 151
Jones, A.M., 328, 351
Joseph, A., 364, 389
Jost, H.A., 30, 54, 346
Jung, C.G., 15, 25

Kadinsky, D., 359, 389
Kahn, M.W., 328, 352, 369, 389
Kallstedt, F.E., 327, 338, 349
Kaplan, A.H., 309
Kaplan, M.L., 388
Karp, S.A., 353
Kates, S.L., 319, 352
Katz, H., 426
Kazaoka, K., 372, 388, 404, 408, 409
Keehn, J.D., 331, 349
Keith, S.J., 417, 426
Kelley, D.M., 12, 25, 29, 30, 55, 62, 78, 89, 135, 152, 160, 313, 332, 341, 342, 349, 366, 390, 405, 409
Kelly, E.L., 60, 80
Kemalof, S., 321, 349
Kennard, M.A., 322, 351
Kerner, J., 425
Kerr, M., 364, 389
Kety, S.S., 416, 426, 427
Khouri, P., 416, 427
Kinder, B., 146, 151
King, G.F., 328, 349
King, S., 317, 350
Kirkner, F., 328, 349
Kirkpatrick, E.A., 4, 25
Kisker, G.W., 367, 389
Klatskin, E.H., 331, 349
Klebanoff, S.G., 319, 349, 359, 389
Klein, D.F., 417, 427
Klein, G.S., 349
Kline, J.R., 328, 343, 348, 360, 387
Klingensmith, S.W., 73, 80

Klopfer, B., 11, 12, 18, 25, 29, 30, 55, 62, 78, 80,
    82, 89, 103, 104, 116, 119, 135, 136, 137, 146,
    151, 152, 153, 160, 303, 310, 313, 319, 322,
    328, 332, 333, 338, 340, 341, 342, 349, 366,
    381, 389, 390, 402, 405, 409
Klopfer, W.G., 12, 25, 89, 135, 152, 328, 341,
    345, 349, 389, 409
Kluckhohn, S., 304, 309
Kluckholm, C., 364, 390
Knapp, P., 426, 427
Knopf, I.J., 366, 390
Korchin, S.J., 366, 390
Korman, A.K., 18, 25
Kostlan, A.A., 60, 80
Kropp, R., 142, 152
Kruglov, I., 366, 387
Krugman, J., 304, 309
Kubovey, M., 35, 56
Kuhn, B., 408

Larsen, R.M., 16, 25
Latesta, P., 350
Learned, J., 30, 53, 345, 386
Lebo, D., 319, 349
LeFever, A., 313, 319, 341, 346
Leighton, D., 364, 390
Leiser, R., 334, 353
Lerner, B., 327, 349
Leura, A.V., 41, 42, 43, 54, 55, 56, 64, 79, 334,
    339, 340, 347, 348, 349, 360, 388
Leventrosser, C., 339, 347
Levin, M.M., 75, 80
Levine, M., 327, 328, 349, 350, 366, 387
Levitt, E.E., 30, 53, 134, 151, 319, 345, 350,
    387, 408
Levy, E., 431, 442
Levy, L., 300, 309
Levy, M.R., 306, 310
Lewis, N.D.C., 417, 427
Liberman, R., 416, 427
Light, B.H., 341, 350
Lindner, R.M., 412, 427, 431, 442
Lindsey, G., 17, 25
Linton, H.B., 332, 350
Lion, E., 345
Lipton, M.B., 329, 350
Lisansky, E.S., 304, 310
Little, K.B., 304, 310
London, H., 45, 55
Lossli-Usteri, M., 70, 80
Lord, E., 63, 80
Lotesta, P., 329
Lotsoff, E., 357, 390
Louttit, C.M., 15, 25
Loveland, N.T., 327, 350
Lowell, E., 350
Lubin, B., 16, 25

Luborsky, L., 61, 80
Ludwig, A., 416, 428

McArthur, C.C., 317, 350
McCandless, B.B., 357, 390
McClelland, D.C., 335, 350
McCoy, R., 396, 408
McFate, M.Q., 338, 350
MacKinnon, D.W., 61, 80
McMichael, A., 351, 390
McReynolds, P., 367, 387, 403, 408
Magnussen, M.G., 31, 55
Majumber, A.K., 317, 350
Mann, L., 332, 345, 350
Margulies, H., 313, 332, 349
Marmorston, J., 328, 346
Martin, H., 412, 427
Martin, L.S., 30, 37, 40, 54, 55, 325, 339, 341,
    347, 396, 397, 408
Marwit, S.J., 65, 81
Masling, J., 64, 80
Mason, B., 46, 51, 54, 313, 317, 322, 324, 327,
    339, 341, 350, 357, 365, 366, 368, 384, 388,
    390, 396, 397, 408, 418, 426
Matarazzo, J.D., 16, 25, 30, 55, 307, 310
Matranga, J., 443
May, P.R.A., 417, 427
Mayman, M., 146, 147, 151, 152
Meadow, A., 61, 80
Meehl, P.E., 17, 25, 306, 310
Meer, B., 27, 30, 56, 431, 442
Meichenbaum, D., 390
Meli-Dworetzki, G., 95, 98
Meltzer, H., 350, 416
Meltzoff, J., 327, 328, 349, 352
Mensh, I.N., 30, 55, 381, 387
Metraux, R., 30, 53, 345, 386, 406
Meyer, B.T., 332, 350
Meyer, M.M., 12, 25
Miale, F.R., 29, 56, 116, 135, 309
Miller, A.S., 53, 318, 335, 345, 347, 401, 408
Miller, D.R., 64, 79
Milton, E.O., 30, 55
Mindness, A., 322, 350
Mirin, B., 328, 350, 370, 390
Mittman, B.L., 31, 41, 45, 54
Molish, H.B., 30, 53, 89, 134, 142, 151, 152,
    318, 322, 328, 345, 350, 366, 381, 387, 390,
    402, 403, 408, 409, 431, 442
Monroe, R.L., 304, 310
Montalto, F.D., 338, 350
Moreland, K.L., 306, 310
Monty, R.A., 35, 55
Morgan, C., 15, 25
Morris, H., 404, 408
Morris, W.W., 402, 409
Mosher, L.R., 426

Mukerji, K., 392, 409
Munoz, R., 426
Murillo, L.G., 313, 314, 325, 336, 347, 359, 367, 378, 388, 390, 394, 398, 408, 417, 426
Murray, H.A., 13, 15, 25, 26, 27, 56
Murray, V.F., 364, 389

Neel, F.A., 317, 350
Neff, W.S., 403, 409
Neisser, U., 35, 56
Nett, E.W., 364, 387
Newton, R., 304, 309, 310

Oaks, G., 417, 427
Oberholzer, E., 135, 304, 310
Ogden, D.P., 327, 350
Orange, A., 44, 56
Orlansky, D., 328, 349
Orlinsky, D.E., 327, 350
Orr, F.G., 338, 350

Page, H.A., 327, 351
Paine, C., 16, 25
Palmer, J.O., 304, 310, 327, 351
Papania, N., 351, 390
Parrill, T., 334, 348
Parsons, C.J., 4, 26
Pascal, G., 27, 56, 431, 442
Paulsen, A., 313, 327, 351, 366, 390
Pearl, D., 386
Perlman, J., 332, 351
Peters, B., 346
Peterson, L.C., 64, 80
Phares, E.J., 64, 80
Phillips, L., 27, 56, 328, 351, 398, 402, 405, 408, 431, 443
Piaget, J., 95, 98
Pierce, G.E., 339, 351
Piotrowski, Z., 13, 26, 29, 56, 60, 62, 80, 82, 89, 103, 104, 105, 106, 114, 119, 135, 146, 154, 159, 160, 168, 169, 303, 310, 317, 321, 326, 328, 331, 334, 336, 340, 351, 367, 370, 381, 383, 390, 402, 404, 405, 409, 412, 417, 427
Pomerantz, J.R., 35, 56
Poser, E.G., 346
Potanin, N., 338, 351
Pottharst, K., 30, 55
Prados, M., 366, 390
Prandoni, J., 431, 443
Pyle, W.H., 4, 26

Rabin, A. I., 30, 56, 313, 332, 351, 359, 390, 408, 431, 442
Rabinovitch, M.S., 322, 351
Rabinovitch, S., 341, 351
Rafferty, J.E., 16, 26
Rapaport, D., 14, 26, 60, 73, 80, 82, 84, 89, 95, 99, 104, 119, 135, 146, 154, 157, 160, 161, 169, 313, 319, 328, 340, 351, 366, 367, 381, 390, 398, 405, 409, 417, 427
Rappaport, M., 417, 427
Ray, A.B., 401, 409
Raychaudhuri, M., 392, 409
Razoni, J.H., 304, 309
Reading, E., 146, 151
Rees, W.L., 328, 351
Reifman, A., 426
Reintz, A.H., 387
Reisman, J.M., 73, 81
Renner, K.E., 17, 26
Richard, S., 332, 346
Richardson, H., 401, 409
Richter, R.H., 327, 351
Rickers-Ovsiankina, M., 157, 160, 331, 351
Ridgeway, E.M., 320, 335, 347, 352
Robins, E., 417, 421, 426, 427
Rorschach, H., 6, 26, 95, 99, 100, 135, 152, 153, 154, 160, 299, 310, 313, 322, 330, 341, 352, 356, 390, 430, 443
Rose, R.B., 409
Rose, R.J., 17, 26
Rosen, B., 417, 427
Rosen, E., 381, 390, 431, 443
Rosenthal, D., 426, 427
Rosenthal, M., 325, 352
Rosenthal, R., 427
Rosenzweig, S., 304, 309
Ross, D.C., 396, 410
Ross, D.M., 428
Rotter, J.B., 16, 26, 313, 349
Roy, A.B., 317, 350
Rubenstein, B.B., 304, 309
Ruesch, H., 27, 56, 442
Rybakov, T., 4, 26

Sakheim, G.A., 396, 409, 412, 427
Salmon, P., 319, 352
Sanderson, M.H., 30, 56
Sapenfield, B.R., 332, 352
Sapolsky, A., 412, 427
Sarason, S.B., 64, 79, 319, 346
Sarbin, T.R., 60, 81, 302, 310
Saretsky, T., 369, 391
Sargent, H., 17, 26
Satorius, N., 416, 427
Sawyer, J., 17, 26
Schachtel, E.G., 63, 81, 304, 310, 331, 352
Schachter, W., 359, 391
Schafer, R., 14, 26, 60, 62, 63, 80, 81, 82, 89, 99, 104, 135, 152, 160, 161, 169, 328, 351, 367, 372, 390, 391, 400, 405, 409, 431, 443
Schlesinger, H.G., 328, 349
Schmidt, H., 142, 152, 328, 352
Schnitzer, R., 427
Schon, M., 319, 352
Schooler, N.R., 426

Schreiber, H., 396, 410, 412, 428
Schreiber, M., 317, 321, 336, 351
Schulman, I., 327, 352
Schulsinger, F., 426, 427
Schumacher, J., 334, 348, 408
Schumer, F., 3, 26, 89
Schuyler, W., 161, 169, 420, 426
Schwartz, A., 425
Schwartz, C., 425
Schwartz, F., 319, 352
Sechrest, L., 431, 443
Seitz, C.P., 328, 349
Sender, S., 11, 25, 104, 135
Senders, J.W., 35, 55
Sendin, C., 34, 56, 157, 160
Shalit, B., 50, 56, 317, 352
Shapiro, D., 331, 352
Shapiro, R., 416, 427
Sharlock, N., 388
Shatin, L., 398, 410
Shavzin, A.R., 64, 79
Sherman, M.H., 313, 352, 366, 391, 402,
    410
Shneidman, E.S., 304, 310, 411, 426, 427
Siegel, E.L., 355, 391
Siegel, M., 304, 310
Silverman, L.K., 304, 310
Singer, J.L., 27, 56, 322, 327, 352, 431, 442
Singer, M.T., 328, 350
Sisson, B., 141, 152
Sloan, W., 366, 391
Sloane, K., 404
Smith, J.G., 27, 56, 328, 351, 431, 443
Snyder, S., 416, 427
Sommer, D., 327, 336, 352, 378, 391
Sommer, R., 327, 336, 352, 378, 391
Spiegelman, M., 340, 349
Spitzer, R.L., 417, 421, 427
Spivack, G., 328, 350
Spohn, H.E., 322, 328, 352
Stanley, F., 361, 388
Stanton, A., 417, 427
Stauffacher, J.C., 417, 428
Steele, N.M., 328
Stein, M.I., 38, 56, 61, 81
Steiner, M.E., 338, 352
Steisel, I.M., 332, 352
Stern, G.G., 61, 81
Sterne, S.B., 334, 353
Sternklar, S., 398, 408
Stewart, L.M., 64, 80
Stiff, M., 345
Stone, H., 431, 443
Storment, C.T., 378, 391
Stotsky, B.A., 73, 79, 329, 348, 353, 378, 391,
    402, 410
Strauss, J.S., 416, 417, 426, 427

Strauss, M. E., 65, 81
Stricker, G., 73, 78, 81, 160, 319, 348, 412, 426,
    431, 442
Sundberg, N.D., 15, 26
Suttell, B., 27, 56, 442
Swarz, J.D., 83, 89
Swift, J.W., 304, 310, 313, 353
Symonds, P.M., 17, 26, 304, 310

Tallman, G., 151
Tamarin, S., 329
Tanaka, F., 327, 353
Taulbee, E., 141, 152, 366, 391
Taylor, M., 417, 428
Theisen, W.C., 408
Thiesen, J.W., 417, 428
Toal, R., 349
Thomas, C.B., 396, 410, 412, 428
Thomas, E.A., 40, 43, 45, 46, 51, 54, 55, 56, 313,
    317, 320, 322, 324, 325, 329, 339, 347, 368,
    388, 396, 399, 406, 409, 410, 418, 426
Thomas, H.F., 328, 353
Thomas, R.W., 348
Thompson, G., 336, 353
Thorpe, J.S., 83, 89
Tougas, R., 000
Townsend, J., 391
Tucker, G., 425
Tuma, A.H., 417, 427

Ulett, G.A., 408
Ulrich, R.F., 426

Van de Castle, R.L., 61, 81
Vannicelli, M., 426, 427
Varvel, W., 142, 152
Vernon, P.E., 44, 56, 61, 81
Vernon, P.H., 304, 310
Viglione, D., 45, 54, 317, 319, 322, 324, 327,
    333, 347, 353, 364, 378, 379, 388
Vinson, D.B., 402, 410
Vives, M., 422, 428
Von Lackum, W.J., 30, 54, 346

Wagner, E.E., 327, 353
Walker, E.J., 50, 54, 318, 335, 347, 408
Walker, E.L., 64, 79
Walker, R.G., 431, 443
Walker, R.N., 30, 53, 345, 386, 406
Wallach, J., 431, 443
Wallen, P., 353
Waller, P.F., 319, 338, 353
Wallis, R.R., 16, 25
Wallner, J.M., 331
Walters, R.H., 401, 410
Warshaw, L., 334, 353
Watkins, J.G., 417, 428

Watson, A., 129, 135, 393, 410
Weber, A., 340, 353
Wedemeyer, B., 403, 410
Weigl, E., 332, 353
Weiner, I.B., 18, 26, 30, 46, 50, 53, 62, 66, 81,
    150, 152, 160, 161, 169, 313, 317, 319, 322,
    324, 327, 328, 348, 353, 357, 364, 367, 368,
    376, 388, 391, 401, 408, 412, 417, 418, 420,
    422, 423, 426, 428, 431, 442
Weiss, A.A., 398, 410
Weiss, L.J., 409
Weithorn, C.J., 353
Welsh, G.S., 41, 54
Wender, P., 426, 427
Werner, H., 95, 99
Wetherhorn, M., 370, 391
Wheeler, W.M., 431, 443
Whippel, G.M., 4, 26
White, M.A., 396, 410, 412, 428
Wickes, T.A., 31, 56
Wiener-Levy, D., 315, 353
Wiggins, J.S., 17, 26
Wilensky, H., 355, 391
Williams, M.H., 000
Wilson, G., 142, 152

Wing, J., 416, 425
Winnik, H.Z., 398, 410
Winnokur, G., 426
Winter, L.B., 395, 410
Winter, W.D., 327, 351
Wisham, W., 328
Wishner, J., 141, 152, 357, 366, 391
Witkin, H.A., 327, 353
Wittenborn, J.R., 357, 391
Wohl, J., 20, 25
Woiska, P.H., 387
Woodruff, R., 426
Wylie, J.R., 37, 38, 55, 334, 343, 348, 368, 370,
    373, 382, 385, 388, 395, 396, 397, 409, 412,
    426
Wylie, R.C., 392, 410

Zalis, T., 334, 348
Zamansky, H.J., 367, 391
Zax, M., 73, 78, 81
Zelin, M., 431
Zolliker, A., 398, 410
Zubin, J., 3, 26, 82, 89, 416, 428
Zuckerman, M., 332, 353
Zukowsky, E., 369, 391

Subject Index

Achromatic Color Response (C′), 116–118,
    339–341
Active passive Movement (a, p), 106–110
Active-Passive ratios (a:p, M^a:M^p), 178–180,
    370–374
    cognitive flexibility, 370–373
    snow-white syndrome, 374
Adjusted D Score, 179, 317–321
Administration procedures, 59–78
    difficult subjects, 75–77
    instructions, 66–67
    inquiry, 70–77
    lengthy records, 68–69
    location sheet, 77
    questions by subjects 67–68
    recording responses, 69–71
    rejections, 68
    response phase, 66–69
    seating, 63–65
    subject preparation, 65–66
Affect, 315–339, 377–386
    capacity for control, 315–321, 377–381
    experience of distress, 337–342
    FC:CF+C ratio, 180, 377–379
    modulation in expression, 330–333, 377–379
    receptiveness to, 332–333, 379–381
    response to loss, 338–339
    use in decision operations, 322–326, 329–333
    white space responses, 381–383
Affective ratio, 180, 332–333, 379–381
Aggressive movement response (AG), 167,
    404–405
    interpersonal perception, 404–405
    self image, 404–405
Ambient, 322–326
Autistic logic (ALOG), 164, 375–377

Blend responses, 93–94, 136–141, 180,
    384–385
Blot difficulty, 30, 35–41
Body concern, 397–398
Brief records, 311–312

Case illustrations, 434–442, 447–510
    L.S. Protocol–tension complaints, 434–442
    Protocol 1–question concerning tension and

    depression, 447–460
    Protocol 2–question of adolescent withdrawal,
        460–473
    Protocol 3–question of somatic involvement,
        473–485
    Protocol 4–question of impulsiveness,
        485–498
    Protocol 5–question of chronic anxiety,
        498–510
Chromatic Color responses (FC,CF,C,Cn),
    110–116, 330–333, 377–379
    color naming, 114
    FC:CF+C ratio, 180, 330–333, 377–379
    pure C response (C), 110–113, 330–333
    weighted sum C, 178
Cognition, 354–377
    complexity, 354–356
    concreteness, 354–356, 362–364
    dysfunction, 362–364
    efficiency, 359–362
    initiative, 354–356
    organizing activity, 354–355
    overincorporation, 360–362
    underincorporation, 360–362
Color Projection (CP), 167–168, 383–384
Color Shading Blends, 384–385
Confabulated response (CONFAB), 166,
    362–364
Contamination (CONTAM), 163–164,
    375–377
Content, 153–156, 397–398, 401–407
    specific categories, 153–156
    specific ratios, 181–182
Controls and stress tolerance, 315–321
Coping styles, 313–315, 322–333

Decision making, 313–333
    controls, 315–321
    response styles, 313–315, 322–333
    stress tolerance, 315–321
Depression, 290–292, 424–425
    affective distress, 337–342
    reference group, 290–292
Depression Index (DEPRI), 182, 424, 425
Detail responses, 91–93, 358–359
    common details (D), 91–92, 358–359

Detail responses (*Continued*)
  unusual details (Dd), 92–93, 359
Determinants, 100–134
  coding symbols, 101–102
Developmental Quality (DQ), 94–97
  and cognitive operations, 355–356
Deviant response (DR), 161–163, 375–377
Deviant verbalization (DV), 161–163, 375–377
Diffuse shading response (Y), 124–127, 317–321
Disordered thinking, 328–329, 374–377,
    419–420
  M- response, 328–329
  six critical special scores, 375–377, 419–420
D scores, 178–179, 315–321

EA:es relationship, 315–322
Egocentricity Index (3r+(2)/R), 180, 392–396
  perceived *vs.* ideal self, 396
Erlebnistypus (EB), 178, 322–333
  ambitent, 322–326
  extratensive, 322–326, 329–333
  introversive, 322–329
  physiological correlates, 323, 325–326
  problem solving approaches, 323–326
  temporal consistency, 324
Examiner influence, 63–65
Experience Actual (EA), 178, 321–322
Experience base (eb), 178–179, 333–342
  achromatic-shading component, 337–342
  FM+m component, 334–337
Experienced stimulation (es), 179, 333–344
Extratensive, 322–326, 329–333
Eye scanning, 35–36

Fabulized Combination (FABCOM), 163,
    375–377
FC:CF+C ratio, 180, 315–321, 377–379
Form Dimension response (FD), 127–129,
    342–344
Form Quality, 146–151, 181, 188–250,
    367–369
  F+%, 181, 365–367
  ordinary, 148
  minus, 148
  superior-overinclusive, 148, 249–250
  table. 188–248
  unusual, 148
  X+%, 181, 367–368
  X−%, 181, 368–369
Form response (F), 103, 313–315
Four Square, 315

H+A:Hd+Ad ratio, 181
H+(H):Hd+(Hd) ratio, 181
History of the test, 3–14
Human content, 153–154, 401–404

Ideation, 369–377, 396–401, 419–420
  defensiveness, 398–400
  disordered, 374–377, 419–420
  fantasy abuse, 374
  flexibility, 370–373
  intellectualization, 398–401
  pessimism, 396–397
Inaccurate perception, 368–369, 418–419
Inadequate controls, 315–321
Incongruous combination (INCOM), 163,
    375–377
Inquiry, 70–72
  direct, 77
  inappropriate questions, 75
  key words, 73–75
  preparing the subject, 70
  range of questions, 72–75
  testing limits, 77–78
Instructions, 66–67
Interpersonal perceptions, 401–407
Interpretation, 299–309, 311–344, 354–386,
    392–407, 411–425, 429–442, 447–510
  based on sequence of scores, 429–430, 438,
    457, 471, 482–483, 496, 508
  based on structural data, 299–429, 434–437,
    455–457, 468–471, 480–482, 493–496,
    506–508
  based on verbal material, 430–434, 438–441,
    457–458, 471–472, 483–484, 496–497,
    408–509
  blind interpretation, 302–306
  computer based, 306–307
  conceptual basis, 299–302
  integration stage, 301–302
  logical progression, 307–309
  propositional stage, 300–301
Interscorer agreement, 133–134, 150–151,
    159–160, 168
Introversive, 322–329
Isolation Index (ISOL:R), 181, 405–407

Lambda, 180, 312–315
  in records of questionable validity, 312–313
  as related to overincorporation, 315
  as related to response style, 312–315
Location coding (W,D,Dd,S), 90–97
  developmental quality, 94–97
  numbering for detail areas, 91–92
Location sheet, 77

Morbid content (MOR), 167, 396–397
  influence on thinking, 396–397
  self image, 396–397
Movement responses, 103, 317–321, 326–330,
    373–375
  active-passive coding, 106–110

animal (FM), 104–105, 333–337
  human (M), 104, 326–330, 373–375
  inanimate (m), 105, 317–321, 333–337
  no form, 374–375
  stress effects, 317–321

Normative data, 252–287
  adults, 257–259
  children, 262–287
  demography, 256, 260
  sampling, 255–257
  socioeconomic differences, 256–257, 260–261
  use of, 252–255
Number of responses (R), 311–313

Organizational activity (Z), 141–146, 354–355,
    359–362
  overincorporation, 360–362
  predicted Zsum, 142, 177, 179
  underincorporation, 360–362
  weighted Zsum, 141–177
  Zd score, 142, 177, 359–362
  Zf, 141–143, 177, 354–355

Pair response (2), 131–133
Perception, 364–369
  conventionality, 364–369
  distortion, 365, 368–369
  encoding, 35–39
  visual scanning, 35–36
Perseveration response (PSV), 164–165,
    362–363
Personal response (PER), 167, 398–400
Popular response (P), 157–160, 251, 364–365
  cultural differences, 159
Projection, 14–18, 27–28, 51–53, 166, 430–434
  as concept, 14–18
  projective hypothesis, 27–28
  in response, 51–53, 166

R, 311–313
Reference groups, 288–295
  character problems, 293–295
  depressives, 290–292
  schizophrenics, 288–290
Reflection responses (Fr, rF), 129–133
Reliability, 44–49
  brief interval retests, 47–49
  internal consistency, 44–45
  interscorer, 133–134, 150–151, 159–160, 168
  lengthy interval retests, 45–46
Response phase, 66–69
Response process, 27–53
  classification of stimuli, 36–39
  decision choices, 29–34
  discarding, 40–44

Schizophrenia Index (SCZI), 182, 416–424
Scoring, 82–89
  vs. coding, 82–87
  as Rorschach language, 82–87
Seating, 63–65
Self image, 392–401, 404–405
Sequence of scores, 170, 176
Shading blends, 385–386
Shading responses, 118–127, 317–321
  diffuse (Y), 124–127, 317–321
  texture (T), 120–123, 338–339
  vista (V), 123–124, 341–342
Special Scores, 161–168, 362–364, 375–377,
    419–420
  aggressive (AG), 167, 404–405
  color projection (CP), 167–168, 383–384
  confabulation (CONFAB), 166, 362–364
  contamination (CONTAM), 163–164,
    375–377
  deviant response (DR), 161–163, 375–377
  deviant verbalization (DV), 161–163,
    375–377
  fabulized combination (FABCOM), 163,
    375–377
  inappropriate logic (ALOG), 164, 375–377
  incongruous combination (INCOM), 163,
    375–377
  morbid (MOR), 167, 396–397
  perseveration (PSV), 164–165, 362–363
  personal (PER), 167, 398–400
Stress tolerance, 315–321
Structural summary, 87–89, 170–183
  frequency tallies, 170, 176–177
  ratios, percentages and derivations, 177–182
Suicide constellation (S-CON), 182, 411–416

Tachistoscopic presentation, 38–39
  input of the stimulus, 35–36
  as problem solving task, 28–29
  range of potential responses, 30–34
  role of projection, 51–53
  role of psychological states, 49–51
  role of traits and styles, 44–49
Response styles, 313–315, 322–333
Retest studies, see Reliability
Rorschach test:
  concept of the method, 27–28
  history, 3–14, 20–24
  intersystem differences, 18–20
  and projection, 14–18, 27–28, 51–53, 166,
    430–434
  systems, 6–14
  and test battery, 60–62

Schizophrenia, 288–290, 416–424
  reference group, 288–290

Temporal consistency, *see* Reliability
Testing decisions, 59–60
Texture response (T), 120–123, 338–339

Unusual verbalizations, *see* Special
    scores

Vista response (V), 123–124, 341–342

W:D ratio, 181
Weighted sum C, 178
White space response (S), 93, 381–383
Whole response (W), 90–91, 356–359
W:M ratio, 181, 357–358

Working tables, 187–251

X+%, 181, 367–368
X−%, 181, 368–369

Zd, 142, 178, 359–362
Z frequency (Zf), 141–143, 177, 354–355
Z scores, 141–146, 250–251, 354–362
    adjacent detail, 143, 250
    distant detail, 143, 250
    estimated, 142, 179, 250–251
    integration of white space, 143, 250
    weighted by card, 143, 250
    whole response, 143, 250

(*continued from front*)

Handbook of Research Methods in Clinical Psychology *edited by Philip C. Kendall and James N. Butcher*

A Social Psychology of Developing Adults *by Thomas O. Blank*

Women in the Middle Years: Current Knowledge and Directions for Research and Policy *edited by Janet Zollinger Giele*

Loneliness: A Sourcebook of Current Theory, Research and Therapy *edited by Letitia Anne Peplau and Daniel Perlman*

Hyperactivity: Current Issues, Research, and Theory (Second Edition) *by Dorothea M. Ross and Sheila A. Ross*

Review of Human Development *edited by Tiffany M. Field, Aletha Huston, Herbert C. Quay, Lillian Troll, and Gordon E. Finley*

Agoraphobia: Multiple Perspectives on Theory and Treatment *edited by Dianne L. Chambless and Alan J. Goldstein*

The Rorschach: A Comprehensive System. Volume III: Assessment of Children and Adolescents *by John E. Exner, Jr. and Irving B. Weiner*

Handbook of Play Therapy *edited by Charles E. Schaefer and Kevin J. O'Connor*

Adolescent Sexuality in a Changing American Society: Social and Psychological Perspectives for the Human Service Professions (Second Edition) *by Catherine S. Chilman*

Failures in Behavior Therapy *edited by Edna B. Foa and Paul M.G. Emmelkamp*

The Psychological Assessment of Children (Second Edition) *by James O. Palmer*

Imagery: Current Theory, Research, and Application *edited by Aneés A. Sheikh*

Handbook of Clinical Child Psychology *edited by C. Eugene Walker and Michael C. Roberts*

The Measurement of Psychotherapy Outcome *edited by Michael J. Lambert, Edwin R. Christensen, and Steven S. DeJulio*

Clinical Methods in Psychology (Second Edition) *edited by Irving B. Weiner*

Excuses: Masquerades in Search of Grace *by C.R. Snyder, Raymond L. Higgins and Rita J. Stucky*

Diagnostic Understanding and Treatment Planning: The Elusive Connection *edited by Fred Shectman and William B. Smith*

Bender Gestalt Screening for Brain Dysfunction *by Patricia Lacks*

Adult Psychopathology and Diagnosis *edited by Samuel M. Turner and Michel Hersen*

Personality and the Behavioral Disorders (Second Edition) *edited by Norman S. Endler and J. McVicker Hunt*

Ecological Approaches to Clinical and Community Psychology *edited by William A. O'Connor and Bernard Lubin*

Rational-Emotive Therapy with Children and Adolescents: Theory, Treatment Strategies, Preventative Methods *by Michael E. Bernard and Marie R. Joyce*

The Unconscious Reconsidered *edited by Kenneth S. Bowers and Donald Meichenbaum*

Prevention of Problems in Childhood: Psychological Research and Application *edited by Michael C. Roberts and Lizette Peterson*

Resolving Resistances in Psychotherapy *by Herbert S. Strean*

Handbook of Social Skills Training and Research *edited by Luciano L'Abate and Michael A. Milan*

Institutional Settings in Children's Lives *by Leanne G. Rivlin and Maxine Wolfe*

Treating the Alcoholic: A Developmental Model of Recovery *by Stephanie Brown*

Resolving Marital Conflicts: A Psychodynamic Perspective *by Herbert S. Strean*

Paradoxical Strategies in Psychotherapy: A Comprehensive Overview and Guidebook *by Leon F. Seltzer*

Pharmacological and Behavioral Treatment: An Integrative Approach *edited by Michel Hersen*

The Rorschach: A Comprehensive System. Volume I: Basic Foundations (Second Edition) *by John E. Exner, Jr.*